D1135057

EDUCATIONAL PSYCHOLOGY

THE MACMILLAN COMPANY
NEW YORK · CHICAGO
DALLAS · ATLANTA · SAN FRANCISCO

THE MACMILLAN COMPANY
OF CANADA, LIMITED
TORONTO

EDUCATIONAL PSYCHOLOGY

GLENN MYERS BLAIR, Ph.D.
PROFESSOR OF EDUCATIONAL PSYCHOLOGY
UNIVERSITY OF ILLINOIS

R. STEWART JONES, Ph.D.
ASSISTANT PROFESSOR OF EDUCATIONAL PSYCHOLOGY
UNIVERSITY OF ILLINOIS

RAY H. SIMPSON, Ph.D.
PROFESSOR OF EDUCATIONAL PSYCHOLOGY
UNIVERSITY OF ILLINOIS

New York
THE MACMILLAN COMPANY

PRINTED IN THE UNITED STATES OF AMERICA

First printing

PREFACE

THE MODERN TEACHER is no longer merely a hearer of lessons or an officer who maintains order in the classroom. Instead he is an individual who is concerned with the total development and adjustment of children. He is, of course, interested in having children acquire knowledge and skills, but he is equally concerned about their health, personal and social adjustment, and their goals and plans. The child who is shy and retiring, underweight, or whose levels of aspiration are too low requires the study and attention of the teacher as much as does the one who is having difficulty with fractions or decimals.

The old adage that "teachers are born and not made" may contain a germ of truth, and may have been useful in characterizing teachers of an earlier date, but it is very misleading and inappropriate today. The present-day teacher who would succeed with such complex tasks as guiding and directing learning, diagnosing and alleviating personality maladjustments, and evaluating the outcomes of his work must be a specially trained expert. Among the subjects of greatest relevance in this program of training is that of educational psychology. Teachers need thoroughly to understand the basic principles of psychology governing the behavior of children, and in addition need to possess skill in methods of child study.

The present book has been written in an effort to supply teachers and prospective teachers with those facts and principles and methods of procedure which have maximal usefulness in the classroom and in other educational situations. The materials have been gathered from many sources including the psychology laboratory, classroom experimentation, clinical experience, and from such related fields as cultural anthropology, psychiatry, biology and sociology.

It is the plan of the book first to present a longitudinal view of the child as he progresses toward maturity; secondly, to show the forces which influence and produce change in the child's learning and adjustment; thirdly, to illustrate how the methods and tools of psychology can be used to evaluate the effectiveness of the educational program; and finally, to discuss some of the psychological factors which influence the professional growth and mental health of the teacher. The book has a developmental emphasis throughout and is particularly oriented in terms of the needs of children and the forces which motivate them to learn and adjust.

A distinctive feature of the book is the deliberate effort which has been made to illustrate psychological theories by using actual classroom examples so that teachers may gain clear insight into the fundamental values which psychology has to offer. Also of a unique nature is the section dealing with the psychology of the teacher. Books in the past have frequently given the impression that all one needs to know in order to teach is to understand children. Recently, however, an awareness has developed that to be effective the teacher must know himself—be able to diagnose his own assets and liabilities, his own personality and his own teaching methods. Hence much attention has been given to the teacher's role in the learning process, and to the nature of teacher-pupil relationships.

Although the book has been written by three authors, it is, in every sense, a joint and integrated effort. G. M. Blair was largely responsible for the preparation of Chapters 1 through 4, and 13 through 15; R. S. Jones for Part III and also Chapter 16; and R. H. Simpson for Chapters 17 through 21. The entire manuscript, however, was read, revised, and put into final shape by all three authors.

The writers are indebted to many individuals for the part they have contributed toward the substance of this volume. These include research workers and colleagues in psychology and related fields who have augmented the rapidly growing body of experimental evidence, and thousands of experienced teachers in the writers' classes who have helped them build a bridge between theory and practice. Gratitude is also expressed to the many publishers who have generously given permission to quote from copyrighted works.

GLENN MYERS BLAIR
R. STEWART JONES
RAY H. SIMPSON

Urbana, Illinois

CONTENTS

PART I INTRODUCTION

Chapter 1. **Psychology and the Work of the Teacher** 3

General Psychology and Educational Psychology 3
Educational Philosophy and Educational Psychology 4
The Role of Educational Psychology in the Work
    of the Teacher 6
Making Educational Psychology Functional 8
Organization and Plan of the Book 10

PART II GROWTH AND DEVELOPMENT

Chapter 2. **The Biological and Social Bases of Behavior** 13

Organic Basis of Behavior 14
Environmental Basis of Behavior 30
Summary 40
References for Further Study 40

Chapter 3. **Growth and Development During Childhood** 42

General Nature of Growth 42
Fundamental Needs of the Child 43
Developmental Tasks of Childhood 44
Mental Development 45
Personality and Social Development 49
Importance of the Period of Childhood 60
Summary 61
References for Further Study 62

Chapter 4. **The Adolescent Period** 64

Why Adolescence Is a Period Requiring Special
    Study 65

Adolescent Needs 67
Developmental Tasks of Adolescence 69
Adolescent Physical Development 70
Adolescent Problems Related to Physical Varia-
tions 71
Mental Growth During Adolescence 73
Adolescent Interests 74
Adolescent Worries and Problems 79
The Adolescent and the Family 82
Sex Education and the Adolescent 84
Adolescent Delinquency 86
Summary 88
References for Further Study 89

PART III   LEARNING

Chapter 5. **An Orientation to Learning** 93

Introduction 93
Ways of Studying the Learning Process 96
Essential Characteristics of the Learning Process 104
Pervasiveness of Learning in the Classroom 107
Summary 111
References for Further Study 112

Chapter 6. **Readiness for Learning** 114

Factors Which Determine Readiness 115
Individual Differences in Readiness 127
The Appraisal of Readiness 138
Building Readiness 142
Summary 146
References for Further Study 148

Chapter 7. **Motivation: The Forces Which Energize and
Direct Behavior** 150

What Is the Motivational Process? 150
Needs and Behavior 152
Effect or Reinforcement in Learning 161
Dynamics of the Motivational Process 164
Goals and Incentives 173

	Summary	187
	References for Further Study	189
Chapter 8.	**Interests and Attitudes**	**191**
	A Working Concept of Attitudes	192
	The Place of Interest in Schooling	194
	The Origin and Development of Interests and Attitudes	195
	Attitudes, Interests, and Teaching	201
	Summary	208
	References for Further Study	209
Chapter 9.	**Organization of Learning and Teaching**	**211**
	Basic Principles of Organization in Learning	212
	Organization and Understanding	222
	Organization and Methods of Teaching	232
	Summary	238
	References for Further Study	239
Chapter 10.	**The Transfer and Application of Learning**	**241**
	Transfer the Ultimate Goal of Teaching	241
	How Does Transfer Take Place?	249
	Teaching for Transfer	256
	Summary	260
	References for Further Study	261
Chapter 11.	**The Social Psychology of Teaching and Learning**	**263**
	The Importance of Social-Emotional Factors in Schooling	263
	Teacher-Pupil Relationships	265
	Relationships Among Pupils	271
	School Staff Relationships	279
	Other Factors in Social Climate	282
	The Effect of Social Climate on Learning	284
	Summary	290
	References for Further Study	292
Chapter 12.	**Discovering and Overcoming Special Difficulties in Learning**	**294**
	What Happens When Difficulties Remain Unsolved?	295

Types of Difficulties and Contributing Factors   296
Early Recognition of Difficulties   299
Psycho-Educational Diagnosis in the Classroom   300
Some General Principles in Giving Special Help   302
Difficulties in Reading   303
Remedial Spelling   311
Remedial Speech   315
Remedial English   316
Remedial Mathematics   317
Use of Available Resources   319
Summary   321
References for Further Study   322

PART IV   ADJUSTMENT AND GUIDANCE

Chapter 13. **Basic Processes of Adjustment**   **327**

Fundamental Human Needs   327
Conditions Which Create Frustration   329
Adjusting to Frustrating Conditions   330
Adjustment Mechanisms   331
Neurotic and Psychotic Adjustments   346
Summary   354
References for Further Study   355

Chapter 14. **Problems of School Discipline**   **356**

Discipline in the Classroom—Past and Present   356
A Show-Off in the Algebra Class   361
Disorder in the Study Hall   362
The School Building Is Defaced   363
Joe—A Slow Learner and a Bully   364
Miss Henry Is Upset   365
Guiding Principles for Keeping Discipline   366
Summary   368
References for Further Study   369

Chapter 15. **Promoting the Personal and Social Adjustment of
            Pupils**   **371**

How Teachers View Adjustment Problems of
    Pupils   371

Detecting Maladjustment   372
Causes of Maladjustment   374
Dealing with Specific Types of Maladjustment   381
School Programs Which Aid Pupil Adjustment   386
Useful Techniques and Materials   388
The School Psychologist   390
Summary   391
References for Further Study   392

Chapter 16. Studying the Individual Child   **394**

The Need for Child Study   394
Pitfalls to Be Avoided in Child Study   396
Which Children Should Be Studied?   400
Sources of Information   401
Tools and Methods for Child Study   409
Summary   417
References for Further Study   418

PART V   MEASUREMENT AND EVALUATION

Chapter 17. Diagnostic Tools   **423**

Intelligence Tests   424
Achievement Tests   432
Measures of Character and Personality   435
Vocational Interest Tests   441
Study Skills   442
Other Diagnostic Tools   445
Selecting the Appropriate Test   446
Teacher-Constructed Diagnostic Tools   449
Summary   455
References for Further Study   455

Chapter 18. Interpreting and Using Test Results   **458**

Cautions in Interpreting Test Results   459
Use of Achievement Test Results   464
Using Tests to Facilitate Social Relationships   472
Summary   478
References for Further Study   479

Chapter 19. Marking, Reporting, and Promoting   **481**

How Marks and Reports May Serve Various
Groups   482
Major Difficulties in Marking and Reporting Sys-
tems   493
Improving Marking and Reporting Practices   495
Factors of Importance in Promotion   .   503
Summary   506
References for Further Study   506

Chapter 20. Appraising the Work of the School   **508**

Evaluating the Effect of Teaching on Out-of-
School Behavior   509
Studies of Pupil and Community Attitudes To-
ward Schools   511
Case Studies of Classes   514
Then and Now Studies   518
Studies Comparing Two Methods   520
Longitudinal Studies   523
Matched Community Comparisons   526
Review of Research Summaries   527
Difficulties in Analyzing Merits of Different Ap-
proaches   527
Summary   529
References for Further Study   530

PART VI   THE PSYCHOLOGY OF THE TEACHER

Chapter 21. Professional Growth of the Teacher   **535**

The Teacher as a Learner   536
Teacher Self-Appraisal   538
Improvement of the Teacher's Class Activities   545
Teacher-Teacher Relationships   548
Improving Teacher-Administrator Relations   552
Professional Reading   553
Teacher-Community Relations   555
Summary   558
References for Further Study   559

**Chapter 22. Personal and Emotional Adjustment of the
Teacher** 561

The Problem 561
Effect of Teacher Maladjustment on Pupils 565
Causes of Teacher Maladjustment 568
Suggestions to Teachers for Keeping in Good
Mental Health 571
Summary 573
References for Further Study 574

Indexes 575

ILLUSTRATIONS

1. Locations of the Principal Endocrine Glands — 21
2. What Is the Length of the Line AO? — 103
3. The Effect of Teaching on the Growth of Spelling Ability — 116
4. Mental Age and Success in Reading — 118
5. The Rate in Growth of Reading Ability for Three Pupils — 128
6. Profile of Aptitudes of a Twelfth-Grade Youth Who Wanted to Study Engineering — 137
7. Examples of Items Used to Measure Reading Readiness — 140
8. Readiness Profiles of Two High-School Students Prior to a Course in High-School Physics — 143
9. How Needs Operate to Produce Tensions — 153
10. How Well-to-do and Poor Ten-Year Olds Estimated the Size of Coins — 156
11. A Child's Conception of Stonewall Jackson Riding Ahead — 213
12. A Theoretical Curve of Retention of Relatively Meaningless Material — 234
13. Group Word Teaching Game — 306
14. The Reading Accelerator — 310
15. A Diagnostic Chart in Arithmetic — 318
16. Pencil Sketch Made by an Emotionally Disturbed Twelve-Year-Old Boy — 408
17. Excerpts from the California Short-Form Test of Mental Maturity — 429
18. Sample Items from the Davis-Eells Games — 431
19. One of the Ten Ink Blots from the Rorschach Test — 439
20. Profile of Reading Skills of the Sixth-Grade Class Described in Table 32 — 466

21. Sociogram for Thirty Eighth-Grade Pupils 475
22. Developmental Report Form Used by One High School 484
23. General Section of a Student Progress Report 500

TABLES

1. Distribution of IQs of 68 Children of Feebleminded Mothers   34
2. IQs of 76 Canal Boat Children Arranged According to Age Groups   35
3. Size of Vocabulary at Different Grade Levels   47
4. Age Norms for the Terman-McNemar Test of Mental Ability   74
5. Twenty-Five Novels Most Popular with Boys and Girls in Grades 10 to 12   77
6. Relationship Between Kuder Scores Made 15 Months Apart   78
7. Problems Checked by Twenty-Five Per Cent or More of Twelfth-Grade Pupils of Either Sex   80
8. Rank Order of Problem Areas Indicated by Twelfth-Grade Pupils   82
9. Typical Adolescents' Complaints Regarding Their Mothers   83
10. Should the School Help Students Obtain Sound Sex Education?   85
11. The Percentage of Children in Each Grade Ready for Each Book Level   115
12. The Scores of 240 Fifth-Grade Boys and Girls on a Variety of Tests and Measurements   132
13. Results of Diagnostic Pretest in High School Biology   141
14. Arithmetic and Intelligence Test Data for Control and Experimental Groups   144
15. A Comparison of Interests of American and Egyptian Children   198
16. Relationship Between Delinquency and Play Interests   200
17. Factors Listed by Youth as Reason for the Choice of Medicine as a Career   201

18. Traits of Well-Liked Teachers 267
19. Types of Leadership, Characteristics of Leaders, and Pupils' Reactions 269
20. Summary of Sociometric Choices in an Eighth-Grade Class 276
21. Symptoms Which May Point to Handicaps and Learning Difficulties 301
22. A Basic Sight Vocabulary of 220 Words 308
23. Prefixes Occurring Most Often in the 20,000 Words of the Thorndike List 309
24. Easy Reading Books for Older Children 312
25. One Hundred Words Most Often Misspelled by Children in the Elementary Grades 314
26. The Ten Problems Most Frequently Reported by Beginning Ohio Teachers 357
27. How 290 Elementary School Teachers Met Classroom Behavior Problems 359
28. Rank-Order Comparison of the Ratings by Mental Hygienists and Teachers of the Seriousness of 50 Behavior Problems of Children 373
29. Errors of Beginning Counselors Observed over a Period of Several Years 406
30. Achievement Tests Listed in the Fourth Mental Measurements Yearbook 432
31. Comparison of Subtests of Two Widely Used Achievement Batteries 433
32. Iowa Silent Reading Data for One Room of Sixth Graders 465
33. Data from Survey of Community Reading 510
34. Some Reactions of Parents, Pupils, and Teachers Toward Their Schools 513
35. Effects of Two Procedures in Changing Food Habits 522
36. What Is the Motivational Level at Which Learners Are Operating? 543
37. The Incidence of Maladjustment of Teachers as Reported in Several Investigations 563

PART I

INTRODUCTION

Chapter 1

Psychology and the Work of the Teacher

THE STUDENT who is beginning the study of educational psychology may not be entirely clear as to the exact nature and purpose of this area of study. He knows that it is a course that is generally required of teachers, but he may not know why. What is educational psychology? How does it differ from general psychology or from other courses in education? What is its unique function in the education of teachers? The answers to these and related questions will be considered in this chapter.

GENERAL PSYCHOLOGY AND EDUCATIONAL PSYCHOLOGY

General psychology is concerned with the behavior of living organisms, and how they react to varying types of environmental stimulation. It is interested not only in human beings, but also in animals. Consequently, we find psychologists devoting much time to experiments in which white rats, cats, and chimpanzees learn to run mazes or perform other types of activities. Maier and other investigators [1] have been able to induce behavior disorders in rats, and Masserman and Rubinfine [2] have studied the "counting" behavior in cats. In its study of human beings, general psychology is interested

---

[1] See N. R. F. Maier, *Frustration*, New York, McGraw-Hill Book Company, Inc., 1949. Also J. McV. Hunt and H. Schlosberg, "Behavior of Rats in Continuous Frustration," *Journal of Comparative and Physiological Psychology*, Vol. 43, 1950, pp. 351–357.

[2] J. H. Masserman and D. L. Rubinfine, "'Counting' Behavior in Cats," *Journal of General Psychology*, Vol. 30, 1944, pp. 87–88.

in observing how people react to all sorts of situations. Many of these situations are set up in a laboratory, and a careful record is made of the responses that the individual makes. Such studies may investigate human reaction time, the pupillary reflex, gustatory sensitivity, or the learning of nonsense syllables.

Educational psychology is interested primarily in children and how they respond to the various conditions they meet in school and in life situations. It selects from the total field of psychology those facts and principles that have a direct bearing upon the growth, learning, and adjustment of children. It draws heavily from such areas as child psychology, adolescent psychology, the psychology of learning, clinical psychology, abnormal psychology, mental hygiene, and social psychology. Educational psychology, however, does not confine itself to the use of principles which have been developed by general psychology or its subdivisions. In recent years it has developed many areas which are relatively unemphasized by general psychology. For example, it has done extensive research in the teaching of reading, spelling, arithmetic and other school subjects. It has developed and evaluated guidance practices and remedial programs, and has contributed notably to the psychology of the atypical child, the social psychology of the classroom, and the measurement of the more intangible outcomes of education. Since the turn of the century educational psychology has probably contributed as much to general psychology as it has had occasion to borrow.[3] Educational psychology also utilizes relevant materials from such fields as social anthropology, medicine, psychiatry, biology, and sociology.

EDUCATIONAL PHILOSOPHY AND EDUCATIONAL PSYCHOLOGY

The nature of educational psychology may be still further clarified by comparing it with the subject of educational philosophy. Educational philosophy is interested in formulating theories as to the purpose of life and of education. It has as its function the establishing of aims and goals to be achieved by education. Why do schools exist? What is the relation of the school to society? What should be the nature of the school curriculum? It is concerned with

[3] Glenn M. Blair, *Educational Psychology, Its Development and Present Status*, Bureau of Research and Service, College of Education, University of Illinois, Urbana, 1948, p. 13.

such questions as these. The objectives of education have been stated in various terms by educational philosophers. One group, the Midcentury Committee on Outcomes in Elementary Education [4] listed nine types of behavior which the schools should endeavor to improve. These included such aspects of development as health, emotional and social adjustment, knowledge of the physical world, and quantitative relationships. Another group of educators [5] listed ten major types of objectives of secondary education. They are (1) the development of effective methods of thinking, (2) the cultivation of useful work habits and study skills, (3) the inculcation of social attitudes, (4) the acquisition of a wide range of significant interests, (5) the development of increased appreciation of music, art, literature, and other esthetic experiences, (6) the development of social sensitivity, (7) the development of better personal-social adjustment, (8) the acquisition of important information, (9) the development of physical health, and (10) the development of a consistent philosophy of life. The setting forth of such aims and objectives as these falls primarily in the province of *educational philosophy*.

What then is the province of *educational psychology?* Whereas educational philosophy is primarily concerned with the question of what should be done in schools, educational psychology attempts to answer the question of how it can be done. Educational psychology is interested, for the most part, in means rather than ends.

Educational philosophy might, for example, suggest that it is desirable for pupils to develop cooperative behavior. Educational psychology should be able to suggest ways and means of producing such behavior. From what has been said it should not be inferred that the functions of these two subjects are mutually exclusive or that each does not influence the other. Many of the theories of the philosophers may be tested by the psychologists. On the other hand, findings of the psychologists may cause the philosophers to modify their theories. How children learn and what they can learn at various stages of development help the philosopher to formulate realistic goals of education. Most teachers are both philosophers and

---

[4] Nolan C. Kearney, *Elementary School Objectives,* New York, Russell Sage Foundation, 1953.

[5] Eugene R. Smith and Ralph W. Tyler, *Appraising and Recording Student Progress,* New York, Harper and Brothers, 1942, p. 18.

psychologists at the same time—they are concerned with where they are going and also how to get there.

THE ROLE OF EDUCATIONAL PSYCHOLOGY IN THE WORK OF THE TEACHER

The activities engaged in and the problems faced by school teachers in the course of their work are both numerous and complex. What to do about retardation in reading, how to provide for the unadjusted child, when to introduce long division into the curriculum, how to identify children who possess physical or sensory defects, how to teach pupils to think critically, how to develop self-initiative in pupils, how to motivate the study of geography or some other subject, and how to evaluate the outcomes of the educative process are a few of the specific problems that might be mentioned. The modern teacher clearly has much more to do than listen to recitations and assign marks to pupils on the basis of their performance. He must be a diagnostician who can discover difficulties both in the learning and adjustment of pupils, and at the same time, possess the requisite skill for carrying forward the necessary remedial work. He may also have important educational and vocational guidance functions to perform. In short, his task is to further the total development of children and young people and to assist them in adjusting both to school and to out-of-school situations.

Three short case studies may serve to illustrate further some of the types of problems that continually face teachers. In the instances described here, the teachers were poorly trained and hence unable satisfactorily to solve the problems.

George—A Potential Delinquent

George is an attractive looking eleven-year-old boy who spends most of his time annoying the teacher or the other pupils in his sixth-grade class. He jiggles the desks, talks out loud, and throws objects around the room. On the school grounds, he pushes little children and throws dirt on their clean clothing. He occasionally breaks windows by throwing rocks. Frequently he brings to his teacher flowers which he has stolen from neighboring yards. George comes from a poor home. He is neglected by his parents. Seldom does he have adequate clothes or food. Although he has an IQ of 110, he is reported to be failing in his school subjects. Recently he has been accused of damaging street lights and of stealing articles from other childrens' lockers. His teacher and principal are considering the possibility of sending him to a reform school. His teacher has never understood what makes George misbehave. She has sent him to the principal to be punished, has asked him to apologize to the class, and has kept him after school, but none of these methods has been effective.

Luella—A Social Isolate

Luella is a nine-year-old girl in the fourth grade who never causes her teacher any trouble. Although her IQ is 139, her school grades are only slightly above average. When the teacher asks questions, she hides her head behind the pupil in front of her to avoid being called upon. She daydreams much of the time, and blushes when she speaks. The slightest criticism brings her to the verge of tears. Luella has no friends and does not play with other children during recess or after school. Her chief form of recreation consists of helping her mother develop a stamp collection. Because her schoolwork is satisfactory, and because she is a "good" girl, her teacher gives her no special thought or attention. Luella, however, is developing in a most unwholesome manner. Every day she is becoming more fearful, shy, and unsocial.

Harold—A Retarded Reader

Harold is a high school sophomore who has serious difficulty in reading. His English teacher was amazed when she discovered that he was unable to answer the simplest questions covering the content of *Silas Marner*. When the class moved on to a consideration of *Julius Caesar,* Harold again showed a complete inability to comprehend what he was reading. Not knowing what to do the teacher took Harold to the principal. She received no help from him other than a suggestion that she consult a Miss X in a neighboring school who was reported to have worked with such cases. After some difficulty, arrangements were made for this teacher to come to Harold's school to study him and to make recommendations.

It is apparent that the many complex duties involved in teaching require specialized training of the highest order. Educational psychology dealing, as it does, with problems of child growth and development, learning, and adjustment clearly occupies a place of paramount importance in any program of teacher education. This point of view has been well expressed in the following words by the Committee on Contributions of Psychology to Problems of Preparation for Teaching.[6]

[6] "Report of the Committee on Contributions of Psychology to Problems of Preparation for Teaching," *Journal of Consulting Psychology,* Vol. 6, Washington, American Psychological Association, Inc., May–June, 1942, pp. 165–166.

Basic in any program for the preparation of teachers must be a thoroughly scientific, broad, and insightful understanding of development in childhood and adolescence. . . . The teacher should be familiar with present knowledge regarding growth in physique, intellect, interests, emotions, attitudes, character traits, social adjustment—and the influences affecting these developments. . . . The Committee would therefore stress as essential parts of any teacher-preparation program the following: (a) an adequate treatment of psychological development—a treatment including the entire life span; (b) a broad treatment of the psychology of learning, including the forming of appreciations, attitudes, concepts, ideals; (c) some consideration of methods of child study, individual differences, and methods of treatment of the individual child.

MAKING EDUCATIONAL PSYCHOLOGY FUNCTIONAL

Traditional textbooks and courses in educational psychology have frequently failed to make the contribution they should to teacher education. Teachers have been known to have taken one or more courses in the field of educational psychology and yet have been unable to apply effectively the knowledge gained to their teaching. Too often they have seen but slight connection between what is discussed in the textbook or in the educational psychology course and what goes on in the classrooms where they work. To them educational psychology has appeared to be just another academic subject whose facts must be learned for test purposes and then just as quickly forgotten. There are probably several reasons for this. In the first place, the topics chosen for treatment in some textbooks in educational psychology have been only remotely related to the actual on-the-job behavior of teaching. Certain fairly recent books, for example, discuss at length such topics as microscopic features of the nervous system, visceral processes, the synapse theory of learning, the neural basis of imagination, the Muller-Lyer Illusion, and the ergograph test. In these books, actual children or teaching situations seldom if ever make their appearance. For the course in educational psychology to function in the work of the teacher, only that content should be selected and emphasized which has maximal educational applicability.

Another reason why courses in educational psychology may fail to influence greatly the behavior of teachers is that principles and theories are often learned apart from their application. *Individuals learn to do what they do.*[7] If teachers or prospective teachers commit to memory facts and principles of educational psychology, they should be able to repeat them verbally at some later date provided forgetting does not set in too rapidly. However, a teacher's ability to recite psychological facts or principles gives no assurance that he will be able to utilize them when educational problems are encountered in the schoolroom. If the educational psychology course is to have important and lasting effects upon teaching procedures and techniques, it will have to tie up theory and practice in a very definite way. Specific educational implications of psychological facts and principles should be pointed out both in the text and in class discussions. Students should be given abundant opportunity to study, from a psychological viewpoint, typical educational problems. The educational psychology class itself may be studied. Public school classrooms may be visited and the activities evaluated in terms of sound principles of educational psychology. Whenever possible, observation and study of individual children should be undertaken by members of the class.

The teacher who would successfully guide the development, learning, and adjustment of children must (1) possess a comprehensive and integrated set of psychological principles which explain human behavior, (2) possess a technique for studying the individual child in order to determine which principles explain his behavior in a given situation, and (3) be able to analyze his own teaching and learning procedures. The teacher who knows psychological principles, but who does not know the particular facts regarding a given child will be ineffective in his work. Equally ineffective will be the teacher who knows numerous facts about an individual child, but who does not possess a well-formulated set of principles to explain behavior. The teacher's position is similar to that of the medical practitioner who must first study his patient before prescribing for him. The teacher who knows his pupils, knows psychological principles, but does not know how to diagnose and improve his own behavior and his relationship with his pupils will also be ineffective. In short, if educational psychology is to function in the work of the teacher, it will have to assist him to develop competence in study-

[7] For a thorough elaboration of this principle see E. R. Guthrie, *The Psychology of Learning*, Revised Edition, New York, Harper & Brothers, 1952.

ing children, in utilizing psychological principles, and in evaluating his own teaching methods.

ORGANIZATION AND PLAN OF THE BOOK

The book contains six units or parts as follows: Part I, Introduction; Part II, Growth and Development; Part III, Learning; Part IV, Adjustment and Guidance; Part V, Measurement and Evaluation; and Part VI, The Psychology of the Teacher. In Parts II, III, and IV, the basic facts and principles of child and adolescent growth, learning, and adjustment are presented together with applications to school practice and problems for psychological study. Part V is devoted to a study of instruments, methods, and procedures teachers may use in evaluating the results of the educational programs with which they are concerned. The purpose of Part VI is to acquaint the student with professional and personal problems of a psychological nature which teachers face in the course of their work. This section is designed to help teachers understand themselves and the teaching-learning situations of which they are or will be a part.

PART II

GROWTH
AND DEVELOPMENT

Chapter 2

The Biological and Social
Bases of Behavior

AN INDIVIDUAL at any stage of his development is the product of organic and environmental factors working hand in hand. What he is; what he does; what he becomes; in short, how he reacts and behaves in all life situations can be explained in terms of these two interacting forces. The teacher should understand the nature and mechanisms of these two bases of behavior in order properly to diagnose and guide the growth and development of children. For example, a child may misbehave in school because of an abnormal glandular condition or he may misbehave because he comes from a home where good manners are not stressed. A child may fail to learn because of a vitamin deficiency or because he is not sufficiently motivated.

The behavior of a human being is obviously, to a large extent, dependent upon his biological inheritance. Children, for example, can perform many acts which are impossible for lower animals to perform just because they have the organic equipment of human beings. "It is man's large and complex cerebrum which makes possible the use of abstraction and enables him to develop symbolization and language." [1]

On the other hand it is equally clear that there could be no development whatsoever without environmental stimulation. No organism could live or grow in a vacuum. A basic property of protoplasm (living substance) is irritability. Without stimulation no modifica-

[1] *Child Growth and Development Emphases in Education*, American Association of Teachers Colleges, 1944, p. 30.

tion or differentiation of protoplasm would be possible. Changes in both structure and function of the body are dependent upon physical and chemical changes within its protoplasm.

A few of the differences which exist between human beings and some of the lower animals may even be traceable to environmental differences. For example, Kellogg's ape when reared in the same environment with a child learned to play ball and tag, and to work with the form board and to scribble.[2] The home-raised chimpanzee of Hayes [3] learned to say "mama" at fourteen months of age and to use in a meaningful manner the words "papa" and "cup." Certainly many of the differences which exist between human beings of a given chronological age can be attributed to differences in environmental conditions. Persons of similar heredity reared in different environments clearly grow differently and behave differently. The African aboriginal who is reared in the United States becomes civilized and takes on many forms of behavior which are unknown to his brother who remains in the jungles of Africa. City children play games which differ from those of country children. People in different geographical locations possess distinctive language accents. Children from different social classes learn different forms of behavior with regard to family relationships, sex, aggression, and work, and acquire different codes of right and wrong.[4]

Although it is probably impossible to attribute any specific act or form of behavior entirely to either organic or environmental causes, it is possible to discuss each separately and to note the important role each plays in the growth of behavior.

ORGANIC BASIS OF BEHAVIOR

The Mechanism of Heredity. Each child begins life as a one-celled organism known as a *zygote*. This first speck of life which is about $\frac{1}{125}$ of an inch in diameter is formed from the union of a *sperm* from the father and an *ovum* from the mother. In this ferti-

[2] W. N. Kellogg and L. A. Kellogg, *The Ape and the Child: A Study of Environmental Influence upon Early Behavior*, New York, McGraw-Hill Book Company, Inc., 1933, p. 314.

[3] Keith J. Hayes and Catherine Hayes, "The Intellectual Development of a Home-Raised Chimpanzee," *Proceedings of the American Philosophical Society*, Vol. 95, 1951, pp. 105–109.

[4] Allison Davis, "Child Training and Social Class," *Child Behavior and Development* (Barker, Kounin and Wright, editors), New York, McGraw-Hill Book Company, Inc., 1943, p. 607.

lized cell there are twenty-four pairs of *chromosomes,* half of which have been contributed by the father and half by the mother. Each chromosome consists of a string of tiny particles arranged in linear fashion known as *genes.* These genes appear to be the ultimate bearers of heredity. The zygote or fertilized ovum contains all the hereditary potentialities the individual will ever realize.

There is considerable evidence that physical traits such as eye color, skin color, blood types, color blindness, and tendencies to be tall, short, heavy, or light follow the laws of heredity. It is not known to what extent mental traits are inherited. A discussion of the factors related to mental growth and development will be found in later sections of this chapter.

The Human Organism. The one-celled organism or zygote, described in the previous paragraph, grows by a process of cell division and specialization, and in time (approximately 280 days) reaches a stage of growth which makes it unnecessary to remain *in utero.* It emerges into the outside world and is known as a *neonate* or new-born child. This human organism is equipped with receptor organs (such as those for seeing, hearing, smelling, tasting, and feeling), effector organs for making movements (muscles and glands), and an integrating system (the nervous system). Without this equipment it would obviously be impossible for the child to grow or to develop new forms of behavior.

Physical Needs of the Child. The individual at birth, and at later stages of development, possesses a wide variety of physical needs or drives which demand satisfaction. These bodily, or tissue, needs create a state of restlessness or tension in the organism which is only reduced when the appropriate goal [5] or satisfier is reached. The physical needs or drives of the individual serve as potent motivators of behavior. A child whose basic physical needs are severely frustrated will not develop or behave normally. Frequently such children become problems in school. Among the major physical needs of the child which teachers and parents should keep in mind are the following:

The need for food, air, liquid. The hungry or malnourished child is frequently restless, irritable, and inattentive. Mid-morning lunches and feedings in schools have been known to greatly reduce the amount of

[5] The term *goal* as used here refers to any object or condition which satisfies a need.

nervousness and restlessness in school children. The child who is denied adequate amounts of fresh air or liquid is also tense and unadjusted and hence unable to carry forward his schoolwork in an effective manner.

The need for proper temperature. A schoolroom which is too hot or too cold creates a condition which interferes with the well-being of the child and makes effective study well nigh impossible. The human organism strives to preserve its body temperature from threatened change. Cannon introduced the word "homeostasis" to apply to those constant states which the organism seeks to maintain.[6] The individual becomes ill or dies when his blood temperature varies a few degrees above or below 98.6.

The need for activity and rest. A rhythm of activity and rest seems to be a biological essential in the development of the child. The young child who is forced to remain inactive very long becomes bored, unhappy, and frequently unruly. On the other hand, too extended periods of activity are detrimental to the child's physical and emotional well-being. The tired or overfatigued child is often cranky, stubborn, irritable, and in no condition to profit from learning experiences. Meek feels that pupils of secondary school age particularly need guidance in striking the correct balance between activity and rest. She says, "Probably this tendency to abandon what appears to be a fundamental biological pattern of living is greatest during the period when young people are in school. The upsurging of new vital power characteristic of the puberal cycle, coupled with increasing independence in planning and doing, causes young people at this stage to resent any interruption of continuous zestful activity. From the point of view of education there is need to guide these emerging adolescents toward an appreciative acceptance of the rhythmic alternation of relaxation and effort not only because it enhances the satisfaction in living at the time but also because it establishes a pattern which becomes increasingly important as life goes on."[7]

The need for elimination. Regular and adequate elimination of the waste products of the body is an important biological need. Children who have irregular habits in this matter and who suffer from constipation are often irritable, physically ill, and unsuccessful with their school work. There are schoolteachers who will not permit children to leave the room to take care of this physical need regardless of the urgency. Other teachers are known to the writer who permit pupils to leave the classroom in case of

[6] W. B. Cannon, *The Wisdom of the Body,* New York, Norton & Co., Inc., 1932.

[7] Lois Hayden Meek, *The Personal-Social Development of Boys and Girls with Implications for Secondary Education,* New York, Progressive Education Association, 1940, p. 24.

necessity, but who require everyone who does so to stay fifteen minutes after school as a punishment. Needless to say, such lack of insight on the part of teachers with respect to this basic need may cause both physical and mental harm to children under their control.

The sex drive. The psychologist Sigmund Freud and others of the psycho-analytic school have held that frustration of this basic need is a chief cause of personality maladjustments and nervous disorders.[8] This contention contains much truth, since we know that the frustration of any basic need may lead to maladjustment. Small children are curious about sex and should receive straightforward and accurate information from teachers and parents. Appropriate sex instruction should also be given to older children who are at more advanced stages of sexual development. In our society, as in most others, numerous conventions and taboos are enforced with regard to expression of the sex drive. It is, therefore, necessary for most young people of adolescent age to "sublimate" or develop substitute outlets for this energy until such a time as marriage is possible. School activities such as sports, parties, dances, and plays provide wholesome outlets of importance.

What About Instincts? At one time it was a very common prac-tice of psychologists and educators to explain much human behavior in terms of "instincts." Instincts were thought of as inborn tenden-cies to respond in certain definite and somewhat complicated ways without previous experience or training. William James,[9] one of America's first great psychologists, listed twenty-eight human in-stincts with nine subordinate varieties. McDougall [10] recognized seven principal instincts in man: the instinct of flight, the instinct of repulsion, the instinct of curiosity, the instinct of pugnacity, the in-stinct of self-abasement, the instinct of self-assertion, and the pa-rental instinct. Thorndike in 1913 [11] enumerated forty or more differ-ent types of instinctive reactions of which the following are samples: hunting, collecting and hoarding, fighting, motherly behavior, gre-gariousness, rivalry, cooperation, greed, ownership, kindliness, teas-ing, imitation, cleanliness, and play.

[8] Sigmund Freud, *New Introductory Lectures on Psychoanalysis,* New York, Norton & Co., Inc., 1933.

[9] William James, *Principles of Psychology,* Vol. II, New York, Henry Holt and Company, 1890, p. 440.

[10] William McDougall, *Introduction to Social Psychology,* Boston, John W. Luce Company, 1923, Chap. 3.

[11] Edward L. Thorndike, *Educational Psychology,* Vol. I, *The Original Na-ture of Man,* New York, Teachers College, Columbia University, 1913.

Recent research on infant behavior and on children in nursery schools seems to point to the conclusion that human instincts are either relatively few or do not exist at all in any pure and unmodified form.[12] John B. Watson, the behaviorist, was one of the first of present day psychologists to question the existence of elaborate and numerous instincts in man. He says,

Everything we have been in the habit of calling "instinct" today is a result largely of training—belonging to man's *learned behavior*. As a corollary from this, I wish to draw the conclusion that there is no such thing as the inheritance of *capacity, talent, temperament, mental constitution and characteristics*. These things again depend on training that goes on mainly in the cradle. The behaviorist would *not* say, "He inherits his father's capacity or talent for being a fine swordsman." He would say: "This child certainly has his father's slender build of body, the same type of eyes. His build is wonderfully like his father's. He too has the build of a fine swordsman." And he would go on to say: "—and his father is very fond of him. He put a tiny sword into his hand when he was a year of age, and in all their walks he talks sword play, attack and defense, the code of dueling and the like." A certain type of structure, plus early training—slanting—accounts for adult performance. . . .

So let us hasten to admit—yes, there are heritable differences in form, in structure. . . . These differences are in the germ plasm and are handed down from parent to child. . . . But do not let these undoubted facts of inheritance lead you astray. . . . The mere presence of these structures tell you not one thing about function. . . . Much of our structure laid down in heredity would never come to light, would never show in function, unless the organism were put in a certain environment, subjected to certain stimuli and forced to undergo training.[13]

A somewhat similar point of view has been taken by Griffith who states: "In brief, it begins to look as though the word 'instinct' should be dropped out of educational theory and practice altogether. . . . Instead of saying that any attitude or action whose history is not known must, on that account alone, be instinctive or original, the teacher ought now to confess that no aspect of human nature should be called native or original until it has been definitely

[12] K. C. Pratt, A. K. Nelson, and K. H. Sun, *The Behavior of the Newborn Infant*, Ohio State University Studies, Contributions to Psychology, No. 10, 1930.

[13] John B. Watson, "What the Nursery Has to Say About Instincts," *Journal of Genetic Psychology*, Vol. 32, June, 1925, pp. 293–327.

shown to be almost, if not quite, wholly independent of the processes of training during the preschool years." [14]

Too often in the past the term "instinct" was used as a cover up
for ignorance as to the precise cause of some specific behavior pattern. If a child or group of children were observed to perform some
act for which a scientific explanation was unavailable, the behavior
was apt to be labeled instinctive. The same general practice prevailed in the past in the field of animal study. Cats were supposed
to have a rat killing instinct because they were observed to have
killed rats. Birds were said to have a migratory instinct because
it was known that they flew away at certain seasons of the year.
Young salmon were supposed to possess some mysterious instinct
or "ancestral memory of the sea" which caused them in their second
year of life to leave the headwaters of inland streams and to journey
downstream to the ocean depths from which their parents came.

As the result of carefully controlled experimentation, it is now believed that rat killing behavior on the part of cats is an acquired response. Kittens who are brought up with rats and who have never
seen their mothers kill rats learn to "love" them and to play with
them, and do them no bodily harm. On the other hand, kittens who
have been raised in a more traditional environment in which they
have observed their mothers killing rats almost always develop into
rat killers. [15]

Controlled experimentation with birds has shown that migration
either in a northerly or southerly direction is caused by endocrine
changes which are controlled by the amount of daily illumination
which acts upon the birds. [16]

In the case of young salmon, it is now known that a loss of skin
pigmentation, which occurs as the result of normal growth, is the
cause for their downstream migration. The disappearance of the
pigment makes their skin extremely sensitive to light. In the shallow
waters of the inland streams, the illumination from the sun becomes
so irritating that the salmon seek relief in deeper pools or are rendered inert and carried by the current tail first downstream. Over a

[14] Coleman R. Griffith, *An Introduction to Educational Psychology,* New
York, Farrar and Rinehart, Inc., 1935, p. 35.

[15] Z. Y. Kuo, "The Genesis of the Cat's Response to the Rat," *Journal of Comparative Psychology,* Vol. 2, 1930, pp. 1–30.

[16] W. Rowan, *The Riddle of Migration,* Baltimore, Williams and Wilkins,
1931, Chap. IV.

period of time they reach the sea where they spend the next three or four years of their life.[17]

The word instinct, at least as it applies to human beings, has become so misused and has carried so many unscientific connotations that it has been almost entirely dropped by psychologists. Instead of labeling certain forms of behavior "instinctive," and closing the matter at that point, there is an increasing tendency to try to discover what environmental or biological conditions produce the activity in question.

The child seems to begin life with a few basic physical needs or drives as have been mentioned earlier, and a few somewhat undifferentiated and not too specific reflexes (sucking, swallowing, etc.). He is also equipped with receptor organs (sense organs), effector organs (muscles and glands), and a nervous system. From this simple beginning more complex behavior is developed as the result of the child's interaction with his environment. This further growth and development involves changes due both to maturation and learning.

The Effect of the Glands upon Behavior. There are two types of glands—the duct glands and the ductless (endocrine) glands. The duct glands or glands of external secretion, as they are sometimes called, convey their secretions through tubes (ducts) to some opening on the surface of the body or the mucous lining. Among the more important duct glands are the following: salivary glands, gastric glands, liver, pancreas, kidneys, sweat glands, sebaceous glands, tear glands, and sex glands. The salivary and gastric glands and the liver and pancreas serve primarily in the digestion of food. The kidneys serve an important excretory function; the sweat glands and sebaceous (oily) glands also excrete waste products from the body, and in addition condition the skin, and help regulate the body temperature. The tear glands lubricate the eyes, and the sex glands serve in reproduction.

The ductless or endocrine glands (glands of internal secretion) are the ones about which so much has been written for popular consumption and which seem to be so strikingly connected with normality and abnormality of behavior. The endocrine glands have no special ducts or outlets, but instead secrete their products directly into the blood stream, which carries them to all the tissues of the

[17] L. Roule, *Fishes: Their Journeys and Migrations* (trans.), New York, W. W. Norton & Company, 1933, Chaps. 2–6.

body. The products of the endocrines are powerful drug-like substances known as *hormones*. The chief endocrine glands are the thyroid, pituitary, parathyroid, adrenal, sex (in part), pineal, thymus, pancreas (in part) and the liver. The location of these glands is shown in Figure 1.

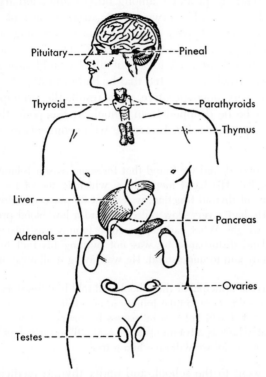

FIGURE 1. Locations of the Principal Endocrine Glands.
(From J. F. Dashiell, *Fundamentals of General Psychology*, p. 295. Copyright, 1949, by Houghton Mifflin Company, Boston.)

The thyroid gland. Of the endocrine glands, probably more is definitely known about the thyroid gland and its effects upon behavior than is known about any of the others. This gland, which is about the size of a walnut, consists of two lobes which are situated in the neck on either side of the windpipe. The functioning of the thyroid gland has marked effects upon the growth of intelligence, on the rate of metabolism, and on behavior in general. If this gland is defective at birth or wastes away while the child is very young, a condition known as *cretinism* results. The cretin is stunted in height, exhibits feeblemindedness at the imbecile or idiotic levels, possesses little emotional color, and is incapable of taking care of himself. Underfunctioning of the thyroid gland in school children and adults tends to produce, among other things, lethargy, diminished metabolism, and overweight. A striking case of a fifteen-year-old boy whose thyroid gland was not functioning properly is reported by Lawrence, a Boston physician.[18] This boy, who had previously done excellent work in school, all of a sudden began to fail miserably. His teachers reported that he had lost interest in his studies, and was very uncooperative. As a result, the principal recommended that he be dropped from school. At this point the parents brought the boy to see Dr. Lawrence who comments as follows on the case:

We went to work and we found that for some reason Johnny's thyroid had left him flat. His basal metabolism, which is one of the important measurements of thyroid function, was about 35 per cent below the normal range. He had a very slow pulse. He had a low blood pressure. He was gaining weight. What had happened to Johnny was this: because of a thyroid gland disturbance he was not burning his fuel to give him energy to study and to understand. He was laying it all away in the form of weight.

I called up the principal of the school, and told him the story, and said, "I wish you would agree to take Johnny in next fall, and just to make this a sporting event, I will bet you he passes his courses all the year long." The principal, who was a friend of mine, said, "If you have got something you think you can do, we will give him a try."

The boy went to the school, and under thyroid medication took honors in every subject.[19]

Mateer describes a six-year-old child whose behavior was also adversely affected by lowered thyroid activity. She says,

This child, reared with the assistance of a pediatrician, properly handled by intelligent parents, and given an excellent environment, had been under preschool and kindergarten training for two years with no per-

[18] Charles H. Lawrence, M.D. "The Endocrine Factor in Personality Development," *The Educational Record*, Vol. 23, Supplement No. 15, January, 1942, pp. 88–89.
[19] *Ibid.*, p. 89.

ceptible gain in self-reliance, initiative, or even normal social responses. Careful scrutiny of every phase of her life revealed only minute deviations of a physical nature that might be due to lowered thyroid activity. The personality traits, however, confirmed the possibility of subnormal glandular functioning. Entrance into first-grade work brought no better response, and after one month in that work a very small daily dose of thyroid extract was started. In three weeks the child was taking a normal and very active part in all group activities, and within the next month she had asserted herself to the point of exercising leadership which was readily accepted by her group.[20]

In the two cases just described marked improvement in behavior was noted as the result of feeding the individuals thyroid tissues or extracts. Many individuals suffering from a shortage of thyroxine, including cretins,[21] have been brought up to normal or near normal as a consequence of such treatment. The feedings, however, must usually be continued in order for the individual to maintain the gains he has made.

Overdevelopment or hyperfunctioning of the thyroid gland creates a condition of "increased nervous tension, accelerated pulse, loss of body weight, and increased oxygen consumption. In short, the body tissues are overstimulated throughout. The results in the life processes are comparable with those of opening the draughts of a furnace. The basal metabolic rate that mirrors this forced draught may be doubled." [22]

A good example of a case of hyperthyroid activity is that of Alice, a fifth-grade child in the Winnetka schools. "She bothered children around her by continually whispering; she talked out loud when the class was supposed to be quiet; she interrupted; she was constantly out of her seat wandering around the room to sharpen her pencil needlessly, to drop a piece of paper in the wastebasket, or perhaps

[20] Florence Mateer, "The Correction of Special Difficulties through Glandular Therapy," *The National Elementary Principal*, Vol. 15, No. 6, Fifteenth Yearbook, July, 1936, pp. 543–544.

[21] A. Gesell, C. S. Amatruda, and C. S. Culotta, "Effect of Thyroid Therapy on Mental and Physical Growth of Cretinous Infants," *American Journal of Diseases of Children*, Vol. 52, 1936, pp. 1117–1292.

A. W. Brown, I. P. Bronstein, and R. Kraines, "Hypothyroidism and Cretinism in Childhood: VI. Influence of Thyroid Therapy on Mental Growth," *American Journal of Diseases of Children*, Vol. 57, 1939, pp. 517–523.

[22] R. G. Hoskins, M.D., *Endocrinology: The Glands and Their Functions*, New York, W. W. Norton and Company, Inc., 1941, p. 91.

without any reason whatever." [23] The teacher worked for months trying to get Alice to be still and to "behave herself," but she was unsuccessful. Treatment of her thyroid gland by a physician and the teacher's improved methods of dealing with her in school, which were suggested by the physician, however, brought marked changes in Alice's behavior. By the end of the school year she had ceased to be a problem child.

In treating hyperthyroidism it is necessary to decrease the amount of glandular secretion that is pouring into the blood stream. The usual method is to remove part of the thyroid gland by a surgical operation, although some practitioners destroy a portion of the gland by means of X-ray or radium treatments.

The pituitary gland. Malfunctioning of the pituitary gland in a child frequently creates conditions which may have important effects upon his personality and behavior. This gland, which is about the size of a large pea, is located in a small pocket in the center of the head. Underfunctioning of the gland leaves the child short, and physically and sexually underdeveloped. Pituitary deficiency also plays a more or less definite part in the production of "Frohlich's disease." Individuals suffering from this disorder are extremely fat. Overfunctioning of the gland may result in *gigantism* and precocious sexual maturity.

It is well known that marked physical deviations of the type just mentioned greatly affect the personal-social adjustment of children. Stolz and Stolz report that lack of size, excessive height or weight and other physical deviations greatly disturb adolescent boys and girls.[24] The same holds true with respect to elementary school pupils. Pressey's statement [25] that "anomalies of physical development are the explanation of many a 'problem child'" is a most apt and accurate observation. There is evidence that the course of physical growth and development may be altered, and that personality

[23] Frances Dummer and Carleton Washburne, "Punishments Recommended for School Offenses: A Reply," *Elementary School Journal,* Vol. 29, June, 1929, p. 777.

[24] Herbert R. Stolz, M.D., and Lois Meek Stolz, "Adolescent Problems Related to Somatic Variations," *Adolescence,* Forty-third Yearbook, National Society for the Study of Education, Part I, Chicago, The Department of Education, University of Chicago, 1944, pp. 80–99.

[25] Sidney L. Pressey and Francis P. Robinson, *Psychology and the New Education,* Revised Edition, New York, Harper and Brothers, 1944, p. 11.

changes may be brought about as the result of medical treatment involving the pituitary gland.[26]

The parathyroid glands. These small glands are located upon the thyroid gland, but have no known connection with the thyroid's activity. Removal of the parathyroid glands or marked deficiency in their function causes cramps and convulsions (tetany) which may result in the death of the individual. Less marked deficiency of function produces hyperexcitability, lack of agreeableness, mental depression, and numerous other disorders. In treating a parathyroid deficiency a solution of calcium salt is usually injected into the subject's muscles or veins. Also used are parathyroid extracts and foods containing high calcium content.

The adrenal glands. The paired adrenal glands are small yellowish bodies located at the top or "pole" of each kidney. Each gland consists of two parts—a central portion known as the *medulla* and a surrounding outer portion known as the *cortex*.

The effects of adrenal cortical deficiency are many. These include fatigue, lethargy, weak heart action, low blood pressure, and general interference with the growth process. Overactivity of the adrenal cortex or the existence of tumors on the gland may create a condition known as *adrenal virilism*. This disorder is characterized by precocious growth and sexual maturity. Girls suffering from this disorder may develop excessive facial hair, a deep voice, and other masculine characteristics. Abnormalities resulting from the dysfunction of the adrenal cortex can be treated and ameliorated by means of medication or surgery.

The *medulla* secretes a substance known as "adrenin" or "epinephrin." According to Cannon [27] this substance acts upon the tissues of the body in such a way as to prepare the organism to meet emergency conditions. The proper functioning of the medulla is thus of the greatest importance for the individual's survival and for his adjustment to an ever changing and sometimes hostile environment.

[26] L. A. Lurie, "Pituitary Disturbances in Relation to Personality," *Research Publications of the Association for Research in Nervous and Mental Disease,* Vol. 17, 1938, pp. 547–560.

R. G. Hoskins, *op.cit.,* p. 64 and pp. 172–173.

[27] W. B. Cannon, *Bodily Changes in Pain, Hunger, Fear, and Rage,* Second Edition, D. Appleton-Century Company, 1929.

The sex glands or gonads. The *sex glands* serve both as organs of internal secretion (ductless) and external secretion (duct). As duct glands their function is reproduction. As ductless glands they play an important role in the development of personality and behavior. The male glands are known as *testes* and the female glands as *ovaries*. Inadequate functioning of these glands in either boys or girls may make normal development of the secondary sexual characteristics impossible. Children, especially of adolescent age, are extremely sensitive to differences which exist between them and their peers. Either precocious sexual development or greatly retarded development is a source of great concern and anxiety to them and may have far-reaching effects upon their adjustment to school and to other life situations.

Other endocrine glands. The functions of the *pineal gland,* which is located at the base of the brain, and the *thymus gland,* which is located in the upper thorax, are at present not well known. It is believed, however, that both produce hormones which help to regulate the rate of bodily growth and the onset of puberty. The *pancreas* have small parts located in them known as the *Islands of Langerhans* which secrete *insulin.* Underfunctioning of these glands causes *diabetes.* The liver also possesses endocrine functions which are of great value in supplying energy to working muscles.

In this discussion the different endocrine glands have been listed one by one, and some of their chief functions have been pointed out. It must not be inferred from this, however, that they work independently of one another. Many bodily conditions are created by the joint actions of several of them. For example, the secretions of the thyroid, pituitary, pineal, and sex glands all seem to contribute definitely to the control of growth. Extreme obesity may result from dysfunction of one of several glands, or it may be caused by the interaction of two or more glands. Similarly, sex development seems to be influenced in part not only by the gonads, but also by the action of the pituitary, pineal, thymus, adrenal, and thyroid glands.

The evidence is clear, however, that the glands do produce marked effects upon the physique and behavior of individuals. Teachers should be on the alert for physical or mental signs of glandular disorders in pupils. Any pupil who is a scholastic or behavior problem in school should, when possible, be given a thorough physical examination which includes an endocrine diagnosis. This examination, of course, must be conducted under the personal direction of a medical expert.

Physical and Sensory Defects. The effects of malfunctioning glands upon behavior have just been mentioned. There are many other physical defects or disorders which greatly influence the learning and adjustment of school children. Among these are the following: poor eyesight, defective hearing, diseased tonsils and adenoids, diseased teeth, physical deformities, skin blemishes, defective speech organs, malnutrition, and encephalitis. The child who possesses some physical defect or disease frequently is as much affected by the psychological consequences of the condition as he is by the physical. A child with a hare lip, for instance, might suffer but little in the way of speech disturbance from the defect, but be greatly tormented by over-sensitivity to imagined rejection by his playmates. He might even withdraw from association with other children and fail to learn the social skills necessary for later adjustment.

Poor eyesight. Statistics show that as many as 30 per cent of all school children possess some defect of vision.[28] Most of these defects are correctable, but in many school systems only a small percentage of the children who need ocular attention receive it.

Some time ago the writer was administering a mental test to a group of ninth-grade pupils in an English class in a high school in the West. He noticed that one little girl had apparently fallen asleep because her head seemed to be reclining on her desk. He, therefore, went to the section of the room where she was, with the intention of waking her up. To his surprise he found that she was not asleep but was working intently on the test. She was so near-sighted that it was necessary for her to place her face not more than an inch from the material she was attempting to read. The writer made a mark on her test blank to remind him not to compute an IQ from data gathered under such unfavorable conditions. He also called the teacher's attention to this pupil. The teacher replied that there were undoubtedly many pupils with severe visual defects in the school but that so far as he knew no tests had ever been given, or no effort had ever been made to find out who they were or to do anything about them.

The child whose eyes do not function properly may have difficulty in learning to read, may suffer from headaches or may in some instances develop unwholesome personality adjustments. Children

[28] Edgar Sydenstricker, *Health and Environment*, New York, McGraw-Hill Book Company, 1933, p. 23.

with crossed eyes or with other forms of vertical or lateral imbalance are often very sensitive about the defect.

Defective hearing. The child with defective hearing may develop undesirable forms of behavior. He may avoid talking to people, be sensitive, aloof and suspicious. Furthermore, he may have difficulty in acquiring effective speech patterns, and have trouble with reading and spelling, especially when these subjects are taught with an emphasis upon phonics. It has been estimated that about 14 per cent of school children have defective hearing. Baker states that in any typical classroom "there would normally be at least five out of thirty-five pupils with some hearing defect." [29] Such children often are unnoticed and neglected by their teachers because of the inconspicuousness of this defect.

Physical deviations, deformities, and blemishes. In a study by Stolz and Stolz [30] it was found that physical anomalies of various types greatly disturb boys and girls of adolescent age. Boys were chiefly worried and upset by such manifestations as: lack of size (particularly height), fatness, poor physique, lack of muscular strength, unusual facial features, unusual development in the nipple area, acne, skin blemishes, scars, bowed legs, obvious scoliosis, [31] lack of shoulder breadth, unusually small genitalia, and unusually large genitalia. Physical conditions which bothered girls were: tallness, fatness, facial features, general physical appearance, tallness and heaviness, smallness and heaviness, eye glasses and strabismus, thinness and small breasts, late development, acne, facial hair, big legs, one short arm, scar on face, and brace on back.

Just how such physical defects or deviations may affect the behavior and adjustment of children can be seen from the following letters [32] which were sent by boys to a doctor who conducts a section in a boys' magazine, which deals with problems of physical development.

[29] Harry J. Baker, *Introduction to Exceptional Children,* New York, The Macmillan Company, 1944, p. 82.

[30] Herbert R. Stolz and Lois Meek Stolz, "Adolescent Problems Related to Somatic Variations," The Forty-third Yearbook of the National Society for the Study of Education, Part I, *Adolescence,* The Department of Education, University of Chicago, 1944, pp. 85–86.

[31] A lateral curvature of the spine.

[32] E. D. Partridge, *Social Psychology of Adolescence,* New York, Prentice-Hall, Inc., 1938, pp. 78–82. These letters are used with the permission of *Boys' Life,* the original publisher.

. . . I have been bothered since the last year of high school with pimples and blackheads on my face, and that is what I want to ask you about. I probably could not tell the whole story to a doctor in person even if I had the opportunity, so I am taking this means to put into effect my determination to suffer no longer, but to do something about it. . . .

Time and time again I had thought that I had rid myself of them, only to have another bunch of pimples break out. I know you have read the advertisement of . . . yeast in . . . magazines. Very likely some people laugh at the idea of a boy's complexion keeping him from mixing with people, going places, having a normal life, but everyone of those ads is a reminder of something I have endured. And it's serious; if I thought that I had to live the rest of my years with my trouble, or even many more years, I would rather die today. I'm not afraid of death. I am afraid of life handicapped with pimples. . . .

I am a boy twelve years of age and am very skinny. I am in the seventh grade. In school when we have gym periods and we get in our gym suits, when they see me with my gym suit on they say, "lookit skinny over there," and I hate them to call me that. So I decided to let the fellow have a sock!

The other fellow grabbed me by the arm and said, "skinny, better take it easy because I might sock you and you'll dry up and blow away."

I want your advice on how to get strong with big muscles, and when I get in my gym suit to look like a second Max Baer. Will you please answer this letter and tell me how to be strong. . . . I don't want the boys to call me skinny. . . .

I am fifteen and a half years old, weigh 96 pounds, and am only five feet in height. I still talk in a high pitched, girlish voice. I am several inches shorter than anyone in my class—third year high school.

I have been told that it is just a case of delayed development, but just the same, I am beginning to worry as I show no signs of "sprouting.". . .

Do you think there is anything I can do besides just waiting?

Although the cases which have just been presented show a connection between physical deviations and behavior patterns, it is clear that the social implications of the physical conditions have played a major role in the resultant adjustment of the individuals involved. Pimples in and of themselves, for example, would have little effect upon the behavior of young people if it were not for the attitudes of other individuals toward this condition. In some societies a scarred face is a mark of distinction and is greatly cherished by the possessor.

Malnutrition and behavior. Undernourished children have been shown to be more irritable, restless, and nervous than children who are adequately fed.[33] It has also been shown that an increase in the learning of school children has followed an increase in thiamine (vitamin B_1) intake.[34] Vitamin A deficiency in human beings produces what is known as "night blindness." Studies of the effect of vitamin deficiencies on behavior are becoming more numerous and may eventually shed additional light on behavior and adjustment problems of children.[35]

Encephalitis. This disease of the nervous system has been known to produce vast behavior alterations in children. The case of Blanche is a good illustration.

Blanche was normal until the age of eight when suddenly encephalitis attacked her with crossing of the eyes, double vision, and sleepiness. Conduct disorders appeared: tantrums, jealousy, overactivity, over-affectiveness, obscenities, and sexual misdemeanors. On admission to the hospital she was wild, stole, broke things, upset dishes and trays, and lied about everything. She fought and kicked, laughed when she caused an older person to fall, and kicked a maid viciously. Following this she got in a tub and "assumed an expression of angelic innocence." [36]

ENVIRONMENTAL BASIS OF BEHAVIOR

In previous pages of this chapter, some of the biological and organic factors which influence the growth, development, and behavior of children have been pointed out and discussed. It has constantly been reiterated, however, that there is a continuous reaction between the organism and the environment.[37] The individual makes

[33] D. A. Laird, M. Levitan, and V. A. Wilson, "Nervousness in School Children as Related to Hunger and Diet," *Medical Journal and Record,* Vol. 134, 1931, pp. 494–499.

[34] Ruth F. Harrell, *Effect of Added Thiamine on Learning,* New York, Bureau of Publications, Teachers College, Columbia University, 1943.

[35] For research on the effects of vitamins on behavior see Nathan W. Schock, "Physiological Factors in Behavior," *Personality and the Behavior Disorders,* Vol. I (edited by J. McV. Hunt), New York, The Ronald Press, 1944, pp. 597–600.

[36] Taken from S. L. Pressey and J. E. Janney, *Casebook of Research in Educational Psychology,* New York, Harper & Brothers, 1937, p. 22.

[37] In this discussion of the effect of environment upon behavior, it is well to remember that environment affects the child as *he* perceives it, not as parents, teachers or others see it. It would not be amiss to say that in a given schoolroom, there is not one environment but forty, and in a given home, not a single set of

changes in the environment and the environment in turn produces profound changes in the individual and in his behavior. In some ways, however, it might be said that the environment possesses the "last word." No organism, regardless of its potentialities and basic qualities, can survive in the absence of a favorable environment. Two children of equal constitutional capacities or characteristics may develop in entirely different ways depending upon the nature of the environment in which they are reared. In this connection the sociologist Lynd makes the following comment:

> Persons in the great modal mass of our population are endowed with what we call "normal (i.e., most customary degrees of) intelligence." From the moment of birth, the accidents of cultural status—for instance, whether one is born "north or south of the tracks"—begin to play up and to play down the potentialities of each person. As life progresses, culture writes cumulating differences recklessly into these individual lives; until in adult life two persons of generally similar native endowment will differ so widely that one is on relief, reads the tabloids, and follows Father Coughlin, and the other is a manufacturer, is hostile to expenditures for relief, reads the *New York Herald Tribune,* sends his sons to Harvard, and votes for Landon.[38]

The average teacher probably does not realize the tremendous significance of environmental and cultural factors as they affect the attitudes, adjustments and behavior of children. In the next few pages a brief résumé will be made of some of these non-biological conditions and the ways they influence behavior and personality of growing individuals.

Effect of the Environment on Prenatal Development. Actually the environment begins to affect the course of development of the individual as soon as he is conceived. This belief is reinforced by studies from the field of experimental embryology which have clearly shown that by altering the chemical environments of salamanders, squids, and other animals, marked changes in bodily structures can

---

external circumstances, but as many as there are persons in the family. It is crucial, in attempts to understand children, that teachers find out how the child perceives the situations that surround him. Such a proceduce should greatly facilitate the prediction and control of youngsters' behavior. For additional discussion of this point, see D. Snygg and A. W. Combs, *Individual Behavior,* New York, Harper & Brothers, 1949.

[38] Robert S. Lynd, *Knowledge for What?* pp. 229–230. Copyright, 1939, by Princeton University Press, Princeton.

be brought about.[39] In the case of the squid which normally has two eyes, a one-eyed specimen can be obtained by exposing the embryo to a solution of one per cent LiCl in sea water from twelve to forty-eight hours.[40] For obvious reasons no such experiments have been performed with human embryos. Several studies have been made, however, of the effects of external stimulation upon the behavior of the human fetus. In one such study it was shown that it is possible successfully to condition the unborn fetus.[41] It is possible that left-handedness and other human characteristics may be in part due to prenatal conditioning.

Some Effects of the Environment on Mental Development. An increasing number of investigations have clearly shown the remarkable way that mental growth may be facilitated or retarded by factors present in the environment. Of particular interest are those studies which have been made of children reared in foster homes, and children reared in isolated and backward communities.

Studies of children reared in foster homes. Studies by Skeels,[42] Skodak,[43] Harms,[44] Snygg,[45] Speer[46] and others have all shown the beneficial effect upon IQs of children who have been taken from poor homes and placed in superior adoptive homes or boarding houses. Two of these studies, the one by Skodak and the one by Speer, will be briefly reviewed.

Skodak's investigation was based upon 154 children, 140 of which were illegitimate, and all of whom were placed for adoption under six months of age, the average age being 2.8 months. The average

---

[39] Paul Weiss, *Principles of Development,* New York, Henry Holt and Company, 1939.

[40] See John J. B. Morgan, *Child Psychology,* Third Edition, New York, Farrar & Rinehart, Inc., 1942, p. 46.

[41] D. K. Spelt, "Conditioned Responses in the Human Fetus," *Psychological Bulletin,* Vol. 35, 1938, pp. 712–713.

[42] Harold M. Skeels, "Mental Development of Children in Foster Homes," *Journal of Consulting Psychology,* Vol. 2, 1938, pp. 33–43.

[43] Marie Skodak, *Children in Foster Homes: A Study of Mental Development,* University of Iowa Studies of Child Welfare, Vol. 16, No. 1, 1939, 156 pp.

[44] Irene E. Harms, *Children with Inferior Social Histories: Their Development in Adoptive Homes,* University of Iowa, Unpublished Master's Thesis, 1941.

[45] Donald Snygg, "The Relation Between the Intelligence of Mothers and of Their Children Living in Foster Homes," *Journal of Genetic Psychology,* Vol. 52, 1938, pp. 401–406.

[46] George S. Speer, "The Mental Development of Children of Feebleminded and Normal Mothers," *The Thirty-Ninth Yearbook of the National Society for the Study of Education,* Part II, 1940, pp. 309–314.

IQs of the true mothers of these children was 88 as revealed by the Stanford-Binet test. The occupational levels of the true fathers were markedly below that found in the general population.

Both true mothers and fathers were found to be on the whole socially inferior, shiftless, and irresponsible. The foster homes in which the children were placed were distinctly superior to the average run of homes, and in each case was rated as a good place in which to rear a child. Since the children were mere infants (average age, 2.8 months) at the time of adoption, no mental tests had been given them at that time. However, they were tested after they had lived with their foster parents nearly two years, and again after they had lived with them approximately four years. On the first test, when the children were about two years old, the average IQ was found to be 116; on the second test, when the children had reached a mean age of four years and four months, the average IQ was 112. Both of these figures are well above the averages for the general population of children of the same ages. In referring to the Skodak study, George D. Stoddard states: "Children like these, if left in their own homes, would on the average show a mental retardation." [47] Yet, we find these children early reaching a most satisfactory intellectual level.

Speer made a study of 68 dependent children all of whose mothers are definitely feebleminded as judged by mental test results and social criteria. He says: "All but one of the mothers were committed to state institutions for the mentally defective. The mean IQ of the mothers is 49.0, with a range from 38 to 64. The children have been placed in boarding homes [48] selected and supervised by the Children's Service League." [49] The Children's Service League is the child caring agency responsible for all dependent children in Sangamon County, Illinois. The fathers of the children are described as being either unemployed or engaged in unskilled labor and as being "irresponsible, alcoholic, epileptic, mentally ill, or venereally diseased."

[47] George D. Stoddard, *The Meaning of Intelligence*, New York, The Macmillan Company, 1943, pp. 356–357.

[48] Speer says: "The age at which these children have been placed has not been influenced by any factor other than the need for care. When the mother died, deserted, or was declared incompetent, *all* children in the family under sixteen years of age were declared dependent and placed in boarding homes." G. S. Speer, *op.cit.*, p. 311.

[49] *Ibid.*, p. 310.

In analyzing the mental test scores of these 68 children, Speer made the amazing discovery that children who were taken from their feebleminded mothers and impoverished environments very early in life had approximately average intelligence quotients while those children who remained in their own homes with their feebleminded mothers for more extended periods of time were either mentally retarded or feebleminded. The amount of mental retardation was proportional to the number of years spent in the unfavorable environments. The exact figures for the Speer study are given in Table 1. It is seen that the twelve children who were taken from

TABLE 1

Distribution of IQs of 68 Children of Feebleminded Mothers *

AGE AT PLACEMENT, IN YEARS	NUMBER	MEDIAN IQ
0 to 2	12	100.5
3 to 5	19	83.7
6 to 8	12	74.6
9 to 11	9	71.5
12 to 15	16	53.1

* From Speer.

their own homes before they were three years old had, at the time of the testing, on the average, IQs of 100.5. On the other hand, the sixteen children who remained from 12 to 15 years in their definitely poor environments scored an average IQ of only 53.1 on the tests.

In commenting upon his study, Speer says: "The data presented here do not support the position of agencies in refusing to place for adoption children of mentally deficient mothers. Insofar as the data of the present study are concerned, there is no reason why physically normal children of feebleminded mothers may not be placed for adoption, from their own homes, provided this is done before the third birthday." [50]

Studies of children reared in isolated and backward communities. The effect of the environment on the mental development of children is further illustrated by studies which have been made of chil-

[50] George S. Speer, *op.cit.*, p. 314.

dren who have been born and reared in extremely atypical communities. Two very striking examples of such studies are those conducted by Gordon [51] and by Sherman and Key.[52]

Gordon tested 76 English canal boat children ranging in ages from 4 to 14. For this purpose he used the Stanford-Binet Scale. In describing these unique people he says, "The Canal Boat population, as a rule, is born, lives, and dies on the boats. . . . These people appear to live very isolated lives with very little social intercourse." "When the boats remain in a town for loading and unloading, the children do not appear to mix readily with other children." He also states that the children only attend school "about once a month for one to perhaps two and a half days."

TABLE 2

IQs of 76 Canal Boat Children Arranged According to Age Groups *

AGE OF CHILDREN	NUMBER OF CASES	AVERAGE IQ
4, 5, 6, 7	21	84.4
8, 9, 10	27	66.1
11, 12, 13, 14	28	58.4

* Adapted from Gordon.

The test data secured for these 76 underprivileged children reveal two most interesting facts. In the first place it was found that the entire group was very much retarded as measured by the tests—the average IQ being 69.6. In the second place, it was found that the extent of the dullness was proportional to the age of the child. Younger children who had spent fewer years in this impoverished environment had higher IQs than their older brothers and sisters. The correlation between chronological age and IQ is usually zero, but for the canal boat children it was −.755, meaning that the older the child the lower the IQ. How the IQs of the children dropped with age can be seen from the data presented in Table 2.

[51] Hugh Gordon, *Mental and Scholastic Tests Among Retarded Children, Physically Defective, Canal Boat and Gipsy Children and Backward Children in Ordinary Elementary Schools*, London, Board of Education, 1923, Educational Pamphlets, No. 44, 92 pp.

[52] Mandel Sherman and Cora B. Key, "The Intelligence of Isolated Mountain Children," *Child Development*, Vol. 3, 1932, pp. 279–290.

At the conclusion of his study, Gordon states: "The fact that there is a marked decrease in 'intelligence' with an increase of age, and that this is especially noticeable among children in the same family, suggests very convincingly that the low average 'intelligence' of these children is not due to heredity. It may be due to environment, or to the lack of schooling,' or to both combined." [53] The present writer would classify schooling as being part of the environment and hence conclude that the trends shown in Table 2 are due primarily to environmental factors.

Sherman and Key [54] tested 102 isolated mountain children and compared their intellectual ratings with 81 children who lived in a little town (Briarsville) only a few miles distant. They also studied the relationship of chronological age to IQ for these groups. The mountain children lived in four hollows—Colvin, Needles, Oakton, and Rigby—which are located about 100 miles west of Washington, D. C., in the Blue Ridge Mountains. In Colvin Hollow, there is no road to the outside world with the exception of a small trail; all the adults are illiterate except three; school is held most irregularly (a total of sixteen months over an eleven-year period), and many of the children do not know their last names. "They identify themselves, for example, as Sadie's Benny or Dicy's Willie." In the other three hollows the conditions though roughly comparable are probably somewhat superior to those of Colvin Hollow. For example, in Oakton Hollow the school term is approximately four months each year; there is a combined general store and post office and "many of the inhabitants receive mail and an occasional magazine." The town of Briarsville is located at the base of the mountains to the south of the Hollows, has hard surface roads connecting it with principal cities of Virginia, has a four-room modern school with three well-trained teachers, has a good general store, telephones, and receives newspapers.

On the mental tests which were administered, the average intelligence quotient of the Briarsville children was higher than that of the mountain children in every instance. For example, on the *National Intelligence Test*, the average IQ of the mountain children (N = 24) was 61.2, while the average IQ of the Briarsville children (N = 50) was 96.1. An analysis of relationship of age to IQ showed

[53] Hugh Gordon, *op.cit.*, p. 44.
[54] Sherman and Key, *op.cit.*

for the mountain children a tremendous drop in IQ with increasing age. For the Briarsville children there was a slight drop in IQ with increasing age but not nearly so marked as for the mountain children. Of the mountain children those living in Colvin Hollow had the lowest mental ratings. From the standpoint of social development it should be remembered that Colvin Hollow also ranked lowest.

Sherman and Key conclude that "the expression of intelligence, as measured by standardized tests, depends in a large measure upon the opportunities to gather information and upon the requirements made upon the individual by his environment." [55]

In both the Gordon study and the one by Sherman and Key, the average IQs of the underprivileged groups were much below the norms for typical children. Furthermore, the older children had lower IQs than the younger children. This of course does not mean that these children were "dull" or "feebleminded" as these terms are generally used. These data, in the opinion of the writer, clearly show instead that these groups were greatly retarded in skills which have been mastered by children reared in more favorable environments.

Effects of the Environment upon Personality. Environmental factors not only play a most important role in the mental development of the individual, but also have much to do with the type of character and personality he will develop. The effects of the culture upon the attitudes, ideals, and behavior patterns of individuals have been clearly shown by social anthropologists [56] who have studied various primitive peoples.

The mountain-dwelling Arapesh of New Guinea,[57] for example, are a highly cooperative, peaceful, docile, and unaggressive type

[55] *Op.cit.*, p. 289.

[56] G. Bateson and M. Mead, *Balinese Character: A Photographic Analysis*, New York Academy of Sciences, Vol. 2, 1942.

Wayne Dennis, *The Hopi Child*, New York, D. Appleton-Century Company, 1940.

M. Mead (editor), *Cooperation and Competition Among Primitive Peoples*, New York, McGraw-Hill Book Company, Inc., 1937.

M. Mead, *From the South Seas*, New York, William Morrow and Company, 1939.

J. W. M. Whiting, *Becoming a Kwoma*, New Haven: Yale University Press, 1941.

[57] M. Mead, *Sex and Temperament in Three Primitive Societies*, New York, William Morrow and Company, 1935.

of people. Their children seldom show temper tantrums or steal and lie. One hundred miles away from the Arapesh, however, lives the river-dwelling Mundugumor tribe. These people are highly competitive, suspicious of one another, aggressive, and violent. Among the lake-dwelling Tchambuli, also a tribe in New Guinea, the roles of men and women are completely reversed from what they are in American culture. The women do the farming, fishing, hunting, and other heavy work, while the men stay at home, look after the children, and devote themselves to artistic pursuits. The women thus develop typically masculine personalities and the men appear effeminate according to our standards. These differences in temperament and personality found to exist between the Arapesh, Mundugumor, and Tchambuli peoples can be traced very definitely to their respective systems of social organization and methods of child rearing.

Even in our own society, we have subcultures or classes each of which leave their marks on the personality of the individuals belonging to them. Allison Davis brings this out very clearly in discussing the relationship of the caste and class structure of American society to the personality development of adolescents. He says:

Lower-class culture, white or Negro, organizes adolescent behavior with regard to aggression, sexual relations, age roles, and family roles, to mention only a few of the basic types of relationships into patterns which differ radically from those of middle-class adolescents. . . . In the middle class, aggression is clothed in the conventional forms of "initiative," or "ambition," or even "progressiveness," but in the lower class it more often appears unabashed as physical attack, or as threats of and encouragement of physical attack. . . . The lower classes not uncommonly teach their children and adolescents to strike out with fist or knife and be certain to hit first. Both girls and boys at adolescence may curse their father to his face or even attack him with fists, sticks, or axes in free-for-all family encounters. Husbands and wives sometimes stage pitched battles in the home, wives have their husbands arrested, and husbands try to break in or burn down their own homes when locked out. Such fights with fists or weapons, and the whipping of wives occurs sooner or later in many lower-class families. They may not appear today, nor tomorrow, but they *will* appear if the observer remains long enough to see them.[58]

[58] Allison Davis, "Socialization and Adolescent Personality," in *Adolescence,* Forty-Third Yearbook of the National Society for the Study of Education, 1944, p. 209. Quoted by permission of the Society.

Much evidence in recent years has also clearly shown the effect of family influences upon the personality development of the child.[59] Neurotic parents are often directly responsible for similar traits found in their children. Children who are rejected by their parents are very likely to be aggressive, negativistic, quarrelsome, rebellious, or untruthful. The over-protected child is likely to be submissive, anxious, and lacking in self-reliance. The Viennese psychologist, Alfred Adler, and his students have also stressed the importance of such other family members as brothers, sisters, and grandparents as factors influencing the character and personality of the child. For example, Dr. Rudolph Dreikurs states:

The child's position in the family entails a great variety of trials and stimulates the development of certain traits and qualities. The second-born child is generally more active in good and in evil; he acts as if he had to make up for lost time. The first-born, on the other hand, may be troubled his whole life long by the feeling that his position is under threat.[60]

Although the evidence with respect to birth order *per se* and personality is somewhat confused and unconvincing, there is little question but that certain situations and relationships resulting from a child's position in the family constellation do have marked effects upon his behavior and personality.

In concluding this chapter, the writer would like to cite the excellent statement of the psychologist Kurt Lewin. He says:

One can say that behavior and development depend upon the state of the person and his environment, $B = F (P, E)$.[61] In this equation the person P and his environment E have to be viewed as variables which are mutually dependent upon each other. In other words, to understand or to predict behavior, the person and his environment have to be considered as one constellation of interdependent factors.[62]

[59] M. M. Bolles, H. F. Metzger, and M. W. Pitts, "Early Home Background and Personality Adjustment," *American Journal of Orthopsychiatry*, Vol. 11, 1941, pp. 530–534.

[60] Rudolph Dreikurs, *Manual of Child Guidance,* Ann Arbor, Michigan: Edwards Brothers, Inc., 1946, p. 27.

[61] This equation is read: behavior (B) is a function (F) of the person (P) and his environment (E).

[62] Kurt Lewin, "Behavior and Development as a Function of the Total Situation," in *Manual of Child Psychology*, Leonard Carmichael (editor), New York: John Wiley and Sons, Inc., 1946, p. 792.

The teacher who would understand, control, and predict the behavior of children must, therefore, (1) know the child, his physical condition, needs, and abilities, and (2) know the environmental, social, and cultural forces which are acting upon him.

SUMMARY

The behavior of a child at any given moment is the result of biological and environmental factors operating simultaneously. The child behaves as he does because he is a human being with needs, and because he is surrounded by environmental and cultural forces which determine how these needs shall be met. In this chapter the effect upon child behavior of various physical, biological, and social conditions has been traced. It has been shown, for example, how the action of the glands affects personality, and how sensory and physical defects may alter behavior. Equal attention has been given to the effects of cultural variations upon personality and conduct. Children from isolated and backward communities have been shown to deviate downward from the usual norms on standard tests of intelligence. Children taken from "poor" homes and placed in "superior" foster homes have shown marked increases in mental test scores. In the realm of personality, evidence has been presented that children from the lower socio-economic classes show characteristics which are markedly different from those of children in the middle class. The effects of interfamily relationships on the child's development have also been noted.

The point has been amply documented that what children are to become depends in no small part upon influences arising from the school and other educational agencies. Human nature is highly modifiable and teachers have a crucial role to play in the process of producing desired changes in children's behavior. To understand the child the teacher must (1) know him as a biological organism with needs and goals, and (2) must know the social and psychological environment of which he is a part.

REFERENCES FOR FURTHER STUDY

Cameron, A. T., *Recent Advances in Endocrinology*, Philadelphia, The Blakiston Company, 1947.

Doob, Leonard W., *Social Psychology*, New York, Henry Holt and Company, 1952.

Frank, Lawrence K., *Nature and Human Nature,* New Brunswick, New Jersey, Rutgers University Press, 1951.

Hayes, Cathy, *The Ape in Our House,* New York, Harper and Brothers, 1951.

Hoskins, R. G., *Endocrinology, The Glands and Their Functions,* New York, W. W. Norton and Company, 1941.

Kluckhohn, Clyde, and Murray, Henry A. (Editors), *Personality in Nature, Society, and Culture,* New York, Alfred A. Knopf, 1949.

Linton, Ralph, *The Cultural Background of Personality,* New York, Appleton-Century Company, 1945.

Mead, Margaret, *From the South Seas,* New York, William Morrow and Company, 1939.

Montagu, M. F. Ashley, *On Being Human,* New York, Henry Schuman, 1951.

Scheinfeld, Amram, *The New You and Heredity,* Philadelphia, J. B. Lippincott Company, 1950.

Sherif, Muzafer, *An Outline of Social Psychology,* New York, Harper and Brothers, 1948.

Stern, Curt, *Principles of Human Genetics,* San Francisco, W. H. Freeman, 1949.

Stoddard, George D., *The Meaning of Intelligence,* New York, The Macmillan Company, 1943.

Swanson, Guy E., Newcomb, Theodore M., and Hartley, Eugene L., *Readings in Social Psychology,* Revised Edition, New York, Henry Holt and Company, 1952.

Whipple, G. M. (Editor), *Intelligence: Its Nature and Nurture,* Parts I and II, 39th Yearbook of the National Society for the Study of Education, Bloomington, Illinois, Public School Publishing Company, 1940.

Chapter 3

Growth and Development During Childhood

THE HUMAN organism during its life, passes through a number of so-called developmental periods. These might be labeled for convenience (1) the prenatal period, (2) the period of childhood, (3) the adolescent period, (4) adulthood, and (5) senescence. Much of value has been written about each of these stages of human growth and development. Although teachers are interested in growth trends at all stages of the life cycle, they are probably most concerned with developments that take place during childhood and adolescence since most of their subjects fall in these two categories. This chapter will, therefore, focus its attention upon the period of childhood, and the succeeding chapter will concern itself with the adolescent period.

Generally speaking, the period of childhood may be thought of as extending from birth to puberty. It is a period which varies in length from individual to individual depending upon his rate of growth. Many individuals reach puberty at such early ages as 10 or 11 while others may not complete the cycle of childhood and reach puberty until they are 14 or 15. Extreme cases are on record of individuals who have attained puberty as early as 3 or 4 years of age [1] or as late as 25 or 26.

GENERAL NATURE OF GROWTH

There are a number of principles regarding growth which should be understood by teachers and others who work with children. In

[1] W. W. Greulich, "Physical Changes in Adolescence," in 43rd Yearbook of the National Society for the Study of Education, Part I, *Adolescence*, 1944, p. 17.

the first place growth is continuous and gradual rather than salta-
tory. Although growth is continuous it may be somewhat more
rapid at certain stages than at others. For example, the child during
the first year of life grows in height more rapidly than in any subsequent one year period. The fact of continuity of growth, however,
makes it possible to project curves and to make predictions regarding future growth with some degree of accuracy. Nancy Bayley [2]
for instance has developed a set of tables which can be used for
predicting adult height from the child's present height and skeletal
age. A child's mental capacity at age 9 or 10 is also a fairly reliable
indicator of what it will be at age 12 or 13 provided the environment is held reasonably constant. Although growth in a given trait
can be predicted to some extent, it is most difficult if not impossible
to predict growth in one aspect of personality from the rate of
growth in another. The typical child has many "ages." Thus a child
who is 10 years old chronologically might have a mental age of 12,
a social age of 8, a dental age of 9, a reading age of 7, and a weight
age of 13.[3] The teacher who wishes to match teaching with the developmental level of the child, must clearly understand that un-
evenness of growth in the several traits is more often the rule than
not. A curriculum based upon chronological age alone or on mental
age alone, for example, will fall far short of ministering to the needs
of the whole child.

FUNDAMENTAL NEEDS OF THE CHILD

In Chapter 2, reference was made to the physical or tissue needs
(drives) of the child, e.g., need for food, air, liquid, activity, and
rest. In addition to these biological needs, every child in our society
(and possibly in all human societies), possesses certain social or
personality needs.[4] These latter needs are sometimes referred to as
sociogenic or learned needs. They are, however, among the most
powerful of the human needs. No child can develop properly or
learn effectively whose personality needs are disregarded. The

[2] Nancy Bayley, "Table for Predicting Adult Height from Skeletal Age and
Present Height," *Journal of Pediatrics*, Vol. 28, 1936, pp. 49–64.

[3] A social age of 8 means that a child is as advanced socially as the average
8-year-old; similarly a dental age of 9 indicates that the child is as advanced in
dentition as the average 9-year-old.

[4] For a good discussion of biogenic and sociogenic needs see Muzafer Sherif,
An Outline of Social Psychology, New York, Harper and Brothers, 1948, pp.
9–90.

teacher should constantly ask himself if the activities of the class-room are ministering to these needs of children. Among the important personality needs are the following:

1. *Need for status.* Every child wants recognition and attention. He craves the esteem of his teachers, parents, and peers.

2. *Need for security.* Children desire regularity and stability in their lives. Too much uncertainty as to how they stand in their group or excessive anxiety as to whether they will pass or fail a course creates a very unwholesome condition for them.

3. *Need for affection.* Everyone craves love. The good teacher is one who genuinely likes his pupils. A child becomes uneasy and restless when he discovers that he is not liked by his teacher.

4. *Need for independence.* Children want to take responsibility and to make choices which are commensurate with their abilities. The wise teacher will give children an opportunity to satisfy this need in the many classroom activities which are arranged.

DEVELOPMENTAL TASKS OF CHILDHOOD

Individuals of every age group have problems which must be successfully solved if normal adjustment is to be maintained. The adolescent, for example, must deal with such tasks as attaining emotional independence from his parents, and developing new relations with age-mates of both sexes. The young adult has such special problems as learning to live with a spouse, rearing children, and securing a place for himself in the occupational world. The middle aged adult has such new problems as living harmoniously with adolescent children in the family, adjusting to physiological changes occurring during the menopause, if a woman, or adjusting to decline in general physical capacity, if a man. Still older people often have such unique problems to deal with as adjusting to retirement, or living alone after the death of a husband or wife. Robert J. Havighurst has made a special study of the typical and somewhat unique problems facing human beings at various stages of their existence. He calls these problems or special learning activities "developmental tasks." He has suggested nine basic problems or tasks of infancy and early childhood, and eight tasks for the period of middle childhood.[5] They are as follows:

[5] Robert J. Havighurst, *Developmental Tasks and Education*, pp. 9–26. Copyright, 1950, by Longmans, Green and Company, New York.

Infancy and Early Childhood
1. Learning to walk
2. Learning to take solid foods
3. Learning to talk
4. Learning to control the elimination of body wastes
5. Learning sex differences and sexual modesty
6. Achieving physiological stability
7. Forming simple concepts of social and physical reality
8. Learning to relate oneself emotionally to parents, siblings, and other people
9. Learning to distinguish right and wrong and developing a conscience

Middle Childhood
1. Learning physical skills necessary for ordinary games
2. Building wholesome attitudes toward oneself as a growing organism
3. Learning to get along with age-mates
4. Learning appropriate sex role
5. Developing fundamental skill in reading, writing, and calculating
6. Developing concepts necessary for everyday living
7. Developing conscience, morality, and a scale of values
8. Developing attitudes toward groups and institutions

Most of the above tasks listed for infancy and early childhood are either mastered or will be along the road toward mastery at the time the child enters school. The tasks of middle childhood, however, face the child during the period he is under the guidance of the school. Teachers have the responsibility of helping the child to solve these and similar problems which are particularly important at this stage of his development. The child who fails to master the important developmental tasks of children of his age group is in for trouble. Such failure will have unfortunate effects upon his personality development and his ability to deal with the more advanced tasks facing him at later stages of development.

MENTAL DEVELOPMENT

Consistency of Mental Growth. School teachers are usually very much interested in the child's IQ. They feel that this information will provide them with a measure of what the child can do at the present and also provide them with an indication of what the child will be able to do in the future. The IQ of a child, however, does not give a sure answer to either of these questions. In the first place, it must be recognized that the correlation between mental test scores and school achievement seldom is higher than .60. This means that many factors other than intelligence enter into school success. Teaching methods, the child's interests, and emotional security have much to do with his performance at all educational levels. A child with an IQ of 100 who is highly motivated and who feels secure may do much better work in the first grade, for example, than a child with an IQ of 130 who is uninterested in school or who has severe personality problems. When it comes to predicting what a child's future IQ will be when his present IQ is known, much difficulty and inaccuracy can also result. It is a well known fact that the test scores obtained on children before the age of two bear little relationship to scores obtained on the same children later in life.[6] Even IQs obtained on children at the first or second grade levels may be quite different from those obtained on these same children when they are in high school. Data obtained in the Harvard Growth Study, has shown that the correlation between mental scores at age seven and age sixteen is only slightly above .50.[7]

Probably the most thorough study of IQ stability is one conducted at the Institute of Child Development at the University of California.[8] Two hundred and fifty-two children were given mental tests at specified periods over a span of several years. The results showed that between ages 6 and 18, the IQs of almost 60 per cent of the group changed 15 or more points; the IQs of a third of the group changed 20 or more points; and the IQs of 9 per cent of the group changed 30 or more points. The IQs of 15 per cent of the group shifted less than 10 IQ points, but the IQs of some individuals changed as much as 50 points. The authors conclude from their study that the "fluctuations in the scores of individual children indicate the need for utmost caution in the predictive use of a single test score, or even two such scores. This finding seems of especial importance since many plans for individual children are made by schools,

[6] F. N. Freeman and C. D. Flory, *Growth in Intellectual Ability as Measured by Repeated Tests,* Monographs of the Society for Research in Child Development, Vol. II, No. 2, Washington, National Research Council, 1937.

[7] J. E. Anderson, "The Prediction of Terminal Intelligence from Infant and Preschool Tests," *Intelligence: Its Nature and Nurture,* Part I, 39th Yearbook of the National Society for the Study of Education, 1940, pp. 385–403.

[8] M. P. Honzik, J. W. Macfarlane and L. Allen, "The Stability of Mental Test Performance between Two and Eighteen Years," *Journal of Experimental Education,* Vol. 17, 1948, pp. 309–324.

juvenile courts, and mental hygiene clinics on the basis of a single mental test score. Specifically it should be noted that a prediction based on a 6-year test would be wrong to the extent of 20 IQ points for one out of three children by the age of 18 years, and to the extent of 15 IQ points for approximately six out of ten children." [9]

Language Development. On the average, children begin to talk when they are about fifteen months of age. Any given child may, however, vary greatly from this general norm. Some children utter their first word as early as eight months of age, while it is not at all

TABLE 3

Size of Vocabulary at Different Grade Levels *

GRADE	BASIC	DERIVED	TOTAL
1	16,900	7,100	24,000
2	22,000	12,000	34,000
3	26,000	18,000	44,000
4	26,200	18,800	45,000
5	28,500	22,500	51,000
6	31,500	18,000	49,500
7	35,000	20,000	55,000
8	36,000	20,000	56,000

* From Smith.

uncommon for others to be as old as twenty months or even two years before this happens. The age at which a child starts to talk has often been regarded as symptomatic of his future mental development. Although there is a positive relationship between onset of talking and later mental development, the correlation is far from being perfect. Any parent who attempts to predict his child's future mental ability from the age at which he began to talk is likely to make a very serious error. It is known, of course, that idiots never learn to talk, but on the other hand it is also not uncommon for very highly intelligent individuals to be slow in developing language. In Terman's [10] group of gifted high school children there

9 This quotation taken from Raymond G. Kuhlen and George G. Thompson, *Psychological Studies of Human Development*, New York, Appleton-Century-Crofts, Inc., 1952, p. 158.

10 L. M. Terman, *et al.*, *Genetic Studies of Genius: Vol. 1, Mental and Physical Traits of a Thousand Gifted Children*, Stanford University Press, Stanford University, California, 1925, p. 573.

were some who did not learn to talk until they were 2, 2½, or even 3 years of age.

Although the development of vocabulary in the typical child appears to proceed rather slowly at first, there is very marked acceleration in this regard during the last few years of the preschool period. Smith [11] has reported that the average child knows 16,900 basic words by the time he enters the first grade. The growth of vocabulary from grade I to grade VIII is shown in Table 3.

Sex Differences. During the elementary school years in our culture, there are some rather striking sex differences with respect to mental development and school achievement. Although the average mental ability of boys and girls seems to be equal or is made by the test constructors to be equal age for age, [12] it is noted that girls exceed the boys on the language parts of the mental tests while boys are superior to girls on mathematical and mechanical parts of such tests. On school achievement tests the results are similar. Girls on the average are superior to boys in reading, knowledge of vocabulary, and use of language. Boys show a superiority in arithmetic achievement. Willard Olson has stated that at the University of Michigan laboratory school comparisons have been made of the growth curves in reading and language for boys and girls from the same family. He states: "Age for age the girls regularly exceed the boys in eight out of ten comparisons where five out of ten would be the result of chance." [13] So far as overall school achievement is concerned, it can probably be said that girls excel boys in the elementary school.

Some of these sex differences are unquestionably related to differences in the ways boys and girls are reared in our society. We expect somewhat different behavior from boys and girls and the results are in line with these expectancies. There is some evidence, however, that girls of elementary school age are slightly more mature from a physiological standpoint than the boys. For example, during this period the average anatomic index of girls exceeds that

[11] Mary K. Smith, "Measurement of the Size of General English Vocabulary Through the Elementary Grades and High School," *Genetic Psychology Monographs,* Vol. 24, 1941, pp. 311–345.

[12] L. M. Terman and Maud A. Merrill, *Measuring Intelligence,* Houghton Mifflin, Boston, 1937, p. 34.

[13] Willard C. Olson, *Child Development,* Boston, D. C. Heath, 1949, p. 134.

of boys.[14] This index is based upon the percentage of the area of the wrist showing ossification. During the elementary school period, girls are also consistently more advanced in their dentition than boys.[15] Olson goes so far as to say that "the differences reported between boys and girls are in a sense not sex differences but maturity differences. . . . Boys of a given age continue to achieve and behave in a manner consistent with somewhat younger girls." [16]

Because of the difference in rate of maturing between boys and girls, it has been suggested from time to time that girls be allowed to enter the first grade at age five while boys would enter at six. This procedure might eliminate some of the disparity which now exists in the relative maturity of boys and girls as they pass through school, and should probably be subjected to experimental study. It should be remembered, however, that the differences which exist among girls and the range of differences which exist among boys of a given age are much greater than the average differences which exist between the sexes. No plan will eliminate individual differences in the classroom. The wise and effective teacher will always have to provide for a wide range of maturity levels in each class which is taught.

PERSONALITY AND SOCIAL DEVELOPMENT

Effect of Early Infant Experience on Personality. Freudians have long held that the experiences of early infancy leave lasting marks on the individual's personality. They have been especially concerned with the effect of infantile suckling, excretory, and genital experience on adult personality.[17] Pediatricians, psychiatrists, and psychologists, who follow Freudian theories have advocated certain systems of infant care which they believe will promote sound personality development.[18] In general, they have advocated breast

[14] B. T. Baldwin, L. M. Busby, and H. V. Garside, *Anatomic Growth of Children,* University of Iowa Studies in Child Welfare, 1928, Vol. 4, No. 1.

[15] Psyche Cattell, *Dentition as a Measure of Maturity,* Cambridge, Massachusetts, Harvard University Press, 1928.

[16] Willard C. Olson, *op.cit.,* p. 134.

[17] S. Freud, *New Introductory Lectures on Psychoanalysis,* New York, Norton, 1933, pp. 135–140.

[18] See L. K. Frank, "The Fundamental Needs of the Child," *Mental Hygiene,* Vol. 22, 1938, pp. 353–379; and M. A. Ribble, *The Rights of Infants,* New York, Columbia University Press, 1943.

feeding rather than bottle feeding, late and lenient bowel and bladder training, and lack of rigid scheduling in feeding. The specific
conclusions of the Freudians, however, are open to some question
in view of the fact that experimental data do not always support
their theories. Orlansky,[19] an anthropologist, has brought together
an excellent summary of existing objective studies dealing with the
effects of such things as nursing experiences, mothering, sphincter
training, and restraint of motion on personality development. He
concluded that there was no evidence that breast-fed babies were
better adjusted in later life than bottle-fed babies, or that children
who received early or late sphincter training were particularly different from other children. What seemed to be important was the
total context in which the child was reared, rather than some specific method of handling the child. Support for this position can be
found in Benedict's [20] study of the effects of swaddling on various
groups of European children. She concluded that the child's character is not determined by the overt details of early infant care, but
by attitudes and motives communicated to the child by the mother
in connection with the practices employed. It would thus appear
that whether a child is to become a well-adjusted adult depends to
a great extent upon whether he is loved, accepted, and is made to
feel secure in the home rather than whether he is fed from the
breast, bottle, or cup.

Family Relationships and Personality Development. The general
conditions existing in homes from which children come have been
shown to have marked effects upon children's behavior and personality. An important study in this area was conducted by Baldwin [21]
at the Fels Research Institute. He explored the consequences of
democracy in the home upon the personality development of 67
children who were approximately four years of age. These children
were observed in free play situations in the nursery school. Their
behavior was recorded on a rating scale by independent observers
who also rated the extent to which the homes from which the children came were democratically or autocratically operated. De-

[19] Harold Orlansky, "Infant Care and Personality," *Psychological Bulletin,*
Vol. 46, January, 1949, pp. 1–48.
[20] Ruth Benedict, "Child Rearing in Certain European Countries," *American
Journal of Orthopsychiatry,* Vol. 19, April, 1949, pp. 342–350.
[21] Alfred L. Baldwin, "Socialization and the Parent-Child Relationship," *Child
Development,* Vol. 19, September, 1948, pp. 127–136.

mocracy in the home was found to produce children who were active, aggressive, fearless, planful, curious, nonconforming, and more likely to be nursery-school leaders than average. Children from authoritarian homes tended to be quiet, well-behaved, socially unaggressive, and restricted in curiosity, originality, and fancifulness. In a California investigation involving the developmental study of 500 nursery-school children over a three-year period, it was reported that children coming from homes where parents *disagree* on methods of discipline are much more often problem cases than are children whose parents *agree* on methods of control.[22]

Further evidence of the effect of family influences upon personality has been found in studies of delinquency. In one such study [23] the investigators found three types of delinquent children, (a) an unsocialized aggressive group, (b) a socialized delinquent group, and (c) an emotionally disturbed delinquent group. The unsocialized aggressive boys predominantly came from homes where they had experienced parental rejection; the socialized delinquents were better accepted at home than the aggressive delinquents and came from larger families, but were reared under conditions of extremely lax discipline. The emotionally disturbed delinquent tended to be the unfavored child in his family and to come from a smaller family than either of the other two groups. In another study of problem children, Sloman [24] analyzed the family backgrounds of 62 individuals who were referred to the Chicago Juvenile Court. All the cases in the particular group were "planned for" children, i.e., children who were originally wanted by their parents and whose births were definitely scheduled. The findings revealed that many of these children had been wanted in an effort to remedy marital difficulties. The largest number, however, were children of compulsive and perfectionistic type mothers who liked to plan everything and who were often disappointed when their children failed to meet their expectations as to sex or achievement. This study seemed to imply that whether a child was planned for or not was of little importance

[22] Ruth Pearson Koshuk, "Developmental Records of 500 Nursery School Children," *Journal of Experimental Education,* Vol. 16, December, 1947, pp. 134–148.

[23] Richard L. Jenkins and Sylvia Glickman, "Patterns of Personality Organization Among Delinquents," *The Nervous Child,* Vol. 6, July, 1947, pp. 329–339.

[24] Sophie S. Sloman, "Emotional Problems in 'Planned for' Children," *American Journal of Orthopsychiatry,* Vol. 18, July, 1948, pp. 523–528.

so far as the child's character and personality were concerned. The really crucial point was whether or not he was wanted and made to feel secure after he arrived!

Personality Change with Age. What changes in personality take place with advancing age? Harsh and Schrickel [25] traced the typical stages of personality development revealed by individuals from infancy to old age. Perhaps the most significant difference they noted between the adult and childhood personality was that the adult personality was more rigid than that of the child. Adults strove for a more limited set of goals than did children or adolescents, for example, and sought a continuously slower and more regular tempo of living. Hartley and others [26] investigated the relation of age to children's ethnic frames of reference. They found that children three and one-half to four and one-half years of age usually replied by giving their own name when asked the question, "What are you?" For the age group four and one-half to five and one-half this type of response was still given by some children, but many began, at that age, to use ethnic designations rather than personal ones. From the age five and one-half on, the child's conception of himself and others tended to be expressed almost entirely in ethnic terms. He considered himself or his neighbor as "American," "colored," "Jewish," "Catholic," "Italian," and "Spanish."

Remmers and Weltman [27] found older children (Grades XI and XII) to be less like their parents in attitude patterns than younger children (Grades IX and X). This is a trend which would be expected in view of the strong drive for emancipation from the family found during adolescence.

Children's Fears. The best available evidence indicates that children are born with few if any specific fears. The psychologist John B. Watson held that the new-born child showed fear or startle reactions only to very loud noises or to loss of support in the act of being dropped. The great number of fears and anxieties held by

[25] Charles M. Harsh, and H. G. Schrickel, *Personality: Development and Assessment*, New York, The Ronald Press, 1950, p. 518.

[26] Eugene L. Hartley, Max Rosenbaum, and Shepard Schwartz, "Children's Use of Ethnic Frames of Reference: An Exploratory Study of Children's Conceptualizations of Multiple Ethnic Group Membership," *Journal of Psychology*, Vol. 26, October, 1948, pp. 367–386.

[27] Herman H. Remmers and Naomi Weltman, "Attitude Inter-Relationships of Youth, Their Parents, and Their Teachers," *Journal of Social Psychology*, Vol. 26, August, 1947, pp. 61–68.

children at the various age levels must, therefore, be attributed to learning. The child learns to be fearful of objects, persons, or situations in a variety of contexts although the basic principle of learning involved is usually the same. This principle is known as *conditioning*.[28] The child who has had unfortunate or terrifying experiences in the presence of some object, person, or situation tends to be fearful of these same objects or situations in the future. Numerous examples could be cited. The child who possesses an irrational fear of dogs may have been jumped upon by a dog and seriously threatened on a previous occasion. The child who fears school teachers may have been humiliated by a given teacher at some earlier time. The child who fears school examinations is one who has had unsuccessful experiences with such examinations or who has been made to feel insecure with respect to such activities. Such a case described in the subject's own words is given by Wallin.

As a child in the public school I developed a most pronounced fear of examinations and tests. I am sure this fear was instilled into me by a teacher who always threatened her pupils with the hard examinations she was going to give, and with the fact that if we did not pass we would not be promoted. . . .

I must confess I have never been able to overcome the fear of tests. To this day examinations and tests almost make me ill.[29]

Through direct contact with disturbing situations or through vicarious experiences such as listening to lurid stories told by adults or by members of one's peer group, children become afraid of an amazing variety of things. These include such things as darkness, snakes, thunder, strangers, high places, dirt, dentists, and water. There is no end to the lists of things which children may learn to fear.

Jersild and Holmes [30] have made an analysis of some of the fears which are held by large numbers of children at different age levels. Jersild has summarized this study and related ones made under his direction in the following words:

During the preschool years, more and more of his (the child's) fears are formulated in terms of imaginary or anticipated dangers. At the ele-

[28] See Chapter 5 for additional discussion of this concept.
[29] J. E. Wallace Wallin, *Personality Maladjustments and Mental Hygiene*, New York, McGraw-Hill Book Company, 1949, p. 80.
[30] A. T. Jersild and F. B. Holmes, *Children's Fears*, Child Development Monographs, Teachers College, Bureau of Publications, 1935, No. 20.

mentary school age, and from then onward, a large proportion of fears concern misfortunes that never materialize. As the child grows older and abler, there is a decline in his fear of numerous events that scared him at an earlier time, such as noises, unfamiliar persons, places and situations, everyday objects, animals and persons. However, individual children may fail to outgrow such fears, by reason of the harrowing shock of the original experience, or by reason of recurring experiences that strengthen the original fear, or by reason of failures to gain in understanding and mastery of themselves and their environment as they grow older. Certain childhood fears, such as fears of animals, the dark, being alone, criminal characters, ghosts and the like, are likely to persist into adult life sometimes in much the same form, sometimes in a modified version.[31]

The teacher or parent should be concerned with ways and means of helping children overcome their fears. How are fears unlearned? The essential circumstance is that the feared object or situation must be associated with pleasantness, security, success or other state of well being. The child who has a deathly fear of cats must gradually be placed in the vicinity of a cat, under conditions where he is secure, happy, and free from threat. After a period of time the cat will lose its terrifying effect. The writer knows of a child who formerly was tense and afraid in the presence of all cats or even little kittens. A kitten was brought in the home. At first the child was unwilling to be in the same room with the kitten. Now the child insists that this kitten, which has now grown into a full sized cat, sleep at the foot of his bed.

A child who fears school examinations or school teachers needs success experiences with examinations or teachers. The child who dreads or is fearful of such a school activity as reading, needs to have satisfying experiences with reading.

A fifth grade boy was once brought to the writer at the educational clinic of the University of Illinois because his parents and teachers considered him to be a non-reader. The boy's reaction when the subject of reading was brought up was one of extreme aversion. He stated that he thoroughly disliked reading and felt most uncomfortable to even discuss the subject. He asked that he not be subjected to the terrifying ordeal of trying to read to the

---

[31] A. I. Gates, A. T. Jersild, T. R. McConnell, and R. C. Challman, *Educational Psychology*, p. 98. Copyright, 1948, by The Macmillan Company, New York. Used by permission.

writer who was interviewing him. The boy further stated that he was definitely a non-reader and no useful purpose would be served by such an exhibition of his weakness. The writer told the boy that many people are non-readers and perhaps he was also, but insisted that the boy prove that he was a true non-reader. This the boy reluctantly agreed to do. The boy was given a pre-primer and asked to begin reading. He did very well on this. He was then given a second pre-primer. He was again successful at reading this most elementary material. By this time, his parents returned to the conference room. They were told that the boy was definitely not a non-reader because he had just finished reading two books. In order to demonstrate this fact to his parents, a third pre-primer was placed in the boy's hands and he was asked to read. After he had read three or four pages successfully, the writer reached over to take the book from him, but he would not give it up. He sat there beaming in front of his parents and refused to stop reading until he had finished the entire pre-primer.

This case illustrates how an aversion, dislike, or fear can often be dissipated in a very short time once the activity is associated with need satisfying experiences. This boy needed success and recognition in connection with reading. His dislike and aversion for reading had developed as a result of his previous humiliating experiences with it. All that was needed to produce a positive reaction toward reading was a sense of achievement and success in connection with the activity.

The efficacy of the method just described for eliminating fears has been subjected to experimental study by Jersild and Holmes.[32] In summarizing this research, Jersild states, "The highest percentage of success was reported for procedures that helped the child to gain increased competence and skill, aided him in finding practical methods of his own for dealing with the feared situation, and helped him by degrees to have active experience with, or successful direct participation in the feared situation." [33]

Children's Prejudices. Prejudices like fears are learned. The very young child is neither a Republican nor a Democrat. He does not

---

[32] See A. T. Jersild and F. B. Holmes, "Methods of Overcoming Children's Fears," *Journal of Psychology*, Vol. 1, 1935, pp. 75–104.

[33] A. T. Jersild, "Emotional Development," in *Manual of Child Psychology* (Leonard Carmichael, editor), New York, John Wiley and Sons, 1946, p. 768.

prefer one racial group to another, one religion to another, or one social class to another. The direction his attitudes take will depend entirely on the experiences he has and the groups with which he later identifies. Horowitz [34] has reported that white children, for example, possess no prejudices whatsoever toward Negroes under the age of three. Between the ages of four to six there is a marked increase in such prejudices. He also noted that there is a close relationship between the attitude of the child at this age and the attitude of the parents. It seems therefore that many prejudices are initiated through the process of the child taking over the general cultural attitudes of his parents. As the child grows more mature the influence of the peer group becomes increasingly more effective in modifying his attitudes. By the time of adolescence the attitude of the "gang" may exert a more profound influence on the thinking of the youngster than that of his parents.

So far as education and psychology are concerned, one attitude can be as easily developed as another. Schools should determine what attitudes they desire children to have and then see that the holding of these attitudes is rewarded. The school teacher or parent who accords a child prestige and status for expressing a given idea or attitude is doing much toward establishing that point of view in the child's frame of reference. Parents who desire their children to hold certain attitudes must also do all they can to insure that their child or adolescent associates and identifies himself with a group of other children who hold the given attitudes or viewpoint. Studies of methods of reducing prejudice have been made by Rosen [35] who found that the motion picture "Gentlemen's Agreement" had the effect of reducing prejudice toward Jews, and by Axline [36] who presented evidence to show that play therapy could accomplish similar results.

Personality Development of Handicapped Children. Johnson [37]

[34] E. L. Horowitz, *The Development of Attitudes Toward the Negro*, Archives of Psychology, New York, No. 194, 1936.

[35] Irwin C. Rosen, "The Effect of the Motion Picture 'Gentleman's Agreement' on Attitudes Toward Jews," *Journal of Psychology*, Vol. 26, October, 1948, pp. 525–536.

[36] Virginia M. Axline, "Play Therapy and Race Conflict in Young Children," *Journal of Abnormal and Social Psychology*, Vol. 43, July, 1948, pp. 300–310.

[37] George O. Johnson, *A Study of the Social Position of Mentally-Handicapped Children in Regular Grades*, Doctor's Thesis, Urbana: University of Illinois, 1950.

using sociometric technics, studied the social position of mentally handicapped children in regular school classes. The 39 children included in the investigation all had IQs of 69 or below as determined by the 1937 Revision of the Stanford Binet Scale, Form L. He found that the majority of the children were socially isolated, and that many of them were actively rejected by their classmates. The percentage of mentally handicapped children suffering social maladjustment in regular classes was found to be statistically greater than that of typical groups which he used as controls. The study was carried out in two communities which had no special classes for mentally handicapped children. Cruickshank and Dolphin [38] investigated the emotional and social characteristics of crippled and noncrippled children using as their instrument of evaluation the *Raths Self-Portrait N Test*. They concluded that crippled children, on the average, differ little if any from noncrippled in so far as social and emotional adjustment are concerned. They did, however, suggest that crippling may have a deleterious effect upon the social adjustment of given children, depending upon the attitudes they hold toward their physical disability.

Individuals with severe sensory defects such as deafness or blindness may in many instances be affected from a personality standpoint by their handicap. It has been shown, for example, that both the deaf and the blind are psychologically more rigid (set in their ways) than individuals with normal sensory equipment. Of the two groups, the deaf show the more rigidity. When the Rorschach test was administered to deaf children the results showed that they reacted, on the whole, as normal children of a somewhat younger age. [39]

Investigations have been made of children who have been affected with poliomyelitis. In one study, [40] the *California Personality Test* was given to 101 Minneapolis children who had had this dis-

[38] William M. Cruickshank and Jane E. Dolphin, "The Emotional Needs of Crippled and Non-Crippled Children," *Journal of Exceptional Children*, Vol. 16, November, 1949, pp. 33–40.

[39] Helton McAndrew, "Rigidity and Isolation: A Study of the Deaf and the Blind," *Journal of Abnormal and Social Psychology*, Vol. 43, October, 1948, pp. 476–494.

[40] Lakin E. Phillips, Isabel R. Berman, and Harold B. Hanson, *Intelligence and Personality Factors Associated with Poliomyelitis Among School Age Children*, Monographs of the Society for Research in Child Development, Vol. 12, No. 2, Washington, D. C. National Research Council, 1948, p. 60.

ease during the year prior to the investigation. On this test, no reliable difference was found between children who were victims of polio and a control group of children. However, in a study [41] conducted in New Haven, Connecticut, some evidence was found that children who had recovered from poliomyelitis tended to be somewhat more hyperactive, irritable, disobedient, and "whiney" than would normally be expected. It was also found that parents showed anxieties which manifested themselves in overindulgence and concern with the problem of incorporating the child in the regular family routine.

The available evidence seems to point to the conclusion that a handicapped child may develop a very wholesome and well-adjusted personality or he may become seriously maladjusted. It all depends upon how he is treated by other individuals and how he views his condition. Since the handicapped child has an extra burden to carry, the task of making satisfactory personal and social adjustments may be somewhat more difficult for him than for average children.

The question is sometimes raised as to whether mentally handicapped children should be taught in regular classrooms or in special ones designed to fit their needs. This is a question which cannot be answered categorically. If classes are small and the teacher is qualified and equipped to provide for a wide range of individual differences, such children may make very satisfactory progress in regular classes. This, of course, would be true only in those cases where stigmatization of the handicapped children could be eliminated. In general, the child with a severe, mental handicap is so atypical that he probably needs more modification of his program than can be provided in regular classes. He feels less inferior when working with pupils who are more at his level of ability. The writer has observed children who have been seriously disturbed in regular classes make excellent personal adjustments when placed in special classes designed to fit their needs.

Childhood Friendships. What are the factors that influence children's friendships? Grossman and Wrighter [42] studied the relation-

[41] Edith Meyer, "Psychological Considerations in a Group of Children with Poliomyelitis," *Journal of Pediatrics*, Vol. 31, 1947, pp. 34–40.

[42] Beverly Grossman and Joyce Wrighter, "The Relationship Between Selection-Rejection and Intelligence, Social Status, and Personality Amongst Sixth-Grade Children," *Sociometry*, Vol. 11, November, 1948, pp. 346–355.

ship between selection-rejection and intelligence, social status, and personality among sixth-grade children. They found that intelligence was related to selection of friends up to a certain point, that of normal intelligence, but beyond that point no relationship existed. Social status was found to be related to popularity, but the association ceased for levels above the middle class. The more popular children were found to be better adjusted than the less popular as measured by the *California Personality Test*. Bonney [43] made an intensive study of five very unpopular children who had been identified by means of sociometric tests. He found that the popular children differed significantly from the unpopular children in conformity and group identification, emotional stability and control, social aggressiveness, adaptability and tolerance, dependability, social service motivation, and several other traits. Thompson and Horrocks,[44] studying the degree of friendship fluctuation for children in Grades VI to XII, found a trend toward greater stability in the friendships with increasing chronological age. Hare and Hare [45] found that the number of friends possessed by a family increases with length of stay in the community and varies with the presence or absence of children in the home. A negative correlation existed between number of friends and amount of expenditure for recreation outside the home.

There are undoubtedly numerous factors which account for children being drawn together with other children in friendly relationships. The most obvious one, of course, is propinquity. It is very difficult for children who are too widely separated by distance to carry on a close friendship. Age, social class, intelligence, and other traits of personality are also clearly related to the process of forming friendships. It can probably be said that the fundamental reason why two children become friends is that each helps the other satisfy some of his basic social and psychological needs. A child who makes another child feel accepted, secure, and important will likely secure a friend. If the relationship is mutual, a close friend-

[43] Mark Edwin Bonney, *Popular and Unpopular Children: A Sociometric Study*, Sociometry Monographs, No. 9, New York, Beacon House, 1947, p. 81.
[44] George G. Thompson and John E. Horrocks, "A Study of the Friendship Fluctuations of Urban Boys and Girls," *Journal of Genetic Psychology*, Vol. 70, June, 1947, pp. 53–63.
[45] Alexander P. Hare and Rachel T. Hare, "Family Friendship Within the Community," *Sociometry*, Vol. 11, November, 1948, pp. 329–334.

ship may be formed and the two children will become confidants—buddies, chums, or pals.

The Effect of Social Class upon Children's Behavior. Although teachers come predominantly from the middle class, the children they teach come in great numbers from the lower classes as well as the middle class. A few children in a school may be from the upper classes. Social psychologists have found that child rearing practices vary greatly among the various social classes, and that the attitudes and modes of behavior of children from the different social classes are markedly different.[46] Particularly important differences between middle class children and lower class children have been noted. Whereas middle class children are taught that it is most important to do well in school, such instruction is rarely given to lower class children by their parents. Thus it is frequently very difficult to interest lower class children in schoolwork. Attitudes with respect to destruction of property, fighting, stealing, and sex practices, also vary considerably between middle class and lower class children. For example, lower class boys are taught to fight any one who insults them or opposes them. Middle class boys are usually encouraged by their parents to avoid fighting whenever possible. In order to get a better understanding of the children under his tutelage the teacher might profitably visit the homes of his pupils to get a picture of some of the cultural forces that are operating to mold their attitudes and practices. Teachers who do this will be less likely to blame children for certain seemingly deviant behavior than otherwise. Instead, a more sympathetic attitude toward such children should result. The good teacher knows the backgrounds, interests, attitudes, ambitions, and problems of his pupils. These facts furnish the basis for instruction which is designed to lead the pupils toward increased effectiveness in living.

IMPORTANCE OF THE PERIOD OF CHILDHOOD

Freudian psychologists have long held that the experiences of childhood are crucial so far as later developments in personality are concerned. In fact, it is their opinion that in the first five or six years the basic life pattern is set. Although it is probable that they have somewhat overstated their case with respect to the all-pervading in-

---

[46] See W. Allison Davis and Robert J. Havighurst, *Father of the Man*, Boston, Houghton Mifflin Company, 1947.

fluence of early childhood experience upon later behavior, no one doubts the extreme importance of the period. Florence Goodenough [47] suggests that there is some evidence "that one-half of an individual's ultimate mental stature has been attained by the age of three years." The pre-school years and the elementary school years do represent periods of most rapid physical, mental, and social growth. Habits formed during this period are difficult to break at later stages of development, and many behaviors left undeveloped during the period are difficult to establish later. Thus the individual who fails to develop consideration for others or self-reliance as a child will be greatly handicapped in developing these traits as an adolescent or adult. The child who fails to learn to read or develop an interest in books during the elementary school years will have the greatest difficulty overcoming these obstacles when he reaches the secondary-school level. Because of the great importance of childhood as a period of learning, probably no group of teachers carry as heavy a responsibility for the development of appropriate behavior in our citizens as pre-school and elementary-school teachers. The complexity of their task requires the most thorough professional preparation and insight into the psychology underlying the learning process.

SUMMARY

The period of childhood is one of rapid growth and learning. Starting as it were almost from "scratch" the individual in a few short years develops a most complicated set of behaviors. He learns to talk, read, write, cooperate, distinguish right from wrong, and make thousands of other adjustments to the society in which he finds himself. All children, of course, are not equally successful in mastering the "development tasks" expected of them. Some develop rapidly in some areas of behavior and slower in others. The wise teacher will realize that the typical child is uneven in his abilities and will endeavor to gear instructional activities not only to each child, but also to his several aspects of development.

In judging what a given child can learn, or in predicting what his future growth will be, tests of "intelligence" should be used with

[47] Florence L. Goodenough, "The Measurement of Mental Growth in Childhood," *Manual of Child Psychology* (Leonard Carmichael, editor), New York, John Wiley and Sons, 1946, pp. 467–468.

extreme caution. Studies have shown marked fluctuations to occur in tested IQs. In one careful investigation it was found that between ages six and eighteen, the IQs of almost 60 per cent of the individuals changed fifteen points or more.

Childhood is the time when the individual's basic outlooks, values, and ideals are to a great extent shaped. The experiences the child has at school and in the home and the larger community during these formative years, will determine, for example, whether he is to be a fearful child or one possessed with confidence in himself, or whether he will be tolerant or intolerant toward others. Handicapped children have special problems which must be faced and which need the sympathetic understanding of teachers.

No period during the life-cycle is more important than childhood from an educational point of view. Teachers who work at this level should understand children—their fundamental needs, their problems, and the forces which modify and produce behavior change. The statement that "the child is father of the man" bears much psychological validity. The patterns of growth, learning, and adjustment established in childhood reach into the future and influence the entire course of life.

REFERENCES FOR FURTHER STUDY

Anderson, John E., *The Psychology of Development and Personal Adjustment,* New York, Henry Holt and Company, 1949.

Ausubel, David P., *Ego Development and the Personality Disorders,* New York, Grune and Stratton, 1952.

Barker, Roger G. and Wright, Herbert F., *One Boy's Day: A Specimen Record of Behavior,* New York, Harper and Brothers, 1951.

Blair, Arthur Witt and Burton, William H., *Growth and Development of the Preadolescent,* New York, Appleton-Century-Crofts, Inc., 1951.

Bossard, James H. S., *The Sociology of Child Development,* New York, Harper and Brothers, 1948.

Cunningham, Ruth, *et al., Understanding Group Behavior of Boys and Girls,* New York, Bureau of Publications, Teachers College, Columbia University, 1951.

Davis, W. Allison and Havighurst, Robert J., *Father of the Man: How Your Child Gets His Personality,* Boston, Houghton Mifflin Company, 1947.

Dennis, Wayne, *Readings in Child Psychology,* New York, Prentice-Hall, Inc., 1951.

English, Horace B., *Child Psychology,* New York, Henry Holt and Company, 1951.

Erikson, Erik H., *Childhood and Society*, New York, W. W. Norton and Company, 1950.

Gesell, Arnold and Ilg, Frances L., *Child Development*, New York, Harper and Brothers, 1949.

Gruenberg, Sidonie Matsner (Editor), *Our Children Today*, New York, The Viking Press, 1952.

Hartley, Ruth E., *et al.*, *Understanding Children's Play*, New York, Columbia University Press, 1952.

Jenkins, Gladys G., Shacter, Helen and Bauer, William W., *These Are Your Children*, Chicago, Scott, Foresman and Company, 1949.

Jersild, Arthur T., *et al.*, *Child Development and the Curriculum*, New York, Bureau of Publications, Teachers College, Columbia University, 1946.

Josselyn, Irene M., *Psychosocial Development of Children*, New York, Family Service Association of America, 1948.

Kuhlen, Raymond G. and Thompson, George G., *Psychological Studies of Human Development*, New York, Appleton-Century-Crofts, Inc., 1952.

Martin, William E. and Stendler, Celia Burns, *Child Development: The Process of Growing Up in Society*, New York, Harcourt, Brace, 1953.

Merry, Frieda K. and Merry, Ralph V., *The First Two Decades of Life*, New York, Harper and Brothers, 1950.

Olson, Willard C., *Child Development*, Boston, D. C. Heath and Company, 1949.

Piaget, Jean, *Play, Dreams and Imitation in Childhood*, New York, W. W. Norton and Company, 1951.

Prescott, Daniel (Editor), *Helping Teachers Understand Children*, Washington, D. C., American Council on Education, 1945.

Ribble, Margaret, *The Rights of Infants*, New York, Columbia University Press, 1943.

Stendler, Celia, *Children of Brasstown*, Urbana, Illinois, Bureau of Research and Service, College of Education, University of Illinois, 1949.

Symonds, Percival M., *The Dynamics of Parent-Child Relationships*, New York, Bureau of Publications, Teachers College, Columbia University, 1949.

Thompson, George G., *Child Psychology*, Boston, Houghton Mifflin Company, 1952.

Chapter 4

The Adolescent Period

ADOLESCENCE is that period in each individual's life which begins at the end of childhood and closes at the beginning of adulthood. It is a period of transition. It is a time when the individual is striving to wean himself from the family and become a self-sufficient and independent person. For girls, the end of childhood and the beginning of adolescence is generally marked by the appearance of menstruation. For boys, the appearance of pubic hair is usually the criterion employed for establishing the onset of adolescence. After these physical changes have taken place, girls and boys not only perceive themselves differently, but other people also begin to look at them in a different light. They have become adolescents. Roughly the adolescent period in our culture corresponds to the ages of the "teens." Some boys and girls do, of course, begin adolescence considerably before they reach the age of thirteen and others do not finish the adolescent phase of their development by the time they are nineteen. A high percentage of the adolescent population, however, is found between these age limits. The bulk of the students in junior and senior high schools are adolescents. It should be kept in mind, however, that many pupils in the elementary school and many students in college are also in the stage known as adolescence. When adolescence is defined as that period between puberty and maturity a great range of ages is obviously included.

The exact length of the adolescent period varies from individual to individual and from culture to culture. In some primitive societies children are transformed into adults almost overnight. At thirteen or fourteen years of age they are given adult responsibilities and quickly weaned from the family. In our own culture in pioneer days it was not at all unusual for young people to marry at fourteen or fifteen years of age and take on family responsibilities. Such individuals probably had at the most one or two years to be adolescents. More recently, particularly during the depression years, it was not at all uncommon for young people to spend as much as ten years in making the transition from childhood to adulthood. During the recent war, great numbers of boys were automatically matured into adults upon reaching eighteen. At this age, they left home and entered the service of their country, thus cutting short the usual period of dependence upon their families by several years. Normally, however, adolescence in America is a long and drawn out period and one fraught with many trying problems of adjustment for the developing individual. In this connection Norman Cameron makes the following comment:

The chasm in our society between childhood and adulthood is very wide. Adolescence is the long biosocial bridge that spans it. The duration and complexity of the adolescent phase of personality development are more or less peculiar to modern industrial society. In other societies the transition from childhood to adulthood seems to be achieved more quickly and simply. Children are able to share progressively in the serious functions of the community life, beginning at a relatively early age. They are not held rigidly, as our children are, to a dependent status that differentiates them sharply from adults. . . . Less delay is interposed also between biological fitness and social privilege than in our culture.[1]

WHY ADOLESCENCE IS A PERIOD REQUIRING SPECIAL STUDY

The general principles of psychology as they relate to growth, learning, and adjustment, apply to individuals at the adolescent stage as well as to individuals in any other phase of development. Yet each stage of life has special problems which must be understood if appropriate applications of psychological principles are to be made. The teacher who works with adolescents needs to understand the nature of the transition period through which adolescents pass, the role of the peer group in influencing adolescent behavior, the nature of adolescent developmental tasks, the effects of somatic variations on adolescent behavior, and many conditions and problems which affect adolescents in more or less unique ways.

[1] Norman Cameron, *The Psychology of Behavior Disorders: A Biosocial Interpretation,* p. 46. Copyright, 1947, by Houghton Mifflin Company, Boston.

The adolescent, for example, is in reality neither a child nor an adult. He is often treated in an ambiguous manner by his parents, teachers, and other members in his society. He may be told one moment by his parents that he is too young to drive the family car; the next moment he may be informed he is too old to be carrying on certain childish antics such as playing leap frog on the parlor rug. Roger Barker has stated that ". . . for the adolescent, the overlapping situations of childhood and adulthood are paramount. Adolescents, by virtue of their frequently ambiguous and rapidly changing physique, are often placed in marginal situations with the physiological, social and psychological behavior determiners of both childhood and adolescence acting upon them simultaneously." [2]

The adjustments adolescents must make to the new problems they face place many of them under severe strain and conflict. What happens to a considerable number is indicated by the following statistics on death rate and incidence of mental disorder given by L. K. Frank. He states:

In this country the period from ten to fifteen years of age has the lowest death rate of all age periods from infancy to senility. But in the age period fifteen to nineteen boys and girls begin to succumb to the stresses and strains of later adolescent life, and the death rate increases 100 per cent. . . . Likewise for mental disorders. In the age period ten to fourteen the first admissions to state hospitals for mental disorders is very low—in New York state only 4.3 per 100,000 children of that age. In the age period fifteen to nineteen the rate is 40.3 per 100,000, almost a ten-fold increase over the preceding five-year period. [3]

It is a well-known fact that delinquency rates soar during this period, that suicides become increasingly prevalent, that drug and alcohol addiction may have their beginning, and that much general unhappiness exists for many. Adolescence is also a period when satisfactory heterosexual adjustments are facilitated or hindered, when careers are planned, and when philosophies of life become molded. Teachers who understand adolescents and the problems they encounter can do much to help them make a successful transi-

[2] Roger Barker, et al., Adjustment to Physical Handicap and Illness: A Survey of the Social Psychology of Physique and Disability; Social Science Research Council Bulletin 55, New York, 1946, p. 33.

[3] L. K. Frank, in The 43rd Yearbook of the National Society for the Study of Education, Part I: Adolescence, Chicago, The Department of Education, The University of Chicago, 1944, p. 5.

tion to adult status. Too often, however, it seems that schools and teachers because of lack of understanding actually frustrate adolescents and contribute to their general maladjustment.

ADOLESCENT NEEDS

The adolescent, of course, possesses the same fundamental physical needs as do children and adults. His social and personality needs also are of the same general nature as those of individuals at other age levels. The strength of some of the needs and their significance for his behavior may, however, be somewhat different at this stage of his development than in other periods of his life. Hence a brief discussion will be given of a few of the powerful human needs as they affect the adolescent.

The Need for Status. Perhaps no need is more important than this one so far as the adolescent is concerned. He wants to be important, to have standing in his group, to be recognized as a person of worth. He craves to achieve adult status and leave behind the insignia of childhood. Thus it is not at all uncommon to see adolescent boys attempting to smoke cigars and act in what seems to them to be other sophisticated adult ways. The adolescent girl wants to wear high heeled shoes, use lipstick, and take on the ways of adult women. Status in the peer group is probably more important to many adolescents than status in the eyes of their parents or teachers, yet recognition from both of these latter sources are cherished by adolescents. The teacher who directs the activities of the adolescent should always ask himself whether or not the experiences of the classroom are status producing ones for each individual. The adolescent who is achieving his goals in school and who is accorded appropriate recognition is seldom if ever a disciplinary problem. He, furthermore, is in the best possible emotional state to continue to profit from the learning experiences of the school.

One of the writers observed the classroom of a teacher who delighted in forcing her pupils, especially boys, to read poetry aloud. In this class in which most of the boys were 14 or 15, just at the age when they were trying to throw off the label of "children" and avoid "sissy" activities, the teacher asked them to read aloud Edgar Allen Poe's, "The Bells." One phrase of the poem was "to the tintinnabulation that so musically wells from the bells, bells, bells, bells, bells, bells, bells." The teacher insisted that each boy rise and read the phrase with a different inflection on each "bells." Finally one of the larger boys slammed his book on the floor in disgust and stamped out of the classroom.

This teacher did not realize how sensitive adolescents are about being treated like youngsters, or engaging in activities they feel to be below their dignity. There is probably no surer way for any teacher to become unpopular with a group of teen-agers than to call them children or to infer in any other way that they are anything but young men and women.

The Need for Independence. The young child exhibits this need when he desires to tie his own shoe laces without help from his parents. With the onset of adolescence, however, this need takes on increasing significance and importance. The adolescent craves to be weaned from parental restrictions and become a self-directing person. He wants his own room in the home where he can be free from younger members of the family and where he can do his own thinking and plan his own activities. He desires to run his own life. Whereas young children have no objection whatsoever to their parents visiting school and enquiring regarding their progress, adolescents are generally very sensitive about this because it implies they cannot handle their own affairs. The adolescent boy who is a member of the tennis or basketball team in high school usually prefers that if his parents attend the matches or games, they not be too conspicuous. The normal adolescent does not want anyone to sense or faintly suspect that he is in any way tied to his mother's apron strings. The adolescent wants to take on responsibility that is in line with his increased abilities and maturity level. Teachers too often, however, treat adolescents much as if they were children. They scold them for little misbehaviors, plan most of their work for them, and expect little of them in the way of responsible behavior. If that is what they expect, that is what they usually get. Adolescents who are treated in a more adult manner will show a more adult behavior, and can be depended upon to take on and carry out highly independent and responsible assignments.

Need for Satisfying Philosophy of Life. The young child asks many questions and does some immature speculating about the nature of the universe, but it is not until adolescence is reached that a persistent and driving concern about the meaning of life is exhibited. The adolescent is concerned with questions about truth, religion, and ideals. Data show that in adolescence religious conversion and initial radical political activity reach their peak.[4] Dictators who establish youth movements, and religious organizations which sponsor young peoples' societies recognize the importance of this period for attitude formation. The school has a great responsibility to help the adolescent find himself, and help him develop the outlooks on life which are consistent with our democratic philosophy.

Sex Needs. The Freudians and others have called attention to the fact that the child has many sex impulses and curiosities. With the advent of adolescence these needs take on an increasingly impelling force. The postmenarcheal girl of thirteen is more interested in members of the opposite sex than are her thirteen-year-old classmates who have not yet reached the menarcheal stage.[5] Kinsey's study of adolescent boys gives strong support to the already known fact that adolescence is a period of strong sexual desires. He makes the statement that over 95 per cent of adolescent males are regularly sexually active by fifteen years of age.[6] Kinsey means by this that they engage in such activities leading to orgasm as masturbation, nocturnal emission, intercourse, petting, and homosexual practice. Facts such as these seem to point to the urgent need for schools to do something of importance about sex education. The adolescent seeks help regarding his sexual problems, and the school can do much, if it will, to assist him to make socially appropriate heterosexual adjustments.

DEVELOPMENTAL TASKS OF ADOLESCENCE

Closely related to adolescent needs are a series of developmental problems which adolescents typically face in their transition from childhood to adulthood. These problems are not entirely unique to the adolescent period, but they are ones upon which the adolescent must work if he expects eventually to achieve an adult role. Robert Havighurst[7] has listed nine tasks which are particularly significant

[4] See S. L. Pressey, and F. P. Robinson, *Psychology and the New Education,* New York, Harper and Brothers, 1944, pp. 271–272.

[5] See C. P. Stone and R. G. Barker, "The Attitudes and Interests of Premenarcheal Girls," *Journal of Genetic Psychology,* Vol. 54, 1939, pp. 27–71.

[6] See A. C. Kinsey, W. B. Pomeroy, and C. E. Martin, *Sexual Behavior in the Human Male,* Philadelphia, Saunders, 1948.

[7] Robert J. Havighurst, *Developmental Tasks and Education,* pp. 30–63. Copyright, 1950, by Longmans, Green and Company, New York.

for the adolescent, and which need much attention during this period. These tasks are as follows:

1. Accepting one's physique and accepting a masculine or feminine role.
2. Developing new relations with age-mates of both sexes.
3. Attaining emotional independence of parents and other adults.
4. Achieving assurance of economic independence.
5. Selecting and preparing for an occupation.
6. Developing intellectual skills and concepts necessary for civic competence.
7. Desiring and achieving socially responsible behavior.
8. Preparing for marriage and family life.
9. Building values in harmony with an adequate scientific world-picture.

If these are, indeed, the important problems of adolescence, schools should gear their curricula to take them into account. The school has traditionally devoted most of its energy to assisting the adolescent achieve the first part of developmental task number 6, namely, developing intellectual skills. Such tasks as achieving socially responsible behavior, preparing for marriage and family life, and developing new relations with age-mates as well as other tasks on this list have been largely neglected.

ADOLESCENT PHYSICAL DEVELOPMENT

Both boys and girls show a spurt in height and weight near the beginning of puberty. Girls, however, on the average, begin this period of rapid development at least a year earlier than boys. Data [8] show that girls, on the average, are taller than boys from age eleven to age fourteen. By fifteen, boys are a little taller than girls and from then on maintain superiority in height. Girls are also heavier than boys at ages 12, 13, 14 and 15. At age sixteen boys have overtaken girls and remain heavier during the rest of the life span. Girls also exhibit the secondary sexual characteristics approximately a year or two before boys. The fifth or sixth grade teacher often has girls in class who resemble mature women in their general physical development, but seldom are boys found in these grades who have attained a comparable level of maturity. During the junior- and senior-high-school years, the greater physical and social development of

[8] See W. W. Greulich, "Physical Changes in Adolescence," in the *43rd Yearbook of the National Society for the Study of Education*, Part I: Adolescence, 1944, pp. 10–11.

girls is also obvious. Freshman high school girls, for example, often feel that the freshman boys are immature and uninteresting. They therefore seek the company of sophomore or junior boys. This leaves the freshman boys at a disadvantage in developing appropriate social skills with members of the opposite sex. In the elementary school the very early maturing girl may feel isolated and out of place and hence develop an unhappy outlook on life.

ADOLESCENT PROBLEMS RELATED TO PHYSICAL VARIATIONS

Human beings at nearly all age levels dislike being too much different from other people. This is true of the child and also of the adult. With the adolescent, however, this aversion to being different reaches perhaps its highest peak. For him, being different is viewed as being a most serious obstacle to social acceptance. Stolz and Stolz have commented on this point as follows:

A child in the elementary school may easily become the butt for teasing or group ostracism because he speaks with a peculiar accent, has cross-eyes, red hair, or wears clothes different from his classmates. With the accentuation which adolescence brings to the need for social acceptance by peers, the wanting to be like and not wanting to be different tends to modify persistently both outward behavior and attitudes toward self.[9]

Being different physically is thus one of the major concerns and worries of the adolescent. Adolescent boys worry, for example, about lack of size, being too fat, poor physique and skin blemishes. Girls are disturbed about being too tall, too fat, lack of well-developed bosom, bowed legs, facial hair, late development, and numerous other defects.

One boy expressed concern over his slow development as follows:

I am 14 years old, weigh 95 pounds, and measure 5 feet 4 inches. A few years ago my pals were the same weight and height as I was, but now they are much taller and heavier than me. I eat lots of good food but I don't seem to gain weight or grow much. It would be swell of you if you could tell me how to catch up with my friends. . . .[10]

[9] H. R. Stolz and Lois Meek Stolz, "Adolescent Problems Related to Somatic Variations," in *43rd Yearbook of the National Society for the Study of Education,* 1944, p. 84.
[10] Taken from E. D. Partridge, *Social Psychology of Adolescence,* New York, Prentice-Hall, 1938, p. 81.

In a study [11] conducted in an Arizona high school it was found that many boys would change themselves physically if they could. Following are some of the verbatim statements of these boys:

I would make my chest bigger than it is now and also my shoulders. I would like to weigh a little bit more, say about twenty to twenty-five pounds more.

I would make myself look handsomer and not fat. I would have wavy black hair. I would change my whole physical appearance so that I would be handsome, with a good build.

I would be taller, more muscular, slimmer, have better posture, lighter and more slowly-growing head of hair, big, broad shoulders and heavier calves.

Well, I would start off by putting on some meat, next would be get rid of my pimples, then get some muscles, then get rid of my glasses.

The way adolescent girls feel about physical deviations can be seen in the following quotations taken from the same study.

My hips and legs are too large and fat. If I could have smaller hips and legs, I'd have a much better figure. I'd also like to be a little more developed above the waist than I am, but I am not too flat. I wish I didn't have so many pimples or have to wear glasses.

I would first of all change my nose, as it is large. I think some day I will go to a plastic surgeon and get my nose changed. . . . I would like a clear, unscarred complexion. I have blackheads and pimples. I may go to a dermatologist.

I would rather not wear glasses. I would like to lose ten pounds.

I would like to be three inches shorter and have smaller feet.

Many adolescents consider themselves to be abnormal in certain physical characteristics when in reality they are well within the normal range. For example, girls are sometimes known to worry because their menstrual cycles vary from the so-called norm of 28 days. A study made by Fleshman [12] of seventy-six healthy young women, showed that their menstrual cycles varied from 11 to 144 days, with the great majority falling between 18 and 42 days. Only

---

[11] Alexander Frazier, "Adolescent Concerns with Physique," *The School Review*, Vol. 58, October, 1950, pp. 397–405.

[12] C. F. Fleshman, "The Length of the Human Menstrual Cycle," *American Journal of Obstetrics and Gynecology*, Vol. 27, 1934, pp. 73–78.

five of the seventy-six girls showed absolutely regular cycles. Adolescent boys are known to sometimes be concerned about the size of their genital organs and to develop personality disorders because of their anxieties.[13] Yet such concern in most cases is groundless because the boys are in all likelihood well within the limits of normalcy. A thorough study by Schonfeld and Beebe provides data with respect to what normal genital development for adolescent boys is.[14] If adolescent boys and girls could be supplied with appropriate information regarding the great range of individual differences which typically exist among individuals of their age, a great deal of personal unhappiness could be eliminated. The teacher, psychological counselor, or athletic coach is in a position to offer sympathetic help and advice to adolescents who are distressed because of real or imagined physical defects or somatic deviations.

MENTAL GROWTH DURING ADOLESCENCE

It was formerly believed that ability to perform on mental tests reached its peak somewhere around fourteen, fifteen, or sixteen years of age. Thus Terman stated with regard to the Revised Stanford-Binet test that "the yearly gain becomes relatively small by the age of fifteen, and mental age score shows but little tendency to improve thereafter. Chronological age beyond this point has, therefore, been disregarded in computing the IQ." [15] Recent research, however, seems to show that growth as measured by intelligence tests continues considerably longer than earlier investigators thought. Age norms for the more recently standardized Terman-McNemar test presented in Table 4 show gains up to nineteen.

It is not clear from these data what happens after age nineteen, but it is likely that increments of mental growth continue beyond this point. Studies of college students [16] have indicated that there are definite gains in intelligence test scores during the college years with students making much higher scores during their senior year than

---

[13] W. A. Schonfeld, "Inadequate Masculine Physique as a Factor in Personality Development of Adolescent Boys," *Psychosomatic Medicine*, Vol. 12, January–February, 1950, pp. 49–54.

[14] W. A. Schonfeld and G. W. Beebe, "Normal Growth and Variation in the Male Genitalia from Birth to Maturity," *Journal of Urology*, Vol. 48, 1942, pp. 759–777.

[15] L. M. Terman and Maud A. Merrill, *Measuring Intelligence*, Boston, Houghton Mifflin Company, 1937, p. 30.

[16] T. M. Livesay, "Does Test Intelligence Increase at the College Level?" *Journal of Educational Psychology*, Vol. 30, 1939, pp. 63–68.

in their freshman year. Thorndike's study of ability to learn in relation to age seems to show a steady rise in learning effectiveness up to about age twenty-two.[17] A thorough review of the literature on mental development during adolescence led Jones and Conrad to conclude that the "bulk of evidence on 'general intelligence' indicates a limit of growth not earlier than eighteen to twenty years."[18]

TABLE 4

Age Norms for the Terman-McNemar Test of Mental
Ability *

AGE IN YEARS	STANDARD SCORE	INCREMENT OVER PRECEDING YEAR
10	77	
11	84	7
12	90	6
13	95	5
14	100	5
15	105	5
16	109	4
17	113	4
18	117	4
19	120	3

* L. M. Terman and Q. McNemar, *Terman-McNemar
Test of Mental Ability: Manual of Directions*, New York,
World Book Company, 1941.

It thus appears clear that there is a steady growth in intellectual capacity during the years of adolescence, and that, near the end of adolescence, learning ability reaches its peak. This high level is maintained with little loss for twenty or more years. Thorndike's [19] investigation shows a decline of only about fifteen per cent in learning ability between the ages of twenty-two and forty-two.

ADOLESCENT INTERESTS

Numerous studies have been made of adolescent vocational interests, reading interests, hobbies, and the like. These studies show

[17] E. L. Thorndike, *et al.*, *Adult Learning*, New York, Macmillan Company, 1928.

[18] Harold E. Jones and Herbert S. Conrad, "Mental Development in Adolescence," in *43rd Yearbook of the National Society for the Study of Education*, 1944, p. 158.

[19] E. L. Thorndike, *et al.*, *op.cit.*

that adolescents hold many of the same interests as do preadolescents and postadolescents, although in some instances fairly definite adolescent trends have been found. There are, furthermore, tremendous variations from adolescent to adolescent and from community to community. Specific interests also shift somewhat from generation to generation. What would interest an adolescent boy today would differ in many respects from what would interest a boy of the same age in 1890, for example. The boy in 1890 would scarcely have been expected to show interest in such activities as piloting an airplane, building a "hot rod" car, or working with radios or television sets. Likewise the girl of 1890 would undoubtedly have expressed no interest in being an airplane stewardess, or motion picture star. What may be a fad today among adolescents may not be so tomorrow. The teacher who would capitalize on adolescent interests as a means of promoting effective learning, must constantly study the individual adolescent under his direction, and also current trends of interests in the adolescent peer group of a given community. Lists of activities which interest boys and girls in a rural community in Texas, for example, may be only of slight value to the teacher who works with urban adolescents in Boston.

Although specific interests vary from adolescent to adolescent, from community to community, and from time to time, there are certain general interests which may be said to be typically adolescent. Adolescent girls, for example, are much more interested in members of the opposite sex than their preadolescent age-mates. They are also more interested in adornment and display of their persons. They are less interested in participation in games and activities requiring vigorous and strenuous activity than their prepubescent classmates.[20] Adolescent boys likewise develop new sex interests which lead to concern with personal appearance. For both sexes there is marked increase in vocational interests.

Studies by E. K. Strong[21] and Roeber and Garfield[22] show that

[20] Calvin P. Stone and Roger G. Barker, "The Attitudes and Interests of Pre-menarcheal and Postmenarcheal Girls," *Journal of Genetic Psychology*, Vol. 54, pp. 27–71.

[21] E. K. Strong, *Vocational Interests of Men and Women*, Stanford University Press, 1943, p. 294.

[22] Edward Roeber and Sol Garfield, "A Study of the Occupational Interests of High School Students in Terms of Grade Placement," *Journal of Educational Psychology*, Vol. 34, September, 1943, p. 358.

boys of adolescent age are extremely interested in such occupations as aviation, engineering, exploring, inventing, mechanics, and athletics. In some areas farming is a major interest for boys. Girls' chief choices of occupations include stenography, nursing, teaching, beauty operator, commercial artist, and housework.[23]

Strong's studies also support the common belief that boys of adolescent age tend to like activities which border on the dare-devilish and which require physical skill. He says, "Fifteen year-old boys like activities expressive of physical skill and daring more than any other type. On the average, 50.7 per cent of such boys like chopping wood, handling horses, snakes, boxing, performing sleight-of-hand tricks, pursuing bandits in a sheriff's posse, playing baseball rather than watching it, driving an auto, hunting, climbing along the edge of a precipice, auto races, secret service man, explorer, aviator, and so on." [24]

Many studies have been made of the reading interests of adolescents. Perhaps the most thorough of these is the one conducted by Norvell [25] and reported in his book, *The Reading Interests of Young People*. In this book, lists are given of the novels, plays, poems, short stories, biographies, and essays which are most popular with pupils in grades 7 to 12. The twenty-five novels most preferred by boys and girls in grades 10 to 12 are presented in Table 5.

Lists such as these are useful to teachers, but it must be remembered that any given adolescent may show no interest whatsoever in any of the books on such lists. This may be because the subject matter does not appeal to him or because his reading abilities are so meager that he can not read such materials with ease and enjoyment. As was mentioned earlier, the wise teacher will search for individual interests of pupils when making curricular adaptations. There are now available several series of books which have been especially designed for adolescents who have very limited reading abilities. Some of these are as follows: the "American Adventure Series," published by the Wheeler Publishing Company, Chicago; "The Thorndike Library," published by D. Appleton-Century Company; the "Simplified and Abridged Classics," published by Long-

---

[23] Edward Roeber and Sol Garfield, *Ibid.*, p. 360.
[24] E. K. Strong, *op.cit.*, pp. 301–302.
[25] George W. Norvell, *The Reading Interests of Young People*, Boston, D. C. Heath and Company, 1950.

mans, Green and Company; the "Classics for Enjoyment" series published by Laidlaw Brothers, and the "Everyreader Library" series published by the Webster Publishing Company, St. Louis.

TABLE 5

Twenty-Five Novels Most Popular with Boys and Girls in Grades 10 to 12 *

BOYS	GIRLS
1. *Huckleberry Finn*	1. *Bent Twig*
2. *Call of the Wild*	2. *Huckleberry Finn*
3. *Treasure Island*	3. *Silas Marner*
4. *Last of the Mohicans*	4. *Turmoil*
5. *Smoky*	5. *David Copperfield*
6. *Arrowsmith*	6. *So Big*
7. *Bishop Murder Case*	7. *Beloved Vagabond*
8. *To Have and To Hold*	8. *Call of the Wild*
9. *Cimarron*	9. *To Have and To Hold*
10. *The Virginian*	10. *Arrowsmith*
11. *Three Musketeers*	11. *Seventeen*
12. *Turmoil*	12. *Cimarron*
13. *Seventeen*	13. *Ethan Frome*
14. *Ivanhoe*	14. *The Virginian*
15. *Spy*	15. *Tale of Two Cities*
16. *Connecticut Yankee*	16. *Three Musketeers*
17. *Tale of Two Cities*	17. *Return of the Native*
18. *Beloved Vagabond*	18. *Crisis*
19. *Babbit*	19. *Oliver Twist*
20. *Moby Dick*	20. *House of Seven Gables*
21. *Ethan Frome*	21. *Green Mansions*
22. *Mr. Brisher's Treasure*	22. *Smoky*
23. *Silas Marner*	23. *Treasure Island*
24. *Green Mansions*	24. *As the Earth Turns*
25. *David Copperfield*	25. *Last of the Mohicans*

* From Norvell.

Stability of Adolescent Interests. Interests at all age levels are subject to change. One of the purposes of the school is to help pupils develop new interests and to forsake others which may not be educationally or socially rewarding. Those who give educational or vocational guidance to pupils of high school age are often concerned, however, with the question of how much faith to put in a pupil's declared vocational choice or his score on the Strong *Voca-*

tional Interest Test or the Kuder *Preference Record.* In the case of the Strong *Vocational Interest Test* [26] it has been shown that interests are surprisingly stable from age 15 years on, the average correlation over a ten-year period being .75. Of the changes taking place between age 15 and age 23, one-third of the change occurs between 15.5 and 16.5 years, one-third between 16.5 and 18 years, and the remainder between 18 and 23 years.[27] A study which has been made

TABLE 6

Relationship between Kuder Scores
Made 15 Months Apart *

INTEREST FIELD	CORRELATION
Mechanical	r = .835
Computational	r = .72
Scientific	r = .77
Persuasive	r = .89
Artistic	r = .755
Literary	r = .77
Musical	r = .77
Social service	r = .82
Clerical	r = .81

* From Reid.

of the Kuder *Preference Record* [28] also indicates that considerable degree of stability exists over a period of time. In this investigation 145 students were given this test at the beginning of their college freshman year and then retested fifteen months later. The results are shown in Table 6. No correlation falls below .72, and for one interest field the obtained relationship is .89. Facts such as these indicate that teachers and counselors can made good use of interest test data when advising adolescents. They must realize, however, that any given score is subject to change and that only by constant appraisal and re-appraisal of the individual's interests can sound guidance be given.

[26] E. K. Strong, *op.cit.,* p. 357.
[27] *Encyclopedia of Vocational Guidance,* New York, The Philosophical Library, 1948, p. 605.
[28] John W. Reid, "Stability of Measured Kuder Interests in Young Adults," *Journal of Educational Research,* Vol. 55, December, 1951, pp. 307–312.

ADOLESCENT WORRIES AND PROBLEMS

Attention has already been given to some of the worries adolescents have regarding physical deviations and defects. Adolescents are also concerned and anxious regarding problems of courtship, sex, marriage, religion, family relationships, school progress, educational and vocational futures, and personality development.

A very thorough investigation of the problems which trouble adolescents has recently been carried out in the state of Illinois.[29] Seven thousand twelfth-grade pupils in 57 high schools were administered the Mooney *Problem Check List.*[30] This is a questionnaire containing 330 problems which often bother adolescents. In the Illinois study the students were instructed to answer the questions anonymously so that an honest opinion of their chief worries and problems would be revealed. In Table 7 the specific problems are listed which were checked by twenty-five per cent of either boys or girls. Some of the major worries and problems of boys concern military service, how to dance, how to save money, "What I'll be 10 years hence," and dull classes. Major concerns of girls include taking things too seriously, wanting better personalities, losing tempers, being easily hurt, afraid of making mistakes, nervousness, and worry about grades. Of course, every problem listed in Table 7 is a major problem for either boys or girls.

At the end of the Mooney *Problem Check List* space is provided for the student to summarize his chief problems in his own words. A few of these statements made by twelfth-grade boys and girls in 1951 in two Illinois high schools [31] are presented herewith:

I would very much like to become a teacher, but since I am not working, and it costs money to go to college, the future doesn't look so good. I worry about what I'll be like in ten years too. Also, if I will find the right mate. (A girl)

[29] Harold C. Hand, *Principal Findings of the 1947–48 Basic Studies of the Illinois Secondary School Curriculum Program,* Circular Series A, No. 51, Bulletin No. 2, Office of the Superintendent of Public Instruction, Springfield, Illinois, 1949, pp. 67–73.

[30] Published by the Bureau of Educational Research, Ohio State University, Columbus, Ohio.

[31] These statements are taken from the Mooney Problem Check Lists administered to students by Harry D. Lovelass in connection with the Illinois Curriculum Program, 1951.

TABLE 7

Problems Checked by Twenty-Five Per Cent or More of
Twelfth-Grade Pupils of Either Sex

	PER CENT	
	BOYS	GIRLS
Military service	46	4
Worrying	30	29
How to save money	29	22
How to dance	29	11
Dull classes	28	29
What I'll be ten years hence	28	25
Too little study time	27	25
Restless in class	26	29
Weak, spelling, and grammar	26	8
Don't know what I want	25	29
Lunch hour too short	25	23
Need occupational decision	25	22
Take things too seriously	24	40
Forgetting things	23	26
Afraid of making mistakes	22	31
Daydreaming	22	26
Losing my temper	21	34
Worry about grades	21	27
Want better personality	20	35
Worry, exams	20	26
Nervousness	17	27
Stubbornness	16	26
Afraid to speak in class	13	25
Have less money than friends do	11	29
Too easily hurt	10	31
Overweight	7	26

I have a feeling that I am always being watched and am always in the wrong even though I didn't do anything. (A girl)

My chief problem is sex and learning to control my urges. (A girl)

I am too concerned about being in love and holding that person. Also I am confused on my moral code as everyone seems to have a different idea of what is wrong and what is right. (A girl)

I have got a low IQ. Many students who get lower grades than I do have got a higher rate of learning or IQ. I am full of faults. I should have checked more problems and worries than I did. (A boy)

I am altogether too shy. I want to date the girls but I am too shy or scared. One reason is I don't have enough money available.   (A boy)

My chief trouble is woman trouble. I go steady with one, but like another better. I am not sure what I should do or how I should do it.
(A boy)

My home life is the source of most of my troubles. My parents do not get along very well.   (A girl)

I am always troubled about my subjects and worried that my grades are not high enough. I think the teachers are too strict with their grades and we don't have enough freedom in class.   (A boy)

My chief problem deals with my disappointment in one love affair. I worry about this because many of the fellows think an ex-engaged girl isn't all she could be. They take advantage of you and expect too much.
(A girl)

I am especially worried because not only are my religious beliefs confused but my life is quite opposite to that which I feel a Christian should lead. Moreover, although I would like to change certain things in my life, I don't seem to have the will-power to do so, especially as all my friends' lives are very similar to mine.   (A girl)

The 330 problems of the Mooney check list are thrown into 11 categories and presented in Table 8.[32] This summary indicates the order of importance of the various problem areas as viewed by nearly 7,000 Illinois youth.

Worries connected with school work rate first with boys and second with girls. Boys also seem to be more concerned about their educational and vocational futures than girls. Girls show more worry than boys in the areas of personal and social relationships.

Both boys and girls during the adolescent period are seemingly overwhelmed with many problems and concerns which the schools could do much to alleviate. Better teaching and effective personal counseling would seem to be urgently needed. The first step a school should take would be to make a study of the problems boys and girls in a given locality and at a given time face. It is most important that the pupils be given as a part of this program a chance to state anonymously their problems. The school will thus be made aware of

[32] Taken from Harold C. Hand, *Principal Findings of the 1947–48 Basic Studies of the Illinois Curriculum Program*, May, 1949, p. 68.

TABLE 8

Rank Order of Problem Areas Indicated by Twelfth-Grade Pupils
1 = Highest Frequency of Mention

| | | RANK | |
PROBLEM AREA	BOYS	GIRLS	TOTAL
Adjustment to school work	1	2	1
Curriculum and teaching procedures	3	4	2.5
Future: vocational and educational	2	5	2.5
Personal-psychological relations	8	1	4.5
Social-psychological relations	6	3	4.5
Social and recreational activities	4.5	6	6
Courtship, sex, marriage	4.5	8	7
Health and physical development	8	7	8
Finances, living conditions and employment	8	9.5	9
Home and family	11	9.5	10.5
Morals and religion	10	11	10.5

the existence of many problems that otherwise would not come to the fore.

THE ADOLESCENT AND THE FAMILY

One of the chief needs of the adolescent is to attain emancipation from the family and become an independent individual in his own right. It is very difficult, however, for most parents to give the adolescent the independence he needs or the responsibility which he can easily carry. This situation produces much parent-child conflict. The sources of conflict between adolescents and their parents involve such matters as the use of the family car, choice of friends, spending of money, hours of getting home at night, grades at school, and ways of dressing. A partial list of grievances adolescents have against their mothers is presented in Table 9. The twenty-five complaints there listed are taken from a longer list of fifty which were registered by boys and girls in grades 7–12.[33] From the adolescent's point of view, parents pester, nag, complain and object. If parents were asked to list anonymously the complaints they have regarding their adolescent children, they would probably mention stubbornness, secretiveness, and unthankfulness. This eternal struggle be-

[33] Virginia L. Block, "Conflicts of Adolescents with their Mothers," *Journal of Abnormal and Social Psychology*, 1937, Vol. 32, pp. 192–206.

TABLE 9

Typical Adolescents' Complaints Regarding Their Mothers *

| | PERCENTAGE EXPRESSING | |
NATURE OF COMPLAINT	BOYS	GIRLS
Won't let me use the car	86	71
Insists that I eat foods which I dislike, but which are good for me	82	84
Pesters me about my table manners	75	64
Objects to my going automobile riding at night with boys	66	87
Teases me about my girl friends	51	0
Brags about me to other people	50	23
Won't let me take the subjects I want in school	33	56
Makes me go to bed at the same time that my younger brothers and sisters do	31	45
Insists upon nagging me regarding what I wear and how I dress	26	51
Objects to my going with boys or girls she doesn't like	19	40
Objects to the books and magazines I read	18	33
Won't let me spend the night with any of my friends	15	43
Refuses to let me buy the clothes I like	13	56
Treats me as if I were a child	5	16
Won't let me attend the church I want to attend	4	53
Accompanies me to parties, movies, etc.	3	30
Objects to my smoking	1	13
Teases me about my boy friends	0	66
Fusses because I wear lipstick	0	65
Objects to my going to dances	0	59

* Adapted from Block.

tween adolescents and their parents during the process of weaning often becomes very painful to all parties involved.

Both parents and adolescents need to recognize the existence of the types of problems which typically exist in families where adults and young people are striving to make new adjustments to a changed situation. They should also make efforts to change their behavior in ways to avoid serious conflict. Parents are sometimes greatly helped by programs sponsored by PTA groups which deal with adolescent problems. Schools can also provide activities which help boys and girls to gain insight into home and family relationships. A number of suggestions in this respect have been made by a group of educators.[34] Four of these are as follows:

1. Provide opportunity for boys and girls to study the role of various members of the family; guide them in analyzing their own problems related to breaking home ties.
2. Help boys and girls learn what their responsibilities are in helping to keep parents informed of their activities.
3. Help them analyze the kinds of situations in which it is important for young people to follow the judgment of their parents.
4. Give counseling on an individual basis to boys and girls who face frustrating problems by reason of over-protection, authoritarianism or inconsistent discipline in the home.

SEX EDUCATION AND THE ADOLESCENT

Sex education should begin in the home before the child starts to school; should be continued during the elementary school years; and should receive much attention by both the home and the school during the adolescent period. Adolescence brings many new problems of a sexual nature which are of only small concern to the child. In a careful study [35] of love problems of adolescents it was found that adolescent boys and girls are greatly concerned with such questions as the following:

Is it all right to make a blind date?

What about pick-up dates?

Is it all right to park after a school dance?

Can a brother and sister get a baby?

What is masturbation?

Should a student go steady?

What is true love and how can one recognize it?

How much difference should there be in the ages of a boy and a girl who are to be married?

Should a tall girl avoid marrying a tall man lest she have children who are abnormally tall?

How far should familiarities increase during engagement?

[34] *Guides to Curriculum Building, the Junior High School Level;* Illinois Secondary School Curriculum Program, Bulletin No. 8, Superintendent of Public Instruction, Springfield, Illinois, January, 1950, pp. 37–41.

[35] Oliver M. Butterfield, *Love Problems of Adolescents,* New York, Emerson Books, Inc., 1941.

Why shouldn't young people feel free to engage in sex relations before marriage if they know safe contraceptive methods?

Why don't they teach more about sex and social relations in school?

These are just a few of the numerous questions raised by boys and girls in the study just referred to. There is much evidence that our young people are eager for instruction in such matters, but that schools have done very little in the way of giving effective guidance in this area.

The amount of interest shown by teachers, parents, non-parents, and students in the question of sex education is revealed in a recent study conducted in Illinois.[36] Sixty-nine secondary schools and their constituents participated in this investigation. The question asked was: "Should the school help students obtain sound sex education?" The percentage of individuals answering yes is shown in Table 10.

TABLE 10

Should the School Help Students Obtain Sound Sex Education?
Percentage Answering, "Yes"

TEACHERS	PARENTS	NON-PARENTS	STUDENTS
83	82	77	83
(n = 2024)	(n = 6455)	(n = 1739)	(n = 20101)

It is there seen that all the groups strongly favor instruction in sex education. Over 80 per cent of parents, teachers, and students feel the need for this type of activity as do also 77 per cent of the non-parents. In this same study additional data show that only 10 per cent of the teachers and 20 per cent of the graduates of these secondary schools feel that sufficient attention is being given to sex instruction in the schools.

Probably the most effective type of sex education program would be one that both integrates sex education study into such courses as biology, physiology, health or hygiene, sociology, home economics, civics, and literature; and also provides a special course dealing with family and personal living problems. Boys need the latter type of course as much as girls, although in many schools it is a course

[36] Kenneth B. Henderson, *Principal Findings of the Follow-Up Study of the Illinois Secondary School Curriculum Program,* Office of the Superintendent of Public Instruction, Springfield, Illinois, 1952.

mainly for girls. The course in sex education should not be labeled as such but should be given a nonemotional title, such as a course in "personal relations," "life adjustment," or "family living."

Any program in sex instruction must have the whole-hearted support of parents and the rest of the community. The PTA group or other parent group can help in the planning of the work, and review from time to time films and other materials which are to be used in the program. The reader who is interested in more detailed discussion of sex education programs will find the following references very useful:

1. Baker, J. N., *Sex Education in High Schools,* New York, Emerson Books, Inc., 1943.
2. Bibby, Cyril, *Sex Education,* New York, Emerson Books, Inc., 1946.
3. Gruenberg, Benjamin C., *How Can We Teach About Sex?* Public Affairs Pamphlet, No. 122, Public Affairs Committee, Inc., 22 East 38th Street, New York, N. Y., 1946.
4. Strain, Frances B., *Sex Guidance in Family Life Education: A Handbook for the Schools,* New York, The Macmillan Company, 1946.
5. Kirkendall, Lester A., "Sex Education in Nine Cooperating High Schools," *The Clearing House,* Vol. 18, March, 1944, pp. 378–391.

Several valuable films have also been produced which can be used in sex education programs at the secondary school level. Two of these are the McGraw-Hill production called *Human Reproduction*[37] and the University of Oregon film called *Human Growth.*[38] A new test with two forms entitled the *Sex Knowledge Inventories*[39] is also now available for use. Materials which have been especially prepared for use by the boys and girls themselves include *Facts of Life and Love* by Evelyn Duvall,[40] *Youth Grown Into Adulthood* by Morey Fields *et al.,*[41] and *Life and Growth* by Alice Keliher.[42]

ADOLESCENT DELINQUENCY

Adolescence is the period when initial criminal activity reaches its peak. Statistical evidence shows that "youths between the ages of sixteen and twenty-one commit serious crimes far out of proportion

[37] McGraw-Hill Book Company, Inc., New York.
[38] E. C. Brown Trust, 220 S. W. Alder Street, Portland, Oregon.
[39] Published by Family Life Publications, Inc., Box 337, Durham, North Carolina.
[40] Published by the Association Press, New York, 1950.
[41] Published by the Chartwell House, Inc., New York, 1950.
[42] Published by the D. Appleton-Century Company, New York, 1938.

to the incidence of this age group in the population." [43] Additional data indicate that 40–60 per cent of inmates in Federal and state prisons are under 25 years of age.[44]

Why is it that young people are so prone to commit delinquent acts? In the first place, with the coming of adolescence the individual, because of less supervision of the home, is able to get out with the gang and follow either his group or his individual inclinations to a greater extent. In the second place, the adolescent's desire for new experiences together with his only partly developed philosophy of life cause him to make many unwise decisions which an older person would not make.

The basic cause of delinquency, however, is frustration of some type. The adolescent's needs for recognition, security, independence, and affection are frequently thwarted to such an extent that anti-social behavior is employed in an effort to reduce the pent-up tensions. Not all individuals become overtly aggressive when thwarted, but many do. Some of the conditions of life which cause frustrations that may lead to delinquency are poverty, low intelligence, conflict in the family, broken homes, lack of affection from parents, humiliation and lack of success in school, and inferiority feelings arising from real or imagined physical deviations.

A boy may break street lights and put paint on the school building because he receives no recognition around school in either curricular or extracurricular activities. A girl may drift into sexual difficulties because, in this relationship, she is really wanted by someone, and what she has to offer is, for the first time as valuable as what anyone else can offer. Delinquent acts would not be committed if they did not help the adolescent satisfy some of his basic needs. The delinquent needs assistance in making adjustments which are socially acceptable and at the same time need-satisfying.

Plant has pointed out that the delinquent through his very behavior is trying to tell us certain things are wrong in our schools and other social arrangements. Plant [45] says:

[43] Bertram M. Beck, "Youthful Offenders," in *Social Work Yearbook*, New York, American Association of Social Workers, 1951, p. 542.

[44] William W. Brickman, "Juvenile Delinquency," *School and Society*, Vol. 68, October 30, 1948, p. 305.

[45] James S. Plant, "Who is the Delinquent?" in *Juvenile Delinquency and the Schools*, Part I, 47th Yearbook of the National Society for the Study of Education, Chicago, University of Chicago Press, 1948, p. 28.

The truant and the delinquent are doing their best to tell us of the places in our social structure that need change—changes that would be for the benefit of all children. The delinquent is trying hard to tell us to give to all children a curriculum that is built for their needs. He is trying to tell us that while we have made a good start on vocational courses, courses in sewing, homemaking, carpentry, and special classes for the retarded, our culture still looks upon these as second-rate—something that the child is not to go into if he can make the grade in the more "proper" course. He is trying hard to force us to give every child a sense of growth and a feeling of success in his school years. He is asking us to give expert help to the child who has one specific disability: e.g., in reading. He is trying to tell us to choose our teachers for their real understanding of children as well as for their academic ability, and not let marriage end the careers of those who would have the most rich and facile communication with children.

The school can not solve all the problems of juvenile delinquency, but it can do much to make children feel worth while and thus lessen frustrations that arise in the home and elsewhere. By requiring certain children to meet requirements that were impossible for them to meet, schools in the past have actually contributed to the delinquency of children. The happy, successful boy or girl who is achieving worthwhile goals is seldom if ever a delinquent.

SUMMARY

Adolescence is the period of transition which extends from the end of childhood to the beginning of adulthood. It may be long or short depending upon the practices employed by families and larger social groups. In our society children are generally given adult responsibilities very slowly. This results in a prolonged period of semi-dependence for many youths which may continue for as long as eight or ten years.

The adolescent, because of his ambiguous status (being neither a child nor an adult), frequently finds himself involved in emotional conflicts with younger children in the family, parents, teachers, and other members of the community. He wants to be grown-up and sometimes feels that he is not understood or not given enough responsibility for his own acts. Adolescents are particularly sensitive with respect to the opinions of their peers and generally value the judgments of their age-mates more highly than those of adults. During adolescence an extreme sensitivity is also exhibited in regard to personal defects, blemishes, or sex inappropriate physical characteristics. Many adolescents give the impression that they feel insecure. Statistics have revealed that during this period, delinquency and emotional problems of many types reach a high peak. There is no question but that adolescence is a trying time for many individuals. Although adolescence presents numerous problems for young people, there is no reason why under favorable conditions these can not be handled without undue stress or crisis. Teachers are in a favorable position to help adolescents resolve their worries, and plan courses of action which will provide for the satisfaction of their needs. Since adolescents so universally resent being treated as younger children, teachers should make an especial effort to give them responsibilities, and freedom which is commensurate with their maturity. Teachers may also find it possible at times to give guidance to parents regarding procedures to be followed in dealing with adolescents in the family.

It has been shown in this chapter that the adolescent has special problems which he did not have as a child and which are somewhat different from those he will encounter as an adult. He has certain needs which are accentuated, and a series of developmental tasks which must be mastered. Teachers and parents alike should understand the nature of the unique problems of the adolescents if they are to help them make a smooth transition into adulthood. Knowledge of basic behavior theory plus specialized information regarding the period of adolescence and the individual adolescent are prerequisites for this task.

REFERENCES FOR FURTHER STUDY

Ausubel, David P., "An Evaluation of Recent Adolescent Drug Addiction," *Mental Hygiene*, Vol. 36, July, 1952, pp. 373–382.

Averill, Lawrence A., "The Impact of a Changing Culture Upon Pubescent Ideals," *School and Society*, Vol. 72, 1950, pp. 49–53.

Barschak, Erna, "A Study of Happiness and Unhappiness in the Childhood and Adolescence of Girls in Different Cultures," *The Journal of Psychology*, Vol. 32, October, 1951, pp. 173–215.

Blair, Glenn M., "What Teachers Should Know About the Psychology of Adolescence," *Journal of Educational Psychology*, Vol. 41, October, 1950, pp. 356–361.

Cruze, Wendell W., *Adolescent Psychology and Development*, New York, The Ronald Press, 1953.

Daly, Maureen (Editor), *Profile of Youth*, Philadelphia, J. B. Lippincott Company, 1951.

Fleming, C. M., *Adolescence*, New York, International Universities Press, Inc., 1949.

Frank, Lawrence K., "Needs of Adolescents in the Area of Emotional Health," *The High School Journal*, December, 1951, pp. 66–74.

Garrison, Karl C., *Psychology of Adolescence*, Fourth Edition, New York, Prentice-Hall, Inc., 1951.

Hamrin, Shirley A. and Paulson, Blanche B., *Counseling Adolescents*, Chicago, Science Research Associates, Inc., 1950.

Hollingshead, August B., *Elmtown's Youth*, New York, John Wiley and Sons, 1949.

Horrocks, John E., *The Psychology of Adolescence*, Boston, Houghton Mifflin Company, 1951.

Jones, Mary C., and Bayley, Nancy, "Physical Maturing Among Boys as Related to Behavior," *Journal of Education Psychology*, Vol. 41, March, 1950, pp. 129–148.

Kirkpatrick, Milton E., "The Mental Hygiene of Adolescence in the Anglo-American Culture," *Mental Hygiene*, Vol. 36, July, 1952, pp. 394–403.

Klineberg, Otto, "How Adult Are Adolescents?" *National Parent Teacher*, Vol. 47, September, 1952, pp. 21–23.

Kuhlen, Raymond G., *The Psychology of Adolescent Development*, New York, Harper and Brothers, 1952.

Landis, Paul H., *Adolescence and Youth*, Second Edition, New York, McGraw-Hill Book Company, Inc., 1952.

Levi, Joseph and Michelson, Barbara, "Emotional Problems of Physically Handicapped Adolescents—A Study of Ten Adolescent Boys," *Exceptional Children*, Vol. 18, April, 1952, pp. 200–206.

Malm, Marguerite and Jamison, Olis G., *Adolescence*, New York, McGraw-Hill Book Company, Inc., 1952.

Reid, Chandos, "The Classroom Teacher and Adolescent Adjustment," *Teachers College Record*, Vol. 52, May, 1951, pp. 500–511.

Segel, David, *Frustration in Adolescent Youth*, Bulletin 1951, No. 1, Washington, D. C., Federal Security Agency.

Stolz, Herbert R. and Stolz, Lois Meek, *Somatic Development of Adolescent Boys*, New York, The Macmillan Company, 1951.

Thorndike, Robert L., "Growth of Intelligence during Adolescence," *The Journal of Genetic Psychology*, Vol. 72, 1948, pp. 11–15.

PART III

LEARNING

Chapter 5

An Orientation to Learning

INTRODUCTION

WHAT IS LEARNING? Any change of behavior which is a result of experience, and which causes people to face later situations differently may be called learning. The person not trained in psychology may conceive of learning in a narrow, academic sense. To such a person learning means acquiring skill in reading, spelling, or a trade. Actually, it is much more! Children learn cultural values; they learn appropriate sex roles; they learn to love and to hate and to fear and to be self-confident; they learn wants and interests and character and personality traits. It is not much of an overstatement to say that a person is what he has learned to be.

Learning is thus the central theme in educational psychology. Whenever one hears or sees terms such as adjustment, emotional blocking, laziness, delinquency, or problem-solving, he may be sure that such words demand a knowledge of the principles of learning for their understanding. Most of this volume is an attempt to give the reader a view of what is presently known about learning, so that teaching may be based upon general principles rather than upon specific rules whose application is limited by the specificity of the teaching situation.

In following the subsequent material and the principles which evolve it is hoped that the student will achieve more than a rote memorization of new words. By noting the illustrative (even though tentative) application of the principles of learning to classroom situations the reader should begin to get an applicational point of view enabling him to apply principles of learning in his own teaching. A specific technique which works in music education may not be appropriate for the teaching of biology, but basic principles of learning can be fitted to both.

What Do Teachers Need to Know About Learning? [1] At one time, the writer was requested by an insurance company to suggest ways of improving its training program for newly inducted salesmen. The writer took the question to his class (composed almost entirely of teachers), and within a short time had received a number of positive suggestions which he passed on to the company.

Teachers should, and usually do, know more about human learning than any other professional group. But as in other fields of work, there are probably certain minimum essentials—which all do not know—and a rapidly growing body of knowledge which challenges even those whose major field of study is the psychology of learning. In the next few paragraphs a résumé is given of essential materials with which all teachers need to be acquainted.

1. *Readiness and individual differences.* Teachers should have a good understanding of the nature of learners and of the importance of considering developmental levels of all pupils. Experienced teachers know the futility of trying to push a child too fast.

2. *Motivation.* Some teachers have expressed the belief that by far the greatest part of a teacher's work centers around problems of motivation. Certainly it is apparent that effective teaching stems from a consideration of children's interests and needs. The child who is motivated to learn is well on his way to learning.

3. *Interests and attitudes.* Out of those activities which satisfy needs, children develop interests and attitudes which may become enduring habits and traits, and which may have a profound effect upon the children's acceptance or rejection of schooling. Interests and attitudes have a double-barreled significance in teaching. Not only are they learned but also they play an important part in all the behavior change which the school tries to produce.

4. *Organization.* What is the most effective way to organize learning experiences? How do the principles of organization affect such things as assignment-making, reviewing, testing, selection of books and the like? These questions can only be answered when the

---

[1] For a more detailed discussion of this section see: G. M. Blair, "How Learning Theory is Related to Curriculum Organization," *Journal of Educational Psychology,* Vol. 39, 1948, pp. 161–166.

teacher knows learning as a process of seeing relationships and purposive integration of ideas and experiences.

5. *Transfer of Learning*. Learning which remains specific to the situation in which it was acquired is almost useless. To be of value, learning must have utility in new situations in and out of school. Consequently, teachers must know the facts regarding transfer of learning, and those methods of teaching and learning which will facilitate the use of learned materials.

6. *Social Psychology of Learning*. A good share of school learning occurs in a group set-up. The group can facilitate learning of an individual or militate against it. Consequently, a teacher must know how to work with groups, how groups learn, and how the behavior of groups affects individual learning.

7. *Special Difficulties in Learning*. No matter how excellent the teaching, there will always be children with special disabilities who need special help. Teachers must know how to diagnose pupils' difficulties when the causes are not apparent, and the principles of remediation which will make learning possible for such children.

Subsequent chapters in this section follow the above outline. The reader must remember that coverage herein represents what these authors consider as minimum essentials in this very broad field. Further work is suggested at the end of each chapter.

How May Teachers Know This Field? Understanding of a field as complex and broad as the psychology of human learning is possible only when educators read widely, form habits of critical analysis, and focus attention upon the processes of learning in their daily work. Following are suggestions which the writer gives students in his class in "The Psychology of Learning for Teachers."

1. Read widely from general sources about learning, and also from current journals in educational psychology and related fields.

2. Use the suggested readings at the ends of chapters.

3. Analyze your own reading, study methods, tests, and discussions.

4. Form the habit of appraising each teaching technique in terms of its effect upon learning. Ask yourself: How will this test, exercise, field trip, movie or demonstration bring about learning?

5. Think of the consequences of school activities not only in terms of academic learning but also as they affect other learnings such as attitudes, interests and the personality of children.

6. Develop an experimental attitude. Try new techniques and evaluate the learning outcomes.

WAYS OF STUDYING THE LEARNING PROCESS

As in other areas of science there are, in the field of learning, various theories which attempt to explain its basic processes. Both in method and conclusion these theories have differed greatly, for they have sharply focused attention on only certain aspects of the total learning process. As a consequence, the behavior which various experimenters and teachers have observed has been different. For example, some workers in this field have so diligently pursued the way in which a stimulus and response are connected that they have ignored the condition of the person, or animal with which they were working.

A few of the kinds of experimental situations which have been used to study learning include: (1) A hungry animal is put inside a puzzle box (food outside) from which release is possible only by striking the latch, (2) An animal is put in a box in which there is a bar connected with a source of food pellets which are released one at a time as the bar is pressed, (3) An animal is placed on a platform and forced to jump towards one of a series of doors which are differentiated by shape or color, (4) Nonsense syllables are paired with geometric designs and a person is shown the pairings a number of times until he has memorized them, (5) A person is given a verbal problem, and asked to describe his solution aloud. Obviously the kinds of behavior which are observed will differ greatly. In one case there may be a wild thrashing about in an attempt to escape, in another a seemingly thoughtful or cautious approach. Furthermore, the variation in what is found is not surprising when it is realized that experimenters have worked with animals of nearly every species from one-celled organisms to man.

These various experimental studies have led to several ways of looking at the process of learning. Each has attempted to derive basic principles. At the present time, however, it would be unwise for a "human engineer" (the teacher) to adopt any one method as *the* way. Dealing with complex human learning demands that one give attention to all aspects of the learning process. As one writer puts it: "Have we any right to classify the learning to high-jump, to get along with alcohol, and to be friendly with other people under the same term, and to expect identical laws to hold for all these processes?" [2]

It is the hope of the writers that the readers of this volume will be able to achieve a meaningful synthesis of the material which follows. In a later section suggested guides to such a synthesis will be given.

Learning as an Associative Process. The oldest and most common method of analyzing the process of learning is through a study of the association of ideas, stimuli and responses. Even the ancient Greeks attempted to describe mental life in this fashion. Aristotle talked of learning as an association of ideas following the laws of (1) similarity, (2) contrast, and (3) contiguity.[3] He believed that people learn and remember those things which are alike, which are striking because of their difference, and which occur together in space and time.

Centuries later, a rebirth of interest in the philosophy of the human mind resulted in a school of thought known as the British School of Associationism. This group had the notion that mind was formed through a lawful process of the association of experiences and ideas. Well-known historical figures such as Thomas Hobbes, John Locke, David Hume, and later, James Mill, and Alexander Bain were represented in this philosophical venture, and the great, revolutionary ideas concerning the original nature of man were developed. For instance, the concept of the newborn as having a blank mind (*tabula rasa*) probably gave impetus to the idea that man is a product of his experiences.[4] From these early beliefs came a great concern for the nature of mental life and in turn this concern led to many of the modern ideas about education, child-rearing, and even democratic ideals.

Not until the turn of the present century, however, did learning, as a process of association, receive experimental analysis. At that time, two widely separated workers, E. L. Thorndike in America and I. P. Pavlov in Russia, established bases for analytical studies of the process of learning.

Connectionism. Thorndike's work for a period of over fifty years

[2] Kurt Lewin, "Field Theory and Learning," in National Society for the Study of Education, 41st Yearbook, Part II, *The Psychology of Learning*, Bloomington, Illinois, Public School Publishing Company, 1942, p. 220.

[3] Gardner Murphy, *Historical Introduction to Modern Psychology*, New York, Harcourt, Brace and Company, 1949, p. 9.

[4] *Ibid.*, pp. 21–29 and pp. 97–110.

is recognized as one of the greatest contributions to the psychology of learning, particularly for its educational implications. His psychology of "Connectionism" has had a profound influence upon American education.[5]

Thorndike demonstrated that learning could be analyzed and furnished practical results to educators when he conducted experiments which led to his statement of the "law of effect." In brief, this law tells those who teach, that learners will acquire and remember those responses which lead to satisfying after effects.[6] A praised response will be retained longer than one which is not praised or one which is called wrong. This is indeed a practical kind of material, and one which has gained such wide acceptance that the reader may think of it as just common sense.

Another practical venture of the "Connectionists" was their study of the effect of exercise or frequency of repetition on learning. Every teacher in certain types of courses is faced with the problem of how much drill to use in teaching. Thorndike's experiments showed that repetition *per se* did not establish a connection, but that the strength of such connections depended upon the laws of effect and readiness and such secondary principles as belongingness.[7]

How did Thorndike go about testing his principles and laws of learning? Following is a typical experiment which was used to test the principle of "belongingness."

A Thorndike Experiment

Thorndike read the following paragraph 10 times to persons who were told: "Listen to what I read with moderate attention as you would listen to a lecture."

"Alfred Dukes and his sister worked sadly. Edward Davis and his brother argued rarely. Francis Bragg and his cousin played hard. Barney Croft and his father watched earnestly. Lincoln Blake and his uncle listened gladly. Jackson Craig and his son struggle often. Charlotte Dean and her friend studied easily."—and so on.[8]

[5] An excellent description of Thorndike's contributions may be found in Peter Sandiford, "Connectionism: Its Origin and Major Features" in National Society for the Study of Education, 41st Yearbook, *op.cit.*, pp. 97–140.

[6] E. L. Thorndike, *The Fundamentals of Learning*, New York, Teachers College, Columbia University, 1932.

[7] E. L. Thorndike, *Selected Writings from a Connectionists' Psychology*, New York, Appleton-Century-Crofts, Inc., 1949, pp. 62–80.

[8] *Ibid.*, p. 63.

After the tenth reading, students were asked such questions as:

1. What word came after rarely?
2. What word came after Lincoln?

Of 240 students to whom the paragraph was read, about 2% (the number who would have guessed the right name) could answer such questions as number 1; while between 70 and 80% were able to answer such questions as number 2. Although the number of repetitions was the same between "rarely" and the word that followed it, and "Lincoln" and the word that followed it, the latter was remembered better because of a connection or "belongingness."

Conditioned Reflex.[9] A precise and clear-cut picture of the way in which associations can occur was demonstrated in the famous experiments of Pavlov. While working on the process of digestion (for which he won a Nobel Prize), Pavlov noted that dogs, which began to salivate when presented with meat powder, also made this response when they heard the sound of the attendant's footsteps approaching their cages.[10] This observation led to a systematic study of the "conditioned reflex," the diagram for which follows:

STEP 1.	Original Natural Relationship	Unconditioned Stimulus or Meat Powder		→ Unconditioned Response Salivation
STEP 2.	Pairing of New Unrelated Stimulus with the Old	Conditioned Stimulus or Sound of a Tuning Fork	Unconditioned Stimulus + Meat Powder	→ Unconditioned Response Salivation

(SEVERAL REPETITIONS OF STEP 2)

STEP 3.	Removal of Unconditioned Stimulus	Conditioned Stimulus Tuning Fork Alone		→ Conditioned Response Salivation

If one uses this scheme to analyze the conditioning of a child to a fear of dogs, appropriate substitution would be as follows:

[9] The reader will appreciate the necessity of brevity in treating a topic such as this when attention is directed to the fact that literally thousands of experiments have been carried on in the area of conditioning. For an introduction to the area see: E. R. Hilgard and D. G. Marquis, *Conditioning and Learning*, New York, Appleton-Century Company, 1940.

[10] Gardner Murphy, *op.cit.*, p. 255.

STEP 1.	Unconditioned Stimulus (Pain—Loud Noise)	→ Unconditioned Response (Fear Responses)
STEP 2.	Conditioned Stimulus (Dog) and Unconditioned Stimulus (Bark or Bite)	→ Unconditioned Response (Fear)
STEP 3.	Conditioned Stimulus (Dog)	→ Conditioned Response (Fear)

It should be clear that children can form connections even though there is apparently no "logical" relationship between the ideas and events which are associated. Conditioning does occur in the classroom. For example, there is no logical relationship between a child's feelings of inferiority and arithmetic *per se*. But when, in arithmetic class, he is made to feel inferior enough times, the activities connected with arithmetic become almost inextricably linked with the emotional responses associated with feelings of inferiority. Teachers of remedial reading have often reported cases in which children flinch, tremble, or show other fear responses at the mere sight of a reading book, while a comic book or newspaper fails to elicit these emotional manifestations.

Learning as a Process of Reinforcement! [11] Another way of looking at the learning process is to focus attention upon the *effect* of the response upon the individual. As was shown in the preceding section on "Connectionism," Thorndike's most important law of learning was his *law of effect*, which has become a basic part of most psychologies of learning. [12]

It is important that educators consider learning in this way, as it is a point of view which alerts them to the characteristics of the learner—the learner's need states, and his past experience (previous reinforcements). There is little doubt that knowledge about the kinds of behavior for which a youngster has been rewarded or from which he has received satisfaction will provide a teacher with the best possible tool for predicting future behavior. Also, this knowledge should offer help in finding ways to change behavior, by changing the patterns of reinforcement.

In a simple form, reinforcement might be illustrated as follows:

[11] When an act reduces a need and leads to satisfying consequences that act is said to be reinforced. As used in psychological literature, the concept of reinforcement is roughly equivalent to the notion of reward.

[12] E. R. Hilgard, *Theories of Learning*, New York, Appleton-Century-Crofts, Inc., 1948.

$$\text{Rat} - \frac{\text{Running}}{\text{Through}} - \text{Food}$$
$$\text{Maze}$$

The receipt of the reward serves to fixate the responses (making proper turns in the maze) so that on subsequent trials the animal will be more able to go directly to the goal object. The same sort of scheme can be thought of in the learning of children. For example:

$$\text{Child} - \frac{\text{Throwing Paper}}{\text{Out of School Window}} - \frac{\text{Laughter and Enjoyment}}{\text{of Fellow Students}}$$

The attention getting response is fixated by the receipt of satisfaction, i.e., by the reduction of the need for peer approval.

When responses do not achieve the desired effect (a satisfying state of affairs or need reduction), responses are not fixated. The child who works hard to achieve a certain goal such as the teacher's approval or a material reward, only to find after his efforts that these are not forthcoming will be much less likely to retain the learnings which have led to the "empty" goal. Many other principles connected with learning viewed in this manner will be taken up in Chapter 7.

Learning as a Perceptual Process. Much of what is called learning really involves a change in ways of looking at one's environment. The impetus for this point of view comes from Gestalt Psychology.[13] The group of psychologists who established this system began working on problems of perception in Germany in about 1912. This group objected to analysis of learning and behavior by breaking it down into specific elements.[14] They contended that such "molecular" analysis destroys the forces which bind experiences into meaningful wholes, and argued that in teaching one must consider the whole situation as a unit, rather than as a series of discrete parts.

For example, these dots and lines: [15]

[13] "Gestalt" means pattern or configuration. A good introduction to "Gestalt" learning theories may be found in E. R. Hilgard, op.cit., pp. 177–208.

[14] They objected particularly to a stimulus-response psychology such as advocated by some behaviorists, and the atomism of the psychology of Wundt.

[15] Kurt Koffka, Principles of Gestalt Psychology, New York, Harcourt, Brace and Company, 1935, p. 164.

appear to unite into pairs. The "pairness" caused by their proximity is a characteristic entirely apart from the nature of the objects, and any analysis which breaks down this configuration destroys this characteristic.

Conceived in this way, learning may be thought of as a change in cognitive structure, i.e., as a change in the readiness of the individual to perceive objects and situations in a new way. The child who has first experienced a loss of breath in a wading pool now perceives water in an entirely different manner. Likewise a youngster who for the first time has seen his own story in print, perceives the job of reading as a much different task than before.

The individual's behavior, when looked at in this way, is seen as a "purposive" striving toward goals, the paths to which are marked by signs or cues. The significant feature of the learning process occurs when the learner ascribes meaning or significance to these signs.[16] Experimentation has shown that interference with response sequences are not sufficient to prevent learners from reaching goals by a new series of responses.[17] This supports the notion that what is learned is not primarily a stimulus response connection, but a changed perception in which various stimuli are seen as pointers toward a goal.

Learning as a Process of Organization and Understanding. For complex learnings, especially when verbal factors are considered, the analysis must include a consideration of such things as meaningfulness, organization and understanding. This type of analysis is quite similar to the study of learning as a perceptual process. The major emphasis is upon the study of relationships and how people learn to see relationships among various items of experience. Learning of relationships may be clearly seen in the phenomenon of insight. Sometimes pupils work for a long time on a problem or skill with little apparent progress. All of a sudden there will be a flash of understanding in which the student sees through the problem, or reforms his responses into a more complex habit. The phenomenon was first widely publicized by the famous German psychologist

[16] E. C. Tolman, *Purposive Behavior in Animals and Men*, New York, D. Appleton-Century Company, 1932.

[17] E. C. Tolman, B. F. Ritchie and D. Kalish, "Studies in Spatial Learning, IV, The Transfer of Place Learning to Other Starting Paths," *Journal of Experimental Psychology*, Vol. 37, 1947, pp. 39–47.

Köhler,[18] who found that apes, when confronted with a difficult problem, might act as if they were surveying the situation; would then go directly to the goal object (banana) by putting two sticks together, or by piling one box on top of another. It appeared that there had been a sudden perceptual change in which these animals saw the relationship of the sticks or boxes to themselves and the goal in a new way.

The reader who wishes to experience insight might consider the problem shown in Figure 2.

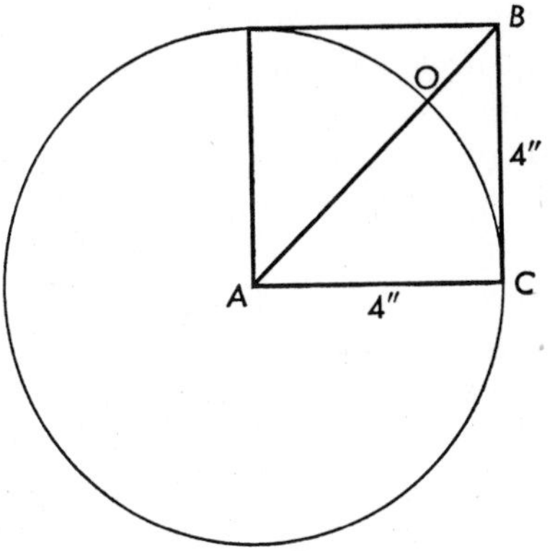

At first glance many people attempt to apply the Pythagorean theorem or some other inapplicable formula to the solution. Immediately after the line AO is seen as another radius of the circle, a perceptual shift occurs and the problem is solved.

FIGURE 2. What is the Length of the Line AO?

Learning in this sense must also be thought of as a process of problem-solving—a way of thinking, creating, and synthesizing. The point of view that learning is much more than the acquisition of specific skills is made explicit by Brownell, who writes:

A problem solving attitude, an inquiring and questioning mind, is a desirable educational outcome and it is possible of development. The practice of "learning" by cramming does not produce this outcome, nor does the practice of accepting from others truths and conclusions which ought to be established by the learner himself. The attitude *is* produced by continued experience in solving real problems, one consequence of which is that the learner comes to *expect* new problems and to look for them.[19]

The important aspect of this view of learning is that it points to the importance of studying the processes in learning—the steps

[18] W. Köhler, *The Mentality of Apes,* New York, Harcourt, Brace and Company, 1925.
[19] W. A. Brownell, "Problem Solving," in National Society for the Study of Education, 41st Yearbook, *op.cit.,* p. 440.

which the learner takes in solving problems, rather than the end-product of learning.

ESSENTIAL CHARACTERISTICS OF THE LEARNING PROCESS

If one looks in retrospect at the various ways of analyzing learning, which have just been discussed, he can find little with which to quarrel, and few principles derived from experimentation which are wholly incompatible. Instead he will find that for the complex learnings in school it is necessary to make use of all these forms of analysis and the principles they offer. Each gives essential elements in the total picture of various kinds of behavior change. By putting these several analyses together, one may obtain a composite view of the essential characteristics of learning, and of the nature of the processes involved.

The fundamental ingredients of learning which emerge from this composite analysis are: needs, incentives, barriers to goals, response potential, selectivity and elimination of responses, and effect of the response. A discussion of each of these six ingredients of the learning process follows.[20]

Needs. Behavior derives energy value from the imbalance caused by needs. Without this important substratum, learning could not occur, because the person would make no responses. Needs are products of stimuli both from without (a dish of ice cream) and from within (stomach contractions). These stimuli become motives in that they literally push the person in the direction of those objects or situations which the person perceives as capable of fulfilling them. Needs are the mainsprings of behavior, and no learning situation can be fully understood without some knowledge of the forces which impel the person to act.

Incentives. Behavior is goal directed—purposive. The child strives for those objects, situations or skills which he thinks will satisfy his needs. Reward, approval, a feeling of achievement and success, and long-time goals such as vocational incentives all serve to stimulate the youngsters. Schools are apt to use grades, tests and various kinds of honors as incentives but often fail to provide for

---

[20] The following characteristics are in part adapted from A. W. Melton, "Learning," in W. S. Monroe (Ed.), *Encyclopedia of Educational Research*, New York, The Macmillan Company, 1950, pp. 668–690.

other important needs such as social approval and the desire of a learner for a knowledge of his progress.

A study of the things a child wants—his daydreams, wishes and ideals, and his play activities outside the classroom should give the teacher a basis for planning activities and teaching procedures which contain the most desirable incentives. Also, the teacher needs to know the abilities of his pupils so that incentives are realistic and within the reach of the learner.

Barriers to Goals. Each learning situation entails effort. Behavior does not materially change if the child already has a well-established path to a goal. Thus constant repetition of an already established response may have little effect other than possibly strengthening the behavior change. (Even this has limits, for if repetition of the response is forced too often the person's perception of the goal may change, fatigue and work decrement may cause a drop in performance.) When, however, there is no clear-cut route to the incentive, the finding of such a path denotes learning. Overcoming obstacles is a characteristic of every learning situation. Melton has given a description of a barrier as:

The notion of obstacle encompasses such varied circumstances as, reactive inadequacy through forgetting, negative transfer, conflict of motives, inappropriate sets and attitudes, perceptual inadequacies, and aberrations and emotional inadequacies.[21]

With respect to barriers which prevent the child's achieving incentives, teachers should:

1. See that a good share of the barriers are within capabilities of the child to surmount.

2. Give guidance, and help children find responses which will achieve incentives.

3. Carefully appraise the obstacles or barriers in a learning situation when a youngster's responses show he is trying to escape from the situation altogether.

Response Potential—Variable Behavior. Learning requires a response potential which is sufficient to allow various kinds of behavior. Lower animals are unable to profit greatly from experience or adapt themselves to changing circumstances, because their responses are stereotyped and somewhat fixed. Those environmental

[21] A. W. Melton, *op.cit.*, p. 670.

forces which *reduce* the youngster's response potential by increasing rigidity and anxiety are deleterious to learning.[22]

Even before entering school, most children have matured sufficiently and have acquired enough experience so that in a given situation they have a large storehouse of verbal and motor responses. They know how to look, point, discriminate, manipulate, use tools— also how to kick, scratch, bite, scream and run and do many many more things. Learning (especially as the teacher conceives it) means associating these various response potentials to the appropriate stimulus situations.

The job of the school is not only to increase a child's response potential (various skills and understandings) but also his effective potential for response. In other words, the youngster must have sufficient self-confidence and desirable attitudes about school so that he will *use* the responses of which he is capable.

Selectivity and Elimination of Responses. As learning progresses, the individual discards certain unessential responses, selects appropriate ones, and reduces the number of signs or cues which are needed to point toward the goal. The learner brings to each new situation something of his experience with similar situations in the past. This means that he makes a readier response—less false starts and random movements. Instead of sounding out each syllable of the word "appreciate" he recognizes it at a glance and pronounces it without hesitation. It is in this process that behavior change is most clearly seen, and it is the one which is most likely to receive attention. However, this is but one phase of the total process of learning, and the nature of what happens here depends upon variation in the other phases.

Effect of the Response. The behavioral cycle which results in learning is not complete until the individual receives some satisfaction, reward, or reduction of tension for his strivings. One rewarded, satisfactory or "right" trial may become so important that it is learned and remembered far better than dozens of "wrong" or unrewarded trials. Although this facet of the learning process has been clearly shown and known for about forty years, it is apt to be most frequently neglected in analyzing learning and in planning for teaching and learning activities.

[22] E. L. Gaier, "Selected Personality Variables and the Learning Process," *Psychological Monographs,* Vol. 66, No. 17, Whole No. 349, 1952.

Each of the six factors just mentioned exist to some degree in every complex learning situation. Analysis must give attention to each. Teaching methods ought to be conceived with *all* these elements in mind.

PERVASIVENESS OF LEARNING IN THE CLASSROOM

Everyone takes for granted certain behaviors as common to every child. It is assumed that when he sees an object in his path, he will step around it, that when he touches something hot, he will avoid touching it again, and that he sees the world as adults see it. Actually these assumptions are not entirely justified—all of these and a myriad of other taken-for-granted behaviors are products of learning and are subject to the variability which is characteristic of learning.

Learning to Perceive. Although everyone is equipped with an elaborate sensory system which orients him to his environment, this system operates in a manner dictated, not altogether by its structure, but as a result of experience. The way we see, feel and hear the world in which we live is largely a matter of learning. Dramatic illustration of how much of our daily lives is subject to learning comes from a study of persons cured of blindness. When sight is first restored to such cases (those blind from birth), the world is apt to appear as groups of unclear shapes and unknown objects, which only take form and meaning as the person learns to perceive his surroundings.[23] Evidence that people have learned to perceive was shown in the classic experiments of Stratton [24] and Young.[25] Stratton equipped himself with eyeglasses which inverted images (meaning the images were right-side-up on the retina instead of inverted as normally). At first the world appeared upside down, but after a time things righted themselves. After he removed the glasses, the world was again topsy-turvy for a period, but straightened as adjustments were made. Young's experiment with auditory localization gave similar results.

[23] From Senden as reported in D. O. Hebb, *Organization of Behavior*, New York, John Wiley and Sons, Inc., 1949, pp. 31–37. Also see N. H. Pronko and J. W. Bowles, Jr., *Empirical Foundations of Psychology*, New York, Rinehart and Company, Inc., 1951, pp. 236–267.

[24] G. M. Stratton, *Psychological Review*, Vol. 3, 1896, pp. 611–617, and Vol. 4, 1897, pp. 341–360 and 463–481.

[25] P. T. Young, "Auditory Localization with Acoustical Transposition of the Ears," *Journal of Experimental Psychology*, Vol. 11, 1928, pp. 399–429.

The influence of learning upon perception is an important consideration for teachers. Cases of reading reversals, distorted visual perception and short perceptual span are common. To dismiss such cases as ones of structural defect may do little in solving such problems (although structural factors may contribute).[26] Without a point of view which emphasizes learning, needed retraining may be hit or miss or not take place at all.

To overcome reversal tendencies one needs to learn new habits of perception, namely, the development of a left to right direction while reading.[27] The importance of perceptual learning—especially as it may apply to the work of the teacher is pointed out in the following statement:

Many children who have great difficulty in learning to read also have great difficulty in being able to quickly and accurately perceive shapes or visual forms.[28]

Learning Needs. The basic need structure of children is but a foundation for the many derived or socially conditioned needs. The goals toward which people strive are learned. Not only are goals learned, but also the methods of reaching toward them are learned. The following diagram will show how the same basic need will, because of experience and learning, produce two entirely different results.

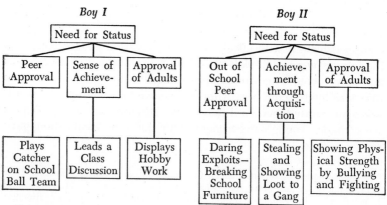

	Boy I			Boy II	
	Need for Status			Need for Status	
Peer Approval	Sense of Achievement	Approval of Adults	Out of School Peer Approval	Achievement through Acquisition	Approval of Adults
Plays Catcher on School Ball Team	Leads a Class Discussion	Displays Hobby Work	Daring Exploits—Breaking School Furniture	Stealing and Showing Loot to a Gang	Showing Physical Strength by Bullying and Fighting

[26] E. A. Betts, *Foundation of Reading Instruction*, New York, American Book Co., 1946.

[27] A. J. Harris, *How to Increase Reading Ability*, New York, Longmans, Green and Company, 1940, p. 106.

[28] Samuel Renshaw, "Reading as a Special Case of Perception," *Visual Digest*, Vol. V, No. 1, 1941.

In both cases, the boys have a need for status. The goals which satisfy this need are also quite similar. But the specific activities utilized are very different.

The all important question in these two cases is *why* the boys learned different methods of satisfying this need. Although this question is discussed fully in later chapters on adjustment, it is suggested that the reader here consider the dynamics of learning in this situation with the following two points in mind:

1. The two boys obviously have different kinds of identification, i.e., their experiences, and the groups to which they belong have been such as to produce differences in the kinds of values they hold.

2. Lack of success by the delinquent in trying to achieve status by socially approved means may have forced him to find recognition by other means.

Learning Attitudes and Values. Among the most important learnings which occur early in the child's life, and continue as an ever-present force in his behavior are the attitudes and values which he acquires. Many attitudes are adopted directly from parents. But even in the pre-school period, influences other than parental training begin to work on him. As soon as the youngster allies himself with other children, he begins to adopt ideas, modes of behavior and points of view which give him access to a childhood group. If his friends think that breaking windows or tearing up shrubbery are bad, so will he. Conversely, if other youngsters value the daring which destruction of property may imply, then he is fairly sure to have like attitudes about this behavior.

Attitudes are quite apt to spring from experiences in which feelings and emotions are brought into play. Highly unpleasant or pleasant happenings in the classroom may lead to long enduring attitudes about the teacher or the school. Other ways in which attitudes may be influenced are through movies, radio, reading, and any other form of communication in which a youngster finds a basis and a reason for being for or against something.

It is important for teachers to know that a verbal barrage of pleas, threats or propaganda may have little effect upon attitudes, especially those which are strongly entrenched. The attitudes which a child now holds do something for him. They satisfy some need, or were adopted to do so, and hence he prizes them—they are a part of him. The meager effect of "telling" upon attitudes is well illustrated by the ineffectiveness of teachers' talks about the evils of alcohol. By law in many states, teachers are required to describe the bad effects of alcohol; yet a few years later, taverns are filled with the people who had listened to these exhortations about drinking. Much more promising as a means of changing attitudes are carefully planned experiences, in which the pupil's own activity leads him to a new point of view. Methods of accomplishing these results are discussed in Chapter 8.

Learning to React to Conflict and Frustration. Even the most intelligent person, with the most favorable environment will meet obstacles and hazards which bring about frustration and conflict. Most unfruitful is the belief that aggression, attack, withdrawal and other such forms of behavior are innate willfulness which should be "pounded" out of children. That children display highly variable behavior in a frustrating situation was shown by studying children in a controlled play situation. In this experiment more attractive toys than the ones with which the youngsters were playing were blocked off with a wire screen. Some children kicked, lifted or tried to climb the net, others attempted to influence the experimenter by requests, threats or coaxing while still others showed only a passive observation of or talking about the prettier toys.[29]

It is the contention here that variable reactions such as these are products of learning—of experiences—of responses which grow through sanction and need satisfaction in the home, schoolroom and elsewhere. The array of such kinds of learnings will be more fully described in Chapter 13. Suffice it to say here that all these reactions have a place in the total response system of the adult. Unfortunately, from the standpoint of learning, children, and teachers too for that matter, sometimes fixate or become habituated to one type of reaction in the face of conflict. For example, every time he has to make a difficult decision, Willie has to talk with his mother (in reality she makes the decision). Willie not only fails to learn how to make decisions, but also his stereotyped response in the face of conflict insures that he will not develop the necessary flexibility which he *must* have if he is ever to deal with life's problems.

Learning a Self Concept. Psychologists, philosophers and educators have known for a long time that the way a person learns to look

[29] R. G. Barker, T. Dembo, and K. Lewin, "Frustration and Regression, An Experiment With Young Children," *University of Iowa Studies of Child Welfare*, Vol. 18, No. 1, 1941.

at himself is basic in understanding his behavior. A child, or group of children told often enough that they are bad, stupid, or failures may act in those ways.

The writer knew a group of soldiers during World War II, who were constantly told by their officers and other men not in their outfit that they were worthless and "no good" as soldiers. This group had more disciplinary problems and more absences without leave than any other company on the post. They were always rated lowest on inspection day, and always brought up the rear in parades. When a new officer was assigned to this detachment, he was pitied by his colleagues. However, during his first day of duty, this officer assembled the men and told them they had every reason, by virtue of training and selection, to be the best group on the post. He followed his belief by action—joined with the men in their activities—and within the space of only a few months, this same group won marching and inspection prizes each Saturday and went for several months without a single case of disciplinary action!

"What a person does, and how he behaves are determined by the concept he has of himself and his abilities. If a man thinks he is Napoleon, he will act like Napoleon; at least like his concept of Napoleon." [30] The guide to behavior is the learned way of looking at one's self, and in the normal well-adjusted person this makes for a unity and consistency of personality. Often the maladjusted youngster is the one who has never learned a consistent positive self-concept, or has a concept of himself that is socially unacceptable.

SUMMARY

Learning has been defined and analyzed in various ways by psychologists and educators. Nearly all are agreed that it involves a change in behavior which causes a person to face subsequent situations differently. Some of the ways of scrutinizing the process of learning are to study it as (1) an associative process, (2) a process of reinforcement, (3) as a perceptual process, and (4) as a process of organization and understanding.

For the teacher no one theory or way of analyzing learning is adequate. All theories are useful for describing some aspects of the behavior cycle, but the teacher as an engineer must be able to work

---

[30] Donald Snygg and A. W. Combs, *Individual Behavior*, New York, Harper and Brothers Publishers, 1949, p. 78.

with *all* phases and types of behavior change. A composite view of the various methods of analyzing learning would picture the learning situation as including these important elements: (1) needs of the learner, (2) incentives, (3) barrier or obstruction of motivation, (4) response potential of the learner, (5) selectivity and elimination of responses by the learner, and (6) effect of the response upon the learner. When teachers plan instructional units or exercises *all* these aspects of learning should be considered.

Learning pervades all the work of the classroom. Children not only learn to read, write, spell, and figure, but they learn to perceive, learn attitudes and values, learn characteristic reactions to conflict and frustration, and learn a self concept. These learnings certainly cannot be relegated to a position of importance secondary to academic skills. On the contrary, each activity in the school day must be appraised in terms of its total effect upon the learner.

REFERENCES FOR FURTHER STUDY

LEARNING—GENERAL INTRODUCTIONS

Anderson, G. L. and Gates, A. I., "The General Nature of Learning," Chapter I in 49th Yearbook, National Society for the Study of Education, Part I, *Learning and Instruction,* Chicago, University of Chicago Press, 1950.

Deese, James, *The Psychology of Learning,* New York, McGraw-Hill Book Co., Inc., 1952, Chapters 1 and 17.

Kingsley, H. L., *The Nature and Conditions of Learning,* New York, Prentice-Hall, Inc., 1946, Chapters I and II.

Melton, A. W., "Learning" in W. S. Monroe (Ed.), *Encyclopedia of Educational Research,* New York, The Macmillan Company, 1950, pp. 668–690.

McGeoch, J. A. and Irion, A. L., *The Psychology of Human Learning,* New York, Longmans, Green and Co., Inc., 1952, Chapter I.

Munn, N. L., "Learning in Children," in Leonard Carmichael (Ed.), *Manual of Child Psychology,* New York, John Wiley and Sons, Inc., 1946.

National Society for the Study of Education 41st Yearbook, Part 2, *The Psychology of Learning,* Bloomington, Illinois, Public School Publishing Co., 1942.

Rivlin, H. N., *Improving Children's Learning Ability,* Chicago, Science Research Associates, 1953.

Tilton, J. W., *An Educational Psychology of Learning,* New York, The Macmillan Co., 1951, Chapters I and XIV.

SUMMARIES—LEARNING THEORY

Dashiell, J. F., "A Survey and Synthesis of Learning Theories," *Psychological Bulletin*, Vol. 32, 1935, pp. 261–275.

Hilgard, E. R., *Theories of Learning*, New York, Appleton-Century-Crofts, Inc., 1948, Chapters 1 and 12.

Kellogg, W. N., "An Eclectic View of Some Theories of Learning," *Psychological Review*, Vol. 45, 1938, pp. 165–184.

McConnell, T. R., "Reconciliation of Learning Theories," in 41st Yearbook, National Society for the Study of Education Part II, *The Psychology of Learning*, Bloomington, Illinois, Public School Publishing Co., 1942.

FILMS

How We Learn, Coronet Instructional Films, Coronet Bldg., Chicago 1, Illinois.

Willie and The Mouse, Teaching Film Custodians, Inc., 25 West 43rd St., New York 18, N. Y. (10 mins.)

Chapter 6

Readiness for Learning

As HE FACES a new class for the first time, the teacher is aware of tremendous differences among his students. But awareness of differences is not enough. He must, if teaching is to be successful, know the nature and extent of such differences, how they affect teaching and learning, and the factors which account for such widespread differences among children. The teacher who knows a great deal about learning, but little about the learner, is only half prepared. This chapter will attempt to show the kinds and degrees of differences in learners, the factors which bring about such differences, and the methods which seem best fitted to appraising readiness, building readiness, and taking readiness into account in teaching.

If one were to select a class at random, he would find that the readiness of pupils for a given task is so variable that it is inadvisable to expect a single or standard series of lessons and work materials to be effective. In Table 11 is presented the picture of a single aspect of readiness in only one subject. There it can be noted, for example, that 16 per cent of fifth graders are not ready for books above the first and second-grade levels; [1] 7 per cent of the sixth graders are also not ready for books above the second-grade level. Seven per cent of the fifth graders are ready for ninth-grade books as are 16 per cent of the sixth graders. It is the belief of the writers that such a wide range of differences in all types of school work make attempts to achieve "standardized performance" futile—that readiness for learning must ultimately be conceived in terms of individual pupils and that the teacher who is aware of differences and

[1] Grade level as used here and elsewhere in this book refers to the level of development of the average or middle pupil in designated grades.

TABLE 11

The Percentage of Children in Each Grade Ready for Each Book Level *

BOOK LEVEL		GRADE LEVEL					
GRADE	AGE	I	II	III	IV	V	VI
Nursery School	5	2	2	2			
Kindergarten	6	23	8	5	7		
1	7	50	24	11	9	7	
2	8	23	33	20	10	9	7
3	9	2	24	24	16	10	9
4	10		8	20	17	16	10
5	11		2	11	16	17	16
6	12			5	10	16	17
7	13			2	9	10	16
8	14				7	9	10
9	15					7	9
10	16						7

* Willard C. Olson, "Seeking Self-Selection and Pacing in the Use of Books by Children," *The Packet*, Vol. 7, Boston, D. C. Heath and Company, Spring, 1952, p. 7.

knows how to teach accordingly will have a greater chance for success.

FACTORS WHICH DETERMINE READINESS

Maturation. Children grow into learning. This simple but important fact is often ignored in the hustle of planning children's activities, because the process of growth may be a subtle change which is erroneously attributed to the effects of teaching. As an illustration of this, one writer has traced the rate of growth of a simple function over the school years as is shown in Figure 3.

These two spelling words, "sincerely" and "customary," were compared over a ten year span. One word (sincerely) was taught as a regular part of the spelling lists, while the word (customary) was not taught. But as evidenced in the figure there is little difference in the eventual position of the words, and apparently there is but a small effect, due to teaching. Courtis, the investigator, contends that it is growth, not teaching which makes the big difference in the shape of these curves.

Maturation or genetically determined growth, "takes place without express efforts to promote it or even in the face of efforts to prevent it." [2] Maturation and learning operate as dual forces in almost all cases of behavior change. As English has indicated, "though they may be distinguished in idea, they can not be separated in actual performance any more than we can separate the speed of a pitched ball from its direction, though we can certainly distinguish them." [3]

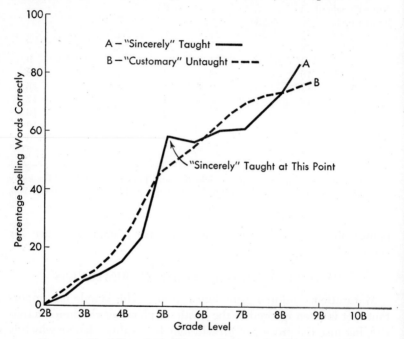

FIGURE 3. The Effect of Teaching on the Growth of Spelling Ability. (From Stuart Courtis, "The Rate of Growth Makes a Difference," *Phi Delta Kappan*, Vol. 30, 1949, p. 323.)

Because of this interdependence, learning cannot transcend maturation. A child who has not reached a sufficient stage of mental and physical development, cannot perform school tasks which require a higher level of development.

The concept of maturation as a factor in producing behavior change raises several important questions for teachers. First, what

[2] H. B. English, *Learning as Psychotechnology*, Mimeographed Manual, Ohio State University, Columbus Ohio, 1949, p. 14.
[3] *Ibid.*, p. 14.

evidence is there that maturation does in fact operate to facilitate such change? How important a factor is it in determining readiness for learning? What is the course of growth in various maturing structures and functions? Most important, is the question of how teaching can be conducted so as to take account of maturation.

There have been a number of studies [4, 5, 6] of the behavior of infants and pre-school children which have shown that such things as sitting up, crawling, walking, bladder and bowel control, and simple manipulative skills are products, mainly, of maturation. Going from infancy to the beginning school years, there is still further evidence that genetically determined growth may play an extensive part in learning.

In Figure 4, for instance, is shown the ages at which various percentages of children (141 first grade children) are able to profit from formal instruction in reading. The figure illustrates that early school performance may depend largely upon mental maturation. It should be obvious that formal reading instruction of a "fixed" type is often started somewhat earlier than it should be considering this maturational factor.

If maturation is considered an essential prerequisite for learning, as Figure 4 seems to show, the question arises as to what teachers can or should do to speed up the maturational process. Do stimulation and practice alter the capacity to learn in any marked degree? In an experiment with kindergarten children, fourteen pairs of youngsters were used to test the effect of practice in memorizing oral digits. The experimental group of children was given 78 days of practice in this work (the controls were given no practice). At the end of the training period, the experimental group was markedly superior to the controls, but after four and one-half months, the superiority due to training had completely fallen away.[7]

Similarly, nursery school children given extensive practice in such

[4] Wayne Dennis and Marsena G. Dennis, "The Effect of Cradling Practices Upon the Onset of Walking in Hopi Children," *Journal of Genetic Psychology*, Vol. 56, 1940, pp. 77–86.

[5] Myrtle McGraw, "Neural Maturation as Exemplified by the Achievement of Bladder Control," *Journal of Pediatrics*, Vol. 16, 1940, pp. 580–590.

[6] Wayne Dennis, *Readings in Child Psychology*, New York, Prentice-Hall Inc., 1951, pp. 104–131.

[7] A. I. Gates and G. A. Taylor, "An Experimental Study of the Nature of Improvement Resulting from Practice in a Mental Function," *Journal of Educational Psychology*, Vol. 16, 1935, pp. 583–593.

activities as buttoning, climbing, and using scissors do little if any better than others who have only short practice periods at a later age.[8] Such experiments raise serious questions about speeding up maturing functions. One is forced to conclude that within normal limits of environmental opportunity there is little that can be done to hasten this process. What then is the value of practice at early

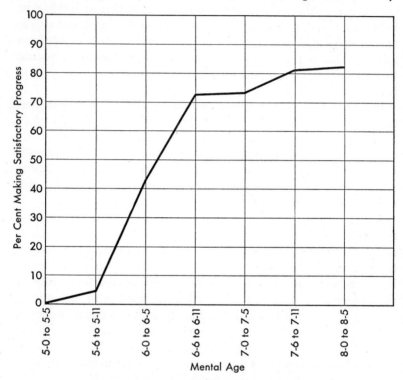

FIGURE 4. Mental Age and Success in Reading.
(From M. V. Morphett and C. Washburne, "When Should Children Begin to Read?" *Elementary School Journal,* Vol. 31, 1931, pp. 496–503.)

ages? For one thing, several investigators have found that such practice results in increased self-confidence and more mature personalities.[9] Also, through the pride of accomplishment, children learn de-

[8] Myrtle McGraw, "Later Development of Children Specially Trained During Infancy," *Child Development,* Vol. 10, 1939, pp. 1–19.
[9] Josephine Hilgard, "Learning and Maturation in Preschool Children," *Journal of Genetic Psychology,* Vol. 41, 1932, pp. 40–53.

sirable motives and interests. Finally, it seems clear that certain skills such as reading, which could be learned just as easily later (say at 10 to 12) are necessary for use by the normal child at earlier ages.

A word of caution, however, should be inserted. The teacher should realize that only a portion of a child's readiness for learning is determined by the maturation of functions measured by mental tests. In one study,[10] the coefficient of correlation between mental age and reading readiness ranged between .50 and .65. Although these correlations show definite relationship, they are low enough to leave a large part of what constitutes readiness unaccounted for. Also, the teacher needs to know that maturation cannot take place in a vacuum. All studies of IQ constancy (and others showing the effect of maturation upon performance) presuppose environmental conditions within a somewhat normal range. There is considerable evidence to the effect that when lack of a normal environmental stimulation is long continued maturing intellectual functions seem to suffer permanent setbacks.[11] Likewise when rich stimulation is provided during early development, mental maturation seems to be given a boost. The teacher who reads this volume is urged not to take a fixed, one-sided view of the nature-nurture controversy.[12] As before stated, maturation and learning operate together in producing behavior change, and focusing attention upon one to the exclusion of the other is not only unscientific but impractical. Hiding behind the rationalization that a child is without capacity, as an excuse for poor teaching, and trying to go beyond a child's limits are equally bad.

The question of limits which are dictated by the level of attained mental and physical maturation is unsolved. Psychologists are sure that for practical purposes such limits do exist but they are not rigid

[10] M. V. Morphett and C. Washburne, op.cit., p. 502.

[11] Mandel Sherman, *Intelligence and Its Deviations*, New York, The Ronald Press Company, 1945.

[12] During the past few decades, there has been a controversy among social scientists about the degree to which intellectual ability is a function of heredity. Some take the view that mental capacity is largely a matter of genetic potential over which society has little control. Others believe that intelligence is greatly affected by environmental conditions. For an excellent discussion of the issue see: National Society for the Study of Education, 39th Yearbook, Part II, *Intelligence: Its Nature and Nurture*, Bloomington, Illinois, Public School Publishing Company, 1940.

limits; for there is evidence that limits assumed to exist are passed in some cases. Two children, ages five and six, who would have attempted to swim the English Channel had the English government permitted, were tested by the physical fitness laboratory of the University of Illinois. These children turned in astounding performances. The older, a boy, was able to hold his breath for four minutes, and could swim under water for about 290 feet. The younger, a girl, had swum four miles down the Mississippi river with her hands tied. Both were able to run without stopping for several hours.[13] Feats of this kind are certainly beyond the point which would be expected under previously assumed maturational limits. The writer knows of a mongoloid-type, mentally defective boy who reads with facility and has an unusual memory for certain current events in which he is interested. Roberts [14] reports a case of a mental defective who had suffered serious birth injury and cerebrospinal meningitis. Although his IQ was below 20, and he was completely unable to care for himself, he reputedly knew the day of the week which corresponded with any date since 1915. There are many such cases of individuals who, in spite of seemingly insurmountable handicaps, develop skills and "knock the top off" the level of achievement predicted by mental tests.

Experience. The second major factor in determining a child's readiness for learning is his previous experience. The whole program of prerequisite courses and sequences of learning are predicated upon the assumption that basic skills are necessary before complex tasks are tackled. A pupil is not ready to read given materials until his previous experience has provided him a proper background for thinking out and interpreting the materials which he has read. Blair has elaborated this point:

> Unless a pupil has read considerably it is inevitable that he will be deficient in reading. Poor readers are invariably individuals who read little. There is no way that a person can become a good pianist without practicing the piano; likewise a person never becomes a good bowler without bowling or a good basketball player without playing basketball. Let us suppose for example, a given boy has no skill whatsoever in playing basketball, and we set out to diagnose the case to find out why he

[13] Unpublished Research Data, T. K. Cureton, Physical Fitness Laboratory, University of Illinois, 1952.

[14] A. J. Roberts, "Case History of a So-Called Idiot Savant," *Journal of Genetic Psychology*, Vol. 66, 1945, pp. 259–265.

does not perform better in this field of athletics. We might start by checking his vision, his hearing, his intelligence, hand and eye preferences, emotional factors which may be involved and his interest in basketball. But it is most likely that when all is said and done it will be found that the reason he is not a better player is that he has never played much basketball.[15]

Given experiences may make a child more ready for new learnings, but there is no assurance that they will do so. Experiences may be relatively meaningless, and the child's compliance by sitting through a course, or reciting rote material should not be misjudged as assurance that the experience has made a real change in his behavior. A boy who was asked to write the pledge of allegiance to the flag (which he had presumably said dozens of times) wrote, "I led the pigeons to the flag." [16] A student in a biology class asked to give the term which describes the tendency of plants to turn toward the earth wrote, "G. O. Tropism." [17]

The home and community background are obviously important factors in readiness. To some parents, school is of minor importance. In fact in some communities nearly all adults look with disdain and suspicion at the business of schooling. Few rewards exist in such cases for the child who steps above his group. In language skills, for example, the "fancy" talking child may be rejected both by peers and adults whom he needs to believe care for him.

That marked community differences do exist is illustrated by the following samples of representative writing drawn from third graders in two widely different communities (age, grade and mental ability controlled).

Community I:

I think Americans are honest, good workers, willing, smart and good citizens.

I think Americans are kind, honest, free and respectful. I think this because they always tell the truth. They are always friendly. It is a free country.

I think Americans are smart, honest, helpful and brave. If they wanted to be mean, we wouldn't be here today.

[15] G. M. Blair, *Diagnostic and Remedial Teaching in Secondary Schools,* pp. 78–79. Copyright, 1946, by The Macmillan Company, New York.

[16] Marion C. Sheridan, "Studying Words," *Teachers Service Bulletin in English,* Vol. 5, No. 4, New York, The Macmillan Company, April, 1951.

[17] Geotropism.

Community II:

I think Americans are kind and hasom. Because the give people stufh.

I think Americans are clean white flasted people.

I think Americans are the Best people in the lind. thay are mice people.[18]

Relevance of Materials and Methods of Instruction. Whereas the innate capacity of a child at a given time for learning reading, algebra or physics is not subject to great change, the methods of teaching and materials used are. When we say a first-grade child is not "ready" to read, we generally mean not ready in terms of the kinds of materials and methods which are generally used.

Evidence that relevance of material to children's interests is a factor in readiness may be found in the superiority of girls over boys in reading achievement. Lecky [19] believes that apparent lack of reading ability of boys may be due to their failure to perceive the consistency between required school behavior and their own self concepts. For example, primers and other readers may have content which is inconsistent with the masculine role as defined by our culture, and as viewed by boys. Perhaps if boys were given more adventuresome and manly materials, sex differences in reading ability would be reduced.

Children are more ready to respond to material which meets their needs and fits their already established interests. The idea that there should be a dual program, one for rote skill materials and one for developing understandings and meaningful relationships is now regarded as fallacious. "Unless skills are learned while being put to use they are uninteresting and difficult to learn, the resulting learning may not be applicable to real problem solving, and the learning may not be permanent." [20] Children are more ready for skill learning, spelling, reading and writing, when they are having fun doing it—and in connection with some meaningful project. They may be ready for *this* kind of learning situation and not at all ready for drill material.

[18] John Gillis, Unpublished Research Data, College of Education, University of Illinois, 1952.

[19] Prescott Lecky, *Self-Consistency, A Theory of Personality,* New York, Island Press, 1945.

[20] Gertrude H. Hildreth, "Skills Develop with Functioning." *Educational Outlook,* Vol. 24, 1949, pp. 13–19.

What is the relationship of method of teaching to readiness? A case in point is the following situation.

Observation of a ninth-grade high school class in so-called general mathematics disclosed a teacher (trained in a field other than mathematics) attempting to present to a slow, dull-normal group, (more than half of them from foreign language backgrounds and many with reading handicaps) certain solid geometry concepts by merely reading from the textbook, appealing solely to auditory impressions.[21]

It is inevitable that little learning or understanding would obtain in such a situation. But can it be said then that this class was not ready for general mathematics, or even solid geometry? Certainly not. A skillful teacher, using relevant materials and methods commensurate with these children's abilities, could undoubtedly bring at least some measure of success to this work.

A striking contrast to the above description is provided in an experiment by Luchins.[22] These experimenters, using a 6B class, set out to teach the concepts of geometric area. First they drew a 15 inch by 5 inch rectangle on the blackboard. Then a pupil was given a one-inch cardboard square and asked to determine the area of the figure in square inches. "The pupil laid off the square along the longer base 15 times, repeated this process to obtain a parallel row and was about to start on a third row when he said, 'I don't have to do it again. It will always go 15 times this way and it goes 5 times the other way, so it's 15 times 5 squares.'" This student, then correctly computed the area as 75 square inches. After all students had practiced this same procedure with various rectangles, they were asked if this was necessary. A number of children replied that the area could be found simply by measuring one side and then the other.

In the next step, each pupil was given a paper parallelogram and asked to find its area. At first they could not solve the problem, but in a few minutes one girl volunteered. She had cut off both ends to make it straight. She was asked what to do with the ends, and after toying with them a moment put them together to form another rec-

[21] E. G. Nolan, "Determining the Most Effective Media of Student Learning," *Journal of Educational Research*, Vol. 43, 1950, p. 549.

[22] A. S. Luchins and Edith H. Luchins, "A Structural Approach to the Teaching of the Concept of Area in Intuitive Geometry," *Journal of Educational Research*, Vol. 40, 1947, pp. 528–533.

tangle. Only after each student made discovery of this process was formal geometric proof presented. The experiment was repeated with nine young girls from five to nine in age, and *all* including the five-year-old learned these processes as above described.

Emotional Attitudes and Personal Adjustment. After capacity, experience and methods of teaching are considered, there still remains a residual of unexplained failure to learn. There are numerous children who have sufficient capacity, and experience, but who are still not ready for a given task in school. A large proportion of pupils who are having difficulties in reading, for example, exhibit forms of emotional instability, and it has been estimated that about a fifth of all retarded readers are rendered so by emotional stress.[23] Thus emotional stress may serve as a factor in lack of readiness or (as is more often the case) be an unfortunate concomitant of a failure to consider individual differences or readiness in setting up school work initially. Emotional disturbance is both cause and effect in children's failure in school. But whichever it is, the chances are that once the pattern of disturbance starts, a circular relationship is built up.

Common provocations which give rise to emotions and block readiness for learning are: unmet needs, overprotection and rejection in the home, previous experiences of school failure, and other home difficulties. "The components of emotional patterns leading to reading difficulties are varied and complex. Sibling jealousy, parental overindulgence, excessive negativism, parental rejection, social class differences, general home insecurity, instability and general feelings of inadequacy have all been listed in the literature." [24]

The way in which an emotional problem stemming from an unhappy home situation may affect a child's readiness for schoolwork is illustrated in the case of Tony.

Tony—A Rejected Child

Tony was born at a very inopportune time for his mother. Just when she had decided she could no longer bear an unhappy marriage with an erratic and quarrelsome husband, and when she was trying to make

[23] A. I. Gates, "The Role of Personality Maladjustment in Reading Disability," *Pedagogical Seminary and Journal of Genetic Psychology,* Vol. 59, 1941, pp. 77–83.

[24] Norman Young and E. L. Gaier, "Implications in Emotionally Caused Reading Retardation," *Elementary English,* Vol. 28, 1951, pp. 271–275.

plans whereby she could take the two older children with her and set up a little business of her own, she discovered that Tony was on the way. To make matters worse, her entire pregnancy was one of illness and discomfort. Submissive and dependent by nature and fearful of a scene, she had not told her husband of her plans to leave him, and now with another child coming, it seemed to her that the doorway to an independent life was permanently closed. Although her life seemed bleak, her husband did provide for her and the children in a feast or fast fashion, and by careful managing she had always saved a few extra dollars during good times to help in hard times.

"While waiting for Tony to come," she said, "I used to think of doing away with myself, and the baby with me. I thought bitterly that I was disillusioned and had no love left to give to anyone, even to a little innocent child who had no blame of his own. And when the baby was put in my arms I had no feeling for him. Those were wicked thoughts and I should not even say them—so I tried to make it up to the poor little babe, and did more for him than I ever did for the other two, who came when I was younger and had hope. Do you think a mother can mark a child by her thoughts? I mean, in his spirit? Because he never developed any feeling for anyone. He wants things only for himself. I am nothing to him. His father and sisters are nothing. School is nothing. Only for play he lives, and such play! Fires, and breaking up expensive toys, and showing off, and bragging."

Tony, the subject of his mother's discussion, proved to be a curly-headed, cherubic-looking boy of nearly six. With an IQ of 125 to give him ideas, and with "no feeling for anyone," he was indeed the terror of the first grade. Quick, when it appealed to him, to take part in the class, he waited for no one but answered out of turn all the teacher's questions whether he knew the answers or not. He grabbed the papers to pass them and buffeted his way to the head of the line in passing to recess. On the days he did not care to participate in the class activities, he stalked around the room glowering, refused to obey requests, and was a law unto himself. Reading made no appeal, and he never entered into the reading classes except to disturb others. He loved art work, however, and the classroom was most peaceful when Tony was sitting at a table alone covering huge sheets of paper with brilliantly colored bombers, battleships, and burning buildings.

Tony's case needed to be approached from many angles. His mother and father were referred to a psychiatrist, and in talking out their problems with the doctor they achieved a better understanding of their marriage. The mother learned to see that her feelings of rejecting the child and her guilt over such feelings were related to her inconsistent treatment of the child—her overindulgence of him but without the warmth he needed. She became more accepting of Tony as she grew more accepting of his father, and she was able to establish better routines for the whole family at home. As she gave Tony more of her real self, she was able to ask and receive more from him. She no longer needed to indulge him with an excess of toys and gifts as peace offerings to her conscience.

Paralleling the treatment of the parents, the reading clinic studied Tony to see if he could learn to read. Since he was so bright, it was hoped that actual achievement would bring him self-respect and ability to gain recognition in legitimate channels. A puppy that he admired was given to him, and the snuggly, dependent little creature won from him real protection and friendship, and served as a basis for many stories which he related to the teacher and which were typed into "his own book." One of his drawings of a burning building was so brilliantly colored and really beautiful artistically that it was chosen for a school poster for a fire-prevention drive. Tony proudly thought of and copied an appropriate caption under the picture. In the playroom at clinic and school his activities gradually shifted from destructive types of play to more constructive activities. By the end of the year, he enthusiastically accepted reading and made real progress.[25]

In a case of this kind, it is a mistake to assume that readiness training or remedial procedures of academic nature alone will prepare the child for learning. As was shown, it was only after a period of intensive psychotherapy with both parents and child that Tony was ready for school work.

The circular relationship between personal adjustment and readiness creates problems more serious than either maladjustment or lack of readiness alone. Difficulties become intensified as failure to solve either problem continues. Consider the child who enters the first grade and is not ready for reading. By the time he gets to the second grade he is ready for first grade reading, but now the class is doing second year work, and so it goes grade after grade until the child is hopelessly behind. This case was reported by a school psychologist:

John H. was reported to the office as an unmanageable boy of fifteen. In English class, where the trouble was most pronounced, he had crawled on his hands and knees in the back of the room playing bear. He growled and bit several youngsters on the legs. Investigation showed that this class was reading and reciting from *Silas Marner*. Tests of the boy's abili-

[25] Marion Monroe, *Growing into Reading*, pp. 41–43. Copyright, 1951, by Scott, Foresman and Company, Chicago.

ties and achievements revealed that he was almost completely unable to read. (The school psychologist reported that John would have been just about taxed to his limit to pick out such words as "is" and "the" on a page of *Silas Marner*.) Faced with an untenable situation year after year, John had become a behavior problem. Adjustment wise, he was probably doing about all that was left for him to do—i.e., getting his share of attention in the only way he knew how.

There are many such cases in our schools today. There are emotionally disturbed and maladjusted children who are products of a schooling which continually fails to start their training at their own level or fails to find areas of competency and potential in which they are ready to progress. In the extreme case the student may even reach high school, with years of school experience behind him, and show little progress in mastering the fundamental tools of education.

It is unfortunate that children who are not ready for given tasks are often made even *less* ready through emotional tension induced in the classroom. When 239 college freshmen were asked to describe incidents in their schooling which undermined self-confidence, they gave frequent examples of "punishment and sarcasm in the presence of others; competition or invidious comparison; and ridicule and scorn of personal attributes or background." A specific report of how a teacher actually *interfered* with a student's readiness for learning follows:

When I was in elementary school, I was rather nervous and high strung. I was tall and very thin. The thing I remember and I shall never forget was an incident that happened in about the fifth grade.

I wasn't a very good reader, and I think that this was partly due to the fact that I was shy and didn't like to be made fun of. I was called upon to read. Things were going along fairly well until I made one mistake and it seemed everyone in the room was laughing at me. This caused me to make more mistakes. My teacher said, "That will do fine, I guess you will never learn to read." [26]

Surely of all the factors contributing to readiness, emotional stability and self-confidence should be the first concern of the teacher.

INDIVIDUAL DIFFERENCES IN READINESS

The factors which make children ready for school operate to create widespread individual differences. Before teachers can plan for

[26] Charles Lyman Smith, *A Study of Factors Contributing to Self-Confidence in School*, Unpublished M.A. Thesis, Columbus, Ohio State University, 1950.

treating such differences, they must have a clear picture of their nature and extent.

So long as a teacher considers his job as that of teaching individual children, it is necessary to know the level at which each individual operates, and to set up school tasks commensurate with each level. Unfortunately, whether they like it or not, a large part of their work as teachers consists in working with groups and not with indi-

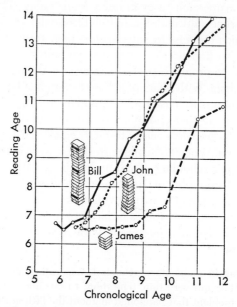

FIGURE 5. The Rate in Growth of Reading Ability for Three Pupils.
(From Willard C. Olson, "Seeking Self-Selection and Pacing in the Use of Books by Children," *The Packet*, Vol. 7, p. 5. Copyright, 1952, by D. C. Heath and Company, Boston.)

vidual students. Thus the problem of dealing with differences among children is complicated by the size and heterogeneity of groups which constitute grade levels or subject matter areas. Primary teachers may have as many as forty or more children in a class. Some first grade classes are so crowded that it has been necessary to change to two half-day sessions of thirty to forty different children in each. An English teacher in high school may have fifty or sixty students in one class, and a physical education or art teacher nearly a hundred. An art teacher in one of the writers' classes has on the average 210 students per day. Under such conditions, providing for differences in the readiness for learning becomes a major problem.

Differences in Rates of Growth. Children and adolescents grow at different rates. This differential growth rate is not simply in terms of physical development but includes mental and personality development as well. Growth in many functions varies from one individual to another and rates vary within individuals. Figure 5 gives an example of the rate of growth in reading ability for three pupils.

There are "slow growers" and "fast growers" in almost every human trait. Each child has his own unique growth pattern. "Some children seem 'slow to catch on' in school for several years yet prove later to be excellent students." [27] In fact there may be only a slight relationship between various forms of mental, physical, and social development. Recognition that each growth system operates somewhat independently of others has led to the concept of "organismic age," [28] which is an arithmetical average of various "ages" such as skeletal age, dental age, reading age, arithmetic age, and others.

Variability within school groups increases with age. (This is especially true of higher mental processes.) For example, it was shown in Table 11 that various children in the first grade were ready for books which covered five grades in difficulty level. But by the time these children had reached the third grade, they varied so much that some were ready only for nursery school books, others for seventh grade books—a range of about *nine* years in difficulty level. Teachers who strive to reduce such differences by insisting on equal preparation for all are bucking against known and immutable facts about growth. Far more effective is effort expended in giving materials and guidance which are commensurate with various rates of development.

The known facts about rates of growth hold several important implications for the educator. Foremost is that each child must be considered in relation to his own level of expectancy (i.e., what is normal development for him) and not in terms of comparisons with other children. Also, it is impossible to predict with anything approaching complete accuracy the extent of terminal development

[27] M. E. Breckenridge and E. L. Vincent, *Child Development*, Philadelphia, W. B. Saunders and Company, 1950, p. 15.
[28] W. C. Olson and B. O. Hughes, "The Concept of Organismic Age," *Journal of Educational Research*, Vol. 35, 1942, pp. 525–527.

from early developmental patterns. It is poor practice to prejudge a child's eventual potential in terms of early achievement. Since growth is uneven, and varies from one individual to another, the teacher may expect school behavior and school learning to show irregularities and regressions. Such fluctuations should not be viewed with alarm but taken as a matter of course, unless they are long continued.

Differences Among Students. To what extent do pupils in various grades differ, and what kinds of differences are there? Aside from the readily observable differences of stature, strength, and gross behavior, there are many other, sometimes subtle, differences among children which must be taken into account in teaching.

Differences in intellectual capacity. The widespread use of mental tests from preschool age through college has provided a wealth of information about differences in mental ability. In summary of some of these differences, Cook has written:

When a random group of six-year-olds enters the first grade, two per cent of them will be below the average four-year-olds in general mental development and two per cent will be above the average eight-year-olds. Disregarding the extreme two per cent at either end, there is a four-year range in general intelligence.[29]

If one were to follow this group of six-year-olds through the sixth grade, when they were twelve, he would find the range to have increased to almost eight years.

Extensive differences persist on into high school and college, although there is probably an increasing dropping out of students from the lower mental ability levels when attendance at school becomes voluntary. Nevertheless, tests of academic aptitude or mental ability reveal that even college students may vary to the extent of 100 IQ points.

Differences in school achievement. In a typical sixth-grade class, tests in reading comprehension, vocabulary, arithmetic reasoning, and arithmetic computation have shown a range of about eight school years for all these subjects.[30] In other words, in almost any

[29] W. W. Cook, "Individual Differences and Curriculum Practice," *Journal of Educational Psychology,* Vol. 39, 1948, p. 141.

[30] W. W. Cook, *Grouping and Promotion in the Elementary School,* Minneapolis Series on Individualization of Instruction, No. 2, University of Minnesota, 1941, pp. 26–30.

sixth-grade class, there will be a pupil with average second-grade reading ability and one with average tenth-grade reading ability. These differences do not decrease much, if any, in later grades. When a General Culture Battery Test (composed of general science, foreign literature, fine arts and social studies) was administered to high school and college seniors, the upper 10 per cent of the high-school seniors scored above the college seniors' median.[31] These differences are not extreme cases, they are the kind which any teacher may expect to find in classes in New York, Chicago, San Diego, or most any other place.

Table 12 illustrates the spread of differences in a number of measured abilities and skills for a group of fifth graders and should indicate how futile it is to expect a "standard" performance of every pupil.

Note in Table 12 how few of these pupils were actually at the average of their own grade level. As the investigator indicates, "All of these 240 students were in 5A at the time of measurement but only thirty-six out of 240 or about 15 per cent are at the 5A standards." In the first column of Table 12 (Chronological Age), it may be seen that only one pupil out of the 240 is old enough to be at the ninth-grade level or above, while twenty of the pupils weigh enough to be considered at or above ninth-grade averages. Note also that in intelligence one pupil was at the 3B level (first half of the third grade), while two were at the ninth-grade level or above—a range of twelve half-grades or six years.

Differences in interests.[32] Perhaps no type of difference among children has been so well recognized and so poorly taken into account in teaching than that of differences among children in interests. The teacher, and rightly so, has seen his job as changing interests, but in order to do this he must start with the child's already existing interests.

Presumably one of the main objectives of schooling is to foster widespread individual interests. In an economy of specialization this is essential, and yet classroom methods more often than not assume common interests. Many teachers still use a single text, a single as-

---

[31] W. D. Learned and B. D. Wood, *The Student and His Knowledge*, New York, The Carnegie Foundation for the Advancement of Teaching, Bulletin No. 29, 1938.

[32] Instruments used to measure interests are discussed in Chapter 17.

TABLE 12

The Scores of 240 Fifth-Grade Boys and Girls on a Variety of Tests and Measurements *

Number of Children Making Each Grade Level Score

GRADE LEVELS	C. A.	HEIGHT	WEIGHT	NO. TEETH CUT	INTELLIGENCE KUHLMAN-ANDERSON	READING Stanford Achievement	READING Thorndike-McCall
9th & Above	1	7	20		2	8	5
8A	2	6	9		0	3	0
8B	0	9	15		0	7	5
7A	5	36	23		7	5	7
7B	6	25	19	18	24	21	10
6A	10	44	29	25	34	22	51
6B	19	18	25	55	64	42	23
5A	34	39	31	44	33	38	31
5B	135	22	23	42	39	43	48
4A	29	19	12	23	17	26	25
4B	7	9	15	14	5	21	17
3A		2	11	7		7	14
3B				9	1		
2A & Below		2	6				
Total Children Measured	248	238	238	237	226	243	236

132

* Stuart A. Courtis, "The Rate of Growth Makes a Difference," *Phi Delta Kappan*, Vol. 30, 1949, p. 320.

signment, and a single class procedure for all. There are, of course, exceptions. In English composition, children are sometimes allowed to write a theme on a topic of their own choosing, and in mechanical arts advanced students often work on their own projects.

Other trait differences. Besides differences in abilities, physique and interests, there are hundreds or even thousands of other trait differences. Although the distributions of these traits are at this time not clearly or definitely known, there is every reason to believe that most of those which have been identified follow the same normal curve as do differences in abilities and physical factors. In honesty and other measures of character for instance, children probably vary as much as they do in intellectual capacity.[33] Some children are so aggressive that they will try to dominate everyone in their class, while others are so meek that they respond only when they are forced to do so. In sheer amount of energy, children may show great differences. One child in a classroom may be so restless that he is unable to sit still, while another will be content to let the lesson go by while he spends hours daydreaming about the things he would like to do but never does. One child may have enough self-confidence to try almost anything. He may make decisions rapidly. Another may approach each new situation with caution and a sense of inferiority.

Sex Differences and Readiness. Beginning in early life, our culture creates roles which are believed appropriate for each sex. These roles are reflected in the kinds of toys and games which are provided children, and in the kind of behavior which is expected. Also, there are biological determinants which may lead to psychological differences (albeit these biological factors have probably been overemphasized in the past).

In general, studies of school achievement agree that girls tend to make consistently better scores than boys (particularly in elementary school). Girls are less apt to be retarded readers and spellers and they are less apt to suffer such speech incoordinations as stammering and stuttering (which are often attributed to pushing a child beyond his capacity).[34] Although on the average girls excel in general school achievement, particularly at the elementary level, boys

---

[33] Vernon Jones, "Character Development in Children—An Objective Approach," Chapter 14 in *Manual of Child Psychology*, L. Carmichael (Ed.), New York, John Wiley and Sons, Inc., 1946.

[34] Leona Tyler, *The Psychology of Human Differences*, New York, D. Appleton-Century Company, Inc., 1947.

seem to have a slight edge in arithmetic, history, geography and science. Such differences as do exist seem to parallel so closely what we know about the interests of each sex that it is safe to conclude that a great part of these differences are products of the roles which are set for children and not due to innate factors. A school environment which favors either sex is likely to produce superiority in achievement for that sex.

In over-all appraisal of differences between sexes in ability, achievement and readiness, one is forced to conclude that any differences are slight, with almost a complete overlap in distributions. As previously shown in Chapter 3, girls in the early years are probably growing somewhat faster than boys, and since they reach puberty earlier, acquire sex-social interests when younger. The slight difference between sexes is certainly not sufficient to warrant grouping of sexes into separate classes, nor the separation of the sexes in elective classes in high school. Even though boys and girls differ more in interests than they do in ability, there is a considerable overlap of distributions even in this respect. It is common in schools today for boys to take courses in home economics and for girls to be interested in physics and mechanical arts. Special provisions for differences in interests should be on the basis of qualitative differences in needs and not arbitrarily determined on the basis of sex.

By far the greatest differences between the sexes are in factors of personality and value systems. For the most part these differences are also culturally produced. Children learn concepts about themselves which are determined by sex. The girl soon learns that affection, neatness, primness and a quiet sense of humor are rewarded by adults and by other members of her peer group. On the other hand, boys find rewarding greater aggressiveness, display of fearlessness, and vigorous physical activity.[35] These differences are not due to any innate factors but come about because the child finds rewards, approval and status in adopting the role which is defined for him.

Present research indicates that men are more aggressive than women, and women are more often neurotic and maladjusted than men.[36] There is little question, however, that the culture is changing

[35] Caroline Tryon, *Evaluations of Adolescent Personality by Adolescents,* Monographs of the Society for Research in Child Development, Vol. 4, Serial No. 23, 1939.

[36] Leona Tyler, *op.cit.,* p. 80.

and some personality differences now apparent may, within a few generations, virtually disappear. Teachers, in planning work to fit the readiness of pupils, need to be alert to such change. It is a mistake to hold to previously conceived values about the "role of women" and thereby exclude girls from activities once thought of as strictly masculine. School girls of today are probably ready for a much wider range of learning materials than was true even a generation ago.

Differences Within Individuals. Teachers may see only a few facets of the total picture of an individual child in school and therefore may not be aware of the great differences in traits and skills within a given school child. The extent of such intra-individual variation has been summarized as follows:

> Trait variability in the typical individual is 80 per cent as great as individual variability in his age group; trait differences are normally distributed. Some individuals are twice as variable as others, and there is no relationship between general level of ability and the amount of trait variability.[37]

Teachers are sometimes astonished to find a child who they think of as a slow learner doing very well in a specific area. An algebra teacher related the following incident: "My car was stalled on a country road near the town in which I was teaching. I tried in vain to get it started. While sitting there, Bill S. came along. He was the bottom man in my algebra class, but within five minutes he had taken the top off my carburetor, made a minor adjustment, and I was on my way." Psychologists have found that errors in judging persons' total abilities and personality because of specific information is an almost universal weakness. This weakness, known as the "halo effect," operates to reduce the accuracy of such things as personal ratings, because one good or bad feature about a person tends to influence judgment about other aspects of the person. Of all professional groups, teachers have the best reason for avoiding this kind of error.

Even in so-called primary mental abilities, children may show distinct intra-individual differences. In one case, a kindergarten child tested with the Primary Mental Abilities Test,[38] had an IQ of 103, but scored as low as four years, nine months MA on one subtest,

[37] W. W. Cook, *op. cit.*, p. 143.
[38] Thelma G. Thurstone and L. L. Thurstone, Chicago, Science Research Associates, 228 South Wabash Avenue.

and as high as seven years, eight months on another—a range of nearly three years mental age on these two subtests of intelligence.[39] It is not infrequent for a child to rank at the ninety-ninth percentile in so-called general ability and below the tenth percentile in such functions as pitch discrimination, aesthetic judgment, art and drawing skills.[40] These differences are apparent also in various school achievements. A junior at the University of Illinois had the following grade record for one semester: Physics A, Integral Calculus B, Descriptive Geometry B, and Rhetoric D. This student's spelling was at the fifth grade level, and he misspelled such words as "upon, fail, awful and wait." [41]

A profile of a student's aptitudes is often a valuable tool not only in planning his instructional program, but also in counseling him about vocational aims. The profile of a college student with an IQ of 115, who was planning to enter engineering school is shown in Figure 6. This profile indicates the status of this student in relation to other college freshmen who had taken the same test. It is clear that, on seven of the eight traits measured, this student was below the median of college freshmen.

In a consideration of individual differences and readiness for learning, the school needs to recognize such wide differences within students, and, as in Figure 6, these differences may be an instructive pattern for guidance. In this case, as a result of proper vocational counseling, the student decided to change his vocational plans.

The Nature and Importance of Qualitative Differences. When differences are stated solely in terms of figures representing IQ, MA, or achievement level, one fails to get a full perspective of the nature of such differences and the consequent problems of teaching which are created. The original writing of an eight-year-old boy with an IQ of 180 who began to write a book on astronomy has been described by Carroll. The following is the first paragraph of his first chapter:

In this book I intend to cover as nearly as I can all that is known of the ten large bodies which form the solar system. But we must remember that the Solar System is only a few tiny specks in space, with their parent

[39] Anne Anastasi and J. P. Foley, *Differential Psychology*, New York, The Macmillan Company, 1949.

[40] Anne Anastasi and J. P. Foley, *ibid.*

[41] G. M. Blair, *op.cit.*, p. 265.

Sun, which in turn, was formed by an immense piece of gaseous nebulae, huge pieces of gas which collect together to form a planet.[42]

When this boy was twelve, he wrote a 75,000 word book on astronomy and when fourteen wrote a letter to an adult friend—part of which is reproduced at the bottom of this page.

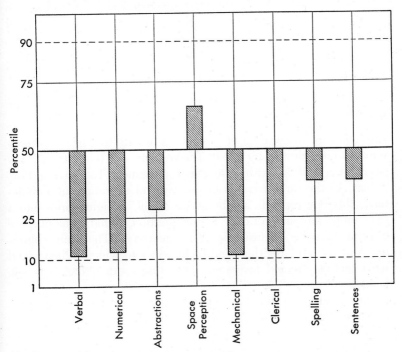

FIGURE 6. Profile of Aptitudes of a Twelfth-Grade Youth Who Wanted to Study Engineering.
(From G. K. Bennett, H. G. Seashore, and A. G. Wesman, *Differential Aptitude Tests*, New York, Psychological Corporation, 1947.)

Dear ———:
I was interested in your ideas concerning the "red-shift" or expansion of the galaxies, but I cannot say I agree with it. According to what I read, certain cosmological theories seem to require a contraction or expansion of the galaxies or island universes. Einstein and de Sitter, a Dutch relativist, have found that a certain cosmical constant is necessary for the

[42] Herbert Carroll, *Mental Hygiene*, Second Edition. Copyright, 1951, by Prentice-Hall, Inc., New York, p. 329. Reprinted by permission of the publisher.

operation of space-time in the universe as they see it. This cosmical constant is known as lambda. Actually, according to relativity, there is no gravitation and no lambda, but the universal curvature and various other factors working together make these two entities act as if they were forces.[43]

Compare with the above, the work of several eight-year-olds who were asked to tell what they thought about Negroes and Jews. (All were of about average intelligence.):

I think negroes are real real kind. Because most of them say nice thing I think Jews are pretty. Because they were juwerely and losts of makeup.

I thank Jews are just about like us. I thank their just like us because they are huming bings.[44]

Also compare the writing of Carroll's case with that of a fourteen-year-old boy with an IQ of 90. The responses of the latter are answers to a test in arithmetic about insurance. To the question, "What are the three hazards of owning and operating an automobile," this boy replied, "might go off a cliff," "might bumb into a pole, bumb into another car." To the question, "What is the purpose of comprehensive car insurance?," he answered, "The windle blures up. And its' hard for the windshield wiper to wipe." When asked what factors affected insurance rates, this youth wrote, "gas, oil, keracine." [45]

Such qualitative differences point clearly to the need for *qualitative* differences in the curriculum. Those who expect a given series of learning experiences to be appropriate for such extremes—or even for less extreme cases—are not facing one of the real issues in teaching. A mere change in speed of presentation, or the assignment of extra work (i.e., more of the same problems or study material) falls far short of providing for such differences.

THE APPRAISAL OF READINESS

In a sense, any measure of achievement or performance, be it a written test or a teacher's observation, is a test of readiness. Pre-

---

[43] *Ibid.*, p. 330.

[44] John Gillis, Unpublished Data, College of Education, University of Illinois, 1952.

[45] Furnished to the writer by Mr. David G. Hunt, Mathematics Teacher, Harlem High School, Rockford, Illinois.

sumably, the final examination in a course is often a check to see if a student is ready for more work in a particular area. A child who cannot add a column of figures is not ready for studying the formal addition of fractions (yet he may be quite ready to work with simple concepts of fractions), and one who cannot read is not ready to study history. However, ordinary measures of achievement fall far short of the requirements of a good check on readiness. A single score on a test or a single letter grade from a previous course or grade level gives very little usable information about a child. In some instances such information may bias the teacher about him before he begins. Often the scores and grades which are available are somewhat meaningless—unless the teacher knows what factors went into the scoring and grading. A grade based on a pupil's standing relative to his group may be of little or no value unless a good deal is known about the group, and a grade derived from some arbitrary standard is useless unless the standard is known and well defined. Even if the teacher knows these things, he still will not know *why* a student is having difficulties, nor the specific areas of weakness.

In assessing readiness the following information is needed: (1) How does each student compare with a well-defined group? (2) What are the specific skills, facts, attitudes and understandings which each student has or does not have? (3) How consistent are the errors which are made? (4) What personal factors, if any, interfere with his work?

Forms of Appraisal. There are numerous ways of getting information about a student's readiness for new material or new experiences. In some areas, such as reading, arithmetic, and spelling, there are well-constructed standardized tests. Also there are various general aptitude and ability tests, and prognostic tests in the sciences, mathematics and language skills. Finally, and perhaps most important, are teacher-made diagnostic pretests constructed for, and used in connection with a specific class.

Tests of readiness. A job analysis of the skills and abilities involved in learning new materials constitutes the background for various readiness tests. Most of the work in this field has been done in reading, although there are hundreds of aptitude tests in such fields as art, medicine, mathematics, mechanical drawing, and many others. In using a standardized test of readiness or of aptitude, a person assumes that the content of the subject or work is sufficiently well-defined so that the test results will predict performance.

In reading and arithmetic, skills and operations are more standardized, whereas in subjects such as geometry, history and the like, courses may vary considerably from any one "standard" content or method. Thus the value of an aptitude or readiness measure for such courses is doubtful.

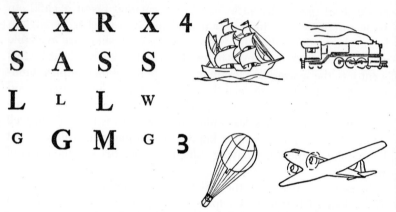

FIGURE 7. Examples of Items Used to Measure Reading Readiness.
In the item on the left, children are asked to find the letter in each line that is not the same as the others and draw a line through it. In the items on the right, the youngsters are asked to put a mark on the airplane, and put a mark on the ship with sails. (From J. M. Lee and W. W. Clark, *Lee-Clark Reading Readiness Test.* Copyright, 1943, by the California Test Bureau, Los Angeles.)

The kinds of items which are used to appraise readiness for reading may be seen in Figure 7.

Mental tests.[46] Mental tests are useful guides in selecting children who might need further diagnostic study, or are helpful in anticipating and heading off difficulties in schoolwork. Usually such tests give only an estimate of rather general abilities, hence are not very useful as an indication of a child's readiness for any particular subject or skill.

Illustrative of the way in which mental tests have been used as predictors of readiness for learning is their use for determining the time of entrance to school. In one school system where tests were used in this way for a period of ten years, criteria for admission,

[46] For a discussion of mental tests, see Chapter 17.

such as mental age (and other factors such as apparent emotional maturity) provided an elastic system of admissions which seemed to work better than chronological age as the sole criterion. In every case, over the ten-year period reported, children who were under age chronologically (but had an MA of at least six years) did as well or better than over-age children, and they were less often held back or put on trial promotion. Furthermore, they were referred for emotional and social adjustment problems less often than their older peers.[47]

TABLE 13

Results of Diagnostic Pretest in High School Biology *

Figures are Percentages Correct in Each Area

STUDENT	I BODY PARTS AND FUNC- TIONS	II NUTRI- TION	III DISEASE AND PA- THOLOGY	IV VOCABU- LARY OF BIOLOGY	V PLANTS AND ANIMALS	VI COMMON MISCON- CEPTIONS	VII SCIEN- TIFIC METHOD	VIII INTER- PRETING DRAWINGS
1. Burch	100	100	100	80	100	100	100	100
2. Nichols	80	60	50	60	90	80	80	100
3. Davis	80	30	40	5	90	80	70	80
4. Rubits	70	0	80	5	40	70	70	20
5. Krailar	50	40	20	0	10	60	50	20

* This test was administered near the beginning of the second half of a semester of biology by Mr. William Gilkey, Science Teacher, South Beloit, Illinois, 1952

Diagnostic pretests. A most important and oft-neglected form of appraisal of individual differences and readiness is the teacher-made diagnostic pretest. Much testing (especially the indiscriminate use of standard tests of ability and achievement) involves the collection of a large body of information about students with little follow-up or use of the information, thus collected, in teaching. Such testing is almost useless. On the other hand, tests designed for a specific appraisal of each student's strengths and weaknesses, and an insight into the working processes of each, can be a valuable aid to instruction. In fact, no teaching can be considered adequate without this necessary first step.

[47] J. R. Hobson, "Mental Age as a Workable Criterion for School Admission," *Elementary School Journal*, Vol. 48, 1948, pp. 312–321.

In Table 13 are some of the results obtained from a pretest in biology which was given in the middle of a first semester in a high school class. Figure 8 shows similar types of results for students just prior to their registration in a high school physics class.

A glance at figures such as those in Table 13 will show the area in which students are most poorly prepared. In this case it appears to be "biological vocabulary." More important, however, is the information about various individual students which is provided. For example, Burch was almost consistently high on every subtest, and Krailar was consistently low. But Davis, who scored 80 per cent on the questions about body parts and 90 per cent on the "plants and animals" section, scored only 5 per cent on vocabulary.

In Figure 8, when two boys are graphically compared on eleven different areas in beginning high school physics, it may be noted that these students who were equal (70 per cent) on the subtest, "molecular structure," were quite different in their scores in arithmetic (60 per cent for John and 100 per cent for Bill). Knowing these differences in advance, the teacher should be able to give help accordingly.

BUILDING READINESS

Preschool Experiences. There are important experiences prior to formal schooling which are needed by all children if they are to adapt to the demands of school. They must learn to work and find acceptable channels for aggression; acquire social skills, such as sharing, cooperating and competing; play group games and follow rules; know about books, pictures and numbers; and have some degree of motor skills, such as drawing and coloring. Readiness for schooling is thus being built long before the child enters school, as is well stated by Monroe:

The earliest efforts at reading do not take place at school in the first grade when children are six years of age. Books, magazines, signs, posters and reading materials of all kinds are so much a part of our American culture that most children have had many experiences with printed materials from early infancy.[48]

That such cultural factors do influence readiness has been shown in numerous studies. Investigators have found that size of family,

[48] Marion Monroe, *Growing into Reading*, p. 3. Copyright, 1951, by Scott, Foresman and Company, Chicago.

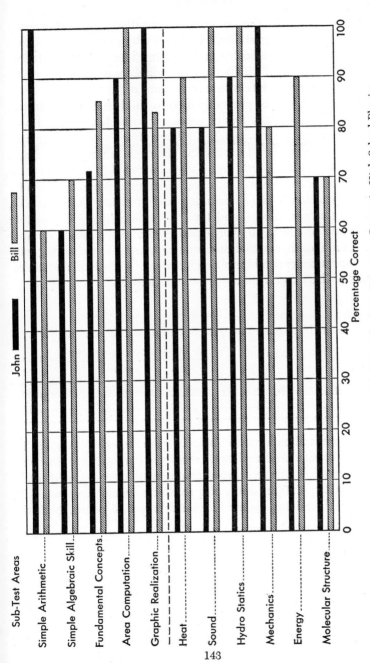

FIGURE 8. Readiness Profiles of Two High-School Students Prior to a Course in High-School Physics.
(This profile was prepared by Mr. Paul E. Mann, Science Teacher, Harlem High School, Rockford, Illinois, 1952.)

143

number of books in the home, and educational level of parents correlate with reading ability.[49] Children who come from "bookless homes" often have difficulty in beginning reading.[50] Such failure should not be blamed wholly upon the home deprivation, but partly upon the school which fails to take account of it.

Kindergarten may be profitably used to build readiness for formal schoolwork without any loss of necessary social learnings (also an important part of readiness). Children from two kindergarten classes were compared to see what effect an arithmetic readiness program would have. One group was conducted in the usual fashion. The other was given a rich and meaningful program which included such things as (1) counting and grouping chairs, pencils, crayons, children, blocks, and toys; (2) comparing and grouping objects and numbers; (3) participating in number games, number stories, number rhymes and number songs; and (4) measuring with ruler and yardstick: childrens' heights, room dimensions, and tables. Results of this experiment are shown in Table 14.

TABLE 14

Arithmetic and Intelligence Test Data for Control and Experimental Groups[51]

GROUP	AVERAGE IQ	AV. ARITH. READINESS SCORES		AVERAGE GAIN
		FALL	SPRING	
Experimental	102.52	13.22	23.44	10.22
Control	102.59	13.59	18.74	5.15

Both groups of children in Table 14 were essentially equal in IQ score and in measured arithmetic readiness (in the fall). However, the group which received special readiness training (experimental) gained 10.22 points in arithmetic readiness, while those who did not get such training (control) gained only 5.15 points. Both the

[49] W. D. Sheldon and Lawrence Carillo, "Relation of Parents, Home and Certain Developmental Characteristics to Children's Reading Ability," *Journal of Elementary Education*, Vol. 52, 1952, pp. 262–276.

[50] See M. C. Almy, "Children's Experiences Prior to First Grade and Success in Beginning Reading," *Teachers College Record*, Vol. 51, 1950, pp. 392–393. This writer found a significant positive correlation between success in beginning reading and opportunity for reading prior to the first grade. In studying homes of 106 children, this investigator found some that were almost "bookless."

[51] R. H. Koenker, "Arithmetic Readiness at the Kindergarten Level," *Journal of Educational Research*, Vol. 42, 1948, pp. 218–223.

teachers and the experimenter were convinced that the children of the experimental group expressed genuine interest and enthusiasm for this arithmetic experience.

So much of a child's psychological development has occurred before the first grade, that it seems obvious that the school's concern for children ought to begin long before school entrance. The school which becomes an influential force in a community can and should act as a service agency for parents of preschool children. Services such as nursery schools, home visitation services, and mental hygiene clinics should all be closely coordinated with public schools.

Readiness Programs in School. Readiness training does not stop as the child enters first grade, but should be continued in the first grade and even on into high school for that matter. Training which follows diagnostic procedures to prepare students for further work has successfully reduced educational mortalities at all levels. Results which may accrue from this type of program are shown in a study by Edmiston and Peyton. Fifty-four first-grade pupils, who had made very low scores on a reading readiness test were selected for special help. Under ordinary circumstances, these youngsters would probably have had considerable difficulty in reading. But in this case they were given a program planned to build their reading readiness.[52] Most of the pupils were, as a result of the training, able to move ahead in the reading program without undue difficulty.[53]

Even in college, remedial programs designed to fill in gaps in students' backgrounds have had a good effect upon course work. It was found [54] that college freshmen failing in chemistry and physics (especially veterans of World War II) were not failing through lack of ability, but because they had forgotten (or never obtained) basic concepts of arithmetic. Remedial work in general mathematics was helpful in a number of such cases.

Building Self-Confidence. The attitude which a child has about himself in relation to schoolwork is a pervasive element in readiness. Children with good ability often have developed such feelings of

[52] E. W. Dolch, M. P. Dolch and B. Jackson, *Readiness for Reading*, Champaign, Illinois, The Garrard Press, 1942, pp. 1–64.

[53] R. W. Edmiston and Bessie Peyton, "Improving First Grade Achievement by Readiness Instruction," *School and Society*, Vol. 71, 1950, pp. 230–232.

[54] J. R. Kinzer and H. P. Fawcett, "The Arithmetic Deficiency of College Chemistry Students," *Educational Research Bulletin*, Vol. 25, 1946, pp. 113–114, 140.

inferiority that they are defeated before they begin to work. Such children are hardly ready for the tasks they face in formal schooling. These youngsters need, more than anything else, experiences which will build their self-confidence and allow them to approach new situations without fear of failure or ridicule.

How is self-confidence won? Here are some suggestions derived from psychological research:

1. Individual instruction in special skills which are valued by child society gives a direct method of providing children the means of winning their own place in the school.
2. Research in nursery school indicates that children who lack self-confidence may gain it by being placed, for a time, with younger children. In this way the shy or fearful child is inducted gradually into a group of his age mates.[55]
3. College students asked to report instances in which their self-confidence was given a boost during their schooling, named most frequently praise by the teacher, winning in competition, being given a position of trust by the teacher, individual counseling with teachers, and statements by teachers which reflected a desire for the student's well being.[56]

The student's self-confidence and attitude about school are among the important, ultimate criteria of how well the school has planned for dealing with individual differences and readiness. The centering of attention upon the learner rather than solely upon subject matter has been one of the great psychological improvements in this century.

SUMMARY

Children differ widely in the many factors which determine their readiness for learning. To understand learning and teaching demands a knowledge of the learner. This understanding implies that teachers know the differences among children as well as the various strengths and weaknesses of each child. It also implies that the teacher understand factors that determine a child's readiness, such as maturation, experience, relevance of materials and methods, and emotional stability.

[55] Florence Goodenough, *Developmental Psychology*, D. Appleton-Century Company, New York, 1934.
[56] Charles Lyman Smith, *A Study of Factors Contributing to Self-Confidence in School*, Unpublished M.A. Thesis, Columbus, Ohio State University, 1950.

Much attention has been given to the problem of readiness in the early grades especially in subjects such as reading and arithmetic. But much less study has been given to the problem as it exists in the higher grades in spite of the fact that for all levels and in all subjects readiness for learning should be a primary consideration. An eighth-grade child who reads at the second-grade level is not ready to work on eighth-grade reading material, and a college freshman who is not a master of arithmetic is not ready for chemistry.

That class procedure which provides a given text which all must read or a set of exercises which all must do, violates the principle of readiness, for there are inevitably great differences among children in abilities, interests, experiences and personality factors. In a given grade, the teacher is apt to find that children vary in mental abilities from as much as four years in the first grade to as much as eight or ten years in high school. In achievement, interest, and other aspects which contribute to readiness, the differences are equally pronounced. Furthermore, children may be expected to show a great deal of intra-individual variation. A given child may be low on some measures of ability and high on others. All these differences produce unique individuals who are qualitatively different. Any instructional program which is to be successful must plan not only for differences in the quantity of material which is presented, but also for differences in the difficulty and kinds of materials.

Facing up to the problem of readiness means that the teacher needs to be able to determine or appraise the child's readiness, and not only teach accordingly, but in many cases build readiness for the work which the child must eventually be prepared to do. The appraisal of readiness entails measuring the factors which determine readiness. This is done through checks of physical factors, mental measurement, aptitude tests, and most important, through the regular use of diagnostic pretests. The latter should be used to get information about each child and to facilitate teaching in line with the individual differences which are found.

A part of every course or grade involves the building of readiness. This process begins before the child ever enters school. Most homes, for example, provide drawing materials, books and other reading and writing materials, and thus in the experience of nearly all children, there is some knowledge about books, pictures and rudiments of writing. From that time on through school, children are learning skills both for their immediate usefulness and for their preparation for new learning.

In essence, the building of readiness necessitates, (1) an analysis of the skills, understandings, and knowledges required to study given material, (2) diagnostic pretests or other devices to determine not only the level of each prospective learner, but also the specific areas of strengths and weaknesses, and the nature and origin of errors, and (3) an instructional program with a good deal of early individual guidance, designed to match teaching with individual needs and abilities.

REFERENCES FOR FURTHER STUDY

Adams, Olga, "Arithmetic Readiness in the Primary Grades," *Elementary School Journal,* Vol. 48, 1947, pp. 91–96.

Anastasi, Anne, and Foley, J. P., *Differential Psychology,* New York, The Macmillan Co., 1949.

Betts, E. A., "Factors in Readiness for Reading," *Educational Administration and Supervision,* Vol. 24, 1943, pp. 199–230.

Carroll, H. A., *Genius in the Making,* New York, McGraw-Hill Book Co., Inc., 1940.

Ellis, R. S., "The 'Laws' of Relative Variability of Mental Traits," *The Psychological Bulletin,* Vol. 44, 1947, pp. 1–33.

Glock, M. D., "Forty Demonstrations in One Class Period," *School Science and Mathematics,* Vol. 52, May, 1952, pp. 359–363.

Harrison, M. Lucille, *Reading Readiness,* Boston, Houghton Mifflin Co., 1936.

Hilliard, F. P., "Children Differ, So Should Programs," *Childhood Education,* Vol. 29, December, 1952, p. 155.

Horst, Paul, "Most Men Are Created Unequal," *Science Monthly,* Vol. 72, 1951, pp. 318–324.

Hunt, J. T., "What High School Teachers Should Know about Individual Differences," *School Review,* Vol. 60, October, 1952, pp. 417–423.

Jensen, B. T., "Suggestion to Teachers Regarding Individual Differences," *Kentucky School Journal,* Vol. 29, May, 1951, pp. 34–35.

Kabat, G. J., "Continuous Education for Varying Needs and Abilities," *Junior College Journal,* Vol. 23, November, 1952, pp. 154–163.

McGraw, Myrtle, "Maturation of Behavior" in Carmichael, Leonard (Ed.), *Manual of Child Psychology,* New York, John Wiley and Sons, Inc., 1946, pp. 332–369.

Monroe, Marion, *Growing into Reading,* Chicago, Scott, Foresman and Co., 1950.

National Conference on Research in English, *Readiness for Reading and Related Language Arts,* Chicago, The National Council of Teachers of English, 1950.

Pastore, Nicholas, *The Nature-Nurture Controversy,* New York, The Columbia University Press, 1949.

Tyler, Leona, *The Psychology of Human Differences,* New York, D. Appleton-Century Co., Inc., 1947.

Vernon, Philip, *The Structure of Human Abilities,* New York, John Wiley and Sons, Inc., 1950.

Wechsler, David, *The Range of Human Capacities,* Baltimore, The Williams and Wilkins Co., 1952.

Weeks, D. F., Macmann, E., and Erickson, I., "Our Programs Are Different," *Childhood Education,* Vol. 29, December, 1952, pp. 160–163.

Witty, P. A., and Kopel, David, "Preventing Reading Disability: The Reading Readiness Factor," *Educational Administration and Supervision,* Vol. 22, 1936, pp. 401–418.

FILMS

Individual Differences, The McGraw-Hill Book Co., Inc., New York. (20 mins.)

Willie and the Mouse, Teaching Film Custodians, Inc., 25 West 43rd St., New York 18, N. Y. (10 mins.)

Chapter 7

Motivation: The Forces Which Energize and Direct Behavior

THE KEY to controlling and guiding behavior is the understanding of needs, motives and interests. Consequently much of a teacher's work centers around problems of motivation. Almost invariably the teacher who fails is the one who is unable to take proper account of motivational factors. Questions such as how to relate school work to pupils' needs and interests, how to appraise the results of teaching methods in terms of their effect upon interest and motivation, how to diagnose interests and motives are persistently raised by teachers. The understanding and proper use of motivational techniques bring interest, good morale, effective learning and a sense of real achievement to the classroom. Lack of understanding and improper attempts to direct and change behavior often result in increased tension, disciplinary problems, boredom and fatigue, inefficient learning, and a sense that the school activities are little more than busy work.

This chapter will outline the forces which influence child and adolescent behavior. It will show how basic and learned needs relate to goals and incentives, and how these needs and incentives operate in the classroom.

WHAT IS THE MOTIVATIONAL PROCESS?

Teachers frequently make such statements as: "How can I motivate my class," "He wasn't motivated," or "His motives were not clear," or "He doesn't read because of improper motivation." A

150

glance at these different usages of the same word illustrates a vague understanding of this term by professional workers. In the first instance it would appear as if motivation were some activity of the teacher, in the second as a general characteristic of the child, in the third as a group of attributes, and in the last as a characteristic of a situation.

Some of this confusion is due to the failure to consider motivation as a whole process involving a relationship between the child and his environment rather than as a choice between either an internal or an external process. Motivation is certainly not something the teacher turns on and off at will, nor can it be thought of solely as an internal push which "will out" regardless of circumstances. Rather it is a process in which the learner's internal energies or needs are directed toward various goal objects in his environment.

One frequent misconception should be noted. Teachers do not motivate! They cannot create needs; they are but one aspect of the social environment. However, due to their strategic position they often serve as the mediator of satisfactions and manipulators of incentives, hence they may cause children to learn needs which might otherwise never have developed.

Arising from our basic needs, motives are the energies which give direction and purpose to behavior. It should be understood, however, that complex behaviors do not usually spring from a single need. For example, John who is editor of his school paper may spend a good deal of time and energy in the newspaper office; he may even work long hours after school. This activity may relate to a number of needs. Growing out of this activity are satisfactions of the need for status and for feeling important, the need for social approval from other staff members and the teacher and parents, the need for heterosexual adjustment, the desire for independence, and possibly many others. Furthermore, the newspaper writing and attendant activities may provide a needed release for tensions which have been built up in other situations.

Motives are highly individualized and, in their surface manifestations, may appear in a highly distorted manner. Thus interpretation of behavior without a knowledge of the needs which give rise to it may lead to error in treatment. The following case will illustrate how needs may lead to behavior which, on the surface, bewilders the teacher:

Bill, an eighth grader, was a small boy who lacked both physical strength and academic ability. He was persistently ignored or laughed at by other boys in the class. In the same class Harold was large for his age, and a person of good ability. He was popular with the boys in the class except for the times when he tried to dominate their activities. One of his amusements, which was enjoyed by other boys also, was to bully Bill. This distressed the teacher, especially as Bill seemed to like it. One day Harold picked up Bill and dropped him on his face, dislodging a front tooth. For several days, Bill displayed the gap with an apparent sense of pride. This was his bid for status and reflected his need to be one of the gang.

The teacher who described this incident to the writer commented that educational psychology was useless in such a situation. Here was a failure to see the pressing need of Bill for status in his peer group. The alert teacher, had she been able to guide the youngsters in other ways of gaining approval, might easily have prevented this event.

Clearly, the first consideration in the motivational process must center around needs, especially those which are frequently unsatisfied. In this category (as needs manifest themselves in the school) fall the needs for status (ego needs) and social needs. The school with competitive academic organization and emphasis upon team sports creates many cases of non-recognition and isolation. Needs which are powerful springs of behavior when properly harnessed become diverted into many channels some of which are undesirable, and operate at cross purposes with the aims of the teacher and school.

NEEDS AND BEHAVIOR

Unsatisfied needs result in increased physiological and psychological tension. Psychologists believe that it is the tension produced by needs which gives rise to behavior. Thus much if not all behavior may be described as tension reducing, as is illustrated in Figure 9.

The diagram in Figure 9 indicates that all behavior is goal oriented. Individuals are constantly striving for goals which will reduce tensions that have been built up from unsatisfied needs. Many times, of course, goals are attained without too great difficulty and the tensions are discharged. Frequently though, in all life situations, including the classroom, obstacles arise (barriers) which make the achievement of goals difficult or at times impossible. A person who is thwarted along the pathway to a goal may do one of two things. First, he may back up and with renewed energy or with a different attack try again to pierce the barrier or overcome the obstacle and attain his goal. If he should repeatedly fail, by using these direct

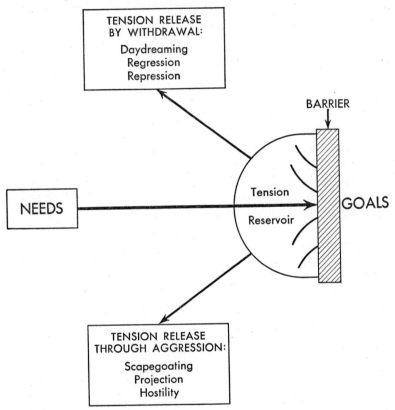

FIGURE 9. How Needs Operate to Produce Tensions.

methods, it is very likely that he will be forced to make a substitute adjustment—find another means of releasing his tensions. Figure 9 illustrates how tensions may be reduced through withdrawal and aggressive behavior. The forms of substitute release shown in the diagram are only a few of those which are used by human beings in their efforts to establish psychological equilibrium.

Behavior, and consequently learning, can only occur when there is some imbalance or tension for the pupil. Thus the teacher cannot consider his task one of satisfying needs, but rather one of manipulating the physical and social environment in such way that desirable tensions, anticipations, and desires are built up and are channeled in the direction of learning those skills and solving those problems which will lead to tension reduction.

In guiding the child's behavior it is of greatest importance for teachers to realize that identical behavior can spring from different motives, or different behaviors can spring from the same motive. Four children may be tardy in arriving at school. For one this behavior may be due to an aversion for school; for the second it may be the result of great pleasure in playing on the way to school; a third may be required to help at home in the mornings; and a fourth may wait until a bully in his neighborhood is inside the building before he enters the school area. It should be obvious that a single treatment (such as detention after school) is hardly the solution to these four problems. True, the detention may change the overt behaviors, but do little in the way of solving the problems. In fact it may increase the problem for any given individual.

A case which illustrates the necessity of considering children's needs in providing remedial training follows:

Steve, a seven-year-old boy was brought by his mother to the psycho-educational clinic as a reading problem. Tests revealed that the boy was above average in intelligence, was free from any gross sensory defects and was physically healthy. Subsequent work with the boy convinced the psychologist that the boy did not want to learn to read. The boy's home and school life were studied for possible causes of this attitude, and it was found that the boy's mother, who worked and had a number of social obligations, gave little attention to her son except at bedtime when she read him stories. She had several times remarked that she would be glad when Steve learned to read so she would no longer have to spend this time reading to him. The psychologist concluded that the boy had failed to read because he saw it as a threat to the little attention he was able to get from his mother. Work with the mother, not the son, soon cleared up the difficulty. She was encouraged to plan regular times when she could play with the boy, and also to plan activities which they would do together when Steve finally learned to read. In a few months, Steve was reading at a second grade level with the rest of his classmates.

It should be clear, that any attempt at education (in this case teaching the child reading) without some understanding of Steve's needs would have been unlikely to succeed. For a large group of the school's most persistent problems the need or motive conditions underlying the problems must be analyzed before effective, corrective steps can be taken.

How Needs Manifest Themselves in Behavior. Many valuable clues to children's needs may be found in their school behavior. How they see things, how they react to the teacher and other pupils, how they perceive themselves and their own activities, their attitudes about classwork and school in general may reflect not only past experience, but also their present needs (especially those which are unfulfilled or frustrated).

Even slight changes in needs seem to change activities. Sanford,[1] using a free-association word test (i.e., giving children a stimulus word or picture and asking them to respond with the first word that came to them) found that children gave about twice as many food responses to words *before* meals as immediately after eating. Bruner and Goodman [2] also showed that perceptions may be a function of needs. Working with ten-year-olds, they asked two distinct socio-economic groups to estimate the size of various coins. One group of children was from a settlement house in a Boston slum area and the other group was from a school attended by children from prosperous business and professional homes. Both groups overestimated the size of coins, but the poor children (to whom the coins presumably represented many unfulfilled needs) consistently overestimated their size more than the rich children, as may be seen in Figure 10.

Aside from changing the perceptual framework, needs may affect other responses of the child—in fact may alter the entire manifest personality. For example, prolonged periods of deprivation such as those reported in the University of Minnesota Semi-Starvation Studies [3] created rather major personality and behavior changes. The way in which these food needs manifested themselves in behavior

[1] R. N. Sanford, "The Effects of Abstinence from Food Upon Imaginal Processes: a Preliminary Experiment," *Journal of Psychology,* Vol. 2, 1936, pp. 129–136.

[2] J. S. Bruner and C. C. Goodman, "Value and Need as Organizing Factors in Perception," *Journal of Abnormal and Social Psychology,* Vol. 42, 1947, pp. 33–44.

[3] A. Keys, J. Brozek, A. Henschel, O. Mickelsen and H. L. Taylor, *Experimental Starvation in Man, Laboratory of Physiological Hygiene,* Minneapolis, University of Minnesota Press, October 15, 1945.

is well expressed in Guetzkow and Bowman's book [4] describing the above studies:

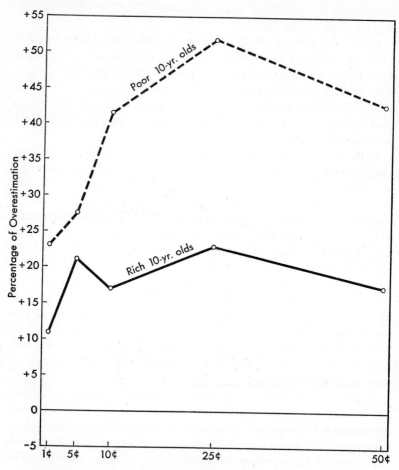

FIGURE 10. How Well-To-Do and Poor Ten-Year-Olds Estimated the Size of Coins.

(From J. S. Bruner and C. C. Goodman, "Value and Need as Organizing Factors in Perception," *Journal of Abnormal and Social Psychology*, Vol. 42, 1947, p. 40.)

The intensive preoccupation with food made it difficult for the men to concentrate upon the tasks they had intellectually decided to work on.

[4] H. S. Guetzkow and P. H. Bowman, *Men and Hunger, A Psychological Manual for Relief Workers*, Elgin, Illinois, Brethren Publishing House, 1946.

If a man tried to study, he soon found himself daydreaming about food. He would think about foods he had eaten in the past; he would muse about opportunities he had missed to eat a certain food when he was at this or that place. Often he would daydream by the hour about the next meal.

Perhaps even more important for its implication in school practice (if we assume that other pressing needs would create like results) was the marked change which deprivation produced in the decreased sociability and increased irritability of this semi-starved group. It was reported that "Petty defects became very important and were the source of much irritation. Standing in line at the diet kitchen before being served was the source of explosive conduct. The men blew up at each other on occasion. Mannerisms which formerly went unnoticed now became sources of friction." [5]

Deprivation, or the frustration of needs often produces marked irritability and hostility. For example, the student who gets insufficient sleep may be highly irritable, overcritical and apt to flare up at the teacher or his classmates. Sherif, a social psychologist, has gone so far as to say that the deprivation of any biogenic need tends to result in frustration mechanisms. [6]

The child who is starved for attention or affection may spend an inordinate amount of school time absorbed in efforts to satisfy these social needs, or when these attempts fail, cut himself off from the teacher and his group, obtaining solace in daydreams, or with other groups, not a part of the school's social situation.

Adjustment to school is fraught with problems created by unsatisfied needs, and consequent distorted social perceptions which in turn give rise to maladaptive behavior. Since an entire section of this book is later devoted to problems of adjustment, such material will not be considered here. At this point it is enough to say that school behavior contains clues of need level which may be valuable aids to the teacher in knowing what kinds of school tasks are needed; what manipulations of the social group are desirable, and what kinds of remedial help are necessary to facilitate learning.

Two Oft Neglected Needs. Among the needs of children there are two which, though important, are often overlooked by teachers. These are sex needs, and the desire for activity. Although each is

[5] *Ibid.*, p. 27.
[6] Muzafer Sherif, *An Outline of Social Psychology*, New York, Harpers, 1948.

definitely founded in physiological or tissue needs, their expression is, to a great extent, culturally determined. Thus they are at once both sources of learning and products of learning.

Sex Needs. The importance of sex needs in energizing the behavior of youngsters should not be underestimated. At the same time, however, there is danger in interpreting all action as the result of a single motivating force. As stated before most school behavior is complex, and likely to be the result of a number of forces (both internal and external).

Teachers who have watched teen agers in school plays, working together on the school paper, or in other groups where boys and girls are together, are often amazed at the rapidity with which youths, under such circumstances, learn. The English teacher may find it difficult to get a boy to remember one stanza of poetry, but in the school play, he learns 500 or a thousand words with little trouble. The coach knows too that when girls' cheers ring out across the football field or the basketball court, there is an improved athletic performance. Undoubtedly a great deal of schoolroom behavior and misbehavior arises from attempts of the sexes to attract favorable comment and attention from each other.

In many cases schools have failed to take advantage of this powerful motivating force—or have attempted to block those activities which are designed to satisfy it. Some of the poorly conceived policies practiced in one midwestern high school are illustrated in the following description:

Boys and girls eat on separate sides of the lunchroom and they have their coat lockers on separate floors of the building. Extracurricular activities except for a few clubs are divided according to sex, i.e., there are girls' and boys' debating teams and glee clubs. One group of students tried to get a program of social dancing started, but this was voted down by the school administration. In some classrooms boys sit on one side of the room and girls on the other.

Not only does this short-sighted policy militate against heterosexual adjustment, but also, it fails to take advantage of a need which can be a rich source of energy in promoting school learning.

Desire for activity—There is considerable evidence to show that every child has a basic need for activity, which manifests itself in the form of curiosity, bodily movements, exploration, games, and problem solving. Of all human needs there are perhaps none which are so directly applicable to motivation in school learning. As one writer puts it:

> Back of particular interests and the source of their energies, are certain physiological tensions or pressures or urges. Of broadest and greatest importance is the urge toward activity normal in any healthy organism. That dogs should run about and bark or children run and jump and shout requires no special explanation; such a "going off" of the healthy organism is simply the normal and inevitable product of structure and organic constitution (failure to be active *would* call for an explanation). Such activity is not limited to mere physical exuberance but also includes mental activity, i.e., curiosity, playing with ideas, imagining.[7]

The sources of potential activity level for a given individual are manifold. Endocrine balance, pathological conditions, general constitutional makeup, sleep and nutritional factors all play a part in determining the strength of the activity drive. It is important for the teacher to recognize the fact that the way this drive is expressed is largely a function of previous training, and of the kinds of tensions which are induced in the classroom. The schoolroom with stationary seats and strict rules governing movement, talking and other activity not related to a teacher's lecture, or recitation clearly blocks this important drive. In a study of 530 elementary pupils from grades one to eight it was found that children spent on the average 57.5 per cent of their time listening, and the greatest part of this, 33 per cent, in listening to the teacher talk. In some classrooms nearly three-fourths of pupils' time was spent this way.[8] Often there is but one pathway open for expression of this important need, namely, the activity determined by the teacher. Lectures or recitations, allow so little individual movement and expression that tensions are inevitably created. Having no other release for such tensions, children learn activities such as daydreaming, drawing on note paper, and passing notes in class, and may indulge in a wild release of tensions through running and shouting after class. The reader who is not familiar with this fact should ob-

[7] S. L. Pressey and F. P. Robinson, *Psychology and the New Education,* p. 149. Copyright, 1944, by Harper & Brothers, New York.
[8] Miriam E. Wilt, "A Study of Teacher Awareness of Listening as a Factor in Elementary Education," *Journal of Educational Research,* Vol. 43, 1950, pp. 626–636.

serve the behavior of a group of high-school students in the school's hallways after they emerge from many of their classes. The crude energy discharge in a short space of time is tremendous! Perhaps this is a healthy release, but one might hope that if learning activities were sufficiently related to needs, a good deal of this energy could be constructively released in the classroom. The description below shows how one teacher known to the writer took advantage of this basic drive by providing ample opportunity for its individual expression.

When Mrs. Sanders came to Central High, her journalism room was set up as a conventional classroom with five rows of stationary seats and one or two tables along one wall. In the back of the room was one desk for the editor of the school paper. Her predecessor had lectured and given practice in writing articles, and helped students after school. Except for the after school work, the class procedure was little different from any one of dozens of other classes in the school. After several conferences with the school principal, Mrs. Sanders convinced him that a real journalism laboratory should be set up. The principal agreed but reminded her that there were no funds for such a venture. The next day after talking to the principal, she explained the problem to her classes, and enlisted their help. First the group decided that the boys who were also enrolled in shop could make some of the equipment which was needed if they had sufficient money for lumber. It was agreed that extra advertising profits would be used to buy these needed supplies, and each student agreed to sell extra advertising space for several issues. As the construction and remodeling fund grew, materials were purchased, and the shop classes produced several tables, news racks, bookcases, etc. Several businessmen donated desks. At a school dance sponsored by the group, sufficient funds were raised to buy a camera and an additional typewriter. Today a visitor to this laboratory might be surprised at the amount of materials which are available for study. In addition to the facilities which were bought and made by students, there is an excellent library of books, periodicals and technical publications in the field of journalism. An excellent liaison program has grown up between this class and the city papers and other city offices, so that these facilities are open for students' use. Needless to say, there is a great deal of work and energy devoted by students to this course. But it is far more than a course. It is a real living experience which takes children into the community, and provides for individual differences by offering a wealth of different kinds of activities. Evidence of the effectiveness of this teacher's work is given by the kinds of people who have developed after taking this course. In one graduating class there were nearly a dozen students who made a life career of journalism. Of these dozen, one is a vice president of one of the nation's large advertising firms, one is an associate editor of a national magazine, and another is a publicity director for a national insurance company.

The application of what is known about the drive or desire for activity may be facilitated if consideration in teaching and curriculum planning is given to these principles.

1. The basic need structure, and crude energy level are in large part, functions of the "internal environment." The healthy child will tend to be the active child. A first principle, of great importance is that the school needs concern itself with the physical health of its pupils.
2. Listening and watching *do not* provide an adequate outlet for this drive—especially for young children. Large blocks of school time which are set aside for these kinds of activities are contrary to what is known about the activity drive.
3. That which is an outlet for the activity drive for one child, will not necessarily serve for another. Whereas one youngster may find adequate release of tension in a laboratory or in reading, another may gain release in talking, or in athletics. School programs will be most successful when they plan for individual difference in modes of expression.
4. Characteristic modes of energy release are learned through reinforcement. Activities toward which the teacher wishes the child to turn his energies must involve some satisfaction and pleasure.
5. Once a characteristic way of energy release is fixed, other incentives to learning may be unnecessary. The child may find sufficient satisfaction in solving problems that he will go on doing this long after the teacher's support is removed.

EFFECT OR REINFORCEMENT IN LEARNING

Perhaps no psychological principle has so much to offer the teacher as the "law of effect" [9]—the idea that behavior which results in a reduction of need, or in satisfaction, causes the responses leading to that effect to be fixated.

The concept of effect in learning has had wide acceptance and a tremendous influence upon education. Some psychologists [10] prefer to think of effect in terms of need reduction, and in such cases they

[9] E. L. Thorndike, *The Fundamentals of Learning*, New York, Bureau of Publication, Teachers College, Columbia University, 1932.
[10] C. L. Hull, *Principles of Behavior*, New York, D. Appleton-Century, 1943.

use the term "reinforcement" to describe this process. Translating this concept of effect or reinforcement in terms of usable school practices, the principle might be stated: *When a child's responses result in need reduction symbolized by such things as reward, approval, or praise, the responses (activities) perceived by the pupil as having led to these pleasurable consequences are fixated or learned.*

A situation from the writer's own experiences is presented to show how reinforcement may operate in a school setting.

Several years ago in a large West Coast high school some of the teachers were having a good deal of difficulty in handling study halls. One particular incident will illustrate the kind of thing which was happening. The students had been in their seats only a short time, when someone in the back of the room rolled a marble down the steps of the aisle. This was greeted with laughter. The teacher stormed to the back of the study hall in a rage, demanding to know who had rolled the marble. When she received no reply she threatened that when she caught the culprit she would make him pay. This was but one in a series of such incidents— all of which elicited the same fighting response from the teacher. What she did *not* realize was that each episode was a reinforcement for the very kind of behavior which she was trying to stop.

The young man who was sent to replace this teacher began by refusing to fight with the youngsters. There were a few trial episodes which failed to get results. In terms of learning, there was a period of *extinction* due to *non-reinforced trials.* At the same time, this teacher began to reinforce a new kind of behavior. Praise was given for students who worked diligently during the period. Help was given with individual lessons. The new teacher also added a few reference books to the study hall which helped give an outlet for some of the tensions which were built up. Group work was not discouraged so long as it did not interfere with others. In some cases groups who wished to study something together were sent down the hall to an empty room, where they were placed on their honor to spend their time studying.

There are probably few practicing teachers who are unaware of this principle of motivation—some might say it is just common sense. However, only in recent years have school experiences been planned to take advantage of this principle to any great degree, and even now, many opportunities for its application are not utilized.

Mistakes in the application of the principle of reinforcement are probably due to failure to consider some the following specific characteristics of the process:

1. The goals and needs of pupils may be quite different from those which the teacher perceives. For example, a child may make a foolish mistake in recitation and be laughed at by his peers. If this child has a strong need for attention, the laughter quite likely will reinforce this activity—namely, making foolish mistakes.
2. Children's needs are sufficiently individualized so that what is reinforcement for one may not be for another. In one instance a teacher's praise may be a strong reinforcement, while in another that praise will have little or no effect. In fact, for some youngsters the teacher's reproof may be a reinforcement in that it signifies a marking of the pupil as one whose behavior is accepted by his age mates.
3. Punishment, and other unpleasant consequences of pupils' activities do not serve as opposites to reinforcements. They do not necessarily weaken response tendencies in the same way that pleasurable consequences strengthen response tendencies.
4. The effect of previous reinforcements is carried into new learning situations. This means that students have an expectation as to what the results of present activities will be.
5. The effect of a particular response must be immediate or at least not long delayed for the reinforcement to be effective. This is particularly true for young children.
6. There must be a consistency in the effect of the response or activity. The learner must not be rewarded for a response one time and then later punished for the same response.

With these principles of reinforcement in mind much of a teacher's guidance of learning should center around the study of the kinds of reinforcement which have previously operated in a student's experience, and also the techniques which he will use as reinforcement in his own teaching program. Understanding of the effect of previous experience is impossible without a knowledge of the kinds of reinforcements which have occurred.

The reader is urged to pause at this point and consider these questions:

1. What are the various ways in which I as a teacher, can reinforce desirable behavior in the classroom?
2. How can the classroom be organized so that the optimum amount of social reinforcement occurs?

3. What ways can I use to prevent the reinforcement of undesirable behavior?
4. How can I infer from present behavior, the kinds of reinforcement which have previously occurred—in the classroom and in the home?
5. How can the effects of undesirable reinforcements be nullified?

Although much of this volume is devoted to just such questions (particularly in this and the following chapter) it is impossible to predict for the reader exactly what kinds of specific techniques of reinforcement will work for every individual. Each child is unique, and requires treatment according to his particular need pattern.

DYNAMICS OF THE MOTIVATIONAL PROCESS

The way in which learning results from goal seeking behavior is perhaps the central theme in present day psychology. The view of behavior as purposive, rather than accidental, has proven productive in the study of how children learn. Teachers, better than they were a generation ago, are trained to seek causes for all kinds of behavior. The modern teacher knows that maladjustment, misconceptions and hostile attitudes are learned, just as anything else is learned, and serve a purpose for the child. Since much that we say about motivation is inferred from the overt behavior of youngsters, it is essential that the teacher understand the way in which internal and external forces manifest themselves in behavior. The important question for the teacher to answer is what, about the motivational process, makes for efficient school learning.

Purpose or Intent to Learn. Without purposeful attention to stimuli, or intent to learn, the student may perform rote activities time after time, without acquiring the skills or learnings which represent the teacher's objectives. One psychologist, Sanford [11] gives an excellent illustration of this fact. He reported that after saying the prayers of the Episcopal service (about 5,000 times in a twenty-five-year period) he was unable to recall them unaided.

On several occasions one of the writers has asked his graduate classes how the name of the pen manufacturer, "Sheaffer" is spelled. Invariably well over 90 per cent of the group are unable to give the

[11] E. C. Sanford, "A Letter to Dr. Titchener," as reported in J. A. McGeoch, *Psychology of Human Learning*, New York, Longmans, Green and Company, 1942, p. 276.

correct spelling, including those who own Sheaffer pens. The radio quiz programs have capitalized upon this fact by asking such questions as "What famous American is portrayed on the cigarette tax stamp?" Few of those who have smoked cigarettes for years have learned that "DeWitt Clinton" appears beneath the familiar engraving.

Little wonder that children can read a given word hundreds of times and yet be unable to spell it, or work mathematical problems under the teacher's guidance and be unable to solve similar problems on their own.

What are the factors operating in this important principle of motivation? First there are attitudes, needs and desires which lead to an interest in given parts of the pupil's environment. These attitudes are products of experience and guidance and like other kinds of learned behavior are primarily the result of reinforcement. Secondly, these attitudes lead to habits of attention and perception which are learned ways of looking at and looking for something. Even with the desire for information, in a particular area, however, there is the additional question of whether students have enough skill to find what they are looking for.

The perceived usefulness of information and skill is a third factor in the purposefulness of a pupil's approach to schoolwork. Teacher's of industrial education, for example, are well aware of increased attention and intent to learn, when class material in motor mechanics relates to the youth's own "hot-rod." An art teacher [12] reports that there was a much greater intention to learn on the part of a settlement house pupil when he had a chance to mould some brass knuckles. In such cases, the learner may be so interested in his own problems that he will go directly to the information of specific concern without bothering to learn other related skills which the teacher may consider essential.

Finally, the kinds of instructions or set given prior to performances such as reading, listening to a lecture, making notes, seeing a demonstration, or taking a test are important variables in determining intent to learn. McGeoch in a summary of considerable experimental evidence has stated that:

[12] As related to the writer by Mr. John Laska, University High School, Urbana, Illinois.

. . . An active set to learn, with its accompanying active response to the material practiced, is a powerful determiner of learning, whether the learning be the fixation of a verbal series, the establishment of a conditioned response, or the discovery and fixation of the solutions of perceptual-motor and rational problems. The set may be established by formal instructions or it may arise from the experimental situation and the subject's own reaction systems.[13]

Knowledge of Progress. Knowledge of progress seems to be essential for effective learning. The beneficial effects of apprising a learner of the results of his learning activity has been well demonstrated from the early 1900's to the present,[14] and as a principle of motivation, it has been experimentally tested in a number of types of school subjects.

There is little doubt that the extent of a pupil's motivation is dependent upon his knowledge of how well he is doing. But probably just as important as this general feeling of attainment is his knowledge of the result of each response, plus some means for the immediate correction of it if he has made an error. This kind of knowledge of progress has been described as follows:

As illustrative of the value of specific knowledge of progress—of knowing just what is wrong, we may take an experiment by English, 1940. A proper trigger squeeze is an important factor in accurate rifle shooting, especially with high powered rifles. Soldiers who were told that they were not properly squeezing the trigger of their guns, showed slow gains with practice; when they were made to feel tactually and kinaesthetically, the difference between adequate and inadequate squeezing, they made much more rapid progress. Likewise it is not enough to be told that ones sentence structure is weak; one needs to be shown where it lacks balance or parallelism.[15]

How may this principle be used in teaching? In one case [16] the simple expedient of showing sixth grade children progress charts of their reading improvement and emphasizing rapid reading for only a short period of twenty-eight days increased the speed of

[13] John A. McGeoch, *The Psychology of Human Learning*, New York, Longmans, Green and Company, 1942, p. 279.

[14] J. B. Stroud, *Psychology in Education*, New York, Longmans, Green and Company, 1946.

[15] H. B. English, *Learning as Psychotechnology*, Mimeographed Study Guide, Ohio State University, Columbus, Ohio, 1949, pp. 35a–35b.

[16] J. A. O'Brien, *Silent Reading*, New York, The Macmillan Company, 1921.

reading over 200 per cent without a loss in comprehension. This experiment was especially significant in that no other special motivations or skills were emphasized during the period of improvement.

The case which follows was reported to the writer by a basketball coach in an Illinois high school, and will show how this principle was applied in one phase of physical education:

> I had a very poor group of free-throw shooters, and I had tried several means of reward and punishment for improving them, but these methods did not work, so I decided to try something different. Each boy was required to shoot 100 free throws each day. My manager and I kept a record of the number of successful shots but the boys did not know about this. To my dismay, *the practice did not improve their percentage.* So I made a huge chart with each squad member's name on it and the number of successful free throws made each day. I posted this in the gymnasium where all the players could refer to it at anytime.
>
> At the end of a week, slow but steady improvement was discernable. I stressed the point that the chart was not to show who had the highest average but rather who was making the most improvement. The chart was continued until the end of the basketball season, and in all but three out of twenty-four cases, the rises were continuous.

Several aspects of motivation are illustrated by this report. First, note that knowledge of progress was effective when other techniques had failed. Secondly, the case illustrates that practice, or repetition, alone, does not necessarily lead to improvement. Finally, it should be noted that the teacher in this case emphasized that pupils should make comparisons with their own previous performance and not with other players.

The Self Concept and Goal Setting. How does the child see himself in relation to his goals and aspirations? What factors determine the kinds of goals and the achievement levels which he visualizes for himself? Studies of levels of aspiration have shown that one of the important factors in determining the level of achievement which a child proposes for himself is his previous experience in like situations.[17] A systematic study [18] of aspirational levels has shown the

[17] R. R. Sears, "Success and Failure: A Study of Motility," in Q. McNemar and M. A. Merrill, *Studies in Personality,* New York, The McGraw-Hill Book Company, Inc., 1942, pp. 235–258.

[18] P. S. Sears, "Levels of Aspiration in Academically Successful and Unsuccessful Children," *Journal of Abnormal and Social Psychology,* Vol. 35, 1940, pp. 498–536.

important effects upon future goal-setting behavior when the child fails to achieve his stated goals. This same investigation found that a child who thus fails is more apt than the one who succeeds to develop unrealistic aspirations for succeeding performances. More specifically, he estimates his future performance so high as to be wholly impossible, or so low that he is sure to attain the mark. Those children who fall near the level which they have set for themselves are prone to be quite realistic about their estimate for future performances.

Certainly a most important factor in the choice of goals and expected level of performance is the child's self-concept. (This is of course conditioned by such things as previous experiences with stated versus attained goals.) Working with orthopedically handicapped young people, Rotter [19] set up a task involving a simple motor skill. The important finding was that this handicapped group had a lower level of aspiration *even though the task being performed was totally unrelated to their physical handicap.* In Chapter 4 it has already been shown how specific deviations of adolescents (such as minor somatic variations) may be destructive of self-confidence. It is a great misfortune when such minor matters come to spread to a person's entire self-concept. It is clear in such cases what the teacher's job is. The child must be made to realize that a slight handicap may limit him *only* in the specific areas where it is involved. Also the development of a healthy self-concept demands that the youth's notion of normality be in terms of a wide range, rather than conceived as a fixed point.

The overidealization of goals and of the self in relation to those goals is a disease of our culture. Young people's goals are often unrealistic because of the inadequacy of our language to describe them, and because words are used to take the place of objects. Also influences such as motion pictures, newspapers, fiction and advertising have given a romantic aura to many goals and ideals sometimes to such an extent that the pupils' aspirations are far from realistic. On top of this idealization of goals, our language is such that we use "either-or" categories in describing, to ourselves, such things as success and attainment. Therefore, if a youth's goals are

[19] Julian B. Rotter, Unpublished information as reported in K. Lewin *et al.*, "Level of Aspiration," in J. Mc.V. Hunt (Ed.), *Personality and the Behavior Disorders,* Vol. I, New York, The Ronald Press Company, 1944.

so idealized as to be non-existent in reality—and therefore impossible of attainment—and if he visualizes success on an all or none basis, he is doomed to be disappointed. One writer describes this process as the cycle of idealization, frustration, and demoralization (IFD). Because he is unable to attain his unrealistic ideals, the youth meets frustration, which in turn leads to demoralization.[20]

Children need to learn to set for themselves goals which are within their ability of attainment and which are realistically perceived. The expectations which build up around goal seeking activities must be met, if reinforcement is to be effective. When achievements fall far short of the learner's expectations the learning process is disrupted. Perhaps even more important, young people need to develop self-concepts which are positive and healthy. In fact this is so important in the person's overall development that counselors and clinical psychologists use, as one measure of the success of their work, the number of positive self references which are made by a client.[21]

The Emotional Aspects of Motives. Motivation always involves an affective component. Both the tension release, when the student has achieved his goal, or the frustration if he is unable to do so, are circumstances which give rise to feelings and emotion. If the reader will look back into his own experience, he will find it impossible to conceive of high energy states and goal seeking behavior as being neutral in feeling. If we consider the school child as under a strong impulsion toward his goals, or goals selected for him by the teacher, there are a number of possible events which may lead to emotional states.

Confronting the child with impossible tasks. When the child, due to lack of ability or training—or because of the nature of the task is unable to perform satisfactorily, strong motivation toward the goal which the task represents may lead to anger, displaced aggression and feelings of inferiority as shown in the following experiment:

Dembo's experimental method consisted in confronting her subjects with an impossible task and demanding completion from them. Her experiment lasted between one and two hours and was usually continued

[20] Wendell Johnson, *People in Quandaries*, New York, Harper and Brothers, 1946.
[21] C. R. Rogers, *Counseling and Psychotherapy*, Boston, Houghton Mifflin Company, 1942.

on the following day. The experimenter and a special reporter were in the same room with the subject, the former sometimes interfering with the action of the subject. In all cases very genuine emotions of anger were aroused, manifesting themselves in swearing, threats, wishes and acts of destruction, and even in one case in the subject's rushing out of the room and being found in tears in another.[22]

The reader should see a clear parallel between these experimental results and some of the anger and aggression which school children display under similar circumstances. These kinds of explosion can not often bring satisfactory tension release, because they do not change the conditions which feed the tension—actually they may lead to further tension, as children may be ashamed and this shame may create additional emotional disturbance.

Saturation. Earlier it was pointed out that various school activities serve as avenues for the release of energy. However, there are some cases in which activity instead of releasing tension, serves to build up tension. This is particularly true when a child is held to one task (by threats or encouragement), to a point of saturation. At this point, the task assumes a negative character, and if continued will induce tension and emotional reaction much as when a child is presented with an impossible task—indeed it becomes impossible for the child to go on. Saturation is particularly apt to occur when the school's tasks are relatively meaningless or rote activities. Teachers should be alert to symptoms of emotionality which accompany saturation. They are:

1. Marked deterioriation in the quality of performance.
2. Apparent fatigue—although the child may not *actually* be tired, he will say that his back aches—he can no longer hold a pen or pencil or his eyes hurt.
3. Irritability and anger often not directed at a person but toward school materials such as books, paper, and writing materials.

Conflict between motives. Increased emotional tension is characteristic of those instances in which the child is faced with a choice between two positive pulls or a positive and negative pull toward the same object or situation. The former is exemplified by the pupil who wishes to go to school, but at the same time wants to go fish-

[22] Kurt Koffka, *Principles of Gestalt Psychology*, New York, Harcourt, Brace and Company, 1935, p. 408.

ing. In the latter would be found such cases as those in which the adolescent wants to be with his gang, but finds the activities of the gang in conflict with his previous training.

In the section of this volume dealing with school adjustment, problems of emotionality will be dealt with in greater detail.

Community Resources and Motivation. The use of materials and ideas from the immediate environment of the school child may be marked as one of the great advances in educational practice in the past thirty or forty years. Activity which a child perceives as useful and productive becomes rapidly self-energized. A high school principal furnishes the following illustration from his own experience:

When I was in high school, I had a learning experience which I shall never forget. It originated in our shop class and involved the study of plywood. We actually made plywood. The problem required reading and assembling of facts. We learned about kinds of wood, their strength, durability, and uses. We learned to plane wood to the desired thickness and we made our own glue, and sandpaper, and found the ingredients of these as well as of the finishing agents such as varnish with which we treated the finished product. Although we bought our paint brushes, I enjoyed learning that in primitive times people set combs in the paths frequented by wild boars thus collecting bristles. To this day I like shop work very much, and I attribute this interest to a very understanding and patient teacher. The articles which we made of wood were useful, and I still have some of the things I constructed including a gun rack made from black walnut. Our class actually went to the standing timber, identified the walnut, felled the tree, took it to the saw mill, dried it, and planed it. I would not part with this rack for anything. Needless to say, absences in this shop class were rare, and there were no problems involving discipline.

Aside from the increased meaningfulness and better learning of material which results from making schoolwork relevant, there is the additional consideration here of how such teaching steps serve to increase motivation. Such considerations are particularly important in schools which are relatively isolated from their community. One writer [23] warns that, isolation from direct experience is a real danger facing our schools. In large cities, especially, he says "talk about things increasingly takes the place of real experience with things."

[23] M. R. Collings, "Exploring Your Community: A Direct Experience Study," *Journal of Educational Research*, Vol. 44, 1950, pp. 225–230.

The community is full of challenging problems and opportunities for learning, and when students are allowed or encouraged to tackle these problems, their interest and enthusiasm may be tremendous. Following is one example of this kind of well-motivated activity in operation.[24]

During a class discussion it was found that over half of the persons present had had malaria. The students were amazed and began to wonder whether they were truly representative of the population of Tuscaloosa. A visit to local health authorities revealed a lack of reliable data. By this time class interest was so high, students proposed that they secure answers to their questions through a direct survey.

A questionnaire was drawn up and plans for administering it were discussed. But the city was large. What was an adequate sampling? How should the information be gathered?

It was finally decided that the students would secure training in interview techniques in school and then visit every fifth house in the city with their questionnaire.

Next the data were compiled and charts were drawn. The class found that they were an atypical group. However, the rate of malarial infection was so high that students decided to take some steps to improve the situation.

The class studied causes and remedies for malaria and prepared literature for distribution in the school and community. The findings of the study were submitted to the local board of health and to the city newspaper, and a complete report of the study was placed in the high school library.

Here is intrinsic motivation in its mature form. There is little need in such cases for the teacher to be concerned with schemes for prodding students into action, or sugar coating the subject matter to make it palatable. In a sense, activity of this sort is the ultimate for which teachers should strive, because it is the culmination of careful planning which accepts students as responsible self-motivated persons who no longer need the teacher except as a guide and who are now ready to go on learning whether they are in school or not.

[24] This is a description of Robert Strang's class in biology in the Tuscaloosa, Alabama High School reported in The American Association for Supervision and Curriculum Development, 1949 Yearbook, *Toward Better Teaching*, pp. 203–204.

GOALS AND INCENTIVES

There is often a wide discrepancy between the way in which a student perceives his goals and the goals which teachers perceive as the learner's aspirations. For instance a teacher may see a child's interest as due to the appeal of the class material, whereas the actual energy which occasions the behavior may be as mundane as the pupil's attempt to impress the girl across the aisle. Likewise, teacher's appeals through praise, threats or other incentive conditions may give rise to behavior which the teacher may then view as self-sustaining interest. This practice has led to the common assumption that if one can get a pupil to do something he will have learned it. But this assumption must be seriously questioned in light of what we have said about reinforcement. It is doubtful if behavior elicited under external pressure and without a child's interest will actually persist (in other words mark a lasting change in behavior). Nevertheless, certain spurs to activity are useful in schooling. Many activities (learning multiplication tables, spelling, memorizing formulae) may be considered important by teachers and parents, but may not be seen as immediately useful by students. Thus as the child sees it the intrinsic worth of the material to be learned is low. One might think of school activities as being on a continuum which represents the intrinsic worth of school material for a given child. For one child this scale might appear as follows:

Scale of Intrinsic Value for a Given Child

Low Intrinsic Value					High Intrinsic Value
	History Dates	Classical Literature	Science	Shop	

Confronted with the task of teaching materials on the low end of this scale, the teacher may find himself forced to resort to the use of incentives which are not clearly related to the learning activity.

Rewards. Whereas reinforcement is generally considered as the pleasant consequence for a specific response, reward is a satisfaction of needs for a whole series of responses. Furthermore rewards (in the form of teachers' rewards to students) may be artificial and somewhat unrelated to the activity for which they are given. The most effective reward (and punishment, for that matter) is that which is a natural consequence of the learning activity. Unfortunately rewards are characteristically given for such things as a well-memorized poem, a correct list of spelling words, or a winning theme.

If reward is thought of in the broad sense of including both material and intangible values which result from performance, such as praise, self-esteem and adulation of one's fellows, it is then secondary only to physiological satisfactions as a force in human behavior. In fact all other forms of motivation may be thought of as subsidiary to it, and in this sense it becomes synonymous with a previous concept—tension reduction. However, there are various types of rewards, and we are particularly concerned here with the rewards teachers give and their effect upon school behavior.

The use of material rewards in school is not common for obvious reasons, but there is some evidence as to how such rewards affect the learning of children. The important drawbacks in the use of material rewards in school learning seem to be (1) in order to keep performance at a high level it seems necessary to increase rewards periodically, (2) the attainment of the material reward becomes the primary goal, and school learning only an incidental means to an end—a means which is quickly cast aside when the reward is attained, (3) other kinds of incentives are just as effective or more effective and do not lead to the relegation of learning to a secondary position. An Illinois principal gave an illustration of the use of material rewards in his school:

One teacher who had an outside income, made a habit of bringing presents (generally candy bars) to her classroom. She distributed these to students who, on a given day worked diligently and stayed out of trouble. She was, according to the principal, well-liked by her pupils, and achieved good results in her teaching. However, the other teachers in the school, financially unable to do the same, complained bitterly to the principal who was thus obliged to ask the teacher in question to find other means of rewarding her class.

If learners are to form attitudes about school learnings in which they like school activities for their own sake, stress on material rewards is distinctly out of place.

The use of marks, percentages, and grades; the giving of honors through assemblies, honor societies and scholarships; and the awarding of prizes in the form of ribbons, cups or trophies are all ways in which the educator attempts to foster desirable behavior and promote a maximum of effort toward school goals. Such incentives may be powerful, as they often symbolize the approval and admiration of parents, teachers or other pupils. However, as is the case with material rewards, these incentives may become the sole purpose or aim of achievement with mastery of subject matter only an incidental step toward the incentive. In such cases, schoolwork itself may be viewed in a neutral way or even as a somewhat unpleasant but necessary task. Even so, the writers take the view that all behavior is purposive or goal directed, hence there is nothing artificial about working for a scholarship or for honors, any more than it is artificial for behavior to be directed toward earning money and the things it will buy. Nevertheless, there is a profound difference between the man who hates his work but does it to earn money and the man who likes his work and also the financial rewards he achieves for it. In the same way there is an important difference between the youngster who dislikes work, but masters it because of honors, and the one who is engrossed and pleased with his work and achieves honors as a consequence. The important difference here to consider is that the learner in the latter case will be much more likely to remember what is learned and better able to apply it in a new situation. What accounts for the differences in the above cases? What is there about learning activity which is of intrinsic value to the pupil? Such factors as the following may operate from time to time in the learning situation which possesses intrinsic motivation.

1. There is a pleasant association between material to be learned and the learning situation, e.g., a friendly social atmosphere.
2. The material to be learned allows for a satisfaction of the drive for activity and curiosity and allows the learner to make discoveries for himself and to solve problems. These consequences are rewarding, but are a more natural consequence of the learning activity than teacher-controlled rewards.
3. The student identifies the learning with persons he admires.
4. The consequences of the learning include the opportunity for the student to see how the subject matter works—see a finished production. For example, he may use a foreign language in another country or with a foreign visitor, or he may build his own radio set.
5. There is novelty or humor in the learning material which serves as a release from boredom and monotony.

6. The learner takes an active part in the planning of the material to be learned thus gaining a proprietary interest in its completion.

The fulfilling of one, or better, several or all of these conditions will almost certainly lead to rewards which are an intrinsic part of the learning situation, and the teacher will not have to depend solely upon extrinsic rewards to achieve the school's goals.

Punishment. Punishment and the fear of punishment are still used as forms of extrinsic motivation in the schoolroom even though the use of punishment has decreased markedly in the last fifty years. There is little question that fear, anxiety and avoidance of pain are powerful motivating forces. Threats, reproof, and sarcasm build up tensions which are released much in the same fashion as those shown in Figure 9. Because of its power, and because of its ease of use, and because it often serves to release tension of the person doing the punishing, this form of motivation, historically, has been among the most frequent forms of man's attempt to train his young. Punishment has been assumed, at one time or another to accomplish these ends: (1) teach the child respect for authority, (2) block undesirable responses, (3) force the child to do something he was not ready to do or did not want to do, (4) set an example for potential offenders, (5) make students pay attention to class work, and (6) motivate students to learn assigned material.

A report of one of the writer's advisees will illustrate the powerful force of punishment:

When I was in the fourth grade I had a teacher whom I just hated. Once she told me that if I did not learn the "9's" in multiplication by the next day I would fail the course. At that time the idea of failure was terrible, and so I stayed up until twelve that night studying them. I just knew I could never face my parents and friends if I failed, so I really worked that night. I think this is one reason I dislike math so much now. Every time I see a page of figures I get that tense feeling.

This example should show two important facts about the use of threats for purposes of motivation. In the first place, it was a powerful force for this particular child, but it should also be noted that the results of its use included more than learning multiplication. There was also the resulting dislike for the teacher and for arithmetic in general. These too are learnings. For this reason, many psychologists have concluded that while punishment is a potential mover, its results are less predictable than other modes of influencing children and also is often accompanied by undesirable results. These undesirable aspects of punishment include (1) resentment and hostility toward the "punisher," (2) increased emotionality often so severe that any learning during the phase of activity elicited by the punishment is unlikely, (3) learning in order to avoid punishment rather than for the intrinsic value of the material to be learned, (4) fatigue due to tension created by anxiety, and (5) disintegration of class morale.

Psychologists today are convinced that punishment has often been overused in schools and homes. They do not, as a general rule take the position sometimes ascribed to them by laymen, that punishment should never be used. It might be said, however, as a general principle for teachers to follow, that as a form of motivation, punishment is crude and relatively ineffective when all factors in the learning process are considered.

Some values of punishment (not primarily for motivational purposes) are shown in the instances which follow:

The first is when punishment is appropriately combined with reward. Punishment may occasionally be used to redirect behavior so that the desired behavior can occur and be rewarded. Even though the effect of punishment is temporarily disturbing, it may under some circumstances permit the more permanent effect of reward to become operative. For example, a shock through mishandling an electrical appliance in science may be effective if supplemented by help in correcting the hazardous condition.

The second situation in which punishment is appropriate is that recognized clinically as one in which the need for punishment is great. A child sometimes tests the authoritative adult by provocative behavior to see how far he can go. If not punished (in order that the limits may be defined for him), his anxiety mounts as he does things which seem beyond the law.[25]

If the teacher who is confronted by a problem considers the *purpose* for which punishment is meted out, he will go a long way toward eliminating undesirable aspects of punishment and will be far

[25] E. R. Hilgard and D. H. Russell, "Motivation in School Learning," in Part I, the 49th Yearbook, National Society for the Study of Education, *Learning and Instruction,* Chicago, University of Chicago Press, 1950, p. 50.

It should be noted that the above writers have used as an example that type of punishment which is a natural consequence of the act, and not punishment by the teacher. Also it should be clear that there are times when punishment and restraint are necessary in emergencies for the safety of children.

less apt to misuse this technique. Thorndike suggests several ways in which teachers might improve the results from punishments. They are: (1) Make sure in each case that the punishment belongs to the behavior in question (2) . . . forestall the punishment in cases where the want which led to the offense can be satisfied innocently, and more frequently reward good tendencies in place of repressing bad ones.[26]

Clearly the consequences of punishment upon behavior will vary greatly from one situation to another. Any guiding principles which the teacher formulates for his own use should give cognizance to the following factors. First, there are social relationships between teacher and pupils which are important determiners of the effect of punishment. The slightest reprimand by a very unpopular teacher may be perceived as an injustice. Secondly, there are personality differences among children which make a difference in the effect of various influence techniques which the teacher uses upon them. In one study,[27] it was shown that children who are apparently extraverted may respond with greater effort following reproof, while children classified as introverts are more apt to suffer in achievement following reproof. In the third place, the teacher must always try to appraise the child's perception of the punishment. If the student feels he is unjustly singled out for punishment (especially when his transgressions are ones common to his group) he is apt to build a resentment toward the teacher and a desire to "get even" which interferes with learning activities.

Lastly and perhaps most important, punishment must be considered in terms of the total learning situation. The teacher should always be sure that correct or desirable activity is made known and rewarded upon occurrence when punishment is used. Punishment for the *only* thing a child knows how to do will not lead to desirable learning, but may cause emotional disturbance and even a fixation of the undesirable responses.

Competition. By placing a high premium upon individual achievement the school generally assists in the development of a keen sense of rivalry among students. There can be little doubt that

[26] E. L. Thorndike, *Selected Writings from a Connectionist's Psychology,* Appleton-Century-Crofts, Inc., 1949, pp. 60–61.

[27] G. G. Thompson and C. W. Hunnicutt, "The Effects of Repeated Praise or Blame on the Work Achievement of Introverts and Extroverts," *Journal of Educational Psychology,* Vol. 35, 1944, pp. 257–266.

competition operates as one of the outstanding incentives in school learning. Competition gets its strength from the ego and social needs of the individual who comes to value his place in a particular group or groups, and who strives to maintain that place or better it. As with other important incentives, its roots grow in the soil of basic needs, but its form and consequences are culturally determined.

Characteristically, American schools have fostered competition without teaching children *how* to compete. Experienced teachers know that many children are afraid to try. To these children, the setback of not winning is such a threat that they would rather refrain from the activity than risk what they perceive as failure. They are victims of the attitude that as a result of *any* task one either wins or loses. The attitude of self-confidence in facing problems and in learning are much more important than any subject matter which the teacher wishes the student to learn. The following example will illustrate how the child may learn to compete, and the effect upon his development when he has *not* learned to do so.

In the first four grades Alfred was considered a failing student, but was passed along because his teachers could find nothing else to do for him. At first he had tried hard to succeed, but in such activities as oral reading, he succeeded only in gaining the ridicule of his fellow pupils who laughed at his mispronunciations. After dozens of such experiences he stopped trying. In the last half of the fourth grade he became a "trouble maker." He was competing in the only way left to him—by physical means, bullying, and attention getting by disrupting the class. His 4B teacher passed him, not because of achievement, but because she was happy to be rid of him. In the beginning of the fifth grade, he again started misbehaving but for once he had a teacher who tried to understand him. She knew that Alfred must learn how to compete, and unlearn attitudes of dislike for school work. A mental test given at this time showed the boy's IQ to be about 80. Also it was noted that he had a slight speech defect. Otherwise he was physically healthy. The fifth grade teacher paid a visit to Alfred's home, and found the mother cooperative but worried about her boy. When asked what Alfred liked to do, the mother showed the teacher several wood carvings which the boy had whittled out in his spare time. The teacher asked to borrow them, and next day showed them to Alfred and asked if he would mind if she displayed them to the class. Fellow pupils were impressed by this work, and in the weeks that followed, the teacher planned several activities (such as cutting out linoleum plates for printing) in which Alfred could be used to help other students. Sometime later in the semester, Alfred began to take part in the class discussion, and on one occasion when he had made a contribution, the students clapped. By arbitrary standards Alfred, even with improvement, was not doing fifth grade academic work, but he had regained a good deal of his self-confidence, and he had learned to compete.

What is the experimental evidence about competition as a school incentive? The first well demonstrated point is that competitive activity and the strength of competition as an incentive increases directly with age in elementary school.[28] In kindergarten there is little indication of a competitive attitude.[29] Thus it is probably a learned function of schooling and other cultural factors. A look at other cultures shows a much different relation between competition and ego needs (to which the competitive incentive is presumably related). For instance Eriksen [30] has described the problems of teachers in reservation schools of the Sioux Indians. Unlike other American children, the Sioux child cannot easily be induced to strive for grades and marks. To do so might cause him to lose status with his peers. Competition, at least in the form in which we know it, is *not* a universal incentive.

A second major finding is that competition may be a rather effective incentive in fostering school achievement. Numerous studies [31] support the view that children, at least in our culture, will learn and perform when there is an optimal amount of friendly rivalry within the group. Pertinent here is the work of Maller,[32] who showed that students tended to work harder for themselves in a competitive situation than they would for a group (*i.e.,* under conditions of group competition). More recent investigations, however, have shown results just the contrary of those described by Maller. These studies [33] show that under some conditions, especially when

[28] Pearl J. Greenberg, "Competition in Children: An Experimental Study," *American Journal of Psychology,* Vol. 44, 1932, pp. 221–248.

[29] T. H. Wolf, *The Effect of Praise and Competition on the Persisting Behavior of Kindergarten Children,* University of Minnesota, Institute of Child Welfare, Monograph Series, No. 15, 1938.

[30] E. H. Erikson, *Childhood and Society,* New York, W. W. Norton and Company, Inc., 1950.

[31] A summary of various studies may be found in J. B. Maller, *Cooperation and Competition, An Experimental Study in Motivation,* Teachers College Contributions to Education, No. 384, New York, Teachers College, Columbia University, 1929.

[32] *Ibid.*

[33] Alexander Mintz, "Nonadaptive Group Behavior," *The Journal of Abnormal and Social Psychology,* Vol. 46, 1951, pp. 150–159.

there is a strong intragroup feeling, individual reward may produce much more inefficient behavior than cooperative effort. It should be clear that the effect of competition upon the performance either of individuals or of groups depends upon factors such as the nature of the task, the structure of the groups involved, and the previous experience and personalities of the individuals who comprise competing groups. Generalizations about the effects of competition can be made only when these various factors are taken into account. It is probable that when a group has little structure or common interests and goals, competition becomes an individual matter. On the other hand, the teacher should consider some of the excellent results and highly motivated conditions obtaining in cases when the work of groups has been directed toward meaningful and challenging materials.[34]

Any school incentive must be considered in terms of its total effect. Even though fair competition may be effective in some circumstances as an incentive in motivating academic achievement, there is still the question as to its effect upon other kinds of learning than subject matter performance. Other influences of intense competition are: (1) discouragement and despair for slow learners, (2) for the average pupil a tendency for either excessive emotional stress and worry, or the development of a "get by" attitude, (3) often a superlative, unwarranted opinion of and optimism regarding their abilities among fast learners, especially those who have a capacity to manage the types of more or less rote learning which characterizes so much of our traditional course of study, and (4) generally an attitude of aggressive non-cooperation marked by a striking indifference to the fate and welfare of other pupils and a strong fear or anxiety of losing status if one fails to maintain his expected position in the class grading scheme.[35] From experimental evidence, and the preceding discussion may be derived the following principles which may guide teachers in their understanding and use of competition in the classroom. Competition may be a desirable school incentive when:

1. All students have a reasonable expectation of reward for their effort.
2. Each student has had training in how to compete.

[34] American Association for Supervision and Curriculum Development, *op.cit.*
[35] Kimball Young, *Personality and Problems of Adjustment*, New York, F. S. Crofts and Company, 1940, p. 437.

3. There are sufficient and varied competitive activities to allow all to experience some area of success.
4. Groups which are somewhat evenly matched compete as groups.
5. Losing is considered not as failure but as a temporary setback.

Competition may result in undesirable conditions when:

1. It is so intense that it leads to emotional disturbance.
2. Success is limited to a small portion of the total group.
3. There is so much stress on winning that other goals of the activity such as group or team cooperation, and intrinsic value of the learning lose their importance.
4. Losing implies failure, and threatens loss of peer and adult approval.
5. It leads to excessive rivalry between the sexes.
6. It interferes with social adjustment.

Feelings of Achievement and Success. The desire for success is derived from ego and social needs. The child craves not only to feel a sense of achievement himself, but also he wants his accomplishments to be admired by others. Success is always perceived in relation to the individual's concept of himself, and in terms of the meaning of various incentives as they spell success or failure in the eyes of others. Thus a child who sees himself as a top ranking scholar may set as his goal the attainment of the highest grade in the class. Anything less than this level of achievement is not perceived as success.

Success is a kind of reward in which the student's achievement results in a finished product associated with feelings of pride and accomplishment. Commonly it includes both, and indeed as a basis of effective learning should include both. Pride of accomplishment without recognition is empty and there is nothing more discouraging than for the student to have something he views with pride unduly criticized or ridiculed or dismissed with no reaction by the teachers.

An advisee of the writer recently stopped in for a conference in which he reported he was considering dropping out of school. (He was a good student and had been doing above average work in all classes.) After some time, this student stated that the harder he worked, the worse he did. When asked to explain this, he reported that in one class he had spent a great deal of time writing a paper into which he had put a lot of his own ideas, and had worked hard in mulling over the problems to be included. He was therefore proud of his work, seeing it as an excellent product. When the paper was returned to him, the instructor had commented that the paper appeared hurriedly done, and as if not much thought had gone into its preparation. The student was so disturbed by this comment that he claimed he was unable to get anything out of the class, and he did not feel as if he could talk with the instructor because of the attitude he had taken.

This case illustrates that we develop expectations of what our performance will achieve, and that when there is considerable discrepancy between our expectations and achievements, there may be emotional disturbances which interfere with learning.

Social Approval. A special kind of reward for achievement is the approval given children by age-mates, teachers, parents and other adults. As an incentive it includes praise, complimentary remarks, acceptance by a group, admiring glances, cheers, publicity, and the like. It might be conceived in a broad sense as including those cases of reward for achievement in which favorable attention is gained.

The strength of social approval as an incentive will be in proportion to: (1) need for attention and social recognition, (2) perceived value of the individual or group which gives the approval (that is how closely the student identifies with these individuals), (3) previous satisfactions from similar situations, and (4) perceived genuineness of the social approval.

The force of this kind of incentive should be clearly recognized by teachers because the way in which they manipulate class structure, group organization, study materials, and work activities can be important determiners of the number and kinds of outlets of the need for social approval. The school-age youngster has an imperative demand for recognition from his age group. This need cannot be ignored. Some notion of its strength is illustrated by the following experiment.

Ten college freshmen who had just gone through "hell-week" were told that part of the consideration for admission to their respective fraternities would depend upon how well they did on a series of arithmetic problems, which were given in 24 five-minute periods. Later fifty-four other students, in regular classroom situations were given the same work. In spite of the fatiguing nature of their experiences during the preceding week, the ten freshmen did significantly more work than the other students. Presumably their incentives for social approval were of sufficient intensity to carry them through.[36]

[36] F. B. Knight and H. H. Remmers, "Fluctuations in Mental Production When Motivation is the Main Variable," *Journal of Applied Psychology*, Vol. 7, 1923, pp. 209–223.

Speaking of the recent cases of teen-age drug addiction, the Board of Education of New York City writes: "Teen-agers frequently adopt forms of behavior which identify them with their group or 'gang.' They often effect special haircuts, wear bizarre clothing or use a particular kind of slang. Some teen-age youngsters have even started the use of narcotic drugs in order to gain acceptance by a particular group." [37] One may see the strength of the desire for social approval in the following words of a teen-age boy who wrote an essay on the topic, "What I Know about Narcotics."

I am a boy going on fourteen. Many of you think that a boy my age and size have probably never had any experiences with narcotics, but if you lived in my neighborhood you would know. I am going to tell you a true fact that happened less than a week ago. My teacher told us of the dangers and the good uses of narcotics. So one night when I was in the candy store around my block, my friends and I were talking about dope. A boy said, "Let's get high, I got a few sticks." So everyone said yes except me. I didn't say anything. To tell you the truth I was really scared. So we all went into a hallway and started snorting. When they got to me I told them to come back to me later. Just then there was a fight in the apartment upstairs and the cops came. The cops came just in time, because I didn't want to take any. We all spread out. Lucky thing nobody was caught. Right now seven of those boys are dope addicts. I guess many of you are wondering why I went into the hallway in the first place. Well the reason is because even tho they were bad, *they were still my friends and I didn't want to lose friendship with them.* Since last week I stopped hanging around with them. Around my block you can buy heroin in a bubble gum wrapper.

It is probable that the craving for peer approval increases during early childhood and reaches a peak at some time during adolescence, when the desire for approval of members of the opposite sex joins already existing demands for age-group recognition. By the time children reach school they are, while still sensitive to adult approval, already in need of recognition from their age group. In early school years, however, the teacher may serve as the mediator of much of the recognition and social approval which a child obtains. The teacher's rejection of a child may become tantamount to group rejection. Later as the child's age group begins to assume paramount

[37] Board of Education of the City of New York, *Suggestions for Teaching the Nature and Effects of Narcotics,* June 1, 1951.

importance, and as the desire for independence grows, students more likely than not will ally themselves with a given offender, rather than with the teacher. In some cases, rejection by the teacher then becomes a signal of group acceptance. Especially is this true when the teacher comes to be perceived by the group as a force *against* them. When a teacher is viewed in this way there is little he can expect in the way of successful motivation or interest as any suggestions he makes becomes associated with the students' concept of him as an enemy. Since the many incentives involved in social approval are powerful in directing or channeling this important social need, teachers should be fully aware of ways in which teaching can use and abuse these incentives. Common errors committed by teachers include: (1) using sarcasm or ridicule, (2) banning school clubs, social groups or social functions, (3) insisting on nothing but individual work, and (4) giving mass punishment in order to discover a single offender, or because they cannot discover the individual offender.

Vocational Goals—Life Interests As Incentives. Often students are impelled to learn by the incentives of vocational aims which may be transitory (but none the less powerful as incentives) or persistent, and which may begin as early as the first few grades in school. In spite of the recognized importance of realistic and clear vocational objectives, there is considerable evidence that parents, schools and society in general, have in large measure failed in helping young people develop these desirable incentives.

Several studies [38] have shown that mature goals, and definite vocational choice are related to academic achievement. As earlier characterized, the motivational process is comprised of both energy and direction. The pupil who has clear goals—a definite direction for the release of energy is obviously more apt to succeed. One of the writers interviewed several dozen students whose achievement in college was far below that of which they were capable. Typical of the comments about vocational plans were the following:

"I don't know what to do in a vocation. I think maybe I'd like to be a psychologist." "My grades are always too low to get in what I

[38] A. B. Crawford, "Forecasting Freshman Achievement," *School and Society,* Vol. 31, 1930, pp. 125–132.

Henry Borow, "The Measurement of Academic Adjustment," *Journal of American Association of Collegiate Registrars,* Vol. 22, 1947, pp. 274–286.

want." The bewildered pupil, the one who is unable to make a decision and to follow a course of action is truly an educational casualty, as the following case taken from the records of a college instructor will show:

His behavior is adolescent. He gives one the impression of not being able to make up his mind. I found out that he is, as a consequence of failing out of college, afraid to go home and face his parents and grandparents. He has been going to classes even though he is not registered and he is not interested in getting a job. He says that he is afraid his failure in college will have "dire" consequences on the health of his grandparents. Their status in the community, he feels, is wrapped up in his going to college and making a success. He did not participate in class discussion and when queried about this, he said that just as he develops an idea, someone else would give it. Asked why this was so, he said "I guess I've been criticized so much by my parents, I'm afraid to say anything." [39]

Youth are often unrealistic in their statements of vocational aspirations. "Young people have been fed upon aspirations according to the American myth of vertical occupational mobility." [40] Thus they may set goals for themselves which are beyond attainment, and, when forced to accept some other work are dissatisfied and unhappy. That the school is relatively ineffective in bringing about more realistic goals is indicated by the fact that there is little change in vocational choice (in terms of less illusory goals) between the ninth and the twelfth grades. In one high school, 58 per cent of one hundred graduating seniors said that they had had no help in planning a vocational career after graduation.[41]

Pressures are sometimes directed toward young people's choice of goals. The ensuing conflict between their interests and adult pressures destroys initiative. A leader in the field of vocational interests writes:

Among college students there are cases of conflict between interest and seeming duty. Some fathers, for example, insist that their sons shall take a certain course or they will not finance the son's education. Loss of interest and poor grades bring some of these cases to the counselor. We do

[39] Letter to writer from Professor Harold Phelps, Ohio State University, 1949.

[40] H. D. Carter, "Vocational Interests and Job Orientation," *Applied Psychological Monographs*, Number 2, Stanford University Press, 1944.

[41] W. E. Moser, "Evaluation of a Guidance Program by Means of Student's Check List," *Journal of Educational Research*, Vol. 42, 1949, pp. 609–617.

not know how many others keep on regardless of personal wishes, nor what price they pay for forcing themselves to do so.[42]

Unquestionably students need help in developing clear cut vocational goals. These are the life interests which mark maturity. One of the best criteria for the success of schools and parents in educating youngsters should be found in the appraisal of students' goals. If these are vague, or practically non-existent, or if they are illusory, the adults have failed one of their most important tasks. The life style which emerges in late adolescence is in large part a function of the kinds of incentives, interests and needs which have been learned in school The teacher who effects real change in behavior must be fully aware of the processes in motivation and further must be a skillful technician in helping youngsters find worthwhile life goals.

SUMMARY

Motivation, contrary to the popular usage of the term, is not a bag of tricks which the teacher uses to produce learning. Rather it is a process which belongs to the pupil. It is similar to vision in that it involves external stimulation, appropriate mechanisms of response, and an internal force which energizes the response. The basic substratum of motivation may be found in the needs of the child. The first important characteristic of motives is that they have an energizing function. They stir up behavior. Besides releasing energy, motives have a character of directionality. Energy produced by needs seeks a discharge in relevant incentives, or goal objects which satisfy needs. In brief, motivation may be described as a process in which energies produced by needs are expended in the direction of goals.

An interesting question is why energies take one direction rather than another. Why does one boy do work after school to satisfy his needs for achievement, while another finds satisfaction in his alliance with a gang of lawbreakers? The answer outlined in this chapter was in terms of reinforcement, that is, responses which satisfy the needs on previous occasions are fixated. When responses do not satisfy needs, the responses are extinguished, or are never adopted.

[42] Edward K. Strong, Jr., *Vocational Interests of Men and Women*, Stanford University Press, 1943, p. 451.

Teachers thus need to find means to reinforce (reward) desirable behavior.

Motivation of school learning depends upon such factors as the learner's purpose or intent to learn, his self-concept and self-confidence, his levels of aspiration, and his knowledge and appraisal of how well he is doing in relation to his goals. It is the job of the teacher to create an atmosphere which provides desirable outlets for needs in the direction of worthwhile incentives—an atmosphere in which interests will as a consequence flourish. How can all this be brought about? This chapter has attempted to answer this question by showing that the teacher should:

1. Treat each child's needs and interests as a unique group of traits, which they are, and plan activities and incentives accordingly.
2. Set up clear-cut goals in which the pupil takes an active part, thereby helping to give the pupil a real intention to learn.
3. Help the child achieve a sense of success and confidence by
   a. providing a clear-cut knowledge of progress.
   b. praising deserving work.
   c. finding special areas of skill, and allowing him to develop these and to display them in the classroom.
4. Give exercises and materials in the context of "real life" so that students see that their work is beneficial and a real achievement.
5. Avoid making school unpleasant by requiring meaningless tasks, by punishment, by over repetition and busy work or too much drill.

The incentives toward which youngsters strive are sometimes quite different from those which the teacher would think desirable. Children work for new gadgets for their cars, for new clothing, trinkets, or other passing fancies. They see themselves as persons working toward some adventurous or romantic goal. Many times these goals are quite distant from school work. Attempts to capture their energy are sometimes fruitless, simply because the teacher does not understand or see the incentives for what they are. Ways which teachers do use to influence children in the direction of desirable incentives are praise, various kinds of reward, punishment and threats, and competition and rivalry. All these incentives may be rather artificial. For example, a gold star for a good test paper may have very little to do with the intrinsic value of the task being learned. On the other hand, these devices may be quite natural consequences of the learning, as when a girl learns to sew and actually makes a dress for which she receives praise and the desired remarks from her friends. In any case, teachers should not consider themselves as the sole mediators of all rewards and punishment in the classroom.

The ultimate goal of teaching should not center around how many facts have been learned but around the kinds of motives youngsters learn. Surely when students begin to like and want school activities for their own sake a milestone of maturity has been reached. Only when schoolwork offers activities which will satisfy the needs of all pupils will this goal be approached.

REFERENCES FOR FURTHER STUDY

Buhler, Charlotte, "Maturation and Motivation," *Personality*, Vol. 1, 1951.

Fuller, J. J., and Baker, J. N., "Competition vs. Cooperation in the Classroom," *Secondary Education*, Vol. 8, 1939, pp. 134–137.

Hilgard, E. R., and Russell, D. H., "Motivation in School Learning," Chapter 2 in Part I, 49th Yearbook, National Society for the Study of Education, *Learning and Instruction*, Chicago, University of Chicago Press, 1950.

Hurlock, E. B., "An Evaluation of Certain Incentives Used in School Work," *Journal of Educational Psychology*, Vol. 16, 1925, pp. 145–159.

Kinney, L. B., and Bell, Reginald, *Better Teaching through the Use of Current Materials*, Stanford University Press, 1947.

Maier, N. R. F., *Frustration: The Study of Behavior without a Goal*, New York, The McGraw-Hill Book Co., Inc., 1949.

Marzolf, S. S., "Motives and Objectives," *Education*, Vol. 65, 1944, pp. 26–29.

May, M. A., and Doob, L., *Competition and Cooperation*, Social Science Research Bulletin No. 25, 1937.

McGeoch, J. A., and Irion, A. L., *The Psychology of Human Learning*, New York, Longmans, Green and Co., 1952, Chapters 6 and 7.

Miller, N. E., "Acquirable Drives and Rewards," in Stevens, S. S. (Ed.), *Manual of Experimental Psychology*, New York, John Wiley and Sons, 1951.

Mowrer, O. H., "Preparatory Set (Expectancy)—A Determinant in Motivation and Learning," *Psychological Review*, Vol. 45, 1938, pp. 62–91.

Mursell, J. L., *Psychology for Modern Education*, New York, W. W. Norton and Co., Inc., 1952.

Ryans, D. G., "Motivation in Learning," in Part II, 41st Yearbook, National Society for the Study of Education, *The Psychology of Learning*, Bloomington, Ill., Public School Publishing Co., 1942, pp. 289–331.

Schmidt, H. O., "The Effects of Praise and Blame as Incentives to Learning," *Psychological Monographs*, Vol. 53, No. 240, 1941.

Sears, R. R., "Success and Failure," *Studies in Personality*, New York, McGraw-Hill Book Co., Inc., 1942.

Sherif, Muzafer, and Cantril, Hadley, *The Psychology of Ego Involvement*, New York, John Wiley and Sons, Inc., 1947.

Snygg, Donald, and Combs, Arthur W., *Individual Behavior*, Chap. IV, "What People Strive For," New York, Harper and Brothers, Publishers, 1949.

Stone, C. P., "Motivation: Drives and Incentives," in Moss, F. A., *Comparative Psychology*, New York, Prentice-Hall, Inc., 1934.

Thomson, M. K., *The Springs of Human Action; a Psychological Study of the Sources, Mechanisms, and Principles of Motivation in Human Behavior*, New York, D. Appleton Co., 1927.

Thorndike, E. L., *Selected Writings from a Connectionist's Psychology*, New York, Appleton-Century-Crofts, Inc., 1949, Chaps. 1 and 3.

Thorndike, E. L., *The Psychology of Wants, Interests, and Attitudes*, New York, D. Appleton-Century Co., 1935.

Tuttle, H. S., *Dynamic Psychology and Conduct*, New York, Harper and Brothers, Publishers, 1949, Chaps. IV, V, and VI.

Wright, Herbert F., "How the Psychology of Motivation is Related to Curriculum Development," *Journal of Educational Psychology*, Vol. 39, 1948, pp. 149–156.

Young, P. T., *Motivation of Behavior*, New York, John Wiley and Sons, Inc., 1936.

FILMS

Motivating the Class, The McGraw-Hill Book Co., Inc., New York. (19 mins.)

Importance of Goals, The McGraw-Hill Book Co., Inc., New York. (19 mins.)

Chapter 8

Interests and Attitudes

SOMETIMES THE behavior of children, their likes and aversions, the things which they want to do seem strange to adults. Teachers are frequently baffled and may be discouraged when a youngster greets a new venture in the schoolroom with defiance. Likewise the teacher may be frustrated by the enigma of the child who hates him for no apparent reason. Following is a typical case which illustrates how a child may show a readiness to oppose the teacher even before the class begins.

Miss Smith, the first-grade teacher was forewarned about Bill. He had been described as the "terror of the kindergarten." Not long after the first period had begun, Bill said, "I don't have to do this, and you can't make me. My mother can't make me do things and neither could Miss Foster," (the kindergarten teacher). Of all problems in teaching, working with children like Bill seems to cause teachers the greatest concern. In a study,[1] in which teachers were asked to describe those forms of behavior which gave them the most concern or which represented the most serious difficulties, it was found that teachers were most concerned about the existence of negative attitudes, attitudes of indifference, and lack of interest in school on the part of their pupils.

In the preceding chapter, motivation was discussed as a process whereby needs create energies which are directed toward goals. The forces which energize and direct behavior (needs, drives, purposes, goals, and punishment or pain) not only create ongoing behavior, but also help to mould more lasting facets of the child's

[1] E. L. Gaier and Stewart Jones, "Do Teachers Understand Classroom Behaviors?" *Understanding the Child,* Vol. 20, 1951, pp. 104–109.

personality. These forces are the bases of long-time interests and attitudes. This chapter will show how attitudes and interests originate,
how they develop, and the methods of controlling and modifying
these fundamental human characteristics. These are basic questions
in education. As one writer has commented:

> Education and society are in many cases concerned with making learn-
> ers want things, which, if left to themselves, they would not normally
> seek, such as interest in good government, intellectual integrity, economic
> welfare of others and the like. How does one, in effect, attach *plus* signs
> to such aims so that the personality will actively and positively orient itself
> in these directions.[2]

A WORKING CONCEPT OF ATTITUDES

Attitudes and interests are closely related concepts. The broader
term is attitude, which subsumes interest. Interests are attitudes
which cause a person to seek more activities in a given area; they
are positive attitudes about selected aspects of the environment.
Both are descriptions of a *readiness* or proclivity of an individual to
respond in a certain way toward something. For instance, a child,
through experience or through the imitation of admired adults, may
have learned to dislike school and academic subject matter. He has
thus acquired a readiness to resist actively school materials such as
books, and school activities. Children have such a readiness to respond to a large group of objects and abstractions. At early ages
youngsters have positive or negative feelings about tangible things
such as games, teachers, animals, and people. As they grow older
children begin to have definite feelings about such abstractions as
honesty, intelligence, and "my country." There are several aspects
of attitudes which have special implications for teaching.

Attitudes Are Learned.[3] Attitudes are acquired through experiences which have a pronounced affective (feeling) component.
More than most other forms of learning, they are transmitted

[2] George W. Hartmann, "Interests, Attitudes and Ideals," *Educational Psychology,* Charles E. Skinner (Ed.), New York, Prentice-Hall, Inc., 1951, pp.
436–437.

[3] For a more thorough discussion of attitudes and the way they are learned,
see L. W. Doob, "The Behavior of Attitudes," *Psychological Review,* Vol. 54,
1947, pp. 135–156, and Ross Stagner, "Attitudes," in W. S. Monroe (Ed.), *The
Encyclopedia of Educational Research,* New York, The Macmillan Company,
1950, pp. 77–84.

through the process of imitation, and many have origins early in life. The parent's revulsion, bodily posture and facial grimaces toward an object such as a kind of food, or an animal, may be transmitted directly to the child who may even ape the same overt symptoms of avoidance.

Attitudes Have Both Perceptual and Affective Components. Attitudes help determine not only *what* the child sees, but *how* he sees it. Suppose a pupil has acquired (through parents, other children, or other adults) certain negative attitudes about a particular teacher. He has thus acquired a readiness to respond with those modes of behavior which are characteristic of his particular way of expressing dislike and defense. He may notice the teacher's slightest gesture or suggestion, while other children are unaware of these details. Furthermore, he may see these behaviors of the teacher as evidences of domination, or unfairness. He ascribes motives to the teacher on the basis of his already existing biases. In some cases, children have had such unfortunate experiences that they may see every new person as a threat, and they are constantly ready to flee or strike back.

Attitudes May Be Enduring. Since they operate in perception, a person tends to see what he is looking for and hence will find reinforcement for already existing attitudes, even though there is evidence to the contrary. They are sometimes highly resistant to change. It is therefore important that desirable social attitudes, attitudes about school, teachers, work and the like be learned early in life.

Attitudes Affect Other Learnings. In several ways, the kinds of attitudes which a child has affects schoolwork and learning. If he has positive attitudes about teachers, and likes schoolwork, it is almost inevitable that he will experience some success and through reinforcement (a feeling of achievement) will work more effectively and achieve more nearly up to his capacity. Conversely, negative attitudes toward school and teachers usually signifies that his interests and energies are aimed elsewhere, and that he will fight attempts to make him learn.

The orienting function of attitudes, i.e., their influence upon perception, leads to the child's seeing tasks to be learned as pleasant and important, as unpleasant and useless, or as colorless and neutral. The feeling which goes along with such attitudes is an important factor in learning, for experiments have shown that pleasant material is retained longer than that which is unpleasant or neutral. The latter type of material is most poorly retained.[4] Another important factor is that attitudes about oneself are determiners of the kind of approach which a learner makes to a task. It should be recalled that in Chapter 6, it was shown that self-confidence played a major role in determining a learner's readiness for school work.

The way in which attitudes may interfere with learning becomes apparent when one considers the kinds of attitudes which result from school failure. It is safe to say that the majority of school failures seem to disorganize rather than to reorient the child.[5] It is in the nature of a person's ego structure not to accept failure as due to personal inadequacy. Instead the child is forced into the position of attributing lack of success to teachers or schools, and this serves to block future learnings. In repeated failures when such personal defenses break down, strong feelings of insecurity and inferiority may result.

THE PLACE OF INTEREST IN SCHOOLING

Only in more recent years have the child's interests been given a place in the planning of school activities, texts and curricula. Earlier ideas of education have been characterized by a leading authority on interests: "The old conception of education based on early philosophy viewed human desires as evil. The first step in educating the child was to break his will. The second step was to force him into the mold of the adult." [6] The present concern for children's interests is a healthy development, but even so, much that goes on in school does not conform with what is known about child development. The beginning teacher could take a lesson in motivation by observing some of the out-of-school activities of youngsters. Under these sometimes near ideal learning situations, which exist outside the classroom, the child's interests are directly related to ongoing

[4] H. D. Carter, H. E. Jones and N. W. Shock, "An Experimental Study of Affective Factors in Learning," *Journal of Educational Psychology*, Vol. 25, 1934, pp. 203–215.

[5] E. R. Hilgard and D. H. Russell, "Motivation in School Learning," in National Society for the Study of Education, 49th Yearbook, Part I, *Learning and Instruction*, Chicago, University of Chicago Press, 1950, pp. 36–68.

[6] E. K. Strong, *Vocational Interests of Men and Women*, Stanford University, Stanford University Press, 1943, p. 4.

play activities. He has spontaneous interests which carry him hour after hour. The boy who wants to drive a car, or shoot a gun will devote hours of attention watching adults and imitating them (sometimes in the fantasy of play), and he will learn and retain skills with almost any kind of teaching. Most classroom learning situations are quite different. The goals may be quite abstract or distant from ongoing behaviors and urges. Schools often try to get children to accept as motives and interests those things which, if left alone, they would not seek. They are trying to develop favorable attitudes toward teachers and subject matter, and to use interests as forces to bolster up subject matter learning. This is as it should be. However, motives and interests are far more than tools to be manipulated to the advantage of academic learning. These are objectives of teaching in their own right. The acquisition of socially accepted and worthwhile motives, attitudes and interests is a major goal of the educative process. Far more than any other factor they determine the kind of a person which the school turns out.

THE ORIGIN AND DEVELOPMENT OF INTERESTS AND ATTITUDES

Attitudes and interests are learned in much the same way that skills, habits, and other kinds of schoolwork are learned. The principles of learning discussed in previous chapters are equally applicable in determining the origin of these behavior determinants. However, the forces which lead to the development of attitudes are not always clearly discernible. Subtle factors such as needs of which the person is not aware, or hidden aggressions and wishes may become cornerstones in the building of attitudes. For example, it was found in one study that young people possessing the most anti-semitism were those who also had a high degree of emotional conflict and insecurity.[7] Commenting about this kind of highly prejudiced individual in the study cited above, Stagner has written, "to such a person, propaganda, educational material, or even casual remarks by teachers suggesting that a certain group is evil or dangerous, provide a welcome outlet for repressed aggression."[8]

The Function of Needs. A common error made in studying chil-

[7] Else Frenkel-Brunswik and R. N. Sanford, "Some Personality Factors in Anti-Semitism," *Journal of Psychology*, Vol. 20, 1945, pp. 271–291.

[8] Ross Stagner, *op.cit.*, p. 80.

dren's behavior is to assume that interests and attitudes are direct indications of needs. The child needs approval, a feeling of importance, security and independence, and he is likely to develop an interest in *any* activity which brings him a satisfaction of such needs. It might just as well be music or basketball or hopping freight trains or sneaking a smoke of marijuana. All these activities might serve basic needs in some particular societies of young people.

It is deplorable that schools do not allow all children an opportunity to satisfy their ego and social needs through approved school activities. But when rewards are limited to a few students and depend upon a narrow range of innate abilities there is little chance that all youngsters will experience the achievement necessary to satisfy basic needs. A major function of the school is to find activities which satisfy needs. These activities will then become areas of interest and should lead to positive attitudes about schooling.

Wishes and Ideals. Valuable clues to what children want and of the factors which influence their modes of behavior and their attitudes can result from a study of their wishes and ideals, their heroes, and their ideas of what is glamorous. The studies which have been made reveal one fact of immediate importance, namely, that what appeals to children most is quite different from the activities which go on in the classroom. Young children's wishes are predominantly for material things such as pets, bicycles and athletic equipment. They also have deep concern for family matters such as wanting a new brother or a wish that father would come home. Only a small number wish for materials or activities directly connected with school work.

In contrast with younger children, high-school students' wishes are more often in terms of personal improvement, ambition, security and professional aspirations. Seventy per cent of a large group who were surveyed, wished for self improvement in some form.[9]

Most likely, attitudes and interests are pretty accurately mirrored in the kinds of people with whom children identify. As would be expected, in the early school grades, children's admiration is for people who are close to them. When a group of 344 grade-school youngsters

[9] A. T. Jersild and R. J. Tasch, *Children's Interests and What They Suggest for Education,* New York, Bureau of Publications, Teachers College, Columbia University, 1949, p. 14.

were asked to name the person they would most like to be, the younger ones answered with names of parents, friends, teachers and other close associates. Older children more often chose characters from books, historical figures, and stars from radio and television. The trend with age of children's identifications away from their immediate environment to the remote environment (radio, books, etc.) is shown below.[10]

	Grade 2	Grade 4	Grade 6
Immediate Environment	72%	47%	42%
Remote Environment	25%	52%	57%

In the study just cited boys and girls differed in the kinds of "heroes" which they chose. This is shown, for example, by the fact that no boys out of the primary group (Grade 2) named the teacher as the person they would like to be, while 27.3 per cent of the girls chose a teacher as the person they most wanted to be like. The individuals chosen reveal the type of person these youngsters admire.[11] High on the list were Gene Autry, Roy Rogers, Margaret O'Brien, and Shirley Temple. Also named were the Lone Ranger, Superman, Dick Tracy, J. Edgar Hoover, and Joe DiMaggio. When these children were asked the reasons for their choice, the most frequent answer was "goodness." For boys, the most important reason was that the character chosen represented adventure. The above choices jibe well with what is known about the reason for children's choices of occupations. Interests revealed in studies of occupational choice show that they are often dominated by the desire for escape, for freedom from humdrum work and for adventure.[12] Children's wishes and ideals seem to stem mainly from three needs, the need for psychological security, the need for status and importance, and the need for approval. These needs find partial satisfaction through the emulation of those adults whom the child perceives as being highly successful in ways in which he would like to achieve.

Cultural Influences and Interests. A notion of the origin of interests may be gained from a comparison of the interests of American

[10] M. L. Stoughton and A. M. Ray, "A Study of Children's Heroes and Ideals," *Journal of Experimental Education*, Vol. 15, 1946, p. 157.

[11] *Ibid.*, p. 159.

[12] P. M. Freeston, "Vocational Interests of Elementary School Children," *Occupational Psychology*, London, Vol. 13, 1939, pp. 223–237.

children with those of children from a quite different culture. Table 15 shows some of the findings when interests of American children were compared with those of Egyptian youngsters.

TABLE 15

A Comparison of Interests of American and Egyptian Children *

CHARACTERISTICS OF INTERESTS COMMON TO BOTH AMERICAN AND EGYPTIAN CHILDREN	MAIN DIFFERENCES IN INTERESTS BETWEEN AMERICAN AND EGYPTIAN CHILDREN
1. Interests in material things declines with age.	1. American children showed more interest in material things.
2. Expressed interest in academic work declines with age.	2. More American children expressed interest in improvement of living quarters.
3. Interests in self improvement increases with age.	3. A large percentage of American children expressed interest in people outside the family circle.
4. There is an increase in interest in out-of-school intellectual activities with age.	4. Arts, crafts and hobbies were reported more frequently by American than Egyptian children.
5. There is more interest in own language and arithmetic than in science or social studies.	5. A much higher proportion of Egyptian than American children expressed wishes pertaining to religious qualities and social graces.
6. There is a greater interest in people with increasing age.	6. Less than 1 per cent of American children reported homework as a favorite out-of-school activity, while 40.1 per cent of Egyptian children mentioned it.
7. Sex differences were common to both cultures. Girls expressed less interests in material things.	7. The American child hardly ever expressed interests pertaining to health, while 12.5 per cent of the Egyptian children did so.
8. There was an egocentric character to interests.	8. More Egyptian than American children expressed patriotic wishes.
9. There was a disinterest in school courses which did not bear obvious relation to a goal.	

* Adapted from El-Demerdash Abdel-Meguid Sarhan, *Interests and Culture,* New York, Bureau of Publications, Teachers College, Columbia University, Contribution to Education, No. 959, 1950.

A study of the experimental literature on children's interests reveals the following trends and conclusions:

1. Interests are in great part a product of the development of the drive for activity and the desire to make use of newly matured mental and physiological functions.
2. Children's wishes, aversions and desires are often the result of cultural pressures—there is a desire to conform to the culture because youngsters thus gain approval and reward from adults.
3. The egocentric character of interests, as well as the correlation between specific abilities and interests suggests that many interests spring from the child's attempts to perform in areas where his chances of success are greatest.
4. Environmental demands lead to the creation of interests. In the study just cited it was noted that there is a great pressure upon Egyptian children to do well on examinations and a system of very limited rewards for school achievement. Consequently there was a much greater interest in homework on the part of the Egyptian children (also a great deal more anxiety about schoolwork).

An over-all principle is that the child's interests will generally center in those activities which have in his experience most satisfactorily reduced his needs and tensions.

Opportunities and Experience. The kinds of opportunities and experiences which a child has are obvious and ubiquitous factors in shaping his attitudes and interests. Even so, it is not uncommon for parents, social workers and teachers to wonder why a child from a "fine" family has the interests and negative attitudes of a delinquent, when even the most casual investigation would reveal that his youth group (gang) has like interests and attitudes. Likewise, it is not rare to find teachers baffled by a child's lack of interest in reading, when the obvious fact is that in the child's home there has been virtually no opportunity for such an interest to develop.

Table 16 shows the difference in the interests of two groups of boys. Sixty-three delinquents and sixty-three non-delinquents were compared with respect to the kinds of activities in which they were interested. It is clear that delinquency is closely related to an interest in such activities as "hopping freights," smoking, and "swiping milk bottles," and negatively correlated with such activities as seeing historical movies and collecting stamps.

Harris who collected the data shown in Table 16 believes that environmental limitations play a major part in the development of delinquent play interests. In speaking of the delinquent he notes:

Such a person inevitably uses the materials and methods available to him in his efforts to have a good time. He lives near the railroad tracks and makes them his playgrounds. Locomotives and cars on sidings are intrinsically interesting anyway. He indulges in throwing contests and, lacking the inhibition developed in children reared in homes where more supervision is given their activities, windows and telegraph insulators

TABLE 16

Relationship Between Delinquency and Play Interests *

QUESTIONNAIRE ITEM	TETRACHORIC CORRELATION †
Hopping freights	.92
Playing hookey from school	.90
Smoking	.88
Running away from home	.84
Swiping milk bottles	.81
Hitching of rides on wagons, autos or street cars	.72
Seeing historical movies	−.36
Studying schoolwork (at home)	−.39
Making collection of stamps	−.39
Making things with hammer, saw, nails, etc. for fun	−.40
Belonging to school clubs (nature, literary, drawing, farm citizenships, etc.)	−.40
Imagining you are an explorer or adventurer	−.46

* From D. B. Harris, "Relationships Among Play Interests and Delinquency in Boys," *American Journal of Orthopsychiatry*, Vol. 13, 1943, p. 633.

† A measure of the extent of relationship between two dichotomous variables— viz. delinquency, non-delinquency vs. "yes" or "no" on the questionnaire used to discover play interests.

become his targets. Dodging the policeman constitutes at once an activity indulged in by his fellows and an act of daring and adventure.[13]

Jersild and Tasch[14] note that there are many "wasted potentials" among children because opportunities have not been provided for their development. These deficiencies in opportunity "leave lasting gaps" in the personality of the adult.

The kinds of experiences which lead to specific interests are often

[13] D. B. Harris, "Relationships Among Play Interests and Delinquency in Boys," *American Journal of Orthopsychiatry*, Vol. 13, 1943, p. 634.

[14] Jersild and Tasch, *op.cit.*, p. 64.

revealed in studies of the reason for students' vocational choices. Table 17 shows the stated reasons for the choice of a medical career by 191 students selected from forty medical schools. They were asked to name the factor which played the dominant role in their choice.

TABLE 17

Factors Listed by Youth as Reason for the Choice of Medicine as a Career *

STATED REASON FOR CHOICE	NUMBER OF STUDENTS
Finances finally available	30
Association with persons other than father in medicine	26
Own ability in science	22
Father practicing medicine	19
Work experiences related to medicine	19
Parental pressure	17
"Early interest"	16
Need of making a decision	10
Influence of a science instructor	8
Influence of other instructors	7
Reading medical literature	7
Other factors	5
No Idea	5
TOTAL	191

* R. E. Scantlebury, "Factors Which Influence Youth to Study Medicine," *Journal of Educational Research*, Vol. 42, 1948, p. 172

Two things immediately stand out in this table. The first is that the most influential factor was association with some person practicing medicine (items two and four). The second is the fact that teachers apparently had relatively little influence in shaping this occupational interest.

ATTITUDES, INTERESTS, AND TEACHING

Appraisal of Present School Practices. Schools vary greatly in the extent to which they take into account the attitudes and interests of their pupils. Certainly attitudes and interests are just as much a part of individual differences as abilities and achievements and as such deserve equal attention in the methods of dealing with individual differences. But in many instances, these important aspects of learning are at best relegated to a position of secondary importance. Some of the questions which should be answered in appraising the practices in a given classroom are:

1. How are subjects taught so as to correspond with what is known about children's interests? (This implies that some appraisal of interests be made.)
2. How are interests used to facilitate learning of subject matter?
3. To what extent does the school provide information and guidance to meet important interests such as vocational goals, and sex-social matters?
4. Does the school consider as a regular function the teaching of and testing for interests and attitudes?
5. Are children's interests considered in making assignments, choosing reading materials, constructing tests, and planning the curriculum?

That such questions are not given due attention is indicated by the findings of Jersild and Tasch, whose survey of over 2000 children's interests led them to the following conclusion:

As the average child moves up through the grades, he seems to become less eager about things that distinctly belong to school and scholarliness, more inclined to complain, more interested in the things that go along with school rather than with work in the classroom. He becomes relatively more interested in recess periods than in class periods. He mentions play and sports more often. There is a greater hiatus between his wishes and what the school offers.[15]

Teachers who participated in this major study of children's interests were asked reasons for this "drifting away" of students with increasing age. The most prominent reason given by these teachers was that they believed students too often have a feeling of lack of achievement. High school students liked best those things which led to a sense of personal worth through accomplishment. There is little question that the school has less influence upon a child's primary attitudes and interests than many other aspects of his life. The blame for this lack of influence must be shouldered, in part at least, by the school because of its failure to meet youths' interests halfway. It is well known that youngsters in high school have an active interest in vocations, yet one survey of high school graduating sen-

[15] A. T. Jersild and R. J. Tasch, *op.cit.*, p. 41.

iors showed that 58 per cent had received no help in planning a vocational career after graduation and a like number had received no assistance in planning to meet college requirements.[16]

A survey of children's interests in various school subjects and activities shows that several important areas lack appeal. Following are the main results: (1) By far the greatest interests were expressed toward so-called extracurricular activities such as athletics, (2) The subject matters scoring highest were reading and other forms of English usage, and number work, (3) Social studies were recipients of a large number of unfavorable comments, yet it was this area in which children desired more information, (4) There was a great preoccupation with people at all ages (even though the questionnaire used in the survey was not worded to encourage such responses).[17]

A given survey of interests, unfortunately, may not have widespread applicability to children in general, since an appraisal of interests in one community or area, or at any particular time may indicate only a temporary or local condition. Lists of favorite books, games, hobbies can have but temporary usefulness, as fads and interests change from one child generation to another. A few short years ago, science fiction was an esoteric reading interest. Today youngsters find in comic books and on the radio and television, such things as space patrols, interplanetary travel, and ray guns. It is highly doubtful, however, that schools are sufficiently alert to such interests or modify activities regularly to take account of the ever-changing interests of youngsters.

Forces Which Change Attitudes and Interests.[18] As earlier noted, attitudes once formed may be highly resistant to change. The reader may recall that attitudes are wrapped up with a person's feelings, needs and self concept. To let them go requires a change in self. Furthermore, attitudes are easy to maintain because a person sees what he wants to see, and may distort reality so as to find evidence to support any position he wants to hold.

[16] W. E. Moser, "Evaluation of a Guidance Program by Means of Student's Check List," *Journal of Educational Research*, Vol. 42, 1949, pp. 609–617.

[17] A. T. Jersild and R. J. Tasch, *op.cit.*, p. 25–40.

[18] For an excellent discussion of the ways in which schools can effect a change in intercultural attitudes, the reader is referred to W. Van Til and G. W. Denemark, "Intercultural Education," Chapter II in *Review of Educational Research*, Vol. 20, 1950, pp. 274–286 (99 item bibliography).

Attempts to modify attitudes will fail unless factors such as the aforementioned are taken into account. Schools often fail in changing attitudes, because their whole program is based on telling and reading. But telling is not teaching. Verbalism alone is not enough. Mere information may do little to change attitudes especially if they are strongly rooted social attitudes.[19] Likewise there may be little relation between attitudes and intelligence. A well endowed and well informed student will not necessarily have desirable social attitudes.

An effective program for modifying attitudes should incorporate one, or several of the following principles in the learning situation.

1. Since attitudes are closely linked with the self concept and with the child's personal identifications, attitudes are more easily changed through group processes (e.g., group discussion and group work of other kinds). The child may readily accept values of his peer group while rejecting those of the teacher.
2. First hand experience is more effective than reading or telling. Delinquent gangs in large cities have changed their attitudes of hate and distrust of the police when these agents of law enforcement have taken part as referees and instructors in athletic programs at youth centers.
3. An appeal to feelings is necessary for change. The affective part of attitudes makes them tenacious, and it is only by eliciting different feelings that change can be accomplished. Dramatic movies which presumably elicit such feelings may have a lasting and deep affect upon attitudes. High school pupils, shown a movie giving a favorable impression of the Chinese, exhibited a marked shift in attitudes toward these people, and the attitudes (at the last measurement a year and a half later) still remained much more favorable than they had been before the movie had been seen! [20] Likewise soldiers in World War II who saw orientation films dealing with the background of the war, and with our allies, had a more clear notion of why we were fighting, and were better disposed toward allies than soldiers who had not seen these films.[21]
4. As teachers become expert in anticipating the forces which produce

[19] W. S. Watson and G. W. Hartmann, "Rigidity of a Basic Attitudinal Frame," *Journal of Abnormal and Social Psychology*, Vol. 34, 1939, pp. 314–336.

[20] R. C. Peterson, *et al.*, *Motion Pictures and the Social Attitudes of Children and Conduct and Attitudes of Movie Fans*, New York, The Macmillan Company, 1933.

[21] J. R. Miles and C. R. Spain, *Audio Visual Aids in the Armed Services*, Washington, D. C., American Council on Education, 1947.

attitudes they may use preventive measures which alert students to propaganda by developing their critical abilities. An experiment with high school students in a unit in child study shows how this may be effective. One group of students were taught the results of studies of various kinds of discipline—a comparable group received no such training. Both groups were then subjected to a radio program favoring the "get tough" method for raising children. The untrained students readily succumbed to the propaganda, while students who had learned experimental evidence about discipline resisted the effects of propaganda.[22]

5. Children are more apt to accept attitudes which are the result of what they believe to be their own thinking—their own original ideas. Skillful leading of group discussion or planning for information seeking in the community offers opportunities for youngsters to make discoveries, which they will rapidly adopt.

6. Community centered schools may make the development and change of attitudes and interests a project shared jointly by teachers and parents. When the school has to buck values learned in the home or through other sources, the student is placed in a position of psychological conflict and he is more apt to retain community fostered notions than those which are obtained in the classroom. The school which is to have a real effect in a community must concern itself not only with attitudes of the child but also of the adult.

Suggested Techniques for Using Interests to Facilitate Learning. Many times teachers are faced with the problem of guiding learning of material which may at first glance not seem to be heavily weighted with intrinsic values for the learner. The teacher must find ways of capturing the energy of his charges and directing it toward desirable school goals. The first-grade teacher who is asked to teach reading may have little choice in the matter. In this situation, there are certain psychological principles in the arousal of interests and the development of favorable attitudes which have been used and found successful by teachers and by experimentation. Suggestions for teaching using such psychological principles are given in the following paragraphs.

The student's perception of the material to be learned may be changed by placing it into a new or different context—one that is

[22] R. H. Ojemann, "Research in Planned Learning Programs and the Science of Behavior," *Journal of Educational Research*, Vol. 42, 1948, pp. 96–104.

pleasant. An example of this principle is found in the reading aids devised by Dolch.[23] One of these is a word bingo game in which the child can play only by recognizing words necessary to complete rows and columns. Another is a "Vowel Lotto Game," which requires the child to know vowels and simple phrases in order to play.

Material to be learned may be placed as a barrier in the path toward a desirable goal. The child may not be interested in reading *per se* but definitely interested in the stories and activities which the skill of reading will allow him to enjoy. Frequently the child is made to understand that he will gain approval of the teacher only when he has mastered a given skill such as spelling or arithmetic, which are made to become symbols of approval. Perhaps in terms of frequency this technique is most widely used. However, the use of it is based on several assumptions which may not be warranted. First, the teacher in this case is largely the mediator of needs. Second, there is an assumption that the learning activity will, by association with desirable goals, take on some of the affective elements of those goals. Actually this procedure may have the reverse effect. The third assumption is that the material in its own right is not interesting enough to be self-sustaining. Experienced teachers know that it is virtually impossible completely to control rewards either in a teacher dominated class or in a permissive one. With regard to peer approval, for example, pupils may find that various attention getting devices such as boisterous behavior, note passing and the like, give sufficient satisfaction of this need without recourse to the means established by the teacher. The assumption that material is not in its own right sufficiently interesting may in some cases be warranted. It is doubtful for instance that arithmetic as sometimes taught, has sufficient relevance to the needs and interests of children. But in this case one should question whether it would not be better to change the whole teaching pattern rather than just the method of arousing interest.

Related material of a high interest value may be inserted into the lesson which is being studied. This technique is based upon the assumption that attention and activity will be maintained at a higher level when the learning material is interspersed with vivid and colorful illustration, demonstrations, anecdotes, personal allusions, and

[23] E. W. Dolch, *The Dolch Reading Materials,* Garrard Press, Champaign, Illinois. One such device is illustrated in Figure 13, Chapter 12.

the pupils' own experiences. The following incident, related to one of the writers by a student, is illustrative of the way such devices may be used to stimulate interest.

After the class was seated, the teacher made his appearance staggering under the weight of what appeared to be a large boulder. When he reached the front center of class he suddenly threw the large object down into the middle of the class. The brief period of pandemonium which ensued subsided quickly when the students saw the "boulder" float harmlessly through the air. It was a large piece of insulating material and the discussion which followed was lively and profitable.

Describing this incident the student remarked that it was this sort of thing which endeared that science teacher to his students. As he put it, "you never knew what was going to happen next. I liked this course better than any I had ever taken." The same student had subsequently taken a science major in college and largely attributed his choice to this particular high school teacher.[24]

Make the classroom atmosphere a permissive and pleasant one. Interests abound, and attention rarely flags when youngsters are given a proprietary feeling about the doings of a class. Even when the values of what is to be learned are not immediately apparent, children may participate eagerly, because the friendly atmosphere and cooperative work helps satisfy their social needs and their need for feeling important and worthwhile. The following description of a high school class should illustrate how a pleasant yet purposeful classroom atmosphere can stimulate interests.

In Mr. Eames' high school biology class students were permitted to help with such things as the preparation of specimens, drawings for class use and the planning of class work. Individual projects were encouraged. One group of students arranged with local dentists for a dental survey of the entire class. Another group took white rats, some fed good diets and others which were malnourished, to nearby grade schools and made talks to the

[24] It might be well here to reemphasize a point stressed earlier, viz., that there is no substitute for the cardinal principle that students' interests center around activities in which they have found need satisfactions. Stimulating episodes created by a teacher may be helpful, but these episodes alone cannot support for long materials and methods which fail to allow each pupil to feel important and to view the learning as worthwhile. It is quite possible in the case just described that for the one student who went on to a career in science, there were dozens of others who had no real interest in science but only in the "antics" of the teacher.

pupils about the effects of various kinds of foods. Classwork included a variety of activities many of which were suggested by students. There were debates, biology spelldowns, diet surveys, and numerous demonstrations made by both the teacher and students. Also there were field trips to local bakeries, dairies, nurseries and the like. The classroom was a center of numerous activities. In a given period one might have found one group of students working with microscopes, another planting seeds in flats, and still another sitting around one of the laboratory tables talking. Mr. Eames traveled from group to group, giving encouragement, making suggestions, and asking help with something he or another student was doing. The total effect of all this was to create an experience which students would never forget. Many believed this the best course they had ever had in high school. Needless to say interest in the work was keen, and there were rarely disciplinary problems.

SUMMARY

Attitudes and interests are learned dispositions or sets to action. They are highly pervasive and influence personality, and personal relationships, as well as having a profound influence upon school learning.

As do motives, interests and attitudes grow out of children's needs. They find voice through children's wishes and ideals. The influence of needs upon attitudes may be seen, for example, in the way children identify with persons such as movie stars or other romantic or adventuresome characters. Their identification reflects a desire for escape from the humdrum activities of school. Apparently much schoolwork fails to capture the interest of pupils, and unfortunately the older they become, the less interest youngsters seem to have in what is going on in school.

The major implication for teachers is that interests and attitudes are goals of teaching in their own right, and this means that teachers must know how attitudes are formed and can be changed, and how interests may be used to facilitate learning. The teacher who would change pupils' attitudes should: (1) give group work and group discussion, and provide for improved human relations in classes, (2) provide first-hand experiences with issues about which attitudes are formed, (3) involve the emotional life of the child through dramatics, stories or episodes, and (4) make the school a real part of the community.

In a number of ways, interests may be used to facilitate learning.

By applying the principles discussed under motivation in the previous chapter, the educator ought to be able to transform schooling from drudgery to an exciting adventure. The results of experimentation and of experience of teachers support the greater use of the following techniques. First, material to be learned should be placed in an interesting and sometimes novel context. Sometimes a game will elicit increased interest. Secondly, material to be learned may become more attractive when pupils see it as a necessary step toward a goal. Finally, the learning situation should be one in which there is ample opportunity for active participation of all pupils, and an atmosphere which is friendly and permissive.

REFERENCES FOR FURTHER STUDY

Anderson, J. E., "Relation of Attitude to Adjustment," *Education,* Vol. 73, December, 1952, pp. 210–218.

Cox, W. M., "Slow Learners Have Normal Interest Spans," *Clearing House,* Vol. 26, April, 1952, pp. 472–473.

Cresci, G., "We Did Something about Attitudes," *Balance Sheet,* Vol. 34, December, 1952, p. 157.

Ellis, A., and Gerberich, J. R., "Interests and Attitudes," *Review of Educational Research,* Vol. 17, 1947, pp. 64–77.

Hawkes, G. R., "A Study of the Personal Values of Elementary School Children," *Educational and Psychological Measurement,* Vol. 12, 1952, pp. 654–663.

Haugh, O. M., "Relative Effectiveness of Reading and Listening to Radio Drama as Ways of Imparting Information and Shifting Attitudes," *Journal of Educational Research,* Vol. 45, March, 1952, pp. 489–498.

Hovland, C. I., "Changes in Attitude through Communication," *Journal of Abnormal and Social Psychology,* Vol. 46, July, 1951, pp. 424–437.

Kilpatrick, W. H., and Van Til, William (Eds.), *Intercultural Attitudes in the Making,* New York, Harper & Brothers, 1947.

Kingsley, H. L., "The Development of Attitudes and Ideals," Chap. XVII in *Nature and Conditions of Learning,* New York, Prentice-Hall, 1946, pp. 425–451.

Mead, A. R., "What Schools Can Do to Improve Social Attitudes," *Educational Leadership,* Vol. 9, December, 1951, pp. 183–187.

Nelson, E., "Attitudes," *Journal of General Psychology,* Vol. 21, 1939, pp. 367–436.

Rokeach, M., "Method for Studying Individual Differences in Narrow Mindedness," *Journal of Personality,* Vol. 20, December, 1951, pp. 219–233.

Strong, E. K., Jr., *Vocational Interests of Men and Women,* Stanford University Press, 1943.

Thorndike, E. L., *The Psychology of Wants, Interests, and Attitudes*, New York, D. Appleton-Century Co., 1935.

Van Til, William, and Denemark, George W., "Intercultural Educational," Chap. II in *Review of Educational Research*, Vol. 20, No. 4, October, 1950, pp. 274–286.

FILMS

Attitudes and Health, Coronet Instructional Films, Coronet Bldg., Chicago 1, Illinois.

How to Develop Interest, Coronet Instructional Films, Coronet Bldg., Chicago 1, Illinois. (11 mins.)

Chapter 9

Organization of Learning and Teaching

IN SOME classrooms children run aimlessly about jumping from one thing to another every few minutes. Lacking guidance, they follow momentary whims and fleeting interests. At the other extreme children are glued to their seats, enthralled by the fear of teacher or of rules. At these extremes may be supporting educational philosophies, but both are blind to important principles of learning. Somewhere between these extremes is an organization of activities mutually shared by pupil and teacher, which will produce optimum learning.

Learning is more efficient and more permanent when there is an organization of materials, methods, and processes. So strong is the tendency to learn in an organized way that even when material is presented in a disorganized or relatively meaningless fashion, pupils tend to develop an organization of their own.[1] But when the child is buried under a vast array of apparently unrelated facts, the tendency to organize into meaningful relationships may be partially thwarted by the necessity of repeating those facts on examinations. In such cases, the facts thus learned are not long retained, nor do they seem to have much effect in changing behavior.[2] There is a large body of convincing evidence which shows how poorly students

[1] William Brownell and Gordon Hendrickson, "How Children Learn Information Concepts and Generalizations," Chapter IV, 49th Yearbook, National Society for the Study of Education, Part I, *Learning and Instruction,* Chicago, University of Chicago Press, 1950, pp. 92–128.

[2] G. M. Blair, "How Learning Theory Is Related to Curriculum Organization," *Journal of Educational Psychology,* Vol. 39, 1948, pp. 161–166.

retain information which is not related to significant problems and which has a low degree of perceived internal relationship. In contrast, results obtained with well-organized and meaningful materials may show actual gain rather than decrease with a passage of time.[3] Meaningful learning may suffer only slightly with a passage of time. Ability to apply principles, solve problems, and interpret experimental data are examples of the kinds of activities which are very resistant to the ravages of the forgetting process.[4]

The principles of organization in learning have many implications for pupils, teachers, and school administrators. Answers to questions about assignment making, problem solving, reviewing, and many others essential to good teaching hinge upon the teacher's understanding of the principles of organized learning. Teachers' activities should be arranged to fit into a coherent pattern with the activities of pupils. They must know when and how to give guidance, correct errors, introduce new materials, and take part in discussion. No single skill or technique will suffice for the many and often unique educational situations in which a teacher finds himself. Rather he must be able to apply principles and generalizations which have wide usefulness in analyzing each new learning situation as it emerges.

BASIC PRINCIPLES OF ORGANIZATION IN LEARNING

One of the writers once visited a biology class in which one of the major activities of students was looking at slides which the instructor projected upon a screen in front of the class. There were about 250 slides representing various plants and animals and their parts, which students were expected to memorize. These slides were grouped into a logical arrangement following standard classification procedures. Later, on a final examination, newly prepared slides identical with the old ones were substituted and several students who had previously done well, did very poorly. An investigation of these individuals revealed that they had learned to associate specimens with peculiarities of the old slides such as cracks and other imperfections. When new slides were used, students had lost their cues and were unable to name the specimens. To these students, the learning of these names had been a meaningless task to which they

[3] Ralph Tyler, "Some Findings from Studies in the Field of College Biology," *Science Education*, Vol. 18, 1934, pp. 133–142.

[4] A. H. Word and R. A. Davis, "Individual Differences in Retention of General Science Subject Matter in the Case of Three Measurable Teaching Objectives," *Journal of Experimental Education*, Vol. 7, 1938, pp. 24–30.

responded with a system which seemed the easiest and best to them. In spite of an organization of materials which seemed very logical and coherent to the teacher, the students learned with an organization of their own. The moral of this story, and a basic principle of learning, is that the teacher's organization is not necessarily taken over by the student. The teacher cannot successfully impose an organization upon students. Instead, the teacher should view his task as that of teaching so that students learn to organize facts and principles into meaningful units of ever-increasing scope.

How can such organizational errors be avoided? In the writers' opinion there are principles of learning which, if applied, will make incidents such as the above much less likely. The teacher must become skilled in providing for meaningfulness in study materials, working with students on tasks of optimal size and scope, and knowing the best distribution of learning activities.

Providing for Meaningfulness. Understanding, ready learning, and retention are products of that teaching which makes material meaningful to the student. Teachers often take for granted that material "makes sense," especially when youngsters give lip service to the material which is taught. That such assumptions by teachers are not always justified has been often and dramatically illustrated. For example,

FIGURE 11. A Child's Conception of Stonewall Jackson Riding Ahead.

(From Howard Kingsley, *The Nature and Conditions of Learning*, copyright, 1946, by Prentice-Hall, Inc., New York, p. 338. Reprinted by permission of the publisher.)

the drawing in Figure 11 was made by a young child after hearing the poem "Barbara Frietchie." She explained to the teacher that it was, "Stonewall Jackson riding a head."

Further illustrations are easy to obtain from the work of pupils in almost any school. The reader may recall, in a previous chapter, that the fourteen-year-old who was asked to give the factors affecting the rates of auto insurance replied, "gas, oil and kerosene." Clearly the work on auto insurance which had preceded this test, as well as the question, as worded, were relatively meaningless to this student. When teaching is characterized by rote learning, meaningless memorizing, and an excessive emphasis upon verbalism, children will almost inevitably make errors such as the following:

"The circulatory system is composed of veins, arteries, and artilleries."

"Socrates died from an overdose of wedlock." [5]

The following well-known anecdote told by William James further exemplifies what happens when meaningfulness is supplanted by meaningless verbalization:

A friend of mine, visiting a school, was asked to examine a young class in geography. Glancing at the book she said: "Suppose you should dig a hole in the ground, hundreds of feet deep, how should you find it at the bottom—warmer or colder than on top?" None of the class replying, the teacher said, "I am sure they know, but I think you don't ask the question quite rightly. Let me try." So taking the book she asked: "In what condition is the interior of the globe?" and received the immediate answer from half the class at once: "The interior of the globe is in a condition of igneous fusion." [6]

The teacher must know how to avoid such nonsensical interpretations and meaningless memorization. He will succeed in proportion as he is able to help youngsters gear material to their vocabulary levels; relate material to their backgrounds; provide activities in context, as they will be used; show relationships among various subjects and concepts; and provide a wide variety of experiences commensurate with the individual differences which he finds in the class.

Meaningful vocabulary. Materials must be commensurate with a pupil's verbal ability. In the past, too little attention was paid to the vocabulary level of school texts. Often grade school texts were too difficult vocabulary-wise for as much as two-thirds of the entire class using them.[7] In 1938 when thirty textbooks of science were analyzed, it was found that both the technical and non-technical vo-

---

[5] H. R. Douglass and H. F. Spitzer, "The Importance of Teaching for Understanding," in the 45th Yearbook of The National Society for the Study of Education, Part I, *The Measurement of Understanding,* Chicago, University of Chicago Press, 1946, pp. 10–11.

[6] William James, *Talks to Teachers on Psychology and to Students on Some of Life's Ideals,* New York, Henry Holt & Co., 1899, p. 150.

[7] E. L. Thorndike, "Improving the Ability to Read," *Teachers College Record,* Vol. 36, 1934, pp. 1–19.

cabularies of general science, biology, chemistry, and physics were too difficult for most of the pupils for whom the books were written. In this study, it appeared also that too many of the difficult words were non-scientific. In addition, the analysis revealed that too small a percentage of words were defined when they first appeared, and when they were defined it was often only after they had already been used in previous material.[8] Even today too little attention is given to the difficulty of words in texts. Fifteen elementary science texts, analyzed for word difficulty proved too difficult for most of the pupils in the intermediate grades.[9]

Recent research has made available to teachers and pupils, methods and materials for increasing the meaningfulness of vocabulary used in schools. Analysis of millions of words which children have used in writing and speaking have given educators several word books, basic vocabularies, and dictionaries written in children's terms. Such sources as Thorndike's list of 30,000 words,[10] The Buckingham-Dolch Combined Word List,[11] the Rinsland List,[12] the Dolch Basic Sight Vocabulary,[13] and the Thorndike Century Junior Dictionary[14] should be available as a part of the school's professional library.

There are several books on the use of language for effective written communication.[15] These sources may be helpful to teachers in showing means of avoiding ambiguity and verbosity in writing. Besides being able to appraise the difficulty of style and vocabulary of textual material, teachers should become apt at direct and clear

[8] F. D. Curtis, *Investigations of Vocabulary in Textbooks of Science for Secondary Schools*, Boston, Ginn and Company, 1938.

[9] G. G. Mallison, H. E. Sturm and R. E. Patton, "The Reading Difficulty of Textbooks in Elementary Science," *Elementary School Journal*, Vol. 51, 1951, pp. 460–463.

[10] E. L. Thorndike and Irving Lorge, *The Teacher's Word Book of 30,000 Words*, Bureau of Publications, Teachers College, Columbia University, 1944.

[11] B. R. Buckingham and E. W. Dolch, *A Combined Word List*, Boston, Ginn and Company, 1936.

[12] H. D. Rinsland, *A Basic Vocabulary of Elementary School Children*, New York, The Macmillan Company, 1945.

[13] E. W. Dolch, *A Manual for Remedial Reading*, Second Edition, Champaign, Illinois, The Garrard Press, 1945, p. 438.

[14] E. L. Thorndike, *Thorndike Century Junior Dictionary*, Chicago, Scott, Foresman and Company, 1942.

[15] For example see R. Flesch, *The Way to Write*, New York, Harper and Brothers, 1949.

composition. Examinations, syllabi, and outlines are all too often vague or poorly written.

An attempt to appraise the difficulty of vocabulary has been made through the application of readability formulae.[16] Lorge has indicated that "factors influencing readability are numerous, and many subtle factors have not been accounted for. However, experimental evidence supports the following important elements as determiners of readability: (1) measure of vocabulary such as percentage of different words or word difficulty, (2) sentence form such as length of sentence, number of clauses, etc., (3) appraisal of human interest by determining personal pronouns or vivid words used."[17]

Experiential background of students. To be most meaningful, school work should be related to pupils' backgrounds. Children cannot do real thinking on the basis of abstractions alone. "As long as words refer to objects or situations at some time present to the senses, the meaning is simple and sure. What causes the difficulty is that the higher-order abstractions go farther and farther from realities or concrete experiences."[18] Often teachers rely upon words to take the place of concrete experience, but concepts and real understanding are not formed in this way. The following definition taken from a high-school geometry text will illustrate how youngsters may fail to understand ideas which are not based upon concrete experience:

"The word area conveys the idea of space on a plane surface."

Not one of these words is above Thorndike's most common 4000 words in the English language, and yet the above definition can have little meaning to most high school readers because the idea is not rooted in any concrete experience which students have had in dealing with area.[19] *Apropos* is John Dewey's comment: "By rolling

[16] See Edgar Dale and J. S. Chall, "A Formula for Predicting Readability," *Educational Research Bulletin*, Vol. 27, January 21 and February 18, 1948, pp. 11–20 and 37–54; Rudolf Flesch, *Marks of a Readable Style*, New York, Teachers College, Columbia University, 1943. (Teachers College, Columbia University Contributions to Education No. 897); and E. W. Dolch, *Problems in Reading*, Champaign, Illinois, The Garrard Press, 1948, Chapter XXI, as representative of readability formulae applicable for appraising reading difficulty of textbooks.

[17] Irving Lorge, "Predicting Readability," *Teachers College Record*, Vol. 45, 1944, pp. 404–419.

[18] Madeline Semmelmeyer, "Extensional Methods in Dealing with Abstractions in Reading," *Elementary School Journal*, Vol. 50, 1949, p. 28.

[19] *Ibid.*, pp. 30–31.

an object the child makes its roundness appreciable; by bouncing it he singles out its elasticity; by throwing it he makes weight its conspicuous distinctive factor." [20]

A student in one of the writers' classes in educational psychology while doing his practice teaching used a number of sailboat problems in his class in physics. He was discouraged by the poor results, but was quick to realize, in class discussion, that the prairies of Illinois offer little opportunity for experience with sailboats.

Following are some suggestions for making material meaningful by gearing it to pupils' experiences: (1) appraise the student's experiences, (2) find problems in the student's immediate environment and help him find solutions to these problems, (3) whenever feasible provide kinesthetic training along with the material presented, (4) use pictorial illustrations, models or examples frequently.[21]

Variety of classroom experiences. Students should engage in a variety of experiences to increase the depth of meaning of important concepts. Today's schools probably depend far too much upon reading as a data gathering technique. The clever teacher should be able to devise many activities which will give concrete experiences instead of verbal abstractions. In one recent teaching experiment [22] in a general science class in junior high school, it was shown that ideas about atomic energy and nuclear physics can be successfully taught with models and demonstrations. In this teaching experiment small building blocks, labeled with appropriate chemical symbols, were used to explain molecular structure. To illustrate the atomic explosion, a number of mouse traps, loaded with corks were placed in a screen enclosure. Then by throwing in one cork, one trap was sprung, hurling its cork to another. This went on until nearly all the traps were set off. This kind of visual analogy, for beginning students, invests school activity with vivid meaningfulness which cannot be achieved solely through the verbal presentation of ideas. Furthermore, the motivation which is apt to occur through such demonstrations is much better than that elicited by a lecture, or even a discussion, where the only tools are words.

[20] John Dewey, *How We Think*, Boston, D. C. Heath Company, 1910, p. 112.
[21] Semmelmeyer, *op.cit.*, p. 35.
[22] J. V. Farrell and J. R. Wailes, "Multi-Sensory Approach to Science in the Elementary School," *Elementary School Journal*, Vol. 52, 1952, pp. 271–276.

Working on Units of Optimal Size and Scope. All subject matter, even in a core curriculum, contains elements of various size and complexity. In reading, for example, there are letters, groups of letters which form certain sounds, words, groups of words, sentences, paragraphs, chapters, and so on. In biology there are cells, tissues, systems, members, and organisms, and organisms are grouped into such categories as species, orders, and phyla. In what sequence and in what sized units should this material be learned? Often considerations of this kind are treated as "whole versus part learning," [23] and the general answer by most authorities is that whole learning is frequently superior to part learning. The phrase whole or part learning, however, is somewhat of a misnomer, for in practice, there are rarely parts of anything which are learned which are not "wholes" in their own right. In memorizing poetry, for example, the pupil might learn a stanza at a time or the whole poem. In this case, the pupil is not making a choice between whole or part learning but between two wholes of different size. A tennis instructor who gives concentrated work on the serve is not instructing by a part method, but has chosen a unit smaller than the total game—a sub-whole.

The key principle in choosing units of various sizes for instructional purposes must be based upon the meaningfulness of the units which are to be learned. The learner must be able to see how units fit into a larger, more inclusive whole. Since smaller units will always have to be welded into larger ones eventually, a general principle might be to use the largest whole which the child's developmental level will permit. But the teacher must not become so enamoured of the "whole method" that he loses sight of the importance of various sub-units and skills. When large units are undertaken, such as a whole game, or a whole chapter in physics, special attention to, and additional guidance in, difficult parts should be given concurrently with the larger unit.[24] Likewise in elementary reading, teachers should not lose sight of the necessity for developing skills in word-attack, in order to develop better and speedier readers.

The size of units to be learned has special implications in the field

[23] For a discussion of the "Whole-part" learning controversy see J. A. Mc-Geoch and A. L. Irion, *The Psychology of Human Learning*, New York, Longmans, Green and Co., Inc., 1952.

[24] R. S. Woodworth, *Experimental Psychology*, New York, Henry Holt, 1938.

of motor learning and physical education. Many games and manual tasks may be quite novel to an individual. Furthermore, new activities can be very fatiguing due to the involvement of little-used muscle groups. Often there is little relation between various parts of a game. Thus in baseball, there is only a slight relation between batting and catching, and either may be practiced as a meaningful whole. On the other hand, long continued practice on specific parts of the game may fail to capture interest. In such learnings (baseball, football, and basketball, for example) the best approach seems to be an orientation and beginning trials with the game as a whole and then a breakdown into meaningful sub-wholes. This practice should not exclude continuing use of the sub-wholes in actual game conditions.[25]

There is no clear-cut superiority for either whole or part learning when closely knit motor units or skills are learned. For instance, in juggling, there is little apparent difference in eventual skill when the person starts with two balls and works up to more, or begins initially with three or more balls.[26]

Criteria which might serve to determine operating principles for teachers are:

1. First consideration should be given to the developmental level of the individual learner. Units which are clear to the teacher may be entirely too broad for the learner. Frequent quizzes, discussions, and interviews can serve as check points of understanding and help pace the speed and scope of the material.

2. The meaningfulness of units to be learned should be weighed against the contexts in which such units of learning are to be used. Units artificially or arbitrarily set up such as a unit on the throwing motions in baseball, bowling, and football passing, could be ridiculous. A unit in history on world rulers, if studied in isolation from the events which transpired during their rules might be just as ridiculous.

3. The gross size of the whole to be learned must be within reason. Blind

[25] For a more complete discussion of "management of practice" in motor learning see C. E. Ragsdale, "How Children Learn the Motor Types of Activities," Chapter 3 in The 49th Yearbook of the National Society for the Study of Education, Part I, *Learning and Instruction*, Chicago, University of Chicago Press, 1950.

[26] C. G. Knapp and W. R. Dixon, "Learning to Juggle: II A Study of Whole and Part Methods," *Research Quarterly of the American Association for Health and Recreation*, Vol. 23, 1952, pp. 398–401.

application of the principle of whole learning to all types of material would find teachers having students learn such things as the multiplication tables as a whole.

4. The pupil's own grasp of units to be learned should be given some consideration. Some self-selection on the part of pupils will give clues and direction to the teacher's plans for material to be covered.

Distributing Learning Activities. Even when learning is made meaningful, and material is presented or studied in the form of comprehensible elements, problems or units, there still remains the question of spacing and placing the activity. Learning efficiency varies with the length of study or practice periods and with the spacing of such periods, and with the rapidity with which material is presented.[27] Theoretically for some types of material more profit will be gained from four twenty-minute periods of study than from one eighty-minute period. Distribution of practice has long been regarded as superior to massed practice (or cramming). There is much evidence to support this general principle. In everything from rote tasks such as learning of nonsense syllables [28] to more complex work such as studying technical materials,[29] a spacing of relatively short practice periods has proven superior to long periods of study— to periods which are jammed together.

However, teachers may err in either direction. One investigator found that two-minute practice periods (in hand-eye coordination) were superior to either a one-minute or four-minute period practice group. The four-minute group was poorest of the three.[30]

Because of the dearth of well-designed experimentation in the classroom it is not possible at this time to determine the optimal temporal distribution of practices in a given school subject. The problem is alleviated when there is a good deal of student-teacher planning. When the organization is one of a subject-centered approach the distribution of activities is determined almost entirely by

[27] J. A. McGeoch and A. L. Irion, *op. cit.*, pp. 138–193.

[28] C. I. Hovland, "Experimental Studies in Rote Learning Theory III, Distribution of Practice with Varying Speeds of Syllable Presentation," *Journal of Experimental Psychology*, 1938, Vol. 23, pp. 172–190.

[29] S. D. McAustin, "A Study in Logical Memory," *American Journal of Psychology*, Vol. 32, 1921, pp. 370–403.

[30] R. C. Travis, "Practice and Rest Periods in Motor Learning," *Journal of Psychology*, Vol. 3, 1937, pp. 183–187.

the teacher. When student and teacher work together in defining tasks and setting about to solve problems, the spacing of activities becomes a much less important issue.

However, there are some general principles which will give guidance in appropriate spacing of school activities. The variables which should be considered in determining the distribution of study and work activities are:

1. Monotony, boredom and fatigue result more quickly, especially in rote learning, than is generally realized. Such factors are obviously deleterious to learning. A college student was able to type errorless speed drills of one-minute duration with an average speed of over fifty words per minute, but when periods of two-minutes were tried speed dropped to about forty-two words per minute, and when five minute periods were used, it was no longer possible to maintain errorless work.[31]

2. Another variable is the retroactive inhibition [32] which results from interference between various parts of a given material or activity. This type of interference increases with the length of the material, the similarity of parts of the material, and the extent to which practice is massed. When there is a good deal of similarity in materials, such as words in foreign language study, practice periods should be short and more widely spaced.

3. The type of material to be learned is another factor. Difficult memorization and complex perceptual motor learning requires short, frequent (more than once a week) practice periods, while well-integrated and interesting material such as problem solving may be studied or practiced for longer periods without a decrement in motivation or efficiency.

4. Since motivation is a key to performance and learning, self-pacing by the learner seems called for. Predetermined schedules imposed upon the eager student in an effort to make learning more efficient may serve just the reverse purpose by killing interest and initiative. Pupils who work at meaningful tasks matched with their interests and needs may work arduously and for long periods without any apparent detrimental effects.

[31] Howard Kingsley, *The Nature and Conditions of Learning*, New York, Prentice-Hall, 1946, pp. 246–249.

[32] Retroactive inhibition is a term which signifies an interference with learned material by subsequent learning. For example, a youngster, who has learned one stroke in swimming, then learns a different stroke, may, when he returns to the first, find some interference and decrease in skill in the original swimming stroke.

Eliciting Student Activity. The involvement of the student as an active participant in the learning process is of paramount importance. So much of this book is devoted to this concept that elaboration here would be repetitious. The value of and applications of this principle of activity are well known. Even in such meaningless tasks as learning nonsense syllables, subjects will learn faster if they can turn the cards upon which the syllables are printed, or the knob on the memory drum, than if someone else does this for them. For more complex and meaningful learnings, one need only to consider the excellent results obtained by schools which have adopted various forms of curricula and methods which allow a maximum of student activity.[33]

Whatever method of organization is adopted by the teacher there is little chance for success unless provision is made for a large amount of activity by students. In most cases "listening" is far short of being an active process. As Guthrie has written, "In order to make listening profitable (or school work of any kind for that matter) it is essential that the student be led to do what is to be learned. . . . A student does not learn what was in a lecture, or in a book, he learns only what the lecture or book caused him to do." [34]

ORGANIZATION AND UNDERSTANDING

Formation of Concepts. By responding to various objects as both similar and different, the individual is able to organize his environment into meaningful categories. For example, the reader by now has formed a concept about learning. He knows that acquisition of skill, changes in attitudes, and alterations in verbal responses all represent learning. Thus he has a concept of learning. Without the ability to form concepts, one would have to face each new situation afresh.

Before coming to school, children have developed concepts such as roundness and magnitude, and are beginning to grasp the concept of time. However, social concepts such as honesty and courage

---

[33] The American Association for Supervision and Curriculum Development, 1949 Yearbook, *Toward Better Teaching,* Washington, National Education Association.

[34] E. R. Guthrie, "Conditioning: A Theory of Learning in Terms of Stimulus, Response, and Association," in 41st Yearbook of the National Society for the Study of Education, *The Psychology of Learning,* Bloomington, Ill., Public School Publishing Co., 1942, p. 55.

are probably not well developed before the average child is in the sixth or seventh grade.[35] Conceptualization is not an all or none proposition, but a gradual attainment with experience. A five-year-old who has a good concept of the size of objects in his immediate environment will have little notion of the size of sections of the earth. In one instance when a kindergarten teacher told her class that the ocean was bigger than the whole city in which they lived, the children laughed, thinking that it was a joke.

The notion that concepts increase in richness or depth of meaning with experience has serious implications for teaching. As it is now, schooling is often organized into a series of rather discrete areas —a horizontal organization. In the grades, children learn world geography, and in many cases this is a terminal point for such study. Geographical concepts which one would expect to increase in meaningfulness with an increase in age may actually decrease, so that sixth graders sometimes have a better grasp of certain geographical concepts than do college students.[36] There are probably several reasons why certain concepts fail to acquire further meaning with the passage of time. For one thing the number of concepts which children are expected to learn in school may be too large.[37] Another is that concepts are often assumed to have been learned when the child can do no more than define words. But as Brownell has indicated, concepts are far more than words or "arbitrary associations." Most important as an explanation of the failure in concept formation is that teachers have not helped provide a vertical organization which is the natural way in which concepts develop. Instead of teaching fractions once and never again referring to this concept, schools should follow through by creating problems which make use of fractions in a wide range and types of situations. In this sense, every teacher, both at elementary and high school levels, should be an arithmetic teacher when the need arises to use arithmetical concepts.

The evidence on how concepts are learned bears directly upon teaching. In fact, the level of conceptualization depends more upon education and experience than upon intelligence. The level of a con-

[35] W. Edgar Vinacke, "The Investigation of Concept Formation," *Psychological Bulletin*, Vol. 48, 1951, pp. 1–31.

[36] E. W. Dolch, Studies on Depth of Meaning in Geographical Concepts, Unpublished Data, University of Illinois, 1951.

[37] Brownell and Hendrickson, *op.cit.*, p. 105.

cept for a given child will be in proportion to the number and kinds of experiences which the child has had with the concept. For example, a child's concept of honesty can grow only as he sees honest behavior in a number of different kinds of situations. Indeed, a child's behavior must be specific to a situation until such abstractions are formed. A child may be honest in one situation and dishonest in another.[38] He has not yet learned the concept of honesty, nor a self-concept which allows discriminations and generalizations. Clearly a teacher can not expect consistent behavior until maturing concepts make such behavior possible. Behavior will become consistent more rapidly when teachers offer many opportunities for honest behavior, allow pupils to make and correct their own errors, and relate one situation to another.

The following experiment [39] of a psychologist with his son, later repeated with a larger group [40] illustrates some of the principles of concept formation and the teaching of concepts. The psychologist asked his son the meaning of the word opposite. He refused to accept the boy's negative response and asked him to name the opposite of "good" and "big." For these the son replied "boy" and "man." These were called wrong, and the boy was given the correct answers, and then asked the opposite of "black," "long" and "fat." The boy immediately knew the correct answers.

In teaching concepts, teachers should realize that, in the main, there is required a reorganization of already existing ideas and experiences. As concepts begin to emerge there should be practice with them in a number of different situations. In this stage, teachers should not be disturbed by errors, as these are inevitable, and may be quite helpful in bringing about clearer discriminations. Finally, teachers should make sure that concepts thus achieved are then welded into larger and more functional units. There is no terminal point in this process! Teaching which gives children the attitude that there is such a final point, certainly must interfere with the depth of meaning which should later be acquired.

[38] Hugh Hartshorne and M. A. May, *Studies in Deceit,* New York, The Macmillan Company, 1928.

[39] K. M. Dallenbach, "A Note on the Immediacy of Understanding a Relation," *Psychologische Forschung,* Vol. 7, 1926, pp. 268–269.

[40] G. Kreezer and K. M. Dallenbach, "Learning the Relation of Opposition," *American Journal of Psychology,* Vol. 41, 1929, pp. 432–441.

Problem Solving. In a rapidly changing world, it becomes imperative that people develop the capacity to adapt to new situations, to make discriminations, think critically and creatively, and make sound judgments. The day to day ability to recognize and solve practical problems as well as the concern with and ability to handle intellectual problems has become a major goal of schooling.

An important consideration for teachers is how children learn to recognize and to solve problems as well as how teaching activities can be organized to elicit problem solving behavior. Problem solving skill is not learned incidentally as children go through the motions of finding answers to the teacher's questions nor is it learned by watching the teacher or other students solve problems. In fact the notion of problem solving activity as memorized steps, as is apt to occur under these conditions, may actually militate against the learning of problem solving. On the other hand, problem solving which is accompanied by examples and explanations, which is marked by active participation of pupils and which stresses an understanding of method, will be likely not only to last, but also to become functional. One noted experiment in problem solving compared groups of students who had learned to solve problems by two different methods. Students in one group memorized the solution to a problem which required the moving of lines to make a new geometrical shape. A second group spent the same amount of time as the first in working on several such problems, the solutions to which were explained. Retests of both groups on similar problems showed a decided superiority for the second group which really understood the nature of the problems.[41] In commenting about this and like experiments, the investigator wrote: "Pupils should learn to learn—that is the best the school can do for them. They should not merely learn to memorize—they should learn to learn by understanding." [42]

What is the case for stressing problem solving? The following paragraph, written for mathematics teachers is of such general value that it is presented here:

If life were of such a constant nature that there were only a few chores to do and they were done over and over in exactly the same way, the case

[41] George Katona, *Organizing and Memorizing*, New York, Columbia University Press, 1940, pp. 82–85.
[42] *Ibid.*, p. 260.

for knowing how to solve problems would not be so compelling. All one
would have to do would be to learn how to do the few jobs at the outset.[43]

It is quite clear that the purposes of schooling go beyond the learning of unvarying routines and details which may characterize training in specific jobs. Furthermore, solutions to school problems may
be of little value to pupils who will likely face much different problems after they leave school. In short, it is not so much the solution
of the problems which is important but the learning of ways to deal
with a wide variety of problems which is crucial. There is much evidence in and out of school to show that few persons ever learn to
handle their problems very effectively and rationally. Instead it is
much more common to find persons facing problems by rote memorization of rules or by affective impulse. In one study only 32 per
cent of a group of college students, all of whom had studied high
school geometry, showed any insight in solving geometrical problems. The rest relied upon habit. Out of 285 test situations, responses
of the "oh I see" type occurred only seventeen times.[44] Again college
students in one of the writer's classes, asked to find the square root
of six digit numbers, attempted to obtain the answer by form (long
since forgotten) instead of attacking the problem by the methods
of logical thinking [45] or even by trial and error.

The failure of many people to make a direct and straightforward
attack upon problems is reflected in difficulties of adjustment, poor
judgment, and inability to make decisions. Writers [46] in the field of
counseling list decision-making as one of the common areas of adjustment problems. Little help comes to such people from rules, bro-
mides and cliches in newspapers and popular books on adjustment.
There is no substitute for actual experience in solving problems, facing difficulties, making errors, and finally discovering a solution
which leads to action. The case for learning to solve problems has

[43] K. B. Henderson and R. E. Pingry, "Problem Solving in Mathematics," in
The National Council of Teachers of Mathematics, The Learning of Mathematics, Its Theory and Practice, 21st Yearbook, Washington, D. C., 1953, p. 233.

[44] L. K. Henry, The Role of Insight in the Analytical Thinking of Adolescents,
University of Iowa Studies in Education, Vol. 9, No. 5, pp. 65–102.

[45] A few students, for example, went from the known to the unknown. They
started with 144 or 625, known squares, and attempted to figure out how the
known square roots of 12 and 25 were obtained.

[46] F. P. Robinson, Principles and Procedures in Student Counseling, New
York, Harper and Brothers Publishers, 1950.

been well summarized by Kingsley,[47] who writes: "A good problem is a good motive for learning. Secondly it is conducive to the building up of confidence in one's ability to work things out for himself. This has definite value for the individual's mental health, for one of the first principles of mental hygiene is that difficulties should be regarded as problems to be solved rather than as emergencies to be evaded."

The nature of the problem-solving process.[48] A description of the problem solving process is little more than a reformulation of the learning process. However, there are differences in emphases. Every situation in which a student has a need and a goal, with a barrier between, leads to some kind of learning. A youngster may have a paper route which covers several blocks. One of his problems is to determine the most economical way to cover the territory. In connection with this problem, a good deal of learning can occur. He might continue in a haphazard manner, or he might ask someone to solve the problem for him. In each of these cases he had learned something, viz., habits of avoiding such issues or of being dependent upon others. But he has not solved the problem until he has recognized it as a problem, turned energy toward it, arrived at a judgment, and checked his final decision.

Various writers have outlined the steps in problem solving, and though there is not a complete agreement among them, there are elements which are common in their descriptions. First, there is a *motive* or identification or recognition phase, in which the student sees that he is faced with a problem and has a desire to do something about it. Secondly, there is generally a *planning* phase in which the person considers several avenues of attack upon the problem. Often this consists in the formation of hypotheses which are later accepted or rejected. The third, or *work* phase, consists of testing hypotheses, collecting relevant materials, talking to others about the problem, etc. Finally, there is an *evaluative, action* phase in which the student appraises his solution or ideas, and takes action as a result. The process does not always follow a neat sequence, and it is quite possible that students will be working upon several fea-

[47] Howard Kingsley, *op.cit.,* p. 379.
[48] For detailed accounts of the psychological nature of problem solving see D. M. Johnson, "A Modern Account of Problem Solving," *Psychological Bulletin,* Vol. 41, 1944, pp. 201–229, 169 titles; and Karl Duncker, "On Problem Solving," *Psychological Monographs,* No. 270, 1945.

tures of a total problem at once. In fact undue emphasis upon form may blind students to the necessity for critical appraisal of all steps in the process as they go along.

Problem solving is a circular process in that facing important issues inevitably leads to further questions. This is especially true when groups as well as individuals work at problems. Various class members should be encouraged to investigate ramifications of questions which individuals raise. As Thorndike notes: "The school is as much concerned with creating problems as it is with solving them." [49]

How do problems arise? A practical question for teachers is where and how problems arise in teaching. A first and obvious source is from the teacher, and texts or other reading materials. From the teacher's viewpoint, such problems may be very important. But there is serious doubt that such problems are always real problems or at least significant ones to the student. Furthermore, if the scope of problem solving activity includes no more than these "set" problems, important steps in the process, namely, recognition and identification of problems are left out. Some problems suggested by the teacher and texts may provide excellent guidance and be a real challenge, but pupils also need activities which cause them to derive problems of their own.

Some of the less obvious but important ways in which problems germinate are through group discussion, trips outside the school, critical self-appraisal, use of a wide variety of class materials, and use of unique equipment. In all these activities there is the underlying assumption of existing needs and interests which can be directed toward awareness of problems and their solution, and that the classroom is the place for this kind of activity.

Suggestions for helping students develop problems which are interesting and at the same time profitable have been made by experienced teachers in a class of one of the writers. These teachers suggested:

1. Ask each student to write a list of problems which are of interest to him or which represent needs for him.

[49] R. L. Thorndike, "How Children Learn the Principles and Techniques of Problem Solving," in 49th Yearbook, National Society for the Study of Education, Part I, *Learning and Instruction,* University of Chicago Press, 1950, p. 194.

2. Have students keep records of difficult words, controversial points, and the like.
3. Provide a rich supply of resource material. One teacher instead of getting fifty copies of the same text ordered fifty different books for study.
4. Use reading interest tests, and provide reading material in the direction of students' interests.
5. Have students score their own quizzes, correct their own written work, and discuss each other's papers.
6. Allow students to participate in making their own assignments.
7. Group students within the class on the basis of common interests and problems.
8. Encourage students to draw problems from the community such as road repair, drainage, police system, and traffic control.

Selection of problems. When an individual child, or a group of pupils develop a number of questions or problems, they must have some guidance in selecting those most appropriate and valuable for further study. It would be questionable to entertain a problem in dating in a course in algebra, and it might be unwise for a child always to work on the first problem which occurs to him. Together, teacher and pupils should develop criteria for the job of selecting good problems which should serve not only for in-class selection, but also in the future when the student is on his own and does not have the benefit of the teacher's guidance.

Each class, and each student with the help of the teacher should develop their own criteria for determining the problems most appropriate for study. In some cases teachers may be unwilling to relinquish this job which they consider their most important prerogative. Other teachers may delegate the whole job to the class leaving pupils without necessary guidance. In either case, children are not learning the important skill of identifying and recognizing important problems in their environment.

Although various class situations are unique, there are several criteria for selection of problems which the teacher should have available. The following are questions which might be asked: Is this the most pressing and important problem at this time? Will solving this problem be profitable and important in developing further learnings? Will there be access to necessary sources of material? Could this problem be more appropriately handled in another class or course? How will solution of this problem benefit the group as a whole?

· *Collecting and using relevant materials.* Students cannot be expected to solve problems without knowing how to find and use appropriate resources. That students are not generally well trained in this respect is well documented. It should be noted that, "even good students do not know how to find and use source material. Some graduating seniors in college have rarely used any other library resource than the reserve desk where one merely has to ask for the book." [50]

When teachers, enrolled in graduate work were given a hypothetical classroom problem dealing with motivation and interests, and asked to show how they would go about solving it, *not one* of 231 graduate students suggested the use of bibliographic materials as resources which would aid in solution of the problem.[51] Wiles found in working with a group in college that neither undergraduates nor graduate students had obtained skills in fact collecting. He says, "The chief weakness revealed by the examination was the inability of students to locate reference material in the library." This "glaring deficiency" exists, Wiles notes, in spite of the fact that many of the students had been in contact with about fifty teachers during the years they had spent in school.[52] It is reported that less than 25 per cent of high schools offer training in how to use a library. Even schools which do offer such courses are highly variable in their practices. In one survey of 100 selected schools, three-fourths of which gave formal training in library usage, only one out of the 100 gave work in how to use textbooks, and how to check in and charge out books. Only about one-half gave information about the *Readers Guide* and the use of encyclopedias.[53]

Evaluating the results of inquiry. Evaluation should be a continuous process during problem solving activity. The acceptance or rejection of hypotheses, the appraisal of various source material, in-

[50] S. L. Pressey and F. P. Robinson, *Psychology and the New Education,* New York, Harper and Brothers Publishers, 1944, p. 608.

[51] R. H. Simpson, E. L. Gaier and R. S. Jones, "A Study of Resourcefulness in Attacking Professional Problems," *The School Review,* Vol. 40, December, 1952, p. 538.

[52] Kimball Wiles, "Are We Developing Skill in Purposeful Fact Collecting," *Journal of Educational Research,* Vol. 38, 1945, pp. 617–623.

[53] W. G. Brink, *Directing Study Activities in Secondary Schools,* Garden City, New York, Doubleday, Doran and Company, Inc., 1937.

corporation of suggestions from teachers and other students are all essential procedures which can be learned only through guided practice in solving problems. The ultimate goal is to develop habits of critical appraisal so that students can solve problems and make discoveries on their own.

How is this skill developed in the classroom? One simple way is a frequent use of questions of how, and why in place of the many what, when, and where questions so often used in our classrooms today. Questions which ask for process and for reasons are challenging, and discourage rote memorization.

Group work, and evaluation by students of each other's ideas is another way in which students learn critically to scrutinize problems. Often the most significant classroom problems are those which affect the whole class or even the whole community. Thus appraisal of progress will become a joint venture, each student learning something of appraisal from the activities of others.

Solution and action. Unless some action results from the solution of problems, students may see the activity as busy work. For some problems no definite answers will be found, but generally such problems (e.g., consideration of racial intolerance in a social studies class) will lead to other problems, and will result in tentative conclusions which can lead to constructive action.

In a previous chapter an example [54] was given of students who were challenged to find a solution to the problem of malarial control in their community. Activities leading to the solution of the problem involved surveys of the health of the community, of the terrain and breeding places of mosquitoes, and of methods of controlling these insects. Had the class, in this instance, stopped at this point, little would have been gained from the experience. The final test of the effectiveness of their work could only be discovered by these students in trying out methods of preventing and controlling malaria.

For more abstract problems, such as problems in mathematics, the same principle applies. The problems with which students work will take on added significance when their solution can be checked in some practical context—e.g., when they can test algebraic solutions in physics and chemistry.

[54] American Association for Supervision and Curriculum Development, *Toward Better Teaching*, 1949 Yearbook, pp. 203–204.

ORGANIZATION AND METHODS OF TEACHING

The teacher should be equipped with working techniques which jibe with psychological principles. A teacher should be an expert in the technology of learning, but as is true of other technologists, must continually appraise techniques in terms of new discoveries, and research. It is literally true that many of today's principles may be outmoded or changed in a few years. It is thus imperative that teachers retain an open mindedness which allows revision of their teaching methods as new discoveries are made.

Consider these specific examples of current school practice. One teacher makes an assignment by giving a number of problems in the text, or a certain number of pages to be read. Another may spend an hour or so planning a new unit of work. One typing teacher begins work with "frf," "juj" drills, another starts off immediately with business letters, and a third allows students to select their own typing material right from the start. Miss Black has pupils add columns up, Mr. Brown has them add from the top down, while a third has pupils add two digits at a time from the beginning. In the face of so many questions about specific teaching plans and techniques, the teacher must be equipped with psychological principles which are general enough to apply in a number of situations.

This section of the chapter will discuss some general principles dealing with the more common workaday problems confronting teachers and pupils such as assignment making, reviewing, testing, and planning a sequence of activities.

Psychology of Assignment Making. The assignment has been considered as a specification by the teacher of material to be read or studied or of work to be accomplished by the student. This somewhat narrow view of assignment making has resulted in almost complete domination by the teacher of assignments. In one study of one thousand high-school teachers 90 per cent of assignments were dominated by the teacher.[55] That this is contrary to the attitudes of pupils about assignments was shown in a study of 1237 high school students who preferred a procedure of democratic assignments to either an autocratic or laissez-faire procedure.[56]

[55] W. G. Brink, "Assignment Procedures of One Thousand High School Teachers," *Educational Trends*, Vol. 1, 1934, pp. 6–14.
[56] R. C. Doll, "High School Pupils' Attitudes Toward Teaching Procedures," *School Review*, Vol. 55, 1947, pp. 222–227.

What of present assignment making procedures? Burton, who has studied such practices in recent years writes:

The meager, vague, unanalyzed, wholly inadequate type of assignment predominates in the secondary school, practically to the exclusion of all other forms.[57]

Still widely used is the procedure of assigning a certain number of text pages or chapters to be read by students and little else. This is done despite the fact that overwhelming evidence supports clear-cut objectives, student participation, and adequately explained assignments as valuable organizing factors in study and learning.

The inadequacy of present procedures may be largely due to a belief that assignments, teaching, practice, and testing are separate entities. These processes are obviously interrelated, and when treated as such should result in better motivation of pupils. The assignment is largely a matter not of information but of motivation, i.e., helping students find a direction for their energy. As such the first principle is that assignments should provide for individual differences.

Assignments should also arouse interest and make for continuing motivation through a unit of work, or problem. Questions, illustrative materials, demonstrations are all a part of the introduction to a new piece of work. Pupils should be involved in the assignment process. The ego involvement which obtains from giving students a proprietary interest in their own course will cause them to identify with the work, and should result in better group morale and enthusiasm. Good assignments give pupils a mental set which makes them anticipate future steps in learning. The youngster learns what to look for, and how to go about doing so. Research has shown that a "set" (i.e., suggestions about how to look at a problem) leads to more rapid and efficient learning.

Placement and Function of Review. Theoretically the curve of retention of material learned might approximate that shown in Figure 12. In actual practice, however, the shape of this curve is a function of many factors. The goal of education is to change the shape, to avoid the rapid drop-off in retention. Following are some of the variables which research has shown to influence the shape of the curve of forgetting:

[57] William Burton, in 49th Yearbook National Society for the Study of Education, Part I, 1950, p. 227.

1. The kind of test of retention used makes a difference. A test of pure recall (e.g., completion) would show a more rapid drop than a test of recognition (multiple-choice).
2. The kind of material which is learned affects the shape of the forgetting curve. The more meaningful the material, the less rapid the drop.
3. The thoroughness of the original learning is also a factor. Overlearning produces a retention curve of an entirely different shape, one which may remain at a high level for an indefinite period of time.
4. The kinds of activity which have occurred after the original learning partially determine how rapidly forgetting occurs.
5. Active involvement of the learner in the learning situation also retards forgetting.

Much of a teacher's work is concerned with altering the shape of this curve. Learning which is put away has little chance of being available when it is needed. Point 4 above, concerned with review, dictates that after learning there must be some use made of material if forgetting is to be retarded. As Figure 12 shows, the greatest forgetting occurs shortly after learning. Hence it would appear wise to place review activities as close to the original learning as practical. Research bears out this supposition. When several thousand grade school children

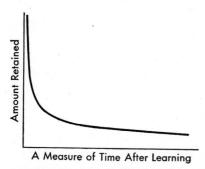

FIGURE 12. A Theoretical Curve of Retention of Relatively Meaningless Material.

read a selection and were given four-minute review tests afterward, the degree of retention was directly related to the placement of the review test. Immediate recall after reading proved the most profitable. Groups which took immediate review tests had over 60 per cent better retention of material read than those who took their first recall test a week later. Furthermore, a group which took an immediate recall test and another one the next day was superior to a group which took an immediate recall test, and a second test a week later.[58] A short test or other form of review at the end of a class period, followed by discussion should do more to retard for-

[58] H. F. Spitzer, "Studies in Retention," *Journal of Educational Psychology,* Vol. 30, 1939, pp. 641–656.

getting than formal reviews which take place several days or even weeks after learning.

Also, since forgetting is due to intervening activity it should be profitable to have new learning make active use of previous learnings. For example, long division following subtraction and addition might easily cause some forgetting (interference) with subtraction and addition, unless the teacher calls attention to the relationships between these processes. Of course, it must be remembered that interference which might result in the academic situation could be dissipated if arithmetical concepts were learned through such meaningful activities as operating a school store.

Testing and Learning. More than any other single factor, the kind of testing used in schools determines the organization of classwork and materials, and the learning of pupils, and often the kind of teaching which is done. Whether teachers admit it or not, the tests they use are statements to students of their objectives and are the forces which direct students activities. One of the reasons why good teaching methods may fail is probably attributable to the discrepancy between the stated goals of a course and the conventional paper and pencil tests which are used as a means of grading. This discrepancy may be destructive of morale, because the avowed purpose of the schoolwork may be the development of understanding and generalizations, while the tests appraise only the number of facts which the student has been able to amass. As teaching methods are improved, so must testing procedures be revised. As before noted, tests may have a beneficial function in learning (perhaps this is their most important function) in addition to their use in measurement of achievement and diagnosis.

Tests should stress process as well as product. Often the results of the ordinary true-false or multiple-choice test reveal little about the reasons for students' mistakes. An analysis of the reasons back of students' choices of multiple-choice alternatives has shown that many students guess, or have a hunch which is the right answer without really understanding why it is correct. Conversely students may miss questions (choose a wrong alternative) and at the same time have a rather good grasp of the issues involved in the questions.[59]

[59] R. Stewart Jones, "Process Testing: An Analysis of Students' Reasons for Choice of Alternatives," *Journal of Educational Research*, Vol. 46, 1953, pp. 525–534.

The teacher who wishes to use tests to facilitate learning should provide a wide variety of testing materials. Also the teacher should make use of the group's appraisal of its own work and self-scoring techniques. Much more frequently than now used should be essay or expository questions which require students to organize material and give reasons for their answers. The effect of various types of tests upon the study which precedes the test is also a factor to be considered. In an experiment with college students, Meyer [60] told previously equated groups to study for *one* of the following types of tests: true-false, completion, multiple-choice, and essay. After study periods of like duration, all of the groups were given *all four* types of examinations. The group which had prepared for the essay test earned better scores on *all* types of tests. Students who had prepared for a completion test made the next highest scores on all tests, and the students who had prepared for true-false and multiple-choice tests scored about the same, and were below both the other groups.

What are the characteristics of tests and test items which give rise to learning? A study of the effect of test items on later performance with similar items showed that items which have a high learning value are: (1) high in arousing student interest, (2) those which pose a specific problem, (3) difficult enough to be a challenge, (4) applicational and practical, and (5) those which call for reasoning or judgment and not just for memorized facts. Tests should contain directions which not only tell the student *what* to do, but explain the reasons for doing it.[61]

Sequence of Activities. Perhaps the most common sequence of activities presently in use is that of—study—teaching—testing, with the first two frequently combined into one process. Generally a reading assignment precedes the study and teaching phase. Sometimes testing follows independent study. This sequence in many ways is contrary to psychological principles of learning. It provides little or no information about individuals prior to the assignment and teaching, and places too much emphasis upon the test as a ter-

[60] G. Meyer, "The Effect of Recall and Recognition of the Examination Set in Classroom Situation," *Journal of Educational Psychology*, Vol. 27, 1936, pp. 81–99.

[61] R. S. Jones, "Integration of Instructional With Self-Scoring Measuring Procedures," Unpublished Ph.D. Dissertation, Ohio State University, Columbus, Ohio, 1950.

minal point in the process. It makes the test the ultimate goal of learning (which it is not) and fails to provide adequate and optimally placed review.

It has been suggested [62] that work revolve around problems and that various skills and parts of the course lead to the solution of these problems. The sequence in this case might well begin with a joint planning session of an hour or so, or even several days, in which students and teacher developed over-all objectives. The individual and group work which follows should be pointed toward these objectives. In such cases testing would be only incidental to the major goal of action or problem solving, and the real testing would become an appraisal of performance—only a part of which would be based upon verbal skills.

No single sequence is appropriate for every case. Buswell points out two extremes which are psychologically undesirable. At one extreme, the subject matter sequence of instruction is so highly compartmentalized that few lateral relationships are seen. At the other, are "radical schools" which let the children decide the curriculum. Neither case results in a desirable coherency of material to be learned.

On the basis of present psychological principles, it would seem that the most desirable sequence of activities would be that which takes account of the individual learner and the eventual goals of the work, somewhat as follows:

Pretest	Assign-ments	Study	Evaluation	Relearning and Re-teaching	Retesting
(Diagnosis of Needs and Abilities)	(Including Pupil-Teacher Planning)	(Individual and Group Work)	(Quizzes, Recitation, Performance, Out-of-School Behavior, Self-Evaluation)	(Remedial Work in Area of Weakness)	(Evaluate the Re-teaching and Effects of Total Learnings)

The above schema is not one which should be rigidly followed but it does represent a series of steps which apply to many teaching-

---

[62] G. T. Buswell, "Organization and Sequence of the Curriculum," Chap. XIII in *The Psychology of Learning*, Part II, 41st Yearbook, National Society for the Study of Education, Public School Publishing Co., Bloomington, Illinois, 1942.

learning situations. In rare cases there may be no need for remedial teaching. Furthermore, some teachers may combine two or more of the steps in one general activity or process. For example, assignments may be made individually in connection with the development of the work indicated under the heading of "Study." It appears, however, that although there may be a merger of some of the above steps, the essential ingredients of each exist in all good teaching.

SUMMARY

This chapter has shown that what is learned is acquired more rapidly and retained longer when it has meaningfulness, structure, and interrelatedness—in short, possesses *organization*. Too often students are buried under an avalanche of unrelated or isolated facts—facts which do not appear to the learner to bear a relationship to any of his important goals or problems. Little wonder that forgetting takes place on a vast scale. It is not uncommon for students to forget two thirds to three fourths of what they learned within a year after a course is completed.

Teaching must take cognizance of the basic principles of organization if it is to produce permanent and usable learning. The implementation of the principles of organization requires that teachers: fit learning activities to what is known about perceptual organization; make instructional materials meaningful to pupils; plan for units of optimal size and scope; distribute learning activities intelligently; and elicit a good deal of student activity.

Young children respond to single objects and single ideas. That lying is bad is a dictum which has no exception for the youngster. As he grows older, his reactions to such concepts as honesty become more complex. Lying in these later stages may then be perceived in its relationships with character, empathy, and social sensitivity. The depth of understanding of ideas and of the degree of interrelationships between facts, probably depends more upon direct experience than upon any other factor—even "intelligence." It would thus appear that insofar as the development of concepts is a goal of education, it is highly essential that the school provide a good many different kinds of experiences.

One may see structure and organization at its best in problem-solving. No great deterioration of learning or drop in retention seems to result when learners engage in activities where the objective is to solve problems rather than to learn facts. Furthermore, increased ability to solve problems should help the student to think critically and creatively and to make better judgments. Problem-solving was shown to be a many-sided process which is capable of being learned. In essence, problem-solving to the teacher should mean helping students choose, study and solve problems through their own discovery in contrast to the popular notion that the teacher should give children "pat" solutions or steps to be memorized.

No one who considers the evidence regarding organization in learning should fail to see the many implications of this evidence for teaching method. Surely questions about how assignments are made, how reviews and tests are carried out, and how various activities are related to each other, must be raised in connection with what is known about the principles of organization. The appraisal of present practices shows that teaching method may be based upon conjecture or belief which, in many cases, is not supported by evidence. For example, such outmoded methods of assignment making as: "Read 30 pages and work problems 6 through 17" still persist in the face of overwhelming evidence against their use.

Finally, organization must be considered as it applies to the students' self-directed activities, particularly their methods of study. At the present time there seem to be all too few programs in which a conscious, well-planned effort is made to teach students how to study. One of the features which most clearly distinguishes good from the poor methods of study is the degree to which the pupil learns to plan ahead for his study. The disorganized pupil is the one who has not yet learned the value of making schedules, and of determining the goals and purposes of study before it begins. Ultimately, one who teaches must, if his influence is to persist, help children attain meaningful and purposeful solutions of their own problems.

REFERENCES FOR FURTHER STUDY

Burton, W. H., *The Guidance of Learning Activities*, New York, D. Appleton-Century Co., 1944, Chap. 18, pp. 449–478.

Duncker, Karl, "On Problem Solving," *Psychological Monographs*, Vol. 58, No. 5, 1945.

Giles, H. H., *Teacher-Pupil Planning*, New York, Harper and Brothers Publishers, 1941.

Guetzkow, Harold, "An Analysis of the Operation of Set in Problem Solving Behavior," *Journal of General Psychology,* Vol. 45, 1951, pp. 219–244.

Heidbreder, Edna, "The Attainment of Concepts," *Journal of General Psychology,* Vol. 35, 1946, pp. 173–223.

Horn, E., "Language and Meaning," Part II, 41st Yearbook, National Society for the Study of Education, *Psychology of Learning,* Bloomington, Ill., Public School Publishing Co., 1942.

Johnson, D. M., "A Modern Account of Problem Solving," *Psychological Bulletin,* Vol. 41, 1944, pp. 201–229.

Kingsley, H. L., *The Nature and Conditions of Learning,* Chap. VIII, "Relationship and Organization," New York, Prentice-Hall, Inc., 1946.

Kinney, Lucien, and Dresden, Katherine, *Better Learning through Current Materials,* Stanford University Press, 1952.

Lancelot, W. H., *Permanent Learning,* New York, John Wiley and Sons, Inc., 1944.

Long, L., and Welch, L., "Reasoning Ability in Young Children," *Journal of Psychology,* Vol. 12, 1941, pp. 21–44.

Maier, N. R. F., "Reasoning in Children," *Journal of Comparative Psychology,* Vol. 21, 1936, pp. 357–366.

Mossman, Lois C., *The Activity Concept,* New York, The Macmillan Co., 1939.

Mursell, James L., *Successful Teaching,* New York, The McGraw-Hill Book Co., Inc., 1946, Chaps. 11 and 15.

Robinson, F. P., *Effective Study,* New York, Harper & Brothers, 1946.

Simpson, Ray H., *Improving Teaching-Learning Processes,* New York, Longmans, Green and Co., 1953.

Vinacke, W. Edgar, *The Psychology of Thinking,* New York, McGraw-Hill Book Co., Inc., 1952, Chap. 9, "Problem Solving," and Chap. 15, "Attitudes."

Weaver, H. E., and Madden, E. H., " 'Direction' in Problem Solving," *Journal of Psychology,* Vol. 27, 1949, pp. 331–345.

Werner, H., "Process and Achievement, a Basic Problem of Education and Developmental Psychology," *Harvard Educational Review,* Vol. 7, 1937, pp. 353–368.

FILMS

How Effective Is Your Reading, Coronet Instructional Films, Coronet Bldg., Chicago 1, Illinois. (11 mins.)

How To Find the Answer—Mathematical Problem Solving, Coronet Instructional Films, Coronet Bldg., Chicago 1, Illinois. (11 mins.)

How To Remember, Coronet Instructional Films, Coronet Bldg., Chicago 1, Illinois. (11 mins.)

How To Study, Coronet Instructional Films, Coronet Bldg., Chicago 1, Illinois. (10 mins.)

How To Think, Coronet Instructional Films, Coronet Bldg., Chicago 1, Illinois. (14 mins.)

Chapter 10

The Transfer and Application
of Learning

TRANSFER—THE ULTIMATE GOAL OF TEACHING

THE ULTIMATE goal of teaching is to produce desirable changes in
behavior which will carry over into new situations. Teachers intend
training in English composition to produce better writing, mathematics to make pupils better able to solve problems, and civics to
lead to better citizenship. At first glance, the attainment of these
aims appears simply a matter of providing sufficient training so that
what is learned is remembered. But achievement of goals such as
these entails much more. Each new situation which confronts the
child contains elements of uniqueness, and requires him to use previous learnings in a new way. The child must not only be able to
remember, but also must be able to select from his experience those
responses which are appropriate in the learning of new and different
ideas and skills. When learning thus carries over into new situations,
the resulting improvement, or in some cases the interference which
is developed, is known as transfer of learning.

There can be little defense of schooling if it does not achieve
these results. Learning for the sake of learning alone is hardly defensible in a system of universal education. All of learning should,
of course, not be judged in terms of its "transfer value." Many skills
are learned for their own intrinsic worth, their immediate value in
the child's life, or for recreational purposes. In such cases proficiency
in relatively unchanging situations may be a legitimate goal of
teaching. However, it is impossible to predict for the pupil in exactly

241

what situations he will use the things he has learned. People who learned to drive automobiles fifteen years ago now have to make adjustments to a changed gear shift location, automatic drives, power steering, and the like. The farmer who once acquired skill in the use of horses has been forced to change to machinery, and the pilot who learned to fly by the feel of the plane has had to learn to use instruments.

The Meaning of Transfer in Teaching. Transfer of learning exists whenever a previous learning has influence upon the learning or performance of new responses. Thus anything which can be learned may be transferred. A simple case of transfer would be the following:

A pupil learns	$4 \times 9 = 36$
This should help him learn	$9 \times 4 = 36$
and	$40 \times 90 = 3600$

Still further removed would be the question of whether the student knowing the above arithmetic computations would be able to use them in long division or in algebra. These simple feats of transfer, which to the reader may appear as being close to identities are not always easy for the beginner. It has been found, for example, that many students who learn to do algebra problems involving x and y as unknowns may not be able to solve the same problems when a and b are used for unknowns. A specific check of the effect of changed symbols showed that 28 per cent of a group of college students were unable to square $b_1 + b_2$, but of the same group only 6 per cent failed to square $x + y$ correctly! [1]

The above examples of transfer are of a highly specific nature. Suppose a student comes to enjoy arithmetic greatly. Will such attitudes transfer to algebra and geometry? Or suppose the student learns to solve problems in geometry. Will he, as a consequence, be more likely to use the methods learned in solving other kinds of life problems? Immediately one sees that transfer of learning is inextricably bound up with the broader objectives of education. How well the schools are achieving these broader goals is considered in the next section.

Appraisal of Present School Practices. Most teaching is done with

[1] E. L. Thorndike, "The Effect of Changed Data upon Reasoning," *Journal of Experimental Psychology,* Vol. 5, 1922, pp. 33–38.

the implicit assumption that what is taught will be available for future use. But research has shown that this assumption is not always warranted. For one thing, the content of school subjects is all too often outmoded and unrelated to students' interests and needs or social usage. For instance, a recent analysis of spellers from grades 2 through 8 has shown that many are filled with spelling words typical of our grandparents' day—words that are rare and difficult and must be studied some years ahead of the infrequent times they will ever be used.[2] Surely analyses of this kind should convince teachers and educators that closer attention be paid to the relation between subject matter and the later use of learned materials.

Besides the lack of functionality, school subjects frequently fail to give proper emphasis to the relationships between various learned materials, or between learning and out-of-school life. As a consequence, students fail to see the relationship between learning and its later usefulness. When the papers (in courses other than English) of 261 college freshmen were analyzed, it was found that only twelve (5 per cent) submitted papers free of misspellings, and 14 per cent contained a number of incoherent sentences. More revealing than this, however, is the fact that when students were given their own papers and were asked to proofread them, they corrected over one-third of their own misspellings and over one-half their punctuation errors. According to Lange, who conducted this investigation, the majority of these students did not expect to be held to good standards of writing in a subject matter assignment. Even more serious is the fact that many of these freshmen not only admitted a lack of communication skills but expressed a fatalistic attitude and believed nothing could be done about it.[3]

The failure of students to see the relationship between English in English classes and English in other subjects or in general everyday usage can often be accounted for by the failure of teachers to make such relationships apparent and to hold students for the use of information acquired in other courses. One has but to examine texts in various subjects to see how infrequently relationships between material and their various applications are pointed out. It has

[2] Gertrude Hildreth, "An Evaluation of Spelling Word Lists and Vocabulary Studies," *Elementary School Journal*, Vol. 51, 1951, pp. 254–265.

[3] Phil C. Lange, "A Sampling of Composition Errors of College Freshmen in a Course other than English," *Journal of Educational Research*, Vol. 42, 1948, pp. 191–200.

been the writer's experience that students who complain about texts give as a most frequent reason the fact that books do not contain sufficient examples, or practical applications.

An appraisal of the results of inadequate teaching for transfer might be sought by asking: How much does learning in school carry over to later years? Enlightening in this respect is a study of over one thousand freshmen entering a large midwestern university. Sixteen per cent could not multiply $.65 \times 32.4$; 11 per cent could not add $2\frac{1}{3} + \frac{1}{7}$; 57 per cent could not express $\frac{7}{8}$ as a decimal fraction, and 38 per cent could not divide 1276.4 by 1000.[4] Deficiencies of this kind are not unique to mathematics, but occur in most other school subjects as well. College students who can barely read or whose spelling is almost indecipherable are not rare, and those who are unable to follow simple rules of grammar are commonplace.[5] Indeed there is evidence on every hand that there is far too little carry-over of school learning to out of school life—or to other school subjects for that matter. That this is a problem of long standing is illustrated by the following anecdote:

I was in a certain junior high school last week and the principal of the school told me the following story. One of the seventh grade pupils took the following problem home to her parents, "Find the product of .08 and ⅛." She came back to the teacher on the Monday following and reported that her father said that the problem could not be done, that it did not make sense. He had worked on it for over an hour and could not do it, so the following morning he took it to his employer, a man who had earned several million dollars in business ventures. The man toyed with the example for some time and asked to take it to a professor friend of his who taught Spanish at a college nearby. The professor could not do the example either, and returned it saying that as far as he was concerned it was ridiculous. The indignant parent sent a note with the youngster to the teacher asking why his seventh-grade daughter was getting work in mathematics which three intelligent adults could not fathom.[6]

Inadequacies in the effects of schooling upon students at all levels and in nearly all subjects are apparent. These inadequacies are not

[4] J. O. Hassler, "What Price Enrichment," *The Mathematics Teacher,* Vol. 34, 1941, pp. 243–247.

[5] S. L. Pressey and others, *Research Adventures in University Teaching,* Bloomington, Public School Publishing Company, 1927.

[6] C. O. Richter, "Readiness in Mathematics," *The Mathematics Teacher,* Vol. 37, 1944, p. 69.

of recent origin. Impermanence of learning, and lack of carry-over of schooling have always been problems of major importance in education.[7] The balance of this chapter will attempt to trace some of the causes of these problems and offer suggestions for their solution through the application of psychologically sound teaching methods.

Common Misconceptions about Transfer. There are a number of erroneous notions about how children's learning carries over to subsequent tasks, a common failure to clarify teaching objectives as they relate to transfer, and inadequate understanding of issues due to poorly defined terms. For example, mathematicians on the one hand defend geometry as a most excellent means of teaching reasoning—on the other hand they admit that there may be little carry-over of this ability to certain non-mathematical fields. Some experiments have found considerable transfer between foreign language study and English vocabulary, others have found little or no effect, and still others have found an actual decrease in understanding of English vocabulary after foreign language study.[8] As positive transfer is the main objective of teaching, it is essential that teachers avoid misconceptions and lay their teaching plans on a groundwork of good understanding of the ultimate purposes of instruction. Some common erroneous views about transfer of training will now be discussed.

The first and most common error in thinking about transfer is that it takes place through a process of "formal discipline." This outmoded idea of education was based on faculty psychology, a theory that separate elements or powers of the mind such as will, memory, and cognition were trained or sharpened by practice. In this view was the assumption that what was practiced was less important than the difficulty or disciplinary value of what was practiced. Also, there was the notion that learning should be somewhat "painful" if it were to achieve the best results. Thus the hard memory work in classical languages and difficult problems in mathematics and science were viewed as the most promising media for sharpening the mind. Instead of defending these subjects for their own intrinsic worth, teachers of classics, mathematics, and sciences frequently defended

[7] See "Then and Now Studies," Chapter 20.
[8] A. R. Mead, "Transfer of Training Again," *Journal of Educational Psychology,* Vol. 37, 1946, pp. 391–397.

them on the basis of their ability (better than other subjects) to improve the mind. Two comprehensive experimental studies which sought to test this hypothesis (that certain subjects or courses are best able to improve the mind) have found no evidence to support it. The first conducted by Thorndike [9] compared the gains in "thinking ability" made by students studying various combinations of subjects. His conclusion was that the subjects studied were of little apparent importance, especially when the influence of the subject was compared with the initial ability of the students. He believed that the apparent superiority of mathematics and science in producing good thinkers was an artifact caused by the fact that better students *take* these courses. If better students were to study vocational arts and social sciences, these subjects would *appear* to produce the best thinkers.

A more recent study (1945) similar to Thorndike's, but in some ways a better designed experiment, found almost identical results.[10] There was no clear-cut superiority for any particular school subject. Students who took the *most* courses made the greatest gains, and (as shown in Thorndike's work) the bright students made greater gains than the slow ones. Even though the idea of mental discipline has long since been discredited by dozens of experimental studies,[11] it is still a part of the thinking of some present-day educators and is still used as an argument to justify the inclusion of various subjects in the school curriculum. It is unfortunate that certain subjects such as geometry, Latin, and English grammar have most frequently been targets of attacks. There is little question that such subjects can be a rich source of learning for some pupils, and may be taught so that much that is learned transfers. On the other hand their defense on the basis of the discredited idea of disciplinary value may lead to unrealistic objectives and methods of teaching which are sterile. (The aforementioned subjects are not singled out as representative of this kind of non-functional teaching, for there is probably not a single subject in our schools which would escape this cen-

[9] E. L. Thorndike, "Mental Discipline in High School Studies," *Journal of Educational Psychology*, Vol. 15, 1924, pp. 1–22, 83–98.

[10] A. G. Wesman, "A Study of Transfer of Training from High School Subjects to Intelligence," *Journal of Educational Research*, Vol. 39, 1945, pp. 254–264.

[11] A. R. Mead, *op.cit.*, p. 394.

sure to some degree.) When courses are conceived in terms of the values of transfer and on the basis of their own intrinsic worth, there is a greater likelihood that they will be taught in a manner which will make them useful.

The second misconception is just the opposite of the first, and probably grew up as a reaction against it. This is the notion that nothing transfers from one situation to another except specific facts or definite identities. In the extreme, this point of view leads to a curriculum composed only of materials which are believed immediately useful. Transfer is minimized and subjects are all learned only for immediate values. What are the results of such a program? One author notes that special trade courses (as in the vocational-industrial curricula) may *not* prepare students to shift from one vocation to another or one job to another because students have never learned to see relationships or look for similarities among jobs.[12] These students are unable to adjust to the rapidly changing industrial scene brought about by technological advances.

If this idea of transfer (that is thinking of transfer in its narrowest sense) were followed, education would become largely rote memorization and skill training—a process almost devoid of understanding, generalization, and problem solving.

A third error which emasculates the effect of teaching nearly as much as the first two, is the notion that transfer of learning is automatic. This view puts the main burden of achieving transfer upon the curriculum builder and neglects the important contribution of teaching method. The arrangement of subject matter into related sequences, plans for common learnings or core curricula, and other curricular plans do not guarantee that children will see relationships apparent to the adults who plan the program. (It is certainly true, of course, that such curricular plans may make more likely the teaching for transfer which is so important a function of school.) It has been noted, for example, that even training which appears most excellent may fail to transfer. In one author's words, "Undoubtedly work experiences may constitute the ideal environment for the development of good working habits; but to postulate that simply by

[12] F. T. Spaulding, *High School and Life,* Report of the Regents' Inquiry Into the Character and Cost of Public Education in the State of New York, New York, McGraw-Hill Book Company, Inc., 1939.

doing part-time work, a pupil will automatically acquire certain general traits associated with good workers is to indulge in wishful thinking." [13]

The acquisition of information does not guarantee its utility. Most teachers have experienced the disappointment of seeing pupils learn in school but later fail to apply information in situations which call for its use. A well-worn story in educational circles tells of three college professors who were building a cabin in the north woods, and were unable to start with a square corner because they did not have a square. While they were trying to solve this problem, a farmer riding by, stopped, and when told the difficulty suggested that they measure three feet along one side, four feet along the other, and if the distance diagonally across the points measured on the sides was five feet, they would have a square corner. All the professors of course were familiar with the Pythagorean theorem, yet were unable to apply it in a practical way. The reader might pause at this point and consider ways in which this theorem could have been taught in the first place so that it would have been more likely to have been recalled under these circumstances.

Finally, the emphasis which books about learning and psychology have given to the topic of transfer has tended to create the impression that somehow transfer and learning are different. Actually transfer is a part of the learning process. There is indeed such a thing as learning to learn,[14] learning how to secure transfer, and learning how to work. There is no learning which does not involve a part of a person's past experience, and in a sense all retention or remembering is a kind of transfer, because original circumstances of learning are rarely, if ever, duplicated in a new situation. Children should learn to expect change—to have the experience of applying even the simplest learnings in a number of different situations. As it is, many times drill precedes understanding and then teachers attempt to teach transfer as a separate step—something different from the initial learning. Actually learning and transfer are best produced when the learning situation all the way through most closely simulates the way in which ideas and behaviors will be used.

[13] T. E. Christensen, "Work Experience and Transfer of Training," *School Review*, Vol. 53, 1945, p. 589.

[14] For a theoretical discussion of this point, see J. A. McGeoch and A. L. Irion, *The Psychology of Human Learning*, New York, Longmans, Green and Company, 1952, pp. 306–309.

HOW DOES TRANSFER TAKE PLACE?

The most obvious form of transfer is that in which an identity carries over from one situation to another. The following are examples:

Transfer of an identity when a single response is appropriate to two stimuli:

Stimulus₁ "Casa" (in Spanish)
Stimulus₂ "Casa" (in Portuguese) → Response—House

Negative transfer or interference when one stimulus requires two different responses:

Stimulus "Mas" → Response 1 (Portuguese) But
Stimulus "Mas" → Response 2 (Spanish) More

This kind of transfer which is a result of stimulus similarity (or identities between two stimuli) was first treated systematically by Thorndike,[15] whose theory held that a function is changed by another only insofar as the two functions have identical or common elements of substance or procedure. Thorndike and his co-worker Woodworth began a series of investigations of the problem of transfer at the beginning of the century. They tested persons in one function, such as estimating the size of geometric figures, then gave practice in another function, such as estimating areas of a quite different magnitude. Finally, they retested them in the first function to see how much improvement was brought about by the intervening practice. They found that the amount of improvement in estimating size was inversely proportional to the degree of change in size and/or shape between the function initially tested, and that which was practiced. They concluded that practice did not lead to a general change in such things as discrimination, attention, quickness, and the like, but that it improved these functions with respect to particular sorts of data.[16]

[15] E. L. Thorndike, *The Principles of Teaching*, New York, A. G. Seiler, 1906.
[16] E. L. Thorndike and R. S. Woodworth, "The Influence of Improvement in One Mental Function upon the Efficiency of Other Functions," *Psychological Review*, Vol. 8, 1901, pp. 247–261; 384–395; 553–564.

Stimulus Generalization. One may see quite clearly in the previous example how an identity transfers (with negative or positive effect) from one situation to another. In this case the only change is in the situation. But how about the case when the actual stimuli themselves are markedly changed?

One term applied to this kind of transfer is *stimulus generalization.* The young child who learns "dada," at first calls all men "dada." He says ball for his own particular ball and later applies this term to numerous other elastic objects regardless of changes in color, shape, and size. Stimulus generalization is not limited to the development of young children. Numerous studies have shown the same phenomenon in older children and adults.

A child who has become conditioned to fear one reading book, or one text, may show similar reactions when confronted with other books or texts. Likewise the dislike of one teacher may transfer to another teacher in a different classroom. In such cases youngsters overgeneralize from specific cases. They have not learned to make necessary discriminations.

From a single incident in the schoolroom, laboratory or playground, a student may find a starting point for either aversion toward or liking of school. The attitudes which are then built may be quite general and all encompassing, so that if they are negative he will actually resist the teacher and if positive will endure many circumstances which would otherwise be odious or boring. The following case will illustrate how a single experience may cause a general change or transfer in attitudes.

In the high school biology class, Jerry was found by a sociometric test to be an isolate, and he had indicated a strong dislike for school and everything connected with it. During the first month of school he did little work for the class and showed no interest in the subject of biology or in other students.

There were some hamsters in the laboratory cages and when one of them became ill, Jerry began coming into the laboratory before school to see how it was getting along. He asked questions about the care and feeding of the animals and the teacher gave him some pamphlets which explained their habits. His interest in the hamsters increased; he was, upon his own request, given the job of feeding the animals and cleaning their cages. From his interest in one phase of the course, Jerry's attitude toward the whole subject seemed to change and his class work improved generally. *There was also a marked difference in his responses in other courses,* and in his attitudes toward other students. At the end of the school year, even though he had been failing in the early work of the semester, his work was acceptable; he had formed several friendships; and he told the biology teacher that he was looking forward to the next school year.

Transfer of Principles. Closely akin to stimulus generalization is the transfer of a general principle from one situation to another. Even before children are aware of it, they begin to generalize or make rules which they apply in several situations. Without ever being told a rule, they learn the generalization that most words form plurals by adding "s," hence "mouses" and "feets" are not uncommon in the speech of young children. Also the fact that "ed" makes the past tense of verbs, leads to such verbs as "runned" and "doed."

One of the earliest experiments (1907) which showed how principles could influence subsequent behavior was that of Judd, who used the principle of refraction of light when it travels from one medium into another.[17] One group of boys was taught this principle, while a second group received no such instruction. Both groups were then given a trial in shooting bows and arrows at underwater targets. Although both groups did equally well when the targets were at a fixed depth, the instructed group excelled the other when the targets were moved to a new depth. The learning of the principle had made them more adaptable under changed conditions.[18] More recently a similar experiment (using air-rifles instead of bows and arrows) obtained like results.[19]

What are the implications of this kind of transfer for teachers? Clearly a general principle has much broader possibilities for use than detailed facts. Also, as shown in the previous chapter, these kinds of learning are more enduring. It would seem then that a major emphasis of schooling should be upon principles and their use in a number of situations, rather than upon memorization of such details as may be quickly forgotten.

[17] When a beam of light passes obliquely from one medium into another it is usually bent at the surface separating the two.
[18] C. H. Judd, "The Relation of Special Training to General Intelligence," *Educational Review,* Vol. 36, 1908, pp. 28–42.
[19] G. Hendrickson and W. H. Schroeder, "Transfer of Training in Learning to Hit a Submerged Target," *Journal of Educational Psychology,* Vol. 32, 1941, pp. 205–213.

Transfer of Set. The way in which a person perceives a new situation is a function of previous perceptual learning. He has a certain expectation or expectations which condition the way he sees a situation and the way he responds to it.

The effect of set has been demonstrated as follows. One group of 80 subjects was told that most of the words in a word list they were to see would be the names of animals and birds—another group of equal size was told that the words had reference to travel or transportation. The following words and pseudo words were then projected tachistoscopically for both groups.

Word List

1. horse
2. baggage
3. chack
4. sael
5. whorl
6. monkey
7. parrot
8. berth
9. dack
10. pengion

The group which had been led to expect names of animals and birds gave 513 "animal-bird" responses such as "seal" for item Number 4 and "duck" for Number 9, while the other group gave only 112 such responses. On the other hand, the group which anticipated items dealing with travel and transportation responded more often (594 to 84) with such terms as "sail" for Number 4, and "dock" for Number 9. Only 4 per cent of the total responses to "unreal" words were seen as what they actually were.

Sometime later, the groups described above were tested with a new kind of list in an attempt to find out if the previously established set would transfer to a new situation. The list (a series of skeleton words), and the expected responses were as follows:

Skeleton Words	Expected Animal-Bird Responses	Expected Travel-Transportation Responses
_ oat	goat	boat
s _ _ l	seal	sail
_ _ _ sel	weasel	vessel

When the groups were compared, the first one, which had been given an "animal-bird" set gave three times as many "animal-bird" responses as the second group, while the second group completed the skeleton words with "travel-transportation" responses four times as often as the first group. Clearly, the kind of set which had been given in the first instruction was an important determiner of responses, and did carry over or transfer even under altered conditions.[20]

How transfer of set may operate in such complex processes as working problems was shown in an experiment conducted by Luchins.[21] Subjects were given a series of problems such as: You have three vessels with capacities as follows, 21 pints, 127 pints, 3 pints. Show how you would obtain 100 pints of water. The problems were given in this form:

$$A = 21 \quad B = 127 \quad C = 3 \quad \text{Obtain } 100$$

The method of solving this problem is B − A − 2C or, 127 − 21 − 6 = 100. A series of six such problems were given, all of which could be solved with the formula B − A − 2C. Then followed the seventh and eighth problems:

	A	B	C	Obtain
7th Problem	23	49	3	20
8th Problem	15	39	3	18

These could be solved either by the same formula as used in the first six problems *or* by the much simpler means of subtracting C from A or adding C to A. Of eleven graduate students and college instructors, including several Ph.D.'s, not one used the shorter method. They had formed what Luchins calls an *"Einstellung"*— a set, which interfered with the easiest solution, and which carried over to new problems. Perhaps the significant thing for school teachers to know about this experiment is that on further experimentation it was found that the simple injunction, "Don't be blind," served to prevent the formation of this set in many of the cases. In other words, there is evidence here (also from other laboratory work) that a simple direction outlining possible difficulties or alerting students to correct expectations may facilitate the discovery of the correct solution to problems.

Transfer of Method. Students who have received practice and guidance in methods of work and study report that such training in one course helps them in other courses. Research dealing with both

[20] E. M. Sipola, "A Study of Some Effects of Preparatory Set," *Psychological Monographs,* Vol. 46, 1935, pp. 28–37.

[21] A. S. Luchins, "Mechanization in Problem Solving: The Effect of Einstellung," *Psychological Monographs,* Vol. 54, No. 248, 1942, pp. 1–4.

elementary and high school pupils showed that time spent in training children how to outline was rewarded with gains in achievement not only in the specific subject in which training was given but also in other subjects as well.[22] Any kind of "how to study" course is predicated on the belief that such training will generalize or transfer to other course material.

As early as 1915 Coover [23] spoke of habits of work and the control of attention as processes which could transfer from one situation to another and since that time numerous research studies have supported this belief.[24] A study which may illustrate how methods transfer was one in which an attempt was made to teach students how to memorize. Three groups of students were given six pretests of memorization. Following the initial testing the groups were treated as follows:

> Group A . . . . . No Training (Control)
> Group B . . . . . Routine Practice in Memorizing
> Group C . . . . . Practice in Memorizing *plus* Instruction
> in the Techniques of Memorizing

Later tests of memorization showed that Group C was clearly superior to the other groups. Practice alone (as Group B had) was not enough to bring a significant improvement.[25]

The pupil who learns a skill in one context should be able to apply it in many contexts. Thus a pupil who has learned in his English class the skills of outlining, note taking, reading, and participation in class discussion should be able to use these proficiencies in all of his courses. These skills are more apt to become generalized when:

1. The teacher uses examples from various subjects and materials as vehicles for the illustration and practice of methods and skills. (The English teacher might ask a student to use his history notes as material to be outlined.)

[22] Rachel Salisbury, "Some Effects of Training in Outlining," *The English Journal* (College Edition), Vol. 24, 1935, pp. 111–116; M. N. Woodring and C. W. Flemming, *Directing Study of High School Pupils*, New York, Columbia University, Teachers College, 1935.

[23] J. E. Coover, "Formal Discipline from the Standpoint of Experimental Psychology," *Psychological Monographs*, Vol. 20, 1916, No. 87.

[24] See J. A. McGeoch and A. L. Irion, *op.cit.*, pp. 330–332.

[25] H. Woodrow, "The Effect of Type of Training Upon Transference," *Journal of Educational Psychology*, Vol. 18, 1927, pp. 159–172.

2. Students are asked (or ask each other) to explain why one method or skill is better than another. In other words, students are led to understand the rationale for various methods of work and study.
3. The class as a whole, with the teacher's guidance, develops criteria for appraising various methods and skills.
4. "Situational tests," which call for application of methods, give direction to students' work and bring more attention to method than tests which deal with facts. A part of the testing program might well involve exercises in which students were asked to point out relationships between solving a problem in geometry and one in social science or physics.
5. Teachers work together toward this important common goal. The English teacher should work with others to determine whether writing skills show improvement in classes other than English.

Transfer of Attitudes. A complex form of carry over from previous experiences is the effect of previously formed attitudes upon new learning. The child who has had unpleasant emotional experiences in an English class will not approach the next class in English with the same attitudes as one whose experiences have been gratifying.

This kind of transfer is a special case of transfer of set or expectancy, but in this case perception of *self* plays an important part. Two children of equal mental potential may differ greatly in their ability to solve problems because one has self-confidence and aggressiveness, the other is shy and has a tendency to withdraw from difficult problems. Obviously their previous experiences with work and problems have conditioned the way in which they perform. Children carry to new problems not only skills, principles, and knowledge, but also attitudes and personality traits. These are truly transferable elements and among the most important.

An indirect but neat piece of evidence on how attitudes transfer may be seen in the results of a test in which directions are given not to guess. When this is done, a large part of the measurement is not of knowledge alone, but of personality traits. Students who have had a good share of success and have self-confidence are apt to leave many fewer blank spaces on their answer sheets than those whose experiences with tests, and with problems in general have been marked by a lack of success.

Since a person's attitude about himself (his self-concept) is quite apt to become over-generalized, it is extremely important that youngsters obtain ideas of positive self-reference—that they see difficulties as problems to be solved rather than troubles which call for retreat. Such attitudes are products of successful and gratifying learning experiences. Insofar as such experiences are within the control of the teacher, pupils should receive due praise for their achievement especially when they solve problems under their own initiative.

TEACHING FOR TRANSFER

Good teaching always involves teaching for transfer. It is another way of saying that good teachers have a definite objective of making learned material a functioning part of the youngster's response system. It is thus essential that teachers think through their own subject matter and study the generalizations, relationships, and methods which may transfer. The extent to which students learn *how* to transfer will depend on how well teachers can lead students to see the similarities between the subject matter and its applications.

Following is a list of suggestions which should form the basis of teaching for transfer:

1. Have clear-cut objectives. Decide what students should be able to *do* as a result of their work.
2. Study the course content to find what it contains that is applicable to other school subjects and to out-of-school life.
3. Select instructional materials which are best suited to the job of making relationships apparent.
4. Let students know when to expect transfer, what kinds to expect, and the benefits which it can bring them.
5. Use methods of teaching (e.g., problem solving, discussion, leading questions) which will facilitate transfer.
6. Provide practice in transfer. It is not enough to point out relationships. Pupils should be given practice in finding relationships on their own. Tests of application, guided discussion and actual class projects ought to provide this kind of experience.
7. Concentrate on the process of learning as well as upon products. Do not be satisfied with a right answer or solution, but probe to find out why a certain answer was given, and discuss with the class the steps which led to their answers.

Setting the Stage for Transfer. Sometimes opportunities for transfer are lost because teachers do not alert students to look for relationships and to see how material which is being learned can be of future usefulness. One study has shown that the simple expedient of telling students that previous learning might be helpful in other situations increased the amount of measured transfer as much as 16 per cent.[26]

It has also been noted that the kind of test directions which are given may significantly affect the amount of learning and transfer which occurs. One group of students in educational psychology was given a short multiple-choice practice test with the directions "See how the principles involved in these questions might apply in various teaching situations." Another group took the same test without these directions. Both groups made equivalent scores on this first test. Later, the groups were given a second multiple-choice test which called for applications of the principles contained in the previous test. The group which had received the directions made significantly better scores, even though the tests, testing procedures and discussions following the tests were almost identical.[27]

In the last chapter it was shown that the way in which assignments are developed probably has a great influence upon the kind of studying which students do. Teachers who help pupils develop specific questions prior to a reading assignment can expect not only better results in the sections of the reading covered by the questions, but also a transfer of this "seeking-while-reading" activity to other sections of the assignment.

Teaching Method and Transfer. Teachers who stress understanding are apt to stimulate learning of a useful and enduring nature. On the other hand, emphasis upon facts and memorization of rules and procedures which are not fully understood by pupils, is apt to result in a superficial lip service which has neither permanence nor utility. A study of the learning of mathematics of three thousand pupils reveals that youngsters learn what teachers stress as important in the classroom. The school which glorifies abstract computation in mathematics is apt to produce pupils who excel in this respect, but who may or may not understand what they are doing or be able to use the computations in changing situations. The author of

[26] M. W. Dorsey and L. T. Hopkins, "The Influence of Attitude Upon Transfer," *Journal of Educational Psychology*, Vol. 21, 1930, pp. 410–417.
[27] R. S. Jones, *Integration of Instructional with Self-Scoring Measuring Procedures*, Unpublished Ph.D. Dissertation, Ohio State University, Columbus, Ohio, 1950.

the study just cited concludes that too great a dependence upon formalized paper and pencil problems robs the student of many of the opportunities for transfer which exist in other kinds of mathematical experiences.[28]

In those instances where teaching is specifically designed to emphasize transfer by stressing applications, relationships, and methods, the amount of understanding and usable knowledge increases. Dozens of experimental studies bear out this conclusion.[29] In studies of the transfer value of foreign languages, for example, it has been discovered that the greatest effect on English vocabulary occurs when relationships between English words and their Latin, French or Spanish roots are shown as a planned part of the teaching procedure. A comparison of four methods of teaching to improve English vocabulary resulted in greater gains for the groups who learned English with word study, or Latin with a study of derivatives, than for the groups taught English and Latin in the conventional manner.[30]

Recent experiments have indicated that the way in which a child learns a generalization will affect the probability of his recognizing a chance to use it. As Hendrix [31] has shown, "persons who know that six times eight is forty-eight, will often count to forty-eight to find the number of chairs in a room containing six rows of eight chairs each." The question of how best to teach a generalization is of utmost importance to the teacher. Evidence shows that one important element may be discovery. One investigator compared methods in which the teacher gave the class a mathematical generalization and then gave several examples of application with methods in which the generalization was a product of the student's own discovery. The latter method proved much more effective in producing trans-

[28] B. A. Sueltz, "Mathematical Understandings and Judgments Retained by College Freshmen," *The Mathematics Teacher*, Vol. 44, 1951, pp. 13–19.

[29] A. R. Mead, *op.cit.*, pp. 394–397; and T. G. Andrews, L. J. Cronbach and Peter Sandiford, "Transfer of Training," in W. S. Monroe (Ed.) *Encyclopedia of Educational Research*, New York, The Macmillan Company, 1950, pp. 1483–1489.

[30] R. I. Haskell, *A Statistical Study of the Comparative Results Produced by Teaching Derivation in the Ninth-Grade Latin Classes and in the Ninth-Grade English Classes of Non-Latin Pupils in Four Philadelphia High Schools*, Ph.D. Thesis, University of Pennsylvania, 1923.

[31] G. Hendrix, "A New Clue to Transfer of Training," *The Elementary School Journal*, Vol. 48, 1947, pp. 197–208.

fer.[32] The reader will recall Luchins'[33] method of teaching geometric area to youngsters. In this investigation pupils derived their
own principles and formulae and gave evidence of a great deal more
understanding than those taught in the usual way. Presumably this
understanding makes much more likely the recognition of opportunities to use information or to adapt it to new situations.

Students actually resent too much supervision.[34] They believe
that it interferes with learning, and there is considerable support
for this belief. It is only natural that teachers should want to help
children—but in the very act of helping they may actually be rob-
bing them of the chance to learn how to solve problems and use information. The learning of a generalization or principle is not complete until pupils have had a chance to practice or use it on their
own. The following description of a geometry teacher's method is
an excellent illustration of how student discovery may be facilitated. At the same time this illustration shows how practice in transfer which is so essential to real understanding may be given.

One of the goals of this teacher's learning experiment was to use geometry as a medium for improving critical thinking. A phase of this involved the study of the criteria of a good definition, and the importance of
such definitions. This study resulted in a marked improvement of definitions in geometry. Not content to wait for this skill to transfer to other
areas (or to assume that it would be automatic), this instructor created
several situations which allowed students to practice their new found
skills. First he asked if rules for good definitions would apply to other
subjects besides geometry. To illustrate the point, he brought to class a
newspaper clipping entitled "Urges Frat Members in Shaker (a city) Be
Barred from Pupil Activities." A lively discussion ensued. In it several
students soon realized that what the school superintendent should do in
the case covered by the newspaper clipping could only be resolved after
he defined what was meant by the phrase "member of a fraternity."

Each member of the class then wrote what he considered a good definition. The results were these:

   12 students wrote: "anyone who belongs to a club which is secret or
                             exclusive"

[32] *Ibid.*

[33] A. S. Luchins and Edith H. Luchins, "A Structural Approach to the Teaching of the Concept of Area in Intuitive Geometry," *Journal of Educational Research*, Vol. 40, 1947, pp. 528–533.

[34] D. H. Fryer and H. A. Edgerton, "Off-the-Job Training," *Personnel Psychology*, Vol. 3, 1950, pp. 261–284.

6 students wrote: "anyone who belongs to a club or society characterized by Greek letters in the name"

5 students wrote: "anyone who is associated with a wild group of boys avoiding adult supervision"

3 students wrote: "anyone who belongs to a social group which just meets at each others' houses to spend the evening playing games and things like that"

3 students wrote: "anyone who belongs to a club which has a name and whose members wear special insignia"

After the definitions were grouped and read back to the class, the students could easily see that the superintendent involved in this school issue would act differently depending upon the kind of definition which he accepted.

This was but one in a series of such experiences which were planned in this particular geometry course, and the results supported the thesis that proper teaching methods can increase transfer and understanding beyond that which generally occurs in such courses. After the course was over, students themselves, parents, and other teachers said that they believed there had been an improvement in critical thinking, reasoning, and objectivity and fairness. Various tests administered during the semester supported these beliefs.[35]

SUMMARY

Transfer of learning is not a new idea to most persons who read this book. It must have occurred to everyone who has given serious thought to teaching, that ultimately classwork is designed to equip pupils to solve effectively the problems of living and to make them happier and more effective citizens. These goals are apparent.

Too often, however, teachers and pupils alike neglect to think through the significance of present activities in terms of future usefulness or applicability. One reason for this is that, although everyone shares the above stated desires about transfer, attempts to reach it are blocked by common, erroneous notions about it. Some of these erroneous notions are: (1) that training *per se* strengthens an ability, (2) that only that which is immediately useful should be taught, (3) that transfer is automatic, in other words, that once a child learns, the learning will lead to transfer, and (4) that transfer and learning are separable elements.

[35] K. B. Henderson, *An Experiment in Teaching Solid Geometry to Provide Training in Thinking*, Unpublished Ph.D. Dissertation, Ohio State University, Columbus, Ohio, 1946.

Transfer may occur when there is a similarity between two activities either in substance or procedure. Anything which can be learned can be transferred including such things as attitudes, a feeling of self-confidence, sets, and interests, as well as skills, facts, and other items generally thought of as constituting school work. Transfer may be quite specific, as when elements of one learning situation occur in identical or similar form in another. In such cases the effects may be either positive or negative, that is, a previous learning may either facilitate a new learning, or may cause interference. Also transfer may be general, in that a given learning such as a principle, a set, or method has influence upon any number of later learning situations.

Teaching for transfer requires that the objectives of schooling be clearly defined, that teachers study content and method to find interrelationships among materials and the applicability to other situations of learned skills, and that the teaching method be such that students are given practice in transfer. Children should learn to expect to see a relationship between present learning and future situations. They should also learn not only to search for such relationships, but also to probe into problems to find reasons for the facts and principles which they are asked to believe. Out of the habit of critical appraisal youngsters will develop the ability to bring past experiences to bear upon new problems and new learning situations.

REFERENCES FOR FURTHER STUDY

Andrews, T. G., Cronbach, L. J., and Sandiford, Peter, "Transfer of Training," in Monroe, W. S. (Ed.), *Encyclopedia of Educational Research*, New York, The Macmillan Co., 1950, pp. 1483–1489.

Barlow, M. C., "Transfer of Training in Reasoning," *Journal of Educational Psychology*, Vol. 28, 1937, pp. 122–128.

Foster, R. G., and Wilson, P. P., *Women after College*, New York, Columbia University Press, 1942.

Kingsley, H. L., *The Nature and Conditions of Learning*, New York, Prentice-Hall, Inc., 1946, Chap. XIX.

Orata, P. T., "Recent Research Studies on Transfer of Training with Implications for the Curriculum, Guidance, and Personnel Work," *Journal of Educational Research*, Vol. 35, 1941, pp. 81–101.

Pressey, S. L., and Robinson, F. P., "Applicational Transfer," *Psychology and the New Education*, New York, Harper & Brothers, 1944, Chap. 18.

Norem, G. M., *Transfer of Training Experiments Revalued,* University of Iowa Studies in Education, No. 6, Vol. VIII, 1933, pp. 3–35.

Stroud, J. B., *Psychology in Education,* New York, Longmans, Green and Co., 1946, pp. 555–597.

Webb, L. W., "Transfer of Learning," in Skinner, C. E. (Ed.), *Educational Psychology,* New York, Prentice-Hall, Inc., 1951, pp. 522–548.

Chapter 11

The Social Psychology of Learning and Teaching

Teachers probably spend about 90 per cent of their classroom time working with groups. Yet, traditionally, little if any of their formal training is devoted to the understanding of groups. In this area, sometimes called group dynamics, there is probably more discrepancy between the requirements of the teacher's work and his training than in any other. The social psychologist who studies the nature and operation of groups has much to offer the teacher, for he has formulated laws and principles about human relationships, group interactions, and their products.[1] The findings of social psychology (and related experimental applications in the classroom) are crucial for the school which wishes to promote efficiency, happiness, and adjustment of pupils. Teachers must learn the principles and techniques which help in discovering and controlling social interaction and social influences within the classroom. This chapter will present a view of principles and research which bear upon this subject.

THE IMPORTANCE OF SOCIAL-EMOTIONAL FACTORS IN SCHOOLING

An intensive study of a single boy's day from the time he got up in the morning until he went to bed at night showed that about a fourth of the 712 episodes in his day occurred in the classroom. Of these 166 schoolroom episodes, 70 per cent were marked by an inter-

[1] Muzafer Sherif, *An Outline of Social Psychology*, New York, Harper and Brothers, 1948, p. 1.

263

action in some way with one or more persons.[2] Clearly an overwhelming amount of a child's total school experience involves social contacts with other pupils. One also finds maladjustment, school failure, and unhappiness closely allied to social difficulties. A major factor causing children to drop out of school is that many are unable to achieve a feeling of belonging to the group.[3] Still further evidence of the importance of social factors in schooling may be found in an appraisal of maladjusted students. In one such appraisal, the investigators found that the single major cause of students' difficulties was lack of social acceptance.[4]

One direct way to see the importance of social factors in schooling is to place in juxtaposition two very different classrooms. Such a "profile" is shown below: [5]

A Profile of Two Classrooms

Miss A_____ was rated as having excellent rapport with pupils. The observers' ratings of central characteristics of the lessons conducted by Miss A_____ stressed: (a) the democratic approach in conducting the lessons with several committees of pupils working on specific problems or projects; (b) the teacher's understanding of pupils and her adaptation of the lesson materials to their abilities and needs; (c) the warm quality of social interaction or rapport between the teacher and pupils; and (d) the poise and apparent emotionally mature personality of the teacher. The observers' ratings of more specific character-

Miss B_____ was rated as having below median rapport with pupils. The observers' ratings of the central characteristics of the lessons conducted by Miss B_____ stressed: (a) the evidence of a lesson planned in detail by the teacher and followed with few significant deviations; (b) the generally formal approach in asking questions and obtaining information from members of the class; (c) the teacher's mastery of subject matter and information related to the topic of the lesson; and (d) the slightly strained emotional atmosphere, or nervousness of the teacher.

The ratings of more specific

[2] H. F. Wright, R. G. Barker, Jack Nall, and Phil Schoggen, "Toward a Psychological Ecology of the Classroom," *Journal of Educational Research*, Vol. 45, 1951, pp. 187–200.

[3] J. A. Lanier, "A Guidance-Faculty Study of Student Withdrawals," *Journal of Educational Research*, Vol. 43, 1949, pp. 205–212.

[4] S. D. Loomis and A. W. Green, "The Pattern of Mental Conflict in A Typical State University," *Journal of Abnormal and Social Psychology*, Vol. 42, 1947, pp. 342–355.

[5] J. W. Wrightstone, "Measuring the Social Climate of A Classroom," *Journal of Educational Research*, Vol. 44, 1951, pp. 341–351.

istics were: (a) cooperation and participation of the pupils were elicited in the initial planning of the lesson; (b) the clear definition of the pupils' role permitted the committee work to progress smoothly; (c) the mildly relaxed atmosphere of the pupil groups helped pupils to adjust to their work; and (d) the sensitivity of the teacher to group needs was evident as she moved from group to group.

characteristics were: (a) a detailed lesson plan and specific questions asked revealed a teacher-centered classroom; (b) infrequent pupil interaction was revealed in the class questioning or discussion; (c) definite teacher control of the class discussion produced a businesslike atmosphere in the class group; (d) a tendency toward orders rather than suggestions was used as a means of class control; and (e) a slightly tense attitude of pupils was revealed by frequent glances in the direction of the observer.

The more permissive, student-centered type of classroom has been contrasted with the more rigid, directive, teacher-centered classroom, and the former characterized as having, "more interest, humor, student participation, student-instructor interaction and commending." [6] Some psychologists have contrasted class groups as dominative versus integrative—others as autocratic versus democratic. In any case, there is overwhelming evidence to show that the social climate, or atmosphere for learning of various classrooms differs greatly. In following sections of this chapter, it is the intention to show how teacher-pupil relationships, interrelationships among pupils, the school's staff relationships and other factors determine the social climate of the school, and how these factors influence learning.

TEACHER-PUPIL RELATIONSHIPS

A first factor of major importance in shaping the social climate of the school is the kind of relationships which exist between pupils and teachers. Students are sensitive to teachers' personalities and methods. Critical statements, threats and sarcasm, for example, create almost immediate change in emotional tension within the classroom. Dramatic illustration of the effect of the teacher's techniques was demonstrated in a series of experiments in teaching at the University of Chicago. Children's reactions were measured by equip-

[6] L. G. Wispe, "Evaluating Section Teaching Methods in the Introductory Course," *Journal of Educational Research*, Vol. 45, 1951, pp. 161–186.

ping them with instruments which recorded their heart beat and palmar skin resistance (measures from which emotional tension is inferred). Under such conditions there was a distinct relationship between measured anxiety and teacher's methods of dealing with students.[7] Under pressure (as existed in teacher-centered situations) students recollected:

> I felt under pressure to adjust to the demands of the teacher.
> I felt the teacher was trying to make me hurry too much.
> I felt the teacher was sarcastic.

Under the low pressure of the learner-centered situations, their comments were of this sort:

> I thought the teacher did his best to make me feel at ease.
> I felt no resentment when the teacher gave me directions.
> I felt that the teacher made sure that I was satisfied.[8]

The effect which teachers may have upon a class over a period of time was illustrated by an intensive study [9] and comparison of the characteristics of second grade children in the classes of two quite different teachers. One was a dominative teacher who more frequently than the other met aggression with aggression and "initiated" contacts with pupils rather than encouraging them to seek contacts with her. The other teacher, who was described by the investigators as "integrative," gave more friendly guidance, and encouraged pupils to join in class activities. At the end of a year there were fourteen statistically significant differences in behavior between the two classes, even though they were comparable in ability and background at the start of the first semester. These differences included such things as more voluntary suggestions, social contributions and responsiveness in the integrative classroom. Teachers who dominate one class seem to retain this characteristic with other classes. Also it should be noted that the amount of conflict between pupils and dominative teachers does not seem to decline as the

[7] N. A. Flanders, "Personal-Social Anxiety as a Factor in Experimental Learning Situations," *Journal of Educational Research*, Vol. 45, 1951, pp. 100–110.

[8] *Ibid.*, p. 103.

[9] H. H. Anderson and J. E. Brewer, "Studies of Teachers' Classroom Personalities II (Effects of Teachers' Dominative and Integrative Contacts on Children's Classroom Behavior)," *Applied Psychological Monographs*, No. 8, American Psychological Association, Stanford University Press, June, 1946.

months of a semester pass. In fact conflict may increase. Even though teachers do not seem to change much semester after semester, it is fortunate that pupils do. When youngsters go from a dominative to an integrative classroom they tend to lose the characteristics which marked their previous behavior. However, when they go from an integrative to a dominative classroom, traits associated with domination are quickly assumed.[10]

What Do Pupils Like About Teachers? Since students rate the teacher's personality and teaching methods as the most important factors in their enjoyment of classroom work,[11] teachers should know what children like and dislike about them. Helpful information was

TABLE 18

Traits of Well-Liked Teachers *

1. Cooperative Democratic Attitude
2. Kindliness and Consideration for the Individual
3. Patience
4. Wide Interest
5. Personal Appearance and Pleasing Manner
6. Fairness and Impartiality
7. Sense of Humor
8. Good Disposition and Consistent Behavior
9. Interest in Pupils' Problems
10. Flexibility
11. Use of Recognition and Praise
12. Unusual Proficiency in Teaching a Subject

* Paul Witty, "An Analysis of the Personality Traits of the Effective Teacher," *Journal of Educational Research*, Vol. 40, 1947, pp. 662–671.

obtained through a national contest in which students were asked to write letters describing, "The Teacher Who Has Helped Me Most." The letters were analyzed to discover what characteristics of teachers were most frequently mentioned. Out of 12,000 letters written by children from grades two to twelve, the traits shown in Table 18 received the most mention. These may or may not be the

[10] H. H. Anderson, J. E. Brewer and M. F. Reed, "Studies of Teachers' Classroom Personalities III (Follow-up Studies of the Effects of Dominative and Integrative Contacts on Children's Behavior)," *Applied Psychological Monographs*, No. 11, Stanford University Press, 1946.

[11] W. B. Michael, E. E. Herrold and E. W. Cryon, "Survey of Student-Teacher Relationships," *Journal of Educational Research*, Vol. 44, 1951, pp. 657–673.

chief characteristics of good teaching but they do represent what youngsters deem important. The wise teacher might well use such a list to partially gauge his own effectiveness.

The Teacher as a Leader. Teaching, in most situations, demands that the teacher assume a role of leadership, and it is through an analysis of the teacher's function as a leader that one sees most clearly how he affects the group.

What happens to a classroom when different kinds of leadership are imposed? Bearing upon this question is a study (one of the first major studies of group dynamics) in which the experimenter set out deliberately to produce two contrasting social climates.[12] In the study, there were two clubs of ten-year-olds who were engaged in making theatrical masks. In one club the leader operated as an autocrat (imposed his goals on the group, frustrated the group's goals and ideas and was not objective in his comments about their work). In the other club the leader operated in a democratic manner by sponsoring group goals, and by giving friendly help and guidance, and objective praise and criticism. Both groups worked at the task of making theatrical masks for a period of three months under these two kinds of leadership. At the end of twelve weeks, the groups voted on (1) whether to continue, and (2) what to do with the masks they had made. All of the autocratic group voted to stop meeting, while most of the democratic group wished to continue. Children of the autocratic group wished to keep, as personal property, the masks they had made. In contrast, all children in the democratic group voted for a group disposal of at least one mask (i.e., to give it to the leader or put one on display). The significance of these findings should be apparent to the teacher. Children who work under the proper kind of leadership and group atmosphere seem to like their work, feel it to be important, and want more of the same or similar activities. Conversely, children whose needs are thwarted by rigid control tend to dislike schoolwork.

In an extension of the above experiment, four groups of boys were organized into clubs and placed under three kinds of leadership: autocratic, democratic, and laissez-faire.[13] The leadership of

[12] R. Lippitt, "Field Theory and Experiment in Social Psychology: Autocratic and Democratic Group Atmospheres," *American Journal of Sociology*, Vol. 45, 1939, pp. 26–49.

[13] K. Lewin, R. Lippitt, and R. K. White, "Patterns of Aggressive Behavior in Experimentally Created 'Social Climates,'" *Journal of Social Psychology*, Vol. 10, 1939, pp. 271–300.

TABLE 19

Types of Leadership, Characteristics of Leaders, and Pupils' Reactions *

TYPE OF LEADERSHIP	CHARACTERISTICS OF THIS TYPE OF LEADERSHIP	TYPICAL REACTIONS OF PUPILS TO THIS LEADERSHIP
Hard-Boiled Autocrat	1. Constant check on students. 2. Expects immediate acceptance of all orders—rigid discipline. 3. Little praise is given as he believes this would spoil children. 4. Believes students cannot be trusted when on their own.	1. Submission, but there is incipient revolt and dislike of the leader. 2. "Buck-passing" is a common occurrence. 3. Pupils are irritable and unwilling to cooperate and may indulge in "backbiting." 4. The work slips markedly when the teacher leaves the room.
The Benevolent Autocrat	1. Is not aware that he is an autocrat. 2. Praises pupils and is interested in them. 3. The crux of his autocracy lies in the technique by which he secures dependence upon himself. He says, "that's the way *I* like it," or "how could you do this to me?" 4. Makes himself the source of all standards of classwork.	1. Most students like him, but those who see through his methods may dislike him intensely. 2. There is great dependence upon the teacher for all directions—little initiative on part of pupils. 3. There is submissiveness and lack of individual development. 4. Amount of classwork may be high and of good quality.
The Laissez-Faire Teacher	1. Has little confidence in dealing with pupils or a belief that they should be left alone. 2. Has difficulty in making decisions. 3. Has no clear-cut goals. 4. Does not encourage or discourage students, nor does he join in their work or offer help or advice.	1. There is low morale and poor and sloppy work. 2. There is much buck-passing, scapegoating and irritability among students. 3. There is no teamwork. 4. No one knows what to do.
The Democratic Teacher	1. Shares planning and decision making with the group. 2. Gives help, guidance and assistance to individuals gladly but not at the expense of the class. 3. Encourages as much group participation as possible. 4. Praise and criticism given objectively.	1. Pupils like work, each other, and teacher better. 2. Quality and quantity of work are high. 3. Students praise each other and assume responsibilities on their own. 4. There are few problems of motivation whether teacher is in the room or not.

* Adapted in part from L. P. Bradford and R. Lippitt, "Building a Democratic Work Group," *Personnel*, Vol. 22, 1945, pp. 142–148. (American Management Association, Publisher).

the first two was like that described above, while the laissez-faire leadership gave unguided freedom to the group. (There were no rules, no apparent group or teacher goals, and little if any help or guidance initiated by the teacher.) Judged by the amount of work accomplished, the amount of identification with the group, group morale and "we feeling," and friendly relations with the leader, the democratic type of leadership was superior to either of the others, which were marked by such reactions as "scapegoating" [14] and attempts to resign from the group.[15] From this and similar studies emerges a picture of the kinds of leadership and the probable results of such leadership in terms of social climate. Table 19 presents a summary of the general findings.

It is apparent that a vital factor in class atmosphere is the way the leadership function of the teacher is used. Inflexible schedules, threats, and autocratic control cut off the communication of pupils with each other, and isolate the timid child from the group. These adverse influences may also create tension, irritability, and aggression among pupils. Also, autocratic control denies leadership training, and training in social learnings to the pupils who need this kind of experience. In appraising his own leadership, the teacher might ask himself the following questions:

1. Do I help the group arrive at clearly stated goals, and allow the group to have some part in planning these goals, or ways of achieving them?
2. Have I helped all members of the class to find satisfaction in class membership through a gratification of social needs?
3. Do I have a sense of objectivity. For instance, do I give praise and reproof in terms of some standard rather than as "you have pleased me?"
4. Am I aware of my own ego needs, or must I dominate the class group or its members to satisfy these needs?
5. Do I encourage students to appraise their own and my activities and to seek improvement in group work?

[14] Scapegoating is an adjustive mechanism, a kind of displaced aggression, in which people release their own hostility by attacking a person or group (usually weaker than they) not connected with the cause of their frustration.

[15] R. Lippitt, and R. K. White, "The 'Social Climate' of Children's Groups," in R. G. Barker, J. S. Kounin and H. F. Wright (Eds.) *Child Behavior and Development*, New York, McGraw-Hill, 1943, pp. 485–506. (These three kinds of leadership have been depicted in a film, made during the experiments described in this reference—See "Films" at the end of this Chapter.)

RELATIONSHIPS AMONG PUPILS

The second major factor in determining the school's social climate is the kind of relationships which exist among pupils. Why is it that some youngsters crave to belong to a class group yet are rejected, others who might belong if they wish instead find undesirable groups outside the classroom, still others find a satisfaction of social needs within the classroom? The answer to these questions has been sought in studies involving observation, clinical analysis, sociometric tests,[16] and studies of personality and group dynamics.

One important finding is that a student may belong to a class group yet be relatively unaffected so far as its values are concerned, being instead affected by the standards and values of some other group (reference group). Or the group to which he belongs may influence him negatively, thus reinforcing a positive influence from an outside reference group. A boy may actually use his dislike of school as a reinforcement for feelings he has about his "gang."

Within a given group only those who conform with group norms have prestige within that group. Thus the boy who strives to be an outstanding scholar in school may be rejected by his peers who believe that schoolwork is for sissies or girls. Many children's relations within the classroom are jeopardized because the school group or groups have values which conflict with values held by other groups of which they are members. Some children have never learned how to satisfy their social needs through contacts outside the home, while others have developed modes of behavior or personality traits which interfere with their relationships with other children. In some cases schools have failed to teach social skills which are necessary for effective group work. Furthermore, the traditional school has actually discouraged social interaction by allowing only individual work and by punishing children who attempt to talk with or help each other.

The way in which social learnings take place is an important consideration in the successful work of the teacher. Crime, insanity, divorce, inefficiency, and failure to learn are among the social catastrophes related to the failure of children to achieve a satisfactory place in social and work groups in the school and community. The following four questions indicate the kinds of information which a

[16] These tests are fully explained in Chapter 18.

teacher needs in order to facilitate desirable interpersonal relationships among pupils.

1. What are the social needs of children, and how are they satisfied?
2. How can teachers diagnose such needs?
3. What are the factors in class organization, teaching, and the behavior and personality of children which lead to acceptance and rejection?
4. How can the teacher handle cases of rejection and isolation, and in general teach in such a way that desirable interpersonal relationships are facilitated?

The above questions are treated in the four sub-sections which follow.

Social Needs. The reader will remember the earlier contention that social and ego needs are basic to human motivation. Children need acceptance by their age mates and by adults. They need to feel important and to have their accomplishments admired by others, and they need to feel that they are a part of a group, i.e., have a sense of belonging. They also need attention and affection. A social structure, or other influence which denies these needs creates misery and maladjustment. Many of the factors which frustrate these needs are present in our schools. Excessive rivalry, limited rewards, favoritism, and retardation are examples of the many conditions which may militate against the satisfaction of social needs.

In the early work of Moreno (one of the first persons to use sociometric tests) many elementary school children were shown to have few if any friends in their classes and many others to be victims of unrequited friendship, i.e., desiring friendship with other youngsters who did not accept them as friends.[17] Some children are not only unpopular with other youngsters but also are odious to their teachers. In fact, more often than not, teachers and pupils agree on whom the problem children are.[18] Statements such as the following are not infrequently made by teachers: "I know I'm not supposed to feel this way, but I just can't like Carl. When he starts something with that smart-aleck sneer, I have to fight myself to keep from shaking him."

[17] J. L. Moreno, *Who Shall Survive?* Nervous and Mental Disorders Monograph, No. 58, 1934.
[18] S. L. Pressey and F. P. Robinson, *Psychology and the New Education,* New York, Harper & Brothers, 1944, p. 436.

Diagnosing Social Needs and Class Social Structure. An adequate picture of the social needs of all children in a classroom, plus the view of the social climate or structure of the class entails the collection of a good deal of information. Yet there is no substitute for these kinds of data. Some of the relationships which exist among members of a group can be inferred from classroom behavior, but many subtle relationships, and frustrated social needs may escape the eye of even the most practiced teacher.[19] A teacher's judgment of the social status of children in his own classroom is far from perfect, and there is rather conclusive evidence that the appraisal he makes is biased by his own feelings about children.[20]

For the teacher who wishes to make a comprehensive diagnosis of the social needs of his class, the following techniques have been suggested by one group of authors.[21]

Analyzing pupils' diaries. A running account of what children do out of school gives clues to social habits, problems, and home and neighborhood influences. If such information is brought together, it may show areas of social weakness and social needs for an entire class. This information is especially important to show peer associations as illustrated in the following excerpts taken from the diaries of elementary school pupils.[22]

> Lunch was swell with Dolores, Bernice, Roberta, Lucille, Charlene, Patty, Greta, and others. We kept up a flow of trading apples for oranges and such. Dolores squealed when the kids tried to "kidnap" her banana. All the fun!

> . . . In the house again, I took off my clothes and got warm, when Mom asked, "Tired?". I replied, Yes, Mom, tired. Tired of not being able to be with kids my own age. Sis and cousins aren't enough.

Holding interviews with parents. Only with some knowledge of home influences can the teacher know what gaps exist in the child's concepts, social beliefs, and values. It is suggested that the interview with parents contain, as a minimum, some information about:

[19] N. E. Gronlund, "The Accuracy of Teacher's Judgments Concerning the Sociometric Status of Sixth-Grade Pupils," *Sociometry Monographs,* No. 25, New York, Beacon House, 1951, p. 5.

[20] *Ibid.,* p. 6.

[21] American Council on Education, *Diagnosing Human Relations Needs,* by H. Taba, E. H. Brady, J. T. Robinson, and W. E. Vickery, Washington, 1951, p. 2.

[22] *Ibid.,* p. 11 and p. 17 respectively.

(1) the parents' aspirations and goals for the child, (2) the young-ster's association with other children, (3) information about the neighborhood in which the family lives, and (4) the child's worries, and pleasures.

Making participation schedules. Questionnaires or schedules which are used to analyze school activities and extracurricular activities may give the teacher a notion of the effect of various school activities upon social or interpersonal relationships. In one such study it was found that 20 per cent of the student body were in no extracurricular activities, while 5 per cent were in six or more such activities. Illustrative of the valuable information which an analysis of students' activities may provide are the findings of the study referred to above.[23]

One out of four students participated in one or more school activity.

One in five of those who participated and one in nine of the total student body were in two or more activities.

Activities which included both boys and girls were three times as popular as other activities.

Most students not participating in activities expressed interest in joining some club, and many suggested new activities.

About 60 per cent of the students believed that clubs should be open to all who want to join.

About 65 per cent of the students thought "big wigs" ran the clubs. The areas which should be explored in participation schedules are the extent of student participation, the range of student leadership, the range of activities in which individuals participate, and the relationship of activities to each other.

Studying sociometric data. Sociometry is the study of the measurement of social interaction in a classroom, or other group. Children are asked to select by vote those whom they would most like to be with in work or play groups or situations (see Chapter 18). Analysis of the voting (often in the form of a sociogram whereby choices are graphically represented) is made in order to find out how well each child is accepted by his classmates. An example of the sort of information which sociometric tests can give is shown in Table 20.

Analyzing pupils' answers to open-ended questions. Sometimes a teacher can gain valuable insights about pupils and classes by ask-

[23] *Ibid.*, p. 67.

ing such questions as: "What I would change about my house" or "What I would do if I had three wishes." A sample of the kind of information which is thus collected is the following statement by a fifth-grade boy, responding to the question, "What people have said they don't like about me."

Like if my mother buys me a pair of shoes or a suit or something my aunts and uncles said I don't like that pair of shoes or suit or whatever she buys me so she tells them if they don't like it they can buy me my clothes. Sometimes my aunt says she don't like my teeth because there green and I don't brush them she says she'll give me a nickel everytime she visits us if I brush them. And another of my aunt and my mother don't like my hair because its messy and I don't comb it. My mother don't like my table manners and neither does my father. They don't like me because I'm bad and I just won't listen and obey.[24]

Acceptance and Rejection. Of great concern to teachers is the fact that some children seem always to be left out of things by their fellows. Disturbing also is the misery of the child who is actually rejected by his classmates. As mentioned earlier, the extent of acceptance and rejection in a classroom is often analyzed through a sociometric test. In Table 20 is presented a summary of the results of one such test given in a small junior-high-school classroom.

Note that choices ranged from 8 for Wayne Z. to 0 for Ernest C. and George S. Perhaps even more significant were the rejections ranging from 12 for Ernest C. to 0 for most of the others. The variability of choices was much less for the twelve girls in this class. Only one girl received a rejection. Teachers who have used sociometric tests know that it is not unusual to find a class in which a person or two are on the bottom (rejected or ignored) on every such test. It is even more disturbing that such unpopularity may remain somewhat stable even in the face of efforts to change it.

Clearly it behooves teachers to find out what characteristics are apt to lead to or be associated with unpopularity or rejection. In one study, when those who were rejected were compared with those who were highly acceptable to their peers, it was found that the former were more quarrelsome, complaining, nervous, aggressive, and dominating.[25] Other investigators have summarized the

---

[24] *Ibid.,* p. 101.
[25] H. H. Jennings, *Leadership and Isolation,* New York, Longmans, Green and Company, 1943, pp. 144–163.

TABLE 20

Summary of Sociometric Choices in an Eighth-Grade Class to the Question,
"With Whom Would You Like (or Prefer Not) to Sit?" *

PUPIL	NO. OF CHOICES RECEIVED	NO. OF RECIPROCAL OR MUTUAL CHOICES	NO. OF REJECTIONS RECEIVED †
Boys:			
Arthur E.	3	2	
Eric H.	6	3	
John C.	6	1	
Wayne Z.	8	3	
Jay B.	5	3	1
Robert H.	1	1	
Ernest C.	0	0	12
George S.	0	0	
Robert S.	4	0	
Roger S.	2	1	
Vance K.	1	0	2
Sebastian F.	1	0	
Russell A.	2	0	1
Girls:			
Janice P.	4	3	
Gloria M.	2	1	
Patricia R.	0	0	
Mary D.	4	2	
Constance B.	4	2	
Rose H.	3	3	
Irene B.	4	3	
Mary Anne B.	6	3	
Evelyn B.	3	3	
June G.	2	2	
Doris R.	2	2	
Jean H.	2	2	1

* Adapted from a Sociogram shown in American Council on Education, *op.cit.*,
p. 78.

† No entry in this column means no rejection.

positive traits associated with popularity as enthusiasm, daring,
pleasing appearance, and cheerfulness.[26]

[26] M. E. Bonney, "Personality Traits of Socially Successful and Socially Unsuccessful Children," *Journal of Educational Psychology*, Vol. 34, 1943, pp. 449–
472.

Youngsters prize qualities which match their concepts of that which gains prestige. For example, the twelve-year-old girl gives highest value in choosing friends to primness, sedateness, and lady-like behavior, while fifteen-year-old girls prefer glamour, and being attractive to the opposite sex. Likewise, the boy of fifteen places high value upon physical skill, aggressiveness, and fearlessness. Woeful is the child who is minus these qualities.[27]

Perhaps the most intensive analysis of children who are not acceptable to their classmates was made by Northway, who took twenty of the least frequently chosen children (on a sociometric test) and subjected them to special clinical study. These children grouped themselves into three patterns—the listless, recessive children; the quiet and retiring, socially uninterested children; and the noisy, rebellious socially ineffective children.[28]

The picture of the rejected child which emerges from these studies is that of a child who is seen by his fellows as different. He is one who does not conform to group norms of behavior, who retreats from social contact, and who attempts to satisfy social needs through the domination of others.

Helping Isolates and "Rejects." Clinical psychologists have recognized social isolates and rejected children as among the most serious of problem cases. Even if this were not true from the standpoint of adjustment and mental hygiene, it would be from an academic standpoint, as such children often lose the benefit of much classwork because they are not active participants in the learning process. Psychological principles and the experience of teachers and those who have worked with such children support the following techniques for helping rejected and isolated children achieve a place in the class group.

Regrouping. In a classroom containing one or several social isolates, it is possible to reseat the class or restructure the work groups in such a way that children may be included in groups which are less likely to be antagonistic or indifferent to them. If sociometric data are available it is helpful to use the "choices" to seat children near

[27] C. M. Tryon, *Evaluations of Adolescent Personality by Adolescents*, Monographs of the Society for Research in Child Development, IV, Washington, National Research Council, 1939, p. 77.

[28] M. L. Northway, "Outsiders, A Study of the Personality Patterns of Children Least Acceptable to Their Age Mates," *Sociometry*, Vol. 7, 1944, pp. 10–25.

those who have accepted them, even though it be on the basis of third-place votes. Unchosen children should not be placed near those who have rejected them. If possible, the teacher should place the isolate in a work group which has need for the particular skill which the unpopular child possesses.

Finding group jobs. Much classwork is of an individual nature, but there are some projects or work which really require group action, and involve a number of different kinds of skills. The isolate may receive much help if allowed to work with a group whose goals transcend petty personal considerations.

Using gradual induction. Sometimes attempts to plunge a timid child into classwork by direct questions, or by asking him to perform before the entire group, fail because the jump from his present withdrawn position to "total immersion" is too great a shock. Thus it may be wise to induct the child into the class group gradually. This may be done by letting him work with small groups at first, finding one person in class with whom he can feel at ease, or in extreme cases, letting him work with younger children for a time.

Finding special skills. Most children have some skill in which they excel. Studies of intra-individual differences have shown that even dull children generally have some skills in which they approach or exceed average performance or potential. One thing which astonishes visitors to a feeble-minded institution is the high level of skills in many vocational areas which are exhibited by inmates. Full use of diagnostic tools ought to provide teachers with information about the interests and special abilities of the withdrawn child. Once found, opportunity for the display of such skills should be given. This should do much toward giving needed self-confidence, and prestige in the eyes of the class.

Training in skills. Children and adolescents often put a high value upon certain skills such as proficiency in games, and basic social skills such as dancing. These skills may take on exaggerated importance in the eyes of the deficient youngster. Thus one straightforward way to help the isolate achieve status is to provide special help in such skills, thus allowing him to participate in group activities on a par with other children.

Discussion. Many times youngsters adopt habits, modes of behavior, and adornment which make acceptance by others unlikely. These characteristics may be retained simply because youths are not aware of the adverse effects of such behavior. Unfortunately young people do not readily change simply as a result of a teacher's statement about such personal habits. They are much more apt to accept ideas about matters of this kind from each other. Hence, a discussion in which students are given a chance to air their views about desirable and undesirable traits (without names being mentioned) may be a worthwhile venture. There are available for teachers' use several films which will introduce such discussions.[29]

Personal guidance. A simple suggestion to a pupil may give him assistance in finding ways to join a social group. Some youngsters lack either the *savoir faire*, or the self-confidence to break into a group. Often they hang back lest their egos be wounded by the rebuff which they so vividly imagine will result from an overture of friendship. In such cases, teachers, counselors, or advisers may offer help by showing ways of getting a start socially. The following incident will illustrate how one instructor was able to help a social isolate.

Mary was a freshman at a large state university. Since she had come to the University from a small town, she had no high-school friends on campus. In talks with her freshman adviser she revealed that she was unhappy and would quit college if not for the disappointment it would bring her parents. She admitted that she had no friends—that her only recreation was going to the movies alone and taking walks. The only time she talked with others was when she and three other girls went from history to gym class. Further conversation revealed that all these girls lived on the other side of campus, while Mary had a room in the dormitory where swimming classes were held. The adviser suggested to Mary that she invite the other girls to hang their coats and clothes in her room, while swimming, thus saving them from having to jam their clothes in gym lockers. Mary adopted the suggestion and soon found a social group which accepted her wholeheartedly. Her adjustment to social life from that time on was adequate and her ideas about leaving the University disappeared.

SCHOOL STAFF RELATIONSHIPS

A third major factor in determining the social climate in any school is the quality of interaction among teachers, and between

[29] Association Films, "You and Your Family," and "You and Your Friends," 79 East Adams Street, Chicago 3, Illinois; and Coronet Instructional Films, "How Friendly Are You?" and "Shy Guy," Coronet Building, Chicago, Illinois.

teachers and administrators. These are important relationships in that they may either lead to cooperative effort and progressive action or to dissension. When tensions are developed these are too often passed on down to the unfortunate pupil. How such tensions operate may be seen in the following record of a committee meeting of a junior-high-school staff.

Our committee is meeting in the late afternoon to consider the problem of homework. Present are Mr. Johnson, the principal; Miss Jones, English teacher and head of the department; Miss Martin, another English teacher; Mr. Brown, a social studies teacher; Miss Smith, mathematics; Mrs. White, physical sciences. (*Some of their thoughts and feelings, many of them unconscious, are given in italics within parentheses.*)

Mr. Johnson: "(*Another meeting, I hope there's no bickering. I'm always glad when the meetings are finished.*) Parents are complaining again about homework. One man called to say his son carried home thirteen pounds of books. Another feels he is doing the teaching teachers failed to do. Miss Jones, what happened when this problem was brought up at PTA?"

Miss Jones: "Many parents felt the school expects too much homework. Some thought this a lazy way of teaching. Others thought it unfair to have to help children do math problems because methods of working are different now. (*That was a swell chance to put Miss Smith in her place. She acts like she owns the school.*) On the other hand, some parents thought that not enough homework was assigned, that students nowadays were spoiled in school. I'm glad to report these parents were in the minority."

Miss Smith: "The trouble with such a meeting is that the few parents with complaints speak so loudly that it looks as though the whole PTA agrees. Most parents are indifferent as to how their children get along. When you try to get their cooperation, you get picayune complaints. If we want to lower our standards, it will be easy to eliminate homework. (*Jones will take any side just so she gets on top. She's determined to run this school.*)"

Mr. Brown: "(*Here we go again. Smithy needs some support before she gets steam-rollered by Jones.*) It's easy enough to talk about eliminating homework. In schools where children have a fine home background, work can be completed during school hours. But with the mixture of children we have, it's impossible to expect standards to be upheld without supplementary study after class hours."

Miss Jones: "Every time we talk about homework, someone brings up standards. Some teachers maintain high educational standards without loading students down with extra homework at night. Good teaching makes children want to read so much that reading becomes pleasure and not homework. (*That shot told.*)"

Mrs. White: "The confusion comes from the lack of basic policy on the part of the school administration."

Mr. Johnson: "We want everyone to give his opinion. Miss Martin, what do you think?"

Miss Martin: "(*He must know that Jonesey pushes me around. She's making a grandstand play with her 'Good teachers don't need to assign homework' stuff. When she says in that sugar voice of hers, 'You don't have to read any of the books on this list but I know you'll all want to,' all her students know they had better read them or else. If I say what I really think about homework, Jonesey will make my life even tougher next month. But I don't like to let Mr. Brown and Miss Smith down.*) Perhaps part of the answer depends upon the subject studied. (*I hate Mr. Johnson for putting me on the spot.*)"

Mr. Johnson: "Now that you have expressed your opinions, I wonder if we shouldn't vote on a final decision."

Miss Smith: "I don't think this problem can be solved by voting. We must get at the real issue of educational standards."

Mr. Johnson: "(*This meeting is getting too hot. If I don't stop it, we'll never have any peace in this school.*) I wonder if we shouldn't appoint a subcommittee to study the problem and report back to us."

Miss Jones: "(*I'd better not let him pull that now. If we can get him to go on, we may get him to decide on less homework, which will put Smith in her place.*) Don't you think, Mr. Johnson, we have most of the facts we need now? It seems to me we can come to a decision pretty soon."

Mr. Johnson: "I'm sure you'll all agree that the sensible conclusion is to expect each teacher to make every effort to reduce homework requirements to the minimum. We will, I am sure, also maintain the high educational standards our school has always tried to uphold. If you wish, I'll be glad to tell the parents, at the next PTA meeting, of our decision."

Miss Smith: "(*We lost this fight. We'll lay for Jones until we get a swell issue where we can push her around.*)" [30]

It is appropriate here to ask what in this teachers' meeting prevented the formation of good working relationships and effective group judgment. An obvious first answer is that this group had little training in group work, and Mr. Johnson apparently was not trained to provide effective leadership. Furthermore, it is apparent

[30] K. D. Benne and Bozidar Muntyan, *Human Relations in Curriculum Change*, Springfield, Illinois, Illinois Secondary School Curriculum Program, Bulletin No. 7, June, 1949, pp. 130–131.

that there was no prearranged plan of procedure, no delegation of tasks and no satisfactory method for either understanding or solving the problem of homework. Likewise the group had developed no satisfactory method of handling the personal animosities and hostilities which subverted the main topic for discussion. Groups such as this one can improve the handling of their problems when they learn to apply the principles of social psychology to their work. Some of the principles which apply to group functioning are discussed in the last section of this chapter.

OTHER FACTORS IN SOCIAL CLIMATE

The teacher's personality and method of leadership, and the organization of interpersonal relationships within the class group are among the important factors in determining social climate. However, there are other factors such as the physical facilities of the school and classroom, the size and composition of the class, and the previous experience of pupils which may also have a decided effect upon social climate.

Consider, for instance, the simple fact that there are dozens of ways in which thirty children may be placed or arranged in a classroom. They may be placed in rows of bolted down desks, sit around one large table, work in small groups of four to five pupils, sit in a circle facing each other, or work at individual projects—as in a laboratory. Besides the physical arrangement of the classroom, one must consider how the size of the class affects its social structure. It is apparent that the social climate in a classroom containing twenty students is different from one which contains fifty or a hundred students. Students are likely to feel freer to participate and take a more active role in group work when they are in small classes.[31] The crude fact that the amount of student participation is limited in the large class makes the small class more advantageous, especially when student participation is deemed an important part of the course. However, class size *per se* is probably of less importance than many other factors. It is probable that the effect of class size varies with the type of instructional method, the grade level of pupils, and the personality of individual teachers. There is some indication, for

[31] G. F. Castore, "Attitudes of Students Toward the Case Method of Instruction in a Human Relations Course," *Journal of Educational Research*, Vol. 45, 1951, pp. 201–213.

instance, that teachers are disturbed by the fact that large classes prevent them from knowing pupils well.[32] On the other hand, if a course consists almost entirely of lectures, class size might make little difference.

Many educators and psychologists have urged teachers to use small subgroups within a class, not only better to provide for individual differences, but also to allow all pupils an opportunity for maximum participation. Such schemes for subdividing a class into work groups also has a decided effect upon social climate and learning.[33] Herbert Thelen, who for several years has worked on the problem of how groups of pupils function, has suggested a principle of "least group size."

In speaking of the optimal size of groups, Thelen notes that the group should be "the smallest group in which it is possible to have represented at a functional level all the socialization and achievement skills required for the particular learning activity at hand."[34] As Thelen notes, an hour's class discussion in which thirty students are participating allows only two minutes per student for active interaction with others. The implementation of the principle of least group size is admittedly difficult in view of the incomplete knowledge presently available about the nature of socialization skills, and about the characteristics of various learning activities. But it is possible to make rough estimates of the optimal size of groups for specific purposes. For instance, when the learning activity consists of skill practice, the most appropriate size is probably two persons. For such tasks as creative thinking about the planning of an experiment or study, Thelen estimates that groups of from four to eight students would be needed. Apparently when groups are larger than needed to fulfill the essential conditions as stated, duplications of abilities and skills result, and there is less opportunity for a pupil to assume full responsibility in connection with a project.

One other important influence upon social climate is the kind of previous training which pupils have had. The child who has adjusted well to an autocratic type of control in previous classrooms

[32] H. L. Baker, "Class Size Does Make A Difference," *Nations Schools,* Vol. 17, 1936, pp. 27–28.

[33] S. L. Pressey and David C. Hanna, "The Class as a Psycho-Sociological Unit," *Journal of Psychology,* Vol. 16, 1943, pp. 13–19.

[34] H. A. Thelen, "Group Dynamics in Instruction, The Principle of Least Group Size," *The School Review,* Vol. 57, 1949, pp. 139–148.

or in the home may be much less able to accept or enjoy group work and interaction, and the responsibilities he is asked to share. In fact, when college students were asked to state their preference for permissive or directive sections in an introductory course in psychology, most of them chose the latter.[35]

Finally, there is the pervasive effect of goals, purposes, and objectives, and the way students believe their work will be evaluated. When a class knows that the goals of a course are centered around the learning of detailed facts which will be tested by recall of such facts on objective examinations, they are likely to prefer a directive, teacher-centered type of classroom. Contrariwise, students who see the objectives of a course as broad understandings, and generalizations which will be evaluated by group and teacher not only on paper and pencil tests, but also through measures of performance, will be apt to prefer a permissive, student-centered type of class.

THE EFFECT OF SOCIAL CLIMATE ON LEARNING

The first part of this chapter was written to show the factors which produce the social-emotional climate of a classroom. It remains to be shown, once social climate is determined, what effects such classroom atmospheres have upon learning. For example, what happens to achievement in spelling, reading, or mathematics when the teacher is sarcastic or overcritical or in other ways abuses his position of leadership? What happens to a child's schoolwork when his classmates reject or ridicule him? In extreme cases, adverse social climate may engender such profound feelings of inferiority, aggression or boredom that learning (at least of subject matter) virtually ceases. Such effect is portrayed in the following case.

Case of Grace W.[36]

Grace had been ill with spinal meningitis when she was just learning to add. When she was well enough to return to school, she was promoted with her grade and was never taught how to borrow and carry. Now in the sixth grade, faced with applying her previous knowledge, she had resorted to a method which had been hastily taught her by her father, only

---

[35] L. G. Wispe, *op.cit.*, p. 184.

[36] From Kimball Young, *Personality and Problems of Adjustment*, p. 440, Copyright, 1940, by Appleton-Century-Crofts, Inc., New York. Used by permission.

to have the teacher ridicule it and send her back to her seat in disgrace. Being a sensitive child, and socially ill at ease, she quickly responded in a negative manner to such treatment and soon gave the teacher the impression that she was stupid. Later, faced with a mental test situation, the girl had retreated into herself and had remained uncooperative. The result was that the psychologist who tested Grace gave a report which tended to confirm Miss Jones' judgment about the child's inherent stupidity.

This girl was sent to a special class where the new teacher soon realized that here was a case of emotional rather than mental difficulty. Under the new permissive atmosphere, Grace began to learn and to participate with others in social life. Eventually she graduated from high school and obtained a supervisory position with a good salary.

In general, the evidence for improving academic learning seems to favor the more flexible, democratically controlled classroom. The use of such procedures on a wide scale, has been appraised in terms of the college achievements of high school graduates who have experienced teaching of this kind.[37] Unfortunately, studies which appraise a whole school, or school system, have the disadvantage of being so broad that it is difficult to isolate the various factors which may have had an influence in shaping their products.

More recently, paired classrooms or groups have been used to test the hypothesis that social climate is an important determiner of the quality of learning. Summarizing one such investigation, Flanders writes, "In all cases, the student's ability to name, elaborate, use, and recall principles in question was greater for learner-centered periods than for teacher-centered periods." [38]

Problem Solving. Problem solving ability is learned best in permissive, learner-centered classrooms. For one thing, considered group judgments are often better than an average of individual judgments. Also many problems, especially those which are significant, are the kind which require group action for their solution.

Various elements of the problem solving process have been found to be developed best in a democratic atmosphere. For instance, two classes in child study, one a teacher-centered class and one a group-centered class, were compared in terms of the amount they had

---

[37] A report of a study of this kind (The Eight Year Study) is shown in Chapter 20.

[38] N. A. Flanders, *op.cit.*, p. 105.

learned. Although both classes were about equal in the number of facts learned, the group-centered class was superior in the use of evidence to support its views.[39] Likewise in sections from the second to the eighth grade (social studies), pupils in classes where teacher-pupil planning prevailed were better able to discriminate between valid and irrelevant reasons to support their views than were those in teacher-centered sections.[40]

Even children in primary grades can (and should) learn to solve problems through group processes. Following is an example of how a socially permissive, yet well-guided group of second graders solved an "ethical problem" during their regularly scheduled "Problem Period."

Henry: "The other day I was painting at the easel. I left the easel to throw my paper in the basket and when I came back, Leland had my place. I tried to tell him that I just went to put my paper in the basket but he wouldn't listen to me. So today when I went up to the easel Leland came and wouldn't let me paint again. He said he just threw a paper in the basket. He made me let him have the easel the other day, but when I did the same thing today he still wouldn't let me paint. I don't think he's being fair about it."

Sandy: "Leland, if you made Henry give it to you, you should have done the same thing when Henry wanted it."

Leland: "Yes, but I had started to paint and I wanted to finish."

Teacher: "Henry wanted to paint, too."

Henry: "Leland, you could take your picture off and finish later."

Cynthia: "Henry, why didn't you put your name on the papers? Then no one could paint on it."

Teacher: "A very good suggestion, Cynthia."

Pamela: "Could we move the waste basket over near the easel? Then you wouldn't have to leave your place. I think it would be better anyway 'cause you wouldn't have to walk so far in quiet time."

Teacher: "We could try that. Leland, what do you think about this problem?"

Leland: "I think, maybe, I should have let Henry paint."

Teacher: "But you are not quite sure?"

---

[39] H. V. Perkins, "Climate Influences Group Learning," *Journal of Educational Research,* Vol. 45, 1951, pp. 115–119.

[40] K. J. Rehage, "A Comparison of Pupil-Teacher Planning and Teacher-Directed Procedures in Eighth Grade Social Studies Classes," *Journal of Educational Research,* Vol. 45, 1951, pp. 111–115.

Leland: "Yes, I am. If I did it to him, I should let him have it. I'll take my paper off, Henry, and finish later." [41]

These children were learning how to solve problems because the classroom atmosphere was permissive enough yet well enough guided so that pupil interaction and cooperative work were promoted.

Social Learning. The kinds of attitudes, roles, characteristic modes of social adjustment, social skills such as taking part in a discussion, and emotional responses which are learned are further important products of classroom atmosphere. The question is how these social learnings come about, and how teaching can facilitate them.

Social interaction, either on the basis of working together toward group goals or in social situations, builds better interpersonal attitudes which may even transcend racial and religious prejudice. In an experiment comparing a group-centered with a leader-centered class, it was found that in the group-centered class there was a greater spontaneity and a better morale and cohesion. Students in this class had a class party, and often remained after class in groups, and several students took part in small get-togethers during the semester following. In the teacher-centered class students were "only too anxious to leave the classroom." [42]

Perhaps attitudes toward people in general, a greater warmth in expression and a greater readiness to accept people are products of group work which fosters widespread interaction. In other words, it is believed that permanent changes in personality may result from the kinds of social experiences made possible in classrooms. Even the way teachers feel about children may be a product of the kinds of class atmosphere which they have experienced in public school, and in their teacher-training institutions. In a controlled study of in-service teachers enrolled in a course in child development, those in group-centered classes were compared in several respects with those in leader-centered groups. It was found that teachers in the former class had more attitudes which were objective and warm, while in the teacher-centered class, the students'

[41] Alice Miel, "Children in Action," *Progressive Education,* Vol. 27, 1950, p. 156.

[42] E. W. Bovard, Jr., "The Psychology of Classroom Interaction," *Journal of Educational Research,* Vol. 45, 1951, pp. 215–224.

attitudes toward children were more often conventional, emotional and cold.[43]

Group Discussion.[44] A final and most practical consideration regarding the effect of social climate on learning is its effect upon group discussion and other forms of group work. Good group discussion involves much more than a decision by the teacher to have a group discussion. There are many forces at work within the group, and within the teacher's relation with the group which determine the nature and efficiency of discussion. Even training and practice in group discussion may fail to produce an efficient work group if social conflicts within the group remain unresolved.

Also the kind of appraisal which is used influences the nature of group work, as was demonstrated in the following study. Ten sections of five students each in an introductory psychology course were studied to find out what effect grading procedures would have upon group work. Five of the groups were told that each member would receive the same grade and that the grade would depend on how well the group did. The other five groups were told that each member would be rated against the other four in his group. All ten groups were then given significant psychological and social problems for discussion. The groups which were to be graded together (the cooperative groups) were superior in the communication of ideas, coordination of work, friendliness and group pride.[45] Apparently, the rivalry within groups engendered by competitive ratings may be sufficient to interfere seriously with group discussion.

The emergence of student leadership and the acceptance of appropriate work roles in a discussion are necessary concomitants to good group discussion. These are factors over which the teacher may exercise some control as both leaders and followers must learn these roles in just such opportunities as group discussion provides.[46]

[43] H. V. Perkins, *op.cit.*, p. 116.

[44] As it is not within the scope of this book to detail teaching methods, no attempt is made here to describe the educational techniques involved in group discussion. Rather this is intended as a presentation of some of the psycho-social factors which influence discussion. See bibliography at the end of the chapter for discussion methods.

[45] Morton Deutsch, "Social Relations in the Classroom and Grading Procedures," *Journal of Educational Research*, Vol. 45, 1951, pp. 145–152.

[46] See Kurt Lewin, "The Dynamics of Group Action," *Educational Leadership*, Vol. 1, 1944, p. 199, and Alice Miel, *Changing the Curriculum*, New York, Appleton-Century-Crofts, Inc., 1946, pp. 156–162.

On the other hand, teachers must realize that leadership is conferred by the group and not by the teacher. As one writer puts it, "the adult's choice of a certain child to be a leader may be a kiss of death to his leadership." In college classes, a group which was allowed to choose its own leader for a group discussion did a better job in a group discussion than a group for whom the leader was picked by the instructor, even though the latter student leader was superior intellectually.[47] It would appear that the teacher's job, rather than assigning roles in discussion, is to help the class pick its own leaders and assign other group positions. In this function the teacher should help the group assess its processes, select its leaders, and train its members.[48]

Unsatisfied needs and unresolved emotional tensions within a group may interfere with group goals. The reader will recall the teacher's meeting described earlier in this chapter. At that meeting, group goals were subverted by the attempts to use the discussion as a means of airing personal issues. The isolated, rejected child, and potential delinquent may not see the group discussion as a helpful activity. Their activities may be limited to attempts to use the discussion as means of gaining attention—of satisfying social needs. Likewise, the teacher's unsatisfied needs may easily interfere with group work. A recent study of junior-high-school students revealed that students were almost completely unaware of the nature of the teacher's social and status needs in the classroom. One student was heard to say, "I never thought about teachers having needs before." [49] The interdependence of pupils, and of pupils and teachers for a mutual satisfaction of needs, would seem to demand that each group receive training in understanding each other's social needs.

The criteria of the goodness of a group discussion are difficult to determine, as the evaluation of a group discussion has to be related to its objective and purposes. It has been suggested that some of the main purposes of group discussion are: "(1) the thoughtful solution of problems considered important by the group; (2) the growth of individual members in the process of discussion in various in-

[47] R. S. Jones, "A Procedure for the Appraisal of the Mechanics of Group Discussion," *Progressive Education*, Vol. 28, 1951, pp. 96–99.

[48] Ruth Cunningham and Associates, "Leadership and the Group," *National Education Association Journal*, Vol. 37, 1948, pp. 502–503.

[49] D. H. Jenkins, "Interdependence in the Classroom," *Journal of Educational Research*, Vol. 45, 1951, pp. 137–144.

sights and skills, particularly those essential to participation and cooperation in group thinking and action; and (3) the growth of the group as a group." [50] The following check list should help groups evaluate their progress.

Measure of Group Progress

1. Does every member make contributions to the discussion?
2. Is every member intensely involved in the discussion at all stages?
3. Does the discussion move toward common agreements in terms of the solution of the problem being discussed? Do all members of the group understand and accept as important the problem being discussed?
4. Is the discussion oriented toward decision and action at all times?
5. Does the group accept and understand the conflicts encountered and move toward their resolution?
6. Does the group recognize its need for information? Does it know how to go about getting such information?
7. Does the group use resource persons or resource material as an aid to its own thinking, not as giving the final action-solution of its problem?
8. Is the group unduly dependent upon its leader or on some of its members? Does the group use its leadership as an aid to common solutions, not as a source of final solutions?
9. Is the leader accepted as a member of the group, with special functions to perform?
10. Is there an atmosphere of friendly cooperation in the group at all times, particularly when conflicts of ideas and points of view are encountered?
11. Does the group resent attempts at domination by its leader, one of its members, a clique of its members or by a visiting expert?
12. Is there a feeling of progress toward common goals?
13. Is the group "realistic" in its choice of problems and in setting its goals?
14. Does the discussion move readily toward decision when decision is required?
15. Does the group find it possible to dispense with the creaking machinery of parliamentary procedure? [51]

SUMMARY

The way in which groups function, the manner in which members of groups interact, and the teacher's role in such activities are sub-

---

[50] K. D. Benne, L. P. Bradford and R. Lippitt, "Stages in the Process of Group Thinking and Discussion," in Illinois Secondary School Curriculum Program, *Human Relations in Curriculum Change,* Bulletin No. 7, 1949, p. 78.

[51] *Ibid.,* pp. 79–80.

jects which have paramount importance in the learning process. Most school learning takes place under conditions wherein the social-emotional climate of the classroom is a major determinant not only of the quality and amount of learning, but also of the way in which children react to classwork, and the attitudes which they develop about school.

Social-emotional climate is the result of at least the following factors: (1) the kinds of teacher-pupil relationships which exist in the classroom; (2) the social interaction or relationships among pupils; (3) the relationships among members of the school staff; and (4) the physical characteristics of the classroom, class size, and the previous experience of pupils.

Analysis of teacher-pupil relationships has revealed that pupils like teachers who are cooperative, democratic, considerate, and who have patience, a breadth of interests, and a pleasing manner. When teachers abuse their position of leadership by being overly autocratic, or shirking responsibility through a laissez faire manner, children are apt to become aggressive, and group morale is likely to be low.

The satisfaction of children's social needs is a crucial consideration for the teacher. The child who fails to achieve a place in the society of his peers is not only apt to become an educational casualty but a community problem as well. A summary of the skills which a teacher needs in order to help such children are: (1) ability to diagnose social needs, (2) ability to study the rejected child and the isolate to find causes of the behavior, and (3) proficiency in setting up programs and work which will allow the induction of such children into the class group.

Experimental evidence favors the flexible, democratically controlled classroom as a means of promoting both academic and social learning. Children under a more permissive type of classroom atmosphere have made as good or better school marks, and certainly have been found superior in ability to solve problems and take responsibility when they have been compared with children in conventional classrooms. Children in pupil-centered classrooms have also been shown to be more critical in their thinking than those in teacher-centered classes. Teaching methods which foster a high degree of interaction among pupils seem to offer unusual opportunities for important social learnings which are left untouched in many classrooms. Educators must find methods which teach children how to work together. Perhaps it is not an overstatement to say that the future of this civilization may depend upon how well children learn the social skills which will enable them to face the crises of tomorrow.

REFERENCES FOR FURTHER STUDY

Benne, K. D. and Levit, Grace, "The Nature of Groups and Helping Groups Improve Their Operation," *Review of Educational Research,* Vol. 23, No. 4, October, 1953, pp. 289–308.

Bollinger, R. H., "The Social Impact of the Teacher on the Pupil," *Journal of Experimental Education,* Vol. 13, 1945, pp. 153–173.

Bossard, James H. S., *The Sociology of Child Development,* New York, Harper & Brothers, 1948.

Bullis, H. E., and O'Malley, Emily E., *Human Relations in the Classroom,* Courses I and II, Wilmington, Delaware, The Delaware State Society for Mental Hygiene, 1947.

Cummings, Howard H. (Ed.), *Improving Human Relations,* Washington, D. C., National Council for the Social Studies, 1949.

Cunningham, Ruth, and Associates, *Understanding Group Behavior of Boys and Girls,* New York, Bureau of Publications, Teachers College, Columbia University, 1951.

Davis, Allison, *Social Class Influence upon Learning,* Cambridge, Harvard University Press, 1949.

Deutsch, Morton, *et al.,* "Leadership in the Small Group," *Journal of Social Issues,* Vol. 4, 1948, pp. 31–39.

Doob, Leonard W., *Social Psychology,* New York, Henry Holt and Company, 1952.

Gouldner, A. W., *Studies in Leadership: Leadership and Democratic Action,* New York, Harper & Brothers, 1952.

Haiman, Franklyn S., *Group Leadership and Democratic Action,* Boston, Houghton Mifflin Company, 1951.

Horwitz, Murray, "The Conceptual Status of Group Dynamics," *Review of Educational Research,* Vol. 23, No. 4, October, 1953, pp. 309–328.

Krech, David, and Crutchfield, R. S., *Theory and Problems of Social Psychology,* New York, McGraw-Hill Book Company, Inc., 1948.

Kuhlen, R. G., and Collister, E. G., "Sociometric Status of Sixth and Ninth-Graders Who Fail to Finish High School," *Educational and Psychological Measurement,* Vol. 12, 1952, pp. 632–637.

Meyer, Herbert H., "Factors Related to Success in Human Relations Aspect of Work-Group Leadership," *Psychological Monographs,* No. 320, 1951.

Miel, Alice, and Associates, *Cooperative Procedures in Learning,* New York, Bureau of Publications, Teachers College, Columbia University, 1952.

Murphy, Gardner, Murphy, Lois B., and Newcomb, T. M., *Experimental Social Psychology*, New York, Harper & Brothers, 1937.

Sargent, S. Stansfeld, *Social Psychology*, New York, The Ronald Press, 1950.

Sherif, Muzafer, *An Outline of Social Psychology*, New York, Harper & Brothers, 1948.

Simpson, R. H., *Improving Teaching-Learning Processes*, New York, Longmans, Green and Co., Inc., 1953.

Slavin, Simon, "Education, Learning and Group Work," *Journal of Educational Sociology*, Vol. 24, 1950, pp. 132–143.

Swanson, G. E., Newcomb, T. M., and Hartley, E. L., *Readings in Social Psychology*, New York, Henry Holt and Company, 1952.

Taba, Hilda, Brady, Elizabeth Hall, and Robinson, J. T., *Intergroup Education in Public Schools*, Washington, D. C., American Council on Education, 1952.

Trow, W. C., Zander, A. E., Morse, W. C., and Jenkins, D. H., "Psychology of Group Behavior; The Class as a Group," *Journal of Educational Psychology*, Vol. 41, 1950, pp. 322–338.

Withall, John, "Assessment of the Social-Emotional Climates Experienced by a Group of Seventh Graders as They Moved from Class to Class," *Educational and Psychological Measurement*, Vol. 12, 1952, pp. 440–451.

FILMS

Changes in Group Atmosphere, Audio-Visual Aids Department, University of Iowa, Iowa City, Iowa. (15 mins.)

Discussion in the Social Sciences, Encyclopedia Britannica Films, 1150 Wilmette Avenue, Wilmette, Illinois. (22 mins.)

Learning from Class Discussion, Coronet Instructional Films, Coronet Bldg., Chicago 1, Illinois. (11 mins.)

Shy Guy, Coronet Instructional Films, Coronet Bldg., Chicago 1, Illinois. (15 mins.)

Social Climate of Groups, Audio-Visual Aids Department, University of Iowa, Iowa City, Iowa. (15 mins.)

You and Your Family, Association Films, 79 East Adam Street, Chicago 3, Illinois. (11 mins.)

You and Your Friends, Association Films, 79 East Adam Street, Chicago 3, Illinois. (11 mins.)

You and Your Parents, Association Films, 79 East Adam Street, Chicago 3, Illinois. (15 mins.)

Chapter 12

Discovering and Overcoming
Special Difficulties in Learning

THE SLOW-LEARNING pupil or the one who fails to learn basic essentials creates major problems for the teacher. The problems are intensified as class size and the range of individual differences increases. School populations are increasing at a greater rate than teacher populations, and school attendance laws are more stringent than in the past. Thus there are not only more children in school, but a greater proportion of them stay in school longer. A few decades ago, a child who had difficulty in learning to read, spell, or figure generally dropped out of school and went to work. Today such children tend to stay in school. The consequent increase in class size and in the range of abilities of children in school forces a greater and greater work load upon the teacher, who may feel that he must aim more and more of his work at the group as a whole rather than at individuals who need special consideration.

What to do with the slow reader, or the child with special deficiencies in arithmetic, spelling, speech, or English represents a major concern of teachers at both the elementary and secondary-school levels. Teachers and schools are attempting to find solutions for these problems in the use of special education for the marked deviate, and in the use of modern diagnostic and remedial methods in the classroom. This chapter is a survey of the principles, techniques, and tools which are being used to overcome special difficulties in learning.

WHAT HAPPENS WHEN DIFFICULTIES
REMAIN UNSOLVED?

The effects of difficulties in learning upon a pupil may be far out of proportion to the apparent seriousness of the problem because emotional pressures build up around his area of weakness. He may fall behind the level which his teachers, parents or administrators have set up as a standard of performance. In reading and arithmetic as many as 10 to 15 per cent of the pupils in a class may be as much as two full grades behind the average grade level for their ages.[1] This is inevitable. But when adults insist upon the achievement of an arbitrary standard for all children, not only will children have difficulties, but also they may suffer emotional disturbances and negative attitudes which can persist long after a given school subject is over. The problem of the slow learner is exaggerated by teachers and parents who cling to unrealistic standards of performance. Perhaps more difficult than the problem of the slow learner is that presented by the child who, as a result of unrealistic and arbitrary demands of the school, rebels and fails to learn even the bare essentials which are well within his capacities.

The number of children who drop out of school is mute testimony to the fact that the school and home have failed to help children solve their scholastic problems. The extent of this condition is indicated by the fact that in 1947–48, approximately 14 per cent of the 24 million children from ages five to seventeen were not in school. Also it was recently noted that about 40 per cent of the students who begin high school never finish.[2] In one city where a study of dropouts was made, students were asked why they dropped out. They listed as important reasons, general dissatisfaction, failure to see the value of material learned, and difficulties with subjects or with teachers.[3]

Finally, the effect of unsolved difficulties in learning may be seen in the number of children who are seriously disturbed as a result of school failure. Many are so frightened and frustrated by the requirements of the schools that they may, and often do, suffer long-time

[1] Stuart Courtis, "The Rate of Growth Makes a Difference," *Phi Delta Kappan*, Vol. 30, 1949, pp. 316–323.

[2] C. E. Skinner (Ed.), *Educational Psychology*, 3rd Edition, New York, Prentice-Hall, Inc., 1951, p. 488.

[3] Harry P. Smith, *Syracuse Youth Who Did Not Graduate*, Syracuse, New York, Board of Education, 1950.

maladjustment, and feelings of inferiority. In cases such as these, parents and school have added to the usual difficulties of learning. It is to be hoped that the greater use of proper diagnosis and individualized remediation will continue to decrease the number of such cases in our schools.

TYPES OF DIFFICULTIES AND CONTRIBUTING FACTORS

Slow maturation, fearfulness and aggression, poor teaching, illness, and bodily defects are samples of the many factors which may add to the problems of learning. Such factors are in addition to the difficulties of the learning itself which may contain inherent barriers that have to be overcome by all pupils. It has become popular in the past few years to speak of children who have some special difficulty as atypical children—but this is a "fuzzy" concept, for in a sense there is no typical child—each is unique in some way, and each has characteristics which make learning easier in some areas than in others. There are, however, certain children whose need for special attention is very apparent. Some of the more conspicuously handicapped types will now be discussed.

The Slow Learning Pupil. Generally youngsters who are slow in learning lack either ability, interest, or experience. It is known, for example, that in large populations such as that represented by the group upon which the Stanford-Binet test was standardized (a sample of 2,904 children used) as many as 9 per cent had IQs of eighty-five or below and 4 per cent had IQs of seventy-five or below.[4] It is thus apparent that in the typical class there will be pupils who should not be expected to proceed at the rate of the average or superior pupil. When such children are ignored or unduly prodded, they may become "learning casualties."

As was shown in Chapter 8, some slow learning results from the fact that children may have little or no interest in the academic part of school. Interests and abilities are of course closely related, but it is quite possible to find in almost any class a child of high ability and an interest level so low that he learns very little about the formal classwork (he probably learns a great deal about a number of other things).

The number of children who have suffered from extreme experi-

[4] L. M. Terman and M. A. Merrill, *Measuring Intelligence*, Boston, Houghton Mifflin Company, 1937, p. 37.

ential deprivation is probably not large when this group is compared with those who have low ability or little interest in schooling. However, it is a sizeable enough group to warrant serious consideration by teachers and the community as a whole. It may be recalled in this connection that in a study of the home life of poor readers, some were found to have come from homes which were almost "bookless." [5]

Children with Sensory Defects. Unrecognized or untreated defects of vision or hearing are among the causes of failure to learn in school. About 30 per cent of all children of school age have some visual defect,[6] (most of which are easily corrected by glasses) and as many as 12 per cent may have some auditory defect.[7] In all such cases, early recognition, corrective measures, and special provisions in the classroom are essential. A failure to recognize such difficulties in early stages may cause the development of emotional disturbances which further interfere with the learning process. In locating children with sensory defects there is no adequate substitute for a medical examination.

Speech Defects. Speech defectives comprise one of the major groups of handicapped school children, (about one to two per cent present serious problems). Speech is such an important part of the communication process, however, that regardless of how commendable the teacher's methods, there will probably be some adverse effects upon learning produced by defective speech. Teachers should know that four or five times as many boys as girls stutter in our culture, and that the majority of speech disorders probably arise from psychological rather than physiological causes.[8] They should also know that the school may be the place where the problem comes into sharpest focus, and that because of attendant emotional involvement may interfere with learning and social adjustment.

Orthopedic Cases. Various crippling diseases, accidents, and structural deviations may interfere with learning in devious ways. Often much schoolwork is missed because of confinement or hospitaliza-

[5] M. C. Almy, "Children's Experience Prior to First Grade and Success in Beginning Reading," *Teachers College Record*, Vol. 51, 1950, pp. 392–393.

[6] Edgar Sydenstricker, *Health and Environment*, New York, McGraw-Hill, 1933, p. 23.

[7] National Society for the Study of Education, *The Education of Exceptional Children*, 49th Yearbook, Part II, 1950, Nelson B. Henry (Ed.), University of Chicago Press, Chicago, Illinois, p. 156.

[8] *Ibid.*, pp. 177–180.

tion. In other instances the handicap may prevent full participation in school activities. The scope of the problem is shown by the fact that about one person in 100 under twenty-one years of age is affected by some kind of crippling condition (about 550,000 in the U. S.), and about an equal number suffer from rheumatic heart.[9] In all such cases teachers may play an important role in identifying symptoms which point to the need for a medical examination. One authority writes:

Among the most important sources of information regarding crippled children are the public schools. Countless undiscovered or neglected handicaps have been reported by alert classroom teachers who have recognized deviations in activity, responses or accomplishment and have related these to untreated physical handicaps.[10]

Social-Emotional Maladjustment. As noted in Chapter 7, perhaps as many as a fifth of reading failures (to take but one subject) are clearly linked with emotional factors, and 80 per cent of cases of reading difficulties have been estimated to be accompanied by strong emotional disturbance. Thus emotional factors not only lead to difficulties of learning, but are a frequent accompaniment of learning difficulties which have other causes.

It is difficult to know how many children are handicapped by maladjustment. The incidence of severe behavior problems and other forms of maladjustment varies with the community or neighborhood and with the times. Undoubtedly there are some classrooms where as many as 20 or 30 per cent of the pupils are emotionally disturbed and upset, but in most situations the number would probably not exceed 5 to 10 per cent. Of these children, boys constitute about 85 per cent of the cases of aggressive behavior which results in delinquency and classroom disturbances.[11] However, it is probable that girls have just as serious problems but that the expression is more often in the form of withdrawal, fantasy, and nervous symptoms. In any event, adjustment problems constitute a very serious source of difficulty in learning. An entire section of this book is later devoted to such problems.

Other Difficulties. There are many other factors which create educational casualties or produce difficulties which require special help.

[9] *Ibid.,* p. 197.
[10] *Ibid.,* p. 195.
[11] *Ibid.,* p. 284.

Malnutrition, frequent debilitating illness, and glandular disturbances are among those which should be mentioned. Sometimes, of course, the difficulty does not reside within the child, but is a result of previous unfortunate experiences. Parents who push the child too hard, or who pamper, overprotect, or neglect him may contribute to his learning failure, as well as teachers who use poor methods of instruction. Since much of this volume is devoted to just such considerations, discussion will not be given here. Nevertheless, it should be reemphasized that unfortunate attitudes, and bad habits which are learned at home or in the school, may interfere with learning to a great degree and for a long period of time.

Summary of the Problem. Although there are no adequate or completely up-to-date figures, it is safe to estimate that there are at least 3,000,000 children in today's elementary schools who are in need of special help.[12] This figure was a conservative estimate in 1930. There is no reason to believe it has decreased. As was indicated at that time, the figure did not include malnutrition and heart cases, nor did it include the many cases in which children were educational casualties because of teaching methods or home care.

It is probable that at least one child in every seven is in need of a certain amount of individual teaching or assistance in addition to group work. Although special classes and other programs of special education take care of more serious cases, there still remains the borderline mental defective, the partially seeing pupil, the hard of hearing child, the slow academic achiever, and many others.

The problem then is of such scope that every teacher must be equipped to diagnose symptoms of slow or impeded learning, and trained to use those remedial techniques which practice has proven effective.

EARLY RECOGNITION OF DIFFICULTIES

One of the most important principles both in the prevention and treatment of learning difficulties is that full-blown problems are preceded by behavioral symptoms or inadequacies, many of which are easily identifiable. The alert teacher should be able to anticipate difficulties and catch them before they become so extreme that there is great emotional involvement.

[12] White House Conference on Child Health and Protection, *Special Education: The Handicapped and the Gifted,* Century Company, 1931, p. 7.

Serious difficulties may, however, be overlooked. In a case known to the writer a child was in the sixth grade at school before a teacher discovered that his eyesight was so poor that not once in the past five years had he been able to read anything which had been written on the blackboard. His eyesight was only 20/200 in the best eye. In another case a freshman at the University of Illinois was astonished to find that he was nearly blind in one eye.

Routine examinations of vision, hearing, and other physical capacities are now a regular part of most schools' programs. Children with partial handicaps are thus identified early. A program of health examinations would seem a minimum essential in any school system. When it is not provided for by the school, however, teachers themselves should administer simple tests of vision and audition when these seem appropriate.[13]

Besides physical checks, it is recommended that children be surveyed in several areas of school achievement and in general ability level.[14] These surveys will reveal children who are having difficulty or are apt to have difficulty in learning.

Tests and checkups may give only a segment of the total picture of the child's problem, and besides some of the instruments may have questionable validity. Therefore, constant surveillance of a class, and alertness for behavioral clues which may be signposts to difficulties are essential. A total list of such symptoms is difficult to compose as it would contain hundreds if not thousands of items. In Table 21, however, is presented a checklist of some of the symptoms which might occur in the schoolroom and indicate the need for further diagnosis.

PSYCHO-EDUCATIONAL DIAGNOSIS IN THE CLASSROOM

Once a child has been identified as a slow or handicapped learner, it is necessary to establish the cause of the difficulty in order to do remedial teaching. In extreme cases the teacher relies upon agencies such as the health office and the psychological clinic. In many in-

[13] For a description of the tests and devices which teachers may use to test for visual and auditory defects see G. M. Blair, *Diagnostic and Remedial Teaching in Secondary Schools*, New York, The Macmillan Company, 1946, Chapter 3.

[14] It would be repetitious at this point to list the intelligence and achievement tests which are available. There are dozens of good tests in each category. Sources are shown in Chapter 17.

TABLE 21

Symptoms Which May Point To Handicaps and Learning Difficulties *

TYPE OF DEFECT	SYMPTOMS
A. Defects of Vision	1. Reading material held too close or too far away. (Normal close work about 8 inches.) 2. Squinting, frowning or shutting of one eye. 3. Rubbing of eyes, eyes red, swollen or eyelids red-rimmed. 4. Dizziness, headaches, nausea.
B. Auditory Defects	1. High-pitched or flat voice (head turned to hear), posture. 2. Very poor spelling, or pronunciation. 3. Incorrect interpretation of a question. 4. Social withdrawal.
C. Motor Defects	1. Uneven posture or gait. 2. Tremors. 3. Rigidity or stiffness of joints. 4. Incoordination. 5. Differences in size of limbs.
D. Malnutrition	1. Puffiness under eyes. 2. Distended abdomen. 3. Lowered vitality and lack of energy. 4. Dull nails, hair and skin.
E. Speech Defects	1. Articulation e.g., (pay for play). 2. Fluency—i.e., jerky, slow or irregular speech. 3. Loudness. 4. Voice pitch—monotones or very high pitch. 5. Hoarse, harsh, or nasal qualities.
F. Neurological Disturbances	1. Chorea (St. Vitus Dance). 2. Tics, such as a jerking of facial muscles. 3. Tremors (especially when fingers are tense). 4. Flights of attention. 5. Brief periods of loss of consciousness.
G. Emotional Disturbances	1. Nail biting, twisting hair, thumbsucking, etc. 2. Crying easily. 3. Exaggerated fears and angers. 4. Responses out of proportion to stimuli. 5. Night terrors. 6. Symptoms of fatigue, such as backaches, tired eyes.

* Parts of this table were adapted from The National Society for the Study of Education, *op.cit.*, pp. 42, 43, 51, 52, 53 and 57.

stances, however, the teacher must conduct a diagnosis himself. When he does so, he should keep in mind some of the principles and practices which will now be discussed.

In the first place, diagnosis of difficulties in school work should include a detailed study of the processes which erring pupils use. There is a marked difference between a survey test which simply shows the areas of weakness and a diagnostic test which traces the source of errors. Often tests made by the teacher for a particular case will give more diagnostic information than a standard test. Teachers should keep a record of the kinds of errors which given pupils make.

Worthwhile information may also be obtained through interviews with individual students. The amount of reliable information gained in such interviews is believed to be a function of the objectivity, acceptance, and rapport which the teacher is able to attain. Following are five rules for interviewing. (1) Do not talk too much. Studies of professional counselors show that the ones who talk too much may discourage the client's talking, and make the interview less effective. (2) Begin the interview with innocuous material. An interview in which the teacher begins by criticizing or scolding a child will put him so much on the defensive that he will not open up; hence will not provide the information for which the interview is intended. Likewise pressing the child too hard or fast may cut off the flow of conversation. (3) Keep the interview pointed toward a central problem. If the talk gets painfully close to a subject (such as a child's feeling of inferiority about acne) the pupil may attempt to throw up a protective barrage of talk which is unrelated to any real issues. (4) Keep the material of the interview in complete confidence. There is no way to dry up the stream of information more quickly than to repeat to other students or parents the information which is given in confidence. (5) Accept what the child says. Censure or value judgments during the interview destroys the rapport which should be maintained. The child's perception of the interview situation as a warm permissive atmosphere should guarantee a decrease in his resistance.

SOME GENERAL PRINCIPLES IN GIVING SPECIAL HELP

Following diagnosis, work should be set up to get the child back into classwork. There will be a variation in the specific techniques used in different subject areas (as will be seen in the next section). However, there are some steps which apply in nearly every instance of remedial teaching.

One of the first of these is to remove negative emotional attitudes. Since a large percentage of learning difficulties are either caused by or accompanied by emotional disturbances it is clear that a major step is to alleviate this situation. A counterpart to alleviating emotional difficulties is to build up the child's self-confidence. A part of the problem of emotional disturbance is the effect upon youngsters of their view of themselves in relation to school work. Feelings of inadequacy in a particular field may persist long after the reason for it ceases to exist. Witness the number of students and adults who say, "I never was any good in arithmetic, I just can't do it."

A second important step is to find materials (in the area of weakness) which are interesting and commensurate with the child's readiness. A retarded reader might have great interest in comic books, and these might well be the media for beginning remedial instruction.[15] Thirdly, the remedial work must be such as to give close attention and guidance to learners in early trials of any new kind of learning, or with new materials. Original difficulties, which may be caused by quite simple mistakes, may grow, become persistent, and affect whole areas of work. Finally, the child should be given an early opportunity to use and demonstrate his new-found skills. In this connection, however, care should be exercised so that the child who is undergoing remedial teaching is not thrown into a competitive situation too quickly, as it may undermine his growing confidence.

DIFFICULTIES IN READING

More children seem to have difficulty with reading than with any other school subject. The causes of reading difficulty may be linked to any of the problems previously discussed, but in addition there may be specific difficulties which will become apparent only with detailed diagnosis. The report which follows is typical of the findings of a remedial reading clinic with respect to causes or concomitant factors in reading difficulties.

[15] Actually many comic books today are picture books. Ones such as *Classic Comics* and *Classics Illustrated* published by the Gilberton Company, New York; and *The Adventure Series* of the General Electric Company, Schenectady, New York, may be valuable supplementary reading materials.

Fifty-four of the seventy pupils needed help in auditory discrimination, twenty were word readers, fifteen had a smart brother or sister. Eleven were troubled with chilling fears, nine thought they were "dumbbells," seven were suffering from insufficient sleep, seven could not see well, four came from broken homes, three had speech difficulties, eight had emotional difficulties due to too much parental pressure, neglect by the mother, overly strict father and a recent death in the family. Five were badly handicapped for physical reasons—thyroid imbalance, scarlet fever, rheumatic fever, bad tonsils, hearing defect, epilepsy, and cerebral palsy. One had learned the sound of individual letters but simply could not blend them.[16]

Diagnosis. When children have unusual difficulty in reading, the following are perhaps minimum diagnostic procedures which should be undertaken.

1. The child should be given a non-verbal intelligence test. (A test which requires reading is obviously of no value in the case of a retarded reader, as such a test tells only what is already known, *viz.*, that the child reads poorly).
2. A check of vision and hearing should be made.
3. There ought to be some notation of the child's previous reading experiences. Such items as records of failures and parents' reactions should be included.
4. An appraisal of the child's interests and attitudes about school should be made. Information thus obtained may serve as a basis for the kind of remedial material that should be used.
5. Finally, the youngster should be given a good diagnostic reading test. Information about a child's reading abilities which may be obtained from various standard tests usually includes appraisal of reading speed and comprehension, and some measure of vocabulary; and often contains sections which test for special reading skills such as map-reading, use of an index, and reading of mathematical or other technical material.[17]

Remedial Reading Instruction. Remedial reading instruction aims to increase reading speed and comprehension by increasing reading enjoyment, and providing for practice with a wide variety of materials. The assumption is made, of course, in giving such instruc-

[16] University of Washington, College of Education, *The Remedial Newsletter,* Vol. 13, No. 2, November, 1951, W. J. Osburn (Ed.), p. 2.

[17] For more detailed discussion and illustration of diagnostic instruments see Chapter 17.

tion that a child is reading well below his level of ability. The slow learner, who is achieving well for his ability simply needs to be guarded from the strain of intense competition and from emotional disturbance, and helped to find materials which are easy enough and enjoyable enough to keep his reading skills growing at a rate which is normal for him.

For the underachiever, on the other hand, a definite remedial or corrective program is necessary. Following are the steps suggested by a leading authority in this field: [18]

1. Go back to where the child is
2. Build sight vocabulary and speed up recognition
3. Teach self-help sounding
4. Develop comprehension
5. Secure much interesting reading at the child's present level

There are hundreds of remedial techniques which have been used successfully in both classrooms and clinics. Most are based on the principle of encouraging children to like reading by providing enjoyable practice. A frequent method of doing this is to make a game of learning. For example, Dolch has a device for improving sight vocabulary called "The Group Word Teaching Game," a sample card of which is shown in Figure 13.

Another method which is used with very difficult cases is described by Fernald.[19] First the child traces a word with "finger contact," saying each part as he traces it. He then writes the word himself, and uses it in a story. After the story is finished he makes a copy of the word on a file card and places it in an alphabetical card case. As a child progresses he is able to pick out new words, spell and pronounce them without tracing them. Some teachers have used with success a method whereby the child tells a story, which is taken down by the teacher, transcribed and typed out, and given to the child to read.

One of the main objectives in remedial reading is to increase the child's self-confidence and decrease fear and anxiety. Fernald's clinic did this by starting a child with big words which gave him a sense of accomplishment and status, especially when he could use them in

[18] E. W. Dolch, *Manual of Remedial Reading*, (Second Edition) Champaign, Illinois, The Garrard Press, 1945, Chapter 2.

[19] Grace Fernald, *Remedial Techniques in Basic School Subjects*, New York, McGraw-Hill Book Company, Inc., 1943, p. 35.

the presence of peers or even adults. The following anecdote related by Fernald illustrates this technique.[20]

Perhaps the most extreme case of positive reconditioning the writer has ever seen occurred at a teachers' institute meeting in California some years

please	just	hold	keep	buy
today		shall	why	
grow	try		drink	kind
six		use	well	
myself	pick	fall		hot

FIGURE 13. Group Word Teaching Game.

Each card has 25 of the 220 words from Dolch's Basic Sight Vocabulary arranged in random order. The rules of the game are the same as in "Bingo." Successful participation necessitates a rapid recognition of words, both as they sound, and as they look. (Reproduced by permission of the author and The Garrard Press, Champaign, Illinois.)

ago. Mrs. Helen Keller [21] was addressing the meeting on the subject of spelling. The children who were supposed to come for the demonstration had not arrived. When Mrs. Keller spoke with regret of the fact that she would be unable to demonstrate the remedial technique, a large and positive woman arose and asked, "Do you want the worst speller in the city for demonstration?" When Mrs. Keller said she would be delighted to have any school child help her out, the woman started down the aisle with

[20] *Ibid.*, pp. 15 and 16.
[21] Co-worker of Dr. Fernald.

a poor scared little eleven-year-old boy held firmly by the shoulder. Everyone gasped at the brutality of so disgracing the child.

Mrs. Keller shook hands with the boy in a matter-of-fact way and told the mother to sit down in the audience. Within a few moments Mrs. Keller had determined how he could best learn words. She then proceeded to teach him *development, university, department, education.*

All the fear and self-consciousness disappeared. As the boy finished the word *education* he turned and grinned at his mother who was staring at the performance in open-mouthed amazement. The audience broke into loud applause. The school reported later that the emotional transformation was complete and permanent. Mrs. Keller worked with the boy and his teacher until they were ready to go on with spelling by the new method. Each day the boy gloated over the words he had learned and went on to new conquests.

Improvement of vocabulary and comprehension. Regardless of the cause, poor readers are frequently retarded in vocabulary, and are often unable to recognize even the most common words. For beginning readers one of the important first steps is the provision of a simple sight vocabulary. From 50 per cent to 75 per cent of ordinary reading matter is made up of 220 very common words immediately recognized by any capable reader. These words are presented in Table 22.

When pupils have difficulties with any of the words from this list, they need practice which will build up their ability to recognize immediately those which they have missed. These words have been printed on flash cards for use with either individual pupils or with groups, and they have been made into games as was shown in Figure 13.

Probably the most effective method of developing both vocabulary and comprehension is through wide reading in a variety of subject matter areas. Words learned in context are much better remembered and also more clearly understood than those learned in isolation. Especially desirable materials for this purpose are those which have immediate usefulness and which help the pupil answer questions and solve problems.

Supplementary methods of improving vocabulary include word study (using dictionaries or building a class dictionary), a study of the derivation of words, and a study of prefixes. The list in Table 23 should be useful in connection with the study of prefixes.

TABLE 22
A Basic Sight Vocabulary of 220 Words *

a	eat	jump	pick	to
about	eight	just	play	today
after	every		please	together
again		keep	pretty	too
all	fall	kind	pull	try
always	far	know	put	two
am	fast			
an	find	laugh	ran	under
and	first	let	read	up
any	five	light	red	upon
are	fly	like	ride	us
around	for	little	right	use
as	found	live	round	
ask	four	long	run	very
at	from	look		
ate	full		said	walk
away	funny	made	saw	want
		make	say	warm
be	gave	many	see	was
because	get	may	seven	wash
been	give	me	shall	we
before	go	much	she	well
best	goes	must	show	went
better	going	my	sing	were
big	good	myself	sit	what
black	got		six	when
blue	green	never	sleep	where
both	grow	new	small	which
bring		no	so	white
brown	had	not	some	who
but	has	now	soon	why
buy	have		start	will
by	he	of	stop	wish
	help	off		with
call	her	old	take	work
came	here	on	tell	would
can	him	once	ten	write
carry	his	one	thank	
clean	hold	only	that	yellow
cold	hot	open	the	yes
come	how	or	their	you
could	hurt	our	them	your
cut		out	then	
	I	over	there	
did	if	own	these	
do	in		they	
does	into		think	
done	is		this	
don't	it		those	
down	its		three	
draw				
drink				

* E. W. Dolch, *A Manual for Remedial Reading*, (Second Edition), p. 438. Copyright, 1945, by The Garrard Press, Champaign, Illinois.

Improvement of reading speed. Generally reading speed increases as children read more, and as they come to enjoy reading. When reading speed does remain relatively slow, it is usually a symptom of difficulty in comprehension, poor mechanics of reading, or of a

TABLE 23

Prefixes Occurring Most Often in the 20,000 Words of the Thorndike * List †

PREFIX	MEANING	FREQUENCY
ab	from	98
ad	to	433
be	by	111
com	with	500
de	from	282
dis	apart	299
en	in	182
ex	out	286
in	into	336
in	not	317
pre	before	127
pro	in front of	146
re	back	457
sub	under	112
un	not	378

(These fifteen prefixes account for 82 per cent of the total prefixes in Thorndike's word list.)

* E. L. Thorndike, *Teachers List of 20,000 Words*, New York, Bureau of Publications, Teachers College, Columbia University, 1932.

† R. G. Stauffer, "A Study of Prefixes in the Thorndike List to Establish a List of Prefixes that Should be Taught in the Elementary School," *Journal of Educational Research*, Vol. 35, 1942, pp. 453–458.

lack of motivation. In the writers' opinion the best way to increase a child's reading speed is to help him find easy-to-comprehend materials which he will enjoy, and encourage him to read rapidly. In those few cases where slow reading is due to bad habits which are persistent (such as pointing with finger to reading material, or regressive eye movements) a series of corrective exercises under the individual guidance of the teacher should be undertaken.

Speed of reading is, of course, closely linked with comprehension.

Many children who read slowly do so because they do not really understand many of the words they are asked to read. Likewise slow readers may not have learned (because of insufficient neural maturation or poor training) to respond to reduced cues, or to use their perceptual abilities effectively. Symptomatic of inadequate percep-

FIGURE 14. The Reading Accelerator.
(Courtesy of Science Research Associates, 57 W. Grand Ave., Chicago 10, Illinois.)

tual ability are poor performance on flash card drills and poor eye movements while reading. Training to produce better understanding and to increase perceptual skills may involve a comprehensive program which enriches the child's experience with words and meanings, and provides exercises such as flash-card drills and reading acceleration. Acceleration has been made possible through the use of machines which uncover printed material at a predetermined rate. One such device, The Reading Accelerator, is shown in Figure 14. This machine adapts itself to all sizes of books or pamphlets, and operates in such a way that the pupil is forced to read at speeds which are appropriate for him.

Often youngsters, and adults for that matter, can read more rapidly than they actually do without any loss of comprehension. In fact, increased speed of reading frequently is accompanied by an increase in comprehension. Since persons are generally not aware that they do have the potential to read more rapidly, devices such as that shown in Figure 14 serve the dual purpose of demonstrating to the individual that he can read more rapidly, and at the same time provides him training in more rapid reading.

Improvement of interest in reading. Many children lose interest in reading because of the type of material which they are forced to read, and because reading materials are of a single difficulty level in a classroom in which reading ability varies as much as seven or eight grade levels (see Chapter 6). One obvious way to heighten interest in reading, therefore, is to provide a variety of reading materials representing not only several levels of reading ability but also several areas of interest. Studies have been made of youngsters' reading interests, including the interests of retarded readers, and books which have been preferred have been listed for the use of classroom teachers.[22] One such list appears in Table 24.

REMEDIAL SPELLING

One of the basic skills of good communication is spelling. At one time, this skill was probably over-emphasized in our schools. The winner of one of the state "spelling bees" in Illinois two decades ago was given individual tutoring by his teacher for three years. During this time the two of them tried to cover the entire unabridged dictionary. Although spelling has been relegated to a position of less prominence in today's schools, it is still essential if understandable writing is to be achieved. Witness the following paragraph written during World War II by an 11th grade student in an English Class in response to the question, "What do you think the chances are for an Allied victory this year?"

I do not think it possible thut under any scarmes they can possible be a vectery this year because the Germans know thut it will do them know good to give up now, so they will sacrfeas ever thing possible to when.

[22] For a list of books for slow learners see G. M. Blair, *op.cit.*, p. 170–174 who has tabulated "the 100 books most enjoyed by retarded readers in high school"; also Beryl McAdow, "Ten Years with Slow Readers," *The English Journal*, Vol. 30, 1941, pp. 573–579 (A list of 250 books popular with slow learners).

TABLE 24

Easy Reading Books for Older Children *

1. The Aviation Readers (first three books) Macmillan Company, New York
   Straight Up, Straight Down, Planes for Bob and Andy
2. The Core Vocabulary Readers, Macmillan Company, New York
   The Ranch Book, Rusty Wants a Dog, Smoky the Crow
3. The Unit Reading Series, Macmillan Company
   Booklets to go along with readers for first three grades, many of them of
   older interest and without pictures of children.
4. The Fairy Tale Series, Chas. E. Merrill Company, Columbus, Ohio
   First Fairy Tales, Giants and Fairies, Magic Tales
5. The Pleasure Reading Series, Garrard Press, Champaign, Illinois
   Fairy Stories, Famous Stories, Bible Stories, and others.
6. The Walt Disney Books, D. C. Heath and Company, Boston. An un-
   marked series of readers from Primer on, with the Disney animal characters.
7. *Robinson Crusoe for Young Folks,* Beckley Cardy Company, Chicago,
   Illinois
8. Picture Scripts, E. M. Hale Company, Chicago, Illinois
   Booklets in Literature, Science, and Social Studies
9. Science Education Series, Row, Peterson and Company, Evanston, Illinois
   Four Primary Booklets, *Spring Is Here, Summer Is Here,* etc.
10. The beginning books of other science series such as by Scribners, Ginn
    and Company, Singer Publishing Company
11. Childhood of Famous Americans Series, Bobbs-Merrill Company, In-
    dianapolis, Ind.
    Abe Lincoln   *Boy of Old Virginia*   *Alex Hamilton*
    Robert Fulton & many others   *Mark Twain*   *Ben Franklin*
12. American Adventure Series: Wheeler Publishing Company, Chicago,
    Illinois
    Davy Crockett   *Kit Carson*   *Buffalo Bill*
    Daniel Boone   *Chief Black Hawk*   & others
13. Easy Reading Books by Scott, Foresman and Company, Chicago, Illinois
    The Box Car Children   Eight Treasured Stories   When Washington Danced
    Lorna Doone   Six Great Stories   Moby Dick
    Tom Sawyer
14. Real People Series, Row, Peterson and Company, Evanston, Illinois
    Booklets of 36 pages, each about some person prominent in American
    history
15. Meadowbrook History Stories, T. Y. Crowell and Company, New York
    On Indian Trails, The First Year, Shipboy with Columbus
16. The Real Book Series, Garden City Books, Garden City, New York
    Animals, sports, pets, inventions, hobbies, etc.
17. The "Initial Biography" Series, Chas. Scribner's Sons, New York
    Washington, Lincoln, Jackson, and others.

* E. W. Dolch, Unpublished Material, College of Education, University of
Illinois, Urbana, Illinois, 1954.

and they are bound to have resous enought to last for at lest 2 to 3 more years.[23]

Poor spellers are easily located, but the causes are not readily apparent. Unlike deficiencies in other school subjects, the major cause does not appear to be closely related to low ability. Fernald claims that most poor spellers are the direct result of poor teaching practices, viz., (1) formal spelling periods, (2) monotonous and uninteresting repetition of meaningless content, (3) lack of adequate attention to spelling, and (4) the use of methods by which certain children cannot learn.[24]

As in other areas, there are available to teachers a wealth of research material upon which diagnosis and remedial teaching can be based. Besides a number of good diagnostic tests, there are several spelling lists which include words commonly needed by the average person. For example, Dolch has composed a list of 2000 words which comprises about 95 per cent of the words needed for ordinary writing.[25] Also there are studies of the kinds of words with which children may be expected to have difficulty. In the Gates list,[26] for example, not only are frequency of errors reported, but also the kinds of errors are indicated so that teachers may know what to stress in their teaching. The list of words in Table 25 comprises the 100 words most often misspelled by elementary-school children as shown by one study. The sample was taken from school children in all forty-eight states, including 190 school systems, and a total of 14,643 children. Words are arranged in the order of their frequency of misspelling. The most misspelled word was *their* (964 times) and the least *money* (54 times).

Any remedial teaching of spelling must take account of the basic fact that children have different kinds of word imagery. Some form visual images, others auditory, and still others motor (the way the word feels when spoken or written). Successful remediation usually entails adding practice in various ways of perceiving words. The most stubborn cases, for example, who have failed to spell using the sight or phonics approach, may show immediate and marked im-

[23] G. M. Blair, *op.cit.*, p. 262.
[24] Grace Fernald, *op.cit.*, pp. 186–192.
[25] E. W. Dolch, *The 2,000 Commonest Words for Spelling*, Champaign, Illinois, The Garrard Press, 1945.
[26] A. I. Gates, *A List of Spelling Difficulties in 3876 Words*, New York, Bureau of Publications, Teachers College, Columbia University, 1937.

provement when given practice in tracing words. In all such cases, important basic causes, such as emotional disturbance, negative conditioning, and physical or mental handicaps must also be given careful consideration.

TABLE 25

One Hundred Words Most Often Misspelled by Children in the Elementary Grades *

their	because	swimming	it's	all right
too	thought	first	started	happened
there	and	were	that's	didn't
they	beautiful	than	would	always
then	its	two	again	surprise
until	went	know	heard	before
our	where	decided	received	caught
asked	stopped	friend	coming	every
off	very	when	to	different
through	morning	let's	said	interesting
you're	something	mother	wanted	sometimes
clothes	named	another	hear	friends
looked	came	threw	from	children
people	name	some	frightened	an
pretty	tried	bought	for	school
running	here	getting	February	jumped
believe	many	going	once	around
little	knew	course	like	dropped
things	with	woman	they're	babies
him	together	animals	cousin	money

* L. W. Johnson, "One Hundred Words Most Often Misspelled by Children," *Journal of Educational Research*, Vol. 44, 1950, pp. 154–155. A similar study has been made of high-school spelling. First reports are contained in Thomas C. Pollock, "Misspelling in the Twelfth Grade," *Teachers Service Bulletin in English*, New York, The Macmillan Company, Vol. 6, No. 1, November, 1952.

One who has studied the principles of learning, and of transfer of training would be forced seriously to question the value of formal spelling exercises in which pupils commit lists of words to memory. In the first place, words so studied are out of context, and, as already shown, material is more easily and effectively learned when in a meaningful context. Secondly, the pupil's goal may be simply to learn the list and keep the spellings in mind long enough to repeat them to the teacher. Finally, it is certain that all children do not need practice in spelling the same words. It would thus appear that the most effective program, and one which might prevent difficulties in spelling would be to concentrate on spelling as an integral part of the pupil's written work. For example, a daily systematic check by the teacher and/or other pupils of all written work done by a particular child should provide a list of misspelled words for him. Work by each child on his own list might avoid much repetitious and needless practice, and in turn increase interest in spelling.

REMEDIAL SPEECH

Defective speech deserves consideration in its own right, but in addition needs special consideration because of its adverse effect upon other school learnings. Furthermore, speech disorders are frequently accompanied by emotional difficulties. The importance of speech is well put by Johnson who writes:

Children and adults, in school and out, do more speaking than either reading or writing. Speech is the most used of all language functions, and the most fateful, day in and day out, in the social and workaday relationships of people everywhere. What is done about speech, and especially speech disorders in our schools is, therefore, of utmost importance to the pupils as individuals and to society which they will help to create as they become adult citizens.[27]

Speech disorders include those of articulation, stuttering or stammering, and voice problems. As there are a number of disorders, so there are a number of causes, including illness, organic defect, hearing loss, injury through the misuse of the voice, and psychological factors. Stuttering, which is probably the most dramatic and common of the classroom disorders is believed to be almost entirely a result of psychological factors. Children who stutter are in many cases made so by parents, early teachers, or other persons having a formative influence upon the child. Parental anxiety about speech and the focusing of undue attention upon the normal nonfluency of children are common causes. It is not uncommon for parents to label, as a stutterer, a child who is having no more than the expected amount of speech difficulty. Speech may, in such cases, become a focal point for children's anxieties and feelings of inadequacy. A speech disorder becomes closely linked with emotional life, and may be made more serious by events which increase emotional tension.

[27] National Society for the Study of Education, *op.cit.*, p. 176.

Emotional strain may magnify the disorder especially in social or group situations.

A leading expert in the psychology of speech has given as general principles for classroom teachers the following points.[28]

1. No classroom teacher or school administrator should ever diagnose any child as a stutterer.
2. Speaking should be fun (a high degree of criticism of speech is bad).
3. Speaking should be encouraged (not forced).
4. Conditions affecting speech adversely should be minimized. In general a more informal, socially permissive classroom is less apt to cause speech difficulty. The more formal, threatening recitation or oral quiz is apt to do little to help and may actually interfere with the adjustment of the speech handicapped person.

REMEDIAL ENGLISH

Studies on a national scale have helped show the frequency of various kinds of errors in written and spoken expression. For example, one survey showed that somewhat over one-half the errors in oral English are in verb forms. A sample list (which in the twelfth grade comprised 70 per cent of all errors) was: [29]

ain't	has rang	done-did
he don't	have did	can-may
I seen	is-are	drawed
have saw	sit-set	blowed

Surveys such as these not only provide teachers with guides to material which should be stressed, but also serve as guides for analyses of errors within their own class. Identification of common errors and of the pupils who make them is a first step in gearing the teaching program to individual abilities, needs, and handicaps.

Errors of pupils in English expression (especially spoken) are apt to be persistent even in the face of efforts by the school to correct them. Ways of expression and colloquialisms from community and family are formed over a long period of time. Furthermore, pupils are apt to see school English and out-of-school English as unrelated. In spite of the effects of early training, and strong attitudes on the part of some pupils against changing to better English usage, there

[28] National Society for the Study of Education, *op.cit.*, pp. 188–192.
[29] G. M. Blair, *op.cit.*, p. 338.

is much that the school can do in remedying poor English. The following points should be fundamental to any remedial program.

1. Give constant examples of correct spoken and written English in a variety of situations. Class discussions, class reports, school clubs and social events will offer opportunities for the use of English which the student may begin to emulate. Youngsters are much more apt to accept change of English expression and attitudes about English from their peers than they are from their teachers.
2. Provide students with a knowledge of specific errors. Show pupils the correct expression and give a rule they can follow in finding it in the future. A paper which is returned with such notes as: "Too many incomplete sentences," "Punctuation poor," or "Capitalization of wrong words" will be of little help to the student who does not realize the specific errors of punctuation, capitalization, and sentence structure he is making.
3. Work on minimum essentials first. Glaring errors such as "He seen them" should be the targets of beginning instruction. Only after the rules which govern such common mistakes are understood and properly applied should teachers begin to stress the niceties of English. If these latter details are pressed too hard, and before the student is ready for them, the whole program may break down.
4. Above all, follow the principles of motivation (Chapters 7 and 8). Have English learned in context; relate it to presently existing interests and needs. The theme topic, selected entirely by the teacher, and covering a subject such as "My Favorite Grandparent," is still widely used in teaching English composition. Such assignments may be justified occasionally, but when they are the only kind which are made, there is little chance that all students will be interested.
5. Enlist the aid of other teachers in the school. English, reading, spelling, speech, and arithmetic are important to all teachers. Learning these things should be considered as a venture for the entire school rather than the responsibility for only one class.

REMEDIAL MATHEMATICS

Perhaps in no other academic subject are deficiencies so persistent, and so needless as in arithmetic. Many surveys have shown that students fail to learn the fundamental essentials of arithmetic even though they have sufficient ability and are not hampered by emotional disturbances. The idea that "I just can't get arithmetic" is common among college students as well as among those in the lower grades who face arithmetic problems daily. There is little doubt that in the schooling of many pupils there have been some experiences with mathematics which have built up habits of avoidance toward any problem or situation which involves even the simplest

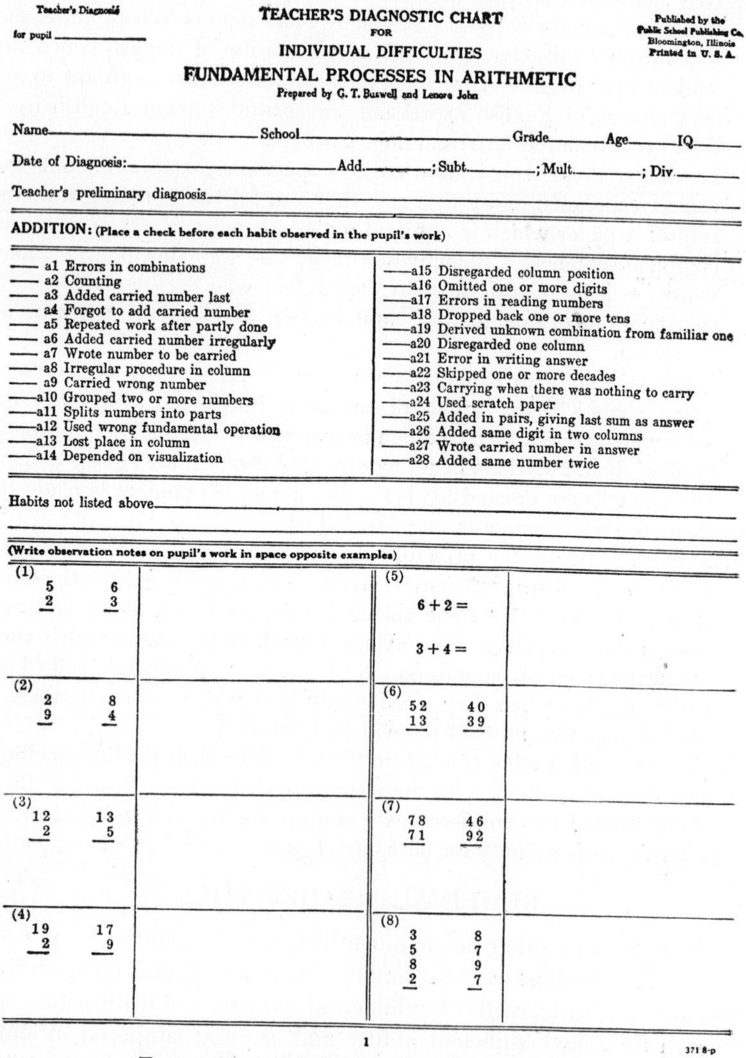

Teacher's Diagnosis
for pupil _____

Published by the
Public School Publishing Co.
Bloomington, Illinois
Printed in U. S. A.

TEACHER'S DIAGNOSTIC CHART
FOR
INDIVIDUAL DIFFICULTIES
FUNDAMENTAL PROCESSES IN ARITHMETIC
Prepared by G. T. Buswell and Lenore John

Name_____ School_____ Grade_____ Age_____ IQ_____

Date of Diagnosis:_____ Add._____; Subt._____; Mult._____; Div _____

Teacher's preliminary diagnosis_____

ADDITION: (Place a check before each habit observed in the pupil's work)

- a1 Errors in combinations
- a2 Counting
- a3 Added carried number last
- a4 Forgot to add carried number
- a5 Repeated work after partly done
- a6 Added carried number irregularly
- a7 Wrote number to be carried
- a8 Irregular procedure in column
- a9 Carried wrong number
- a10 Grouped two or more numbers
- a11 Splits numbers into parts
- a12 Used wrong fundamental operation
- a13 Lost place in column
- a14 Depended on visualization
- a15 Disregarded column position
- a16 Omitted one or more digits
- a17 Errors in reading numbers
- a18 Dropped back one or more tens
- a19 Derived unknown combination from familiar one
- a20 Disregarded one column
- a21 Error in writing answer
- a22 Skipped one or more decades
- a23 Carrying when there was nothing to carry
- a24 Used scratch paper
- a25 Added in pairs, giving last sum as answer
- a26 Added same digit in two columns
- a27 Wrote carried number in answer
- a28 Added same number twice

Habits not listed above_____

(Write observation notes on pupil's work in space opposite examples)

(1)
5   6
2   3

(5)
6 + 2 =

3 + 4 =

(2)
2   8
9   4

(6)
52   40
13   39

(3)
12   13
2   5

(7)
78   46
71   92

(4)
19   17
2   9

(8)
3   8
5   7
8   9
2   7

1

371 8-p

FIGURE 15. A Diagnostic Chart in Arithmetic.
(From *Buswell-John Diagnostic Test for Fundamental Processes in Arithmetic,* The Public School Publishing Company, Bloomington, Illinois. Used by permission of the publishers.)

arithmetic. It is therefore crucial that early identification and remedial work be undertaken before such adverse attitudes are formed. In this task the teacher will find many useful diagnostic tools. Some of the tests available identify the specific processes involved in the several skills in each of the basic computational areas. A good example is the Buswell-John Teacher's Diagnostic Chart for Individual Difficulties in the Fundamental Process of Arithmetic, which is shown in Figure 15.

There is no substitute for practice in learning the essential combinations in arithmetic. Practice of these combinations in a pleasant, nonthreatening atmosphere is the mainstay of remedial work in this field. In order that this activity be specific to the student's weaknesses, it is advisable for teachers to keep an individual record of students' errors. To make the work pleasant, teachers should know of a variety of exercises and games which might appeal to the student who needs special help. Some of the schemes which have been developed for this purpose are: (1) self-practice work books with graded step-by-step exercises (available for all levels from early elementary grades through adult levels), (2) number combination flash cards, (3) games using basic combinations in the four arithmetic areas: addition, subtraction, multiplication and division, and (4) play situations (make believe stores or banks) which allow practice in a pleasant and meaningful context.

The verbalization (working the problem out loud) by the pupil of the processes he uses in arithmetic gives the teacher an insight into the way he goes about his problem solving. Also, it gives the child a better understanding of what he is doing. Equally important is the use of concrete objects in beginning arithmetic experience. Subtraction (at least for the majority of children) should be learned by taking some things away—not just by taking away an abstraction which may have no root in the concrete experience of the youngster. Likewise, problems (especially the so-called thought problems) should be geared to the meaningful experiences of pupils.

USE OF AVAILABLE RESOURCES

Throughout this chapter there have been references to specific tests, and instructional materials for use in diagnostic and remedial work. No teacher can be expected to know of all the tools which are available. He should, however, know where he can find out about them and the general psychological principles involved in their use. Some of the sources available are the following.

Free and Inexpensive Materials. Booklets, posters, maps, recordings, scripts and other resources are available for little or no cost to the teacher who cares to write for them. Comprehensive lists of such materials have been published.[30] Also several book companies have free professional-service bulletins, as well as supplementary materials for classroom use.

Bibliographic materials. In every subject matter field in elementary school and in most of those in high school there are books which give specific techniques of remedial work for that particular subject (see the references at the end of this chapter). In addition there are professional journals, indexes, encyclopedias, and abstracts which should be available in the school's professional library. In planning the school or classroom library so that it will offer materials suitable for all abilities and interests, the teacher should know also that there are several good annotated bibliographies of books for children.

Other Facilities and Agencies. In several of the writers' classes in educational psychology the question has arisen regarding local, state and Federal agencies which are available to help teachers with special problems. For the most part, teachers show a surprising lack of awareness of such facilities (even in their own community). The U. S. Office of Education, The National Education Association, The Office of Vocational Rehabilitation, the U. S. Public Health Service all make publications available through the Superintendent of Public Documents. Most states offer consulting service and printed information through their state departments of public instruction, plus information and help through child welfare and juvenile research organizations.

Assistance which may be obtained in most communities includes consultative help from local physicians, ministers, and employers. Information may also be obtained from local offices of juvenile research or child welfare agencies, and from social case workers. These are but suggestive of the resources of which a teacher may

---

[30] Examples of such lists are: Division of Surveys and Field Service (George Peabody College for Teachers, Nashville, Tennessee), *Free and Inexpensive Learning Materials,* 1948; and Educators Progress Service: *Elementary Teachers Guide to Free Curriculum Materials,* J. G. Fowlkes and D. A. Morgan (Eds.), Annual Editions, Randolph, Wisconsin.

avail himself. Often feelings of helplessness which accompany a very serious problem case could be overcome and remedial work undertaken if available resources were known and put to use.

SUMMARY

A sizeable percentage of the school-age population is either not in school or profits little from its school experience. Many of the latter group (perhaps as many as 40 per cent) will drop out before they finish high school. In the face of increasing class size, teachers may feel they are forced to give less time to individual pupils even though the range of abilities has probably increased in the past few decades.

Although there is no single answer to the problem of educational casualties, it is virtually certain that many pupils, who would otherwise have failed or dropped out of school, are being helped by teachers who have discovered children's difficulties early enough and have provided appropriate remedial teaching. Alert teachers have recognized that anything which interferes with reception of stimuli (sensory defects in vision and hearing), the child's responses (such as disease, low mental ability, or injury), or with motives and energy (such as negative attitudes and emotional instability) interferes with learning. Any such interference whether it be a speech defect, a slight loss of hearing, or a feeling of rejection must be recognized and treated before the child's full potential is released. Remedial teaching begins with a discovery of pupils who are having or are apt to have difficulties. Once these cases have been identified, a more thorough diagnosis to discover the cause of the difficulty is undertaken.

Learning difficulties may be detected by routine physical checkups, mental tests, achievement tests, and clues which the teacher may notice in observing children at work.

The causes of difficulties are found through a more intensive analysis which includes the use of diagnostic tests, interviews, and case studies. It is especially important in this step that teachers study the *processes* which pupils use in solving problems or in going about their work.

Principles of diagnosis and remedial teaching apply to all subjects and grade levels. But there are individual problems in each of the school subjects. In the teaching of reading, for example, there are common errors such as reversals, regressive eye movements, and inability to discriminate between letters and words. In each subject, the teacher should apply the basic principles of remedial teaching, but in addition should make use of the special techniques which research has found to be effective. Remedial teaching in essence is just good teaching which takes the learner where he is, and through well motivated activities leads him to increased competence in his areas of weakness.

REFERENCES FOR FURTHER STUDY

Anderson, I. H., and Dearborn, W. F., *The Psychology of Teaching Reading*, New York, The Ronald Press Co., 1952.

Backus, Ollie, and Beasley, Jane, *Speech Therapy with Children*, Boston, Houghton Mifflin Co., 1951.

Betts, E. A., *Foundations of Reading Instruction with Emphasis on Differentiated Guidance*, New York, American Book Co., 1950.

Blair, G. M., *Diagnostic and Remedial Teaching in Secondary Schools*, New York, The Macmillan Co., 1946.

Dolch, E. W., *Helping Handicapped Children in School*, Champaign, Illinois, The Garrard Press, 1948.

Dolch, E. W., *Manual for Remedial Reading*, Champaign, Illinois, The Garrard Press, 1945,

Dolch, E. W., *Problems in Reading*, Champaign, Illinois, The Garrard Press, 1948.

Dolch, E. W., *Psychology and Teaching of Reading*, Champaign, Illinois, The Garrard Press, 1951.

Durrell, D. D., *Improvement of Basic Reading Abilities*, World Book Co., Yonkers, New York, 1940.

Featherstone, W. B., *Teaching the Slow Learner*, New York, Bureau of Publications, Teachers College, Columbia University, 1951.

Fernald, Grace M., *Remedial Techniques in Basic School Subjects*, New York, The McGraw-Hill Book Co., Inc., 1943.

Foran, T. G., *The Psychology and Teaching of Spelling*, Washington, D. C., The Catholic Education Press, 1934.

Garrison, Karl C., *The Psychology of Exceptional Children*, New York, The Ronald Press Co., 1950.

Gates, A. I., *The Improvement of Reading* (Third Edition), New York, The Macmillan Co., 1947.

Harris, A. J., *How To Increase Reading Ability*, New York, Longmans, Green and Co., Inc., 1947.

Heck, A. O., *The Education of Exceptional Children*, New York, McGraw-Hill Book Co., Inc., 1953.

Johnson, Wendell, *Speech Problems of Children: A Guide to Care and Correction*, New York, Grune and Stratton, 1950.

Kirk, S. A., *Teaching Reading to Slow-learning Children*, Boston, Houghton Mifflin Co., 1940.

Kirk, S. A., and Johnson, G. O., *Educating the Retarded Child*, Boston, Houghton Mifflin Co., 1951.

Levinson, Abraham, *The Mentally Retarded Child*, New York, The John Day Company, 1952.

National Society for the Study of Education, 34th Yearbook, *Educational Diagnosis*, Bloomington, Illinois, Public School Publishing Co., 1933.

National Society for the Study of Education, Part II, 48th Yearbook, *Reading in the Elementary School*, Chicago, University of Chicago Press, 1949.

National Society for the Study of Education, Part II, 50th Yearbook, *The Teaching of Arithmetic*, Chicago, University of Chicago Press, 1951.

Robinson, H. M., *Why Pupils Fail in Reading*, Chicago, University of Chicago Press, 1946.

Thorndike, E. L., *et al.*, *The Psychology of Algebra*, New York, The Macmillan Co., 1924.

Thorndike, E. L., *et al.*, *The Psychology of Arithmetic*, New York, The Macmillan Co., 1924.

Traxler, A. E., and Townsend, Agatha, *Another Five Years of Research in Reading*, New York, Educational Records Bureau, 1946, 527 Item Bibliography.

Tredgold, A. F., *A Text-Book of Mental Deficiency*, Baltimore, William Wood and Company, 1937.

Triggs, Frances O., *Remedial Reading*, Minneapolis, The University of Minnesota Press, 1943.

Werner, Lorna S., *Speech in the Elementary School*, Evanston, Illinois, Row, Peterson, and Co., 1947.

West, Robert, Kennedy, Low, Carr, Anna, and Backus, O. L., *The Rehabilitation of Speech*, New York, Harper & Brothers, 1947.

FILMS

Education of Exceptional Children, University of Illinois, Division of University Extension, Urbana, Illinois. (25 mins.)

PART IV

ADJUSTMENT AND GUIDANCE

Chapter 13

Basic Processes of Adjustment

EVERY PERSON, man or child, spends twenty-four hours a day satisfying or attempting to satisfy his physical, social, and personality needs. We see people eating, drinking, resting, striving for social approval, seeking affection, trying to achieve mastery of a vocation, and striving for independence. Anyone who observes small children will note that they are always wanting something. Older children and adults are always on the go, attempting to reach the goals which will reduce the tensions created by their needs. It is important for teachers to recognize that every activity of the child or pupil satisfies some need which he possesses. Whenever a pupil is restless, aggressive, impudent, cooperative, delinquent, or in fact doing anything, he is making an adjustment to life. The adjustment he makes may not be a good one so far as society is concerned, but it is an adjustment just the same, and its purpose is to satisfy some organic or personality need of the individual.

FUNDAMENTAL HUMAN NEEDS

Many lists have been given of human needs. Murray [1] divided all needs into two groups: (1) viscerogenic needs, and (2) psychogenic needs. His list of viscerogenic needs include: air, water, food, sex, lactation, urination, defecation, avoidance of injury, etc. His list of psychogenic needs include achievement, recognition, autonomy, affiliation, and some twenty-two others which could well be grouped under two or three basic needs. Freud in his later years advanced the notion that man has two basic drives—the life instinct and the

[1] H. A. Murray, *et al.*, *Explorations in Personality*, New York, Oxford University Press, 1938.

death instinct. The life instinct includes all sexual impulses as well as the urges for self-preservation. The death instinct would include not only self-destructive tendencies but also aggressive and hostile feelings toward others. Alfred Adler made the desire for status the key urge in man. People want to be important, and most of their life activities are devoted to satisfying this need, he believed. Herbert Carroll has stated that the "preservation and enhancement of the phenomenal self are achieved through satisfaction of four fundamental needs: the need for physical security, the need for emotional security, the need for mastery, and the need for status." [2] Other lists could be given. In previous chapters of this book (Chapters 2, 3, 4, and 7) discussions of the needs of children have been presented together with a listing of some of the basic needs. Most lists of needs overlap with each other to a great extent and there is usually considerable overlapping between the needs presented on a single list. It is most important, however, for the teacher to have some list in mind when analyzing the behavior of children. It helps the teacher realize that all behavior is motivated, and assists in clarifying the causes of behavior.

A List of Human Needs. The major physical needs (drives) include:

1. Hunger
2. Thirst
3. Activity-rest cycle
4. Sex
5. Temperature regulation
6. Evacuation (urination and defecation)
7. Avoidance of pain and injury

It is somewhat more difficult to draw up a satisfactory list of social and personality needs, but there is general agreement that individuals, at least in our culture, exhibit the following:

1. Need for status
2. Need for security
3. Need for affection
4. Need for independence
5. Need for achievement

[2] Herbert A. Carroll, *Mental Hygiene,* Second Edition, New York, Prentice-Hall, Inc., 1951, p. 43.

In addition to these somewhat universal physical and social needs, every individual develops habits of a personal nature which possess driving force and act in much the same fashion as a basic need. A person who has learned to drink coffee, play golf, or attend the opera possesses a series of drives to action which differ from those of a person who has not developed these particular habits. In understanding why children are motivated to do what they do, the teacher must take into account not only the fundamental physical and social needs (drives) of all children, but also the particular habits and interests of each individual child.

How Needs Operate. When a need exists and is unsatisfied, the individual becomes restless and tense. He seeks some goal which will reduce the state of imbalance which exists within him. The hungry person seeks food; the thirsty individual wants liquid; the tired person craves rest; the cold individual seeks warmth; the unnoticed person strives for attention and status; the unloved one wants affection; and the over-protected individual desires and strives for independence. When a need is completely satisfied, a temporary or momentary state of equilibrium is established and activity toward the appropriate goal ceases. After eating a hearty meal, the individual does not crave food for several hours. A student who has been complimented by his teacher or peers for some worthy performance may not need further vocal approval for several hours or even days. He does, however, need to feel constantly that he belongs, has status, and is a worthwhile person. Most of the social and personality needs remain in a somewhat unsatisfied state. Seldom does a person achieve too much status, security, affection, or achievement.

CONDITIONS WHICH CREATE FRUSTRATION

In many ways this world is unfriendly to man and the satisfaction of his needs. Too much rain or too little rain may result in flood or drought which may create a shortage of food. Extreme heat and cold are also examples of physical factors which may thwart the satisfaction of man's needs. Society has passed many regulations which may or may not be good for the group as a whole, but which invariably restrict the satisfaction of the needs of some individuals. Laws which discriminate between races, requirements of admission to medical schools, standards of what constitutes appropriate dress in the summer time, all are examples of situations which cause frustration for given people. In some communities on the warmest days men are required to wear their coats on occasions when they would be much more comfortable with them off. School regulations which insist that all pupils meet certain prescribed levels of achievement may be very thwarting to children of limited background or ability. Poverty may seriously limit what a person may do, and thus create numerous frustrations which must be met by some sort of adjustment on the part of the individual.

The individual with a personal defect or physical ailment may not be able to engage in activities open to others. Poor eyesight, lameness, a damaged heart, all may produce frustrations of a serious nature for some persons. Conflict with resulting frustration inevitably ensues also when an individual strives to attain two goals which are not compatible. The student who desires to be a playboy and a Phi Beta Kappa candidate at the same time may run into difficulties as will also the individual who tries to please two groups which have widely differing ideals. The Biblical statement that "Ye cannot serve God and mammon" is true from a mental hygiene viewpoint. A final source of frustration results when an individual's moral standards, which have been developed as a child, come in conflict with subsequently developed behavior patterns. Thus the child who has been taught that it is wrong to smoke, dance, or play cards may have severe guilt feelings when he engages in these activities as a college student. The Hebrew child who has been taught that he should not eat pork may spend a sleepless night after having partaken of this food, and the Seventh Day Adventist child may feel very worthless and uncomfortable after having played ball or attended a movie on Saturday.

ADJUSTING TO FRUSTRATING CONDITIONS

As has been stated earlier, the individual whose needs are thwarted is tense and uncomfortable. He is in a state of disequilibrium. Some adjustment must be made to reduce this state of hypertension, and make the situation tolerable for him. There are numerous adjustment mechanisms which are typically used by persons who are thwarted in reaching their goals. These include aggression, direct and indirect; compensation; sublimation; identification; rationalization; projection; repression; reaction formation; egocentricism; negativism; withdrawal; regression; developing physical ailments;

and expiation or atonement. The neurotic or psychotic person, in addition, has ways of behaving in the face of frustration which include hysterias, amnesias, obsessions, phobias, hypochondria, delusions, and hallucinations.

ADJUSTMENT MECHANISMS

Aggression. A typical reaction to frustration is aggression. In fact, the thesis is held by Dollard *et al.*[3] that aggressive impulses are inevitably set in motion by frustration. The individual does not always show overt aggressive responses, but instead may suppress and restrain them. It is very normal, however, to attack directly the frustrating object. The boy who is insulted by a classmate not uncommonly attacks his tormenter physically. School yard fights may not be as much in evidence as formerly, but they have by no means become extinct. Children from the lower social classes tend to exhibit their aggressive feelings somewhat more directly than those from the middle and upper classes. The psychologist Karen Horney has indicated that to repress all hostile and aggressive feelings is bad from a mental hygiene viewpoint. The repression of such feelings may lead to anxiety and neurosis. She would suggest that it is good for a person to express his hostile feelings occasionally, to blow off steam.

Much aggression, however, which is engaged in by people is not direct. Particularly in middle class culture, the pattern is to relieve aggressive feelings in indirect ways. The man who is humiliated by another man may not suggest that the two of them have a fight. Instead, he may take out his feelings of hostility by making disparaging and critical remarks regarding the man he dislikes. Innocent bystanders are often the targets for people who have aggressive feelings which must be relieved. The teacher who has had an argument with her husband before coming to school in the morning may vent her aggressive feelings upon the children in her room. The boy who has been thwarted by his teacher in the classroom may, during the recess period, push into a mud puddle some child he chances to see on the playground. People who are frustrated also frequently relieve their feelings of aggression by attacking inanimate objects. We have

---

[3] John Dollard, N. E. Miller, L. W. Doob, O. H. Mowrer, and R. R. Sears, *Frustration and Aggression*, New Haven, Yale University Press, 1939.

all seen people break dishes, kick chairs, or slam a door as a means of releasing pent-up feelings of aggression.

Students of social psychology have suggested that aggressive feel-- ings also form one of the bases for prejudice toward certain minority groups. A large group of people or given individuals who are frustrated may make attacks or show unfavorable attitudes toward some group which has never done them any harm. A scapegoat is made of the minority group as a means of reducing the tensions resulting from group or personal frustration.

Every individual will have aggressive feelings at times. The teacher should expect to encounter this behavior on the part of pupils. It is perfectly normal. Hilgard and Russell comment on aggression as it affects the classroom teacher as follows:

> Every child needs to find some way to give expression to anger, hostility, and destructiveness which arise out of the thwartings which he faces. . . . One of the lessons to be learned is that we do not, as teachers, always achieve the consequences we seek by an overemphasis upon wholesomeness, propriety, and adult standards of cleanliness and order. . . . Occasional permissiveness, that allows a frank expression of resentment, that takes feelings at their face-value rather than forcing their denial or disguise may result in a child's coming out more spontaneous and friendly and in the end, actually more socially conforming.[4]

Some of the socially acceptable channels for relieving aggressive feelings which can be used by the school include athletic contests, finger-painting, dramatic plays, and so on. The pupil who has no socially acceptable outlet for his hostile feelings will either repress them and possibly develop anxieties, or he may become aggressive in non-socially acceptable ways and find himself in trouble with constituted authority.

Compensation. Every individual must feel important. If he cannot attain distinction in one way, he will try to attain it in some other way. The boy who is a failure in his course in Latin may save his ego or self-esteem by making a success of his efforts in athletics. The boy who has suffered as a child from infantile paralysis may not go out for athletics but instead become unusually proficient as a

---

[4] Ernest R. Hilgard and David H. Russell, "Motivation in School Learning," in Part I, the *49th Yearbook of the National Society for the Study of Education,* 1950, pp. 41–42.

writer or speaker. The boy who cannot dance may brag of his prowess in football, and the pupil who is never given any scholastic recognition may attain distinction as the school's biggest rowdy. The term compensation as used in the foregoing illustrations really means substitution. Attainable goals are substituted for non-attainable goals or goals difficult to attain.

The term compensation has also been used to apply to the situation where a person attempts to succeed in the very line where his handicap lies. Thus a child with a speech defect may, through outstanding effort, become famous as a speaker. A weakling may through strenuous training become a great athlete. A man with very ordinary ability may through hard work rise to the top of his profession. Examples of this type of compensation are numerous. It has been reported that such outstanding athletes and "strong men" as Eugene Sandow, Charles Atlas, Bernarr Macfadden, and Johnny Weissmuller were sickly in their youth. Glenn Cunningham was crippled by burns when he was seven years old, yet he was able to overcome his physical handicap to become one of the greatest mile runners of all time.

Both types of compensation which have been mentioned serve to satisfy the individual's ego and make it possible for him to atone for inferiority feelings he may have. It is generally accepted that compensation is a mechanism which grows out of a feeling of inferiority. Since everyone feels inferior at times it is inevitable that everyone compensates. The person who is relatively secure, however, probably does not engage in compensatory activities to as great an extent as the very insecure individual. It should be stressed, nevertheless, that compensation may be a valuable aid to adjustment. It reduces tensions and anxiety feelings and promotes in many cases good mental health. Teachers should help pupils find activities in which they can excel and thus compensate for weaknesses they may possess. The child who is a success in something is much more apt to be developing in a wholesome manner than one who has been continuously thwarted in reaching his goals. It is important, however, that socially approved compensatory activities be resorted to rather than those which are disapproved. The child with inferiority feelings may compensate by engaging in delinquent acts to gain the attention he desires, or he may satisfy his fundamental need for status by putting forth effort to succeed in worthwhile activities. The way the child is treated by the school will to a great extent determine which type of compensation he will employ.

Sublimation. Sublimation is really a form of compensation. As used by the Freudians the term meant the substitution of a socially accepted non-sexual goal for a goal which is sexual in nature. The individual who was thwarted sexually might resolve his frustration by developing interests in art, sports, scientific research, social service work, etc. More recently, the term has been used in a somewhat broader sense. Cameron and Magaret define sublimation as "the substitution of socially approved reactions, particularly if they have an altruistic flavor, for socially discredited or taboo behavior." [5] This latter definition, of course, would include the substitution of non-sex activities for sex activities. Children of adolescent age according to the Kinsey report are by no means sexless. Sex curiosity and sex drive probably reach their peaks during the teens. In our society with its prolonged period of adolescence, young people need many non-sexual outlets to relieve sex tensions which are built up. Schools with their programs of athletics, social dancing, music and art, woodwork, etc., undoubtedly contribute activities which serve this purpose. The child who is kept busy in such ways has considerably less energy to devote to direct sexual activity or to fantasy in this realm. Helping children develop hobbies, scientific interests, and vocational plans are also among the things the school can do to assist children in sublimating their basic sexual drives.

Identification. Identification is a mechanism by which an individual satisfies certain of his basic needs by allying himself emotionally with or feeling himself one with another person, group of persons, or institution. The individual may have many personal limitations and be quite unsuccessful in reaching his own goals, but by associating himself with successful people or institutions he may receive some reflected glory.

Children often identify themselves with their parents, a successful relative, or with characters in movies, novels, or plays. Through this process adventure may be had, and the desire for power and status may be partially gratified. A common sight around a high school is a non-athletic youth walking arm in arm with a successful athlete or at least trailing close behind. Individuals like to talk about

[5] Norman Cameron and Ann Magaret, *Behavior Pathology*, Boston, Houghton Mifflin Company, 1951, pp. 377–378.

the important people they know or have met. Graduate students when asked what professors they have studied under, give the names of the most distinguished professors and omit the less distinguished. People strive to shake the hands of famous personages or to collect their autographs. It is a great source of pride to the citizens of a community to be able to say that the governor of the state lives in their town or that Abraham Lincoln once slept there. To be associated with a famous business firm, if only in a very minor capacity, or to be a student at a well known university gives the individual involved a sense of prestige and importance and helps reduce any feelings of inferiority he may have. Colleges with successful athletic teams or with distinguished faculties have little trouble drawing students.

Individuals want to be important. If they cannot achieve distinction in their own right they can at least identify with someone who has. When a child identifies himself with a given person or group the tendency is for him to emulate the characteristics of that person or group. Identification thus becomes a powerful dynamism in the formation of personality and character. The school by providing worthwhile models in the form of teachers, personages in literature and science, and appropriate school traditions can do much to assist pupils in making proper identifications. The child who identifies with characters from the realm of gangsters, hoodlums, and rich gamblers is likely to turn out to be quite a different person from one who establishes strong emotional ties with respected and worthwhile people.

Rationalization. It is very difficult for one to admit that he has failed to reach a cherished goal or that his behavior falls short of what is expected of him by others or himself. The situation of not achieving one's goals or not living up to one's expectations may leave the individual not only frustrated but also with feelings of guilt. This is, of course, very undesirable for the person's state of mental health. An adjustment mechanism which is widely used to reduce guilt feelings and tensions arising from this condition is known as *rationalization*. Rationalization has been defined as a "mechanism by which the individual justifies his beliefs or actions by giving reasons other than those which activated or motivated him." [6] By rationaliza-

[6] Louis P. Thorpe, *The Psychology of Mental Health,* New York, The Ronald Press Co., 1950, p. 724.

tion the individual is able to excuse his shortcomings and maintain the defense of his ego.

The pupil who fails in his school work may insist that his teachers are unfair or that a recent illness was the basis of his difficulty. The student who fails to gain admission to medical school may take the position that he did not want to be a doctor anyway—since the work is so strenuous and unpleasant. The girl who is unsuccessful in being invited to join a sorority may argue that sororities are snobbish and not worth belonging to. This type of rationalization has been referred to as the *sour grapes* mechanism. It gets its name from the story of the fox in Aesop's Fables who saved his pride by insisting that the unattainable grapes were sour and hence not worth the effort required to reach them.

Another form of rationalization bears the name of *sweet lemon* or Pollyanna mechanism. The individual is unsatisfied with what he has attained but maintains that everything is lovely. A school teacher may have taken a position which is most grueling and unpleasant, yet he may maintain that he likes his work immensely and that he would not change to another position for anything. A man may buy an automobile which is so inferior that inwardly he is most unhappy. Outwardly, however, he may argue that it is a fine car—one of the best on the market. The pupil who is given a minor part in a school play, though secretly disappointed, may loudly proclaim how happy he is with the type of role he has obtained.

Everyone rationalizes his failures to some extent. If people did not do so the world would contain many more people in poor mental health than it now has. Rationalization is a face saving device which keeps people in a relatively sound state of mind who otherwise would be quite unhappy and maladjusted. As with most other adjustment mechanisms, however, it may be overused. The college student who plays twenty-seven holes of golf every day while receiving failing grades in his courses, may rationalize that one's health should always come first. Yet this student's approach to his problem is far from being realistic, and greater conflict and frustration may result in the future if he does not change his routine of college life. Many problems and situations in life have to be met directly and solved rather than rationalized away.

Projection. Another method used by individuals to excuse their shortcomings and relieve guilt feelings is known as projection. This is a mechanism by which an individual may ascribe to others his own weaknesses, faults, and impulses. The individual judges others by himself. The stingy person more often than would be expected by chance will accuse others of being stingy. The person with a weakness for alcohol will call attention to this defect in others. The dishonest person will assume that everyone else is dishonest.

The term projection is also used to apply to the process by which an individual blames other people or inanimate objects for his own failures. In this sense, projection is essentially another form of rationalization. A school boy involved in a fight will usually blame the other boy for starting the fight. The tennis player who drives the ball into the net will look at his racket as if something were the matter with it. The person involved in an automobile accident almost invariably accuses the other person of being responsible for the mishap. School children caught committing offenses frequently reply, "George made me do it." Projection is an age old method of shifting responsibility and passing the buck which goes back to the garden of Eden when Adam blamed Eve for his own deficiencies.

Although projection is extremely common and undoubtedly reduces tension in the frustrated individual, its constant use is by no means to be commended. In the first place, it does nothing to solve the basic problem or difficulty, and in the second place, when carried on in an extreme form, its use may eventuate in hallucinations. School teachers should aid children to make adjustments which will protect and enhance their egos in ways other than those which involve projection. The child who makes excessive use of this mechanism can appropriately be thought of as needing help and attention.

Repression. Repression is a dynamism which is fundamental in the Freudian system of psychology. It is a process by which the individual attempts to protect his ego by pushing into the unconscious those thoughts and experiences which are in conflict with his moral standards or which are painful to contemplate. Freudians account for much forgetting in terms of repression. Experiences which end in failure or humiliation, or which cause the person to have guilt feelings are more frequently forgotten than those which are of a more happy nature. The individual escapes from his troubles and conflicts by forgetting them.

Redl and Wattenberg have given an example of how repression is used by children to bury feelings of guilt and anxiety. They say:

Nothing is more normal than occasional feelings of rivalry or hostility between brothers and sisters. Under ordinary circumstances youngsters will be aware of these emotions, express some of them openly but gain control of their more harmful wishes just as they gain command over anger-producing inclinations in other areas. In some cases, however, where parents put such a heavy demand on "loving" a brother or sister, the child cannot even allow himself to perceive such hostile feelings as he may have. He will have to repress them all. That means he will not be aware of having them even when they color his actual behavior or appear disguised in his dreams.[7]

There is no question but that repression is used by all individuals at times as a tension reducing mechanism. It is generally believed, however, that this method is one of the most undesirable of the adjustment devices. Vaughn[8] has stated that although it may provide temporary relief, it ultimately serves to perpetuate the emotional disturbance by concealing it. Karen Horney believes that repressing hostile feelings is the chief cause of anxiety and eventually neurosis.[9]

So far as the school is concerned the point should be made that repression may be minimized by providing for children a permissive atmosphere—one in which fear and personal threats are largely eliminated. This will give children a chance to work out their problems rather than forget them or deny their existence. Carroll has suggested that "children should be taught not to force back their desires, not to try to forget their fears and the experiences which they have had which have been accompanied by feeling of guilt, but to face their needs frankly and to work out socially acceptable means of satisfying them."[10] In any event, opportunities should be provided for children to let off steam once in a while, to give vent to their pent-up emotions. The successful teacher will allow pupils to disagree with him on occasion and to express openly contrary opinions and feelings. It is possible for children to develop self-control without

[7] Fritz Redl and William W. Wattenberg, *Mental Hygiene in Teaching*, p. 53. Copyright, 1951, by Harcourt, Brace and Company, New York.

[8] Wayland F. Vaughn, *Personal and Social Adjustment*, New York, The Odyssey Press, 1952, p. 289.

[9] Karen Horney, *New Ways of Psychoanalysis*, New York, W. W. Norton and Company, 1937.

[10] Herbert A. Carroll, *Mental Hygiene*, Second Edition, New York, Prentice-Hall, Inc., 1951, p. 234.

the harmful consequences which may result from continually repressing or bottling up normal emotions.

Reaction Formation. Reaction formation or reversal formation, as it is sometimes called, is the process of substituting an opposite reaction for one which is frustrating or anxiety-inducing. A mother, for example, originally wished very much not to have a baby. The baby was born nevertheless. The mother disliked the baby and rejected it. This rejection, however, aroused in her serious feelings of guilt, for mothers are not supposed to dislike their babies. She repressed these emotions of hatred toward her baby, and substituted in its place an extremely overprotective attitude. She guarded the baby's health with the greatest of care. As the child got older, she insisted that he always be kept absolutely clean. She would not let him play with other children for fear that he would get dirty or would be hurt. She took him to school regularly when other children his age were able to go alone and showered him with excessive affection and attention. Some people might regard this woman as being a wonderful mother. Her overprotection which resulted from reaction formation, however, actually made the child feel insecure and led to his social maladjustment.

Whenever an individual is observed to go to great extremes in expressing a viewpoint or advocating a course of action—when he is all steamed up over a situation which is of relatively little concern to average adjusted persons, the presence of reaction formation may be suspected. The individual who is extremely prudish, inordinately polite, or outstandingly sanctimonious, may actually be covering up for powerful feelings in the opposite direction. The writer once knew of a minister in the West who preached every Sunday morning for a period of several months on the evils of women wearing short skirts and low necked dresses. He emphasized that such attire was dragging America to its doom, and was the basis for most sexual crimes in our society. He seemed to be unusually concerned over this particular subject. It was not long, however, after this series of lectures was delivered that this particular preacher was expelled from the denomination he represented because he was found guilty of numerous sexual indiscretions. Another person of the writer's acquaintance, a young man 33 years of age, died of acute alcoholism after having suffered numerous attacks of delerium tremens. When he was sober he had been a powerful temperance lecturer. Neither of these persons was insincere. Each was trying desperately to repress undesirable feelings he recognized in himself and used the mechanism of reaction formation to help him succeed in this task.

School children are sometimes observed to be extremely favorable toward or opposed to certain types of behavior which is just the opposite of their repressed feelings. A high school boy, for example, may declare that it is disgraceful for boys and girls of high school age to have dates or to walk around arm in arm. Actually this is exactly what he would like to do if his conscience or circumstances would permit it. School teachers should be on the alert to detect such individuals and help them if at all possible to make more appropriate discharge of their fundamental feelings.

Egocentricism. The individual who feels insecure will often strive to establish himself as the center of attention. He may show off, ask numerous questions, talk loudly, try to be witty, and play all types of mischievous pranks. School children who fit this description are numerous and are not difficult to identify. The writer knows of a ninth-grade youngster who released a snake in the back of the room while his English class was in session. Needless to say he received attention not only from his classmates but also from his teacher who soon arrived on the scene. This particular boy had been very unsuccessful in his English course, largely because of low scholastic ability and poor home background. As the course was taught there were very few ways, if any, that he could attract attention through normal channels. Engaging in the type of prank he played was, however, well within his abilities and it gave him a feeling of importance to be noticed.

Everyone, of course, needs regular and satisfying reinforcement of his ego. School activities and curricula should be so designed that every child has some opportunity to receive attention and acclaim for creditable achievement. If this is done, many so-called misbehavior problems will automatically disappear from classrooms.

Negativism. Another ego enhancing and attention getting device is known as negativism. The individual may be opposed to almost everything. In school when a group decides upon a course of action the negativistic child may stubbornly refuse to go along with the decision. He will often sulk, rebel against authority, and refuse to be bound by rules. Negativistic behavior in the home is also a frequent reaction of children who feel thwarted or insecure. Such children may refuse to eat, to talk, or follow any idea propounded by a sibling or their parents. Negativism on the part of children is difficult to deal with but may be lessened by teachers and parents if such rules as the following are adherred to:

1. Avoid situations which are known to produce conflict.
2. Do not make issues of minor sources of disagreement.
3. Reward positive behavior when it occurs.
4. Look at one's own behavior to see if it may possibly be the type which is producing negativistic reactions. Teachers and parents frequently assume that the blame rests with the child. Actually, the alteration of adult behavior will tend to produce marked changes in the child's behavior in so far as negativism is concerned. When a child refuses to do an assignment required by the teacher, the teacher might well analyze the assignment in terms of its relevance to the child's needs, interests, and capabilities.

Withdrawal. In the face of thwarting and distressing situations some individuals find that the easiest way out is to withdraw. Withdrawing probably does not take as much energy as some of the other adjustment mechanisms, e.g., aggression or compensation. One merely removes himself from the world of action and conflict and obtains the satisfaction of his needs in less strenuous ways. Among the several forms of withdrawal are daydreaming, becoming sleepy or drowsy, escaping into work, and using alcohol or other narcotics.

In the process of daydreaming the individual achieves a certain amount of relief from tension and frustration through imaginative thinking. The boy who has failed his course in algebra may imagine that he is a successful boat captain or aviator, and that throngs of people are waiting to give him acclaim as he steps from the parlour car of the Century Limited. The girl who has failed to get a date for the high-school dance may sit for hours dreaming of her success as an opera singer or dancer. Everyone daydreams to some extent and no harm may result if the person keeps in good touch with reality. An individual, however, who habitually achieves his successes in the world of fantasy is in for trouble. He may withdraw into the world of dreams to such an extent that he does not recognize that people are around him. He may develop hallucinations and carry on the major part of his living in a world of make-believe.

The case of a boy who was given to excessive daydreaming but who was helped by his teacher to overcome this tendency is described by Bernard as follows:

> The danger of excessive daydreaming is apparent in the case of a boy who wanted to be a hero in the eyes of his playmates. His conception of the hero role was that of an outstanding athlete. As his participation in the boys' games did not bring him immediate stardom, he forsook the difficult route of actual accomplishment for the easier path of daydreaming. Withdrawing from the group, he devoted his time to the construction of imagined successes on the playing field. Here his success was unchallenged. Since he controlled all the imaginary players, he could always assume the hero's role, and he dreamed that he received the adulation and praise which he desired. Luckily, he came into contact with a teacher who was concerned with his withdrawal and was willing to help attack the problem. By slow stages the teacher secured the confidence of the lad, learned of his daydreams, and used them constructively, showing the boy the necessity of going through a learning period preparatory for successful participation in sports. He helped him develop his latent capacities and the boy actually did become competent, though not a star. After a time, the degree of accomplishment afforded enough satisfaction so that the boy gave up his world of fantasy for the thrill of real participation.[11]

Individuals who have an unpleasant or distressing task to perform also are known to try to escape from it by becoming drowsy and falling asleep. Students occasionally are found sound asleep in a class which has been a source of frustration. Students who have examinations scheduled for the next day and who plan to study on the evening before the examination, often report that they become very tired right after supper and have to go to bed early.

Other escapes from trying situations which were mentioned earlier involve going to the movies, devoting oneself to hard work, and using narcotics. Our motion picture theaters and taverns are full of people every evening, and on Saturdays and Sundays, who are trying to get away from themselves or from some problem they face. To stay at home would be most painful because time would be provided to think of their troubles and to rehash their old anxieties. Alcohol and other narcotics may so benumb the thought processes that worry is impossible for a period of several hours. Some individuals who throw themselves into hard work whenever spare time is

[11] By permission from *Toward Better Personal Adjustment,* by Harold W. Bernard. Copyright, 1951, McGraw-Hill Book Company, Inc., New York, p. 317.

available do so as a means of escaping from a personal problem which generates conflict.

Some of these withdrawal devices which have been mentioned are, of course, more hazardous for the personality than others. All of them, however, may be highly non-adjustive in character in that the real source of the difficulty is left untouched. The individual who can be induced to face and solve his problems probably obtains more satisfaction from living and is of more use to society than the one who withdraws in order to escape the perplexities of living.

Regression. Another form of retreat which might well have been included under the heading of withdrawal is regression. It is a mechanism by which an individual returns to a less mature level of development or adjustment in order to maintain his personal integrity. An adult unable to solve the problems that face him may resort to childish or adolescent tactics in an effort to get what he wants. Adolescents may use childish methods, and children may take on characteristics which served them well as babies.

The process of regression in a young woman is illustrated in the following case:

A young girl was in love and very anxious to marry. The young man she loved was not ready to marry. He wanted to run around and have what he considered a good time for a while before he settled down. This led the girl to fear the consequences of marriage with such a care-free youth and, aided by the disapproval of her fiancé expressed by her relatives and friends, she tried to decide that she would stay single. Yet she could not bear the thought of remaining single indefinitely. She was in a strange dilemma. She wanted to marry and she was afraid to do so. This led to the wish that she did not have any of the tendencies toward love life. If she were only a child again she would not want to marry and the trouble would be at an end. So she tried again to be a young innocent girl who knew nothing of love. She took the same attitude toward the whole affair that she would have taken when she was a pre-adolescent girl, and she seemed to get satisfaction from this for a time. When this satisfaction did not continue, her physiological maturity eventually forcing her to recognize that she was a woman, she attempted to commit suicide. After gaining insight into what she was doing, the girl adjusted her attitude, took a forward view instead of wishing to revert to a childish stage, and has made a satisfactory adjustment ever since.[12]

[12] John J. B. Morgan, *The Psychology of the Unadjusted School Child*, pp. 144–146. Second Edition, copyright, 1924, by The Macmillan Company, New York. Used by permission.

Adults have been known to cry and throw temper tantrums when they do not get what they want. Boys and girls of adolescent age sometimes lisp or engage in "baby talk" as a means of securing attention or affection which they feel is denied them. Living in the past is also a form of regression widely used by individuals whose present successes are not satisfying. This is known as the Old Oaken Bucket Delusion. To the individual, things were better in the old days. This technique may be of value to people getting along in years because the review of successes of earlier days helps to maintain and reinforce their egos. The discouraged person may also derive some sense of encouragement by retrospecting on his past successes. In young people, however, such tendencies should be viewed with suspicion. Regression and all other forms of withdrawal, when carried to extremes, may be symptomatic of such a future behavior disorder as schizophrenia. Regarding this point, Morgan states:

Since regression often begins at the age of adolescence, the teacher should be on the lookout for first signs. Early discovery is especially important in this disorder on account of the fact that in later stages the patient may become so inaccessible that no one can do anything for him.

In the mildest type of schizophrenia, known as *simple schizophrenia*, the onset is hard to discern. The symptoms may appear gradually in a boy or girl who has been getting along satisfactorily in school. At first there is seen a lack of interest in things; the child ceases to go out and associates less and less with other children. There comes over him a general listless, apparently lazy and tired-out attitude toward life. Lessons are neglected and the child begins to fail in his studies. . . .

Even if this form does not progress into more severe forms, the adult that is produced finds it very difficult to adapt himself to life. It is quite likely that a great many criminals, hoboes, prostitutes, pseudo-geniuses, cranks, and eccentrics of various types are cases of permanent and nonprogressive simple schizophrenia.[13]

Escape Through Physical Ailments. The individual who is in conflict or in a difficult situation may make a somewhat graceful withdrawal by developing symptoms of physical disability. Technically this adjustment mechanism is known as *hysteria*. In the neurotic person the symptoms of paralysis, blindness, deafness, and invalidism may appear. Being ill provides a way out for the individual.

[13] John J. B. Morgan, *The Psychology of the Unadjusted School Child*, Revised Edition, pp. 228–229. Copyright, 1936, by The Macmillan Company, New York. Used by permission.

There is, of course, nothing organically wrong, but the illness may persist until the personal problems of the individual are solved. Minor forms of hysteria are sometimes referred to as *hysteroid reactions*. School teachers have ample opportunity to observe such reactions on the part of their pupils. On the day of an examination some children will become so ill that it is necessary for them to return to their homes. The day after the examination they will be perfectly well. Students scheduled to make a talk before a class or before the other students in the auditorium have been known to mysteriously lose their voices and be unable to appear. As soon as the crisis period is over the physical ailment disappears.

Redl and Wattenberg have stated that "one thing for teachers to remember is that a child who has frequent absences, especially where parents report that doctors are having a hard time finding the cause, is probably emotionally troubled. To punish him for his absences or to make school more unpleasant for him is more likely to add to his troubles than to solve them." [14]

Teachers should be sympathetic to pupils who develop headaches, eye trouble, sinus trouble, colds, sore throats, and fainting spells in their attempts to avoid unpleasant situations. At the same time, every effort should be made to make pupils feel so competent and adequate that such defense mechanisms will be unnecessary. The child who has a major or minor success with a school examination or with a talk before the class is on the road to developing such personal adequacy that hysteroid reactions in such situations will be unlikely to appear.

Expiation or Atonement. A final mechanism used by many individuals to establish personal adjustment and to relieve guilt feelings is referred to as expiation or atonement. Challman says that "when other means fail to alleviate painful conflict over an act that is repugnant to the conscience, the individual may endeavor to find a way of atoning for it. The difficulty involved in many forms of restitution, however, is that the individual is subjected to social disapproval. Thus he seeks a way of solving the conflict without running this risk." [15]

Pupils who have neglected their studies or who have violated

[14] Fritz Redl and William W. Wattenberg, *Mental Hygiene in Teaching*, New York, Harcourt, Brace and Company, 1951, p. 64.

[15] R. C. Challman, in Gates *et al.*, *Educational Psychology*, Third Edition, New York, The Macmillan Company, 1948, p. 678.

school regulations may be severely worried over their misdeeds. Some relief has been obtained by such individuals through the process of punishing themselves in one way or another. Individuals have been known to do penance such as fasting for a week to compensate for wrongs they have committed. The writer knew of a high school boy who had extreme guilt feelings which resulted from his practice of masturbation. This boy reported that he had pricked his arm with a pin until it bled in several places in an effort to ease his guilty conscience.

The method of atonement as a reducer of tensions is probably used by all individuals at times. The man who brings his wife flowers when he has been late at the office, or the student who studies unusually hard after having failed an examination are examples of individuals who are expiating for their shortcomings. Atonement produces some sort of a balance for the individual, since good deeds are substituted for bad deeds. Like all compensatory mechanisms its use can probably be overdone. It would, of course, be much better if the individual could so steer his life that he did not have many shortcomings for which it would be necessary to atone. Making appropriate restitution, however, is to be preferred to carrying around a load of guilt and the inevitable anxieties that result from the conflict between the person's ideals and his behavior.

NEUROTIC AND PSYCHOTIC ADJUSTMENTS

The fourteen adjustment mechanisms which have been described in the previous pages are all used by normal people to a greater or lesser degree in response to the various frustrations of living. The more serious the frustration the more one may depend on some escape mechanism to relieve pent-up tensions. Neurotics and psychotics employ the usual adjustment devices in much the same manner as do so-called normal people. The extent to which they use them, however, greatly exceeds that of normal individuals. The neurotic, for example, may withdraw into complete invalidism in order to escape from a conflict situation, whereas a more normal person might develop only a temporary and much less severe physical ailment. The psychotic may have delusions that he is Napoleon or Alexander the Great, whereas a normal person might only think of himself "more highly than he ought."

Despite the fact that neurotics and psychotics are subject to the general laws of behavior the same as anyone else, these individuals do develop somewhat unique techniques and symptoms in the process of solving their problems of adjustment which should be mentioned. The average teacher will probably not encounter a great many neurotic or psychotic children in his classes, although from time to time, some may be identified. Such children should be referred to the school psychologist if one is available, or to medical personnel. It should be remembered that neurotics and psychotics were all once normal individuals. The teacher who can prevent minor maladjustments from becoming more serious and who can detect incipient cases of neurosis or psychosis is one who can make a great contribution to the mental hygiene program of a school.

Neurotic Adjustments. The neurotic or psychoneurotic, as he is sometimes called, maintains his ego by developing certain functional disorders. These include hysteria, obsessions, compulsions, phobias, hypochondria, and anxiety disorders.

Hysteria. It was mentioned earlier that normal individuals may sometimes develop physical ailments of a minor sort to escape unpleasant situations. The neurotic may go to great extremes in this respect. Menninger cites the case of a little girl who developed hysterical lameness:

There was a dispute among the doctors over the case of a pretty little nine-year-old girl. The girl had developed a limp in one leg and it appeared to be hip-trouble. Along with it she had become pale and lost weight. She complained of pain in the hip, and X-rays suggested some changes in the bony structure. It looked very much as if she might have tuberculosis of the hip-joint. For this reason some of the doctors advocated a plaster cast.

Certain things about the case, however, gave some of the doctors another notion about it. For example, the child complained of a variety of pains, and sometimes when touched ever so gently by her mother she would scream out of all proportion to the justification. She would have limp spells in which she would drop into her mother's arms and lie motionless. At other times she would grow bitter toward her mother, make faces at her, and even throw things at her.

The mother was sure the child had tuberculosis of the hip as some of the doctors had suggested. This we assured her was not true. A week after the child had been placed under treatment the leg was perfectly well![16]

[16] Karl A. Menninger, *The Human Mind,* Third Edition, pp. 142–143. Copyright, 1945, by Alfred A. Knopf, New York.

The treatment consisted of helping the little girl become adjusted to a very difficult home situation in which "the father and mother had staged any number of dramatic fights in front of all the children."

A case of hysterical blindness is reported in the *Journal of the American Medical Association* as follows:

Helen D., a charming, curly-headed girl of 14, was the only daughter in a rather large family of boys. On her shoulders fell the drudgery of housework. She resented doing the dishes and the cleaning, and came home every day from school unwilling to perform her tasks. One day she was scolded by her mother; she replied sharply, and received a stinging smack across the face. Immediately she became blind.[17]

This again is an example of a person solving a personal problem by escaping into a disability. In the case of the person suffering from hysteria, nothing is organically wrong. When the individual personal conflict is solved, the disability disappears.

Other symptoms sometimes exhibited by persons suffering from hysteria are paralysis of the arms or legs, deafness, loss of voice, continuous vomiting, fits, sleep walking, and loss of memory.

Obsessions. An obsession is an irrational idea which keeps recurring to the individual. It may persist until the person develops a feeling of subjection to it and until he cannot do much useful thinking or work. Thorpe has illustrated an obsession in the following case:

The nature of obsessional neurosis may be seen in the case of a seventeen-year-old high school student who could not keep from repeating the phrase, "I am not wicked." He was unable to concentrate on his studies and would mutter this phrase to himself hundreds of times a day. A study of the boy's case showed that he had been treated harshly since early childhood by his father, a dominating, sarcastic man who showed him no affection, and who frequently threatened to lock him out of the house if he did not do as he was told. To add to his troubles, the boy had some years previously been severly scolded and whipped for playfully moving his younger sister's chair at dinner with the result that she fell and fractured her back. During her three-month stay in the hospital and for some time afterward the boy dwelt morbidly on the incident, continually blaming himself for his sister's partial paralysis. For years afterward he could not keep from repeating the phrase, "I am not wicked." Following several

[17] J. Fetterman in the *Journal of the American Medical Association*, Vol. 91, No. 5, August 4, 1928, p. 317.

months of therapy, during which he was given the opportunity of talking freely about his sister's accident and other unhappy experiences, as well as being assured of the full respect of the therapist, he was able to make an almost complete recovery.[18]

Compulsions. Some neurotics feel compelled to carry out certain acts regardless of the fact that they are unreasonable. When leaving the house, the neurotic may go back several times to see whether the front door is locked or the gas heater has been turned off. Some people feel they have to touch all the gate posts they pass, or step on every crack that appears on the sidewalk. One neurotic endured for years the compulsion of dressing and undressing three times before he felt comfortable in his clothes. Another neurotic had to wash his hands with soap, and then with alcohol every time he touched a doorknob. The writer knows of a neurotic who hates to see medicine wasted. Every time half a bottle is left around the house by any member of the family, he feels compelled to finish it. Some people will not throw away anything. A little old lady who recently died left among her belongings a little box which was neatly labeled "string too short to use."

There is a group of compulsive reactions which are referred to as *manias.* Among the well-known manias are *kleptomania, pyromania, dipsomania, nymphomania,* and *homicidal mania.* Kleptomania is characterized by an overpowering impulse to steal; pyromania, by an irresistible urge to set fires; dipsomania, by an uncontrollable desire for alcoholic beverages; nymphomania, by excessive sexual desires in females; and homicidal mania, by a compulsion to kill.

Compulsive reactions have been described by Cameron [19] as "techniques of controlling intermittent anxiety reactions. They are the product of incomplete repression, and they provide only temporary control of intolerable anxiety." In treating compulsive disorders it does little good to deal directly with symptoms. Instead it is necessary to discover the conflicts and frustrations of the individual and attempt to help him resolve them.

Phobias. Phobias are irrational fears. There is virtually no end to the list of objects and situations that may bring panic or fear to some

[18] Louis P. Thorpe, *The Psychology of Mental Health,* pp. 385–386. Copyright, 1950, by The Ronald Press Company, New York.

[19] Norman Cameron and Ann Magaret, *Behavior Pathology,* Boston, Houghton Mifflin Company, 1951, pp. 358–359.

neurotics. There is *acrophobia,* fear of high places; *agoraphobia,* fear of open places; *claustrophobia,* fear of closed places; *misophobia,* fear of contamination; *ochlophobia,* fear of crowds; *toxophobia,* fear of poisons or being poisoned; *zoophobia,* fear of animals or of some particular animal; and *phobophobia,* fear of fear, fear that one will be afraid.

The writer knows a young man who has an irrational fear of cats. Whenever a cat or even a little kitten is met on the street this person crosses over to the other side of the street in great haste. This individual could not possibly bear to be in the same room with a cat.

Unreasonable fears are usually explained in terms of early unfortunate experiences with the object feared, or in terms of some personality conflict or anxiety which expresses itself in the form of a fear.

Hypochondria. The person suffering with hypochondria is abnormally preoccupied with his health. He wakes up in the morning feeling exhausted. He runs from one doctor to another without being benefited. His medicine cabinet is usually full of patent medicines. He can be said to be a person who enjoys his ill health. He may bitterly resent anyone telling him that he looks well. The hypochondriac's imagined illness serves as an escape mechanism to relieve him of anxieties which result from personal frustrations. Hypochondriacs whose lives have been reorganized and whose personal problems have been solved are known to have improved miraculously so far as their health is concerned.

Anxiety neurosis. The person suffering with an anxiety neurosis is in an almost constant state of fear, apprehension, and worry. He is afraid he will lose his money, that he will not be successful in his work, or that he will go "crazy." If he is a student, he may worry unduly about his grades or his ability to make friends or get a girl or boy friend. The neurotic with acute anxiety feelings will go to great lengths to protect himself from his anxieties. Karen Horney [20] has pointed out that the neurotic tries to protect himself from his anxiety in four principal ways:

1. By securing affection—He has an inordinate need for this type of reassurance. His motto seems to be: "If you love me you will not hurt me."

[20] Karen Horney, *The Neurotic Personality of Our Time,* New York, W. W. Norton Company, 1937, pp. 96–99.

2. By being submissive—The neurotic argues: "If I give in, I shall not be hurt."
3. By trying to achieve power, possessions, and status—He reasons: "If I have power, no one can hurt me."
4. By withdrawing—His motto is: "If I withdraw, nothing can hurt me."

In addition to these methods, the neurotic suffering from severe anxiety may try to escape from his worries by over-eating, over-working, or resorting to alcohol or other narcotics.

Psychotic Adjustments. The neurotic is characterized by possessing minor nervous disorders. He usually goes about his work and does not cause his friends or his family too much trouble. He is in relatively good touch with reality and very seldom is treated in a mental hospital. Many of our greatest inventors, poets and scientists have been pronounced neurotics who have compensated for their inferiority and anxiety feelings by producing something outstanding. The *psychotic*, on the other hand, possesses a major mental derangement. His mental functions are so profoundly disturbed that he is unable to participate in everyday activities. He is usually confined to a mental hospital. One of his chief characteristics is loss of contact with reality. He may almost totally retreat into a world of make-believe and receive his satisfactions through delusions and hallucinations. Space will not permit detailed discussion of the adjustment mechanisms of the psychotic. A few of the characteristics and symptoms of this group of maladjusted persons will, however, be mentioned.

Schizophrenia. "Schizophrenic disorders are syndromes of disorganization and desocialization, in which delusion and hallucination are prominent, and in which behavior is dominated by primary fantasy." [21] For many years this functional psychosis was known as dementia praecox because it was believed that it had its beginning during adolescence. When it was discovered that this maladjustment was not limited to young people, the older term dementia praecox was dropped in favor of the newer term schizophrenia which means "split mind." Schizophrenia has usually been divided into four somewhat overlapping types: simple, hebephrenic, catatonic, and paranoid.

[21] Norman Cameron and Ann Magaret, *Behavior Pathology,* Boston, Houghton Mifflin Company, 1951, p. 494.

Simple schizophrenia. The simple type shows lack of interest in human affairs; has little ambition and ultimately withdraws from practically all social contacts. He may become careless about his dress, refuse to shave or bathe and give himself over to daydreaming. The child who is extremely shy, lethargic, and withdrawn in school should be particularly a cause of concern to teachers, and every effort should be made to cause him to participate socially. Children of this type may ultimately develop simple schizophrenia.

Hebephrenic schizophrenia. This type is characterized by giddiness, silliness, various tics, and some hallucinations. One hebephrenic claimed that he received radio messages through the gold fillings in his teeth. Some hebephrenics regress to childish behavior, crawl on all fours, urinate on the floor, and show little or no concern for others. The hebephrenic comes close to filling the layman's conception of "crazy" or "insane."

Paranoid schizophrenia. This form of psychosis is characterized by delusions. The individual so afflicted may either have delusions of persecution or delusions of grandeur or both. The individual who feels persecuted may hold to the belief that people are trying to follow him, poison him, or undermine his character. He is suspicious of everyone. The person afflicted with grandiose delusions may claim that he is Christ, Queen Victoria or some other famous personage. Through these delusions the individual attains some of the satisfactions of his basic needs, e.g., status, that have been denied him in real life. The writer had a college student in his class who developed extreme disorganization of his thought process and delusions of persecution and grandeur. Before the course was over it was necessary for him to be committed to a state mental hospital. An example from a note he wrote to the writer while in the course is reproduced as follows:

I and God (one spiritually) reveal from prophetically sealed scriptures my dreams from the perfect subconscious mind that knows, observes, interprets, and records all phenomena as no man can and never will, as I do now. . . . I wrote to the admirals next and told them to hide the great navy and to hold Australia for a base, to march across the River Euphrates with me and the liberated princes of the East to the battle of Armageddon to knock out the 10 restored major powers at the very hub of 3 continents. "To win," I said, "you will still need me or else loose." Pal, some day I will tell how the world runs—means my sex life. You can never tell what is walking in a man's pants. They will never believe you. But you will believe us and see. Look at the movies and the mice. Break them all up. Dirt on all of them.

After leaving the University and while in the mental hospital this man sent the writer numerous disorganized letters which were signed in such ways as the following: George Washington, Valley Forge, % Mother MacCrea; Julius Caesar, Appian Way, Rome, Italy; Montezuma of the White Incas, Atlantic, Michigan.

Although teachers do not often encounter cases as serious as this in their classes, it is important for them to have some knowledge of this type of maladjustment in order to recognize children whose symptoms may be drifting in this direction.

Catatonic schizophrenia. The catatonic is characterized by negativism, phases of excitement and stupor, muscular rigidity, stereotyped and impulsive behavior, and some hallucinations. Some catatonics can be pushed around as one would push a dummy. In the condition known as *waxy flexibility* the individual's arms, legs, or other parts of his body may be placed in the most grotesque positions and these positions may be maintained for long periods of time. With regard to the prevention of catatonia, Morgan makes the following statement:

> If teachers and parents are to detect the symptoms of this disorder in its early stages it will necessitate a careful study of the nature of the emotional cycles of the children in their care. If the excitement and depression are highly emotional in nature and if the child gives other evidence of being extrovertive then the procedure should be to help him adjust to his source of conflict. If on the other hand the evidence points to an introvertive reaction, a sort of senseless activity or meaningless stuporous withdrawal from the environment, effort should be directed toward making the individual more extrovertive. This can be accomplished by managing affairs so that it will be to his advantage to mix with others. Teach him to get pleasure from his social contacts and, insofar as this is successful, he is being guarded against any tendency to withdraw into himself.[22]

Other Forms of Psychosis. Besides schizophrenia other recognized types of psychosis include manic-depressive disorders, involutional melancholia, and (true) paranoia. The manic-depressive swings from the highest levels of elation to the lowest levels of despair.

[22] John J. B. Morgan, *The Psychology of Abnormal People*, Second Edition, pp. 564–565. Copyright, 1936, by Longmans, Green and Company, New York.

When in the excited phase the individual may be hilarious, extremely talkative, unable to sit still. When he swings to depression he becomes very slow in his responses. If a question is asked him it may be two or three minutes before he answers. He may sit and weep for long periods of time and accuse himself of all sorts of wrongdoing. An involutional melancholic is a person who is perpetually sad and depressed. His feelings of dejection, hopelessness, and sorrow may reach the point where suicide seems to him the only way out. The paranoid individual reacts in some respects much like the person afflicted with schizophrenic paranoia. His delusions which are usually of a persecutory nature, however, are much more highly systematized than the schizophrenic paranoid. He is a most suspicious individual but may otherwise appear quite normal. Teachers should be on the alert to detect children who are developing paranoid tendencies. Such children should be immediately referred to a clinical psychologist or child psychiatrist who may be able to suggest measures to arrest the development of this serious disorder.

SUMMARY

Human beings, adults and children alike, possess a great array of needs which are constantly demanding satisfaction. Some of these are physical, others are psychological and social. The physical needs are generated by deficits in the organic structure and chemical balance of the body, the psychological and social needs are learned. Both types of needs create tension in the individual which lead to action (goal seeking). When an individual is blocked in reaching a goal, he may seek to reach the goal with renewed vigor, adopt a substitute goal, try to reach the original goal by devious means, or withdraw into a world of fantasy.

When a teacher observes a child using to an excessive degree such mechanisms as aggression, compensation, identification, rationalization, projection, or daydreaming, he may be sure that the child is trying to satisfy some need which has been thwarted. Since all individuals are thwarted to some extent in satisfying their needs, the various adjustment mechanisms can be observed in everyone at times. The adjustment devices described in this chapter are not all necessarily bad since they do relieve to some extent tensions which have been built up, and help restore equilibrium.

Teachers, however, should assist pupils to set realistic goals which can be achieved. Too great frustration or habitual and exaggerated use of a defense mechanism may greatly reduce an individual's social effectiveness and also his personal happiness. Extreme and prolonged frustration is also believed to be the forerunner of neurotic and psychotic behavior.

REFERENCES FOR FURTHER STUDY

Bernard, Harold W., *Toward Better Personal Adjustment*, New York, McGraw-Hill Book Company, Inc., 1951.

Cameron, Norman and Magaret, Ann, *Behavior Pathology*, Boston, Houghton Mifflin Company, 1951.

Carroll, Herbert A., *Mental Hygiene*, Second Edition, New York, Prentice-Hall, Inc., 1951.

Kaplan, Louis and Baron, Denis, *Mental Hygiene and Life*, New York, Harper & Brothers, 1952.

Lindgren, Henry Clay, *Psychology of Personal and Social Adjustment*, New York, American Book Company, 1953.

Menninger, Karl A., *The Human Mind*, Third Edition, New York, Alfred A. Knopf, 1945.

Redl, Fritz, and Wattenberg, William W., *Mental Hygiene in Teaching*, New York, Harcourt, Brace and Company, 1951.

Steckle, Lynde C., *Problems of Human Adjustment*, New York, Harper & Brothers, 1949.

Symonds, P. M., *Dynamic Psychology*, New York, Appleton-Century Company, 1949.

Thorpe, Louis P., *The Psychology of Mental Health*, New York, The Ronald Press Co., 1950.

Vaughan, Wayland F., *Personal and Social Adjustment*, New York, The Odyssey Press, 1952.

Young, Kimball, *Personality and Problems of Adjustment*, Second Edition, New York, F. S. Crofts and Company, 1952.

Chapter 14

Problems of School Discipline

MANY TYPES of maladjusted children are found in our school class-rooms. The symptoms they exhibit are numerous. These include shyness, suspiciousness, untruthfulness, tattling, cruelty, bullying, cheating, truancy, impertinence, tardiness, stealing, profanity, bois-terousness, showing-off, masturbation, heterosexual activity, and all sorts of classroom disorderliness. In this chapter and the one to fol-low practical suggestions will be given for dealing with a wide range of behavior problems of children. The present chapter will concern itself with behavior problems which might be labeled disciplinary.

DISCIPLINE IN THE CLASSROOM—PAST AND PRESENT

School teachers have reported that the keeping of discipline in their classes represents one of their most difficult tasks. In fact, a study made in Ohio [1] shows that 165 beginning teachers rated the maintaining of discipline as their number one problem. The list of ten pressing problems reported by these teachers is presented in Table 26. This same study also shows that school administrators consider the keeping of discipline to be the greatest problem of school teachers.[2] Problems of discipline are listed by the administra-tors three times as often as any other problem of teaching.

Although the importance of discipline in schools has never seri-ously been doubted, marked changes have taken place over a period of years in the methods of keeping discipline, and in an understand-ing of the psychological principles underlying the process.

[1] W. R. Flesher, "The Beginning Teacher," *Educational Research Bulletin,* Vol. 24, January 17, 1945, pp. 12–18.
[2] *Ibid.,* p. 17.

Horace Mann described the method of keeping discipline in his day as follows:

In one of the schools . . . consisting of about two hundred and fifty scholars, there were 328 separate floggings in one week of five days, or an average of 65 each day. In another, eighteen boys were flogged in two hours in the presence of a stranger.[3]

An elderly man who had formerly been a school teacher told the writer that the first day he taught school he whipped every boy in

TABLE 26

The Ten Problems Most Frequently Reported
by 165 Beginning Ohio Teachers *

| | NUMBER OF TEACHERS REPORTING | | |
PROBLEM	MEN (50)	WOMEN (115)	TOTAL (165)
Discipline	31	83	114
Evaluation	27	69	96
Material and Equipment	33	63	96
Individual Differences	24	66	90
Assignments	30	59	89
Teaching of Classes	23	65	88
Promotions	22	57	79
Testing	25	46	71
Teaching Schedule	25	42	67
Recitations	17	47	64

* From Flesher.

the room. Thrashings were very common in the public schools attended by the writer during the period 1914–1922. On one occasion a sixth grade woman teacher and a large unruly boy wrestled on the floor in full view of the rest of the class.

In 1848, a secondary school in North Carolina published a list of punishments which were in effect in the school.[4] A few of them were:

[3] This quotation taken from Pickens E. Harris, *Changing Conceptions of School Discipline*, New York, The Macmillan Company, 1928, p. 53.

[4] Taken from S. L. Pressey, *et al.*, *Life: A Psychological Survey*, New York, Harper & Brothers, 1939, p. 91.

1. Boys and girls playing together — 4 lashes
2. Quarreling — 4 lashes
3. Playing cards at school — 10 lashes
4. Telling lies — 7 lashes
5. Swearing at school — 8 lashes
6. For drinking liquor at school — 8 lashes
7. For wearing long finger nails — 2 lashes
8. For blotting your copy book — 2 lashes
9. For not making a bow when going home — 2 lashes

As recently as 1928 an article [5] appeared in the *Elementary School Journal* which classified school offenses into seventeen different types and recommended specific punishments for each type. The author stated, "It is not intended that all punishments listed under an offense should be used at each violation. The punishments are arranged in order of severity and should be used in order as far as it is necessary to control the situation." Some examples of the disciplinary procedures which are recommended in this article are as follows:

1. Truancy
   a. Keep pupil in after school to make up work
   b. Report case to parents
   c. Report case to public officer
2. The "show-off" attitude
   a. Put offender in place by a remark that will enlist pupils on your side
   b. Removal of privileges
   c. Public acknowledgment of fault
3. Dishonesty in assigned work
   a. Removal of credit
   b. Assignment of extra work
   c. Seat pupil apart from the group
4. Overzealousness in recitation
   a. Assignment of extra work
5. Bullying
   a. Oral reproof
   b. Removal of privileges

The other twelve types of misbehavior listed in the article are handled in an equally unsound psychological manner as those which have just been presented. It is hard for a student who has been

[5] H. W. James, "Punishments Recommended for School Offenses," *Elementary School Journal*, Vol. 29, October, 1928, pp. 129–131.

trained in the principles of mental hygiene to conceive that such an article could have been written by a professional educator at so recent a date.

A fairly up-to-date description of how teachers currently handle disciplinary problems can be gathered from an examination of Table 27.[6] The material presented in this table is based upon the replies of

TABLE 27

How 290 Elementary School Teachers Met Classroom Behavior Problems

HOW SITUATIONS WERE MET	FREQUENCY
Physical Force (spanked, shook, tied in seat, etc.)	134 (1%)
Censure (scolded, warned, shamed, hushed, used sarcasm, embarrassed, soaped mouth, etc.)	1088 (11%)
Overtime or Extra Work	486 (5%)
Deprivation (deprived recreational time, isolated, rearranged seating, removed from class, etc.)	1044 (10%)
Sent or Referred to Office	65 (0.6%)
Penalties (demerits, money fines, non-promotion)	99 (1%)
Rectification or Reparation (required payment, required giving up of personal article, etc.)	214 (2%)
Ignored or Did Nothing	512 (5%)
Verbal Appeal (used reasoning, reminded, requested cessation, in behalf of the group, etc.)	2586 (25%)
Group Reaction	143 (1%)
Constructive Assistance (tried to create opportunity for successful participation, conferred with parent, assigned special responsibility, arranged for play with peers, etc.)	3167 (31%)
Commendation (personal, public, etc.)	57 (0.6%)
Searched for Reasons of Behavior	620 (6%)
Tried Many Things Unsuccessfully	29 (0.3%)

290 elementary teachers representing eighty-six counties in a midwestern state. Although this study was reported in the year 1950, it is clear that teachers still use many outmoded and psychologically unsound procedures. Physical force, censure, and penalties of one sort or another are much in evidence and probably used more often than the situations would justify. It is encouraging to note, however, that constructive measures were employed in a substantial proportion of the cases.

[6] Frank Slobetz, "Elementary Teachers' Reactions to School Situations," *Journal of Educational Research,* Vol. 44, October, 1950, pp. 81–90.

In the past, discipline in the classroom was too often maintained by using essentially police methods. The child who misbehaved was regarded as "bad" and in need of punishment to make him "good." The newer point of view with respect to discipline gives cognizance to the basic processes of adjustment which have been outlined in the preceding chapter. Children are not regarded as being naturally bad or depraved, but as individuals that have definite needs which must be met in one way or another. Whenever a child misbehaves the teacher should ask himself such questions as: What is it the child is gaining by this particular behavior? or What needs of the child are being met by doing what he is doing? Teachers should realize that there are causes behind every type of behavior exhibited by children.

In many schools a typical method of dealing with misdeeds is to keep the offending pupils after school. If a pupil is tardy he is kept after school, if he doesn't do his geography lesson he is kept after school, if he whispers he is kept after school, if he throws paper wads he is kept after school. There is obviously no connection in these instances between the offenses and the punishment. Such a procedure is similar to that followed by old time doctors who prescribed little pink pills for the patient regardless of what ailed him.

If a pupil is tardy, the teacher should try to find out why. Perhaps the family does not own an alarm clock. Maybe the child works before school, or the mother is ill and the child must do the dishes. If the pupil doesn't do his geography lesson, the teacher should again try to find out the reason. Perhaps he cannot read, or has lost his book. Maybe he doesn't see how studying geography will do him any good anyway. If he whispers, there is a reason also. Perhaps he has nothing to do. Maybe the work is too difficult for him. Perhaps he is uninterested or bored. Maybe he whispers to attract attention. Or maybe he is whispering to find the answer to an important question which he must have in order to proceed with his work. If the pupil throws paper wads, there is also a reason. People just do not throw paper wads for nothing. Some pupils secure attention and recognition in this manner which is denied them in more legitimate activities. If a pupil cannot succeed in conjugating Latin verbs, he may achieve distinction among his peers as the roughest and toughest pupil in the room. Other pupils will look up to him. That makes him somebody.

In the sections to follow, illustrations of classroom disciplinary problems, and the methods used by teachers in dealing with them are presented.

ILLUSTRATIVE DISCIPLINARY PROBLEMS

A Show-off in the Algebra Class

Mr. Smith was teaching his first day of school in a medium sized high school. The subject was Algebra I. Mr. Smith began to call the roll. All went well until he came to the name of Max Howard. When this name was called a large boy began to wave his arms in the air and shouted with ear splitting volume: "I'm here, see I'm right here —old Max Howard is right here." All the rest of the class began to laugh and general disorder temporarily swept over the classroom. The next day when roll was called, the same incident took place. The teacher then sent the pupils to the blackboard to do some problems. Max again began to talk in loud tones which could be heard all over the classroom and even in adjourning rooms. Mr. Smith was greatly worried about what to do. He, however, said nothing to Max about his behavior, but when an opportunity was presented later in the period to speak to Max privately, Mr. Smith asked him if he would like to come in for a little visit later in the day during his conference hour. Max was told that all the pupils in the class were to make similar visits. Max said he would come, and sure enough he kept his appointment.

When Max entered Mr. Smith's room for his private conference, the first thing he said was, "You know, I am a pretty tough customer, I ran a teacher out of the high school I attended last year." Mr. Smith made no comment. Max went on talking. He said, "You know, I have a very loud voice." Mr. Smith replied that he didn't particularly mind loud noises as he used to work in a box factory and had become accustomed to noise. Max then said, "You know, I can also talk softly if I want to." Mr. Smith did not comment directly but gave the impression that he was not particularly concerned with how loudly a pupil spoke. He told Max that he just wanted to get acquainted and help him plan his future or assist him with any problem he might have. He also told Max that he thought it was unnecessary to call the roll every day and wondered if it wouldn't be better to make a seating chart as a means of checking the roll. Max agreed that this might be a good idea. Mr. Smith then asked Max if he would be willing to take charge of the seating chart and make a record of attendance for the ensuing week. Max consented to do this.

The next day, Max took over his duties in connection with taking the roll. His behavior changed remarkably. Mr. Smith reported to the writer that from that time on Max ceased entirely his loud talking and became a very cooperative pupil.

Disorder in the Study Hall

Pandemonium reigned very frequently in the study hall at Oakville High School. Miss Steiner, the teacher in charge, was doing her best to provide a quiet place for pupils to study, but her efforts were futile. On one occasion a mouse was brought into the room and released. On another, a "stink bomb" was burst. During such periods the entire study hall was in an uproar. Miss Steiner's procedure was to try to locate the culprit in each case. She would dash to the section of the room where the disorder seemed to break out and would look for a pupil who gave the appearance of being guilty. When she spotted a promising suspect she would often pounce upon him and give him a good shaking or send him from the room. The children loved this, for seldom did she ever apprehend the real culprit. When she could not find a guilty looking pupil she would turn upon the entire group with threatening statements of what would happen if such disorder should happen again.

Each study hall period began to degenerate into an exciting game of seeing what Miss Steiner would do next. She tried to police the room, but it was so large and there were so many pupils that she simply could not cover her "beat." Finally one day Miss Steiner did not appear at school. The principal received a report that she had had a nervous breakdown and probably would be gone for the rest of the year.

A new teacher was brought in to take over the study hall—a Miss Wilson. Miss Wilson's concepts of disciplinary methods differed radically from those of Miss Steiner. After introducing herself to the pupils, Miss Wilson explained that she had no fixed ideas on just how a study hall should be run. She said that she wanted the type of conditions and atmosphere in the study hall which were desired by the pupils. She asked them if they would like to elect a committee to draw up procedures which all could follow. The pupils liked the idea, and suggested that the elected committee submit their tentative plan when finished to all the pupils in the study hall for their approval or amendment. This course of action was carried out and rules of conduct for the study hall were developed entirely by the pupils. Miss Wilson then made it clear that she was not at all interested in serving as an officer to carry out the rules which the pupils had enacted. She suggested that the pupils design a system for enforcing the rules they had made. The pupils set about to do this, and finally came forward with a system which included a standing committee on study hall procedure. A separate committee was elected for each period of the day. Pupils who were dissatisfied with any condition existing in the study hall were encouraged to report their grievances to this committee which would recommend appropriate action. Membership on the committee was rotated in such a way that many pupils were given the opportunity to serve. Cases of improper study hall conduct on the part of pupils were vigorously dealt with by this committee. Strong social pressure soon developed among the pupils to maintain a place of study that was in line with their expressed wishes.

Many suggestions for improving the physical appearance and educational facilities of the study hall were also sent in to the committee from time to time by pupils. As a result, bookshelves were built along one entire wall of the previously bare hall and these were filled with newspapers, magazines, and numerous interesting books. Some movable tables and chairs were added and potted plants were placed in appropriate places. The pupils began to take an interest in their study hall. So far as discipline was concerned, it ceased to be any real problem at all. Miss Wilson continued to work in the study hall, but her duties consisted of helping pupils with whatever problems they cared to bring to her. She worked with the pupils and not against them.

The School Building Is Defaced

Arriving at Union High School one morning, pupils and teachers found red paint smeared all over the white pillars which stood at the entrance of the building. Several light globes in the front of the high school were also broken. Investigation produced evidence that this was the work of George Stevens, a high school junior, who was considered a general nuisance and problem around school. When confronted with the evidence George admitted his guilt, but was unable to give a reason for his behavior. A group of teachers met with the principal that evening after school to decide what to do with George. It was suggested by several teachers that this was the last straw to break the camel's back. George had committed so many misdemeanors that there was no use putting up with him any longer. A recommendation was made that he be expelled from school. One teacher, however, disagreed with the group and refused to concur in this recommendation. She stated that in her opinion, George was a boy who had been beaten down around school, had been unsuccessful in his studies, and had received nothing in the way of commendation for even the small efforts he had made to do well. She maintained that his desire for recognition and status had been almost entirely thwarted in every avenue of the school's activities. "What George needs," she said, "is a chance to be significant and worthwhile in some activity connected with the school." What activity this might be she was unable to see. One of the other teachers, however, now came to the rescue and stated that there was a need for an assistant to help the regular janitor of the building. Some small compensation would be made available for this work. After much discussion it was agreed that this idea be presented to George for his reaction. This was done and George accepted the job with great enthusiasm. The principal who related this incident to the writer stated that the next morning after George had received this appointment he (George) arrived at the school building one hour before classes began and insisted that every pupil wipe off his shoes before entering the building. George had now found an activity which satisfied his need for attention and status.

Joe—A Slow Learner and Bully [7]

"Joe was larger than his classmates, a fact he was never allowed to forget. Nor was he allowed to forget that he was less intelligent than his classmates. The brilliant method used by Joe's teacher to 'keep him in line' was to send him to the board to do an arithmetic example beyond his mental reach. A carnival air always permeated the class-

[7] Paul E. Chapman, "Sarcasm: Pedagogical Poison," *The Clearing House*, Vol. 23, December, 1948, pp. 219–220.

room during these incidents. Joe would slouch to the board and try the impossible. Then, accompanied by much giggling, a 10-year-old girl would be sent up to complete the example. Joe would slink to his seat with hatred in his heart and another little piece of his soul destroyed. He naturally became quite bullyish and tried to achieve success the only way he thought he could.

"When Joe left school he found that he was no longer physically superior to his associates and his 'education' had convinced him that he was mentally inferior to everyone. What hope had he? More money than his companions was one possibility which he tried to accomplish by stealing. This led to his being sentenced to life imprisonment when he was 19—and a fourth offender. Obviously there were many other contributing factors—but is there any doubt but that some of Joe's sentence should be served by that teacher?"

Miss Henry Is Upset

Miss Henry was an English teacher about 50 years of age. Her students considered her to be a very poor teacher and almost completely scatterbrained. She was referred to as "the ol' battle ax." On several occasions students asked each other—"Wonder what color the ol' lady's hair is gonna be today?" The university student who described this case to the writer stated that the class spent more time laughing at her than trying to learn anything.

At any rate, one day the phone rang. The phone, as it happened, was in a small closet-like affair that served both as Miss Henry's wardrobe and as a phone booth. Miss Henry got up to answer the phone and closed the closet door halfway so that the students could not hear what she was saying.

The half-opened door and the entire set-up proved to be a temptation which Jim Hansen could not resist. Stealthily he crept from his desk and on noiseless feet he work his way up behind the door. In a moment he had slammed the door and snapped the lock. The students who had been sitting in silence during this escapade now burst into a tremendous uproar, applauding what he had done and howling like a pack of coyotes.

Soon the expected banging from the inside of the booth and the frenzied voice of the teacher were heard. She first demanded, and then implored that the students open the door immediately and set her free. Her pleas fell on deaf ears. Some of the pupils began to feel sorry for her and would have unlocked the door but the social pressure from the group kept them from doing so.

Finally after a considerable length of time, Jim unlocked the door and got back to his seat so quickly that Miss Henry had no notion who had done it. When she emerged she was close to being hysterical. Her hair was flung about her in strings and knots; plainly she had been sobbing, and her movements showed that her nervous restraint was nearly gone. "Who did this?" she demanded. "Who dared do such a thing? Why you could have killed me, locking me in there with no air." "Class," (and now she changed her tone), "we are going to have to maintain discipline. You're all going to have to be good little children and mind what I tell you or I'm going to do something drastic." She pointed to the window which was on the third floor of the high school. "If you ever misbehave again I'm going to open that window and throw myself out. Then you'll be sorry for what you have done."

Details are somewhat lacking with respect to further events that took place in this classroom. There is, however, no record that Miss Henry fulfilled her threat. Instead, she continued to nag, make other threats, and have occasional crying spells until the semester finally came to an end.

GUIDING PRINCIPLES FOR KEEPING DISCIPLINE

Teachers should bear in mind that children generally behave in about the only way it is possible for them to behave considering the hereditary characteristics they possess, the kinds of experiences they have had, and the social pressures which are operating upon them at the moment. This is another way of saying that *behavior is caused*. This statement also indicates some of the causes. This principle implies that teachers have an opportunity to alter the behavior of children by helping them restructure their environment and by creating new social arrangements. Teachers are in a strategic position to assist pupils to develop new ideals and patterns of conduct. Realization of the fact that children behave in about the only way they can considering the factors in their backgrounds and present conditions surrounding them, should cause teachers to be sympathetic toward misbehaving children. Seeking for the cause of the misbehavior should replace the pronouncement of blame.

E. K. Wickman [8] has given a succinct explanation of why children misbehave. He says: "Behavior problems can best be explained in terms of discrepancies between the individual's capacities to behave and the requirements for behavior that are imposed upon him by social forces. By capacities we refer not only to biological (physical and mental) capacities but also to experiential factors (conditioned responses, social attitudes, etc.) that extend or limit the individual's possible behavior responses." A seventh-grade teacher, for example, who expects all the children in the room to do work requiring an intellectual level of say twelve or thirteen years is inviting disciplinary episodes. Those children who fall considerably below this level of ability may respond to these excessive requirements by truancy and aggressive behavior or they may withdraw and become introvertive. Similarly children whose abilities far exceed the twelve or thirteen-year-old levels may respond to the discrepancy between their capacities and the requirements by exhibiting symptoms of boredom or engaging in many types of annoying behavior.

It has been mentioned earlier that all children desire to be significant and to achieve status in the eyes of their peers, teachers, and other members of their society. The teacher who can help children reach this goal will have few if any problems of discipline.

Teachers should remember furthermore that older children and adolescents can take considerable responsibility for their own discipline if given a chance. Recently the writer visited a classroom from which the teacher was temporarily absent. She had stepped down the hall to make a telephone call. The pupils continued to work on their projects just as if the teacher were present. This teacher left the room whenever the occasion demanded it. She never expected disciplinary problems. The children knew she trusted them and considered them responsible people. Other teachers in the same building did not dare leave their classes unattended. They had treated their pupils as immature individuals and as a result got immature behavior from them.

Some generalizations and suggestions for keeping discipline which seem to be valid are the following:

1. Praise and social approval are more effective in promoting good standards of conduct than are censure, blame, and punishment.

[8] E. K. Wickman, *Children's Behavior and Teachers' Attitudes*, New York, The Commonwealth Fund, 1928, p. 151.

2. It is unwise to punish a whole group for the misconduct of an individual or a small group.

3. Sarcasm should be used sparingly if at all. Children are sensitive and may become severely hurt by such procedure.

4. The teacher should never consider misconduct as a personal affront. Instead the teacher should adopt the attitude that his interests and those of the pupil go in the same direction. The teacher should work with pupils not against them.

5. Whenever possible necessary rules and regulations should be formulated either by the pupils or by the pupils assisted by the teacher.

6. Discipline is most difficult to maintain unless pupils sense the real worth of the activities in which they engage.

7. Whenever disciplinary episodes arise, the teacher should ask himself such questions as: What is wrong with the course of study? What is wrong with my teaching methods?

8. When a child misbehaves, he should be studied in an effort to determine which of his needs have been thwarted. An attempt should be made to make the child's school experiences satisfying to him.

9. A child may misbehave because he is physically ill or suffering from a glandular disorder. Some restless and annoying children may have hyperthyroidism which needs medical attention.

10. Prevention of disciplinary situations is to be preferred to remedying difficulties that arise. If pupils have sufficient readiness for their work, are highly motivated, and if they are given sympathetic and understanding treatment by their teachers and peers very few problems of a disciplinary nature will develop.

SUMMARY

Teachers consider the keeping of discipline to be their number one professional problem. More teachers probably fail in their work because of inability to maintain a well-ordered classroom than for any other single reason. Although the importance and need for providing a classroom atmosphere that is conducive for effective learning has never been doubted, methods of keeping discipline have changed radically over the years. Formerly, it was considered standard practice to bring an offender into line by corporal punishment, ridicule or the removal of privileges. Discipline was something imposed upon the child by the teacher. Today, the goal is to avoid clashes between pupils and teachers by making the children as responsible as possible for their own behavior and by providing learning experiences which are highly motivated.

When children misbehave there is a reason. The teacher should try to find out what it is. Children frequently show-off in class, are impudent, or are negativistic because they want attention. The wise teacher will attempt to see that such children obtain the attention they crave from more fruitful types of activities. As a matter of fact, frustrated children may show almost any number of unhealthy symptoms which indicate that needs are not being met. When disciplinary episodes arise, the teacher should make a study of the children involved in order to determine their motivations. He should also carefully evaluate his own teaching methods, and the curricular arrangements of the school to ascertain to what degree they are responsible for creating frustration in children.

The need for keeping discipline will diminish when children are happy and are busily engaged in activities that appear to them as being of real worth. Disciplinary problems will increase when the goals of children and the goals of the school are at cross purposes.

REFERENCES FOR FURTHER STUDY

Baruch, Dorothy W., *New Ways in Discipline*, New York, McGraw-Hill Book Company, Inc., 1949.

Bernard, Harold W., *Mental Hygiene for Classroom Teachers*, New York, McGraw-Hill Book Company, Inc., 1952, Chapter 8.

Cellar, Sidney L., "Practices Associated With Effective Discipline, A Descriptive Statistical Study of Discipline," *Journal of Experimental Education*, Vol. 19, June, 1951, pp. 333–358.

Crow, L. D. and Crow, A., *Mental Hygiene*, New York, McGraw-Hill Book Company, Inc., 1951, Chapter 15.

Crow, L. D. and Crow, A., "Basics in Discipline," *Minnesota Journal of Education*, Vol. 30, January, 1950, p. 19.

Daniels, Lawrence, "New Objectives for School Discipline," *School and Community*, Vol. 38, January, 1952, pp. 14–16.

Dyer, J. Pope, "An Experiment With Problem Boys," *Clearing House*, Vol. 20, 1945, pp. 360–361.

Henning, Carol J., "Discipline, Are School Practices Changing?" *Clearing House*, Vol. 23, January, 1949, pp. 266–273.

Kanya, J. R., "Maintaining Classroom Discipline," *California Teachers Association Journal*, Vol. 47, January, 1951, pp. 13–14.

Ludeman, W. W., "Discipline Becomes Guidance," *The Grade Teacher,* Vol. 64, April, 1947, pp. 19+.

Miller, Van, "Dominic Takes a Hand With Discipline," *Clearing House,* Vol. 23, December, 1948, pp. 237–239.

Sheviakov, George V. and Redl, Fritz, *Discipline for Today's Children and Youth,* Washington, D. C., Department of Supervision and Curriculum Development, N.E.A., 1944.

Stendler, Celia B., "Climates for Self Discipline," *Childhood Education,* Vol. 27, January, 1951, pp. 209–211.

Taylor, Leo, "Discipline, A Principal's Interpretation of an Old Meaning," *California Teachers Association Journal,* Vol. 47, December, 1951, p. 17.

Van Pool, Gerald M., "Student-Court Versus Student-Council Policy," *Clearing House,* Vol. 23, March, 1949, pp. 397–400.

Viele, John A., "Guidance Through Class Discipline," *Kentucky School Journal,* Vol. 25, May, 1947, pp. 31–33.

Chapter 15

Promoting the Personal and Social Adjustment of Pupils

THE PRECEDING chapter has given attention to some maladjustments of children which give rise to disciplinary problems in the classroom. There are, however, many children who do not create overt classroom disturbances but who are nonetheless unhappy, insecure, and maladjusted in various ways. Teachers should have an understanding of these children—should be able to diagnose as far as possible their troubles and should in addition be able to create situations designed to improve their condition.

Information from the White House Conference on Child Health and Protection would indicate that one out of every three school children is maladjusted in one way or another. It has also been estimated that 12 per cent are so emotionally upset as to require the services of guidance specialists and psychiatrists.[1]

HOW TEACHERS VIEW ADJUSTMENT PROBLEMS OF PUPILS

Twenty-five years ago, E. K. Wickman [2] found a marked discrepancy between the ratings of teachers and mental hygienists on the relative seriousness of behavior problems in school children. Wickman reported that "teachers stress the importance of problems relating to sex, dishonesty, disobedience, disorderliness and failure to learn. For them, the problems that indicate withdrawing, recessive

[1] C. Morley Sellery, M.D., "An Organized Mental-Hygiene Program in the Schools," *NEA Journal*, Vol. 37, December, 1948, p. 586.

[2] E. K. Wickman, *Children's Behavior and Teachers' Attitudes,* New York, The Commonwealth Fund, 1928.

characteristics in children are of comparatively little significance. Mental hygienists, on the other hand, consider these unsocial forms of behavior most serious and discount the stress which teachers lay on anti-social conduct." [3] Very recently, however, the Wickman Study has been repeated by Stouffer.[4] He finds that today's teachers and mental hygienists are in much closer agreement as to the seriousness of children's behavior problems than they were back in 1928. The extent of the present agreement can be seen from an examination of Table 28. The actual degree of correlation between the teachers' ratings and those of the psychological experts was found to be .61. The fifty classroom behavior problems listed in Table 28, although not of equal seriousness, are all ones which require the attention of teachers. None of them can be said to be entirely unimportant. The well-trained teacher should be prepared to deal with each using the best psychological techniques available.

DETECTING MALADJUSTMENT

There are a number of tests, rating scales, and inventories which are useful to teachers and school psychologists in the process of discovering children who are personally and socially unadjusted. Among these are the *Haggerty-Olson-Wickman Behavior Rating Schedules*,[5] the *Bell Adjustment Inventory*,[6] the *California Test of Personality*,[7] the *Rogers Test of Personality Adjustment*,[8] the *Mooney Problem Check List*,[9] and the *SRA Youth Inventory*.[10]

Many symptoms of maladjustment are readily observed by watching the child. His facial expression may indicate unhappiness or anxiety. He may be restless, hyperactive, tense, give evidence of being neglected, seem self-conscious about physical defects, be easily upset, depressed, or angered by frustration, have nervous habits such as twitching or nail biting, or be constantly engaged in

[3] *Ibid.*, p. 129.

[4] George A. W. Stouffer, Jr., "Behavior Problems of Children as Viewed by Teachers and Mental Hygienists: A Study of Present Attitudes as Compared with Those Reported by E. K. Wickman," *Mental Hygiene*, Vol. 36, April, 1952, pp. 271–285.

[5] Published by the World Book Company, Yonkers, New York.

[6] Published by the Stanford University Press, Stanford University, California.

[7] Published by the California Test Bureau, Los Angeles, California.

[8] Published by the Association Press, 347 Madison Avenue, New York.

[9] Published by the Bureau of Educational Research, Ohio State University, Columbus, Ohio.

[10] Published by Science Research Associates, 57 West Grand Avenue, Chicago.

TABLE 28

Rank-Order Comparison of the Ratings by Mental Hygienists and Teachers
of the Seriousness of 50 Behavior Problems of Children *

BEHAVIOR PROBLEM	RANKING BY MENTAL HYGIENISTS	RANKING BY TEACHERS
Unsocial, withdrawing	1	6
Unhappy, depressed	2	3
Fearfulness	3	23
Suspiciousness	4	35
Cruelty, bullying	5	4
Shyness	6	34
Enuresis	7	30
Resentfulness	8	11
Stealing	9	2
Sensitiveness	10	24
Dreaminess	11	40
Nervousness	12	18
Suggestible	13	13
Over critical of others	14	27
Easily discouraged	15	10
Temper tantrums	16	16
Domineering	17	15
Truancy	18	7
Physical coward	19	33
Untruthfulness	20	5
Unreliableness	21	1
Destroying school material	22	12
Sullenness	23	32
Lack of interest in work	24	22
Cheating	25	9
Selfishness	26	17
Quarrelsomeness	27	28
Heterosexual activity	28	14
Restlessness	29	45
Inattention	30	36
Impertinence, defiance	31	8
Tattling	32	47
Slovenly in personal appearance	33	31
Obscene notes, talk	34	29
Laziness	35	20
Stubbornness	36	37
Attracting attention	37	43
Thoughtlessness	38	41
Imaginative lying	39	46
Disobedience	40	19
Carelessness in work	41	25
Masturbation	42	26
Impudence, rudeness	43	21
Inquisitiveness	44	44
Disorderliness in class	45	39
Tardiness	46	38
Interrupting	47	48
Profanity	48	42
Smoking	49	49
Whispering	50	50

* Adapted from Stouffer.

daydreaming, or again, the maladjusted child may be a truant. The social activities of the child will also reveal much. He may be left out of play groups; he may bully or be bullied by other children. He may be resentful of criticism, be fearful, quarrelsome or defiant, or be given to temper tantrums.

The teacher may sometimes find out what is bothering a child by having him tell a story or write a theme on such topics as "What I Dreamed Last Night," "If I Had Three Wishes," and "When I Was Most Afraid." Sociometric questions such as "With whom would you like to sit?" "With whom would you like to work?" or "With whom would you like to attend a movie?" when answered by pupils may give the teacher an indication of whom the "isolates" or rejected children in a room are. The child who steals, cheats, lies, or engages in heterosexual activity sooner or later identifies himself by becoming involved in conflicts with other people.

CAUSES OF MALADJUSTMENT

In previous chapters it has been pointed out that every child in order to develop in a normal and wholesome manner must achieve reasonable satisfaction of his physical, social and personality needs. Problem behavior, delinquency and personal unhappiness are fundamentally due to frustration of these needs. There are, of course, numerous conditions in and out of the school which create frustrations which lead to maladjustment. Included among these are poverty, broken homes, personal inadequacies, rejection or over-protection by parents, and numerous unhygienic school practices.

Poverty. Sociological studies [11] have shown the close connection which exists between poverty and personal maladjustment. Not all children who come from underprivileged homes are problems by any means, but statistically speaking low socio-economic status breeds conditions unfavorable to sound adjustment. How this works is illustrated in the case of two brothers, Gene and Clyde.

Our acquaintance began when two forlorn little fellows were brought in by the police for stealing from a neighborhood grocery store. Gene was the elder by a year, but it is hard to remember that because he has never been as large as his brother. Undersized, Gene was also undernourished and an extremely nervous little fellow with facial twitches, a shoulder and

[11] See Sheldon Glueck and Eleanor Glueck, *Unraveling Juvenile Delinquency,* New York: The Commonwealth Fund, 1950.

arm that jerked involuntarily, and he could never sit still. Clyde was not so undernourished as Gene, but was a moody, sensitive boy. He cried easily, and could not face censure, expressed or even implied, and he was never to blame. He felt insecure and unloved, said the boys at school picked on him and called him names that he hated. Even then, at the age of ten, Clyde was smarting under the injustice of his lot. Other boys had better homes; other fathers had better jobs. They could have things Clyde and his brother could not have; and their folks were not beaten by life. With very superior intelligence, neither boy was interested in school nor was either doing more than barely passing work. At home the situation was dispiriting. . . . When Clyde's father worked, it was at housecleaning jobs that Clyde and his brother were ashamed of. Resenting the necessity and the implications of charity the family complained bitterly about the amount and character of the aid given them by the county. Health conditions were perilous. The mother was found to have active tuberculosis, and Gene's undernourished condition threatened to develop into the same disease. The parents were listless and indifferent. The school and welfare department complained that they were uncooperative. Keeping the house clean and looking after the children was too heavy a burden for the always-tired mother, but she and her husband could forget about it all when they had had enough alcohol to deaden their sensibilities.[12]

Broken Homes. Statistics have shown that children who come from homes which have been broken by death, divorce, desertion, and separation are more often maladjusted than children who come from more stable homes. In reporting on delinquent boys, Glueck and Glueck state that "no fewer than six out of every ten of the homes of the delinquents, as compared with three of the homes of the nondelinquents, had been broken by separation, divorce, death, or the prolonged absence of one of the parents."[13] It is, of course, the insecurity caused by the breaking of the home that has the deleterious effect upon children. Homes which are not broken but in which there is much parental conflict also provide more than their quota of nervous, unhappy, problem children. To understand why some children behave as they do, it is essential for teachers to engage in home visitation. Such experiences will be most rewarding to the teacher and will furnish a perspective for dealing with the child which cannot be obtained in any other way.

[12] Maud A. Merrill, *Problems of Child Delinquency*, pp. 80–82. Copyright, 1947, by Houghton Mifflin Company, Boston.
[13] Sheldon Glueck and Eleanor Glueck, *Delinquents in the Making: Paths to Prevention*, New York: Harper & Brothers, 1952, p. 60.

Personal Inadequacies. The child who is physically or mentally inadequate for tasks which are expected of him is certain to experience frustration. Equally frustrated is the child who sets goals for himself which he cannot reach. One important function of the teacher is to help each child set aspiration levels which are commensurate with his abilities.

The child who is crippled or disfigured has problems of adjustment to face which are more complicated than those of the average child. Barker and his coworkers state that "studies by means of interviews, observations, and reports of informants indicate rather consistently that physically disabled persons are more frequently maladjusted than physically normal persons." [14] They point out that the resulting maladjustment may take such forms as the following:

a. Withdrawing, retiring, reticent behavior
b. Shy, timid, self-conscious, fearful behavior
c. Serious, thoughtful behavior
d. Refusal to recognize real condition, concealment, delusions
e. Feelings of inferiority
f. Emotional and psychosexual immaturity
g. Friendless, isolated, asocial behavior
h. Paranoid reactions, sensitivity, suspiciousness
i. Craving for affection, love of praise, seeking attention
j. Too high goals
k. Extremely aggressive, competitive behavior
l. Anxiety, tension, nervousness, temper tantrums [15]

Sheldon [16] in one of his studies has noted the fact that delinquents are not as high in the *t* factor (a measure of good looks) as nondelinquents.

Children and adolescents are very sensitive about being different from what is considered typical or normal. They want to be like their peers. The teacher who can make each child feel significant regardless of whether he is tall, short, crippled or disfigured can do much to alleviate inferiority feelings created by what the child may consider to be personal inadequacies. It is not the condition *per se*

[14] Roger G. Barker, Beatrice A. Wright, and Mollie R. Gonick, *Adjustment to Physical Handicap and Illness: A Survey of the Social Psychology of Physique and Disability,* New York: Social Science Research Council, 1946, pp. 72–73.

[15] *Ibid.*, p. 73.

[16] William H. Sheldon, *Varieties of Delinquent Youth,* New York: Harper & Brothers, 1949, p. 762.

which causes maladjustment, it is the way the child views himself that determines his reactions. The teacher can cite many examples to show that people with all sorts of deficiencies have made outstanding successes of their lives. This approach may help the child to forget some of his personal limitations and aid him to make the most of the positive characteristics he possesses.

The Rejected Child. Many children come from homes where they are neither loved nor valued by their parents. Such treatment threatens the child's need for affection and security and may leave him feeling helpless and alone. The forms that parental rejection may take are many. These include neglect of the child; separation from the child; withholding gifts from the child; threatening, nagging, and punishing the child; humiliating him before other people; and comparing him unfavorably with other children in the family.

Children who are rejected by their parents may show a variety of unhealthy symptoms when in the classroom or in other situations. One of these is excessive attention-getting behavior. Many a child who is hyperactive, restless, and who seeks attention through nonconformity or wisecracking is merely striving in the classroom to attain the satisfaction of a need which has been denied him at home. Symonds has pointed out that children who are much neglected or harshly treated by their parents may develop psychopathic and unstable tendencies. He describes the behavior of the psychopathic child as follows:

> The psychopathic child is one characterized by utter disregard of rules and conventions of society, by shallow feeling, by lack of reactions of guilt, and by emotional instability. He has not learned self-control nor developed behavior which is socially acceptable. Rejected children have low frustration tolerance. Since the parents have not exercised restraint or control, the child himself acquires no conscience or restraints from within. His superego is embryonic and consequently he is without feelings of guilt or remorse.[17]

The child who feels rejected also very often tends to be withdrawn or if he is able to find a friend, he may be extremely jealous of him and desire that no one else share his affection. Children who have met with little or no emotional response on the part of parents,

[17] Percival M. Symonds, *The Dynamics of Parent-Child Relationships,* New York, Bureau of Publications, Teachers College, Columbia University, 1949, pp. 27-28.

more often than not, have the greatest difficulty in forming genuine attachments for anyone. It is hard for them to give affection when they are not certain that it will be reciprocated.[18]

Although teachers are not in a position to do much to alter parent-child relationships, they can do much to make children feel accepted, loved, and significant when at school. Acceptance by any adult who is respected by the child or by the child's own peers may at least partially compensate for rejection experienced in the home. This source of need satisfaction may help many a child from becoming a severe behavior case.

The Over-protected Child. Just as children may be rejected, they may be overindulged by their parents. Parents who are themselves insecure and anxious often lavish affection and attention upon their children. They crush the child with solicitude and excessive gratification. Every whim of the child is catered to. He may eat whenever or whatever he wants, or may have any toy or other material object he desires. He, however, may be protected and restricted from playing with other children or from going out into the weather because his parents feel he may suffer thereby.

Children who are overindulged show numerous characteristic behavior traits. These include selfishness, aggressiveness, lack of responsibility, and general infantile behavior. Children who are overprotected often exhibit such nervous habits as thumb-sucking, enuresis, and temper tantrums. "The overindulged child has poor social adjustment. He is known as the child with bad manners, the impolite child who will say the saucy thing and who will be rude and boorish. He is also known as the undisciplined child, and parents and teachers call him disobedient. When they make a request of him, he will obey it or not according to his whim and if it is something disagreeable, he may become impudent when an attempt is made to coerce him. With other children he is demanding, bossy, selfish, cocky, and a show-off." [19]

The overprotected child is greatly in need of socialization. The school can do much to help him take responsibility and overcome his self-centered infantile behavior. He will receive many hard knocks both from teachers and other children but it will be greatly

---

[18] Louis Kaplan and Denis Baron, *Mental Hygiene and Life*, New York, Harper & Brothers, 1952, pp. 244–245.

[19] Percival M. Symonds, *op.cit.*, p. 55.

to his advantage if he can learn to develop tolerance for frustration. This is something that he has never developed at home and something which he will greatly need in life if he is to be successful. Care should be taken, however, that his rough edges are not removed more quickly than he can stand. He will need sympathetic but firm and realistic treatment. Over a period of years the over-indulged child through association with individuals outside the family may develop very socially acceptable behavior.

Unhygienic School Practices. There is no question but that unfavorable home conditions play a large part in maladjustments which children exhibit at school. It is not so apparent, however, that conditions existing in the school may also contribute much to a child's unwholesome development. Teachers who are inadequately trained in psychology and mental hygiene unwittingly commit many serious errors and carry forward practices which are extremely detrimental to the good mental health of their pupils. Requiring all children in a given grade to satisfy the same requirements regardless of their abilities is one such practice. For example, a twelve-year-old child with a mental age of eight may be required to undertake tasks which are appropriate only for normal children of his age. In this case, the child's response to these excessive requirements may be expressed either by withdrawing (e.g., daydreaming) or by attacking the situation (e.g., disobedience). Many children are made to feel insecure, uncertain and afraid because the teacher constantly threatens them with unexpected examinations or with failure in the course.

Many teachers use stringent autocratic controls in their classrooms which have the unfortunate effect of reducing children's resourcefulness and initiative. Children who are impertinent or who "show off" are publicly humiliated and forced to make apologies. Children who are tardy or who play truant are required to stay after school. Children who lie or steal are accused and threatened with expulsion from school.

Altman describes a teacher who told her pupils that "everything in the classroom was charged with electricity, and that they might be electrocuted at any moment if they misbehaved because she, the teacher, could pull a switch to kill them all." He also related a case of an eight-year-old boy who developed a severe case of St. Vitus Dance, because of his fear of his teacher. The boy's nervous symptoms entirely disappeared when he was transferred to another school.[20]

Healy and Bronner have suggested that the school may in some instances directly contribute to the delinquency of children. A quotation from their discussion of what makes a child delinquent will show how this may occur.

Slurs, taunts, cutting remarks, evidences of social and racial prejudice may arouse or accentuate feelings of inferiority which in turn, are reflected in reckless antisocial behavior. If a teacher, without thinking, asks in the classroom, "Why doesn't your mother send you to school cleaner?" or "Are you a placed-out child?" or "What does your father do for a living?"—questions that possibly imply social inferiority—he little realizes how the child may be touched to the quick. We could give vivid illustrations of how such remarks have set off whole trains of explosive behavior. A strong, determined boy of thirteen, already sensitive about his home life, met a teacher's slurs about his mother's lack of care for his appearance with immediate truancy. He stubbornly evaded school for weeks, steadily refusing to return to this teacher's room. When the principal rejected the idea of transferring him to another school, he ran away, made his way to Texas, and was gone a whole year. Returning while still of school age, he continued to be truant, committed other delinquencies and was always embittered about the earlier school experience.[21]

Wendell Johnson has pointed out that in some schools "children are singled out as defective, and even though no official announcements are made, the children themselves, their schoolmates, their families and neighbors become vaguely aware of what they feel to be an unsavory and disturbing label. Then nothing constructive is done. They simply wait and worry. The simple fact is that branding a child as defective and then ignoring or neglecting him intensifies his problem both for him and his family." [22] The practice of labeling children as "dumb," "bad," "stubborn," "disobedient," or a "stutterer"

[20] Emil Altman, "Our Mentally Unbalanced Teachers," *The American Mercury*, Vol. 52, April, 1941, pp. 391–401.

[21] William Healy and Augusta F. Bronner, "What Makes a Child Delinquent?", in *Juvenile Delinquency and the Schools*, Forty-Seventh Yearbook of the National Society for the Study of Education, Part I, Chicago: University of Chicago Press, 1948, pp. 37–38.

[22] Wendell Johnson, "Teaching Children with Speech Handicaps," in *The Education of Exceptional Children*, Forty-Ninth Yearbook of the National Society for the Study of Education, Part II, Chicago: University of Chicago Press, 1950, p. 184.

may actually contribute toward making a child display the characteristics of his label.

Many additional examples could be given of school procedures which promote poor mental health on the part of pupils. The picture, however, is not all dark. As was shown in the study by Stouffer, cited earlier in this chapter, teachers are becoming more conscious of mental hygiene than ever before and as a result the number of unhygienic school practices are undoubtedly decreasing.

DEALING WITH SPECIFIC TYPES OF MALADJUSTMENT

In Table 28 which was presented earlier in this chapter are listed fifty types of behavior problems encountered by teachers. It will be impossible to discuss ways and means of dealing with each of these. As a matter of fact, there is no specific technique that applies to one that may not apply to others as well. These fifty problems are largely symptoms which indicate that all is not well with the pupils who exhibit them. A child who shows one or more of these symptoms should be studied. This study should attempt to discover what is back of the behavior—what needs of the child are thwarted, etc. Frequently many symptoms or problem behaviors of a child can be traced to one given cause.

In this section a few typical behavior problems will be discussed. It is hoped that these illustrations will present a point of view that may be useful in dealing with other similar problems of adjustment.

The Child Who Steals. Behind the act of stealing there is always a cause or motive. The teacher should try to find out what need or needs of the child is being met by this type of behavior. A child may steal because he is hungry, needs clothes or because he needs money to impress his friends. Perhaps he can buy the social approval of other children if he has money to procure gifts for them. Sometimes children steal in order to get revenge upon another child or the teacher, or to vent hostile feelings toward their parents. Just what should be done in the case of the child who steals would depend upon which of the foregoing motives were operative. The child who steals because he is hungry should certainly first of all be supplied the necessities of life. The child who steals in order to buy gifts which will win him acceptance into a social group needs help in gaining social recognition through more legitimate channels.

The child who steals in order to express feelings of hostility toward his teacher probably needs more affection and response from his teacher and opportunity to release his emotions in such activities as school plays, music, art, or athletics. From the mental hygiene point of view it would be very unwise to demand a confession from a child who steals or to publicly accuse him of such an act. Such procedures do not get at the basic cause of his trouble and may only aggravate the case by causing him to lie or gain a bad reputation for an act he may not commit again.

The Child Who Cheats. Cheating on the part of pupils is a problem which confronts a great many teachers. It is true, however, that children cheat in the rooms of some teachers, but do not do so in their other classes. Children cheat for a variety of reasons. Thorpe has suggested four possible causes of this behavior. They are as follows:

1. The task is too difficult
2. Parent, teacher or child standards are too high
3. Parent, teacher, or child has placed a premium on marks or grades rather than on understanding
4. Child feels inadequate or insecure in many situations [23]

The child who cheats is usually under severe pressure to make good or has a fear that he will fail in his studies. The teacher who gears learning tasks to the abilities and interests of pupils will find that cheating drops off drastically. Many times children do not see how the subject they are studying will help them personally. They thus take the shortest possible route to secure a passing grade. Units of work and problems directly related to real life activities often so intrigue pupils that the possibility of cheating never occurs to them. Much cheating can, however, be expected in dull and tense classes where a premium is placed upon the acquisition of subject matter which has doubtful value in the minds of the pupils. Even in such situations, the honor system as employed by some schools, has had a marked effect in reducing cheating. When children are given full responsibility for their own conduct and when peer group pressures are brought to bear, it is a rare child who will break the rules of the game. Under the honor system there may be thirty or forty

[23] Louis P. Thorpe, *The Psychology of Mental Health*, New York, The Ronald Press Co., 1950, p. 538.

pairs of watchful eyes supervising an examination instead of just one pair of eyes—those of the teacher.

The Lazy Child. It is not uncommon to hear teachers characterize certain of their pupils as being "lazy." The writer once taught a high-school geometry class. In this class was a big husky boy named Bill who seemed to be about the most "lazy" pupil the writer had ever encountered in his several years of public school teaching. Bill never did his assignments, and during class periods he would drape himself over the desk in a most lackadaisical manner. One Saturday, however, the writer had occasion to do some shopping at a large chain grocery store. Whom should he see but his geometry pupil, Bill, directing the operations of one of the departments of the store. Although Bill was only a junior in high school, he had been placed in charge of one of the largest divisions of the store. The writer asked the manager how Bill was getting along with his Saturday job. He was told that Bill was one of the most efficient, energetic, resourceful and ambitious students the store had ever employed. The writer blinked his eyes in amazement. It seemed impossible. Bill apparently was not "lazy" at all. About all that could be said was that he was unmotivated when it came to studying geometry.

Many so-called lazy children come to life and exhibit real enthusiasm and competence when school activities are slanted toward goals which the children themselves consider to be important. Too often, however, the goals of the school and the goals of pupils are at cross-purposes. In such situations there will inevitably be many unmotivated or "lazy" pupils on the class rolls.

The Truant. According to Table 28, truancy is ranked seventh in order of seriousness by teachers. It is, however, ranked only eighteenth by mental hygienists. Teachers consider truancy, for example, to be a more serious behavior problem than fearfulness, shyness, enuresis, nervousness, and suspiciousness. Mental hygienists, on the other hand, rate all these symptoms above truancy. The truant is an individual who just does not want to go to school and makes plans to do something else. He may go fishing, attend a movie, visit the circus, take a trip, or work on some interesting project in a friend's basement. He may or may not have a serious problem of personal adjustment. It is clear, however, that he has a real problem of school adjustment. If the activities at school challenged him as much as those outside school, it is certain that he would be no truant. Basketball coaches have no problem of truancy among their players. In fact, they often have great difficulty keeping the boys out of the gymnasium even when practices are not scheduled. The child who is successful in school—whose needs are being met—is unhappy if events prevent him from attending his classes. Teachers should consider truancy on the part of pupils a sign that something is wrong with the school as well as with the pupil. When changes have been made in school programs, truancy has been known to drop off. One teacher commented upon one of her boys as follows: "K. is one of our truants. We have previously had great difficulty in keeping him in school. He is now in one of the remedial reading clubs where he is responsible for telling other children when the group meets. His truancy first disappeared on the days the club met, but recently he has been attending every day." [24] This boy cannot afford to be absent from school because he would then miss the opportunity of being a valued member of his reading club.

The Unsocial, Withdrawing Child. Of all the problem types of classroom behavior, mental hygienists rate this one the most serious. Teachers are also becoming conscious of the unsocial, withdrawing child in their midst as is seen by the fact (Table 28) that they now rate this problem sixth in importance out of a list of fifty behavior deviations. The shy child, although he causes the teacher no inconvenience, may be most unhappy and suffering from feelings of insecurity and inadequacy. He may daydream excessively, refuse to mix with other children, and withdraw into a world of his own. It is this type of child, mental hygienists believe, that is in the most danger of developing schizophrenia if nothing is done to check his unsocial trend. All shy children, of course, do not become psychotic; perhaps only a few do. Yet the fact that some may and that others often develop into adults who are socially ineffective and unhappy is sufficient cause for concern.

An example of such a child is Dodie, a fourteen-year-old girl, who is described by Buhler as follows:

Dodie was an unobtrusive and quiet girl. In school she passed from grade to grade as an average to good student until now she was in the ninth grade of a junior high school. Nobody had paid much attention to her except one physical education teacher who had asked her, in front of

[24] Marion Monroe and Bertie Backus, *Remedial Reading: A Monograph in Character Education,* Boston: Houghton Mifflin Company, 1937, pp. 155–156.

all the children, why she had inferiority feelings about games and athletics. This was an unfortunate remark in the circumstances.

Dodie never talked in class unless asked to. She went around with one or two girls whom she called her friends. She never talked with boys and never participated in group activities or was elected to any office.

The first time any teacher concerned herself with Dodie was when her grades began to drop considerably. The teacher discovered that in the ninth grade Dodie sat daydreaming and rarely spoke to anyone or participated in class.

Calling the mother to discuss Dodie's work, the teacher learned to her surprise that the mother a few weeks earlier had taken the child to a doctor and to a psychologist, but had not wanted the school to know because she felt the school might think there was "something wrong" with Dodie. (This unfortunate idea that the school might be prejudiced against a child seen by a psychologist is not unfrequently encountered in parents.)

The teacher was now interested and worked with mother and psychologist to understand this child. She learned that Dodie, after coming home from school, never talked to anybody outside the house if she could help it. She participated in no games with the many neighbor children as did her brothers and sisters. . . .

Most of her time was spent among books and magazines; she liked to draw dress models and model dolls. She put much imagination into these drawings and her absorption let the mother feel that Dodie, who herself was plain, identified with these beautiful models in her long periods of daydreaming. When asked whether she wanted to be a dress designer, she declared that she just wanted to marry and have children. As she refused to meet anyone, particularly to date with boys, or to talk with them, her marriage wish appears an unreal dream similar to her dreams about beauty and models.[25]

Children like Dodie are not at all uncommon in the classrooms of this country. Efforts to socialize them should definitely be made by teachers. The kindly, sympathetic and understanding teacher is in a position to maneuver things so that the withdrawn child is drawn into more school and social activities. If such a child can experience one success in a group activity, a good start is made. The isolated child needs to feel that he is essential to the happiness of others— that he is a valued member of some group. If satisfaction can be achieved in real life activities, there is no need for the child to withdraw into the realm of dreams to satisfy his basic wants. The wise

[25] Charlotte Buhler, *et al., Childhood Problems and the Teacher,* pp. 141–142. Copyright, 1952, by Henry Holt and Company, New York.

teacher may observe that a withdrawing child has some special competence or ability that can be used in a group activity. By indirection the child may be induced to participate. If his contribution is appreciated by the other children, he will be encouraged to repeat his successful performance in group situations. The writer knows of a home economics teacher who induced one of her very shy and poorly adjusted girls to have a cooking party in her home. Other children in the class were invited. The success of the enterprise greatly increased the girl's confidence in herself and resulted in a changed attitude of the other children toward her.

SCHOOL PROGRAMS WHICH AID PUPIL ADJUSTMENT

The Case Study Conference. Some schools have worked out a plan whereby time is set aside each week for the careful analysis of a given pupil's adjustment problem. At this time all the pupil's teachers gather along with such other interested individuals as the principal, counselor, school nurse, and school social worker. All the pertinent information available regarding the pupil and his problem are presented, and a recommendation is made which is designed to facilitate the pupil's adjustment. This device not only serves to alleviate problems of children but provides valuable in-service training for teachers.

The Delaware Human Relations Class. One of the widely known plans for aiding pupil adjustment is the Delaware Human Relations Class. Bullis has described how this operates in the following words:

Our weekly class generally starts with the teacher reading a stimulus story which features emotional problems. The students are then encouraged to discuss freely the emotional problems presented in the stimulus story, to give an appraisal of the story, and then most important of all to indicate from their own personal experiences parallel situations to those presented in the story. In this retelling of emotional experiences—often bringing out into the open problems they have never discussed before—a better understanding of their actions often results. The students also gain insights by listening to their classmates tell freely of how they meet certain emotional problems.[26]

[26] H. Edmund Bullis, "A Positive Mental Health Program," *American Journal of Public Health*, Vol. 40, September, 1950, p. 1114. For description of the Delaware program also see H. Edmund Bullis, "Are We Losing Our Fight for Improved Mental Health?" *Progressive Education*, Vol. 30, February, 1953, pp. 110–114.

The Delaware program has been designed especially for use in grades seven, eight, and nine. The originator of the plan (H. E. Bullis) has prepared and published three teachers' handbooks— *Human Relations in the Classroom,* Courses I, II, and III.[27] Each book contains thirty lesson plans and six teacher aids together with additional information for conducting the classes.

The Tulsa Personal Relations Course.[28] This course is designed for boys and girls at the eleventh grade level. Among the topics covered are: "Understanding Ourselves," "You and Your Family," "Boy and Girl Friendships" and "Looking Toward Marriage." It is suggested by the designers of the program that the teacher may stimulate interest in the first of these topics, for example, by:

1. Having students list personal adjustment problems
2. Discussing behavior observed, or conversations overheard, which indicate adolescent problems
3. Showing and discussing films, slides or recordings which present adolescent problems.

The work of the course involves a thorough consideration of the basic principles of mental hygiene and their application to everyday living. Regular credit is given for the course. Over the years, the course has been so popular with pupils that many ask to repeat it a second time without additional credit.

Remedial Classes. Children who are extremely retarded in reading, arithmetic, English usage, and other tool subjects often find themselves bewildered, frustrated, and discouraged in regular classes which are geared many levels too high for them. Theoretically a master teacher with unlimited resources in materials, and small classes, could minister to the needs of these children. Actually, however, this is very difficult to accomplish. As a result the very slow learning child is frequently humiliated to such an extent that he develops aggressive, withdrawing, and other antisocial behaviors. A great number of schools have set up remedial classes to fit the needs of such children.[29] By giving the slow learner success ex-

[27] These may be obtained from the Delaware State Society for Mental Hygiene, Wilmington, Delaware. ··

[28] Course in Personal Relationships, Eleventh Grade, Tulsa Public Schools, Tulsa, Oklahoma, 1949.

[29] For description of remedial classes in schools see Glenn M. Blair, *Diagnostic and Remedial Teaching in Secondary Schools,* New York, The Macmillan Company, 1946.

periences rather than failure experiences a big step is taken toward rebuilding his morale and integrating his personality. Reports indicate that as a result of remedial classes many resistant children have become cooperative, apprehensive children have become self-confident, discouraged children have become hopeful, and socially maladjusted children have become acceptable to the group.[30]

In teaching such classes it is imperative, however, that teachers create an atmosphere which makes their pupils feel important and significant and not inferior to other pupils. The pupils should be made to feel that they are normal—that every individual is good in some things and not so good in other things. If it is a special class in reading, the teacher should convey the idea that anyone can learn to read just like anyone can learn to tap dance or play the piccolo. The teacher might cite cases of famous men such as President Andrew Johnson who did not learn to read until after he was married. If a pupil is really made to believe that there is nothing peculiar about him, he will generally be enthusiastic about improving his reading skills even if the lessons are conducted in a class especially designated for that purpose. On the other hand, if teachers and school administrators tend to regard special classes for poor readers as essentially "dumb-bell" classes, the pupils quickly sense this and very unsatisfactory results are bound to occur. Under such circumstances, slow-learning pupils would probably be better off in regular classes.

If properly taught and administered, however, these unfortunate results need not occur. The writer has visited special classes in which children were beaming with success. They were finding out for the first time in their lives that they could learn to read, write, spell, and do arithmetic. Such achievement had a marked effect upon their self-confidence and their entire outlook on life.

USEFUL TECHNIQUES AND MATERIALS

Techniques. The major part of this chapter has been devoted to consideration of ways and means of helping the maladjusted child. Essentially the technique advocated has been that of understanding what his needs are and providing a school atmosphere and curriculum which will make possible their satisfaction. This, of course, is fundamental and all devices utilized should have as their aim a

[30] *Ibid.*, pp. 13–14.

similar purpose. Techniques reported in the literature which have been used or suggested for use by classroom teachers to aid maladjusted children include group therapy,[31] play therapy,[32] non-directive counseling,[33] and psychodrama.[34] Teachers who desire to improve their skills in dealing with maladjusted children should make a careful study of these methods by reading the available literature and pursuing specialized courses in these areas.

An example of how play therapy was used by one teacher to help a disturbed, little boy is reported in a recent article.[35]

John

John was a sturdy, handsome eight-year-old with a violent temper. One of the big causes of friction in his home was his inability to read. He was continually reminded of his inadequacy and his reaction was usually a temper tantrum in which he smashed his own play things and stormed and screamed . . . He tried this same behavior in school, demanding immediate attention whenever he had any difficulty and tearing up his pictures or breaking his clay or wooden handwork when there was any delay in getting help. He did beautiful handwork and was very proud of it so its destruction was a measure of his troubled twisted thoughts. His sullen face and bursts of anger kept him from having any friends. He was a most unhappy little boy.

John's teacher induced him to make puppets as a means of releasing his tensions and developing status among his classmates. This method apparently worked for after a few months it was noted that his classwork was improving, he was beginning to read, and his personality was changing for the better. He lost his sullenness and fiery temper and became a friendly, well-liked, sociable boy.

Haas [36] gives the following examples of types of pupil problems which afford opportunity for use of psychodrama in the classroom.

[31] Henry S. Maas, "Group Therapy in the Classroom," *Mental Hygiene*, Vol. 35, April, 1951, pp. 250–259.

[32] Virginia Mae Axline, *Play Therapy*, Boston, Houghton Mifflin Company, 1947.

[33] Kathleen Fawcett, "Psychotherapy in Your Classroom," *Texas Outlook*, Vol. 32, August, 1948, pp. 19–20. For detailed description of this method see Carl R. Rogers, *Client-Centered Therapy; Its Current Practice, Implication, and Theory*, Boston: Houghton Mifflin Company, 1951.

[34] Robert B. Haas, *Psychodrama and Sociodrama in American Education*, New York: Beacon House, 1949.

[35] Florence Liss, "How Puppets Helped John," *Childhood Education*, Vol. 26, January, 1950, pp. 214–216.

[36] Robert B. Haas, *op.cit.*, pp. 101–102.

1. Boy calls on a girl in the home of her parents. He is instructed to ask her for a date to a coming school dance. Purpose is to explore the kinds of social skills required in such a situation.
2. A girl comes into a schoolroom and discovers two of her friends in a violent gossip session about her. The nature of the gossip is varied to suit the level of the pupils. Excellent motivation is provided for discussion of the psychological meaning of gossip.

Those who advocate the use of psychodrama in schools feel that through the process of acting out a situation (role playing) there will be a release of tension on the part of the pupil and a more complete understanding of his problem. Psychodrama has been recommended for all grade levels of the school.

Materials. An increasing number of good books and films are being produced which can be used in mental hygiene programs of the school. Books which have been prepared for pupils include: *Getting Along with Others,*[37] *How Personalities Grow,*[38] *Personality and Youth,*[39] and *Ways to Improve Your Personality.*[40]

Films that may be used include such titles as *Developing Self-Reliance, Shy Guy, Developing Your Character, Developing Friendships,*[41] *The Other Fellow's Feelings,*[42] *Understanding Yourself,*[43] and *You and Your Family.*[44] Films such as these may frequently be rented from state or university visual aid libraries.[45]

THE SCHOOL PSYCHOLOGIST

Some schools have a psychologist on the regular staff. This person helps to supplement the mental hygiene program of the school. He works with teachers, assists with the testing program, and may con-

[37] Published by Science Research Associates, 57 West Grand Avenue, Chicago, Illinois. This publisher has a whole library of Life Adjustment Booklets which have been designed to help teen-agers solve their problems.

[38] Helen Shacter, *How Personalities Grow,* Bloomington, Illinois, McKnight and McKnight, 1949.

[39] Louis P. Thorpe, *Personality and Youth,* Dubuque, Iowa, William C. Brown Company, 1949.

[40] Virginia Bailard and Ruth Strang, *Ways to Improve Your Personality,* New York: McGraw-Hill Book Company, Inc., 1951.

[41] These first four are all Coronet Films.

[42] Young America Films, Inc.

[43] Church Screen Productions.

[44] Association Films.

[45] The Audio-Visual Aids Department of the Division of University Extension, University of Illinois, Urbana, Illinois, carries many films of this type.

sult with individual children who are seriously disturbed. Although he may render extremely valuable service of a specialized nature, he is just one cog in the total program. Teachers in the classroom will always have to carry the brunt of the counseling and guidance work regardless of whether a specialist is or is not available. When mental hygiene principles are extensively applied in classroom practice the number of children needing the attention of a psychologist will become progressively fewer. The well-trained teacher should be able to recognize children whose problems are of such a nature that outside help is needed.

In some communities child guidance clinics are in operation which may be used by schools with limited specialized personnel. These clinics are often directed by a psychiatrist who has psychologists on his staff. Severe problem cases which require deep psychotherapy should be referred to such agencies.

SUMMARY

Not all maladjusted children create disciplinary problems for the teacher. Some children who are unsocial, withdrawing, unhappy, depressed, suspicious, fearful, and nervous, actually attract very little attention to themselves. These children, according to mental hygienists, need as much if not more sympathetic help from teachers as do the "trouble makers."

The causes of personal unhappiness, inferiority feelings, shyness, and other socially ineffective behavior can be traced to the same sources of conflict that create more aggressive types of maladjustment. Both the shy child and the aggressive child have thwarted needs, but each adopts a quite different method of resolving his problem. Conditions in the environment which create frustrations leading to personal maladjustment are poverty, broken homes, personal inadequacies, rejection by parents, overprotection, and certain unhygienic school practices.

In this chapter some common types of cases encountered by teachers are discussed, and suggestions are given for helping personally and socially unadjusted children. The truant, for example, is described as being a child who finds few satisfactions at school. School is such an unpleasant place to go that nonattendance is preferred. Truancy, however, can be made to disappear when the child finds that he is really needed at school and that what he has to offer is appreciated by others. Likewise the shy and socially in-effective child can be made to show more confident behavior and to take part in more group activities when arrangements are more for him to experience success rather than failure in connection with social activities.

Schools are beginning to give increased attention to problems of mental hygiene. In some instances, special classes or programs have been developed which deal directly with adjustment problems of children. Examples of these are the Delaware Human Relations Class, and the Tulsa Personal Relations Course. Teachers as a result of more sound psychological training are becoming increasingly skillful in using therapeutic devices which formerly were employed only by a few experts. Such procedures include group therapy, play therapy, non-directive counseling, and psychodrama.

Problems such as have been presented in this chapter obviously require for their solution the highest levels of psychological train-ing and insight. How to deal with children who present personality difficulties is a skill which must be mastered by all who would suc-ceed in the difficult task of teaching.

REFERENCES FOR FURTHER STUDY

Bachhaus, Vyonne, "Rehabilitation of Herman," *Wisconsin Journal of Education*, Vol. 83, February, 1951, pp. 9–10.

Baron, Samuel, "Limitations of the Teacher in Guidance," *American Journal of Psychotherapy*, Vol. 6, January, 1952, pp. 104–110.

Bernard, Harold W., *Mental Hygiene for Classroom Teachers*, New York, McGraw-Hill Book Company, Inc., 1952, Chapters 9, 10, 11, 12.

Bettelheim, Bruno, *Love Is Not Enough: The Treatment of Emotionally Disturbed Children*, Glencoe, Illinois, The Free Press, 1950.

Buhler, Charlotte, Smitter, Faith, and Richardson, Sybil, *Childhood Problems and the Teacher*, New York, Henry Holt and Company, 1952.

Cohen, Samuel S., "Building a Curriculum for Adjustment Classes in the Junior High School," *High Points*, Vol. 33, December, 1951, pp. 37–47.

Fenton, Norman, *Mental Hygiene in School Practice*, Stanford University, Stanford University Press, 1943.

Fiedler, Miriam F., *Deaf Children in a Hearing World, Their Education and Adjustment*, New York, The Ronald Press Co., 1952.

Fostering Mental Health in Our Schools, Washington, D. C., 1950 Year-book, Association for Supervision and Curriculum Development, N.E.A.

Glueck, S. and Glueck, E., *Delinquents in the Making: Paths to Prevention*, New York, Harper & Brothers, 1952.

Havighurst, Robert J., "A Community Youth Development Plan," *School Review*, Vol. 59, November, 1951, pp. 457–466.

Kirk, Samuel A. and Johnson, G. Orville, *Educating the Retarded Child*, Boston, Houghton Mifflin Company, 1951, Chapter 15.

Krugman, Morris, "Guidance and Mental Hygiene Services in the New York City Schools," *Journal of Educational Sociology*, Vol. 24, May, 1951, pp. 517–527.

Maas, H. S., "Applying Group Therapy to Classroom Practice," *Mental Hygiene*, Vol. 35, April, 1951, pp. 250–259.

MacKenzie, Louis T., "Group Action in Personality Development," *School Review*, Vol. 56, 1948, pp. 484–488.

Merrill, Maud A., *Problems of Child Delinquency*, Boston, Houghton Mifflin Company, 1947.

Parry, Douglas, "Experimental Practice in Improving the Emotional Health of Secondary School Students," *High School Journal*, Vol. 35, December, 1951, pp. 80–88.

Pearson, Gerald H. J., *Emotional Disorders of Children*, New York, W. W. Norton and Company, 1949.

Redl, Fritz and Wineman, David, *Controls from Within: Techniques for the Treatment of the Aggressive Child*, Glencoe, Illinois, The Free Press, 1952.

Shuman, Shirley N., "Teacher and the Overmothered Child," *Grade Teacher*, Vol. 66, January, 1949, p. 17.

Slavson, S. R., *Child Psychotherapy*, New York, Columbia University Press, 1952.

Ruth Strang, "Mental Hygiene of the Gifted Child," in *The Gifted Child*, (Paul Witty, Editor), Boston, D. C. Heath and Company, 1951.

Chapter 16

Studying the Individual Child

IN A SENSE this whole book is a study of children—how they develop, learn, and adjust. This chapter, however, will focus upon the study of the individual child rather than deal with facts about children in general. No child is simply a summation of many traits, characteristics, interests, and ideals. Rather each is a unique, indivisible organism and each must be appraised separately and *in toto*. A leading authority in the psychology of personality aptly expressed the need for individual study when he wrote: "The only way to make a certain prediction of effect from cause is to study the life in which the causes operate and not a thousand other lives." [1]

This chapter will present the need for child study, some of the sources of information available to teachers and others who work with children, and the methods and tools which psychologists and teachers have found useful.

THE NEED FOR CHILD STUDY

The need for child study, especially the intensive study of individual children becomes clearly apparent in those cases where teachers made judgments and take action with insufficient knowledge about a child. The pathos of some such mistakes is illustrated in two cases which follow.

In the first case, the teacher who was giving a timed test told the class that when she said "go" all pupils should begin immediately. All pupils started work on the signal except Mary who delayed a few seconds and (according to the teacher) gave her an impudent

[1] G. W. Allport, *The Use of Personal Documents in Psychological Science*, New York, Social Research Council, 1942, p. 210.

stare. The teacher collected all the papers, passed them out a second time, and again said "go," but Mary was still late in starting. At this turn of events, the teacher slapped Mary's face several times. Shortly afterward, a medical examination diagnosed Mary's case as "post-encephalitic epileptiform behavior." In short, damage to motor nerves made this girl's reaction time slow. She would have been unable to start on the word "go" no matter how hard she tried.

The second case was that of a girl, Doris, who was accused of stealing from her classmates' lunch boxes. Investigation revealed that large quantities of sandwiches and fruit had been hidden in the school's basement, and Doris was found guilty. The teacher was aggravated by this apparent willful waste of food and suspended the girl from class. A clinical study of this case turned up the fact that Doris was extremely malnourished. Her lunches generally were nothing more than an ungarnished slice of bread or a few saltines. Other children had made fun of her lunch and she retaliated by taking tidbits and hiding them. When she was asked why she had not eaten any of the sandwiches, apples, and other "goodies," she replied, "Eat their lunches, that would be stealing." [2]

Each Child is Unique. Even though people have much in common, there is also much which makes each unique. Children with identical IQs may be very different in other traits and may even be radically different in the distribution of their mental abilities. For example, two children may both score an IQ of 120 on the *Stanford-Binet* test. Yet one may be an excellent reader and the other almost a non-reader. One of these children may have unusual musical talent and the other possess almost none. Furthermore, on the test itself, one child may score highly on the memory items while the other child will make his strongest showing on the problem solving tasks. Even identical twins may, and generally do, have different personalities. [3] When identical twins are reared apart, differences in temperament, and personality may be even more pronounced. [4]

[2] D. E. Lawson, "Development of Case-Study Approaches," *Educational Forum*, Vol. 16, March, 1952, pp. 311–317.

[3] Evelyn Troup, "A Comparative Study by Means of the Rorschach Method of Personality Development in Twenty Pairs of Identical Twins," *Genetic Psychology Monographs*, Vol. 20, 1938, pp. 461–556.

[4] H. H. Newman, F. N. Freeman, and K. J. Holzinger, *Twins: A Study of Heredity and Environment*, Chicago, The University of Chicago Press, 1937, p. 192.

Children Have Individual Problems. The most useful way to answer the question as to "why" a child is behaving in a certain way is to study that particular child. "A problem child is one who has a problem that has not been solved." [5] That child and that problem are unique. An illustration of the way in which individual study and treatment may help youngsters solve their problems is shown in the following case described by Thornley. [6]

The boy, who was 17, had a mental age of 14.3, and an IQ of 89. His achievement test scores were: vocabulary 5.4; [7] reading comprehension 7.9; arithmetic reasoning 8.3; arithmetic fundamentals 6.1; language 5.3; and total grade equivalent 6.2. Intensive individual interviews with this boy revealed that he had considerable drawing ability, and that he wanted to study women's clothing design but was hesitant to make this known. With encouragement from the teacher, he began making sketches and drawing designs. Presently, the teacher suggested that he go to the clothing teacher and talk with her about designs but he found that he was unable to understand her, and returned to the English teacher somewhat discouraged. It was then suggested that he read about design and clothing, and make a list of words that he did not understand. He did this and continued his drawing. Within a few months, he had produced several dress designs which, according to the clothing teacher, were better than the commercial designs which she was buying. Not only had this boy gained self-confidence, and made achievement in this specific area, but in the short space of a semester read nearly 2000 pages—a feat which was unduplicated in his previous work.

The greatest value in the study of the individual child is that such study may show the causes of behavior problems which give rise to concern about the child. Only with a knowledge of these causes does a teacher have a sound base for remedial action. [8]

PITFALLS TO BE AVOIDED IN CHILD STUDY

The arch enemy of good child study is the "typing" of children on the basis of too limited data. Contrary to the specific information

[5] T. L. Torgerson, *Studying Children,* New York, The Dryden Press, 1947, p. 26.

[6] W. R. Thornley, "Unlocking Resources of Retarded Students," *The English Journal,* Vol. 39, 1950, pp. 302–306.

[7] "Vocabulary 5.4" means that the boy achieved in vocabulary as well as the average pupil in about the middle of the fifth grade.

[8] The reader who wishes to find examples of such cases is referred to G. M. Blair, *Diagnostic and Remedial Teaching in Secondary Schools,* New York, The Macmillan Company, 1946, pp. 382–404.

which comes from individual study is the kind of generalization which is implied in such remarks as: "all smart kids are like that." By pigeonholing people, it is possible to brush off differences and treat all children alike. The reaction of a school principal to types of children, and the consequent distortion of his perceptions about the individual children involved is illustrated in the following incidents described by Hollingshead.[9]

Elmtown High was having trouble with tardiness so decided all children should get "detention" for further infractions, and that there would be no excuses. So a decision to this effect was made, and announced to the school and to the office staff. The following Wednesday morning Frank Stone, Jr. (Class I) [10] parked his father's Cadillac in front of the high school at a quarter after eight. When he came into school, the principal said:

"What's the story this time?"

. . . "I didn't wake up, I guess."

The boy was told to report for detention. He failed to do so and when the principal called his father (a very prominent man in the community), the son was sent to school, but the superintendent interceded and got him off, with the mild warning that he try not to let it happen again.

Three weeks later, "Boney" Johnson who was a Class IV boy came late. Before "Boney" could say a word the principal said:

"So my pretty boy is late again! . . . I suppose you took a bath last night too. New shoes and they're shined." "Boney" said nothing, but his face flushed and he bit his lip. The principal walked back to his desk, sat down, and wrote out an admission slip. He put "Boney's" name on the detention list and handed over the excuse with the remark, "I want to see you in detention tonight. Now go on up to class and show the girls what a pretty boy you are."

After the boy left the principal said:

"Now there's a hot one. He's one of our *wise guys*. He thinks he's a *hot shot*. His old man is a laborer out at the fertilizer plant, and the kid thinks he's someone umph! He'll be on the W.P.A. if they have one twenty years from now. There's one guy I'm going to see put in detention."

[9] The incidents described here were taken from A. B. Hollingshead, *Elmtown's Youth*, New York, John Wiley and Sons, Inc., 1949, pp. 188–192.

[10] In Elmtown, the fictitious name of an actual town in Illinois there seemed to be five distinct socio-economic classes. Class I represented the monied land-owning group, Class V were the impecunious "squatters" who worked irregularly and who lived for the most part in homes which were more like shacks than houses. "Boney" Johnson was in the Class IV group, which rated just a little higher than the Class V group just described.

That night after school when "Boney" tried to escape, the principal seized him and when the boy tried to fight loose, hit him several times. The superintendent who was also on hand joined in and together they threw "Boney" out the front door with the threat not to come back till he brought his father. After he was gone, the principal and superintendent spoke of "Boney" as a "sassy kid," a "trouble making type," a "smart kid."

"Boney" quit school. Undoubtedly some might add that he was the type who would.

Here was a case in which prejudgment based on typology, plus sarcastic action were probably influential in producing an educational casualty which could have been averted by individual attention and study. Likewise, the case of Frank Stone, Jr., although on the surface he fared better, was nevertheless shrugged off on the basis of typology. That "kid" was the "rich" type about whom the school could do nothing. Some of the dangerous and misleading kinds of typing which are often employed by teachers are given in the next five paragraphs.

IQ Typing. Frequently used terms are "dull," "average," and "bright." These are based on an arbitrary criterion such as an IQ score. Teachers should know that the error of measurement on tests could easily throw a person from one class into another. Also it must be remembered that there are great differences within the individual, and typing on the basis of IQ might have little connection with abilities in other areas. Another source of error is that excessive weight is given to single items of behavior or single scores. The way to avoid this kind of typing error is to fight the "halo" [11] effect by the use of objective tools of appraisal, the recognition of the limitations of tools of measurement, and the avoidance of the use of stigma words with regard to children who lack one kind of academic proficiency.

Hereditary Typing. "He'll never amount to anything, look at his father. He's shiftless, and the boy's a chip off the old block." Statements such as this illustrate a kind of erroneous thinking which certainly should not be practiced by school teachers. Attributing

[11] The halo effect is an error of judgment about a person which results from overgeneralizing on the basis of a limited amount of specific information. For example, a youngster who has committed one misdemeanor may be viewed as a "bad" boy; or a child who makes one high score may be seen as having over-all high ability.

bad characteristics to the influences of heredity may be a convenient way to shrug off a problem, but it does not solve any problems.

Associational Typing. This kind of typing represents a variety of thinking which is characteristic of the generalizations of small children. It is exemplified by such reasoning as: "One man with a mustache cheated me, therefore all men with mustaches are cheaters." Although no teacher should be guilty of this kind of logic in dealing with children, one suspects that this kind of overgeneralization was working when teachers made these statements: [12] "Dirty children are careless in school," and "aggressive boys are girl-crazy," or the statements that children who masturbate are "mentally unbalanced" or "usually dull and thin."

Social Class Typing. No one can question that there are relationships between social class and behavior. But to judge behavior on social class alone is wrong because there is considerable variation of behavior of children coming from a given social class. Much of the cause of misbehavior is probably due to just such typing and the rejection and unfairness it creates. For the most part, teachers are middle class persons with the values and mores of that group. It is thus difficult for them to look at behavior of lower class children objectively. There is a tendency to excuse the lack of study of such children by the implicit belief that it would be hopeless anyway.

Racial and Religious Typing. This is a most pernicious and psychologically unsound kind of typing. Nevertheless it is sometimes used by teachers as is shown by these statements:

Negro children remind me of an odor
Jewish children think they are better than other children

From a large group of nearly 200 teachers who completed the sentence "Italian boys ———" the following responses were not rare:

have a hot temper
are handsome
are busybodies
are dirty and nasty
are cute
are usually fine athletes, and not too bright [13]

[12] Unpublished data collected by E. L. Gaier, Psychology Department, University of Illinois, Urbana, Illinois, 1951.
[13] *Ibid.*

WHICH CHILDREN SHOULD BE STUDIED?

All children should receive some degree of individual study. The intensity or thoroughness of the study should be a function of the following criteria:

1. The degree to which present behavior is likely to affect adversely a a child's development.
2. The amount of help the child will probably need in solving his problems.
3. The amount of competence the teacher has in dealing with such problems.
4. The degree to which the problem behavior interferes with the work of the teacher and of the class.

The choice of children for study may be biased by the social class to which they belong, although it is obvious that this is not a valid criterion for deciding whom to study. Another factor (number one above) the seriousness of the behavior, is probably the one most frequently used. This is as it should be. However, many teachers probably do not know which varieties of problem behavior are the most serious, and often make their choice of children to study on the basis of number four above, which is probably the least important factor.[14]

The beginning teacher may be aided by knowing what kinds of problems to expect. Relevant here is a survey made by Torgerson. He found in a study of 1270 pupils from grades one to eight the following percentages of children having these difficulties: [15]

31 per cent had scholarship difficulties
27 per cent suffered from reading disabilities
20 per cent had social behavior problems
15 per cent had speech problems
13 per cent had health problems and physical disabilities

The kind of child who is studied is probably also determined by the types of problems which teachers expect, and the sorts of "problem" behavior for which they search. For instance, the referrals from a traditional school, which followed strict routines, and in which there was a crowding of pupils, were almost all disciplinary

[14] See the discussion of the work of E. K. Wickman and George A. W. Stouffer, Jr., in the preceding chapter.
[15] T. L. Torgerson, op.cit., p, 45.

cases or subject matter failures. A "progressive school" with which the former was compared sent to the school psychologist considerably more cases in which children suffered from fear, shyness and social maladjustment.[16]

Finally, it is interesting to note that the sex of children often enters into the question of whom should be studied. In a survey of 1,357 children in Detroit about one per cent were classed as having serious behavior problems, and 85 per cent of these serious cases were boys.[17] In referrals to clinics for problems of reading, speech, and delinquent behavior, boys lead. It is to be noted, that the aggressive behavior, which leads to study is less likely to occur among girls, who nevertheless may be having other difficulties which are just as serious. In the writer's classes over the past few years, when teachers have turned in case studies of their problem pupils, well over 90 per cent have been studies of boys.

SOURCES OF INFORMATION

Where do teachers obtain information about a child? This is an important, but nonetheless difficult question. A child may act very differently in various situations. Furthermore, there are places and ways of obtaining information which are often overlooked in the study of a child.

A child may be extremely aggressive in a permissive play situation and well controlled, even over-inhibited, in the classroom or home.[18] The model child at his mother's knee might, when mother is not around, be the one who would be found squeezing his little brother's fingers with a pair of pliers. To acquire data for a dependable child study requires the gathering of material from many places and in various circumstances. This section will attempt to show how a study of the home, community, and school may furnish information about a child's problems.

Parents and Home Conditions. One of the most successful teachers the writer knows is one who regularly visits the homes of every pupil in her class. This teacher has a third grade in the "toughest"

---

[16] R. G. Anderson, "Two Schools and Their Problem Cases," *Progressive Education*, Vol. 11, 1934, pp. 484–489.

[17] H. J. Baker and V. Traphagen, *The Diagnosis and Treatment of Behavior-Problem Children*, New York, The Macmillan Company, 1935.

[18] A. F. Korner, *Some Aspects of Hostility in Young Children*, New York, Grune and Stratton, 1949, p. 167.

section of a large industrial city, yet she has fewer disciplinary problems than most teachers in the city, and is well liked by both pupils and parents. This teacher attributes her success to knowing how the parents and children live, and dealing with the problems of each child in the light of the*information thus collected.

An important question is what to look for in the home, and what to find out from parents. Parents can be a rich source of information, but simply going to a home or talking to parents will not automatically unlock this source. The teacher may be so busy trying to avoid being called "nosey" or concealing the shock he feels on seeing bad conditions in a home that he misses some of its important psychological conditions.

In teachers' visits to homes, classroom visits by parents, interviews with parents and in group meetings, teachers should be alert to and seek for information in the following areas:

1. The emotional reactions of the parents toward the child
2. The parents' understanding of the child and his problems
3. The parents' ideals, values, and aspirations with respect to the child
4. The parents' control techniques and disciplinary measures
5. Parents' attitudes toward the school, teacher, and learning

Successful work with parents hinges on the same psychological principles which operate in dealing with the problems of motivation, readiness, and individual differences of pupils. Just as children can be alienated by unfavorable comparisons, harsh criticisms, and sarcasm, so parents may become emotionally disturbed and refuse to give information or cooperate when these techniques are used.[19]

Community. At first glance it would appear that a teacher might easily acquire information about a community simply by virtue of living in it. Not so for the middle class teacher who may see the community and its neighborhoods through middle-class eyes. Even small towns may have a number of fairly distinct sub-cultures each with its own values, ideals, and ways of living. In one town of only 6,200, for example, there appeared to be at least five separate socioeconomic classes and about eight rather distinct neighborhoods.[20]

[19] For a good discussion of "The Teacher's Work With Parents," see Charlotte Buhler, Faith Smitter, Sybil Richardson, Franklyn Bradshaw, *Childhood Problems and the Teacher*, New York, Henry Holt and Company, 1952, Chapter 12, especially page 251.

[20] A. B. Hollingshead, *op.cit.*, p. 462.

In studying communities and neighborhoods, teachers should ask these questions:

1. How does the community feel about itself? Does it consider itself to be composed of distinct classes?
2. What are the community's influences upon its youth? What youth serving agencies are there? What do the people who staff these agencies think about the community?
3. Who are the community leaders and how do they feel about the community?
4. How does the school fit into the community? How do the citizens feel about the school?
5. How does the child feel about his community and neighborhood?

Observations. Direct observation of a child under a number of different circumstances has promise of offering more valuable information for the time spent than any other diagnostic activity. On the other hand, when observations are biased or incomplete, they may be worse than useless, as they may lead to either the wrong action on the part of the teacher or give a distorted notion to others when reports of the behavior are made. Two teachers can look at the same behavior in the same child and make very different reports and interpretations of the child's behavior.

The accuracy of perception of observed behavior as well as the empathy which a teacher has for a child's problems and behavior are both important in observation and the action which follows. Ways of improving the accuracy of observation as well as increasing identifications (empathy) with a particular child are suggested in the numbered points which follow.

1. Observations should be planned. One way of implementing the planned nature of observations is to time-sample behavior. This means that at planned (and randomized intervals) observations of a certain length (e.g., 15 minutes) be made of a given child. If such a formalized planning is not feasible for the teacher, it is suggested that he might plan to observe a little of the behavior of the child in each of the various activities during the day on various days of the week for a period of time.
2. Interpretation should *follow* the collection of data. Tentative interpretation, before the data are in, especially when it is made explicit in writing or discussion may ego-involve the observer so that he makes future observations conform to the original diagnosis. In this regard,

the teacher could take a tip from the advice given counselors and clinicians, "Only when he has all the data he is going to have, should he make his public commitment on paper or to the patient or in any other communicated form." [21] Even such an apparently small consideration as the order in which a teacher obtains information may color the interpretation of observed behavior.[22]

3. A written record (if one is to be made) should be made directly after an observation. The longer material is kept in mind, the more details are lost and the greater is the tendency for distortion. But as shown in 2 above this record should not, at least initially, contain interpretive material.

4. Teachers ought to learn how to play the role of the child, i.e., put themselves in the child's place. This was neatly expressed by Cottrell, who wrote:

> Just the simple device of saying to himself, "Now I am X facing this situation and having to deal with this problem," seems to enhance the observer's comprehension of the perspectives, attitudes, and overt behavior of his subject. Deliberate role-taking practice also seems to increase these observational skills.[23]

5. One should look for symptoms of difficulty. H. B. English, who for many years has regularly required the study of an individual child by students in his classes in child psychology, recommends that they look especially for: the "child's relationship with other people," and he adds, "anything that makes the child a little different is always interesting and important." [24]

Interviews. A special kind of observation is the interview. Here the teacher tries to observe the child's behavior (mainly verbal) in a face-to-face relationship. Some interviews are counseling sessions in which the main goal is one of therapy, but most conferences in the classroom are for the purpose of gaining information which will help in cooperatively planning learning experiences that are not necessarily therapeutic. The educator may not be a psychotherapist, but at the same time he may have more powerful tools for influencing the social setting of the classroom than does the psychotherapist.

[21] N. L. Gage, "Explorations in the Understanding of Others," Paper read at the Sixteenth Annual Guidance Conference at Purdue University, Lafayette, Indiana, April 10, 1951.

[22] S. E. Asch, "Forming Impressions of Personality," *Journal of Abnormal and Social Psychology*, Vol. 41, 1946, pp. 258–290.

[23] L. S. Cottrell, Jr., "Some Neglected Problems in Social Psychology," *American Sociological Review*, Vol. 15, 1950, pp. 705–712.

[24] H. B. English, *Child Psychology*, New York, Henry Holt and Company, 1951, p. 21.

Careful analyses of interviews and of the interaction in counseling situations has revealed that the amount and validity of the information obtained is governed to a degree by the rapport or good relationship existing between the client and counselor—or in this case between the teacher and pupil. It should also be noted that interviews may be useful for shedding light on a variety of problems extending from process errors in arithmetic to deep seated problems of maladjustment or personality disorders.

Too common is the notion that a conference with a pupil means having the youngster "on the carpet." In fact there is some question that a teacher can play the dual role of grader and "boss," and at the same time be a confidant of a troubled pupil. Much depends not upon the interview alone, as it does in clinics where the counselor and child meet for the first time, but on the kind of relationships which previously existed in the classroom. In this sense, an interview is merely an extension of an everyday relationship, and should offer no problem for the good teacher.

Opening the interview. This is a very important phase, for it may set the stage for resistance or open the way for a warm relationship and the gaining of much information. Following are some examples of interviews poorly started and those well opened:

Poor Openings	Good Openings
Well, I guess you know why you're here, John.	Won't you sit down here, John.
Take off your hat.	Hello, Mary. Come in and help me move this desk off the light cord.
Did you forget about the rules we had made, Mary?	Well, I'm glad to see you, Edward. Have a seat.

One should avoid putting a child on the defensive in the beginning of an interview as this closes off the source of information. If the purpose of the interview is to discuss some misbehavior, one should not refer to this immediately. Since an interview is not a "third degree," a teacher should never overly press a point when emotional disturbance is detected.

Securing information. Teachers must listen! They may learn very little by talking, but may learn a great deal about a child by listening to everything he has to say. They must also avoid too rapid

TABLE 29

Errors of Beginning Counselors Observed over a Period of Several Years *

ERRORS IN TECHNIQUES

Not giving counselee responsibility	114
Talk too much	103
Too many questions	90
Questions too specific	89
Judicial authoritarianism	88
Missing cues	79
Urging, moralizing	78
Breaking in on counselee	73
Explanation long-winded	55
Counselor pulling counselee too fast	54
Assuring	45
Too much on what counselee says	34
Counselors meaning unclear	18
Reproving	17
Leads too general	14
Silences too long	13

ERRORS IN PROGRAM MAKING

Plans too vague	68
Into program too fast	11

ERRORS IN PATTERN OF CONFERENCE

Counselor structures too much	124
Counselee resistance	90
Tutoring too much	58
Counselee parrying	53
Unstructured wandering	44
Counselee not cooperative	33
Social visiting	33
Too much on skills	21
Counselee resents conference plan	19
Bell ended interview	10
Counselee mystified	5

* From F. P. Robinson.

probing. The creation of a warm, permissive, and confidential atmosphere will help more than anything else in facilitating the flow of information. The surest way to create resistance and bewilder a child is to ask him a question he is unable or afraid to answer. (Many times teachers ask questions which no one could answer.)

The writer recently heard a teacher tearfully ask, "How could you do this Mike?" To ask a seven-year old, "Why did you do such a terrible thing?" not only is a threat, but also may force a response which has only protective purposes. The child may learn to try to escape rather than to face problems.

Resistance. How well the interview is going can be estimated by the amount of resistance which is produced. Some of the indicators of resistance which practiced counselors have noted are: (1) the avoidance of detail or specific plans, (2) use of monosyllables, (3) intellectual discussion of topics, (4) rejection of the teacher's ideas, (5) hostility, (6) apathy, (7) blocks in thinking, and (8) attempts to leave before the interview is concluded.[25] The teacher, as a professional interviewer ought to become familiar with these symptoms of resistance, and know that they are signals which indicate the need for less probing, or less rapid leading.

The beginning teacher, who has not yet done much interviewing or counseling should profit from the material in Table 29 which shows some of the errors of beginning counselors. The data were taken from supervisor's ratings of over 370 interviews.

In brief this table emphasizes that beginning counselors take too much responsibility—they are neither good listeners nor are they able to use their own leads, summaries, and clarifications to the best advantage.

Gaining Information From Creative Activities. Unwittingly and without conscious awareness children may reveal many of their needs and much of their frustration through such things as themes, stories, drawings, paintings, and play. In fact, young children who are not able to verbalize well, or to use abstractions, may have no other means of telling adults their problems. Such is the case of Carl who made the sketch shown in Figure 16.

A study of this case revealed the following facts. Carl, just under age twelve when he made the above sketch, was a pupil in a special classroom for retarded children. He was one of four boys in a lower-middle class family. The mother was very much disappointed because Carl was a boy, and often expressed her resentment by dressing him as a girl. She had kept him in long curls and dresses for several years after his birth, and even continued the practice up to

[25] F. P. Robinson, *Principles and Procedures in Student Counseling*, New York, Harper & Brothers, 1950, p. 107.

the time of the incidents described here. Carl's tested IQ was 75 on the Stanford-Binet and 72 on the Grace Arthur Point Scale. In a Progressive Achievement Test most of his scores were just below

FIGURE 16. Pencil Sketch Made by an Emotionally Disturbed Twelve-Year-Old Boy.

the third grade level. A description of Carl written by his special class teacher follows:

When Carl first came to us he was a trouble maker, and still frequently reverts back to his bad behavior. He is large for his age, height 61 inches and weight 102 pounds. He tried to gain recognition by crawling around on the floor, whining, snickering, and acting very immature. He shoves, pushes, tattles, is destructive, inattentive, denies failures, bullies, acts smart, teases, giggles excessively, is nervous and restless, and indulges in temper tantrums.

The sketch shown in Figure 16 was but a sample of many such sketches and drawings,[26] made by Carl dealing with the same theme. These drawings portrayed Carl killing, boxing, hanging, shooting, frightening Jerry, and other younger children, especially effeminate boys and girls. In these drawings Carl always allied himself with the most masculine boys in class.

If Carl had been able to verbalize what his problems were, he would probably have said something like this:

I hated being treated like a girl when I was younger. I should have hated my mother for doing this to me, but I know children must love their parents. The least I can do now is to prove that I am not a girl in any way—not like Jerry who is a big sissy. I'm like Bill and John. We are tough guys.

It seems obvious that Carl was releasing tension and fighting against a girl's role which had been thrust upon him. In Carl's mind Jerry had come to symbolize the type of boy which represented the feminity which his mother had tried to create in him.

In creative activities one should look for such mechanisms as projection, compensatory activities, and daydreams. In this way the teacher may begin to get a glimpse of a child's real needs, which may emerge only briefly out of his disturbed emotional depths.

TOOLS AND METHODS FOR CHILD STUDY

The exploitation of the sources of information described in the previous section is facilitated by the use of appropriate tools and methods. What are the tests, rating scales, inventories and records which will most efficiently provide teachers the information they need in working with children?

Home and Community Rating Scales. Some professional workers have found a standard rating scale [27] for appraising the socio-eco-

[26] In one water color Carl and his pal John were shown shooting down Jerry in a plane over Korea (Carl's story). In another Carl depicts himself as a ghost chasing several younger children most of whom were girls.

[27] An example is the "Home Environment Inventory" of T. L. Torgerson, *op.cit.*, pp. 136–139.

nomic level of the home or community a helpful device. This is probably too formal a procedure for most teachers' purposes. However, some of these scales can be administered to pupils without the necessity for a home visit, and they seem to have considerable reliability when so used.[28] One such scale, *The Kerr-Remmers American Home Scale* has items such as the following: [29]

Does either of your parents belong to a parent-teacher organization? . . . . Yes No

Does your family own (not rent) the home in which you live? . . . . Yes No

Does your family have an automobile? . . . . . Yes No

Another scale which is filled out by pupils themselves is the *Sims SCI Occupational Rating Scale*.[30] It contains listings of various occupations and the student is asked to rate his own family level as the same, lower, or higher than the social class represented by the given occupations.

Somewhat less formal than the above scales is one suggested by English [31] as a guide for the teacher or case worker who wishes to study the home. This *Items-in-the-Home-Index* asks questions such as:

Is there an electric or gas refrigerator in the home?
Is there a bathtub in the home?
Does the family leave town every year for a vacation?
Does the child have his own room at home?
How many books does the family have?

Socio-economic rating covers but one aspect of the home. The most difficult and important task is that of appraising the psychological climate of the home, and there is no way of doing this simply by administering a questionnaire to the child. Direct observation of the goings on in the home is the best method, but if this is impossible a teacher may be able to get pertinent information from the

[28] H. H. Remmers and N. L. Gage, *Educational Measurement and Evaluation,* New York, Harper & Brothers, 1943, p. 439. *The Kerr-Remmers American Home Scale* is published by Science Research Associates, Chicago, Ill.
[29] *Ibid.,* pp. 439–440.
[30] Published by World Book Company, Yonkers-on-Hudson, New York, 1952.
[31] H. B. English, *op.cit.,* p. 45.

child, interviews with parents, neighbors, social case workers, and other adults who know the family.

For the unusual case in which a really intensive study is made, there are scales which can be used to rate many factors in parents' relationships with children. Such an instrument is the *Fels Parent Rating Scale*. One of the ten paragraphs from this scale is shown here: [32]

Paragraph IV

How emotional is the parent's behavior where the child is concerned? Is the parent highly emotional; or is he/she consistently cool and objective?

A. Constantly gives vent to unbridled emotion in reaction to child's behavior.

B. Controlled largely by emotion rather than by reason in dealing with the child.

C. Emotion freely expressed, but actual policy seldom much disorganized.

D. Usually maintains calm, objective behavior toward child, even in the face of strong stimuli.

E. Never shows any sign of emotional disorganization toward child, either directly or in policy.

Behavior Inventories and Rating Scales. When people try to force the description of a child into a check list of adjectives (which may only add to an already existing bias) there may be a danger of defeating the very purpose of the child study. For example, note the following items which might have been taken from any one of several rating scales: [33]

_____Bluffs in class	_____Scowling
_____Excitable	_____Excessive giggling
_____Acts "smart"	_____Temper tantrums
_____Quarrelsome	_____Selfish

All these items require a qualitative judgment by the rater. Raters without training will not reliably use such instruments, as one rater will describe a behavior as excitable, while another may label the same behavior as aggressive, or as a temper tantrum. Thus, if such scales are to be used it is essential that caution be employed, and

[32] From H. B. English, *op.cit.*, p. 493.
[33] These items were taken from a rating form used by a school counseling service (name withheld for obvious reasons).

that raters agree beforehand with regard to the behavioral referents of the terms which are used in the scale.

Some rating schemes have been developed which attempt to overcome such errors.[34] By and large, however, they have not yet been adapted to use for rating children, and for the present, the most profitable way of improving ratings would seem to be in providing proper training of teachers who will make ratings.

Systematic Records of Behavior. Each semester, teachers in the writer's classes discuss problem children they have encountered in their classrooms. In one instance, a teacher described a boy who had a "temper tantrum." Without further description, the writer asked all students in the class (most of them teachers) to jot down what a temper tantrum was, and what, in the case under discussion, this behavior was likely to have been. In essence they were asked to give a "mind's eye" picture which the term "temper tantrum" had evoked in this case. When the papers were collected, no two had like definitions or descriptions. One student's description was, "I'd say he fell to the floor screaming, kicking and waving his arms." Others believed that he might have struck the teacher, run from the room, or attacked other children. Very revealing, was the description of the behavior as it actually occurred. In the words of the teacher who had originally used the term "temper tantrum," the boy had, "torn up a test paper on which he had received a low grade."

It should become apparent immediately that one of the purposes of good objective records of behavior is to facilitate communication. Teachers are members of a professional staff, much as are a group of doctors in a hospital. Both groups have the problem of communicating their findings and observations to others if they expect to receive the benefits of this staff relationship.

It was previously noted that data must be recorded, and recorded without delay if they are to be accurate and contain the necessary detail. Informal records of observed behavior are often referred to as "anecdotal records." Several summaries and descriptions of these records have been made,[35] and rules have been devised for their use.

---

[34] There are graphic, numerical, man-to-man, and forced-choice rating schemes. The student who wishes to study the details of such scales is referred to H. H. Remmers and N. L. Gage, *op.cit.*, pp. 365–376; and E. B. Greene, *Measurements of Human Behavior*, New York, The Odyssey Press, 1952, pp. 455–472.

[35] Summaries of the description and uses of anecdotal records may be found

Some of the principles which have been suggested for increasing skill in the use of anecdotal records are:

1. Start by selecting one or two cases for intensive study.
2. Describe as many significant events each week as possible.
3. Do not try to interpret every incident. Make a summary analysis at convenient periods and look for developmental trends.
4. Concentrate on describing those types of conduct problems of cause-effect relationship which you know have a bearing on the child's difficulties.[36]

There is little reason to believe or even hope that mere lip service to a kind of record keeping will bring any significant change in the quality of child study, nor is there anything especially unique about anecdotal records. There are other ways of securing behavioral records. Inventories and rating scales have already been mentioned. A self-rating or record kept by the child might also be useful. A diary or log kept jointly by the teacher and pupil to record what each perceived to be significant experiences is used in some schools. Whatever form the record takes, the cardinal rule is that it contain description of behavior, and not merely a series of descriptive adjectives which are often once or twice removed from what the child actually does.

Cumulative and Personnel Records. Behavioral records (anecdotal or otherwise) plus all other pertinent material which is available should be included in the pupil's personnel folder. This record should be cumulative and developmental, and its accretion a planned process rather than the business of stuffing into the folder anything which happens to come along. Since records from a psychological and educational standpoint are so important, the authors would argue that records should be kept even if pupils have to help write them themselves. One system has been described for having each pupil fill out a record card once each semester in his home-

in A. E. Traxler, *The Nature and Use of Anecdotal Records.* Supplementary Bulletin C., New York, Educational Records Bureau, 1939; and L. L. Jarvie and Mark Ellingson, *A Handbook of the Anecdotal Behavior Journal,* Chicago, University of Chicago Press, 1940. For a discussion of how anecdotal records help in "Knowing the Child" see Helen Bieker, "Using Anecdotal Records to Know the Child," in Association for Supervision and Curriculum Development, *Fostering Mental Health in Our Schools,* Washington, National Education Association, 1950.

[36] T. L. Torgerson, *op.cit.,* p. 85.

room. The card contains a good many details, yet any pupil of junior-high-school age should be able to fill it out. It has spaces for courses taken, grades, reaction to school activities, readings, vocational choices, and the like.[37]

The Case Study or Case History. When the causes of children's difficulties, either in school work or in adjustment, are not readily apparent from the usual data contained in personnel records, a more intensive study should be made either by the teacher or the school psychologist to whom the child is referred.

There is little virtue in making a case study just to be making a case study. A case study should have a definite direction and purpose, and the details included should have relevance to the behavior which initiated the study. Nearly a dozen sources [38] give as essential material to include in a case study the following:

1. Data about the family, neighborhood and community, and the sources from which such information is obtained.
2. Physical characteristics and selected items from the medical record of the child.
3. The developmental history of the child (mental and physical).
4. The school record (academic, extracurricular and behavioral).
5. Recommendations.

In addition to such data as these, it is equally important to obtain information about:

1. The child's needs and the barriers which thwart them.
2. A record of the action taken as a result of the case study, and a follow-up report at later periods.

As before noted, teachers in the writer's courses have, over a period of several years, submitted case studies of selected children in their classes. Since these studies are under scrutiny of their classmates and the instructor, they may not be representative of what teachers actually do. On the other hand, they illustrate certain strengths and weaknesses which may provide insights for other teachers. A summary of some of the things which were done poorly and some which were done well is given in the following analysis.

[37] E. C. Roeber, "Cumulative Records Plan Lifts Burden from Teachers," *Clearing House*, Vol. 24, 1950, pp. 534–535.

[38] Good examples of case studies and suggested outlines for making them are found in the Buhler, English, and Young references at the end of this chapter.

Analysis of Case Studies Written by Teachers
in a Graduate Course in Mental Hygiene

Things Done Poorly in Case Studies

1. Inadequate or missing diagnosis. Even when diagnosis was given, the cause was not probed.
2. Little evidence about pupils' peer relationships.
3. Seldom were other teachers contacted about the child.
4. Too little use of a behavioral record—too much opinion.
5. Very little about the child's interests and wishes (or anything positive about the child).
6. Virtually no self criticism by teachers of the school, its practices, or of their own teaching methods.
7. Practically nothing about children's needs and how they were fulfilled or thwarted.
8. Rarely were child's own feelings and ideas about his problems noted.

Things Done Well in Case Studies

1. Statement of the school problems encountered by the youngster.
2. Recommendations were good and practical.
3. General home conditions of the child were fairly well described.
4. Presentation of measurement data done reasonably well.

What teachers did, they did well for the most part, but their omissions were numerous. Largely these omissions resulted from failures to exploit all the sources of information about the child, and his teachers. Many of these sources were close at hand. Pupils' relationships with each other, the reaction of other teachers, and the way the child himself feels are important materials which can be secured if an effort is made.

Some specific errors in collecting information and in writing case studies are illustrated below:

1. *Failure to follow leads.* Teacher's Report—"However, on one home visit the mother told me Carole was terribly afraid of her father." This was the only reference to this matter in the whole case history. In the writer's opinion, this glimmer of information was of sufficient importance to warrant further pursuit. This illustrates the point that a case study involves more than a passive reception of information. It is an active seeking of that information which is important.

2. *Burying important matter*. Teacher's Report—"Monte is not a behavior problem in any way, shape, or form. He only earned one and one-half credits in his entire freshman year. His grade in those subjects were only D's. *He seldom smiles or is happy.* He is of a serious nature, but is a gentleman in every respect." The writer italicized what is probably the most important bit of data about Monte. The teacher in his complete report made no further mention or use of the fact that Monte was unhappy, but dealt exclusively with his academic difficulties.

3. *Use of opinion in place of evidence*. Teacher's Report—"I think he is well-liked by his classmates." or "He seems to understand what I want him to do, but I think he just doesn't care." Some opinion in a case study is desirable, especially in the interpretation and recommendations, but in the factual presentation opinions should be held to a minimum.

4. *Overly abbreviated presentation*. Teacher's Report—"In talking with Carmen about her typing she made known the following:
   1. She was tense at the machine—was trying too hard.
   2. She enjoyed her typing, but was getting discouraged with her inability to do as well as she wanted to.
   3. She wanted to do office work when she finished school."

Here the report of the interview might well have provided some of the actual statements of the girl.

Lest the presentation of these errors and omissions discourage the reader, it should be said that most of the hundreds of case studies which teachers have submitted to the writer were excellent, and stand as evidence that many teachers are well equipped to study individual cases intensively, make diagnoses, and take the remedial or therapeutic action which is indicated. On the other hand most of the studies could have been improved if some of the suggestions of this chapter had been more widely utilized.

The most frequent objection which teachers raise regarding the case-study method of studying children is that it takes too much time—more time than is available in the working day. However, there are methods which will reduce the amount of time necessary to collect and interpret information. In the first place, it is probable that too little attention is given to training children how to assume the responsibility for self-evaluation. Children's own self analyses could well become an integral part of a case study. Secondly, it would seem feasible and desirable for schools to set aside regular meeting times when teachers could have staff conferences in which they would pool information about various children.

SUMMARY

Intensive, individual child study enables the teacher or other professional worker to probe for the causes of a child's behavior—causes which often exist in the form of motives or needs not clearly apparent on the surface. When problems of behavior, either in school learning or adjustment, are treated by teachers who have not given sufficient study to a case, the corrective measures may do more harm than good. Individual study is necessary because each child is a distinct individual who cannot be judged on the basis of what holds true for another child.

Anathema to good child study are the biases or prejudices which may either cause a teacher to pick the wrong children for intensive study, or distort the studies which are made. Often these errors occur when teachers "type" children as "dull" or "lower class," or overgeneralize about children on the basis of limited data.

One must learn *how* to collect accurate information about a child. In the task of probing for information, the teacher can find help in a variety of recommended instruments and methods. Standard rating scales to appraise the home, the parents' relationships with the child, and the child's behavior are available. The use of such scales necessitates training of the teacher in making ratings, however, as all are somewhat subjective in nature. Also of value to the teacher are anecdotal behavior journals, and cumulative records which are a collection of all pertinent material about a child.

The case study generally includes information about the child's home and family, his physical and mental characteristics, his school record, a statement of his problem, and the recommendations which result from a study of these materials. When teachers make case studies, they are apt to give too little information about causes of behavior, reactions of other teachers, the child's relationships with other pupils, or the child's own feelings and ideas about himself.

No teacher can expect to fulfill his obligations in the modern classroom if he is unacquainted with methods of studying individual children. This does not mean that teachers should be amateur psychiatrists, but it does mean that teachers should learn to look for and study basic causes of behavior. This cannot be done without adequate information regarding each child.

REFERENCES FOR FURTHER STUDY

Ackerson, Luton, *Children's Behavior Problems, II,* Chicago, The University of Chicago Press, 1942.

Bentley, J. E., *Problem Children,* New York, W. W. Norton and Company, Inc., 1936.

Bernard, Harold, *Mental Hygiene for Classroom Teachers,* New York, McGraw-Hill Book Co., Inc., 1952, Chap. 12.

Bettelheim, Bruno, *Love Is Not Enough: The Treatment of Emotionally Disturbed Children,* Glencoe, Illinois, Free Press, 1950.

Buhler, Charlotte, Smitter, Faith, and Richardson, Sybil, *Childhood Problems and the Teacher,* New York, Henry Holt and Co., 1952.

Cohen, F. J., *Children in Trouble,* New York, W. W. Norton and Company, 1952, Part II, "Six Case Studies."

Deutsch, Albert, *Our Rejected Children,* Boston, Little, Brown and Company, 1950.

Eissler, Kurt R., *Searchlights on Delinquency,* New York, International University Press, 1949.

English, H. B., *Child Psychology,* New York, Henry Holt and Co., 1951, Appendices and Chaps. 1, 2, and 3.

English, H. B., and Raimey, Victor, *Studying the Individual School Child,* New York, Henry Holt and Co., 1941.

Faegre, Marion L., and Anderson, John E., *Child Care and Training,* Minneapolis, The University of Minnesota Press, 1940.

Glueck, Sheldon, and Glueck, Eleanor, *Delinquents in the Making,* New York, Harper & Brothers, 1952.

Goff, Regina M., *Problems and Emotional Difficulties of Negro Children,* Teachers College, Contributions to Education No. 960, New York, Columbia University Press, 1949.

Hildreth, Gertrude, Brumbaugh, Florence N., and Wilson, F. T., *Educating Gifted Children,* New York, Harper & Brothers, 1952.

Konopka, Gisela, *Therapeutic Group Work with Children,* Minneapolis, University of Minnesota Press, 1949.

Mann, Frank A., "The Frequency of Unmet Emotional Needs as Evidenced in Children's Behavior," *Journal of Educational Sociology,* Vol. 24, 1951, pp. 414–432.

Powers, Edwin, and Witmer, Helen, *Prevention of Delinquency,* New York, Columbia University Press, 1951, especially Chap. XVII.

Sayles, Mary B., *The Problem Child at Home,* New York, The Commonwealth Fund, 1932.

Stone, L. J., "Recent Developments in Diagnostic Testing of Children," Chap. V in Harrower, Molly R. (ed.), *Recent Advances in Diagnostic*

Psychological Testing, Springfield, Illinois, Charles C. Thomas Publisher, 1950.

Strang, Ruth, *An Introduction to Child Study* (3rd Edition), New York, The Macmillan Company, 1951.

Symonds, Percival, *The Dynamics of Parent-Child Relationships,* New York, Columbia University Press, 1949.

Tappan, Paul W., *Juvenile Delinquency,* New York, The McGraw-Hill Book Co., Inc., 1949.

The Journal of Educational Sociology, Special Issue, "Juvenile Delinquency Prevention," Vol. 24, September, 1950.

Tuttle, H. S., *Dynamic Psychology and Conduct,* New York, Harper & Brothers, 1949, Chap. I.

Witty, Paul (ed.), *The Gifted Child,* Boston, D. C. Heath and Company, 1951.

Young, Kimball, *Personality and Problems of Adjustment,* New York, F. S. Crofts and Co., Inc., 1946, Appendix, pp. 819–824.

FILMS

Learning to Understand Children: Part I, "Diagnostic Approach," (21 mins.) and Part II, "Remedial Approach," (23 mins.), McGraw-Hill Book Co., Inc., Text-Film Department, New York.

Psychological Testing, Springfield, Illinois, Charles C. Thomas, Pub-
      lisher, 1950.

Strang, Ruth, *An Introduction to Child Study* (3rd Edition), New York,
      The Macmillan Company, 1951.

Symonds, Percival, *The Dynamics of Parent-Child Relationships*, New
      York, Columbia University Press, 1949.

Tappan, Paul W., *Juvenile Delinquency*, New York, The McGraw-Hill
      Book Company, 1949.

"The Journal of Educational Sociology, Special Issue," *Juvenile Delin-
      quency Prevention*, Vol. 24, September, 1950.

Thorpe, L. P., *Planning Adjustment and Conduct*, New York, Harper &
      Brothers, 1945, Chap.

Witty, Paul (ed.), *The Gifted Child*, Boston, D. C. Heath and Company,
      1951.

Young, Kimball, *Personality and Problems of Adjustment*, New York,
      F. S. Crofts and Co., Inc., 1946, Appendix, pp. 819-824.

                                    TESTS

California *Test of Mental Maturity*, Part I, "Diagnostic Approach," (12
      forms), and Part II, "Analytical Approach" (24 forms), McGraw-Hill
      Book Co., Inc., Test Division Department, New York.

PART V

MEASUREMENT
AND EVALUATION

Chapter 17

Diagnostic Tools

When early in the century, Edward L. Thorndike said, "Anything that exists can be measured," he became a spokesman for a movement which ushered in a new era in education. At first, tests were crude and covered only a few aspects of behavior, but in the years that followed, literally thousands of diagnostic tools were constructed by educators, psychologists, and personnel workers. At present, standardized tests of intelligence, achievement, personality, and interests are accepted as an essential part of the school's materials and equipment.

The scope of the field of evaluation may be seen in the fact that one recent bibliography of printed tests lists 5294 measuring instruments.[1] *The Fourth Mental Measurements Yearbook* (which includes only widely used and well-known tests) lists 793 tests together with a bibliography of thousands of articles written about these tests.[2] There is a great array of types of tests. Measurement can be made of everything from poultry raising to proficiency in aircraft hydraulic systems. There are tests of sensory acuity, strength, coordination, sales aptitude, handwriting, etiquette, sex knowledge, health, religion, honesty, and of a host of other skills and aptitudes. Every teacher should be aware of the great number of diagnostic tools which can assist him in his work.

To test simply for the sake of testing, however, has little virtue. It is not the purpose of this chapter to encourage the indiscriminate use of tests. Indeed, the very fact that there are so many different

[1] Gertrude Hildreth, *A Bibliography of Mental Tests and Rating Scales*, New York, The Psychological Corporation, 1939 and Supplement 1945.

[2] O. K. Buros, Editor, *The Fourth Mental Measurements Yearbook*, Highland Park, New Jersey, The Gryphon Press, 1953.

tests—so many ways of carrying on diagnostic work—makes it essential that teachers be critical in their selection of appropriate methods of evaluation. It should be apparent that the teacher needs to understand the purposes of tests and the information which they yield. It should be remembered that the basic purposes of diagnostic tools are to help determine what is needed for the pupil and to assess the effect of various teaching procedures in achieving the teacher's and pupil's goals.

The following sections of this chapter will contain discussions of intelligence tests, achievement tests, measures of character and personality, vocational interest tests, and the appraisal of study skills. Also brief mention will be made of certain other useful diagnostic devices. Suggestions will then be given for selecting the appropriate diagnostic tools. Finally, consideration will be given to tests which the teacher himself constructs.

INTELLIGENCE TESTS

What Are Intelligence Tests? Intelligence tests are designed primarily to determine a person's capacity to learn, or his ability to adapt to life's tasks. For practical purposes, mental tests in school are generally used to estimate how well children will achieve in school work.

Essentially, such tests are made up of items or tasks which are designed to elicit the quality or efficiency of an individual's behavior in situations for which he has not been specifically trained. The first intelligence scale to appear anywhere in the world was devised by two Frenchmen, Binet and Simon. This test, which was brought out in 1905, contained among other things material for the measurement of word meanings and for the evaluation of memory through the repetition of digits. The original purpose of the test was to screen out youngsters who could profit little or not at all from regular Paris schools. Since the time of Binet and Simon, literally scores of intelligence tests have been devised. Some of these are complete batteries of tests which can be administered to only one individual at a time; others can be given to large groups; still others have been designed especially for the measurement of the deaf, the blind, the illiterate, and peoples of various ages from early infancy to senescence.

In a sense, of course, intelligence tests are nothing more than achievement tests. They differ from regular achievement tests in that they attempt to sample those achievements which are somewhat independent of formal schooling. The reader may obtain an idea of the contents of intelligence batteries by examining the following lists of points which are covered in well-known intelligence tests:

1. Following directions	9. Memory of form
2. Ideational memory	10. Analogies
3. Vocabulary	11. Number series
4. Space perception	12. Aesthetic judgment
5. Memory of numbers	13. Drawing
6. Memory of sentences	14. Abstract reasoning
7. Memory of stories	15. Completion
8. Abstract ideas	16. Reorganization

Individual Intelligence Tests. Perhaps the most widely used individual test of intelligence is the *Revised Stanford-Binet Scale*. It comes in two forms (L and M), and was standardized on a large group of children carefully selected from eleven states and from representative geographical areas and cultural levels. The kinds of behaviors measured may be seen in the following sample items taken from Form M of this scale. The items shown are some of those which are given at the five-year old, ten-year old, and average adult levels.

Form M—Year V [3]

1. *Picture Vocabulary*
   Material: Seventeen 2″ x 4″ cards with pictures of common objects.
   Procedure: Show the cards one at a time. Say, "What is this?" "What do you call it?"
   Score: Child must get 14 or more correct to pass at this age level.

2. *Number Concept of Three*
   Material: Blocks and beads.
   Procedure: Place the blocks before S. and say,
             (a) "Give me 3 blocks." Then place the box of beads before him and say,
             (b) "Give me 3 beads."
             (c) "Give me 2 blocks and 1 bead."
   Score: 2 correct. For (c) the order of presentation is disregarded.

[3] Lewis M. Terman and Maud A. Merrill, *Measuring Intelligence*, p. 151. Copyright, 1937, by Houghton Mifflin Company, Boston.

3. *Comprehension II*

Procedure: Ask,

         (a) "What do we do with our eyes?"

         (b) "What do we do with our ears?"

Score: 2 correct.

Form M—Year X [4]

1. *Verbal Absurdities III*

Procedure: Read each statement and after each one ask, "What is foolish about that?" If the response is ambiguous without further explanation, say, "Why is it (that) foolish?"

         (a) "In the year 1915 many more women than men got married in the United States."

         (b) "A man wished to dig a hole in which to bury some rubbish, but could not decide what to do with the dirt from the hole. A friend suggested that he dig a hole large enough to hold the dirt, too."

         (c) "They began the meeting late, but they set the hands of the clock back so that the meeting might surely close before sunset."

Score: 2 correct.

2. *Abstract Words I*

Procedure: Say, "What do we mean by _____?" or "What is _____?"

         (a) Pity, (b) curiosity, (c) grief, (d) surprise.

Score: 2 correct.

3. *Repeating 6 Digits*

Procedure: Say, "I am going to say some numbers and when I am through I want you to say them just the way I do. Listen carefully, and get them just right." Pronounce the digits distinctly and with perfectly uniform emphasis at the rate of one per second.

         (a) 2–9–4–8–1–6, (b) 9–6–2–7–3–8, (c) 5–1–7–2–6–9.

Score: 1 correct. The series must be repeated in correct order without error after a single reading.

Form M—Average Adult [5]

1. *Abstract Words III*

Procedure: Say, "What is _____?" or "What do we mean by _____?"

[4] *Ibid.*, pp. 163–166.

[5] *Ibid.*, pp. 177–180.

(a) Generosity, (b) independent, (c) envy, (d) authority, (e) justice.

Score: 4 correct.

2. *Opposite Analogies III*
   Procedure: Say,
   (a) "A rabbit is timid; a lion is _____"
   (b) "Trees are terrestrial; stars are _____"
   (c) "A group made up of dissimilar things is heterogeneous; one made up of things which are alike is _____"

Score: 1 correct.

3. *Essential Differences*
   Procedure: Say, "What is the principal difference between _____ and _____?" Repeat for each item.
   (a) Work and play.
   (b) Ability and achievement.
   (c) Optimist and pessimist.

Score: 2 correct.

Although it would be impossible here to give the details of the scoring and administration of the Stanford-Binet, it may be noted briefly that the child's mental age is determined by the number of tests which he passes at each age level. After the mental age is determined, an IQ or intelligence quotient is obtained by dividing the mental age by the chronological, or actual, age and multiplying by 100. Supposing a child had a mental age of nine years and was twelve years of age. His IQ would be:

$$\frac{MA}{CA} \times 100 \quad \text{or} \quad \frac{9}{12} \times 100 = 75$$

The score is meaningful, of course, only insofar as the child's performance can be judged to be well motivated. Also, if the score is to mean anything, certain other assumptions such as the absence of verbal limitations, correct administration, and the absence of disturbing emotional factors must be met. It cannot be too strongly emphasized that IQ scores are but guides or estimates of ability, that they are subject to error, and that they should not be taken as a final judgment about a child. When used with these limitations in mind, they can provide valuable diagnostic information.

Sometimes, schools wish to test youngsters with speech or hearing difficulties, or other verbal disabilities. In such cases, the Stanford-Binet, or other tests which rely heavily upon verbal skills, are not appropriate. Hence there are a number of performance tests which require a minimum of verbal facility. These tests require youngsters to fit pieces into puzzles, construct designs, draw pictures and designs, use building blocks, etc. A battery of such tests is the *Arthur Point Scale of Performance Tests*.[6] This battery is often used to test children who are suspected of having difficulty with words and also is frequently used as a check when a child's obtained IQ with one of the other tests is out of line with the judgment of the teacher or school psychologist.

For upper level high-school students, and particularly for adults, the Stanford-Binet scale may have limitations, as the scale was devised for younger children. There is, however, an excellent instrument, the *Wechsler-Bellevue Intelligence Scale*,[7] which can be used for ages from ten to seventy (with adjustments for deterioration in old age).

All three of these scales, the Stanford-Binet, the Arthur Point Scale, and the Wechsler-Bellevue, are widely used and were introduced only after the most careful selection of items and standardizing procedures. Each has been the subject of intensive research, so that in the hands of a trained examiner they will provide not only an IQ score, but a wealth of other diagnostic clinical information.

Group Intelligence Tests. The major advantage of group intelligence tests is that they permit the examination of large numbers of individuals. Also, the administration of a group intelligence test takes somewhat less training than the administration of an individual test.

To give the reader an idea of the types of directions and questions which may be asked in a group intelligence test, examples from the *California Short-Form Test of Mental Maturity* are shown in Figure 17. This test which takes fifty-two minutes to administer is designed to measure mental abilities in the following areas: spatial relationships, logical reasoning, numerical reasoning, and verbal concepts.

[6] Grace Arthur, *Arthur Point Scale of Performance Tests;* Ages 5 to Superior Adults; 1925–1947, two forms, Chicago, C. H. Stoelting Company.

[7] David Wechsler, *Weschler-Bellevue Intelligence Scale*, published by the Psychological Corporation, New York, 1947.

DIRECTIONS: Mark as you are told the letter, R, for each picture that shows a right; mark the letter, L, for each picture that shows a left.

17

19

R L

R L

DIRECTIONS: In each row find the drawing that is a different view of the first drawing. Mark its number as you are told.

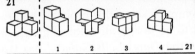

21   1   2   3   4 ___ 21

29   1   2   3   4 ___ 29

DIRECTIONS: In each row of numbers below, there is one that does not belong. Find the number that should be omitted from each row among the answer numbers on the right, and mark its letter as you are told. When you have finished as many as you can from 66 to 75, read the Directions in the middle of the page and proceed with rows 76 to 80.

(73). 21 20 18 15 14 12 10   9   8   6   3   a21 b10 c9 d8 e6 ___ 73

(74).   2   3   5   8 12 17 22 23 30   a3 b8 c12 d17 e22 ___ 74

DIRECTIONS: Mark as you are told the number of the word that means the same or about the same as the first word.

109. predatory   1 soft   2 stationary
          3 plundering   4 lasting   ___ 109

135. antecedent 1 actual   2 pretended
          3 previous   4 genuine   ___ 135

FIGURE 17. Excerpts from the California Short-Form Test of Mental Maturity. (Courtesy of the California Test Bureau, Los Angeles.)

The test from which examples have just been given in Figure 17 yields two main scores—language and non-language. The *language* score gives an indication of how well the individual understands relationships expressed in words, such as instructions, conference discussions, statements of logical principles on courses of action, and the like. *Non-language* results are designed to indicate how well the individual understands relationships among things or objects when no language or a minimum amount of language is involved, such as physical or mechanical relationships. The manual which accompanies the test gives extensive suggestions for use of various combinations of the sub-test scores.

One of the ever present problems in the measurement of intelligence is the difficulty of determining how much the performance is due to innate potential and how much is due to cultural factors. It is known, for example, that middle-class children make higher scores on the Stanford-Binet scale than do lower-class children. Is this an artifact of the selection of items which favor middle-class children, or do they in fact possess a higher potential?

A recent test has made an attempt to solve this problem by providing items which are designed to be fair to all cultural groups in urban areas. This test, known as the *Davis-Eells Games*,[8] has two levels, Primary for grades 1 and 2 and Elementary for grades 3–6. The sample items from the elementary level of the test are presented in Figure 18.

The directions which accompany sample B of the *Davis-Eells Games*, shown in the upper right hand corner of Figure 18, are as follows: "Now look at the *next* picture; it is beside the one you just did. It shows a boy and girl, waving their hands. Look at the picture while I tell you about it. Which number is right? Be sure to look at the picture.

No. 1 Box: They are waving at a *boy*

No. 2 Box: They are waving at a *girl*

No. 3 Box: We *cannot tell* from this picture *whom* they are waving to

In the test there are 62 sets of questions related to pictures. The total time needed for administration of the test is about 110 minutes which is to be divided into two periods. From the test may be obtained the pupil's "index of problem-solving ability," a score which is roughly comparable to an IQ score.

Since there are dozens of group tests of mental abilities, it is not practical to attempt to discuss each one. Most of them, as the two just discussed, have distinctive features which make them appropri-

[8] Allison Davis and Kenneth Eells, *Davis-Eells Games*, Yonkers, World Book Company, 1952.

FIGURE 18. Sample Items from the Davis-Eells Games.

ate for certain purposes. For example, the *American Council on Education, Psychological Examination for College Freshmen*,[9] and the *Ohio States University Psychological Test*[10] are tests of mental

[9] Published by the Educational Testing Service, Princeton, New Jersey.
[10] The Ohio College Association, H. A. Toops, Ohio State University, Columbus, Ohio.

ability which are particularly useful in predicting academic success in college. Other tests which are widely used in school are the SRA *Tests of Primary Mental Abilities*,[11] the *Henmon-Nelson Tests of Mental Ability*,[12] *Kuhlman-Anderson Intelligence Tests*,[13] *Terman-McNemar Tests of Mental Ability*,[14] the various forms of the Otis group intelligence tests,[15] and the *Kuhlmann-Finch Tests of Mental Ability*.[16]

ACHIEVEMENT TESTS

In nearly every field of study or school subject there are achievement tests available. Of the 793 tests listed in *The Fourth Mental*

TABLE 30

Achievement Tests Listed in the Fourth Mental Measurements Yearbook

26	Achievement Batteries	5	Safety Education Tests
30	English Tests	50	Reading Tests including 7
2	Composition Tests		Reading Readiness Tests
18	Literature Tests	11	Study Skills Tests
15	Spelling Tests	7	Science Tests
16	Vocabulary Tests	11	Biology Tests
6	Art Tests	16	Chemistry Tests
6	Music Tests	7	General Science Tests
34	Foreign Language Tests	1	Geology Test
15	General Mathematics Tests	2	Miscellaneous Science Tests
18	Algebra Tests	11	Physics Tests
24	Arithmetic Tests	8	Social Studies Tests
17	Geometry Tests	4	Economics Tests
3	Trigonometry Tests	5	Geography Tests
2	Agriculture Tests	19	History Tests
21	Business Education Tests	10	Political Science Tests
4	Etiquette Tests	2	Sociology Tests
13	Health Tests	16	Education Tests
12	Home Economics Tests	6	Engineering Tests
2	Industrial Arts Tests	2	Law Tests
2	Philosophy Tests	1	Medicine Test
3	Psychology Tests	6	Nursing Tests
3	Religious Education Tests		

[11] Published by Science Research Associates, Chicago, Illinois.
[12] Published by Houghton Mifflin Company, Boston, Massachusetts.
[13] Published by The Personnel Press, Princeton, New Jersey.
[14] Published by the World Book Company, Yonkers-on-Hudson, New York.
[15] *Ibid.*
[16] Published by the Educational Test Bureau, Minneapolis, Minnesota.

Measurements Yearbook,[17] well over half are achievement tests distributed as indicated in Table 30.

Some of these tests have been carefully drawn up and standardized while others, which also may be useful for some purposes, are in less refined stages of development.

  Achievement Batteries. Some of the tests listed in Table 30 are designed to give a general over-all picture of the pupil's achievement in a great variety of skills or subjects. These tests are called achievement batteries. Because of the wide and extremely varied nature of what an achievement test battery might include, many differences exist between what is included in one battery and what

TABLE 31

Comparison of Subtests of Two Widely Used Achievement Batteries

IOWA EVERY-PUPIL TESTS OF BASIC SKILLS * (GRADES 3–5, 5–9)	METROPOLITAN ACHIEVEMENT TESTS † (GRADES 5–7.5)
1. *Silent Reading Comprehension* including reading comprehension and vocabulary.	1. *Reading*
	2. *Vocabulary*
2. *Work-Study Skills* including map reading, use of references, use of index, use of dictionary, and alphabetizing (Elementary Battery) or graphing (Advanced Battery).	3. *Arithmetic Fundamentals*
	4. *Arithmetic Problems*
	5. *English*
3. *Basic Language Skills* including punctuation, capitalization, usage, spelling, sentence sense (Elementary Battery only).	6. *Literature*
	7. *Geography*
	8. *History and Civics*
4. *Basic Arithmetic Skills* including fundamental knowledge, fundamental operations, problems.	9. *Science*
	10. *Spelling*

  * H. F. Spitzer and others, *Iowa Every-Pupil Test of Basic Skills,* Boston, Houghton Mifflin Company, 1940–1947.

  † Gertrude H. Hildreth and others, *Metropolitan Achievement Tests,* Yonkers-on-Hudson, New York, 1932–1950.

[17] O. K. Buros, Editor, *The Fourth Mental Measurements Yearbook,* Highland Park, New Jersey, The Gryphon Press, 1953.

is included in another. For example, in Table 31 note differences in the contents of two widely used achievement batteries.

Each of these batteries may do a good job of measuring what it measures. Whether either of these batteries or any of the other two dozen achievement batteries measures the complex abilities which a particular school or teacher believes should be measured depends largely upon the educational goals and educational philosophy held.

Achievement Tests in Specific Subjects. Subtests of achievement batteries are sometimes used, or expanded and used, to measure achievement in specific subjects such as arithmetic, reading, spelling, handwriting, and English usage. There are other achievement tests which are set up without relation to any achievement battery. An example of one such tool is the *Diagnostic Tests of Achievement in Music*.[18] Its subtests include diatonic syllable names, chromatic syllable names, number names, time signatures, major and minor keys, note and rest values, letter names, signs and symbols, key names, and song recognition. This test has to do with the rudiments of music and contains mostly factual material. One of the serious difficulties in this type of test is that only a part of what constitutes musical ability may be measured. When one attempts to measure global capacities, such as musical ability, he must recognize that specific knowledge and mechanical skill are but a part of the total picture. There are other important factors such as musical appreciation, rhythm, aural perception, and mental imagery. It is probable that most subject matter fields involve many factors presently not adequately measured. For example, one important factor common to most fields is the ability to study which is probably not measured in most achievement tests. (A later section of this chapter will show tools used to measure study skills.)

The Nelson Biology Test Evaluation and Adjustment Series [19] is another illustration of a subject achievement test. The objectives of this test as stated in the manual are:

---

[18] M. Lela Kotick and T. L. Torgerson, *Diagnostic Tests of Achievement in Music*, Los Angeles, California Test Bureau, 1950.

[19] Clarence H. Nelson, *Nelson Biology Test: Evaluation and Adjustment Series*, Grades 9–15, Yonkers, New York, 1951–1952. Additional data indicate: (1) it can be scored by machine (IBM); (2) it has two forms, AM ('51), BM ('52); (3) cost: $2.50 per 25, separate answer sheets must be used—80¢ per 25 IBM answer sheets, postage extra, 35¢ per specimen set postpaid; (4) working time is 40 minutes, total time to administer is 50 minutes.

This test has been developed primarily to measure understanding and the ability to apply knowledge in the interpretation of situations and the solution of problems. Testing of ability to recall minute, isolated facts has been minimized. Rather the student is given an opportunity to demonstrate how well he can discern relationships between what he has learned and the world of living things which he encounters every day.[20]

Since tests tend strongly to influence course objectives and procedures, a test with the types of goals implied in the preceding paragraph is likely to have a healthy influence on course objectives and activities.

As can be seen in Table 30, there is no dearth of achievement tests for the specific teaching fields. The teacher of art, foreign languages, home economics, business education, or in fact almost any other subject in the elementary and secondary curricula will find tests of use to him in his work.

MEASURES OF CHARACTER AND PERSONALITY

The importance of diagnosing personality and character cannot be questioned. But difficulties involved in making appraisal in this area are probably greater than in the field of achievement testing. Nevertheless, during the past twenty years tremendous advances have been made in assessing personality and character traits. The increasing attention which psychologists and educators are giving to personal and social development is indicated by the fact that 40 per cent of the tests listed under "Character and Personality" in the *Fourth Mental Measurement Yearbook* are new tests while only 30 per cent of achievement tests listed fall in this category.

The measurement of character and personality has been attempted in four basic ways; *viz.*, through the use of (1) inventories or questionnaires answered by the person himself, (2) rating scales, (3) situational tests, and (4) projective techniques. Each of these methods, together with examples, will now be discussed.

Personality Inventories and Questionnaires. There are currently available almost one hundred character and personality tests designed to measure a multitude of factors such as aggressiveness, emotional adjustment, curricular adjustment, level of aspiration, sociability, social adaptability, home adjustment, dependability, gen-

[20] O. K. Buros, *op.cit.*, p. 606.

erosity, creativity, grace, psychosomatic symptoms, and attitude toward a disciplinary procedure.

Generally such tests ask questions about a person's feelings, behavior, and attitudes in an attempt to measure personality and adjustment. For example, note the following items taken from the *Personal Index*.[21]

Do you like to tease people till they cry?	YES NO
Do you find school a hard place to get along in?	YES NO
Do any of your teachers mark examinations too severely?	YES NO
Do you ever wish that you were dead?	YES NO

A test similar in form to the *Personal Index*, but with slightly different emphasis, is the *Washburne Social-Adjustment Inventory*.[22] It is designed to test the degree of social and emotional adjustment and gives scores on truthfulness, happiness, alienation, sympathy, purpose, impulse-judgment, control, and wishes. Each of the 122 items on the eight-page booklet is answered by "yes" or "no." Illustrative questions are: "Did you ever act greedily by taking more than your share of anything?" and "Do you sometimes enjoy the sight of an animal or a person being hurt?"

The breadth of material which may be covered by various questionnaires may be sensed by comparing the two questionnaires just illustrated with a very different kind of instrument—the *Social Distance Scale*.[23] This test, together with its adaptations, is probably the most used single test of social attitudes. The test itself is one of the simpler of those now available. Original instructions went like this: "According to my first feeling reactions, I would willingly admit members of each race (as a class, and not the best I have known nor the worst members) to one or more of the classifications under which I have placed a cross: (1) To close kinship by marriage, (2) To my club as personal chums, (3) To my street as neighbors, (4) To employment in my occupation in my country, (5) To citizenship in my country, (6) As visitors only to my country, (7) Would ex-

[21] G. C. Loofbourow and Noel Keys, *Personal* Index, Minneapolis, Educational Test Bureau Inc., 1933.

[22] John N. Washburne, *Washburne Social-Adjustment Inventory;* Ages 12 and over; 1932–1940; non-timed, takes about 30–50 minutes; Yonkers, New York, World Book Company.

[23] Emory S. Bogardus, *Social Distance Scale;* ages 15 and over; 1925–1951; takes about 25 minutes to administer; 3518 University Avenue, Los Angeles.

clude from my country." [24] Under these seven points as column headings are spaces to rate a large number of ethnic and nationality groups.

This test like most other questionnaires depends on voluntary self-description by the person being tested. If for some reason or another he does not want to cooperate, the results are useless. Hence, proper rapport between tester and subject is of prime importance.

While most questionnaire-type personality measures are easy to score, and deal with important information about a child, they also have serious limitations. Little claim can be made for the validity of such instruments,[25] and they are appropriate only for children old enough and bright enough to have a clear understanding of the questions.

Rating Scales. Personality questionnaires ask for self-ratings which, as noted above, may be unreliable (give inconsistent results) and of questionable validity. Another method of securing information about a child is by having teachers or other persons make the ratings. One such scale, which is suitable for appraising young children as well as grown ups is the *Vineland Social Maturity Scale*.[26] It is made up of 117 items of performances "in respect to which children show a progressive capacity for looking after themselves and for participating in those activities which lead toward ultimate independence as adults." The functions measured are: self-help (general, eating, dressing), self-direction, locomotion, occupation, communication, and social relations. A person who knows the subject well answers the interviewer's questions on the subject's demonstrated performance of the 117 items included in the scale. Test results will yield a social age and a social quotient if these are desired. It also has value as an interviewing device with parents.

Probably the most widely used rating scale for school children is the *Haggerty-Olson-Wickman Behavior Rating Schedules*.[27] In two schedules, this rating form combines a check list and a graphic

---

[24] Emory S. Bogardus, "Measuring Social Distances," *Journal of Applied Sociology*, Vol. 9, May–June, 1925, pp. 299–308.

[25] Albert Ellis, "The Validity of Personality Questionnaires," *Psychological Bulletin*, Vol. 43, 1946, pp. 385–440.

[26] Edgar A. Doll, *Vineland Social Maturity Scale;* Ages, birth to maturity; 1935–1947; 1 form; Minneapolis, Educational Test Bureau.

[27] Published by the World Book Company, Yonkers-on-Hudson, New York.

rating scale. There are spaces in Schedule A for checking how frequent is the occurrence of such behaviors as cheating, lying, bullying, and sex offenses. In the second part, Schedule B, are a series of 35 questions set up as follows:

Is his personality attractive?

Repulsive   Disagreeable   Unnoticed   Colorful   Magnetic
Colorless

All rating devices are subject to errors some of which were discussed in Chapter 16. Chief among these is the error due to overgeneralization (halo effect). There is a tendency for a teacher who rates a child high or low on one trait to continue to rate him the same on other traits. Furthermore, it has been shown that four or five independent ratings are necessary in order to secure adequate reliability and validity.

Situational Tests. Situational tests are measures of actual conduct in the face of difficulty, or when the stimulus situation is such that character traits are revealed by the choice or reaction which a child makes. These tests have been useful in the measurement of such behaviors as stealing, lying, sharing, cheating, and reactions to such conditions as psychological stress, pain, shock, and humor.

For example, in a very extensive investigation of children's character, Hartshorne and May [28] devised such test items as:

1. A situation in which a storekeeper returns too much change to a child.
2. Arithmetic problems involving the use of coins. Coins were placed in boxes each of which contained an identifying mark (not apparent to the child). Since children were not aware that boxes could be identified, many kept some of the money.
3. A situation in which children scored their own papers, unaware that the teacher had scored them the night before.

As with other types of personality and character measurement, there are difficulties in the use of conduct measures. It is hard to obtain a representative sample of behaviors and still retain the experimental or test controls which are necessary to make comparisons among children. Also, the time spent in devising situations and in

[28] H. Hartshorne and M. May, *Studies in Deceit*, New York, The Macmillan Co., 1928.

observing each child in these situations is great. However, in the final analysis, segments of actual behavior under controlled conditions probably offers a type of information which can be obtained in no other way.[29]

Projective Tests. One of the most interesting approaches to personality measurement is the projective method. In the projective test a highly unstructured or ambiguous set of stimuli are presented to the individual. In such a situation, the person being tested is encouraged to bring his own unique meanings and organization to the situation. He does not know what inferences the tester intends to make, and so may reveal some of the hidden reaches of his personality.

FIGURE 19. One of the Ten Ink Blots from the Rorschach Test.

(From H. Rorschach, *Psychodiagnostics*, Hans Huber Publishers, Berne and Stuttgart.)

The Rorschach test, the best known and most widely used projective test makes use of ten cards each of which contains an ink blot similar to that shown in Figure 19. The person being tested is given the following instructions:

You will be given a series of ten cards, one by one. The cards have on them designs made up out of ink blots. Look at each card, and tell the examiner what you see on each card, or anything that might be represented there. Look at each card as long as you like; only be sure to tell the examiner everything that you see on the cards as you look at them. When you have finished with a card, give it to the examiner as a sign that you are through with it.[30]

While the teacher should know about the Rorschach test, it should be emphasized that it is a technique to be used only by thoroughly trained clinicians. In this type of test, the interpretive work of the examiner is as important as the test itself.

Another widely used projective test is the TAT (*Thematic Ap-*

[29] For a comprehensive discussion of situational tests, see: L. J. Cronbach, *Essentials of Psychological Testing*, New York, Harper & Brothers, 1949, pp. 413–432.

[30] S. J. Beck, *Rorschach's Test*, New York, Grune and Stratton, 1944, p. 2.

perception Test).[31] In this test, the subject is asked to interpret a series of twenty pictures by telling a story about each—what is happening, what led up to the scene in the picture, and what will be the outcome. As in the Rorschach test, the subject is required to set up his own answer structure. The person projects himself into each picture and presumably brings to it his own problems, conflicts, wishes, needs, and attitudes toward self. In addition to evaluating stories themselves, the examiner observes the subject during the test. Behavior shown may indicate emotion, eccentricities, habits in problem attack, and other cues pertinent to an analysis of personality. As with the Rorschach test, use of the TAT without much training and guided experience is unwise.

A projective test, similar to the TAT, is the *Children's Apperception Test* [32] which uses pictures of animals instead of people to elicit the stories. Other projective tests designed specifically for children are mentioned in the following numbered points. (1) *The Blacky Pictures: A Technique for the Exploration of Personality Dynamics.*[33] This test uses eleven cartoons of a dog, Blacky, and is used to test the child's psychosexual development. (2) *The Driscoll Play Kit.*[34] This kit is a cutaway of an apartment and contains furniture and a doll family which the child can manipulate. It is believed useful for revealing family relationships. It has a dual purpose of providing both diagnostic information, and material for play therapy. (3) *The Machover Draw-a-Person Test.*[35] This test requires only 10 to 20 minutes to administer. The child is asked to draw a person, and then to draw another of the opposite sex. It is believed that conflicts may be revealed in the drawing of bodily parts.

It is probably not an overstatement to say that in all of a child's creative work (writing, drawing, making things) there are elements of projection. There are ways in which he puts himself into the task at hand. Thus a child's English theme, an oral story he tells, or a game he plays with imaginary companions may reveal much about his needs, conflicts and personality. Sims clearly recognized this in

[31] H. A. Murray, *Thematic Apperception Test*, ages 7 and over; individual; nontimed but takes about 120 minutes; Cambridge, Mass.; Harvard University Press, 1944.

[32] Published by the Psychological Corporation, New York, N. Y.

[33] *Ibid.*

[34] *Ibid.*

[35] Published by Charles C. Thomas, Publisher, Springfield, Illinois, 1949.

his thought provoking article, "The Essay Examination Is a Projective Technique," in which he defines an essay test as follows:

> The essay examination is a relatively free and extended written response to a problematic situation or situations (question or questions), which intentionally or unintentionally reveals information regarding the structure, dynamics and functioning of the student's mental life as it has been modified by a particular set of learning experiences.[36]

Although most projective tests are only in their infancy, they do represent an approach to the study of personality which has great promise. With further refinement of scoring methods and continuing efforts to establish their validity, the time may not be far off when they may be widely used in classrooms. Already school psychologists are employing them to a limited extent in helping teachers better understand their children.

VOCATIONAL INTEREST TESTS

Vocational interest tests are widely used for occupational guidance. The *Kuder Preference Record,*[37] one of the interest tests most widely employed with high school students, is used, for example, to (a) point out vocations with which the student may not be familiar but which involve activities of the type for which he has expressed preference, and (b) check on whether a person's choice of an occupation is consistent with the type of thing he ordinarily prefers to do.

The unusual form and appearance of the booklets and the special "pin-prick" device for marking responses have considerable interest value for students and aid in getting careful and thoughtful responses. In the test, the pupil is asked to choose which of certain activities are preferred. For example, he is asked to choose between "work mathematical puzzles" and "play checkers," and between "study physics" and "study public speaking."

The most recent form gives eleven scores: mechanical, computational, scientific, persuasive, artistic, literary, musical, social service, clerical, outdoor, and verification. The manual classifies occupations

[36] Verner M. Sims, "The Essay Examination Is a Projective Technique," *Educational and Psychological Measurement,* Vol. 8, Spring, 1948, p. 17.

[37] G. Frederic Kuder, *Kuder Preference Record,* Grades 6–16 and adults, IBM; editions 3; 1934–1946; time to administer—about 50 minutes; Chicago, Science Research Associates.

according to the profiled interest areas. Such classifications are to be considered tentative and suggestive only.

A second widely used vocational interest inventory is the *Vocational Interest Blank for Men, Revised.*[38] This test indicates whether subjects mark the test the way successful people in various occupations mark it. There are now fifty scorable categories of which the following are examples: artist, psychologist, osteopath, veterinarian, mathematician, production manager, aviator, mathematics-physical science teacher, policeman, certified public accountant, purchasing agent, mortician, realtor, and president of a manufacturing concern. There is also a form of this test for women which rates interest in twenty-five occupations.

The instrument is very time consuming to score, unless machine scoring is used.[39] It can be a valuable instrument for vocational counseling if used as a supplement to other significant types of data such as demonstrated level of mental ability or special proficiency in given fields of study.

A final word of caution is probably appropriate. Neither the Strong blank, nor the Kuder record, nor any other vocational interest inventory is designed to show into what occupation a person should go. They are only intended to give a picture of vocational *interests.* There are many other facts which should be carefully considered when vocational choices are made.

STUDY SKILLS

Children no longer spend a whole year reading one book as they did in the days of the McGuffey Reader. Instead, in the average classroom today, pupils are bombarded with multiple texts, supplementary readings, magazine articles, and newspapers. There are a number of different study skills required to meet the demands placed upon the present-day learner. Thus the evaluation of a student's study habits is a matter of great importance. Fortunately a number of methods for diagnosing study skills are now available to teachers.

[38] Edward K. Strong, *Vocational Interest Blank for Men, Revised;* ages 17 and over; 1927–1951; Stanford, Stanford University Press.

[39] Schools may have their Vocational Interest Blanks machine scored by Testscor, 100 Metropolitan Building, Minneapolis, Minnesota, or by several other testing agencies and university testing bureaus located throughout the country.

Traxler's *Survey of Study Habits* [40] is one such device. It not only gives the pupil a basis for analyzing his own study habits but also serves as a basis for counseling by the teacher. The survey consists of 85 items grouped under the following 17 headings:

Keeping in physical condition for study
Understanding the assignment
Planning a study schedule
Efficient finding of the necessary materials
Applying one's self consistently
Fixing material in mind
Reflecting
Working independently

The prompt completion of work
Persistence in overcoming difficulties
Paying attention in class
Participation in class activities
Reviewing
Memorizing
Increasing vocabulary
Improvement of reading rate
Maintaining an attitude of study

In the Traxler survey the items are statements which do or do not characterize the pupil. He responds by checking "seldom or never," "sometimes," or "usually or always." The total score is not nearly so important as the diagnostic information which the test reveals.

A tool for analyzing a quite different type of study skill is the *Interpretation of Data Test*.[41] In this test the learner in grades 7–12 is presented with various sets of data and asked to discriminate, on a 3-point scale, whether the accompanying statements are (1) true, (2) false, or (3) uncertain as to the truth or falsity because of insufficient information in the data. The test is designed to reveal such factors as a pupil's accuracy, tendency to be overcautious, tendency to be undercautious and go beyond the data.

Although scoring and interpretation is somewhat more difficult than with most tests, the *Interpretation of Data Test* does provide a unique and educationally stimulating departure from traditional methods of pupil evaluation. The use of this type of test can provoke a healthy re-examination of educational goals and procedures.

Other valuable study skills tests include the following:

1. *Bennett Use of Library Test.* High school and college; 1947; Forms A and B; 55 minutes to administer; Alma Bennett and H. E. Schrammel;

[40] Arthur E. Traxler, *Survey of Study Habits, Experimental Edition;* grades 8–14; nontimed—30 minutes; New York 32, Educational Records Bureau, 1944.

[41] Evaluation Staff (R. W. Tyler, Director) of the Eight-Year Study of the Progressive Education Association, *Interpretation of Data Test: General Education Series;* Grades 7–12, 12–14; 1939–1950; 40 minutes to administer; Cooperative Test Division, Educational Testing Service, Princeton, New Jersey.

Bureau of Educational Measurements, Kansas State Teachers College of Emporia, Emporia, Kansas.

2. *Cooperative Dictionary Test.* Grades 7–12, 1951–1952; 5 scores: alphabetizing, spelling, pronunciation, meaning, total; IBM; Form A; S. D. Melville with the editorial assistance of Clarence Derrick and Anne W. Henry; Cooperative Test Division, Educational Testing Service, Princeton, New Jersey.

3. *Logical Reasoning Test: General Education Series.* Grades 10–12; 1939–1950; 2 forms; 10 scores: right conclusions, wrong conclusions, relevant judged relevant, irrelevant judged relevant, irrelevant judged irrelevant, relevant judged irrelevant, accuracy with definitions, accuracy with indirect arguments, accuracy with *ad hominem* arguments, accuracy with if-then arguments; Evaluation Staff (R. W. Tyler, Director) of the Eight-Year Study of the Progressive Education Association: Cooperative Test Division, Educational Testing Service, Princeton, New Jersey.

4. *Test of Critical Thinking.* Grades 7–9; 1951; 7 scores: inquiry, interests, relationships, openmindedness, generalizations, accuracy, total; 1 form; test may be reproduced by users; nontimed, takes about 50 minutes to administer; M. T. Macy and Hugh B. Wood, University of Oregon Press, Eugene, Oregon.

5. *Test on the Use of Books and Libraries: General Education Series.* Grades 7–12; 1939–1950; 8 scores: the parts of a book, use of encyclopedias, use of the dictionary, sources of information, use of an index, use of the library card catalog, use of the *Readers' Guide to Periodical Literature*, total; Forms A and B; nontimed, takes about 60 minutes to administer; Evaluation Staff (R. W. Tyler, Director) of the Eight-Year Study of the Progressive Education Association; Cooperative Test Division, Educational Testing Service, Princeton, New Jersey.

6. *The Use of Library and Study Materials.* Grades 9–16; 1939–1941; 3 scores: finding information, interpreting information, total; IBM; Forms A and B; Mary S. Kirkpatrick, Lola R. Thompson, and Helen Tomlinson; Steck Company, Austin, Texas.

7. *Use of Sources of Information: Iowa Tests of Educational Development, Test 9.* Grades 9–13; 1942–1951; IBM; edited by E. F. Lindquist; K. W. Vaughn; Science Research Associates, Chicago 10, Illinois.

The teacher who is considering the use of any of the tools listed above would do well to acquire and carefully examine a specimen set including the manual, one or more forms of the test, and the key. Before ordering any large number of tests it is frequently wise to try out the test with a small number of pupils to see whether in actual practice it meets the needs of teacher and pupils.

OTHER DIAGNOSTIC TOOLS

For practically every psychological trait or characteristic, one or more tests are available. The teacher who is interested in diagnosing the behavior of his pupils in any specific area should consult the catalogues of test publishers [42] and bibliographies of tests such as those of Hildreth [43] and Buros.[44] No attempt can be made here to give even an incomplete listing; however, to illustrate the range and variety of tests available six representative tests are presented.

Handwriting

Self Corrective Handwriting Charts; Include ten diagnostic handwriting charts analyzing color, size, slant, letter spacing, beginning and ending strokes, word spacing, alignment, and letter and figure forms. Distributed by the Farnham Printing and Stationery Company, Minneapolis, Minnesota.

Vision

Eames Eye Test; Grades 1–16 and adults; 1938–1950; 8 pass-fail scores: visual acuity, lens, near vision, coordination fusion, astigmatic chart (optional), eye dominance (optional), total; 1 form; Thomas H. Eames; World Book Company, Yonkers-on-Hudson, New York.

Clerical

Psychological Corporation General Clerical Test; Grades 9–16 and applicants for clerical positions; 1944–1950; 4 scores: clerical speed and accuracy, numerical ability, verbal facility, total; 1 form; 50 minutes to administer; Psychological Corporation, New York 18, New York.

Mechanical Ability

Revised Minnesota Paper Form Board Test; Grades 7–12 and adults; 1930–1948; IBM; 2 editions; original test by D. G. Paterson, R. M. Elliott, L. D. Anderson, H. A. Toops, E. Heidbreder; revision by Rensis Likert and William H. Quasha; Psychological Corporation, New York 18, New York.

[42] See references at the end of this chapter.
[43] Gertrude Hildreth, *op.cit.*
[44] O. K. Buros, *op.cit.*

Education

National Teaching Examinations; Applicants for teaching positions and prospective teachers; 1940–1951; an examination program for use in selection of teachers and the appraisal of teachers-in-training; IBM; 2 parts; tests administered annually in February at centers established by Educational Testing Service; application form and bulletin of information may be obtained from publisher; prepared under the direction of the Staff of Educational Testing Service with the consultation of the Committee for the National Teacher Examinations; Educational Testing Service, Princeton, New Jersey.

SELECTING THE APPROPRIATE TEST

Out of the thousands of available tests, the teacher must find those which are the most appropriate for his purposes. Before tests are chosen, a necessary first step is that of defining clearly the objectives which the teacher or school is trying to attain. Such objectives must be specific and straightforward if one is to have a reasonable basis for selecting tests. Relatively meaningless phrases such as, "an understanding of," or "an appreciation of," may be of little use in describing the school's aims unless the educator spells out in detail what he wants children to understand and appreciate. When tests are selected on the basis of poorly conceived or overgeneralized objectives, the results of measurement are apt to be disappointing both to the teachers and pupils.

Each teacher or school administrator will have to solve for himself the problem of selecting from the vast array of available diagnostic instruments, those which are most related to his goals. However, there are a number of criteria which will aid him in making wise choices. The questions which follow should provide some of the important criteria to be used in finding the appropriate test.

Is the Test Reliable and Valid? Most good standard tests have a high consistency of measurement (reliability), and measure or discriminate well in the areas which they are supposed to cover (validity). In the examiner's manual accompanying most tests there is usually some statement of the test's reliability.[45] Also there is usually

---

[45] This is usually given as a correlation coefficient such as .93. There are several formulae used to calculate the degree to which a test gives consistent results. It should be emphasized that although most standard tests have a high reliability, .90 or above, they may have little or no validity. The latter, of course, is the more crucial factor.

some evidence about its validity. Validity, however, involves the appraisal of educational outcomes which are themselves very difficult to measure. Thus in many cases, a test will have a high reliability, but there will be incomplete evidence as to its validity. In such cases, the teacher will have to scrutinize the test itself to find out if it gives a useful index of the outcomes which he wishes to measure. For example, an English teacher may wish to measure appreciation of literature. If the test he surveys contains only factual items about literature, the test is probably not valid for this purpose, since it is possible for a pupil to have considerable information about novels, poetry, and stories, and still hate literature. The question of the validity of a test is not only of highest importance, but is also a most difficult one to answer. Sometimes the best a teacher can do is to try out the test with a small group of students. Results on the trial run can then be appraised to see if they yield the type of diagnostic information which will be helpful.

Does the Test Have Alternate Forms? In some situations, it is helpful to the teacher and pupil if one form of the test can be given early in the learning experience for diagnostic purposes, and a second form administered after a period of training or development. This second test can then provide a basis for evaluating the effectiveness of the instruction which took place. Also in cases of error, or when the results of a test seem out of line with what the teacher knows about a child, it is good to have a second form to administer.

What is the Cost of the Test? Even tests which are quite similar in content may vary greatly in cost. One reading test may be twice as expensive as another without yielding better results. In estimating the cost of a test, however, there is more than just the cost of the test booklets to be considered. Some tests are answered directly on test booklets, so that new tests must be purchased for each class. Others are so constructed that the blanks can be used over and over again, since students' answers may be put on separate answer sheets. It may be possible for a teacher to get one complete set of test booklets and mimeograph answer sheets. Such a procedure permits the school to use many more tests at less cost than is involved if a new test is purchased for each student.

What Competence Is Needed for Administration? The administration of most achievement tests does not require extensive training.

However, it is well for the teacher to study a test manual before giving a test. Also it may be helpful in anticipating difficulties if the teacher himself takes the test.

What Is the Interest Value of the Test? Most tests depend for their accuracy of measurement upon highly motivated performance of pupils. Test makers generally take this into account by trying to write items which have a high interest value. For younger children, tests may even be set up as a game. It should be noted, however, that what is interesting for one age group may not be for another. Hence, a test of achievement or intelligence for retarded children may be inappropriate, in that items were chosen to match the interests of a younger group. Likewise a test for his own age group may be of little interest to a pupil of superior ability.

How Much Time Is Required for the Test? Typically this information is given in the test catalogue and certainly in the test manual, and should be investigated before purchase of more than a sample of the test. Some tests require an amount of time that is difficult to fit into the school schedule. Most schools seek tests which can be administered during one class period or can be broken into parts which fit into a class period.

Is the Difficulty Level of the Test Appropriate? A test may be labeled as appropriate for a given group, but if a teacher has a very accelerated class, the test may be too easy for most of the pupils. On the other hand, if the teacher has a relatively retarded group of pupils, most of the test items may be much too difficult. Sometimes, actual administration of the test is necessary, at least to one of the best and one of the poorest students, in order to estimate the difficulty range of the instrument.

How Many Pupils Can Be Tested at One Time? Most achievement tests can be given to fairly large groups of students. Some tests, however, such as reading readiness tests, may require extensive supervision and the breaking of the class into smaller groups which are tested one at a time.

Are There Likely to Be Difficulties in Scoring? Tests vary greatly with respect to ease of scoring. The teacher should, therefore, before ordering the test in large numbers, score a sample test or two to determine how long the scoring will take and how difficult it will be. Some tests have quick scoring stencils and answer keys which reduce the work of correcting papers to a fraction of that required for other tests.

In What Form Are Test Results Given? Frequently, this question is not investigated by the teacher until after the test is given, but it is a matter of sufficient importance to be considered before tests are ordered. Some tests provide a helpful record form which gives a profile of achievement. All test manuals should give a clear description of the test's norms and the group used to standardize the instrument. Most of the better tests provide both grade norms and percentile norms.

Does the Test Measure Extraneous Factors? A mathematics test, for example, may have in its questions many words which the student may not understand. Hence, the student may get a low score not primarily because of weakness in mathematics, but because of the vocabulary used in the test.

How Diagnostic Is the Test? Some comprehensive achievement tests give a single score in reading, a single score in arithmetic, and a single score in other aspects of achievement which are tested. This type of result although useful for survey purposes does not provide the specific information needed for certain teaching purposes. It is often desirable to break down achievement in reading, for example, into various kinds of reading, such as, getting the facts, interpreting what has been read, vocabulary, and critical reading. One way of appraising the diagnostic value of a test is for the teacher to plan in advance the ways in which he can use the information provided by a given test.

TEACHER-CONSTRUCTED DIAGNOSTIC TOOLS

Regardless of the fact that there are hundreds of commercially available diagnostic tools, the teacher is frequently faced with the task of making some of his own evaluative instruments. In the following paragraphs suggestions are given for helping the teacher construct such tests.

Preparing to Construct Tests. To do a sound job of constructing tests for educationally defensible purposes, the teacher should first identify the specific behavioral goals that a particular course or set of learning experiences is supposed to achieve. Unless this is first done, testing is likely to be a hit or miss affair without any well-defined orientation. Sometimes it is helpful if the general goals for a specific class or set of educational activities are defined and then more specific behaviors are listed under each of the general goals.

In preparing to construct a test, it is desirable to consider the possible types of test approaches which might be used. Sometimes testing can be done in the actual situation where the behavior occurs. For example, teachers might observe whether good citizenship is being practiced by noting whether paper is being thrown on floors of the hall rather than in wastebaskets. Likewise, the effect of a safety education program could be judged by keeping a record of traffic violations committed by students.

It cannot be too strongly emphasized that much of the work of constructing a test should take place before any items are written, or before any specific instrument is planned. As previously stated one must first determine the objectives of the course. Secondly, and also very important, a content analysis of the course or unit should be made. This analysis should include (1) the major facts and principles of the course or learning unit, (2) the skills which should be provided, (3) the behavioral changes which are intended to occur as a result of the course, and (4) common misconceptions, errors, or trouble spots which exist in the field being measured. Only when such an analysis is completed does the teacher have a sound basis for making out a test plan and beginning the construction of test items. In other words, items should not be chosen because they are easy to write or score, but because they definitely fit into the analysis which has been made of the goals and content of the course of study.

Tests will be more closely related to the goals of schooling and to the important content of school subjects when pupils are given an opportunity to help with the analysis described in the above paragraph. If pupils and teachers plan assignments together, and if pupils are given an opportunity to set goals for themselves, the preparation of tests may well become a joint project.

Directions for the Test. The problem of test directions assumes importance inasmuch as the pupil's orientation for the test or his mental set is likely to be determined by the type of directions that are given.

Travers suggests that the directions to the students should contain statements concerning the following matters: "(1) the purpose of the test, (2) the time allowed for answering questions, and the speed at which the student should work, (3) the extent to which the student should guess or not guess when he is not sure of the answer, (4) instructions concerning the way in which the student is to record his answers." [46] In addition to these four minimum essentials, directions might also be improved by including sample items in the testing instructions and by explaining what the student should do if he encounters unclear or ambiguous items.

General Principles of Test Construction. It is difficult in a brief space to discuss all the important issues involved in the construction of tests. Several volumes and hundreds of journal articles have been devoted to the problems of constructing and analyzing tests. However, every teacher must be prepared to construct instruments of appraisal, and there are some principles of such major importance that all should apply them in their evaluative work. The suggestions which follow, if applied by teachers, should result in a marked improvement in the quality of their measuring instruments.

1. Choose items whose difficulty level is appropriate for the task at hand. Items at the 50 per cent difficulty level (half of those answering the item pass and half fail) give maximum discrimination. For teaching purposes, it may be appropriate to have items of greater ease. However, youngsters will generally find a test more interesting if it is sufficiently difficult to challenge them.
2. Occasionally have two or three students take a test in advance of its general use. Ask these students to explain each step in the solution of a problem and to give detailed oral reasons for their answers. Such a procedure may be very helpful in revealing ambiguities or other unanticipated flaws in the instrument.
3. Avoid insofar as possible all of the following: (a) trivial details, (b) textbook phrases, (c) phrases which may unintentionally give clues to the correct answer such as "always" and "may" in true-false questions, (d) trick or catch questions so phrased that the correct answer depends upon a single, obscure key word, (e) questions which give answers to other questions in the test, (f) items which have no answer upon which experts will agree, and (g) questions which depend strictly upon rote memory.
4. Constantly strive to improve existing tests. By going over tests with a class after they have been scored, a teacher will find questions which

[46] Robert M. W. Travers, *How to Make Achievement Tests*, New York, The Odyssey Press, 1950, p. 132.

are ambiguous or for other reasons poor. Such questions should be deleted or revised. Many test experts recommend keeping a file of good test questions on file cards. Data such as the number of pupils who missed the item or other forms of item analysis [47] may be included on this card.

5. Use various types of test items. Some pupils do better on one type of item than on another. Furthermore, the use of a variety of types of test items is apt to result in better testing of a variety of skills and understandings than is a single type.

Preparing True-False Items. There are special precautions to be followed in connection with different types of test items. True-false items are widely used in schools but have serious limitations as well as some unique advantages. When to use true-false items and how to phrase such items are important points to be kept in mind by teachers who make their own tests. Greene has stated that true-false items are most appropriately used in the following situations.

1. If one is faced with a situation in which time is short for composing, administering and scoring a test.
2. If the test will have to be scored by clerical helpers who are ignorant of the subject.
3. If complexity of thinking and recall of information are not considered as important as a wide range of information.
4. If occasional chance successes and failures are not too serious.[48]

Suggestions for constructing true-false items are as follows:

1. Avoid excessively long and involved statements, and make the average length of true items and false items approximately the same.
2. If items which express opinions are included, attribute the opinions to some source.
3. In arranging the items, do not establish a pattern or rhythm of true and false answers. For example, do not make every other item true.
4. Avoid double negatives and use single negatives very sparingly if at all.
5. Doublebarreled statements in which one part is true and one part is false should not be used.
6. Do not use ambiguous statements which may be either true or false depending upon the interpretation which is made.

[47] For one approach to the problem of item analysis see: F. B. Davis, *Item Analysis Data*, Cambridge, Mass., Graduate School of Education, Harvard, 1946.

[48] Edward B. Greene, *Measurements of Human Behavior*, New York, The Odyssey Press, 1952, pp. 61–62.

7. Have the number of true items and the number of false ones approximately equal.
8. Although the time required for scoring is greatly lengthened, a highly desirable procedure is to provide space following each question, and request pupils to tell why the item is true or false.

Writing Completion Test Items. In completion test items, words or phrases are omitted and these are to be supplied by the person taking the test. To be useful, such a test must involve a nice balance between what is given and what is omitted. In scoring, complete adherence to a set key is unsound. The following procedures should improve the construction of completion items.

1. Avoid the omission of too many words. Long phrases, particularly should not be left out. Frequently in a short sentence, only one key word should be omitted.
2. Statements should not be taken verbatim from textbooks, particularly ones the students being tested have used. A test should not encourage blind memorization of phraseology.
3. Avoid making the items merely a test of general reasoning or intelligence, unless these are the factors which the test is designed to measure.
4. Make a key when the test item is constructed. Revise the key, adding alternative, acceptable answers as experience with the test item is gained.
5. Leave enough space for writing responses, but do not tailor the space to the length of the answer.

Constructing Multiple Choice Questions. The multiple choice type of test item usually includes the presentation of three or more words, phrases, or sentences from which the best or most logical alternative is to be selected. Items may also be constructed which ask the pupil to select the worst or poorest alternative. Use of the following suggestions will help teachers in constructing multiple choice questions.

1. Many items should present problems which require critical thinking on the part of the pupil.
2. Distractor alternatives (wrong answers) should be sufficiently plausible and attractive so that uninformed pupils will frequently select them. Far-fetched and patently wrong answers should be avoided.
3. In general, the correct alternative in a test item should be about the same length as the incorrect ones.
4. The position of the best answer should be varied. That is, it should not almost always be first, last, or in the middle.

Making Essay Examinations. The much maligned essay examination has again achieved status in the eyes of measurement specialists. It is realized that certain outcomes of education can be more validly assessed by this technique than by any so-called objective test items. Some of the values of the essay examination have been summarized by Sims in the following statement:

The essay examination appears to be particularly well suited for obtaining evidence related to certain "higher order" intellectual outcomes of education. Although most essay testing actually done is primarily concerned with the recall of information learned, the value of the essay for testing ability to organize, relate, and "weigh" materials learned has been long appreciated.[49]

In making specific test questions of the essay type, the teacher may find the following recommendations useful.

1. First, write down what is to be measured and then phrase questions to evaluate this.
2. Phrase questions so as to permit a relatively free response, but be specific enough so that pupils know what they are supposed to do.
3. The problems posed in an essay question should have a "reasonable" separation from the students' original learning situation.
4. The student answering the questions should be encouraged to use his own "frame of reference," to reveal his method of reasoning, to show reasons for his choice of material, and to defend any position he takes.
5. So far as possible, arrange questions in order of difficulty with the easier questions appearing first.

Most of the criticism leveled against essay examinations has centered around problems of scoring. Under certain circumstances, tests of this type have proved to be very unreliable. However, adherence to the following suggestions in scoring should increase both the reliability and validity of the tests.

1. Do not have pupils write their names on their papers but instead have them use an identifying number. This will help the teacher maintain objectivity in scoring the test.
2. Some teachers feel that more accurate results are obtained by marking question one for all pupils before moving to question two, etc.
3. First scan a few papers to obtain an estimate of the quality of answers. This will help to preclude the possibility of the first papers read being more rigorously scored than succeeding ones.

[49] V. M. Sims, "The Essay Examination Is a Projective Technique," *Educational and Psychological Measurement*, Vol. 8, Spring, 1948, pp. 15–31.

4. Determine a scale of points in advance of the reading which will be used to rate the quality of the answers. For example, an outstanding response might be given a value of five points, a superior response four points, and so on to zero points for an omitted question.

SUMMARY

Teachers who have not made a special study of tests and measurements would be very much surprised at the number and scope of evaluative and diagnostic instruments which are available at all levels and in all fields of education. One bibliography lists over 5,000 tests and rating scales. Although the existence of intelligence and achievement tests is relatively well known to teachers and laymen alike, the availability of devices for measuring such aspects of behavior as character, critical thinking, study skills, and interest patterns is not so generally known. Regardless of the field in which a teacher works, he will find helpful measuring tools at his disposal.

In this chapter, some of the better tests in the following areas have been presented and evaluated: (1) intelligence (group and individual), (2) achievement (batteries and special subject matter examinations), (3) character and personality, (4) vocational interests, and (5) study skills. Various types of tests and their uses have also been discussed. These include rating scales, inventories, situational tests, and projective tests. Sources the teacher may consult in connection with testing problems were also recommended.

Throughout the preceding pages it has been emphasized that the indiscriminate use of tests, simply for the sake of testing, is undesirable. Each test that is used should contribute to the attainment of some specific goal of education. A set of criteria which teachers may use to enable them to select appropriate tests was included.

Although a wealth of standardized and published tests is available, teachers will still have to construct many of their own evaluative devices. Suggestions for doing this, constituted the concluding section of the chapter.

REFERENCES FOR FURTHER STUDY

Adkins, Dorothy C., with the assistance of others, *Construction and Analysis of Achievement Tests*, Washington 25, D. C., Supt. of Documents, 1947.

Blair, G. M., *Diagnostic and Remedial Teaching in Secondary Schools*, New York, The Macmillan Company, 1946.

Cronbach, L. J., *Essentials of Psychological Testing,* New York, Harper & Brothers, 1949, Chapters 1, 2, 4–8, 13, 14, 15, 17, 18, 19, 20.

Cunningham, Ruth and others, *Understanding Group Behavior of Boys and Girls,* New York, Columbia University, Teachers College Bureau of Publications, 1951.

Donahue, W. T. and others, *The Measurement of Student Adjustment and Achievement,* Ann Arbor, Michigan, University of Michigan Press, 1949.

Dressel, Paul L. and others, *Comprehensive Examinations in a Program of General Education,* East Lansing, Michigan State College Press, 1949.

Greene, E. B., *Measurements of Human Behavior,* New York, The Odyssey Press, 1952, Chapters 2–11, 20, 21, 22, 23, 24.

Greene, H. A., A. N. Jorgensen, and J. R. Gerberich, *Measurement and Evaluation in the Secondary School,* New York, Longmans, Green and Company, 1943.

Hildreth, Gertrude H., *A Bibliography of Mental Tests and Rating Scales,* New York, The Psychological Corporation, 1939 and Supplement, 1945.

Lindquist, E. F., Editor, *Educational Measurement,* Washington, D. C., American Council on Education, 1951, Chapters 5–13.

Micheels, W. J. and M. Ray Karnes, *Measuring Educational Achievement,* New York, McGraw-Hill Book Company, Inc., 1950, Chapters 2, 3, 4, 5, 11, 12, 13, 14.

N.E.A., Association for Supervision and Curriculum Development, *Fostering Mental Health in Our Schools,* Washington 6, D. C., National Education Association, 1950, pp. 181–313.

National Society for the Study of Education, *The Measurement of Understanding,* Forty-Fifth Yearbook, Part I, Chicago, University of Chicago Press, 1946.

Odell, C. W., *How to Improve Classroom Testing,* Dubuque, Iowa, Wm. C. Brown Company, 1953.

Remmers, H. H. and N. L. Gage, *Educational Measurement and Evaluation,* New York, Harper & Brothers, 1943, Chapters 8–20.

Smith, E. R. and others, *Appraising and Recording Student Progress,* New York, Harper & Brothers, 1942.

Simpson, Ray H., *Improving Teaching-Learning Processes,* New York, Longmans, Green and Company, 1953, Chapters 5, 7, 8, 11.

Taba, Hilda and others, *Diagnosing Human Relations Needs,* Washington, D. C., American Council on Education, 1951.

Terman, L. M. and M. A. Merrill, *Measuring Intelligence,* Boston, Houghton Mifflin Company, 1937.

Tiedeman, H. R., *Elementary School Tests Classified,* Bloomington, Illinois, Public School Publishing Company, 1951.

Travers, R. M. W., *How to Make Achievement Tests,* New York, The Odyssey Press, 1949.

Traxler, Arthur E. and others, *Introduction to Testing and the Use of*

Test Results in Public Schools, New York, Harper & Brothers, 1953, Chapters 1–6.

Weitzman, Ellis, and W. J. McNamara, *Constructing Classroom Examinations,* Chicago, Science Research Associates, 1949.

PUBLISHERS OF TESTS

Bureau of Educational Research and Service, State University of Iowa, Iowa City, Iowa.

Bureau of Publications, Teachers College, Columbia University, New York 27, New York.

California Test Bureau, 5916 Hollywood Boulevard, Los Angeles 28, California.

Educational Test Bureau, 720 Washington Avenue, S. E., Minneapolis 14, Minnesota.

Educational Testing Service, 20 Nassau Street, Princeton, New Jersey.

Houghton Mifflin Company, 2500 Prairie Avenue, Chicago 16, Illinois.

The Psychological Corporation, 522 Fifth Avenue, New York 18, New York.

Public School Publishing Company, 509–513 North East Street, Bloomington, Illinois.

Science Research Associates, 57 West Grand Avenue, Chicago 10, Illinois.

Stanford University Press, Stanford, California.

C. H. Stoelting Company, 424 North Homan Avenue, Chicago 24, Illinois.

University of Minnesota Press, University of Minnesota, Minneapolis 14, Minnesota.

World Book Company, 2126 Prairie Avenue, Chicago 16, Illinois.

The reader is also urged to consult a good sampling of the headings in the *Education Index* which are listed at the end of Chapter 18.

The Fourth Mental Measurements Yearbook (O. K. Buros, Editor, Highland Park, New Jersey, The Gryphon Press, 1953) deserves special mention. It lists 793 tests, 596 original test reviews, 53 test review excerpts, 4,417 references on the construction, validity, use and limitations of specific tests, 429 books on measurements and closely related fields, and 758 excerpts from book reviews. This yearbook supplements rather than supplants earlier yearbooks in the series. In the yearbook an attempt is made to list all commercially available tests—educational, psychological, and vocational—published as separates in English-speaking countries in the four-year period, 1948–1951.

Chapter 18

Interpreting and Using
Test Results

PROPER SELECTION, administration, and scoring of tests may be of little value unless there are appropriate interpretations and uses of test results. Consider, for instance, a large school system, known to the writer, which gave a comprehensive, standardized achievement test to all of its seventh-grade pupils in the spring of the year. Results from the test indicated that the median (middle) grade equivalent of the seventh graders taking the test was 9.2. This means that half of the pupils taking the test in this school system did as well or better than a typical (median) ninth grader in the country as a whole does in October. Since the median-grade level of an average group of seventh graders in April would be 7.7, on the surface, it appeared that the pupils tested in this school system were 1.5 grades above pupils upon whom the test had been standardized. As the result of this showing, self-satisfaction verging on smugness was the typical reaction of both teachers and administrators in the schools of this system.

However, when some of the factors which produced these results were carefully examined by outside test consultants serious doubts were raised regarding the quality of the educational achievement in the school system. What had happened was that the teachers and school administrators failed to take into account numerous conditions which may have influenced test results. They neglected to ask several important questions, which if raised, would have accounted for the seeming superiority of the pupils on the test. In the next few pages some of the factors which this school system should have examined, and which should be kept in mind by any educator using test results, will be discussed. Following this, suggestions are given for effectively employing achievement tests and sociometric measures in classroom situations.

CAUTIONS IN INTERPRETING TEST RESULTS

An essential first step in properly interpreting and wisely using information given by tests is to know what factors influence test performance and test scores. It is obviously unfair to compare two children or two classes on the basis of an improperly administered test. Likewise it is ridiculous to consider seriously the IQ earned by a retarded reader on a test which requires much reading ability. The person giving a test, school policy which determines who will be in school to take the test, the attitudes of pupils toward testing, and the conditions under which the test is given are some of the variables which alter test scores. Cautions in test interpretation related to these and other factors will now be discussed.

Teacher Motivation and School Policy. *Are teachers given pay raises on the basis of test results?* Some superintendents, principals, and supervisors, casting about for an objective basis for giving promotions or salary increases, have settled on the idea of giving monetary rewards to those who can produce the best test results. The goal of giving salary increases on the basis of merit is admirable but this particular method has resulted in many unprofessional practices which should be eliminated in any place where they exist. In the school system used in our illustration, the school supervisor apparently did give the pay increases to those whose pupils had the highest median scores. This was particularly unfair to teachers in schools serving pupils of low socio-economic status and poor home background.

Is the primary goal of the teachers to help the pupils or to get good test results? In some school systems it is unfortunately true that in the struggle to have "my class" come out on top the teacher has almost forgotten the primary purpose of education, to help the learner. In these schools, test results have, unfortunately, sometimes tended to become an end in themselves. When this occurs, "good" test results may be accompanied by basically poor education.

Has the attention of the teacher been focused on improving the test results of those just below the median at the expense of the rapid and slow learners? If a teacher knows that his group and his teaching are likely to be evaluated on the score of the middle learner (median score) of his group, he may gear his teaching to the level of the middle third of the group, feeling that the highest third will get fairly good scores anyhow and that the lowest third or at least the lowest fifth will in all probability have little effect in moving the median upward.

How much retardation is there in the school? It is quite possible for a school system that is doing a relatively poor instructional job to reach or even to exceed the national norms on tests by having a rigid policy of promotion. For example, the writer is familiar with a school system which takes great pride in its "standards." With very few exceptions no pupil is promoted until he has reached the "norm" for his grade on a standardized achievement test. This means that a child in the fifth grade is not promoted to the sixth grade until he can make a score equivalent to 6.0 on the comprehensive achievement test. This policy has resulted in excessive retardation with about 50 per cent of the seventh-grade pupils being held back at least one year. Obviously, a comparison of the median score of this group with the younger group on which the norms of the test were based is unsound. With excessive administrative retardation even an inefficient school system may seem to have a good achievement record when its results are compared with national grade norms. One way of determining the amount of administrative retardation is to see how many pupils are over-age for their grade.

How much elimination is there in the school? Some schools have a deliberate policy of "weeding out" the weakest pupils, particularly in the upper grades; other schools just fall into the habit. Consider two schools each of which originally had 200 pupils entering the first grade. In school *A* only 60 per cent, or 120 pupils, ever reached the seventh grade—the others were eliminated in one way or another. In school *B* 95 per cent, or 190 pupils, entered the seventh grade. Since it usually is the poorer achievers who are eliminated in a school such as *A*, it is obvious that school *B* with a lower median score than *A* might still be doing a much better job of educating the children in its community. The holding power of a school needs to be carefully considered in interpreting test results. The twin evils of excessive elimination and excessive retardation demand thoughtful consideration, and test makers and publishers should be encouraged to give figures indicating the extent of the elimination and retardation in the schools on which norms are based. Actually, in the school system described at the opening of this chapter, there were both unusual "holding back" and elimination. In some elementary schools in the system there were fourteen-year-old students languishing in the third grade. If only the average or above average students are measured in the seventh grade, a basically poor school can look good insofar as test results are concerned.

Learner Background and Training for Test. *Did the teachers teach the test directly or indirectly?* It may seem undignified even to suggest that such an unprofessional practice might be carried on. But in certain school systems the practice *is* carried on by some teachers, and those who interpret test results need to be aware of this possibility. Of course, any time a group of learners is coached on a test the use of norms accompanying the test becomes meaningless. Unfortunately some administrators and supervisors have unwittingly encouraged this practice, partially through the procedure, already discussed, of tying teacher promotions to the test results obtained by their pupils. One type of teaching of the test which borders on questionable practice may involve teaching exactly the same kind of items as the test is expected to contain.

An example, of what can happen if this caution is not observed recently came to the writer's attention. In an air force base in Texas during the Second World War a test of 275 items was developed from a longer list of several thousand items. Scores on this test were highly correlated with bombardier performance in actual combat. After the test had been used with several classes on the base, test results on the new groups were again matched with combat efficiency. This time the correlations turned out to be low. Further investigation revealed that bombardier instructors were teaching the test items to their students. A test can thus become worthless or even lead to disastrous consequences if improperly used.

How many years has the test been given in the school? Undue familiarity with a particular test will tend to produce artificially high results on that test. For example, the writer is familiar with a school which, twice a year, has used some form of the same test for five years, which means that some of the pupils in the upper grades in that school may have had ten very similar tests and some repetitions of the same test. Too great familiarity with a test will indicate the need for using a different test. In the school system described earlier the *Metropolitan Achievement Tests* had been used for some ten years. This school obviously should make use of some of the other excellent achievement tests available.

What is the potential ability of the learners as compared with those upon whom the tests were standardized? While this probably cannot be determined exactly, some clues to the answer can be obtained through the use of good intelligence tests, particularly ones which do not themselves depend upon reading or other achievement skills for successful performance. The occupational level and socioeconomic status of the parents will also frequently give a very rough indication of the answer.

What are the primary motivators of the students? Threats, fear of punishment, marks, extrinsic rewards and the like can produce what seem to be fairly good temporary results but the net result is likely to be undesirable in the long run. An extreme illustration of this was reported to the writer by one of his students. A teacher of American history had given his final examination, the scores of the examination were quite acceptable to the teacher, and the final marks in the course had been prepared. On the final day of school when the report cards were passed out the pupils in a dramatic demonstration of their attitude toward American history tore their history books to bits and tossed the pieces of paper out of the school windows. When high test scores are obtained through motivation that produces antagonistic attitudes, the scores themselves may be of minor significance.

What has been the effect of home training, travel, and other nonschool factors? Some schools take credit for doing a great deal more than they are responsible for. Schools with learners coming from homes with good "educational opportunities" should give the home credit for many learnings which the pupils demonstrate. A healthy community environment including a well-run public library, where youngsters have many opportunities for informal educational experiences outside both the school and the home, may have considerable influence on achievement test results.

What is the annual amount spent per child for education? The time spent with the child and the wherewithal for educating him should be considered in evaluating and interpreting test results. For example, in some school districts in the United States more than

$900 per child per year is spent. In others the amount is below $50. Obviously one could not reasonably expect similar results in two districts, where one spends eighteen times as much per child as does the other.

Are test results in certain learnings being achieved at the expense of other equally important learnings? The basic importance of this point can not be overemphasized. In the preceding paragraph attention was called to differences in the amount of money spent by the community for education. Here the focus is on the emphasis the school gives to different kinds of learnings. There are schools where the teaching is so slanted by standardized tests, that many learnings not touched by the tests, but considered at least equally important by outstanding educators, are being neglected. This neglect may produce negative and undesirable attitudes as illustrated by the book-tearing episode described earlier. Such neglect may also produce antisocial pupils, or ones who take a passive attitude toward teachers in general, schools, testing, or specific subjects.

Administration and Scoring Problems. *Was test administered in standardized manner?* In some schools "standardized" tests are given in a very unstandardized fashion either through lack of knowledge of sound testing procedures or because the person administering the test desires to influence the results. If lack of knowledge of good testing procedures is the difficulty, study of test administration is, of course, strongly indicated. If directions are only partially read or not followed, if the timing is inaccurate, or if unauthorized help is given to testees, then the norms for the test become meaningless and it is probable that much pupil and teacher time has been wasted.

What were conditions under which test was taken? Some of the conditions against which the teacher must guard are: excessive noise, frequent interruptions by outsiders, inappropriate desk equipment for writing, and too high or too low temperatures in the testing room.

Was the standardized test scored according to directions in manual? Most test manuals give complete directions for scoring a test. These must be followed carefully if the test results are to be meaningful.

Reliability and Validity of the Test. In both standardized and unstandardized tests the concepts of test reliability and test validity must be considered. As an extreme example consider a teacher who claimed he had a new measure of intelligence—the circumference of the head. Since a test and subsequent retest would probably show similar results on a particular individual, the test would have a high degree of reliability, i.e., consistency from one measurement to another. However, if head circumference for individuals were compared with some accepted criterion of intelligence little relationship would be found. Hence, one would say the new test is not valid. Reliability indicates how consistently a test measures what it does measure. Validity represents the accuracy with which a test measures what it is supposed to measure. A reliable test that is not valid is likely to be useless.

USES OF ACHIEVEMENT TEST RESULTS

The improvement of teaching and learning activities should, of course, be the primary purpose for understanding the uses to which tests may be put. Every teacher has a responsibility for knowing some of the uses which may be made of test results. To aid the reader in recognizing some of these possibilities, a summary of actual scores from one reading test is given in Table 32. This material is based upon data gathered in a class of thirty-four sixth-grade pupils.

The teacher who is to use such data as presented in Table 32 might well, at the outset, ask himself the following questions: (1) How can the test results help in analyzing the major strengths and weaknesses of the class as a whole? (2) What are some ways of planning improvement on a class-wide basis? (3) How can the test results facilitate individual learner diagnosis? (4) How can the results of the individual diagnosis help individual learner improvement? (5) How can the test results be used to stimulate school-wide diagnosis and plans for improved teaching and learning?

Finding Strengths and Weaknesses of Class as a Whole. Each teacher, or even better a teacher-learner committee, can find the average grade score for students on each test and each sub-test to see on which tests the students as a whole are high and on which tests the students as a group are low.

When the data from Table 32 are summarized and averages are computed, material is available for making a class profile. Such a profile has been drawn in Figure 20 for the class under discussion. The profile reveals some interesting things about the class. It is

Table 32

Iowa Silent Reading Data for One Room of Sixth Graders *

PUPIL NUMBER	ACTUAL AGE	READING AGE	GENERAL READING	READING RATE	READING COMPRE-HENSION	DIRECTED READING	VOCABULARY LEVEL	CENTRAL IDEA	DEVELOP-MENT	SENTENCE MEANING	USE OF INDEX
							GRADE LEVEL				
1	12–4	13–2	8.4	9.6	6.3	9.0	5.6	10.6	6.6	7.3	10.8
2	12–8	12–10	8.0	4.2	5.3	10.6	12.0	8.7	7.3	4.5	9.8
3	11–10	12–5	7.6	7.5	7.5	7.6	6.6	7.3	9.6	7.3	12.0
4	11–10	12–5	7.6	6.9	8.2	12.0	6.6	8.7	8.0	7.8	8.2
5	14–3	12–4	7.5	5.7	7.5	7.3	4.7	10.6	6.6	8.4	8.2
6	12–8	11–10	6.9	6.6	6.9	7.6	5.1	7.3	5.5	6.9	5.6
7	12–9	11–10	6.9	6.5	5.7	8.0	5.1	8.7	7.3	5.1	5.9
8	12–6	11–8	6.9	5.5	6.3	6.6	6.9	5.9	8.0	5.1	12.0
9	12–7	11–7	6.6	6.2	6.9	6.2	4.6	8.7	7.3	6.6	9.0
10	12–6	11–7	6.6	7.1	5.7	6.8	4.7	8.7	6.6	5.1	6.2
11	12–6	11–5	6.5	5.5	6.3	7.1	4.0	8.7	6.6	3.9	9.8
12	13–9	11–4	6.3	5.2	4.5	6.8	5.9	4.8	6.6	6.9	8.0
13	12–2	11–4	6.3	5.5	9.0	7.3	7.3	7.3	9.6	4.6	4.0
14	12–11	11–1	6.2	6.9	5.7	7.3	5.5	4.8	7.3	5.5	8.2
15	11–9	11–1	6.2	6.2	6.9	6.2	7.8	8.7	7.3	6.0	5.6
16	12–10	11–1	6.2	8.0	4.1	7.1	3.4	4.7	3.8	6.6	7.6
17	14–7	11–1	6.2	6.5	3.4	5.7	5.6	7.3	6.6	7.8	5.2
18	11–11	11–0	6.0	6.6	4.5	6.5	4.8	7.3	6.0	4.6	5.6
19	12–2	10–10	5.9	4.7	5.7	6.8	5.9	7.3	6.6	5.7	4.0
20	12–10	10–10	5.9	6.2	5.7	9.0	5.1	4.8	6.6	5.5	8.2
21	13–9	10–10	5.9	3.8	6.3	6.5	6.2	7.3	5.5	3.6	4.5
22	14–10	10–10	5.9	6.9	7.5	5.7	6.2	4.8	6.6	5.5	6.2
23	12–2	10–10	5.9	6.2	5.7	4.7	5.5	7.3	7.3	4.8	12.0
24	11–10	10–8	5.7	6.0	6.9	5.2	6.0	6.0	6.6	5.2	5.6
25	13–7	10–9	5.7	5.5	5.7	6.5	4.0	5.9	6.0	5.5	5.2
26	15–8	10–5	5.3	3.6	4.9	6.0	4.7	5.9	6.2	7.8	8.2
27	12–7	10–0	4.9	4.2	5.3	6.0	5.1	3.9	5.5	4.0	6.6
28	14–12	9–6	4.5	4.5	4.1	5.7	3.9	5.9	6.0	4.2	4.8
29	12–0	9–5	4.4	3.6	4.1	4.7	3.3	5.9	3.9	3.9	6.2
30	14–11	9–5	4.4	3.4	4.9	5.2	3.0	4.7	3.8	4.5	3.7
31	15–6	9–3	4.2	8.2	4.9	3.9	3.1	1.0	2.0	4.5	5.2
32	15–9	9–3	4.2	3.4	6.3	3.7	3.6	4.8	6.0	3.6	4.8
33	14–3	8–10	3.9	4.2	4.1	5.7	3.7	5.9	6.0	3.7	4.7
34	14–6	8–5	3.5	2.0	4.1	3.4	4.8	3.8	4.4	4.1	3.4
Average	13–2	10–9	6.0	5.7	5.8	6.6	5.0	6.6	6.4	5.5	6.9

* Scores from two subtests, Poetry Comprehension and Selection of Key Words, are omitted because of space limitations.

strongest in the "Use of the Index" and weakest in "Vocabulary," and has an over-all reading grade level of 6.0.

A very helpful procedure is also to compare the results on a reading test with achievements in other areas. For example, another class profile which included reading along with arithmetic, spelling, hand-

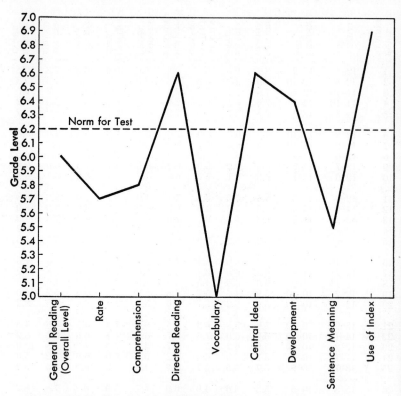

FIGURE 20. Profile of Reading Skills of the Sixth-Grade Class Described in Table 32.

writing, English usage, and other aspects of the school program would be of much assistance to the teacher in understanding the over-all progress being made by a class.

The data in Figure 20 answer some questions regarding pupils' reading abilities, but not all. The teacher and pupils also need to raise such questions as these: What are the attitudes of the majority in this class toward reading? To what extent is the reading ability demonstrated on the test actually being used in situations where the reading might appropriately be used? What interest do the youngsters take in reading out of class where the ordinary school pressures are not being exerted? To what extent are they able to find and select appropriate reading materials for particular problems and in particular situations? What are the processes which they use in reading (as opposed to the products of reading shown on the test)?

Teachers interested in ways of utilizing such data as presented in Table 32 may wish to study such additional questions as the following:

1. Out of 34 pupils listed in Table 32, how many are reading up to actual age? (Use Columns 2 and 3.)
2. How many have average beginning seventh-grade reading ability or more?
3. What is the range of ability in vocabulary?
4. What is the range in the use of the index?
5. What is one of the first things that should be done to meet such great individual differences?
6. What does the table indicate about using the same texts and materials for everybody in the same grade?
7. How many grade levels of material are needed for this class?
8. How many in this group can now read average seventh-grade material with comprehension?
9. What level of material does pupil 26 need? Pupil 30? Pupil 1?
10. Which of these youngsters probably reads too fast for his comprehension?
11. Which pupils should probably be encouraged to speed up their reading?
12. Which of these youngsters apparently needs training in using the index?
13. In the light of these and other data, what would it be reasonable to expect of pupil 20 with respect to reading improvement this year? What is a reasonable goal for him? What might be a reasonable goal for pupil 32?
14. What types of professional problems does it appear the teacher of this class should be studying?

Planning Improvements on a Class-Wide Basis. The average levels of attainment as shown on different reading scales and the class profile and individual profiles may indicate some of the places or points where instruction has been strong or weak (at least, as compared with classes on which the test was standardized). The teacher, as well as students, should be able to act in the light of such information by engaging in activities designed to correct areas of weakness.

The elimination of the weaknesses revealed by the test may involve many activities, some of which will now be discussed. (1) A study of how other teachers in the same school have worked on such problems. (2) A study of relevant published materials. Extensive use of the *Education Index* and the *Psychological Abstracts* will probably be desirable. Annual summaries of reading studies are given in the *Journal of Educational Research*. For example, in Volume 46, February, 1953, there is a "Summary of Reading Investigations, July 1, 1951 to June 30, 1952."[1] Other helpful sources are the summaries and bibliographies printed by the Educational Records Bureau, 437 West 59th Street, New York 19, New York. These summaries and annotated bibliographies are of value in helping the teacher find studies which relate to a particular reading problem such as developing reading interest, activity programs in reading achievement, developmental reading, and remedial and corrective teaching of reading. (3) Finally, weaknesses spotlighted by the tests may be eliminated through revised teaching methods. Those methods which are effective should be capable of validation by a continuous testing program.

For instructional purposes some teachers and teacher-pupil planning groups may find it advisable to group children for particular types of reading or other learning activities. Referring back again to Table 32, the question might be asked: What subgroups may be organized to facilitate the learning of various reading skills? Pupils may be grouped according to the areas of the greatest need as indicated by a study of the diagnostic test results. Subgroups should vary according to the pupil's needs in the different school subjects and their membership should shift as conditions change.

In the matter of grouping it should be kept in mind that some pupils need to develop into leaders in the community and one way of promoting such development is to help individuals assume some responsibility in handling groups. Simply to turn the leadership job over to the student is not enough. The teacher must systematically

[1] By William S. Gray, pp. 401–437.

make a study of ways of developing student leaders [2] and actively engage in promoting the process.

Diagnosis of Individual Difficulties. The teacher should make a systematic study of outstanding strengths and weaknesses of each pupil with the aim of giving appropriate individual help. Questions such as the following point the way toward the effective use of test results for individual diagnosis: Do a pupil's answers on a test indicate that he is weak in following directions? Does his test show that he works quite accurately but too slowly? Does he seem to reverse words or letters and read them from right to left rather than left to right? An analysis of the pupil's errors and the processes he used in making them often sheds much light on the type of remedial work needed.

Another important factor to keep in mind in the diagnosis of individuals is the need to study achievement not in terms of an absolute standard but rather in terms of expected and reasonable *individual* achievement. As reading has consistently been used as an illustration in this chapter, one might pursue the matter of reading achievement a step further by asking who are retarded readers? Can the question be answered from the data shown in Table 32? Some years ago the writer asked several teachers and administrators to define retarded readers. The answers, as will be shown by the following illustrations, were far from constant.[3]

"A retarded reader is one behind his age norm in comprehension and speed in reading ability." If this definition were used, approximately 50 per cent of the youngsters in our schools would always be retarded since the norm simply represents the average achievement at a particular age or grade. Other definitions were: ". . . one who may be in the fourth grade, but has the reading ability of the average second grader." ". . . one who is at least a grade level below his class norm when given a standard test." ". . . one who does not read as well as the average member of his class." Each of the four definitions given in this paragraph implies that every child should be up to average. This is certainly an impossible and unrealistic goal.

---

[2] See Ruth Cunningham, *Understanding Group Behavior of Boys and Girls,* New York, Teachers College, Columbia University, 1951.

[3] Ray H. Simpson, "Who Are Retarded Readers?" *The Journal of Education,* Vol. 124, March, 1941, pp. 91–93.

What, then, should be meant by the term "a retarded reader?" Consider three students aged 11 years, 2 months, who are all in the sixth grade. Mary has a reading age of 9.5; John's reading age is 11.4; and Jean has a reading age of 12.5. It is difficult to tell which of these is retarded in reading until the approximate mental age or *reading capacity* of each is known. When mental test data are included the following figures are obtained:

Pupil	Chronological Age	General Reading Age	Mental Age [4]
Mary	11–2	9.5	9.5
John	11–2	11.4	11.6
Jean	11–2	12.5	15.0

Assuming that both the reading test and the capacity test are reasonably valid, we are now in a position to say that Mary, the poorest reader, is reading apparently about as well as should be expected in view of her mental test score; John is slightly retarded; and Jean, who is the best reader of the three, shows the greatest amount of basic retardation. Thus, the slowest and poorest reader may actually be the least retarded, while the fastest and best reader is apparently retarded about three grades in reading ability.

Before we can intelligently approach remedial reading, we must know which youngsters are most retarded. That child is most retarded whose reading achievements are farthest below his reading capacities. He is the child who someone has neglected or trained improperly in reading. He is the child who now needs remedial assistance with particular emphasis on the kinds of reading in which he is weakest.

Helping Pupils Improve. Achievement test results combined with some measure of basic intellectual capacity will help give a more realistic basis for determining appropriate class, course, and other educational goals. From the achievement tests can be secured an indication of present accomplishments; from mental capacity tests come an approximation of the *speed* with which one may expect the pupil to progress. With these factors in mind it should not be ex-

---

[4] It should be understood, of course, that mental age as measured by intelligence tests is not a perfect indication of reading capacity, especially if the mental test requires the subject to read. Nevertheless, measured mental ability adds an important ingredient to the study of the so-called retarded reader.

pected that a sixth-grade youngster whose mental capacity is much below average and whose present achievement level is that of the average fourth grader will be able to do *average* sixth-grade work. Neither should one expect him to be ready to begin *average* seventh-grade work one year later.

For instance, in an activity such as reading, the average reading grade level of a pupil can be used as a basis for helping him select and use reading materials. This would mean that each classroom would need to have available for use reading materials which vary in difficulty and in areas of interest to the same extent as the reading capacities and interests of pupils. Likewise, diagnostic arithmetic tests may be used to find levels of arithmetic experience which are needed and will be meaningful for each pupil. In essence, the optimum usefulness of diagnostic tests can be achieved only when a major share of the assignments and exercises represent a planned follow-up of the individual test results.

For recreational reading it is at times desirable for the pupil to have reading materials which are considerably easier than those he can comprehend as indicated by test results. For sheer enjoyment and to promote the desire to do much reading, it is sometimes desirable to have materials which are so easy that the pupil does not have to struggle with new words in his reading.

The great spread of ability within each grade level, as indicated by tests, means that if the development of each pupil is to be provided for, the teacher must gear instruction to several grade levels within his class. The data which were shown in Table 32 are typical of what would be found in classrooms the country over—and similar data would be found in subjects other than reading. Within one grade, a range of ability of eight or nine grades frequently appears on test results. It is apparent that a teacher should not only be familiar with materials and methods suitable for *average* pupils of his grade, but should also know about materials and be able to use methods adapted to both less and more mature pupils. This is, obviously, an extremely difficult task, but one which can be faced with considerable optimism if the teacher is willing to study and experiment, and if the teacher is willing to use the learners themselves, so far as is possible, in diagnosing their own difficulties, and in planning their own activities.

USING TESTS TO FACILITATE SOCIAL RELATIONSHIPS

The previous section of this chapter showed some of the many ways in which achievement tests could be used as a basis for improving teaching. If learning were governed strictly by capacity for achievement, an explanation of the use of achievement and mental tests might suffice. However, successful schoolwork depends equally as much upon such characteristics as the pupils' personal adjustment, attitudes, and social or group skills. It is therefore essential that teachers know how to measure and interpret these personal and social factors, and to use the test results in planning classroom activities. One of the most practical and useful types of evidence about children is obtained by appraising their interpersonal relationships.

The term which is generally used to describe a study of patterns of inter-relation existing in a group of people is *sociometry*. From the measure of inter-relationships it is possible to draw up a chart which gives a pictorial representation of some aspects of interpersonal relations. As with any other type of testing procedure, the purposes and uses of the technique are matters of major concern. In the initial part of this section procedures for gathering sociometric data will be discussed. Following this an illustrative sociogram will be presented. Finally, uses which may be made of sociometric approaches will be listed and briefly discussed.

Gathering Sociometric Data. In collecting sociometric data it is desirable not to suggest to pupils that they are taking a test. A superior procedure would be to begin with a statement such as the following:

Yesterday it was decided by our class that we should set up some committees for various purposes in our next unit of work. There are various ways in which these committees might be set up, but it is desirable that you have an opportunity to work on committees with students whom you feel you work with best. If each of you will put on one of these sheets of paper your own name and names of three other students with whom you would like to work, I will attempt to summarize these over the weekend and set up some committee groups based on the recommendations which our planning committee made today.

Obviously the information gained from the voting for committees sheds light on the kind of interpersonal relationships existing within a class. Any number of additional questions could be phrased and presented to the pupils for their reactions. Following are some questions which teachers have found useful:

Will you write on a piece of paper the names of your three best friends?
With which classmates (two or three) do you like best to play?
Whom would you like to have sit next to you in class?
With whom would you like to discuss personal problems?
Who is your choice as student leader for this class?
Whom would you like most to invite home to dinner?
With whom would you like to go to a party?

In this type of testing it is extremely important that the pupils be frank in stating what their preferences are. One way of assuring this, of course, is for the teacher to keep information so gained in strictest confidence. Usually it is wise for the teacher to mention that these data will not be shown to other students in the room or revealed to any other individual.

There is some difference of opinion among experts as to whether it is ever wise to ask for negative reactions or dislikes on the part of pupils. One argument for attempting to get such information is that if there are dislikes it is well to know where they exist and against whom they are directed so that something can be done to better the situation. If it is decided that it is wise to attempt to obtain sociometric rejections, then any of the questions already suggested could be used by placing "not" appropriately in each question. Statements like the following may also be used:

What three pupils do you like least?
Who are the pupils nobody likes very much?
Which children get into a lot of trouble?
Which children are afraid of everything?
Which children do you think are bossy?
Which children act like sissies?
Which pupils cause you trouble?

In the primary grades where pupils are too young to write the names of other children, teachers may obtain similar information through personal interviews with the youngsters themselves. When this is done it is clear that such interviews should be conducted outside of the hearing of other pupils.

Finally, the teacher should keep in mind the following suggestions. It is well to: (1) build up desirable relationships with pupils before requesting the information; (2) collect and use sociometric measurement in situations where the need for such data is or can be made obvious to the pupils; [5] (3) word questions so that they can easily be understood by the pupils.

Pictorial Representation of Interpersonal Relationships. After students' nominations have been collected, the teacher will want to convert the data into some usable form. There are many possible ways of graphically representing the information gathered.[6] One such plan is presented in Figure 21.

The diagram in Figure 21 [7] is constructed to show *mutual relationships* between pupils in the same grade and *mutual relationships* with pupils in other grades. Each child in grades four to eight was asked to indicate: (1) with whom would he like best to play; (2) with whom would he like best to work; and (3) whom would he like best to have sit next to him. Three choices were possible for each question, although this number was not required. On the basis of the answers of the eighth-grade group, the sociogram in Figure 21 was constructed. The dotted lines in the diagram show reciprocated choices—show that a pupil not only likes a pupil but is liked by him in return. These are mutual relationships. Pupils are placed into one of four concentric circles according to the extent of their popularity.

Six of the facts or implications indicated by this sociogram follow. (1) Pupils 5 and 9 not only are chosen fewer than five times but their own choices of other students were in no instance reciprocated. Although pupils 19, 15, 23, and 1 were also chosen less than five times, at least one mutual choice was found in each case. Two of these five pupils, 15 and 23, chose each other. One of these pupils, 1, had his choice reciprocated by a pupil in another grade. (2) In or near Area II seem to be found the pupils with the most satisfactory mutual relationships. (3) One pupil, 29, although receiving more than fifteen votes apparently has no reciprocated friendship with any other girl in her own classroom and crossed room boundaries to

---

[5] For illustrations of such situations see the *Ohio Social Acceptance Scale* published by the Ohio Scholarship Tests and Division of Elementary Supervision, State Department of Education, Columbus, Ohio.

[6] For an analysis of approaches see S. W. Cook and others, *Research Methods in Social Relations*, New York, The Dryden Press, 1951.

[7] E. A. Flotow, "Charting Social Relationships," *Elementary School Journal*, Vol. 46, May, 1946, pp. 498–504.

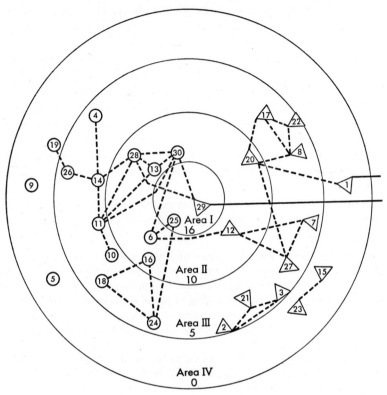

FIGURE 21. Sociogram for Thirty Eighth-Grade Pupils.

This shows the mutual relationships with pupils in same grade (broken lines) and mutual relationships with pupils in other grades (straight lines). Small circles represent boys; triangles, girls. Area I includes pupils chosen as friends by other children 16 or more times; Area II, pupils chosen 10–15 times; Area III, pupils chosen 5–9 times; and Area IV, pupils chosen fewer than 5 times. (From E. A. Flotow, "Charting Social Relationships," *Elementary School Journal,* Vol. 46, May, 1946, pp. 498–504.)

establish a mutual relationship with another girl. (4) Most of the social relationships are with pupils of the same sex. (5) The boys seem to represent a somewhat more tightly knit group than the girls. (6) In general, pupils who receive the most choices also have the greater number of reciprocated relationships.

The teacher of the pupils shown in Figure 21, with these and other data available such as marks and intelligence test scores, should be able to develop and study other facts and hypotheses and gain insights not mentioned in the points above. The way a teacher will pictorially represent data will depend primarily on what relationships he is trying to study.[8]

Uses of Sociometric Data. It is a well known fact that teachers are poor judges of the social roles of many of their pupils. Teachers frequently feel that if a child is bright and doing excellent academic work he is also equally effective in his social relationships. By means of sociometric procedures teachers can get some checks on their own impressions regarding the social relations in their classrooms. Sociometric procedures help the busy teacher avoid the danger involved in neglecting children who are rejected or ignored by their classmates.

In the following list are specific values the teacher can derive from various measures of interpersonal relationships. Sociometric data can:

1. help the teacher identify cliques and cleavages in class groups.
2. focus the attention of the teacher on social goals and on tangible ways in which interpersonal relations can be improved.
3. help improve pupil understanding of social relations and problems, if discussed with class without names on sociogram.
4. help identify rejected pupils—those who are actively disliked by some or many classmates.
5. detect pupils who *feel* themselves to be social outcasts in the classroom. (This feeling may not, of course, be accurate, but may still have educational significance.)
6. give teacher basis for comparing class with published social norms.[9]
7. indicate those who are out-of-school leaders but do not show leadership in school. (Such pupils would frequently have great potentialities as classroom leaders if teacher guidance were appropriate in this regard.)
8. provide clues as to ways of dealing with disciplinary cases. (Can show with whom the problem case would like to work and whom he respects.)
9. show how newcomers in a school or class are faring and can help the teacher check on the effectiveness of various procedures for integrating newcomers into classroom groups.

[8] For other illustrations of sociogram construction see: (1) Horace-Mann Lincoln School of Experimentation, *How to Construct a Sociogram,* New York, Bureau of Publications, Teachers College, Columbia University, 1947; (2) E. Forsyth and L. Katz, "A Matrix Approach to the Analysis of Sociometric Data," *Sociometry,* Vol. 9, November, 1946, pp. 340–347.

[9] H. H. Jennings, *Sociometry in Group Relations,* Washington, D. C., American Council on Education, 1948, p. 21.

10. show which students have friends in the classroom but are also thoroughly disliked by one or more students.

11. help identify the isolates in the classroom—those who are ignored by peers and who have no friends in the classroom.

12. help identify those who are presently classroom leaders. (These individuals can be taught to assume some of the roles now assumed only by the teacher in many classrooms.)

13. aid in determining interracial or interreligious relations and problems.

14. show the direction of changes in interpersonal relationships which are continually taking place in classroom groups.

15. show degree of individual maturity on one dimension by indicating level of interest in those of the other sex.

16. help the teacher through pretests and post-tests to determine the effects of specific procedures which have been tried out in the classroom.

17. give the teacher significant data upon which formal or informal research may be based.

18. show how many mutual or reciprocated choices of friends there are in the classroom.

19. show which class members are in greatest demand as friends.

The values of sociometric testing can be realized only when tests are followed by further diagnostic work or appropriate remedial action. As already noted, sociometric data should point out isolates, rejected children, potential leaders, cliques, and perhaps the general conditions of group morale and group interaction. Some of the uses of such information may be implemented by the techniques described in the following paragraphs.

First of all, the data may provide a means for reseating or reconstituting groups within the classroom. If two near isolates choose each other, for example, it would seem desirable to see that these two youngsters be given the opportunity to work together. Group work of some sort is essential if the full value of sociometry is to be achieved.

Secondly, the information gleaned from sociometric voting should provide a basis for further diagnosis. Interviews, diaries kept by pupils, personality measures, observations, and case studies may be indicated in cases where children are very unpopular. The unpopular child who is identified early in his school career may be helped immeasurably. The writer knows a case in which a girl was rejected almost unanimously by her classmates. She was most unhappy and maladjusted. Further study showed her to be the unfortunate product of an oversolicitous mother who went so far as to bring this teen-age youngster to class each day, and to wait for her after school outside the classroom door. The teacher followed sociometric testing by interviewing the girl and her classmates, and eventually, through the use of group work and several parties which were held at the rejected girl's home, helped her achieve a place in her peer group.

Finally, sociometric information may be used in a more general way to make changes in group procedures and to involve the class in problems which sociograms bring to light. Such matters as needed recreational activities, prejudices, personal inadequacies, tightly knit cliques, and the like are problems which youngsters themselves can help solve. Class discussions in which pupils are encouraged to raise such problems may be one solution. Also, group project work in which youngsters investigate the very problems which exist in their group may lead to better self-insight. The key to good group morale is in the hands of the teacher. Whenever sociograms show an inordinate amount of rejection and group disintegration, the teacher needs to take account of his own teaching methods. Youngsters who are handled in a democratic fashion, who are challenged by significant problems, and who feel that they are making an important contribution to the class are most likely to have a high degree of group morale.

SUMMARY

The giving of standardized tests of many sorts has become an almost universal practice in the schools of this country. So far as many schools are concerned the giving of the tests constitutes an end in itself with little thought being given to the uses to which they may be put. Other schools use their test results, but commit serious errors in so doing.

Those who use tests for instructional and guidance purposes need to observe many precautions. In the first place the validity of any test used should be questioned. Is there evidence that the test measures what it purports to measure? Many tests on the market claim to measure certain important outcomes of education, but in reality appraise something quite different from that announced in their titles. A test of critical thinking, for example, should measure something other than general intelligence or reading ability. In the second place, the reliability of each test employed should be given careful scrutiny. Does the test give consistent results? A reading test which places a pupil at the fifth-grade level one day and at the seventh-grade level the next, is obviously very unreliable.

In this chapter numerous common uses and misuses of tests have been considered. Also included are detailed illustrations of specific help which teachers may obtain from diagnostic achievement tests and sociometric devices.

The perspectives of educators must go beyond the view of a test simply in terms of its accuracy or technical construction. Useful interpretations of test results depend not only upon the goodness of the test, but also upon a careful appraisal of the whole school program and of the children whom the test is supposed to measure. When teachers teach test items, or bring undue pressure to bear upon children's performance; or when schools have a large amount of retardation and elimination, the consequences are clearly mirrored in test results. In short, all testing must be viewed in its relation to the objectives, methods, and administrative policies of the school.

The modern teacher must know much about tests and instruments of appraisal if he is to succeed in his work. He must understand how tests can contribute to effective learning, and how they can point the way to satisfactory individual and group guidance. Testing devices in the hands of inexperienced or inadequately trained teachers may in many instances do much more harm than good. When cautiously and intelligently employed, however, many of the testing devices now available may become indispensable aids in teaching.

REFERENCES FOR FURTHER STUDY

Instead of listing all of the excellent articles in educational periodicals on tests and their uses, the writer recommends for this chapter that students obtain practice in locating these by using the *Education Index*. The following headings, taken from the *Education Index*, are illustrative of ones which merit exploration:

Attitudes, Tests and scales
Behavior, Tests and scales
Educational measurements
Evaluation
Higher education, evaluation
Intelligence
Intelligence quotient
Intelligence tests

Interest (psychology), Tests and scales
Personality tests
Practice teaching, evaluation
Prognosis of success
Psychological tests
Public schools, rating
Questionnaires

Readability tests
Reading, tests
Research, educational evaluation
Self appraisal
Social acceptability tests

Sociometry
Surveys
Testing programs
Tests and scales

Also see subhead, Tests and scales, under school subject, e.g., *Reading*, Tests and scales; *Music education*, Tests and scales; *Science*, Tests and scales.

The Index Numbers of *Psychological Abstracts*, December issues of each year, are excellent sources.

The *Encyclopedia of Educational Research*, (Walter Monroe, Editor, Revised Edition, New York, The Macmillan Company, 1950) represents a useful source of ideas and references on many problems related to diagnostic tools and their uses.

Cronbach, L. J., *Essentials of Psychological Testing*, New York, Harper & Brothers, 1949, Chapters 3, 16.

Cunningham, Ruth and others, *Understanding Group Behavior of Boys and Girls*, New York, Columbia University, Teachers College Bureau of Publications, 1951.

Greene, E. B., *Measurements of Human Behavior*, New York, The Odyssey Press, 1952, Chapters 12, 13, 14, 20, 21, 22.

Greene, H. A., Jorgensen, A. N., and Gerberich, J. R., *Measurement and Evaluation in the Secondary School*, New York, Longmans, Green and Company, 1943.

Lindquist, E. F., Editor, *Educational Measurement*, Washington, D. C., American Council on Education, 1951, Chapters 1, 2, 3, 4.

N.E.A., Association for Supervision and Curriculum Development, *Fostering Mental Health in Our Schools*, Washington 6, D. C., National Education Association, 1950, pp. 181–313.

Proctor, C. H. and C. P. Loomis, "Analysis of Sociometric Data," in Part II of *Research Methods in Social Relations*, S. W. Cook and others, New York, The Dryden Press, 1951, pp. 561–585.

Remmers, H. H. and N. L. Gage, *Educational Measurement and Evaluation*, New York, Harper & Brothers, 1943, Chapters 21, 22.

Smith, E. R. and others, *Appraising and Recording Student Progress*, New York, Harper & Brothers, 1942.

Simpson, Ray H., *Improving Teaching-Learning Processes*, New York, Longmans, Green and Company, 1953, Chapters 5, 7, 8, 12, 14.

Taba, Hilda and others, *Diagnosing Human Relations Needs*, Washington, D. C., American Council on Education, 1951.

Traxler, Arthur E. and others, *Introduction to Testing and the Use of Test Results in Public Schools*, New York, Harper & Brothers, 1953, Chapters 2, 3, 7, 8, 9, 10.

Chapter 19

Marking, Reporting, and Promoting

THE GIVING of school marks to pupils is a trying experience for many teachers. The writers have heard numerous teachers state that they would enjoy teaching if they did not have to make out and issue grades. Much of the difficulty is due to the fact that teachers are never quite sure what purpose the grades are supposed to serve, as is indicated by the following comments: "I gave John a low mark because he continually irritates me in class. . . ." "Jane doesn't learn much but she tries so hard I just can't discourage her by giving her a low mark." "Thorn almost always gets the highest score on the test, but since he never seems to do any work I feel guilty in giving him a high mark for doing no studying." Unfortunately, not only teachers but also pupils and parents are frequently confused about the meaning and uses of the marks and reports now being used.

The primary function of this chapter is to help the teacher and prospective teacher (1) understand the purposes which marks may serve, (2) perceive some of the major difficulties tied up with marking and reporting systems, (3) visualize some ways in which marking and reporting may be improved, and (4) consider the psychological factors related to promotion, a problem closely tied up with marks and reports.

If marking and reporting systems are to make a contribution to the work of the school, it is of utmost importance that a careful study be made of the possible purposes which they may serve. Due to differences in communities, in school systems, in backgrounds of pupils and teachers, as well as to other factors, a marking or reporting system that is extremely appropriate for one school system might be quite inappropriate for another system where the combination of factors is different. This means, in effect, that when one considers a desirable reporting system for a particular school or community, he must take into account the present level of development of those affected by the marking or reporting system. For example, a group of schools which has been experimenting with different marking and reporting systems might profit greatly from descriptive reports to students and parents in lieu of traditional letter grades. However, in a system where only letter grading has been used in the past, an abrupt change to descriptive reporting would probably be unwise. Parents, students, and teachers would all be accustomed to a certain type of marking and reporting, and it would seem to be sound in terms of readiness for those concerned to move gradually from the older system to the newer one. If changes are to be effective they cannot be imposed by administrative decision but should result from study of the problems by teachers, pupils, and parents.

There are various ways in which the purposes of marking or reporting systems might be considered. The organization in the following section of this chapter is based on the fact that marking is designed to serve particular individuals or specified groups. For example, a reporting system designed to inform parents about the school's objectives, activities, changes, and proposed changes has a decidedly different purpose from a system which aims only at informing parents about the relative standing of their son or daughter. Likewise, a mark indicating a learner's progress in relation to his ability has a quite different aim than a mark designed to show how a child's achievement compares with others. Consequently, marking purposes may be in conflict with each other. Those who get and use marks, if they are to use them intelligently, must recognize the aims of the system. Otherwise, marks intended to mean one thing by the maker may be misinterpreted to mean something quite different by the user.

HOW MARKS AND REPORTS MAY SERVE VARIOUS GROUPS

There are at least four groups whom marks and reports serve: pupils, teachers and administrators, parents, and employers. Variations in reporting to meet the needs of these groups will now be discussed.

Marks and Reports Serve the Student. Frequently the teacher's purpose in giving a mark to the pupil is simply to inform him of his status. Too often the instructor has in mind no planful procedure as to how youngsters can or should constructively use such information. There are several ways in which teachers, through marks, may impart information to pupils. One of the most common is to show the pupil his level of achievement, as compared with others in his class or with pupils who comprised the population used to standardize a test. For example, the mark may tell the pupil that he was in the lowest one-tenth of his class on a test in critical reading.

The mark may also show the youngster the amount of progress he has made in a designated period of time. The well-designed report card should, furthermore, make it possible to keep the pupil constantly informed about his progress in a wide variety of behaviors. If the child has improved in his ability to handle fractions, or in his skill in word attack, he should be made aware of this fact.

Reports of pupils' progress may be very brief and attempt to compress much information into a letter grade, or they may be general and cover a wide range of behaviors and attributes as is illustrated by the report form shown in Figure 22.

It will be noted in Figure 22 that the student and parent are given more diagnostic information than percentage or letter grades yield. It is also possible to see whether the teacher thinks there has been progress or lack of progress in each category from one quarter to the next.

The instructor may also attempt to communicate to the student his progress in relation to his estimated ability. For example, consider the following data on two students:

	IQ	Year's Progress in General Reading Ability
James	100	1.3 average grade levels
Robert	102	.5 average grade levels

A report on James might indicate satisfactory progress in general reading ability while the report for Robert might raise questions as to why he, with average ability, had apparently only made about half as much progress in this skill as does the average student. In giving such information to the student, the teacher must recognize

LAKEVIEW JR.-SR. HIGH SCHOOL
DECATUR, ILLINOIS
STUDENT PROGRESS REPORT
1951-1952 SCHOOL YEAR

STUDENT   COURSE

1 2 3 4
QR. QR. QR. QR.   **RESPECT FOR OTHERS**   INSTRUCTOR

Is very respectful and courteous.
Is usually polite to others.
Tries to be considerate and thoughtful, sometimes forgets.
Needs to show improvement.
Is impolite and inconsiderate.

SELF-DIRECTION

Demonstrates superior progress according to his ability.
Shows good progress.
Shows some improvement but is capable of doing better.
Is not working up to his capacity - needs to make more effort.
Makes little or no progress.

PARTICIPATION IN GROUP ACTIVITIES

Is eager to cooperate and works well with group.
Cooperates willingly in working with group.
Limits his participation in group activities.
Seldom cooperates or works with group.
Fails to accept necessary responsibilities.

COMMUNICATIONS

Expresses and shares worthwhile ideas in good form and interesting style.
Strives always for improvement.
Understands simple relationships between words and ideas.
Needs to overcome carelessness.
Has poor communications skills.

CARE OF MATERIALS AND EQUIPMENT

Has highest respect for materials and equipment.
Is usually respectful of materials and equipment.
Handles materials and equipment with reasonable care.
Is careless with materials and equipment.
Deliberately wastes and destroys materials and equipment.

KNOWLEDGE OF FACTS

Knowledge of facts consists of a student's understanding and mastery of the
subject matter as demonstrated by oral and written examinations

Ranks high scholastically.
Completes assignments accurately and on time.
Average scholastic ability.   Usually completes assignments.
Needs to make extra effort to progress.
Often fails, seldom completes assignments.

TOTAL DEVELOPMENT

Taking into consideration each of the above items, a definite level of progress
can be assigned the student as he adjusts himself to this particular course during
the past grading period.

Superior development.   **CREDIT GRANTED**
Above average development.
Average development.   Yes_____
Below average development.   No_____
Poorly Adjusted - failing.   Incomplete_____

FIGURE 22. Developmental Report Form Used by One High School.

that the figure on estimated ability is difficult to determine with great accuracy. Intelligence tests, measures of socioeconomic background, measures of amount of time the pupil spends in school, and other similar factors will give some basis for helping the teacher determine what might be reasonably expected of a particular learner.

Marks as motivators of learning. Teachers often use marks or reports in an effort to stimulate the learner to improve his work. A very common but questionable practice from a psychological standpoint is to punish, discipline, or penalize the learner by giving him poor grades for past mistakes. Such a procedure has to be used on the assumption that the pupil will work harder when his past failures are emphasized. But such an assumption is not warranted by existing evidence.

In an experiment by Sears,[1] the work of subjects who experienced continuous failure steadily deteriorated while a group with success experiences made steady and persistent gains. This type of experiment throws much doubt on the belief frequently held by teachers that continuously failing a student will improve his learning.

In the hands of some teachers, a red pencil becomes a whiplash used to keep pupils tractable, docile, or "in line." Low grades are often a last ditch attempt at motivation. When marks are used as threats, they typically indicate a failure by the instructor to help the pupil see basic or intrinsic values he may obtain from his work. Marks used in this fashion are usually found in autocratically controlled classrooms.

A much more defensible use of grades for motivating pupils is one in which the teacher capitalizes on the diagnostic values of marks by guiding the pupil to see his own strengths and weaknesses. The goal of such a diagnosis will be to stimulate future study through helping the learner identify behaviors needing improvement. To be effective, this type of reporting needs to be rather specific. For example, it probably is not very helpful to the pupil for the teacher to indicate a weakness in sportsmanship. On the other hand, if the teacher can indicate those behavioral aspects of sportsmanship in which the learner is strong and those in which he is weak, there will be a better basis for the learner to plan activities, to capitalize on the strengths, and to eliminate the weaknesses. The following are illustrations of behaviors which might be given attention under the heading of sportsmanship: To what extent (1) does the pupil observe game rules? (2) is he a good loser? (3) does he treat visiting players and officials with respect? Generally, when the diagnostic function is uppermost in the mind of the teacher, he will attempt to maintain a balance in emphasis between the weak and strong points

[1] R. R. Sears, "Initiation of the Repression Sequence by Experienced Failure," *Journal of Experimental Psychology,* Vol. 20, 1937, pp. 570–580.

of individual pupils. Excessive emphasis on weaknesses may lead to discouragement, and continued failure will result. Conversely, excessive emphasis on an individual's strong points may either lead to self-complacency, or give him little indication of where self-improvement is needed. When detailed diagnostic information is emphasized in a reporting system, it may be said to be *future oriented*. When the emphasis is on punishment, discipline, or penalties, the system is *past oriented*.

When pupils are encouraged to see report cards or progress reports as diagnostic aids for learning they are likely to develop desirable self-evaluative abilities. Hence, marking and reporting usually need to be related to goals which pupils have helped to set for themselves.

Giving the student practice in reporting his own progress. Some teachers have thought of reporting functions as the exclusive responsibility of the teacher. However, in some schools students have also been given certain opportunities and responsibilities for recording and reporting their own progress. Following are excerpts from a weekly report which was written by Frank, a pupil in a ninth-grade mathematics class:

During the past week I have been working on the values and costs of different kinds of car insurance. Since I completed driver's training last semester Mr. Hall (the mathematics teacher) and I together decided this would be a good math problem for me to tackle. . . .

In addition to doing quite a bit of figuring this week I have learned such things as the following: My dad's insurance policy is no good if I am driving. This must be changed right away even if I have to use some of the money I made setting pins (in the bowling alley) to pay the extra amount. A $50 deductible policy now means something to me. Some states require every driver to have insurance. . . .

I find I need more practice in doing percentages and must give more study to the different kinds of insurance policies and their purposes. Next week I want to do some figuring on car maintenance, depreciation, trade in values of various makes, miles per gallon of various makes in town and in country driving. . . . Over the week end I must try to get dad in a good humor and then get him to see the local agent about changing our car policy so I can drive! This report should pave the way.

Reports of this sort have several values. They give the student practice in writing on subjects of concern to him. They give parents some picture of what the child and the school are trying to do. They can improve public relations and they can easily be included in the pupil's permanent record. Perhaps even more important, they can help the youngster assume additional responsibility for his own learning. They give both the pupil and the teacher a basis for evaluating past work and for planning future work. Pupils' goals and purposes tend to become clear. These goals, when defined and more clearly structured, form a basis for future educational, vocational, and recreational activities.

When a youngster is encouraged to take a hand in recording his own progress and appraising his own work, his personal adjustment is likely to be improved. For example, if he is having difficulties in inter-personal relations, his troubles may be alleviated by writing a description of the situation as he sees it. He may also try to indicate what types of things he might consider doing to improve the situation. The self report also gives him practice in verbalizing his difficulties and in expressing them in such a way that others may give him help.

Marks and Reports Serve Teachers and Administrators. Teachers sometimes use marking and reporting to make life easier for themselves. In some cases, grades or unfavorable reports are used to purge pupils who are difficult to handle. Some teachers feel that unless a student is docile in obeying without question their directions, he should not receive a high mark. From a psychological standpoint, a use of marking for the convenience of the teacher is extremely questionable if not actually dangerous.

One of the writers recently visited a large Midwestern high school to talk with a principal about his school problems. During the conversation, the principal proudly drew from his desk a report which he was just getting ready to submit to the school board. This document gave the name of each teacher, the subject he taught, the percentage of pupils in his course who "passed" the subject for the semester just closed, and the percentage who "failed." He commented regarding three algebra teachers who were listed. The first teacher, a Miss Olson, had "failed" 53 per cent of her pupils. He remarked that she was a fine teacher—one with high standards. The second, a Miss Burnham, had failed only 26 per cent of the members of her class. He noted that she was also quite acceptable. The third teacher, Mr. Brownfield, however, was not held in high repute! The principal pointed to the fact that he had only "flunked" 8 per cent of his algebra pupils. He stated that nearly any pupil could pass his course. In general, the principal was proud of his teaching staff because they maintained one of the highest records of "washing out" students to be found anywhere in the state.

An extremely high percentage of failures in a class can usually be traced to one or more of the following causes: (1) improper placement of pupils in the class in the first place, (2) inappropriate course content for individual students, (3) unsound standards or goals which take no account of individual differences, and (4) poor teaching. The reader will note that each of these four contributing causes of failure is primarily if not entirely in the hands of the teacher or school.

At times teachers boastfully may use marks as indicators of their own teaching ability. Sometimes there is overemphasis on pencil and paper tests and little concern for individual needs, goals, and important skills not easily measured by current tests. It should be emphasized that grades in such a situation indicate how well the learner did in relation to teacher-structured assignments. The mark or report frequently does not indicate how well the pupil could do if he were ego involved. Unknown under these circumstances is the level which might be achieved if the student were permitted to have a considerable share in setting up his study goals and those of the class and in helping to plan activities needed to achieve these goals.

Administrators or teachers sometimes use grades to determine the eligibility of students for sports, musical activities, other extracurricular activities, the honor roll, or an honor society. When so used care must be taken lest the pupil be excluded from activities in which he can succeed in school. Forcing a pupil to spend all of his time on activities in which success is unlikely may cause him to leave school, or result in other adverse effects.

Potentially, one of the most valuable, but frequently overlooked, uses of marks is that of helping the teacher evaluate his own work, his strengths and weaknesses. For example, the teacher might find that pupils did well on certain individual tests, but rather poorly in group discussion or in other group activities. Such information might well constitute a challenge which would lead to systematic study by the teacher. If this value is to be achieved marks must be based on rather detailed analysis of various aspects of student behavior.

Some schools have successfully used reports as a means of getting parents' reactions and involvement in the schools' work. Where this is done, the reporting system is thought of as a *two-way* reporting or communication system rather than the more common *one-way* school to home system.

In the Cincinnati School system a two-way report card was made available in 1949.[2] The form, a 4″ x 6″ sheet, has the following note to parents:

> "*To Parents:* We hope the information below will be of value to you. We in turn shall be pleased if you will let us know any information which can be used in helping your child get the most out of school."

There is a space below this printed explanation for teachers and principals to report information on the pupil's school progress. The form is intended as a supplement to the report card to be used as needed for reporting information for which there is no provision on the report card.

The reverse side of the sheet is for parents' replies. It states:

> "*To Parents:* Please use this side for sending any information or suggestion which you believe would be helpful. (If you think it would be helpful for us to talk together, we shall be glad to arrange a time that will be convenient to both of us.)"

This printed matter is followed by space which can be used by parents. The form can be inserted in the regular report card or may be sent separately. It was developed by the Report Card Committee.

Where the two-way communication system is established, an attempt is made to get parents to write their reactions to either the behavior of their child or to the goals and activities which are a part of the school. The reactions of parents are considered a key factor which the teachers need to take into account in deciding what will be done in school. For example, if parental reports indicate that a high school student is expected to give much help in supporting the family, it is questionable whether he should be expected to do as much homework as another youngster who has no such obligation. Two-way communication may also give the teachers a picture of how parents are reacting to school programs and may facilitate such things as building bond issues, salary increases, and other

---

[2] *The Elementary School Journal*, "Two-Way Report Card," Vol. 49, March, 1949, pp. 375–376.

forms of community support which will increase the school's facilities.

Marks and Reports Serve Parents. Good reporting practices should improve relations between the school and the home. The effective report will not only show a youngster's status and progress but should also attempt to show changing school goals, procedures, and techniques. Such things as new methods, revised grouping procedures, or reasons for using various texts may be explained through the reporting system. Through such school reporting it is also possible to emphasize school needs in terms of personnel, salaries, equipment, and school buildings. Such a continuous interpretation going to the home provides parents some evidence which can be used in evaluating the work of the school and tends to promote more sympathetic attitudes on the part of parents.

In some schools letters from the teacher to the parent make up for some of the deficiencies of older report forms. The following two letters were sent to the mother of a shy first grader who found it hard at first to make friends and who was not ready for book reading until the middle of the year.[3] The first letter was mailed to Mrs. Harris in November, and the second followed in February of the same school year.

Dear Mrs. Harris,

You may remember at our mothers' meeting in September, it was explained that instead of report cards our school sent letters to tell parents of their children's progress in school. We believe we can give you more information about Roy in this way.

When Roy started to school in September he had the problem, like the rest of the children, of adjusting himself to a large group of children, and of making friends. This was hard for Roy to do, for he is naturally a quiet boy. He and John Miller have struck up a friendship which seems to give both of them satisfaction and which I believe should be encouraged.

Roy worries a great deal about whether or not he is doing a job exactly right. Many young children have similar worries, but I think there are things you and I might plan that would help Roy gain confidence in himself more quickly. Can you come in soon for a conference where we might talk over the problem?

Because of the many adjustments Roy is having to make, I am being careful not to push skills at him too fast. Now that he is feeling more at

[3] C. B. Stendler, "Revising Our Report Cards," *Illinois Education*, Vol. 35, 1947, p. 184.

home in school, he is beginning to enjoy reading. He likes listening to stories, he goes of his own accord to the library table to look at books, he reads labels, signs, and directions we have up in the room. This is satisfactory progress for Roy.

Writing is coming slowly. It is hard for his muscles and for his nervous system to do fine work; so I am not encouraging him to do much writing at present. In a few months co-ordination will be easier.

Roy gets real satisfaction out of our trips and they are helping to make him feel comfortable in the group. Last week he took charge of one of our new boys when we went out and did it very nicely. He enjoys the paints, clay, and wood he has had a chance to use, and these are helping him to express himself freely.

Dr. Wood's report on Roy's physical examination will be sent you separately.

Sincerely,

Adele Woodward

Dear Mrs. Harris,

I am very glad to be able to report that since our conference Roy is much improved in his work habits. He is able to tackle a job independently and no longer feels that he has to ask for my approval at every step of the way. I am sure the added responsibilities and approval you have been giving him at home have helped a good deal. Roy has told us about them and is very proud of his accomplishments.

Roy started reading from books early in January and is moving along at a very satisfactory pace. He has read the best parts of one pre-primer and is starting on a second. He tries to sound out new words for himself and knows many of the beginning sounds. The little words like 'was,' 'were,' 'which,' etc., still give him trouble, but these are often the hardest words for children and will come in time.

I am sure you are as pleased as I with Roy's progress in writing. Do you remember his scrawl in October? He is still writing very large and should for another month or so.

Roy tells time very accurately. He counts by rote, but counting real objects is hard for him. He needs to develop a feeling for number by having many experiences with it. Can he do some shopping for you and count change, etc.?

Please feel free to come in and see me at any time. You can make an appointment through Roy.

Sincerely,

Adele Woodward

The writing of meaningful reports takes time. Some procedure such as liberal use of special or helper teachers, or freeing the teacher two afternoons a month, should be worked out so that report writing can be done under optimal circumstances. Unless time is allotted for the writing, the reports are likely to become so general as to be meaningless.

Reports as suggested by the two letters to Mrs. Harris may also be used as a basis for parent-teacher conferences about the child's progress, difficulties, and needs. Consideration of the desirability of the child's promotion, retention, or acceleration may also be taken up in such conferences.

When a detailed report of a pupil's behavior is given, information should be of such a nature that it helps the parent assess strengths and weaknesses of his child. This can facilitate appropriate child guidance at home. Indications of specific ways in which the parent can help the child are also desirable. Some schools attempt to use the reporting system as a motivational lever for the parent. Generally speaking, the goal here is to provide the parent with a basis for giving guidance to his youngster. Appropriate information might help the parent answer such questions as the following: In what subjects has the child shown a particular interest? What are occupational areas for which the child probably has particular aptitude? Should the boy or girl go to college? If so, to what kind of college? If he goes to college, what course of study would it probably be desirable for him to consider taking?

Marks and Reports Serve Employers. Although not so utilized in many schools, marking and reporting systems may aid employers in getting the type of employee which will be suited to the job. Such a service may not only help the employer but can also improve a pupil's motivation by calling his attention to factors of significance in preparing for employment. Attention to employer needs may also aid the broader social group of which both the employer and the school are a part by economically and wisely matching individuals to jobs which are available.

There are several types of information that employers usually are interested in obtaining. Following is a list of students' traits which are of concern to employers: [4]

[4] This list is a composite derived from data supplied by several placement agencies.

Scholastic average
Initiative
Dependability
Speaking ability
Writing ability
Ability to work with others

Extracurricular activities
Part-time work experience
Grooming
Promptness
Emotional stability

The student who knows that employers may have access to his records and will consider things such as those listed will sometimes develop increased concern for his progress in school.

MAJOR DIFFICULTIES IN MARKING AND REPORTING SYSTEMS

As has been emphasized in the earlier pages of this chapter, one of the greatest weaknesses of present marking systems is their failure to be sufficiently diagnostic. The omnibus letter grade still plagues many school systems. For example, in a school system where the five-letter marking system is used (A, B, C, D, E) a student in English may have an A in oral expression and an E in written composition. A second student may have an E in oral expression and an A in written composition. If a teacher attempts to give a mark indicating the status of these two learners in English expression, the mark for each might be C. Obviously, this type of compromise, in attempting to describe different things with the same mark is most unsatisfactory.

Improvement in marking and reporting systems is difficult because of the hold which tradition has upon teachers, pupils, and parents. While many teachers feel that they would like to have improved marking and reporting systems, they maintain, sometimes with justification, that it is extremely difficult to change because parents and other teachers are not in sympathy with any type of change.

The hold of tradition is further illustrated by the attitude on the part of many parents, and even teachers, that there is some magic, in terms of passing or failing, about a score of 70 or 80 per cent right on a test. Those suffering under such a delusion certainly have not clearly analyzed the fact that a teacher can make a test on which no pupil will make more than 70 per cent correct. And the same teacher can make another test for the same group of learners in which all students will make more than 70 per cent correct on the particular test. The idea of a fixed yardstick or absolute measure for marking purposes disregards the essential fact that marks always depend to a high degree upon subjective factors such as the types of questions which the teacher constructs, the areas covered by the questions, the difficulty of the questions, and the directions given to learners prior to and while taking the test. These are but a few of the subjective factors which influence the eventual numerical score which the pupil gets.

Marks frequently are not adjusted to individual differences in needs, abilities, and goals. Sometimes the teacher's goals and standards are based largely upon his own experience in school. A high-school instructor, for example, may base the standard of achievement he expects in a particular class upon what he himself could do without too much difficulty when in high school. Such a point of view was expressed by one teacher who said: "Well, I didn't have any trouble doing that in high school. I didn't have to work overly hard. It's plain that 60 or 70 per cent of my students are just plain lazy. If they would get down to work and really tackle these problems, they would not have difficulty. Consequently, I am justified in giving them failing marks." Since most teachers were undoubtedly superior pupils when in school and differed in many other important respects from many of the pupils they teach, the practice just described is clearly most unrealistic.

The unreliability of teachers' marks on examinations is well known. In classic experiments conducted by Starch and Elliott, two final examination papers for ninth-grade English were graded independently by 142 English teachers. On the first paper marks ranged from 64 to 98 with a total of nine grades above 95 and five grades below 75. On the second paper there were eight marks above 90 and fourteen marks below 70. The range on the second paper was from 98 down to 50. Using a somewhat similar approach, grades on a final examination paper in geometry marked by 114 mathematics teachers ranged from a high of 92 to a low of 28. The latter is particularly significant in view of the fact that one might expect that papers in mathematics could be marked with precision. Marks on a history examination treated in a similar fashion and scored by seventy history teachers ranged from 43 to 90.[5] More recent experiments on mark-

---

[5] D. Starch, *Educational Psychology,* New York, The Macmillan Company, 1924, Chap. 22.

ing have tended to support the conclusion that teachers' grades are extremely unreliable.[6]

It must be recognized that the great emphasis upon marks has focused attention upon extrinsic values in which pupils are much more concerned about labels [7] put upon learning rather than upon the real values of the course. Thus, one of the pressing problems educators face in attempting to study marking and reporting systems is how to swing the attention of the learner away from the symbols represented by marks and toward the intrinsic values and achievements which can be obtained from his schooling.

Finally, a major criticism that can be directed toward present marking and reporting systems is that they result in a large number of emotional upsets on the part of pupils. According to research studies [8] fear does not seem to be a particularly desirable motivating device and yet in too many school systems the student is plagued continually with failure or the fear of failure. This excessive strain militates against educational effectiveness. The emotional atmosphere which surrounds examinations, marks, and reporting has tended to upset many students and make them nervous. If the emotional tension thus induced led to improved learning, it might be justified. But the evidence seems to be that anxiety is likely to produce just the opposite results. Pupils are encouraged to try to get by, to see if they can fool the teacher, and to worry over past experiences in connection with marks rather than to plan intelligently for future improvement in learning and evaluative activities. If marks produce many emotional disturbances, and the evidence seems to be that they do, then it would appear that attention should be given by teachers, administrators, and students to ways of eliminating these undesirable concomitants which sometimes accompany marking and reporting.

IMPROVING MARKING AND REPORTING PRACTICES

Marking and reporting are integral parts of the total instructional process. They not only reflect what teachers consider important but

[6] P. Hartog and E. C. Rhodes, *An Examination of Examinations,* London, Macmillan and Company, Limited, 1935; A. E. Traxler, "Note on the Accuracy of Teachers' Scoring on Semi-Objective Tests," *Journal of Educational Research,* Vol. 37, 1943, pp. 212–213.

[7] Such as marks, awards, stars, ribbons, and honor lists.

[8] For example, see R. R. Sears, "Initiation of the Repression Sequence by Experienced Failure," *Journal of Experimental Psychology,* Vol. 20, 1937, pp. 570–580.

also direct the activities of students. More specifically, school and course purposes tend to be reflected in the type of marking and reporting practices which are used. Such practices also are likely to reflect the amount of attention or lack of attention given to individual differences. The clarity with which the instructor has thought through his goals in a particular course is likely to be shown by the report or record of progress. For example, if a report card only contains spaces for letter grades in academic subjects this would appear to indicate that the school's objectives are very limited in scope. On the other hand, if space is provided for evaluating such behaviors as critical thinking, social adjustment, and study habits, it is evident that the school is concerned with a much broader set of objectives.

In the past too much attention has been given to grades and report cards as instruments for looking at the present status of the pupil rather than as ways of influencing his behavior in the future. Suppose a superior pupil gets A grades without very much work. Another student gets D's or F's after hard work. The first youngster soon acquires the idea that he can get good marks without work. The second child is likely to develop an attitude of defeatism, that even with hard work it is impossible for him to get recognition. Obviously neither situation is desirable. Whatever marks are used or grades given, they should serve to encourage the child to work better in the future rather than to discourage him and force him into repeated failure.

Attention should be given to such factors as the student's capacity to learn, his attitudes, his purposes, his readiness for a particular kind of activity, and his probable needs in connection with the area being studied. A major number of marking difficulties would be resolved if both teaching and marking took account of individual differences. An illustration of a report which attempts to present much individual diagnostic information to youngsters and their parents is shown in Figure 23. This figure which is presented on pages 500–501 shows the general section of the student report form used at the University High School, University of Illinois. This general section is used in all courses which a student takes.

In this school the reporting system has been carefully studied and the part of the report shown in Fig. 23, plus other parts which relate only to specific subjects, have been developed. Those now using the report forms in their present stage of development feel that they do not represent an ultimate "best" report. However, the forms are an improvement over conventional report cards and are so designed that further innovations and improvements can be made.

In addition to the general report shown in Figure 23, each course has a special page on which the teacher appraises the student on items specific to such subjects as English, science, and mathematics. For example, in English the teacher in addition to filling out the general section shown in Figure 23 also rates each youngster on such factors as reading, writing, reporting (speaking and listening), and sense of achievement. One of the forms used for such rating is shown in the scale below:

Writing

| Needs improvement in mechanics, organization, style, form, handwriting, spelling, vocabulary, punctuation. | Adequate in use of mechanics, organization, style, form, handwriting, spelling, vocabulary, punctuation. | Uses the following well: mechanics, organization, style, form, handwriting, vocabulary, punctuation. | Writes with clarity, logical organization of thought, appropriate style and mechanics. |

The teacher using the form can check and/or cross out items to give a diagnostic picture to the student.

In science one of the goals and the form used to aid in evaluating this goal follows:

Scientific Attitude

| Show little or no curiosity; fails to question what he reads or hears. Is willing to make decisions without sufficient evidence. | Shows some curiosity; should show more initiative and originality; should seek more information on his own. | Shows active curiosity, keen observation and critical evaluation of materials. Bases statements and conclusions on sufficient evidence. |

In addition the University High School report form takes into account the need, primarily for guidance purposes, of some prediction of future academic success in each field and of out-of-school applications of course skills and knowledge. Each course report also contains the following:

NOTE: The following evaluations, based upon the objectives of this course, are predictions of (A) the student's success in further academic work in the area and/or (B) his application of the skills and knowledge gained in this course to life situations:

(A)	(B)
__6 With distinction	__6 Shows deep understanding and makes wide application
__5 Very well	
__4 Fairly well	__5 Makes wide application
__3 With average grade	__4 Can use adequately in real situation
__2 With passing grade only	
__1 Present knowledge inadequate for success in next advanced course	__3 Can use to a limited degree
	__2 Can use only rudimentary learnings
__0 No basis for judgment	__1 Unable to apply in practice
	__0 No basis for judgment

To be completed at close of course (and at close of seventh semester):

Credit granted for college entrance: Yes__ No__   Credit granted for high school graduation: Yes__ No__

COMMENTS:

Descriptive marking and reporting help the student see the intrinsic values of the material being learned. When marking and reporting systems become more diagnostic they also tend to emphasize meaningful situations and goals for the individual pupil. Increasingly, diagnostic descriptions in marking and reporting are likely to decrease the emphasis upon grades *per se* and increase the emphasis upon learning for intrinsic values and for the improvement and self-satisfaction that can be attained through study.

Real improvement in a school's marking and reporting program requires that teachers join efforts to study the program intensively. For example, if teachers decide that more attention should be given to pupils' social development, a study should be made of the behavioral characteristics which indicate desirable or undesirable social development. Next, pupils and teachers should work together in determining specific goals in this area. Plans can then be made for teachers and pupils to report progress toward the achievement of these goals.

One of the major sources of help in improving marking and reporting practices, which has been relatively little utilized in most schools, is the enlistment of the help of pupils. Youngsters can cooperate not only in helping to set up goals but can also assist in measuring and reporting progress toward these goals. Pupils can be helped to see how the achievement of the goals will help them individually, and they can also be aided in setting up check lists and other types of measurements for determining the extent to which their own goals are being achieved. Such practice helps the learner to appreciate what is being attempted in the school and in the particular class. It also teaches him to do the types of things that he needs to know how to do if he is to continue systematic learning after school is over.

Such self-progress reports also give tangible bases for reviewing and evaluating what has been done in past school activities, and such evaluation can form a basis for a realistic planning of future activities upon the part of both the student and the learning groups of which individual students are a part. If teachers try to monopolize reporting and evaluative activities, it is doubtful whether major improvements can be made in marking and reporting systems. On the other hand, if teachers are willing to work with the students and train them in diagnosing their own needs, in keeping a record of progress that they have made toward these goals, and in planning future work on the basis of descriptions of what has been done in the past, then we can be optimistic about the amount of improvement which can be expected in current marking and reporting systems.[9]

The only time some parents see the teacher is when he is explaining a misbehavior or a low grade. This is unfortunate. Marking and reporting systems can be improved in most communities if individual teachers and administrators talk with parents *before* undesirable incidents occur. Such conferences establish desirable rapport with those in the home. They develop good public relations and tend to pave the way for less pleasant conferences, if needed, when the child is having some kind of difficulty. Parent-teacher conferences and home visits are costly in terms of teachers' time. Sometimes a good number of visits may be justified, but the administrator or committee of teachers who is planning such visits should attempt to have them scheduled during the teacher's working day rather than during nonworking hours.[10]

[9] For example, see W. Wallace, J. Chreitzberg, V. M. Sims, *The Story of Holtville*, Deatsville, Alabama, Holtville High School, 1946, pp. 63–65, 74–83.

[10] For a description of a way of conducting parent-teacher conferences see T. K. Muellen, "A Means to an End," *Education Digest*, Vol. 17, 1951, pp. 28–30.

As indicated before, the "report card" can be improved if a space is given for parents' comments. If such has not been done before in a community, it would be desirable to educate parents as to uses that might be made of such a space. One way of doing this is through mass guidance sessions with parents. In these sessions teachers can indicate to parents types of comments which would facilitate the

---

UNIVERSITY HIGH SCHOOL   URBANA, ILLINOIS

STUDENT PROGRESS REPORT

Student _____   Subject _____

Teacher _____   Grade Period Ending _____

NOTE: The statements checked below are descriptions of the student's performance based upon the teacher's judgment of this student's capabilities as well as what is usually expected of students of his grade.

CONCERN FOR OTHERS

___Needs to improve his tolerance of others.

___Needs to improve his tolerance of others outside his own group.

___His concern for others is evident but not consistent.

___He usually shows unselfish concern for the welfare of others.

WRITTEN AND ORAL EXPRESSION

___Content incomplete and inaccurate. Writes, speaks with poor mechanical skills.

___Minimum content acceptable. Writes, speaks with minimum acceptable skill.

___Content usually complete. Organization and presentation of oral, written work good.

___Content excellent. Writes, speaks with clarity, logical organization, and appropriate style.

LEARNING TO THINK

___Fails to recognize and define problems; makes little or no use of available resources; observations inaccurate or misinterpreted; seldom evaluates progress of his work.

___Without supervision, experiences difficulty in recognizing and defining

FIGURE 23. General Section

work of teachers in helping their children. Another way to encourage such parent comment is to have on the report card specific questions which each parent may be asked to answer. Short answers to such questions can lead into more extensive comments on the part of parents and gradually develop into a two-way communication system.

---

problem, organizing work from available resources, making careful and accurate observations and critically evaluating progress of his work.

___Recognizes and defines problems, organizes work from available resources, makes careful and accurate observations, critically evaluates progress of his work.

STUDY HABITS

___Has much difficulty in notetaking and locating materials. Wastes time, needs constant supervision. More careful and complete preparation needed.

___Finds materials and takes adequate notes. Is inconsistent in using time profitably. Makes careful, complete preparation regularly with considerable self direction.

___Uses ingenuity in finding materials. Needs minimum of supervision. Makes excellent preparations which go beyond the required work.

CLASS PARTICIPATION

___Needs to contribute more to class activities. Frequently disturbs class activities.

___Is inconsistent in contributions to class. Makes hasty irrelevant remarks. Interrupts others.

___He takes an active part in class but sometimes monopolizes or objects to opposition to his point of view.

___Makes sound intelligent contributions to class activities.

ACQUISITION OF FACTUAL KNOWLEDGE

___Retains inadequate factual knowledge from lectures, discussions, texts, outside materials.

___Usually tends to memorize assignments with no clear idea of relationships among facts.

___Has good factual understanding. Usually sees relationships.

___Makes sound conclusions from broad knowledge of facts.

of a Student Progress Report.

Schools need to educate the public about school and course purposes and how particular marking and reporting systems are designed to help the individual child. Obviously each parent is interested in the welfare of his own child. If he can be shown how a particular system will help his child, he should be in a better frame of mind to reveal his reactions and to cooperate with the school. If the mark is designed to indicate progress of the individual child in relation to his ability, then both parent and learner should be conscious of this and not misinterpret the mark. Unless such steps are taken many parents are likely to think that the mark represents the standing of the learner in relation to other learners in his class. If the latter mistake occurs, then the report on a relatively slow learner who does well in terms of his ability may give his parents the impression that he has the ability to become a doctor or to enter some other professional occupation. Actually the mark may simply indicate that this learner is doing well in terms of what seems to be his potential ability. To mark in relation to ability seems to be desirable from many standpoints, but it may have undesirable repercussions if both parents and the learner himself are not clear as to what purpose the mark is designed to serve. In some reports both status and progress in relation to ability are shown on the report. Status marks, indicative of educational achievements and sometimes based largely upon standardized tests, can be extremely valuable when parents and teachers are trying to help the pupil decide what his future educational plans will be.

Rapid changes in reporting practices can be made if appropriate public education is carried on before, during, and subsequent to the changes. For example, in one school system [11] teachers and administrators decided that trying out a new card in only one grade at first and using it in an additional grade each year would only give the opponents of change more ammunition to block progress. School leaders reasoned that in many homes both the new and the old cards would be arriving simultaneously and this, it was believed, would make public acceptance of the revised reports more difficult. Acceptance of the new reporting system was promoted through the school board, PTA meetings, parent-teacher conferences, and bulletins answering parents' questions. The emphasis in

[11] Walter Crewson, "Boldness Sells Hamilton's New-Type Report Card," *The Clearing House*, Vol. 26, November, 1951, pp. 146–148.

the discussions was on ways in which the new reporting system helped parent and child more than the old.

When individual instructors or teacher committees wish to study and improve a marking and reporting system, a set of evaluative criteria is sometimes a helpful starting device. An illustrative set of criteria for doing this has been drawn up by the writer.

1. Does the system clearly reflect the specific educational objectives of teachers and learners?
2. Does the current system represent an improvement over the one(s) used in the last few years?
3. Have both students and parents helped to formulate the present system?
4. Is the reporting procedure a two-way communication system (school to home, home to school)?
5. Does the system put emphasis upon areas for future development of the student rather than on errors of the past?
6. Is sufficient working time given teachers for adequate marking or reporting in the system currently being used?
7. Is the behavior of learners desirably affected by the system?
8. Does the marking and reporting system put sufficient emphasis on social and emotional development?
9. Are the specific purposes which the system is designed to serve clearly understood by those affected (i.e., pupils, parents) by the marking and reporting?
10. Does the system give sufficient attention to *ways* the student is learning as well as to what he has learned?
11. Does the system encourage thinking rather than memorization?
12. Are the marks and reports sufficiently diagnostic in nature?
13. Are the differences among individual students in purposes, abilities, and needs adequately handled by the system?
14. Does the marking and reporting system tend to encourage learners to overcome weaknesses rather than discourage added effort?
15. When weaknesses of the learner are stated, are they accompanied by suggested ways of improving?
16. Does the system help the student plan for future vocational activities?
17. Does the system promote self-evaluation on the part of the student?
18. Does the marking and reporting system promote desirable public relations?

FACTORS OF IMPORTANCE IN PROMOTION

As a general policy it is well to keep in mind that promotion should be thought of as placement rather than as punishment or reward. Before judgments are made regarding promotion such questions as the following should be raised: What promotion decision is likely to be best for the individual student, taking into account all significant factors in the situation? With what placement is the student likely to learn most profitably in the next year? How is this placement likely to affect other pupils? How are teachers likely to react to a particular placement? What will be the probable reaction of parents?

The child's attitude toward retention, promotion, or double promotion is of utmost importance. The possibility, of course, should be kept in mind that the child's attitude can be changed. If steps are taken sufficiently early the child will sometimes see that being retained is actually the best thing for him, and he may accept this as being quite desirable. On the other hand, if pupils have been trained to think of lack of promotion as a stigma, it is difficult to use this placement policy without modifying their attitudes. When it appears desirable to retain a pupil, groundwork for retention must be laid through conferences with him. Too great attention cannot be given to the morale of the learner. "Nothing fails like failure," and certainly if the child believes that his placement is an indication of failure he is not in a very good mental state to carry on learning activities profitably in a subsequent year.

Although the effect of each of the various alternatives in connection with promotion upon the individual learner is unquestionably of primary importance, attention must always be given to the likely effect of the placement of a particular learner upon other students. If pupils have been taught that the youngsters in a particular class should reach the same standards regardless of ability, they may feel that promotion of a particular child is a compromise with the "standards" of the school. If the school seriously attempts to base promotion policies upon good placement practices for learning purposes, then pupils must be helped to understand this policy.

The probable effect of promotion, retention, or acceleration upon each teacher with whom the pupil might be placed also demands serious consideration. This must be done because the new teacher can "make or break" the child. If an instructor is likely to be irritated or to react adversely to the placement of the learner, then the latter is placed in an extremely difficult position and successful learning is not likely to ensue.

In considering promotion alternatives this question must be faced: If a below-average child is promoted does the prospective teacher's method provide for individual differences? If a sixth-grade teacher, for example, expects all learners to read the same text regardless of the fact that reading ability is likely to range from average second-grade level to average tenth-grade level, a sound promotion policy for the fifth-grade English teacher becomes very difficult. On the other hand, the problem becomes easier if the fifth-grade teacher knows that the sixth-grade teacher not only recognizes individual differences but is able to a considerable degree to meet these in such activities as assignment making, standard setting, testing, and use of resources. Similar considerations need to be kept in mind when a given child is retained for two years in one grade. A realistic promotion policy must always take into account the fact that there are great variations among teachers in their ability to operate classes in terms of individual differences.

How is "passing" a course or grade likely to be interpreted by administrative officials? Will they conclude that passing a particular course or grade implies achievement of a particular standard? The attitudes of administrative officials and department heads are of significance in deciding on promotion or retention of a particular learner.

What are likely to be parental attitudes toward promotional practices in general? What are likely to be particular parents' reactions toward the promotion or retention of their child? These are types of questions which finally need to be considered. It should be kept in mind of course that parental attitude toward promotion and toward the possible stigma of nonpromotion can be definitely altered if the school starts soon enough and has a desirable type of communication with parents. Obviously parents are primarily concerned about the welfare and growth of their children and can usually be helped to see and approve of an appropriate promotion policy if parental education on this point starts when Johnny enters school.

In conclusion it should be stated that there is no easy answer to the question of whether a pupil should be retained, promoted, or accelerated. Each individual case must be handled on its own merits. All relevant factors should be considered, and then an attempt should be made to place the learner where he is likely to get the most out of his schooling. The important consideration is not promotion or nonpromotion as such, but rather what is done with individual pupils in the classes where they find themselves.

SUMMARY

There is a great deal of confusion about the aims and values of various marking and reporting practices. Much of the confusion stems from a failure to realize that marks and reports can serve various groups such as children, parents, teachers and employers in different ways. The values one group may hope to secure from marks and reports may conflict with those desired by another group. Hence clarity of purpose in using these evaluative devices in particular situations is a consideration of utmost importance.

Marks may militate against desirable educational activities if used for unsound purposes. For example, when marks and reports are used to punish a child for misbehavior, to make the life of an harassed teacher easier, and to help teacher and pupil escape from serious consideration of the intrinsic values of courses, they are likely to be harmful. On the other hand if grading and reporting procedures are used to orient future work, to give youngsters practice in evaluating and expressing themselves, to establish two-way communication with parents, to individualize goals and procedures, and to focus attention on significant intrinsic values of courses, they can be extremely valuable.

Promotion policies should be designed to place the pupil in the class or grade that will be best for him rather than to punish or reward him for past activities. In deciding on promotion for a particular pupil the emphasis should be upon looking forward rather than backward.

REFERENCES FOR FURTHER STUDY

Association for Childhood Education, *Records and Reports*, Washington, D. C., Association for Childhood Education, 1942.

D'Evelyn, K. E., *Individual Parent-Teacher Conferences*, New York, Bureau of Publications, Teachers College, Columbia University, 1945.

N.E.A., Association for Supervision and Curriculum Development, *Toward Better Teaching*, Washington 6, D. C., National Education Association, 1949, Chapter 8.

Smith, E. R. and Tyler, R. W., *Appraising and Recording Student Progress*, New York, Harper & Brothers, 1942.

Strang, Ruth, *Reporting to Parents*, New York, Bureau of Publications, Teachers College, Columbia University, 1947.

Traxler, A. E., *The Nature and Use of Anecdotal Records*, New York, Educational Records Bureau, 1939.

Wrinkle, W. L., *Improving Marking and Reporting Practices in Elementary and Secondary Schools*, New York, Rinehart and Company, 1947.

The reader is also encouraged to use the following headings in the *Education Index:*

Marking systems
Marks, students
Promotions
Report cards
Reports and records

Chapter 20

Appraising the Work of the School

THE ULTIMATE criterion of the effectiveness of schooling is not to be found in test papers, rating scales, or the teacher's grade book, but must be sought in the school's broader contributions to the community at large. No problem which educators face is more difficult than that of appraising the effectiveness of various educational procedures. Opinion and belief, based upon tradition alone, are poor substitutes for experimental evidence and systematic appraisal; yet much of what is done in today's schools finds no other justification.

Far too little experimentation and study have been devoted to the validation of educational procedures, but a number of techniques, which have been used to appraise certain aspects of the school's work, do offer some valuable leads for immediate action and for further study. Such experimentation and study have given firm support to the break with many traditional teaching methods. It is hoped that the reader will find, in the studies and examples which follow, enough evidence so that he will be able to appraise more critically not only his own teaching, but also the broader school policies which he does or should help to formulate.

In the balance of this chapter there will be presented some of the techniques teachers may use in gathering useful data for appraisal, some of the ways in which educators and psychologists have attempted to appraise the schools, and finally some of the difficulties in making such appraisals.

EVALUATING THE EFFECT OF TEACHING
ON OUT-OF-SCHOOL BEHAVIOR

Some instructors are almost exclusively concerned with in-school behaviors, particularly those demonstrated by writing on a piece of paper in response to questions formulated by a teacher. The importance of such responses is not questioned. However, many educators are becoming increasingly concerned with the improvement of out-of-school behaviors. Such concern has resulted in the development of evaluative techniques for estimating the extent to which goals related to out-of-school behaviors are being achieved.

One of the major difficulties in developing evaluative devices related to these goals is the commonly accepted way of describing course purposes. Unfortunately such expressions in statements of objectives as "understanding of . . . ," "appreciation of . . . ," "recognition of . . . ," and "considerable familiarity with . . ." when only couched in vague and general terms, do not encourage teachers to objectify their goals by stating them in behavioral terms. Since teachers should be concerned with what their students do after school, on weekends, in the summer, and after they permanently leave school, it is vital that the specific behaviors to be produced or improved be clearly identified. In addition to the identification of the behaviors, procedures are needed for continuous checking in the community on the extent to which desirable behaviors are actually being demonstrated.

The issue may be clarified through the description of one part of the experience of an agricultural education teacher who became concerned with the "carry-over" effectiveness of his teaching. He set up a comprehensive list of the out-of-school behaviors he had been trying to develop in his students. Then, with some of his current students, he visited the farms of all of the last year's high-school seniors who had taken his courses, and a check was made on the extent to which they were practicing what he thought (or hoped) they had learned. Some of the results were encouraging. Others were both disappointing and at the same time challenging. For example, one of his goals had been to teach the boys to build guard rails around the farrowing pens to protect new born pigs from being crushed when the sow lies down.[1] An actual check of the pens on

[1] About 10 per cent of the newborn pigs probably would be killed without such rails.

farms of recent high school graduates who had taken vocational agriculture showed that only 20 per cent of pens had the guard rails. Interviews further revealed that even these rails apparently had been put up because of the influence of the county farm agent, not because of school training. The check revealed *no* favorable effect on any graduate in this respect. Needless to say this agriculture teacher changed many of his approaches to teaching agriculture as a result of his use of an out-of-school evaluative device.

Another illustrative study of out-of-school behavior was one in which data on community reading were collected and analyzed.[2] The teachers who carried on this study questioned the assumption

TABLE 33

Data from Survey of Community Reading

QUESTIONS	JUNIOR HIGH SCHOOL				SENIOR HIGH SCHOOL
	A	B	C	D	
Subscribe to bulletins telling how to choose best value for your money?	19%	39%	31%	30	10%
Average number of plays read per family per month?	0.5	0.7	0.3	0.7	0.7

that if the child *could* read well when he left school he *would* read often and well after he left school. These teachers in a midwestern junior high school decided they needed to try to get (1) some check on the extent to which their teaching goals were being achieved in the community, (2) some clarification of their out-of-school reading goals, and (3) some indication of the degree to which home situations are likely to facilitate the achievement of reading goals. With these general objectives in mind a committee of teachers set up a list of fifteen specific goals on which they could initially agree. They also listed forty-one questions to be asked of parents by means of a questionnaire.

How these parents, acting for their families, responded to two of the questions is shown in Table 33.

As shown in Table 33, there was a marked difference between the

[2] Ray H. Simpson and K. L. Camp, "Diagnosing Community Reading," *School Review*, Vol. 61, 1953, pp. 98–100.

responses from junior and senior high-school families to the question: "Do you subscribe to any magazine report or bulletin which emphasizes how to tell the value of any given article, and how to choose the best for your money?" Since reading of this type had been emphasized in the junior and not in the senior high school, it would appear that the specific instruction given was having an effect on out-of-school behavior. In this community the teachers were spending considerable time teaching drama in the schools. The results showing play reading behavior (or its lack) in the families caused some of the teachers to reconsider and re-evaluate the effectiveness of their drama teaching. This led to the trying out of revised teaching procedures.

Teachers were found to vary greatly in their ability to get and use meaningfully results of this sort. As with most techniques, the value of such a procedure depends greatly upon the resourcefulness of the teacher using it. One teacher emphasized and thoroughly explained the purpose of the questionnaire to the pupils before sending the forms home. This teacher and class decided that they would study the returns, using the results as one measuring stick in planning their future literature work. This teacher reported that the amount of zeal and zest which his students showed in planning new literature units alone made the study well worth the time and effort.

STUDIES OF PUPIL AND COMMUNITY ATTITUDES TOWARD SCHOOLS

The degree of satisfaction which those in school, parents, and other community members have with respect to the school's goals and procedures has a significant bearing on the improvement of teaching-learning situations. Some of the community attitudes can, of course, be obtained and appraised through informal talks with parents, pupils, and other interested individuals. However, to depend entirely on such nonsystematic techniques is not sufficient. There are now available several types of techniques for determining attitudes toward schools which are designed to substitute systematic consumer research for guessing. Unless youngsters and their parents understand and largely agree with what schools are doing, basic progress in the improvement of education is extremely difficult if not impossible. A thorough appraisal of existing attitudes reveals not only the degree of dissatisfaction or satisfaction, but also the specific areas in which attitudes have crystallized.

What are some of the dimensions to be investigated in getting evidence of parent satisfaction and dissatisfaction with the schools? Hand,[3] for example, has developed specific questions to investigate parent attitudes toward some twenty-three aspects of the school's work. Illustrative of the areas covered are the following: (1) treatment of children by other youngsters, teachers, and other school officials, (2) discipline, (3) help in resolving personal problems, (4) value of schoolwork, (5) adequacy of the school's offerings, (6) participation in student activities, (7) homework, (8) teaching methods, (9) overcrowded school buildings, (10) most liked feature of the school, (11) most disliked thing about the school, and (12) over-all rating of satisfaction or dissatisfaction.

The attitudes of children toward what goes on at school—in the class, on the playground, and in the library—are of major importance. Hand[4] has listed nineteen components of pupils' satisfaction-dissatisfaction. Some of these are: (1) feeling of "belonging," (2) pupil-teacher bond, (3) fair treatment by teachers, (4) attitudes toward discipline, (5) relationship of schoolwork toward real life needs, (6) work requirements in school courses, (7) most liked feature of the school, (8) most disliked feature of the school, and (9) general rating of satisfaction. To measure attitudes toward school, Hand has devised a check list. On this form is also provided space for constructive suggestions.

What are some of the specific questions which may be asked in assessing pupil and parent (and teacher if this is desired) attitudes in such areas as those indicated in the preceding paragraphs? Five illustrations of questions used and data gathered from a senior high school in an Illinois community [5] are given in Table 34.

Many implications may be gathered from these and similar data. For example, they may indicate that more attention should be given to public relations, and perhaps to adult education. They also may suggest some new emphasis which would improve the work of the school. The answers to item 4 in Table 34 imply that more effort should be made to take care of individual differences in needs,

---

[3] Harold C. Hand, *What People Think About Their Schools*, Yonkers-on-Hudson, New York, World Book Co., 1948, pp. 33–44.

[4] *Ibid.*, pp. 48–57.

[5] *Ibid.*, pp. 143–147.

TABLE 34

Some Reactions of Parents, Pupils, and Teachers Toward Their Schools *

1. In general, are you satisfied or dissatisfied with your (child's) school?

	PUPILS	PARENTS
Definitely satisfied	62%	57%
Partly satisfied, partly dissatisfied	30%	28%
Definitely dissatisfied	8%	12%
No response	0%	3%

2. How many of your (child's) teachers know you (him) as well as they should?

	PUPILS	PARENTS
All or most	31%	30%
Half or fewer	67%	63%
No response	2%	7%

3. In general, is the discipline in your school too strict or not strict enough?

	PUPILS	PARENTS	TEACHERS
Too strict	20%	5%	0%
About right	66%	58%	34%
Too lax	13%	27%	63%
No reply	1%	10%	3%

4. How much are you (or your child, or your pupils) getting out of your (or his, or their) schoolwork?

	PUPILS	PARENTS	TEACHERS
All one could reasonably expect	74%	56%	44%
Less than one could reasonably expect	26%	41%	51%
No response	0%	3%	5%

5. How much work do you (or your child, or your pupils) have to do in order to "keep up" in your (or his, or their) studies?

	PUPILS	PARENTS	TEACHERS
Too little	5%	9%	19%
About the right amount	59%	61%	74%
Too much	36%	20%	1%
No response	1%	10%	6%

* Adapted from Hand, pp. 143–147.

abilities, and interests through different amounts and types of assignments for pupils, even for those in the same class. Such data at least give the school a fairly adequate picture of where it stands with parents and pupils.

CASE STUDIES OF CLASSES

Evaluation of class operations may be facilitated if the teacher, with the help of his students, makes a careful record of what happens in a class. The study of such a record of plans and procedures in ongoing classwork should not only provide a foundation for additional planning in the immediate class, but can also form a substantial basis for future improvement in teaching and learning.

Preplanning for Class Case Study. In preparing for a class case study it is desirable for the instructor to lay some initial groundwork. For example, he might very profitably write down the assumptions upon which he will attempt to operate. In doing this, one teacher developed the following guiding principles:

1. Usefulness of knowledge and subject matter in life situations should be a primary criterion for their selection.

2. Pupils should study those problems which they recognize as being worthy of their efforts. (One important role of the teacher is to try to make student problem identification and selection increasingly wise.)

3. What, for each learner, is an appropriate learning experience should be given primary weight. "Ground to be covered" should be de-emphasized.

4. The development of effective ways of identifying and solving problems is to be expected as a product of method.[6]

This type of approach may, of course, be used cooperatively by a group of teachers or even by the whole school staff. Preplanning not only helps the teacher plan more effectively for the immediate course, but also forms a partial framework for evaluation of the course after it is over. Such evaluation, if persistently employed, will tend to produce improved teaching and learning.

Student Plans. Since the plans of the individual learner are of major importance in appraisal of his work, these can profitably be kept and subsequently compared with progress made, and goals attained. Following are the plans made at the beginning of the school year by Elizabeth, a high school senior, who perceived certain needs and goals, but had no definite vocational plans.[7]

[6] Adapted from E. A. Waters. *A Study of the Application of an Educational Theory to Science Instruction,* New York, Bureau of Publications, Teachers College, Columbia University, 1942.

[7] W. Wallace, J. Chreitzberg, and V. M. Sims. *The Story of Holtville.* Deatsville, Alabama. Holtville High School. 1944, pp. 28–29.

This year there are two main goals I hope to attain. The first is to learn how to live, and the second is to learn how to think and reason clearly.

I'm looking forward to learning or doing something new or different each day. I intend to plan my work and not jump at conclusions or into something until I am ready and willing to do a good job of it, because I realize that the willingness to assume responsibility is the chief qualification for success.

From the subjects I have chosen to take this year, I want to get a varied and practical view (as well as important facts, and details). It has been a little hard to decide what subjects I wanted to take this year, because I haven't fully decided what I want to do as a future vocation. After a bit of consideration of the facts relating to this problem, I came to the conclusion that no matter what work we may follow, we should not neglect the cultivation of our minds, for knowledge is a very precious possession.

This year I plan to improve my attitude and personality by applying the rules of life to school, home, and community work. I plan to improve my general fitness and initiative, and a wholesome attitude toward my life and work is very essential in reaching this objective.

The things that I plan to study this year are English, biology (zoology), algebra, French and personal relationships. I plan to begin taking typing the second semester.

English grammar and literature have always been interesting to me. I plan to take grammar the first semester and literature the last semester. I expect to increase my vocabulary and spelling ability through this and all other subjects. I'm taking English because it is essential in forming the foundation for any vocation or profession. It is interesting and is used every day in every vocation. In literature I want to study about great writers and their works.

The study of biology is fascinating, and there are so many phases of it. I plan to take up the study of zoology or animal life.

Mathematical subjects have always been my favorites, and that is why I'm taking algebra this year. I had algebra about two weeks last year, and I liked it. I want to learn how to solve problems by easier and shorter methods in algebra. I intend to learn how to analyze facts and by careful thinking and sound reasoning draw some conclusions.

I wanted to take some foreign language in high school, so I chose French. I like to read books with French backgrounds, and they are not very easily understood if I can't translate French into English. I plan to learn to read and translate French.

I am also planning to have some free time to call my own in which I can read magazines and books.

In personal relationships, I plan to learn how to get along with people, how to meet the public, how to improve my manners, and how to meet other everyday problems.

This year, I shall be a member of the Glee Club. I like both vocal and instrumental music. Although I can't sing or play an instrument, I like to hear others sing and play.

I hope to carry out these objectives so my work will not be found lacking at the end.

Plans of this sort can and should be modified during the year. They do serve to induce the student to consider systematically his school goals.

Keeping a Record of What Happens. In addition to having a record of the plans of both teacher and student, it is desirable to secure a follow-up of what happens in order to evaluate how well plans have been carried out. Such records can be kept by the teacher or the student or, preferably, both.

The teacher's record is probably most useful if kept on a day to day, or week to week basis. It should usually contain a record of such things as: the longtime and immediate goals, resources used by teacher and pupils, ways in which class procedures were planned and how these succeeded. Also, suggestions for modifications of goals, plans, procedures and resources in subsequent classes might be included.

The pupil's record may be similar to that of the teacher but should be geared to the purposes of the youngster who is keeping the record. It may be a daily or weekly summary of plans or activities or it may involve a comprehensive summary of one or more years of work. Inspection of such summaries can help the teacher improve in his work. The following paragraphs are excerpts [8] from one year of a three-year report by a senior in high school:

This year I did not go to school the first few weeks of the first semester. I worked for the school, operating farm machinery. The work is a help to our community and to other communities. The machinery has been out of the county. The machines the school now has are three tractors, a binder, threshing machine, combine, hay baler, peanut picker, power spray, two distributors, a cutaway harrow, and a flat-bottomed plow. I have worked with them all. This fall we worked at the Dam, Lightwood, Deatsville, Coosa River, Elmore, and Crenshaw. Almost all of these machines made this round. They have even gone as far as Millbrook. We baled about

[8] *Ibid.*, pp. 132–135.

500 tons of hay this year besides the peanut vines we baled behind the peanut picker. We picked off 82 tons of peanuts. We threshed about 20,000 bushels of oats and wheat. The binder didn't go far from this community, but we cut about 200 acres of wheat and oats.

We have been plowing some for the community, cutting and turning land. We turned the school farm and planted vetch.

With the power spray we sprayed several hundred peach trees in the spring. We spray them for scale, worms, and dry rot. We spray them with oil emulsion mixed with water for scale, arsenate and lime for worms, and sulphur and water for dry rot.

I started to school in November. I made my plans as follows: first block, agricultural mathematics; second block, current history, and English; third block, biology; and fourth block, feed mill.

Our mathematics class has been working on adding, subtracting, and dividing of fractions; dairying; feeds; soil fertility; percentage, and formulas.

Students in our current history group have been discussing the world today, the wars, and the foreign countries. I wrote a report on Nova Scotia and on England at war, which was part of English work. I have also worked on English in a workbook. I have worked on parts of speech and their uses in a sentence, capital letters, and paragraphs. I am now writing more reports on history work. . . .

The fourth block of time I worked at the feed mill, where we have a feed mixer, a hammer mill, and a grist mill. I have learned to operate these. With the feed mixer we can mix our own chicken feed, which is cheaper than the ready-mixed feed. We crush different kinds of feed such as corn, beans, hay, and peanut vines. We can take a hard feed and crush it into a meal. . . .

I have accomplished more this year by working out with the farm machinery than I would have by being in a classroom, because I take an interest in that kind of work. I can operate all of the machines which the school has. This is a help to the community because these modern machines do not take so much labor. When you do work with these power machines, people can cooperate and help each other. This will save them from hiring labor. These power machines not only take less labor, but they are also faster. You can take a power hay press and bale 250 to 300 bales of hay a day, whereas a mule-drawn press would bale only 100 to 125 bales a day. I did this work to learn and to get experience. It helps me in English, as I have to meet the public and speak correctly. At the feed mill, especially, we have lots of figuring to do in selling feed by the pound, and we meet and deal with lots of people there.

Looking back at my work, I think I did not get as much English as I would have liked. In that and some other things I think I could have done more book work. Working does not give you as much book knowledge as being in classes all day, but it gives you experience. You really should have both.

I feel that my schooling has fitted me for farming and for living a successful and happy life. I am in the draft age now and would have gone to the Army, but because I was needed to farm I was deferred. Farming is the basis of all our war effort. If we did not raise food, everyone would starve. Food is not the only thing that farm products are used for. If all the farms were stopped, everything would stop.

Drawing Some Conclusions. To reap most benefit from the types of data which have been mentioned, the teacher will want to draw some conclusions after a course is over. These conclusions can form a sound basis for continuous improvement in teaching. One high-school English teacher reached the following conclusions:

Goals. The formal grammar work does not seem to appreciably affect pupils' speech and writing. A consultant we had at one of our faculty meetings said research has indicated a similar thing. I am going to give more attention to the functional speaking and writing (expression, punctuation, spelling, and speech in realistic situations) and see if this will not give better results.

Resources. We need to plan to get and use more easy reading material. The regular text was too difficult for about 60 per cent of my last class. I am afraid that instead of appreciating literature some of the students were actually turned against it because I started them out on too difficult material.

Class Procedures. The small group discussions of "a short story I like and why" worked out well and served to arouse much interest in reading. Attempts at improving speech for actual situations through role playing of these situations seem to have many possibilities. I must study this procedure more myself and plan for trying out more types of situations.

Although I feel I made progress in getting individuals and groups to help set up their goals, plans and activities, I still do too much dictating and am front-center-stage too much of the time for democratic class operation. Perhaps some study of democratic leadership and group dynamics would help both me and the other students.

THEN AND NOW STUDIES

In most communities questions like the following are periodically raised: "Are not the schools deteriorating with the introduction of fads and frills?" "Why don't the schools teach the '3 R's' like they did when I was in school?" "Since it is obvious that graduates today don't know how to read or spell like graduates once did, why don't we make teachers discipline their pupils and teach them like we were taught?" The alert teacher must be able to answer these and similar questions. This requires him to know the facts which have been gathered through careful investigations.

The criticisms of schools and schooling now being made are not new at all. Perennially parents have cast a nostalgic look behind to the schools of their youth. Even in ancient times they were complaining.

A clay tablet of great antiquity records the lament of a merchant whose son has come home from school into the shop. Alas, the boy cannot keep the money and accounts straight, cannot write his hieroglyphic legibly, cannot deal with customers. The money spent on his schooling has been wasted. . . .[9]

In 1856 we find attacks and criticisms in the same vein:

. . . little attention is paid to penmanship, very little attention is manifest in this important branch—writing is very poor and does not by any means compare with the general condition of the art in former years.

. . . an evil resulting from the fast spirit of the age—scholars cannot find the time to study and expect the teachers to do it for them.

Our schools are in a feeble and backward state. We think the modern mode of instruction is decidedly bad.[10]

In 1894 a committee on composition and rhetoric reporting to the Board of Overseers of Harvard said:

At Harvard, as the committee demonstrates, the unhappy instructors are confronted with immature thoughts, set down in a crabbed and slovenly hand, miserably expressed, and wretchedly spelled, and yet the average age of admission is nineteen.[11]

In the same year newspaper editors were also active in their criticisms of the schools. *The Boston Herald* carried these lines:

[9] William H. Burton, "Get the Facts: Both Ours and the Other Fellow's!" *Progressive Education*, 29:82–90, January, 1952, p. 89.
[10] *Ibid.*
[11] *Ibid.*, p. 90.

It is really a rare thing to find young people at from fifteen to nineteen years of age who can write or spell out of the common, or prepare a composition correctly.[12]

In a Massachusetts town, the school committee complained bitterly, also in 1894, as follows:

Where are the scholars that modern systems of improved methods are producing? I do not see them. We used to think something had been done when pupils had gained proficiency in the three R's, with few or no ornamental attachments. Even in modern days, if you could find a pupil that could read *well*, write a fine legible hand and master a written arithmetic, what would you think? [13]

An example of an attempt to substitute facts for opinion on these issues is reported by Finch and Gillenwater.[14] As a part of a comprehensive survey of the Springfield (Missouri) schools, the investigators made a comparison of past and present reading achievement of pupils. Form 3 of the Thorndike-McCall Reading Scale, a standardized reading test, had been given in sixth-grade classes in six elementary schools in the spring of 1931. The same test was administered in the spring of 1948 to all sixth graders present in the same six schools. Test conditions closely duplicated those prevailing at the time of the original testing. The test itself had been designed especially to measure the learner's ability to understand the meaning of words, sentences, and paragraphs.

When the scores of the 1931 sixth graders were compared with those of the 1948 sixth graders, it was found that the average 1948 pupil did slightly better than did his 1931 counterpart. All in all, the results of the study did not support the opinion of a group in the city which had been lamenting "the degeneration" in the teaching of reading and other basic skills.

STUDIES COMPARING TWO METHODS

If education is effective it changes behavior. One persistent and continuing problem the teacher faces is that of attempting to compare the relative effectiveness of different methods in producing de-

[12] *Ibid.*, p. 90.
[13] *Ibid.*, p. 90.
[14] F. H. Finch and V. W. Gillenwater, "Reading Achievement Then and Now," *The Elementary School Journal*, Vol. 39, April, 1949, pp. 446–454.

sired behavior. Techniques employed by Bavelas [15] and Lewin [16] are suggestive of a type of informal study which teachers or groups of teachers might successfully employ in evaluating their work.

Acquiring knowledge alone may suffice for pencil and paper test purposes, but may be totally inadequate for more significant behaviors. Recognizing this, Lewin and Bavelas set up an investigation to determine which of two methods of teaching, the lecture or the group decision method, would produce more changes in certain food habits. The immediate goal of the teaching in this experiment was to produce greater use of three types of food (kidneys, brains, and hearts) against which there was known resistance.

Six groups of women were used in the experiment, two of low economic level, two of middle, and two of high economic level. Each of three of the groups, one from each economic level, participated in a discussion led by a skillful teacher with an expert nutritionist as consultant. Members of these groups were led to regard the subject being discussed as important to themselves, and began to assume responsibility for carrying forward the discussion. Finally, after some of their objections and attitudes had been talked over, they reached a decision concerning action to be taken.

In the other three groups the lecture method was used. The expert nutritionist in charge talked for approximately half an hour about the nutritional advantages of using the meats, and described how the meats could be prepared in order to avoid unpleasant odors, textures, and appearance. Visual aids were used by the lecturer to emphasize the vitamin and mineral value of the meats. The amount of time used in each of the six groups was the same. Mimeographed recipes were distributed to the members of all six groups.

The relative effects of the lectures and the group discussions were tested seven days after the experiment began. Through an interview at home with each participant a determination was made of the extent to which the foods were actually served, and what the reactions of the families were.

Although the frequency of using these meats by the participants

[15] A. Bavelas, *Group Decision,* paper read before a meeting of the S.P.S.S.I., 1943.

[16] K. Lewin, *The Relative Effectiveness of a Lecture Method and a Method of Group Decision for Changing Food Habits,* Committee on Food Habits, National Research Council, Washington, D. C., June, 1942, Mimeographed.

of the two groups was about equal *before* the experiment, striking differences appeared at the end as shown in Table 35.

Note that after the experiment 52 per cent of the discussion group members served one or more of the three meats, while only ten per

TABLE 35

Effects of Two Procedures in Changing Food Habits *

Method of induct-ing the change in food habits	GROUP DECISION				LECTURE			
Economic Level	LOW	MIDDLE	HIGH	TOTAL	LOW	MIDDLE	HIGH	TOTAL
Number of participants	17	16	13	44	13	15	13	41
% of individuals serving one or more of the three meats	35	69	54	52	15	13	0	10
% of individuals serving a meat they had *never* or *hardly ever* served before	20	53	54	44	0	8	0	3
% of individuals serving a meat they had never served before	13	36	50	32	0	8	0	3
% of participants serving one or more new meats who had *never* served *any* of the three meats before the experiment				29				0

* Adapted from Lewin.

cent of those in the lecture group did so. Thirty-two per cent of those who had been in the discussion groups, and only three per cent of those who had been in the lecture groups served a meat they had never served before. In short, this investigation seemed to show that the discussion approach was much more effective in producing changed behavior than the lecture technique.[17]

LONGITUDINAL STUDIES

Appraisal of long-time, comprehensive aims of education may require cooperative planning by representatives of a large number of educational institutions, and may demand inquiry over a period of months, semesters, or even years. Illustrative of such an investigation is the Eight-Year Study. This study, initiated in 1930, represented an extensive attempt to answer, upon a factual basis, such questions as the following: Can secondary schools be trusted to use wisely their freedom from traditional college requirements? How can improvements be made in high schools without jeopardizing students' chances of being admitted to colleges or of doing well after admission to college? Is the commonly made assumption sound that success in a college depends upon the study in high school of certain subjects for certain periods of time? How well do high school students who went to college from experimental schools succeed?

Procedures. At the outset, a planning committee selected thirty representative high schools who were willing to experiment educationally provided their students would be freed from the usual college entrance requirements. Starting in 1933 plans for changes in curriculum, organization, and procedure were set up in these schools. Representatives of the thirty schools met annually for mutual stimulation in thinking and planning.

When the Study started the schools all sought to adapt work to individual needs, and to provide for greater mastery of skills, and for release of creative energy. More continuity in learning, and greater unity of school experiences were also provided. Two major principles guided the work of the thirty schools. The first was that the general life of the school and methods of teaching should conform insofar as possible to what is now known about the ways in which human beings learn and grow, and the second was that the

---

[17] It is possible the "lecture group" women might have made as good or even better scores on a pencil and paper test on nutrition than the "discussion-group" women. The educator continuously faces the problem of considering what kind of behavior he is trying to produce. Considerations regarding short-time school behaviors should not crowd out consideration of equally or more important out-of-school behaviors.

high school in the United States should re-discover its chief reason for existence. Leaders in the study concluded that the school itself should become a *demonstration* of the kind of life in which this nation believes. They felt that the spirit and practice of experimentation and exploration should characterize secondary schools in a democracy. The Thirty Schools [18] early in the study became known as experimental schools. Much attention from the beginning was given to recording and reporting the results of their work. Special emphasis was given to the development of testing instruments to meet new purposes of teachers and administrators. Devices designed to appraise critical thinking, sound attitudes, and social sensitivity were among the many which were constructed.

Results. Graduates of the thirty schools were studied to determine how well they succeeded in college. A basis of comparison was established by matching, with utmost care, the graduates from the thirty high schools with graduates from high schools not participating in the study. This latter group had met the usual college entrance requirements. Factors included in the matching were college attended, sex, age, race, scholastic aptitude scores, home and community background, interest, and probable future.[19]

In a careful comparison of the 1,475 matched pairs which were intensively studied, the College Follow-up Staff found that the graduates of the Thirty Schools surpassed the non-experimental group in the following ways:

1. earned a slightly higher total grade average
2. earned higher grade averages in all subject fields except foreign languages
3. specialized in the same academic fields as did the comparison students
4. did not differ from the comparison group in the number of times they were placed on probation
5. received slightly more academic honors in each year
6. were more often judged to possess a high degree of intellectual curiosity and drive
7. were more often judged to be precise, systematic, and objective in their thinking

[18] This was the name given in the study to the schools which agreed to experiment.

[19] W. M. Aiken, *The Story of the Eight-Year Study,* Harper & Brothers, 1942, p. 109.

8. were more often judged to have developed clear or well-formulated ideas concerning the meaning of education—especially in the first years in college

9. more often demonstrated a high degree of resourcefulness in meeting new situations

10. did not differ from the comparison group in ability to plan their time effectively

11. had about the same problems of adjustment as the comparison group, but approached their solution with greater effectiveness

12. participated somewhat more frequently, and more often enjoyed appreciative experiences, in the arts

13. participated more in all organized student groups except religious and "service" activities

14. earned in each college year a high percentage of non-academic honors (officership in organizations, election to managerial societies, athletic insignia, leading roles in dramatic and musical presentations)

15. did not differ from the comparison group in the quality of adjustment to their contemporaries

16. differed only slightly from the comparison group in the kinds of judgments about their schooling

17. had a somewhat better orientation toward the choice of vocation

18. demonstrated a more active concern for what was going on in the world.[20]

While some of the indicated differences in favor of the experimental schools were not large, they were consistent for each class. When one finds even small margins of differences for a number of large groups, the probability greatly increases that the differences are not due to chance alone. When judged by college standards, by the students' contemporaries, or by the individuals themselves, it appeared that the students from the experimental schools did a somewhat better job on the average in college than students with similar backgrounds and basic abilities who were trained in traditional high schools.

The graduates of the "most experimental schools" were strikingly more successful than their matchees. Differences in their favor were much greater than the differences between the total Thirty Schools and the comparison group. Conversely, there were no large or consistent differences between the "least experimental graduates" and their comparison group.

[20] *Ibid.,* pp. 111–112.

The College Follow-up Staff commenting on these facts stated:

If the proof of the pudding lies in these groups, and a good part of it does, then it follows that the colleges got from these most experimental schools a higher proportion of sound, effective college material than they did from the more conventional schools in similar environments. If colleges want students who have developed effective and objective habits of thinking, and who yet maintain a healthy orientation toward their fellows, then they will encourage the already obvious trend away from restrictions which tend to inhibit departures or deviations from the conventional curriculum patterns.[21]

MATCHED COMMUNITY COMPARISONS

One helpful technique which has been used to a limited extent is to compare the educational results in two communities whose population and ability to support education are similar but whose educational practices differ strikingly. Illustrative of such studies is one by Wrightstone [22] who made an extensive appraisal of achievement of pupils under described experimental teaching practices in one group of communities, and compared their achievement with that of matched pupils under conventional teaching situations in similar communities. In addition to using conventional tests of knowledge, instruments were designed to measure work skills, abilities to organize, interpret and apply facts, and such variables as civic beliefs and attitudes.

Because of the complexity of the study a complete picture of it or of all the results obtained will not be given here.[23] However, the implications of the findings are well summarized by its author who notes, "The comparative measurement of certain intellectual factors, dynamic factors, and socal performance factors in selected experimental and conventional schools (in matched communities) indicate *equal or superior* achievement for the experimental practices. Such evidence may be interpreted as tentative proof of the validity of the educational theory and principles upon which the newer-type

[21] *Ibid.*, p. 113.

[22] J. Wayne Wrightstone, *Appraisal of Experimental High School Practices,* New York, Bureau of Publications, Teachers College, Columbia University, 1936.

[23] *Ibid.* For descriptions of conventional and experimental practices see pages 3–116. For appraisal of conventional and experimental practices see pages 117–194.

practices in the selected schools are established.[24] While the matched community procedure is a technique which has been used for research it should be emphasized that it could be misused. It is difficult to match communities. Intercommunity comparisons may cause jealousies and other complications. What one community can or should do may not necessarily be best for another community. However, the results from carefully designed community comparisons may give clues as to the effectiveness of certain educational procedures.

REVIEW OF RESEARCH SUMMARIES

Also fruitful, for the time spent, is the review of research report which summarizes a number of experimental studies. In such summaries an attempt is made to analyze and partially "digest" for the reader dozens of individual studies such as the one by Wrightstone which has just been mentioned. An illustration of the research summary is one made by Leonard and Eurich with the cooperation of others which summarized the results of 154 investigations of progressive practices in teaching.[25]

Probably the most extensive and thorough synthesis of research of interest to teachers is to be found in the *Review of Educational Research* [26] which periodically covers such topics as: "Educational and Psychological Tests," "Methods of Research and Experimentation," and "General Aspects of Instruction, Learning, Teaching and the Curriculum." Also of value to the teacher is the *Encyclopedia of Educational Research*,[27] which brings together in one volume the accumulated research on educational problems of the past half century.

DIFFICULTIES IN ANALYZING MERITS OF DIFFERENT APPROACHES

The techniques which have just been described represent attempts to base educational procedure upon fact rather than merely on opinion. It must be recognized that no technique or procedure gives a final or complete answer to the educational questions that

[24] *Ibid.*, page 193.

[25] J. P. Leonard and A. C. Eurich (Editors), *An Evaluation of Modern Education*, New York, D. Appleton-Century, 1942.

[26] American Educational Research Association, National Education Association, 1201 Sixteenth St., N. W., Washington 6, D. C.

[27] Walter S. Monroe (Editor), New York, The Macmillan Co., 1950.

teachers want to have answered. Some of the practical difficulties which must be kept in mind in assessing the results of most techniques will now be discussed.

Goals Differ. One of the major difficulties in comparing different educational approaches is that teachers, pupils, parents and communities are not agreed with respect to the goals of particular educational procedures. It is very difficult to compare the results of teaching which stresses the learning of detailed factual material with the results obtained when teaching emphasizes critical or analytical thinking, unless it is known which is the more desirable.

A New Method May Stimulate a Teacher to Be More Creative. In attempting to assess the comparative values of older and newer methods the results have typically indicated some advantage of the newer method over the older method. This does not necessarily mean that the newer method is in and of itself superior to the older method. It may be that the teacher who tries out a new procedure is stimulated to work harder and to be more creative than he otherwise would be. If this hypothesis is correct, administrators, supervisors, and others might encourage teachers to try out new approaches with the idea that by so doing their teaching will be invigorated.

It is also possible that the type of teacher or the kind of school staff which tries new or different approaches may be of better quality than those who do not try out innovations. Such complications as these make it extremely difficult to evaluate the effectiveness of schools using different approaches.

Adequate Description of Teaching-Learning Situation Difficult. While most experimenters who try to determine the relative merits of two or more educational approaches attempt to describe as adequately as possible the differences between the competing approaches, it must be recognized that such descriptions are extremely difficult. In fact, it may be almost impossible to describe adequately the multitude of factors which can have a vital bearing on the success of an educational venture. Because of this fact, the student or teacher reading about the results of experiments must be extremely cautious in making interpretations and drawing conclusions.

Readiness of Participants for a New Method. Most educational psychologists recognize that there is probably no best method for all situations and all conditions. One reason for this fact is that those involved in a particular teaching-learning situation may not be ready for a specified method. For example, if neither teachers, learners, nor parents are ready for a particular method to be used, it is obviously impossible to give this method a fair trial. Readiness of participants for a certain method or for aspects of the method is hard to determine. Consequently, an approach that may appear to give inferior results initially may, if persisted in, give better results later on.

Short-Term and Long-Term Gains. It is sometimes difficult to assess the efficacy of a given educational method or organizational plan because there may be a conflict between immediate and long-time goals. For example, the learner who has been practicing tennis for three years while holding his racket the "wrong way" may find that he cannot hit the ball at first after he is shown how to hold his racket in the "right way." Unless the teacher and learner are willing to give a procedure or method a fair tryout it may be eliminated too quickly because it is "too confusing," "too frustrating," "too disorganized," or "too time consuming." Also, studying a subject in a particular way may make it possible for a pupil to pass a particular kind of test immediately after the study, but may cause him to dislike the subject and thus militate against future learning in the area. In assessing the results of educational experience, it is critically important to attempt to identify both short-term and long-term gains and losses.

"Newer Methods" Vary Widely. Sometimes an attempt is made to differentiate between newer methods and older methods. In general, of course, there probably can be established certain major differences between what might be labeled the new emphases in education and the older points of view. However, it must be clearly recognized that newer methods differ widely among themselves and that even two classes believed to be using the same procedures may actually differ considerably in the teaching-learning situations involved. Differing teacher and pupil perceptions, furthermore, create differences in situations where no difference would be noticed by an outside observer.

SUMMARY

Evaluating the total effects of schooling upon children's immediate and later behavior is one of the most difficult and complicated processes the educator faces. The marks which are registered in the principal's office only partially indicate important changes which have been made in children's behavior. In order to appraise the effectiveness of their programs, schools should employ a wide variety of measuring devices and approaches.

In this chapter techniques for evaluating some of the broader and less easily measured outcomes of education have been described. These include measures of out-of-school behavior following formal instruction, scales for determining pupil and community attitudes toward school practices, case studies of classes, and matched community comparisons. Much information regarding what is superior educational practice may also be secured from such longitudinal investigations as the Eight-Year Study, "then and now" studies of achievement, comparisons of teaching methods reported in the professional literature, and research summaries such as those found in the *Review of Educational Research* and the *Encyclopedia of Educational Research.*

Some of the sources of difficulties likely to be encountered in appraising different educational approaches are: (1) Goals of educators may differ, (2) A new method may stimulate a teacher to be more creative, (3) Adequate description of a teaching-learning situation is difficult, (4) Participants in a new method may differ in readiness for it, and (5) Conflicts may exist between short-term and long-term goals and gains.

Pencil and paper tests given in school have their place in an appraisal program. However, the ultimate appraisal must be made on the basis of the out-of-school behaviors of those whom the school seeks to influence.

REFERENCES FOR FURTHER STUDY

Aiken, W. M., *The Story of the Eight-Year Study*, New York, Harper & Brothers, 1942.

Barker, Roger; Tamara Dembo; Kurt Lewin; and M. E. Wright, "Experimental Studies of Frustration in Young Children," in *Readings in Social Psychology*, New York, Henry Holt and Company, 1947, pp. 283–290.

Chamberlin, D. and others, *Did They Succeed in College?*, New York, Harper & Brothers, 1942.

Helbing, Mary E., "Evaluation of the Procedures of a Modern Elementary School in Terms of the Subsequent Adjustment of Its Pupils,"

California Journal of Elementary Education, Vol. 8, February, 1940, pp. 137–146.

Jersild, A. T. and others, "An Evaluation of Aspects of the Activity Program in the New York City Public Elementary Schools," *Journal of Experimental Education,* Vol. 8, December, 1939, pp. 166–207.

Kvaraceus, W. C., "Delinquency—A By-Product of the School," *School and Society,* Vol. 59, May 13, 1944, pp. 450–451.

Leonard, J. P. and A. C. Eurich (Editors), *An Evaluation of Modern Education,* New York, D. Appleton-Century, 1942.

Lewin, K. and others, "Patterns of Aggressive Behavior in Experimentally Created 'Social Climates,' " *Journal of Social Psychology,* Bulletin for the Society for the Psychological Study of Social Issues, Vol. 10, May, 1939, pp. 269–298.

Monroe, Walter (Editor), *Encyclopedia of Educational Research,* Revised Edition, New York, The Macmillan Company, 1950.

Moreno, J. L. and Helen H. Jennings, "Sociometric Control Studies of Grouping and Regrouping," *Sociometry Monographs,* No. 7, Beacon House, 1947, pp. 20–29.

Progressive Education Association (Informal Committee on Evaluation of Newer Practices in Education), *New Methods vs. Old in American Education,* New York, Bureau of Publications, Teacher College, Columbia University, 1941.

Quillen, I. James and Lavone Hanna, *Education for Social Competence,* Chicago, Scott, Foresman and Company, 1948.

Wallace, W., J. Chreitzberg, and V. M. Sims, *The Story of Holtville,* Deatsville, Alabama, Holtville High School, 1944.

Wrightstone, J. W., "Evaluation of Newer Instructional Practices," *Twelfth Yearbook* of the National Department of Supervisors and Directors of Instruction, Washington, D. C., National Education Association, 1939, pp. 307–327.

The student is also urged to study current issues of educational and psychological periodicals. The following are illustrative of magazines which sometimes have articles on appraising the work of the school:

Elementary School Journal
Journal of Educational Psychology
Journal of Educational Research
Journal of Experimental Education
Journal of Experimental Psychology
Journal of Psychology
Journal of Social Psychology
Review of Educational Research
The School Review

PART VI

THE PSYCHOLOGY OF THE TEACHER

Chapter 21

Professional Growth of the Teacher

EDUCATIONAL PSYCHOLOGY is just as much a psychology of the teacher as of the pupil. The professional growth of the teacher involves not only a continuous effort to understand children better, but also constant self-appraisal in which the teacher carefully scrutinizes methods of increasing his own learning. The teacher's professional growth, or lack of it, will be reflected in his methods, in his willingness to change, in his working relationships with children, and in his over-all efficiency as a teacher. It is clear that children's behavior as individuals, and more especially as individuals interacting with the teacher and with other pupils, will depend to a great extent upon the kind of a teacher they have.[1] The teacher whose intellectual growth terminates upon graduation from college or whose work is stultified by monotonous, inflexible routines, will most certainly be an unhappy and ineffective classroom leader. A professionally maturing teacher, on the other hand, is not only better able to diagnose and meet his own needs, but also sets a worthwhile example of growth and learning for students with whom he works.

Some of the paramount issues which merit consideration in studying and promoting teacher development are contained in the following questions.

---

[1] For example, see H. H. Anderson and others, *Study in Classroom Teachers' Personalities*, III, "Follow-Up Studies of the Effects of Dominative and Integrative Contacts on Children's Behavior," Stanford University, California, Stanford University Press, 1946.

What is the teacher's role as a learner?

How can the teacher diagnose his own classroom activities?

What are some approaches the teacher may take in improving his own class activities?

How can the teacher diagnose and improve his relations with other teachers and with administrators?

By what means can the teacher analyze and improve his relations with the community?

What is the relation of the teacher's happiness to his increasing professional efficiency?

These and related issues will be discussed in this chapter.

THE TEACHER AS A LEARNER

As a professional person, a teacher's learning should continue throughout his professional life. However, even in teacher-training institutions some of the practices would seem to indicate that there may be two quite distinct concepts related to the role of the teacher as a learner. The one concept is based on the implicit but frequently unrecognized assumption that the teacher practically finishes his systematic learning as soon as the coveted degree or diploma is obtained. The opposing concept is based on the assumption that the instructor's own systematic learning is only well started when he is graduated from his formal program of teacher training. Only the latter approach can be supported by educational psychology and it implies training for continued learning.

The genesis of the differences in these concepts can probably best be understood by considering the differing emphases in college courses, depending upon which point of view the instructor supports. In the one case the course is highly structured by the instructor; in the other case considerable attention is given to helping the student learn how to plan his own systematic learning. The college instructor who assumes that systematic learning will be finished at the end of the teacher-training program must attempt to impart all information the student (potential teacher) will need on the job. The instructor who is greatly interested in training the future teacher for systematic learning after the course is over is not only concerned with building up the student's informational background, but he is also equally concerned that the prospective teacher develop the attitudes, skills, and abilities necessary to continuously increase and appraise his store of information while he is on the job. Too often the traditional teacher largely completed his education when he graduated. The modern teacher is one who looks upon his teacher training as preparation to start teaching, and *preparation to continue systematic learning after his formal course work is over.*

There are many reasons why the modern teacher cannot afford to stop growing professionally once he gets on the job. In the first place, stagnation may lead to grumpiness, unhappiness, and irritation. Furthermore, there is danger that continuous repetition of the same assignments and discussions will make the teaching job a boring one instead of the challenging one it can be. Continuous systematic learning by the instructor can make teaching a very pleasant and exhilarating experience.

Not only does the assumption of an active role as a learner give great satisfaction to the teacher, as has already been indicated, but such a role is also indispensable in setting an example for students. It is probable that the teacher in most situations has more influence on learners through his example than through the precepts he expounds or the information he teaches. Pupils can usually sense the basic attitudes the teacher takes toward learning. Does the teacher believe enough in systematic learning to practice it himself? Does the teacher who encourages pupils to read actually use his own skill in reading in order to do a better job of teaching? Pupils quickly catch the enthusiasm of a teacher who is constantly growing in knowledge and in its utilization. Some educational administrators, keenly aware that teachers should grow on the job, aid them in doing so by helping them develop in-service training programs and professional libraries. Financial recognition is also given in some school systems for continued professional development.

In addition to in-service training programs and use of professional books and magazines, the teacher can promote his role as a learner through such media as professional meetings of local, state, or national organizations, summer schools, evening classes, and workshops. The stimulating teacher also learns a great deal in working *with* students and colleagues. The importance of the teacher's role as a perennial learner cannot be overemphasized.

Learning and Professional Problems. A host of unsolved problems confront the teaching profession. The teacher who stays abreast of the field is continually aware of its challenges. Unfortunately many teachers do not or cannot work toward the solution of important educational problems in the classroom. Frequently they are not aware of the most important issues, simply because they have never practiced critical analysis of their own teaching methods.[2] Those who have worked with large groups of teachers in workshops or special training programs have noted that this lack of critical analysis is one of the outstanding weaknesses of teachers as a professional group.

The fact of the matter is that most teachers have had limited experience in systematically identifying and analyzing the major professional problems which they face. Probably far too much of their training has been in terms of acquiring subject matter only and too little in developing their abilities to identify and select for study the problems they will inevitably meet in teaching.

TEACHER SELF-APPRAISAL

It is apparent that the development of the teacher and improvement in what he does necessarily involves changes. It is also clear that not all change results in improvement. To set the stage for systematic change in activities which will result in improvement, it is desirable for the instructor continually to diagnose what he is doing, why he is doing it, and how it is succeeding. The remainder of this chapter suggests approaches the teacher may use in diagnosing and improving some of his behaviors.

The Teacher's Diagnosis of His Own Classroom Activities. If the idea is accepted that the chances of happiness and success as a classroom teacher are enhanced by continuous self-diagnosis of his own behavior, then the question immediately arises: What are possible ways of planning such a diagnosis? There is much variety in approaches which may be used with profit.[3]

[2] Verner M. Sims and others, "Problems Relating to Effective Study for Workshop Participants," *The Southern Association Quarterly*, Vol. 7, 1945, pp. 419–421.

[3] It should be emphasized that the approaches discussed here are recommended for the self-improvement of the teacher, not specifically for pay or promotion ratings. The latter issue may be studied in such references as: (1)

Diagnostic instruments for self-evaluation provide the teacher with evidence of a more objective nature than that which is given by judgment alone. The teacher's self-appraisal must involve the collection of evidence sufficient in quantity and detail to allow for reorganization in teaching theory and practice. It is assumed that the self-evaluation will eventually result in more desirable learning on the part of students as a direct result of improved instruction.

Teachers, inveterate testers of their pupils, are invited by Simpson [4] to apply the testing processes to some of their own activities. For self-diagnostic purposes, the individual teacher is encouraged to evaluate himself on thirty-three questions. Questions relate to three main areas:

I. Provision for individual differences in academic ability. Examples: In the last school year did I have as much concern about the very rapid learner as about the very slow learner? Did I help provide reading materials for daily use which had a spread in difficulty of at least five grades?

II. Provision for professional development. Examples: During the last year did I participate *actively* in teachers' meetings? Did I read at least four professional magazines in the average month?

III. Provision for aiding youngsters in developing socially. Examples: During the last year did I encourage pupils to study and work out many of their problems together? Did I discuss more than once with pupils the problem of how to work more effectively with others in a committee?

Herrick [5] has contributed some scales which aid teachers in diagnosing interrelationships in the classroom, including teacher-pupil relationships and the interactions of pupils. He has constructed forty-seven descriptive scales under nine main categories. Two illustrative categories, together with a scale under each, follow:

NEA Research Division and Department of Classroom Teachers, *Teacher Rating*, Washington, D. C., National Education Association, 1946. (2) Association for Supervision and Curriculum Development, *Better than Rating*, Washington, D. C., ASCD, National Education Association, 1950.

[4] Ray H. Simpson, "Teachers, Here is Your Final," *Clearing House*, Vol. 16, September, 1941, pp. 47–48.

[5] Virgil E. Herrick, *Handbook for Studying an Elementary School Program*, Chicago, Department of Education, The University of Chicago, 1943.

Classroom Atmosphere, Use of Democratic Procedures, Kinds of Control

RESPONSIBILITY FOR PLANNING

1	2	3	4	5
Teacher makes assignments. Pupils expect direction in everything they do. Teacher prepares and follows a rigid daily schedule.		Teacher proposes a new project or unit. Pupils may offer suggestions. Teacher prepares a daily schedule but freely varies it on basis of pupil suggestion.		Children plan projects, units of work, activities under teacher's guidance and in some measure the daily schedule. Under pupil leadership, plans are made in general outline first and later details are filled in. Teacher participates as a working member of the group.

Individual Differences

DISCOVERY AND DEVELOPMENT OF SPECIAL ABILITIES

1	2	3	4	5
One course of study for everybody.		Children not discouraged from developing special abilities but little encouragement is given. Teacher incidentally interested. Little concern about records, instruments of appraisal, and the providing of opportunities for creative expression which would serve as a basis for the discovery of special abilities.		Teacher seeks for special abilities, encourages and aids in their development. To provide opportunities for their discovery and development is conceived as a function of the school.

The individual teacher, using a handbook such as that from which these illustrations came, can diagnose some of his current practices and so take an important first step toward improvement.

Another instrument for self-appraisal is one developed by Simpson.[6] This device consists of twelve scales which cover a wide variety of teaching practices. The scales are based on the assumption that key factors in the evaluation of the teacher are the learnings being practiced by his students. The practices analyzed are indicated below:

I. General factors evaluated.
  A. What is the motivational level at which learners are operating? (Scale A)
  B. How are assignments handled? (Scale B)

II. Problem areas evaluated.
  A. What practice is given in guided problem identification? (Scale C)
  B. What practice is given in guided problem selection? (Scale D)
  C. What practice is given in guided problem solutions? (Scale E)
  D. What guided practice is given in trying out possible solutions to problems? (Scale F)

III. "Service Learnings" evaluated.[7]
  A. How are evaluative abilities developed? (Scale G)
  B. What opportunities for guided practice of effective record keeping are provided the learner? (Scale H)
  C. What opportunities in learning how better to find resources needed in identifying and solving problems are provided the learner? (Scale I)
  D. What opportunities for learning abilities connected with selecting appropriate resources are given when resources are at hand? (Scale J)
  E. What opportunities are given for practice in democratic group discussion? (Scale K)
  F. What guided practice in purposeful reading to identify, select, and solve problems is being given? (Scale L)

In using the scales, each of which contains seven alternatives, the teacher decides which alternative in each scale best describes the level at which most of his pupils seem to be operating. In the light of such a diagnosis the teacher may decide to take steps to raise the level of the different learnings being practiced. For illustrative

  [6] Ray H. Simpson, "An Evaluation of Motivation, Assignment-Making, Problem Procedures, and 'Service Learnings' in a School System," *Journal of Educational Research,* Vol. 44, September, 1950, pp. 1–13.
  [7] "Service Learnings" refer to those learnings which support the major processes of problem identification, problem selection, and problem solution.

purposes, one of the complete scales (Scale A) is presented in Table 36, together with a picture of ratings of classes secured in an urban school system. In the school system rated in Table 36 it may be noted that none of the elementary or senior high-school classes obtained the highest rating while 14 per cent of junior high-school classes did. It can also be noted that the junior high-school classes also had the highest average rating, 4.6, while the senior high-school classes received the lowest rating, 3.9.

There may be some disagreement among different teachers as to the level at which it is best for learners to be practicing. However, in ordering the different levels on this scale the assumption is made that the difference between good and not so good learning from the standpoint of motivation is that sound, dynamic learning is dependent upon internal, self-motivation, while in relatively poor learning the stimuli for action have to come continuously from someone else. In the one case the learner is practicing self-generated learning; in the other he is dependent upon someone else for the push necessary to get learning underway. Activity which is primarily dependent upon the teacher is not likely to be continued when the teacher is absent. If learnings being practiced are diagnosed as unsatisfactory, then both study on the part of the teacher and some changes in teaching are usually indicated.

Keeping a Record of What Happens. A comprehensive record of what goes on in the classroom furnishes one of the best sources for a diagnosis of strengths and weaknesses in the teacher's classroom activities. In connection with this record it is helpful for the teacher to keep a list of his own recognized difficulties encountered from day to day.

A systematic collection of student reactions to class activities and methods employed can also be studied for clues as to ways of improving the teaching-learning situation. Methods for administering and interpreting questionnaires which solicit student reactions to teaching procedures have been described by Bryan.[8] He points out that "pupils are not competent to pass on teacher's methods, but they are competent to report their feelings stimulated by any method used." A study of such reactions can stimulate the teacher to reconsider and restudy some of the approaches he has been using.

[8] R. C. Bryan, *The Evaluation of Student Reactions to Teaching Procedures,* Kalamazoo, Michigan, Graduate Division, Western Michigan College of Education, 1945.

TABLE 36

What Is the Motivational Level at Which Learners Are Operating *

	CLASSES RATED				
RATING	ELEMENTARY	J. H. S.	S. H. S.	ALL CLASSES RATED	
		PER CENT			
7.	0	14	0	8	Learner assumes the major share of responsibility for setting up his goals and for self-improvement, the teacher serves as a guide and at appropriate times checks to see that learning is continuing.
6.	27	18	19	21	Teacher and learner together assume responsibility for setting up sound goals and purposes and together take responsibility for carrying ahead activities.
5.	18	18	4	14	Teacher takes major responsibility for identification and selection of goals and purposes but encourages learners to have minor share in this process.
4.	18	22	44	25	Learner sees goals set up by teacher, accepts them as good and is working enthusiastically to achieve them.
3.	27	23	9	20	Learner recognizes goals set up by the teacher, largely rejects them as valueless for him but works because by meeting teacher-set goals he thinks he can achieve his own goals such as getting a passing mark for the course or grade.
2.	10	5	24	12	Learner sees little or no value in what is done in school and so only does as little as possible to keep from being embarrassed or punished.
1.	0	0	0	0	Learner is antagonistic to procedures and resents teacher efforts to work with him. Does practically no work.
Average Rating	4.2	4.6	3.9	4.4	

* From R. H. Simpson, "An Evaluation of Motivation, Assignment Making, Problem Procedures, and 'Service Learnings' in a School System," *Journal of Educational Research*, Vol. 44, 1950, p. 3.

Some Results of Self-Diagnosis. What will a teacher's diagnosis of classroom activities likely show? What areas frequently are revealed as being in need of improvement? Each teacher in the writer's classes during one summer session was asked the question: "What are specific weaknesses which you think have characterized your most recent teaching and learning?" A summary of the results indicated that the following nine areas were mentioned as ones where improvement is much needed. For each category one example of a teacher's comments is given.

Smugness or complacency. "Since I have been teaching, I have utilized the 'information giving and checking method' exclusively and have been complacent with its use. A teacher usually teaches as he has been taught, and I was subjected only to this method when I was a student. Perhaps I should not blame myself too much for starting out as I did, but I cannot excuse myself for not continuing to learn professionally and systematically since I should be setting an example to my pupils. I plan to study and improve my procedures."

Objectives and standards. "Perhaps my most serious weakness is that of unconsciously attempting to standardize my group of fifth graders. I set up a standard that I expected all pupils to meet, yet I now realize this puts undue pressure on the lower group and does not provide a rich enough program for the upper group."

Class control. "As a teacher of history, it is somewhat ironic that I have *talked* so much about democracy and have been so clearly *practicing* extreme autocratic control in the direction of assignments and class activities. I am going to study how to make my practices more consistent with the theories I have so assiduously expounded."

Assignment making. "Too often this past year my assignments filled no need other than keeping students busy in study hall. In some cases, particularly in the grammar unit, I was even guilty of 'page to page' assignments."

Planning class activities. "In my classes the planning for activities has been done entirely by myself. I can see now that pupils could not be expected to gain much self-control as long as I held a monopoly on the making of decisions."

Class activities. "In the past my students have been required to absorb the information presented to them through the media of formal lectures and teacher assigned outside readings. The activities of students in class have tended to be characterized by passive absorbing of information rather than by active participation in a variety of cooperatively planned activities."

Taking care of individual differences. "My neglect of individual differences was shown by my:

1. presenting the same subject matter to all pupils
2. giving the same assignments to all pupils
3. requiring the same reading of all pupils
4. using the same standards of evaluation for all pupils"

Resources. "In my science classes I have made assignments from two textbooks. The pupils have received no experience in finding their own references and in evaluating resources. I have not encouraged pupils to use sources other than these two textbooks."

Evaluation. "Another weakness of which I have been guilty is that of not letting pupils evaluate themselves or their group when working on a problem or when they have completed it. The evaluation is usually done entirely by me. In receiving his grade the pupil has no idea what his weaknesses were if his grade was low and what his strong points were if his grade was high. Being kept in this type of darkness the pupil has no knowledge of how he can improve himself. If each pupil kept his own record and helped evaluate himself as well as the others this would lead to more learning and a more complete understanding of what was being done."

IMPROVEMENT OF THE TEACHER'S CLASS ACTIVITIES

After a teacher has made a tentative diagnosis of his own classroom activities, what can he do to eliminate weaknesses? The points of attack for each teacher will vary depending on such factors as his present practices, the type of self-diagnosis made, and the perceptions of the teacher regarding the areas where improvements are both needed and feasible. Some changes teachers can make will now be discussed.

Experimentation. After diagnosis, the teacher frequently finds his class activities are ones he has just "fallen into" rather than ones whose soundness has been demonstrated. Such a conclusion will, sometimes, lead him to experiment with new or different procedures. Such experimentation, usually started cautiously, may involve changing the way assignments are made or modifying the type of resources used, or trying out various ways of giving students guided practice in leadership. Preceding and accompanying such experimentation will be study of experimentation in similar areas by others. Careful tryout of newer approaches is no more dangerous to the learner than the routine using of traditional practices whose values and limitations have never been experimentally determined. With systematic checking of what is done, one should expect better and more satisfying teaching and learning experiences.

Assignment-Making. One of the areas which study reveals to be in need of improvement is assignment-making. Improvement in this activity frequently involves moving from assignments exclusively planned by the teacher toward assignments cooperatively originated by the teacher and learners. For example, one instructor reports:

After consideration of my assignment-making practices I am forced to admit they are clearly autocratic and dictatorial. Learners have usually done the work, but apparently the motivation has been almost entirely a desire to get a respectable grade and pass the course. There is little evidence the students have really understood *why* they were studying particular assignments. There has been a rather passive interest in the work. I have started to involve the learners in the planning of assignments. This, I believe, will result in more active interest on their part in the work. We are attempting to have assignment-making more democratic.

When learners are given some opportunities to help plan their work, a movement away from the same assignment for everyone usually occurs. Individual differences in such factors as purposes, goals, reading abilities, needs, interests, and mental capacities are likely to result in multiple rather than uniform assignments. For example, Jim Martin, after listing the words he had misspelled in his written work during a particular week (the teacher and other students helped him identify these words) decided with the guidance of his teacher that this list should constitute his spelling assignment for the following week. Increasing responsibility is placed upon the individual learner to help decide what assignment is best for him at a given time. Children in the upper grades and in high school are particularly competent to assist in such activities. Incidentally, such emphasis helps prepare the student for increasing self-responsibility in initiating learning activities.

Control of Activities. Many teachers are fearful that unless they keep strict control, pupils may get out of hand. However, strict control does not give pupils the share in planning activities which is educationally defensible. Beginning teachers often report discipline as a major problem. Improvement in discipline usually involves some shifts in class control. As with assignment-making, control of many classes has been clearly autocratic. Improvement here typically involves study and experimentation designed to give students considerable practice in managing individual and small group activities and in analyzing the advantages and disadvantages in various plans of action. With more student responsibility for what is done in classes comes more active interest in learning activities. As a consequence of acquired student dependence on teachers and lack of teacher familiarity with democratically operated class procedures, improvement may come slowly at first.

Use of Resources. Improvement in the use of resources is intimately related to the ways in which a teacher handles individual differences. The teacher should ask himself the following questions: Have I given students sufficient practice in learning how to select and *acquire* books, magazines, and other resources they will need for individual and group learning activities? Have I put too much dependence upon a single text, particularly when it was probably inappropriate for certain pupils in each class? Have I underemphasized the use of such non-reading resources such as films, pictures, and the wealth of resources found in community activities? Has the money spent on texts or other resources resulted in a plethora of a few resources and a paucity of varied resources? Have I told learners too often exactly what resources to use, giving them little or no practice in making such decisions themselves?

Evaluation. Systematic evaluation in the classroom has long been considered the exclusive job of the teacher. Such control of evaluative processes has led to extreme pupil dependence on the teacher for evaluative activities. It has also resulted in the learner being ill-equipped to evaluate for learning purposes. Evaluation for learning purposes involves practice in setting up objectives, in diagnosing needs through measurement, and in planning future activities. Improvement of teacher activities in this regard will involve helping learners (1) determine their own goals in various areas; (2) diagnose their own individual and group needs; and (3) set up plans for learning activities designed to mitigate or eliminate weaknesses revealed by the diagnosis. The teacher's role in this improvement will shift from one of complete responsibility for evaluation to one of helping students improve their learning through increased facility in self-evaluation. Jim Martin, the boy referred to on a previous page who had a hand in planning his spelling assignments, also learned how to evaluate his success in learning to spell the words he used. Each week a fellow classmate pronounced Jim's individual spelling list to him. Jim checked the words he misspelled and practiced on these the following week.

TEACHER-TEACHER RELATIONSHIPS

In times past it has been assumed by too many teachers that the only major front for improvement of professional activities was in the classroom. While it is true that the teacher's behavior in the classroom is of paramount importance, it is now recognized that there are key areas outside the classroom where potentialities are great for professional improvement. One of these is the working relationships between teachers.

Let us contrast the attitudes of teachers toward each other in two school systems. In the one school a general spirit of cooperation prevailed. Materials were generously shared, including professional books and magazines. Staff members discussed the problems of their pupils. Teachers told others what they were doing in their classes, the difficulties and successes they were having. Things sometimes did not run smoothly in the school, but an attitude of mutual helpfulness characterized the working relationships within the staff. This attitude, incidentally, also seemed to be contagious and favorably affected teacher-learner and teacher-administrator relationships as well.

In the other school the characteristic inter-personal attitudes existing within the staff ranged from an outright antagonistic attitude to one of watchful neutrality. Each teacher's motto seemed to be: "If you keep out of my way, we will get along fine." Below the surface in staff meetings there was an air of suspicion. A teacher would occasionally drop hints to students that certain other teachers took too much student time, or were too easy markers, or that they let pupils get away with too much. There was little sharing of ideas and materials. Some teachers talked as if their subject was the only one of real importance. This lack of cooperation was also spread to teacher-learner relationships. Students quickly sensed that all was not well. Many disciplinary problems developed. In general the atmosphere was not a happy one in which to work.

Much of the success of the modern school depends upon the willingness and the ability of its teaching staff to work together. There are many areas which demand such cooperation. One of these is curriculum revision. Unless the educational experiences of a student are continuously coordinated it is possible that the experiences encouraged by one teacher may work at cross purposes with those recommended by another. For example, it is a too common experience in some schools for a student, particularly one of below average ability, to have an amount of homework assigned which makes it impossible, if he takes all of the assignments seriously, for him to have time for adequate recreation, outdoor activity, and sleep.

Teachers also need to cooperate in dealing with such problems as marking, promoting, and reporting the activities of pupils. Continuous improvement in a school program involves gradual changes in the purposes and specific goals in teaching-learning situations. Such changes can and should be reflected in the bases upon which marks are given and in the school's reporting and promoting practices.

The initial training of most teachers has usually placed all too little stress on the importance of working with other teachers and on developing the skills necessary to work with teaching peers successfully. There is presently an increasing tendency to give added attention to this social aspect of educational psychology. Fortunately, the arousal of interest in inter-personal relations among teachers has developed concurrently with increased research related to the functioning of groups.[9]

Contribution to the improvement of the professional activities of colleagues has too frequently been neglected by teachers. Reciprocal training by teachers of each other has unlimited possibilities as an approach to educational advance.

In-Service Training Programs. For the inter-personal relations within a school staff to remain on a healthy and constructive level some type of in-service training program is most desirable. What form it should take for the individual teacher and for the school

[9] For example, see Kenneth Benne and Bozidar Muntyan, *Human Relations in Curriculum Change,* Springfield, Illinois, Superintendent of Public Instruction, 1949.

staff will, of course, depend to a considerable degree upon the backgrounds of the individuals involved. However, some characteristics of a useful in-service program can be pointed out.

In the first place it should be thought of as a cooperative staff effort designed to bring about specific improvements in the school activities. Mere courses or lectures for the staff will not fill the real need. Active study by teachers and attacks on actual school problems is needed if substantial improvement is to result.

Those working on a particular problem may be the whole staff or this group may divide itself into smaller subgroups, each of which studies and plans improvements. Illustrative problems are these: How can we improve the curriculum in our school? What are ways of meeting individual differences in more effective ways? How can the basic causes of disciplinary cases be identified and eliminated? How can we improve our marking and reporting practices?

The individual teacher, to profit most from the program, must not only be able to accept but should also welcome ideas and suggestions of fellow teachers concerning ways to improve his teaching and other professional activities. A permissive air should be developed in which the teacher is willing to expose some of his difficulties, weaknesses, and confusions so that others can help him eliminate these.

Individuals involved in an in-service training program will find it desirable to study ways of improving their functioning in groups. This is particularly true, since many teachers in their pre-service training have had little or no careful study of the social psychology underlying the behavior of individuals in groups. Furthermore, most teachers have had insufficient practice in working democratically with peers on important professional problems. For example, too many teachers in a group situation tend to have too great a dependence on the group leader.[10] There is a tendency to sit back and wait for the leader to initiate and carry through the activities of the group. Other teachers with all good intentions sabotage group activities since they have only trained themselves to study and plan individually and have not developed the skills and abilities necessary for desirable professional activity.

Finally, in considering the psychological soundness of an in-serv-

---

[10] K. D. Benne and B. Muntyan, *Human Relations in Curriculum Change,* Springfield, Illinois, State Superintendent of Public Instruction, 1949, pp. 214–219.

ice program we may ask such questions as these: Do teachers in a friendly fashion continuously exchange constructive criticism, involving professional goals, plans, and procedures? Does each teacher budget a certain amount of time each week for work with other teachers to get and give professional help? Do teachers realize the fact that helping other teachers learn may be more economical teaching than only teaching pupils? Committee work and departmental meetings offer the teacher opportunities for gathering and giving professional ideas. Trading ideas on an informal basis can constitute a profitable source of professional stimulation. Helping new teachers adjust to the multitude of problems which inevitably face and sometimes threaten to overwhelm them is a service which not only may help the new teacher but can also provide new points of view for the more experienced teacher.

Workshops and Pre-School Planning Conferences. Those studying in workshops are likely to come from more than one school. Members of the pre-school planning conference are usually from a single school or school system. However, the purposes and procedures of workshops and pre-school planning conferences tend to be similar. The general purpose of both of these approaches to in-service training is to improve the educational program through concentrated staff study on realistic school problems. The work of each teacher is pointed toward the solution of problems which he has encountered or visualizes he will encounter in his professional work.[11] Both the workshop and the pre-school planning conference are based on the assumption that teachers learn best when they work together in an atmosphere which encourages critical thinking, free discussion, and systematic planning for future activities.

One of the chief values of workshops and pre-school planning conferences is that they encourage teachers to work with and get the points of view of teachers in other subjects and on other levels. The mathematics teacher may study underlying causes of disciplinary problems with the English teacher. The social studies teacher may study and plan how to improve pupil reading abilities with the fifth-grade teacher. The interaction of teachers which characterizes pre-school planning conferences and workshops tends to broaden the points of view held by the individual teacher.

[11] E. C. Kelley, *The Workshop Way of Learning*, New York, Harper and Brothers, 1951, pp. 6–11.

Generally workshops and pre-school conferences are run on a more democratic basis than more conventional institutes. Instead of being fairly passive participants in an imposed program, the teachers themselves help formulate the framework in which they study and plan. After activities have started the individual teacher has an important role in helping to determine the problems he will attack and the procedures he will use in furthering his study and planning.

Many of the participants of a workshop or planning conference are likely to continue their study during the ensuing school year. Tentative plans resulting from study are to be tried out on the job. The amount of transfer-of-training from the study situation to the teaching situation should be greater than from the ordinary professional class or course.

IMPROVING TEACHER-ADMINISTRATOR RELATIONS

Causes of Difficulties. Whenever difficulties in inter-personal relations are encountered, it is natural to project the troubles on someone else.[12] Bradford and Sheats [13] found that administrators were likely to try to place failure of staff meetings upon teachers. Teachers tend to reciprocate by blaming administrators for lack of cooperation. A more sound approach from a psychological standpoint is to say: What weaknesses on my part have contributed to the difficulties I have in working with administrators (or teachers)? Such a self-diagnosis can pave the way for eliminating many of these weaknesses and for developing needed inter-personal skills which may have been neglected in early professional training.

Active Role Needed. If the teacher feels professional relations with the administrator need improvement he may decide to take a more active role in the operation of the school. Such a role is likely to bring the teacher into more working contact with the principal or superintendent. Evidence from social psychology suggests that such cooperative work is one of the best ways of establishing mutual respect. The teacher sees in most cases that it is possible to work with the administrator after all. The principal (or superintendent) finds that the teacher is a worker who sometimes makes mistakes, as he does, but who is willing to try to help improve the school

---

[12] See pp. 336–337 for discussion of projection.

[13] Leland Bradford and Paul Sheats, "Complacency Shock as a Prerequisite to Training," *Sociatry*, Vol. 2, 1948, pp. 38–48.

program. Each is a bit more tolerant of the other as he gets more acquainted with the other's point of view.[14]

Exposing of Weaknesses. When mutual respect and cooperation between teacher and administrator have been developed each is willing to divulge some of his weaknesses to the other. Fear that such exposure may itself be labeled a weakness is minimized. Each begins to see that it is through mutual trust and cooperative attack on these weaknesses that they can be gradually eliminated. One clue as to the quality of teacher-administrator relations lies in the answer to this question: Is the teacher willing to expose some of his weaknesses to the administrator so that he can give help or suggest where such may be found? In many situations the principal is to the teacher as the teacher is to the child. If the administrator is to help the teacher in professional learning, he must treat confidentially many matters which have been discussed with him.

PROFESSIONAL READING

A rich source of help for teachers lies in the extensive professional literature which is now available. Practically every problem a teacher meets has been met with some success by hundreds of other teachers. The key to viewing the experiences of other instructors is often available through the medium of professional reading.[15]

When the issue of reading disabilities is discussed, educators sometimes forget that they themselves may suffer from such liabilities. For example, in a large urban school system it was found that 3 per cent of the twelfth-grade pupils actually read better than 100 per cent of the teachers.[16] This conclusion was reached after the teachers and administrators, who were planning a reading improvement program, asked one of the writers to administer to them a comprehensive reading test. It was also found that 75 per cent of twelfth-grade pupils read better than 15 per cent of these adminis-

[14] For an additional discussion on this point see: Roberta Green, "The Obstacles to Democratic Administration as Seen by a Teacher," *Progressive Education*, Vol. 30, 1952, pp. 35–37.

[15] For many teachers professional writing constitutes an important activity. Two primary values of such expression are these: (1) it helps the teacher clarify what he believes, what he is doing, and how he can improve; and (2) it can stimulate other teachers to attempt to improve through the tryout of new ideas.

[16] Ray H. Simpson, "Reading Disabilities among Teachers and Administrators," *The Clearing House*, Vol. 17, September, 1942, p. 12.

trators and teachers. The educators were found to be particularly low on these subtests of the Iowa Silent Reading Test: Selection of Key Words, Use of Index, and Directed Reading.

An even more challenging picture was revealed in this same study when an analysis was made of the reading these school men and women did during a typical month.[17] A reasonable amount of leisure-time reading was done, but little or no professional reading to help solve school problems was engaged in by the typical teacher or administrator. *Even those teachers who scored high on the reading test, which indicated they knew how to read well, made little if any more professional use of this ability than did those who scored low.*

The crux of the matter is that many teachers and administrators know *how* to read on a satisfactory level but make extremely little use of this skill in attacking professional problems. In a study of 746 teachers and administrators made by one of the writers, the following results related to professional reading were revealed for a particular month:

No magazine articles read	14 per cent
One magazine article read	10 per cent
Two magazine articles read	13 per cent
Three to five magazine articles read	29 per cent
More than five magazine articles read	34 per cent

40 per cent had not even looked at one professional book.
17 per cent had sampled one book.
24 per cent had read parts of two books.
15 per cent had read parts of three to five books.
 4 per cent had read parts of five or more books.

Clearly reading of professional books is not something which is done to any great extent. How can administrators and teachers really develop a vital reading improvement program in their schools unless they believe in reading enough to use it as an aid in solving their day-to-day problems?

Causes of Failure to Read Professional Literature. Why do teachers and school administrators not make more use of reading? The following causes may partly account for this situation:

1. The experiences of many schoolmen in colleges and universities have led them to think that their professional growth ends when the coveted degree is received. This doctrine stunts growth.
2. Many administrators and teachers are hired largely on the basis of

[17] *Ibid.*, pp. 12–13.

past credit-getting rather than on present abilities and upon probable self-education and growth on the job.

3. Many administrators have not expected their teachers to continue to grow professionally while on the job.
4. Teachers and administrators have not been taught how to get the printed materials which will be of definite help in solving their day-by-day problems.

Improving Professional Reading Habits. Administrators with the aid of their school boards can improve the professional reading habits of teachers by utilizing the following suggestions:

1. Set aside a small sum of money each month for professional materials.
2. Establish with the aid of the teachers and librarians active professional libraries in each school.
3. Make salary increases partially contingent upon evidences of professional growth. One evidence of this would be a consistent use of professional materials.
4. In faculty meetings and elsewhere encourage the discussion and consideration of new ideas relating to methods, materials, and evaluation which are being tried in other school systems.
5. Help teachers isolate the specific professional problems which they feel are the most pressing and make it a point to suggest some sources from which they might get help.
6. Ask individual teachers periodically what they are reading and what ideas they are using from such reading.
7. Encourage publishers to send notices of new professional materials to librarians and teachers for their consideration.
8. Make provisions in work schedules of teachers so that some time each week can be utilized for studying new practices and trends.

TEACHER-COMMUNITY RELATIONS

Teachers not only need to establish good rapport with pupils and administrators but also find it essential to create sound relationships with parents and other community members. Such relations are likely to have considerable effect upon the success of student efforts and upon the effectiveness and happiness of the teacher. Without appropriate school-home understanding and communication the learnings teachers are trying to encourage in school may actually be discouraged, directly or indirectly, by the parents. Poor or inadequate school-home relations too frequently result in a lowering of respect for the role of the teacher and are likely to decrease the financial support the community will give to its schools. Obviously this latter result is likely to keep the salaries of teachers at a low level. Thus, we see that healthy school-home relations not only contribute to better education for learners but also tends to make the status of the teacher a more desirable one.

School Program and Community Needs. Nothing gives a school a sounder foundation for the development and establishment of appropriate relations with the community than to have a dynamic program attuned to community needs. School activities are likely to become more meaningful if students receive guided practice in attacking community problems.[18] The probability of getting transfer of learning from school situations to out-of-school activities is also greatly enhanced. The following are some of the problems which schools in various communities have found useful as vehicles for increasing motivation, getting transfer of learning, and improving school-community relations: How can an unsanitary waterway in the community be changed to improve health and recreation? What improvements can and should be made in parks and playgrounds? How might race relations be bettered? What are ways of getting more active participation in civic activities?

Homework. Instead of being a profitable learning experience for the student and a contribution to improved school-home relations, homework has frequently damaged such relations. Parents are too commonly kept in the dark about the purposes of homework. The child himself is in no position to help the parent understand the work when the purposes of assignments are not clear to him. This lack of understanding by either the parent or child often results from the common practice of having all assignments autocratically imposed on the learner rather than having them developed through teacher-pupil cooperation. Ventures by the teacher in the direction of democratically developed assignments will go a long way toward helping students, and in turn their parents, appreciate the school's objectives. In addition such changes may improve motivation and interest in school work through eliminating busywork and non-meaningful activities.

Frequently the homework can complement rather than merely duplicate the in-school work. For example, if the meaning and skills involved in multiplication are being studied, the pupil might be

[18] For a description of successful joint school and community practices from kindergarten through adult education see E. G. Olsen, *School and Community Programs,* New York, Prentice-Hall, Inc., 1949.

asked to determine such things as the cost of the bread bought by his family in the next week. This will probably involve determining the cost per loaf and multiplying this by the number of loaves purchased.

Sometimes the parent can be given an opportunity to cooperate in guiding the homework. The parent might be asked, for example, if he would supply the amount of bread or other items purchased and let the child determine the cost per item at the grocery story. Budget-making, figuring income tax, planning purchases, using consumer research data are other illustrations of problems where skills can be developed through parent-teacher cooperation.

Using Criticism. All teachers can develop the ability to use criticism in a constructive fashion. Too often suggestions given in a friendly fashion are taken as personal affronts rather than as clues for needed change. Because of their close contact with children, parents can sometimes supply such clues if they feel teachers welcome them. Teachers also need to study how to offer constructive criticism in such a way that parents and colleagues accept and use it rather than resent the teacher's suggestions. Even open disagreement of a friendly sort may be a healthy sign at times.

Adult Use of School Facilities. If the community is to get its money's worth out of the big investment it has in its school plant, such facilities must not be unused three whole months a year plus Saturday, Sunday, and weekday nights. One way of improving school-community relations is for teachers to take the lead in promoting adult use of school facilities. For example, one group of teachers was interested in furthering good reading in the community. They arranged to have the school library open several nights a week. This lead to discussion or "seminar" groups being formed. The community thought more highly of its school and the educators in charge of it when the school started giving taxpayers more for their money.[19]

Other Ways of Improving Communication and Understanding. Use of parents' nights, fathers' nights, and parent visiting weeks have been found helpful in some communities.[20] Of course, parents should always be welcome in the school but special invitations are not out of place.

[19] *Ibid.*, pp. 63–73.
[20] *Ibid.*

Active parent participation in such organizations as the Parent-Teachers Association is to be encouraged. To be virile, PTAs must be willing to face and grapple with significant issues even though at times the matters may be of a controversial nature. Too often such meetings have been innocuous and boring affairs attended out of a sense of duty.

Surveys of community problems jointly conducted by parents and teachers, as well as active participation by students in local projects outside the school are additional ways in which healthy relationships between the home and school can be promoted. In the last analysis, good professional development demands that teachers so involve themselves in community affairs that schoolwork meets the needs and best interests of pupils. There is perhaps no better way to attain this involvement in the community than to make studies of community problems and local issues a regular part of schoolwork.

SUMMARY

Teaching is a professional field where changes are constantly taking place. New discoveries in psychology and in methods of teaching are the rule rather than the exception. The graduate of a teacher-training institution of ten years ago, if he has not kept up to date, would be astonished by advances which have been made even in that short time in the techniques of his profession. Changes and new developments in subject matter fields also are moving ahead at a fast pace. The teacher who is to be a challenging leader of children must learn how to keep abreast of such changes and in a very real sense continue to be a learner after his formal education has been completed.

In this chapter, methods have been presented which enable the teacher to appraise and evaluate his professional activities and teaching procedures. Suggestions are given for improving teacher-pupil relationships, teacher-teacher relationships, teacher-administration relationships, and finally teacher-community relationships.

The professionally maturing teacher is one who not only reads widely in journals dealing with teaching methods and his field of specialization, but also keeps closely in touch with expanding knowledge in all fields. He learns to be a critic of his own performance, and stimulates progress among his colleagues and other professional workers. Most important of all, the continually developing teacher affects the behavior of his pupils who learn by example and profit from the enriched and up-to-date program of studies which almost inevitably ensues.

REFERENCES FOR FURTHER STUDY

Baxter, Bernice, *Teacher-Pupil Relationships*, New York, The Macmillan Company, 1943.

Beecher, Dwight E., *The Evaluation of Teaching, Backgrounds and Concepts*, Syracuse, New York, Syracuse University Press, 1949.

Bond, Guy L. and Handlan, Bertha, *Adapting Instruction in Reading to Individual Differences*, Minneapolis, University of Minnesota Press, 1948.

Giles, H. H., *Teacher-Pupil Planning*, New York, Harper & Brothers, 1941.

Glencoe Public Schools, *Together We Build a Community School*, Glencoe, Illinois, Glencoe Public Schools, 1944.

Jenkins, F. C. and others, "Cooperative Study for the Improvement of Education," *Southern Association Quarterly*, Vol. 10, February and August, 1946, pp. 1–139, 369–488.

Kelley, E. C., *The Workshop Way of Learning*, New York, Harper & Brothers, 1951.

Krech, D. and R. S. Crutchfield, *Theory and Problems of Social Psychology*, New York, McGraw-Hill Book Company, Inc., 1948.

Miel, Alice, *Cooperative Procedures in Learning*, New York, Columbia University, Teachers College Bureau of Publications, 1952.

N.E.A., Association for Supervision and Curriculum Development, *Toward Better Teaching*, Washington 6, D. C., National Education Association, 1949.

N.E.A., School Public Relations Association, *It Starts in the Classroom; a Public Relations Handbook for Classroom Teachers*, Washington, D. C., National Education Association, 1951.

Olsen, E. G., *School and Community Programs*, New York, Prentice-Hall, Inc., 1949.

Olson, C. M. and N. D. Fletcher, *Learn and Live*, New York, Alfred P. Sloan Foundation, 1946.

Rasey, Marie I., *This Is Teaching*, New York, Harper & Brothers, 1950.

Simpson, Ray H., *Improving Teaching-Learning Processes*, New York, Longmans, Green and Company, 1953.

Swanson, Guy E., T. M. Newcomb, E. L. Hartley, and others, *Readings in Social Psychology*, New York, Henry Holt and Company, Inc., 1952.

Wiles, Kimball, *Supervision for Better Schools*, New York, Prentice-Hall, Inc., 1950.

Wiles, Kimball, *Teaching for Better Schools*, New York, Prentice-Hall, Inc., 1952.

560   THE PSYCHOLOGY OF THE TEACHER

The reader is also urged to utilize the following headings in the *Education Index:*

College professors and instructors, Rating, Rating by students
Orientation programs for teachers
Principals and teachers
Professional books and reading
Professional education
Professional growth
Public relations
Social adjustment and development
Teacher training
Teacher training in service
Teachers, Rating, Rating by students
Teachers' workshops
Teaching methods; also subhead Teaching methods under school subject, e.g., Human relations—Teaching methods.

Chapter 22

Personal and Emotional
Adjustment of the Teacher

IF PSYCHOLOGY has any practical value, it ought to help teachers with their own personal adjustment. Teachers need this help. It has been noted that, "All day long, the teacher is dealing with emotionally toned activities—hostility, defiance, dependency, demands, destruction of property, dishonesty. . . ." [1] The energies of children, and the turmoil of the classroom inevitably create tensions within the teacher. These tensions must find healthy release in work and recreation. Teachers who are unable to discover mechanisms of release are apt to become irritable, emotionally disturbed, and maladjusted. The teacher who screams, cries, threatens, or ridicules pupils is the one who has failed to attain other means of relieving pressure and uses the children in his classroom as scapegoats for his own frustrations.

This chapter will present the problem of maladjustment among teachers, the causes and effects of this maladjustment, and finally suggest ways in which teachers may remain in good mental health.

THE PROBLEM

If one were to survey the population of teachers, describe their state of mental health and compare his findings with similar results for other professional groups, he would probably find teachers just as healthy, perhaps more stable, than other people. [2]

[1] National Society for the Study of Education, *Learning and Instruction,* Part I, 49th Yearbook, Chicago, University of Chicago Press, 1950, p. 180.

[2] J. L. Malloch, "A Study of State Hospital Commitments of Teachers in Comparison with Other Occupations," Unpublished Master's Thesis, Stanford University, 1941; and *Fit to Teach*, Washington, D. C., Department of Classroom Teachers, National Educational Association, 9th Yearbook, 1938, p. 77.

Even though this is true, however, it is disquieting to note that in the population as a whole, serious personal problems and maladjustment take an alarming toll. Teachers are not exempt. They, as millions of others, have their work efficiency and happiness impaired by personal problems and emotional unrest. But unlike many other groups, teachers' mental health is an integral part of the job itself. In no other work is good mental health more essential than in teaching. The profession demands stability—a capacity to withstand pressures, and most important the skill of working aggressions off into channels different from the work situation. In other words, the teacher must learn to keep his aggressions and personal difficulties out of the classroom. Most teachers succeed, but a sizeable percentage, to some degree, allow personal maladjustment to interfere with their work. The number of teachers who succumb to pressures of work, or fall victim to nervous disorders and the form which these deviate behaviors take will now be discussed.

How Many Teachers Are Maladjusted? The various studies of the condition of mental health and adjustment of teachers have differed to a considerable extent in their findings. All seem to agree that many experienced teachers could profit from psychological or psychiatric assistance. Table 37 outlines the results of some of the major studies of teachers' adjustment. It is clear that although samples used, methods, and findings differ, there is an agreement that a significant percentage of the teacher population are so maladjusted that their teaching suffers.

Perhaps the most comprehensive study of any shown in Table 37 was that of Fenton. Both Fenton and Hicks (the first study shown in the table) estimated that about 20 per cent of the teachers in their sample were in need of mental hygiene assistance. More serious disturbances—those which would warrant immediate study and therapy—are spotted by Blair, and by Altman as comprising a group somewhere between 4 and 8 per cent. These data would tend to support the conclusion that one-fifth or more of teachers need psychological help while as many as five out of a hundred are mental cases, and need immediate professional treatment.

How is Maladjustment Manifested? The personal difficulties of teachers is often revealed in their treatment of pupils. One investigator found the following examples of cruel and unusual punishments being practiced by experienced teachers:

TABLE 37

The Incidence of Maladjustment of Teachers as Reported in Several Investigations

INVESTI-GATION	FINDINGS	SAMPLE	METHOD
Hicks * 1934	17.5 per cent of teachers unduly nervous or psychoneurotic. 10.5 per cent had had nervous breakdowns.	600 Teachers 124 men 476 women	Analysis of questionnaire filled out by teachers themselves.
Peck † 1936	37.5 per cent subject to persistent worries.	5150 teachers	Analysis of questionnaire filled out by teachers.
N.E.A. Yearbook Committee ‡ 1938	About 17 per cent in need of psychiatric service.	100 women teachers	Administered the Thurstone Personality Schedule.
Altman § 1941	4 per cent described as mental cases. 13 per cent in need of treatment.	35,000 New York teachers	Estimate from clinical practice.
Fenton ‖ 1943	22.5 per cent in need of mental hygiene help and 15.4 per cent handicapped in their work by maladjustment.	241 teachers from small communities	Conferences with supervisors, and classroom observation of all teachers in the sample.
Blair ¶ 1946	8.8 per cent maladjusted to such an extent that they should be screened for psychological study.	205 experienced teachers	Administered the Multiple-Choice Rorschach. Used the Harrower-Erickson norms to determine a cutting score.

* F. R. Hicks, *The Mental Health of Teachers*, Contribution to Education, No. 123, George Peabody College, Nashville, Tennessee, 1934.

† Leigh Peck, "A Study of the Adjustment Difficulties of a Group of Women Teachers," *Journal of Educational Psychology*, Vol. 27, 1936, pp. 401–416.

‡ *Fit to Teach*, Washington, D. C., Department of Classroom Teachers, National Educational Association, 9th Yearbook, 1938, p. 77.

§ Emil Altman, "Our Mentally Unbalanced Teachers," *The American Mercury*, Vol. 52, April, 1941, pp. 391–401.

‖ Norman Fenton, *Mental Hygiene in School Practice*, Stanford University, California, Stanford University Press, 1943, p. 288.

¶ G. M. Blair, "Personal Adjustment of Teachers as Measured by the Multiple-Choice Rorschach Test," *Journal of Educational Research*, Vol. 39, May, 1946, pp. 652–657.

1. A child jerked from his seat by his hair.
2. Kicking child.
3. A child forced to push chalk around the room with his nose.
4. Child forced to apologize on his knees.
5. Mimicry of stuttering child.
6. Coining of descriptive names such as "spaghetti, lard, garbage, and tattler." [3]

Such examples lead one to believe that further training of many teachers is necessary. But when teachers lose control or resort to almost sadistic forms of punishment there is little doubt that their behavior springs not from lack of training but from emotional instability. Altman described a case in which a teacher in a frenzy of rage attacked a girl of nine and came very close to severing her jugular vein. In still another of Altman's cases, a teacher, clearly a psychotic, believed that the school janitor was trying to freeze her, so she insisted on wearing her overcoat in the schoolroom. In fact, according to Altman one teacher commuted back and forth to her school from a mental hospital where she was being treated.[4] These are clear cut cases of profound disturbance. But not all personal problems and emotional disturbances so clearly manifest themselves in the classroom. Many teachers complain of persistent worries, sleeplessness, and nervousness. In the comprehensive study of the N.E.A. Yearbook Committee shown in Table 37, teachers listed nervousness as the third highest ailment in a list of seventeen.[5] And in a survey of 300 beginning high-school teachers in Illinois, it was found that 20 per cent had difficulties which they were unable to solve.[6] Apparently many teachers are beset by difficulties which do not markedly interfere with their teaching but nevertheless do interfere with their adjustment and happiness. And it is safe to say that such difficulties, if they remain uncorrected, may eventually lead to more serious disturbances which will certainly manifest themselves in the classroom.

Early Symptoms of Maladjustment. What are danger signals in the behavior of the teacher which indicate maladjustment or emo-

[3] C. R. Adams, "Classroom Practice and the Personality Adjustment of Children," *Understanding the Child,* Vol. 13, June, 1944, pp. 10–15.

[4] Emil Altman, *op.cit.,* pp. 391 and 396.

[5] *Fit to Teach, op.cit.,* p. 77.

[6] H. L. Wellbank, "The Teacher and His Problems," *Educational Administration and Supervision,* Vol. 38, 1952, pp. 491–494.

tional immaturity? How can an observer or the teacher himself be alerted to the symptoms which indicate a need for precautionary mental hygiene measures? Such questions are crucial since it is well recognized that preventive steps are more effective than later therapy.

Crossness and general irritability are perhaps the most general and frequent early symptoms. Loss of temper is sometimes a reflection of underlying emotional difficulties. For example, the teacher who says: "Who made that noise? You won't tell? All right, all of you will stay in one hour after school," is probably showing either poor judgment or is allowing his work to create mental health hazards. Indulging in sarcasm or incessant scolding, or subjecting children to cruel or unusual punishments are, as previously noted, clues which indicate unhealthy reactions to difficult or frustrating conditions.

The teacher who finds fault with other staff members or departments frequently suffers from a lack of personal security which he tries to ventilate by trying to tear down the reputations of others. Such a teacher also frequently feels too insecure to experiment and try out teaching innovations, and may make fun of colleagues who attempt to improve teaching-learning situations. Sometimes such behavior is accompanied by an attitude of cynicism toward the world in general and toward the possibilities of improvement in education in particular. Such teachers not only try little to improve themselves but may actually strive to keep others from improving.

Sometimes teachers' mental ill health is also reflected in an inability to accept normal aggressions of youngsters. One who cannot stand noise or horseplay, or who becomes unduly disturbed over the exaggerated braggadocio which many adolescents display, should consider a career other than teaching.

A complete list of the symptoms which disturbed teachers might exhibit would be difficult to compose. The few which have just been listed are representative of those which the alert school administrator or teacher should be able to recognize. As a general guide, it might be stated that bizarre methods of striving to be important, or loss of emotional control are symptomatic of maladjustment.

EFFECT OF TEACHER MALADJUSTMENT ON PUPILS

That many personally maladjusted teachers are to be found in our classrooms no one will deny. The extent to which such teachers affect the lives of the children under their tutelage, however, has not been fully determined. Several research studies conducted to date seem to indicate that the effects may be very far-reaching. For example, an early study by Boynton and others [7] carried out in the classrooms of 73 fifth- and sixth-grade teachers showed that pupils of the teachers in the best mental health were more stable than pupils in classes taught by teachers who were rated as being in poor mental health. In a somewhat more recent study [8] it was shown that kindergarten children, taught by a teacher considered to be poorly adjusted, changed for the worse while a comparable group, taught by "an adjusted teacher," suffered no such loss. Baxter's [9] investigation clearly showed that the way teachers conducted their classes was reflected in the security and freedom from tension of pupils, and that much of the teacher's behavior appeared to be tied up with factors of adjustment.

The fate of a pupil who had the misfortune to have a maladjusted teacher is presented by Wallin.[10] This case is described by the individual involved some years after the unfortunate incident occurred.

My friends are always talking about my inferiority complex. I have always considered myself dumb and had little confidence in my ability to get high grades or to achieve much in school, in spite of the fact that I continue to find my university courses very interesting. I think my inferiority feelings sprang up in the third grade, when I had a teacher whom I hated. She is the one who mocked and made fun of my thumb sucking. . . . She said I was naughty, inattentive, and unable to get my work, and kept me in the third grade for three years, while my classmates with probably no more ability than I had were advanced. When the fourth-grade teacher got hold of me and became aware of the injustice done me, she shoved me on as fast as she could, so that I made up about a year that way. Although I advanced a grade every year there after, as long as I was in that particular school I always felt I was a dumbbell. When I transferred to another school, where I had no bad record, I worked with

[7] P. Boynton, H. Dugger, and M. Turner, "The Emotional Stability of Teachers and Pupils," *Journal of Juvenile Research*, Vol. 18, 1934, pp. 223–232.

[8] M. Nichols, J. Worthington, and H. Witmer, "The Influence of the Teacher on the Adjustment of Children in Kindergarten," *Smith College Studies Social Work*, 1939, Vol. 9, pp. 360–402.

[9] Bernice Baxter, *Teacher-Pupil Relationships*, New York, The Macmillan Company, 1941.

[10] J. E. W. Wallin, *Personality Maladjustments and Mental Hygiene*, Second Edition, New York, McGraw-Hill Book Company, Inc., 1949, p. 105.

real zest and during the last few years of grammar school I was among the first six or seven in the class. But this did not entirely eliminate my deeply implanted inferiority feeling. In my heart I felt that I was dumb but the teachers in this school didn't know it, and I felt I was putting something over on them. My inferiority feeling is still with me, although my later successes have helped some to overcome it.

In summarizing numerous studies of the effects of teacher adjustment on child development, Snyder [11] states that there is no question but that the teacher's state of mental health influences the behavior of children under his care. He goes on to say:

Adjusted teachers do much to bring about pupil adjustment, and the converse is also true. Probably the most satisfactory way of measuring whether or not a classroom is smooth-running and effective would be to measure the degree of personal adjustment of the teacher.

Some interesting case studies bearing on this point have recently been collected by the psychologist Laycock [12] who visited 157 different classrooms in an effort to study the effect of the teacher's personality on the behavior of pupils. Although his data do not permit of statistical treatment, Laycock ventures the opinion that "the effect of many teachers on the mental health of their pupils is definitely bad." Two of the fifteen cases he described are reproduced as follows:

Teacher A

This man is an elderly veteran. He is dirty and untidy. He is nervous, jittery and dashes about. He berates pupils who don't know the answers. He complained about the pupils to the superintendent. His teaching is didactic and authoritarian. He makes no attempt to develop his class as a cooperative group. The pupils appear fearful, timid, insecure, and repressed. The teacher's mental health is obviously so bad that he should not be permitted to continue in the classroom.

Teacher B

This teacher is in charge of Grades one to four. Her attitudes are not suited to children. She frowns a great deal and never smiles. She is unanimated, prosaic, and unenthusiastic. She does not appear to be a happy,

[11] William U. Snyder, "Do Teachers Cause Maladjustment," *Journal of Exceptional Children,* Vol. 14, December, 1947, pp. 76–77.
[12] S. R. Laycock, "Effect of the Teacher's Personality on the Behavior of Pupils," *Understanding the Child,* Vol. 19, April, 1950, pp. 50–55.

well-adjusted person. She does not appear to like her pupils or to enjoy teaching. She drives her pupils and may succeed in getting them to acquire certain facts and skills. Her "discipline" judged by the standards of a generation ago was good. The pupils appeared repressed and unhappy. The general effect of the teacher on the mental health of the children is judged to be poor.

There probably is little doubt but that the friendly, enthusiastic, secure, and well-adjusted teacher can contribute much to the well being of his pupils. On the other hand, the irritable, depressed, hostile, tired, and neurotic teacher can create tensions which are disturbing to pupils, and which may permanently alter their outlooks on life.

CAUSES OF TEACHER MALADJUSTMENT

Teachers become maladjusted and develop mental ill health in the same manner as do pupils or other individuals. The fundamental cause is frustration resulting from blocked goals. Teachers have all the needs of other people. They desire security, recognition, new experience, and independence, for example, and become tense when these needs remain unfulfilled. The schoolteacher who does not feel that he is appreciated by the school administration may relieve himself of his tense emotions by gossiping about other teachers or engaging in daydreams which give imaginary success experiences. The teacher who has had a violent quarrel with her husband before coming to school may take out her hostile feelings on children in her classes. The many adjustment mechanisms described in Chapter 13 all apply to teachers.

Special Occupational Hazards. There are frustrating conditions in any occupation or profession. The traveling salesman must not only "put-up" with all types of queer and unreasonable customers, but must also run the risk of missing trains and failing to obtain hotel reservations. The doctor must leave the football game or party he is attending, or get up at all hours of the night to minister to the needs of patients. The ticket agent in a railroad station or clerk in the post office must answer thousands of unreasonable questions and try to be serene when he is insulted by some members of his public. Employed people in many walks of life complain that their work is mentally fatiguing and that they very much need prolonged vacations if they are to avoid mental breakdowns.

Schoolteaching is thus not unique in providing an atmosphere which may be conducive to poor mental health or nervous disorders. Living itself is hazardous, and whether a person succeeds in meeting the problems he faces depends not only on the problems themselves but also how he regards them and how he adjusts to them. Nevertheless, there are special restricting conditions in teaching which may lead to frustrations not encountered equally often in certain of other professions. Kimball Young [13] has drawn up a list of ways in which communities attempt to regulate the lives of their teachers. Some of these are as follows:

1. Frequent indication as to preference of the kind and location of residence.
2. Prescription of appropriate dress, facial make-up, and use of cosmetics.
3. Close definition of leisure-time activities; drinking alcoholic beverages, smoking, dancing, and card-playing are especially taboo in most communities.
4. Restrictions of association between teachers and members of the opposite sex who may be students, townspeople, or other teachers.
5. Considerable pressure to take part in religious or other community-approved activities.
6. Expectation that teachers will give strong support to any extracurricular functions which the community likes, such as competitive sports and musical festivals.
7. Restrictions in many communities on the frequency of trips to other localities during weekends.
8. Taboos against joining labor unions and running for political office or otherwise participating in local politics.

School communities, of course, vary greatly with respect to the degree to which they supervise the private affairs of teachers. In larger cities teachers often have the freedom of almost any citizen, while in smaller places rules and regulations which teachers must follow may be unusually severe. The writer was recently told of a young woman teacher who was dismissed from a small Illinois high school because her landlady found an ash tray in her room. Another teacher in a midwestern town lost his job because he bought his new car from a dealer in a community eighteen miles away. Beale [14] has re-

[13] Kimball Young, *Personality and Problems of Adjustment*, Second Edition, New York, Appleton-Century-Crofts, Inc., 1952, p. 445.
[14] Howard K. Beale, *Are American Teachers Free?*, New York, Charles Scribner's Sons, 1936, pp. 395–396.

produced a contract which one community required its teachers to sign. It read as follows:

I promise to take a vital interest in all phases of Sunday school work, donating of my time, service, and money without stint for the uplift and benefit of the community. I promise to abstain from all dancing, immodest dressing, and other conduct unbecoming a teacher and a lady. I promise not to go out with any young men except in so far as it may be necessary to stimulate Sunday school work. I promise not to fall in love, to become engaged or secretly married. I promise to remain in the dormitory or on the school grounds when not actively engaged in school or church work elsewhere. I promise not to encourage or tolerate the least familiarity on the part of my boy pupils. I promise to sleep at least eight hours a night, to eat carefully, and take every precaution to keep in the best of health and spirits in order that I may be better able to render efficient service to my pupils. I promise to remember that I owe a duty to the townspeople who are paying me my wages, and that I owe respect to the school board and the superintendent that hired me, and that I shall consider myself at all times the willing servant of the school board and the townspeople and that I shall cooperate with them to the limit of my ability in any movement aimed at the betterment of the town, the pupils, or the schools.

Frustrations which beset teachers do not all come from the community. Some come from professional relationships with other teachers and administrators, and some from the pupils themselves. One writer [15] has stated that—

Despite tenure, regardless of contracts, many teachers live in a state of perpetual insecurity. They are fearful of the principal, of the superintendent, of the head of the department, of examiners, of tests, of their failure to meet teaching norms, of unexpected demands, of new arrangements, and of impending changes. Some of them are afraid of their students.

The fact that teachers are usually not in a position to fight back when they are unjustly accused, mistreated, or dismissed from their positions, causes many to adopt a very submissive attitude which in the long run may be at the bottom of a great many "anxiety neuroses." The psychiatrist Karen Horney [16] believes that one of the

[15] Margaret J. Synnberg, "Why Teachers 'Blow Their Tops'," *The Nations Schools*, Vol. 41, March, 1948, p. 47.

[16] Karen Horney, *The Neurotic Personality of Our Time*, New York, W. W. Norton and Company, Inc., 1937, pp. 60–78.

surest ways to develop deep-seated fears and anxieties is to repress hostile feelings. From this point of view, teachers who would remain in good mental health should not continually give in to pressure groups or to superiors, but should at times stand up for their own rights. Expressing hostile feelings once in a while is believed to have excellent therapeutic value.

SUGGESTIONS TO TEACHERS FOR KEEPING IN GOOD MENTAL HEALTH

Since there are many causes of maladjustment among teachers, there are also many ways in which their personal and emotional difficulties may be alleviated. Progress toward better mental health is a goal which must be sought not only by teachers and educational organizations, but also by the community as a whole.

Perhaps no point has been more greatly stressed in this volume than the principle that needs, wants, and drives must come to fruition if people are to be well adjusted. Consequently, the starting point for helping teachers maintain good mental health must be the determination of their drives and goals. Two needs immediately stand out as important in the job of teaching. The first is that teachers want to be liked and respected by their pupils. The second is that teachers need to feel a sense of professional accomplishment. As previously shown, several things stand in the way of the satisfaction of such needs. Pupils are not aware of the needs of teachers. To some extent, they share the community's stereotype about teachers as being a group apart—a little different from other people. Under such circumstances, it might be wise for teachers to make known to pupils what some of their own needs are. Perhaps the simple statement by the teacher that he wants all pupils to like him, and wants help from the class when he does things which the pupils do not like, would be an effective first step.

A further barrier which blocks the attainment of professional goals is that teachers may have erroneous notions about the way in which such goals may be achieved. It is apparent that teachers ought to know the characteristics of teachers which children like.[17] It is also clear that a failure to realize professional goals calls for a reexamination of the teaching situation and one's objectives, as was pointed out in the preceding chapter.

[17] See chapter 11.

Much of the progress toward the better mental health of teachers is in the hands of the larger community whose dictums about salary, teachers' conduct, school buildings, and the size of classes determine not only the kinds of teachers that are recruited, but also the morale of those presently engaged in this profession. Great strides have been made toward bettering the teacher's social status and working conditions in the past twenty years. But even under good teaching conditions there are many problems which teachers must learn to solve for themselves. These are feelings of pressure and inferiority, gnawing anxieties, fears and depressions, and inevitable frustrations and conflicts.

There is no panacea for the solution of these problems; yet much is known about the general conditions which foster good mental health. Principles from the field of mental hygiene would seem to support the following suggestions to teachers:

1. Recognize that differences of opinion are healthy and learn how to use the criticisms of others constructively.
2. Expect a certain amount of aggression and rebellion in young people. Such expression is a normal developmental pattern in our culture.
3. If you do not feel well get a medical examination. Some of your aches and pains may be real.
4. Become so absorbed in teaching and avocational activities that there is little time for worrying about petty problems and engaging in unhealthy preoccupation with yourself.
5. Put yourself periodically into a position where you must learn something new. It may be typing, ping pong, a foreign language, or anything else which keeps you active.
6. Become a member of some organization—church, community, civic, or professional. Belonging to a group tends to make one feel secure and to satisfy a need for belonging and status.
7. Develop some close personal friends. Complete self-sufficiency is undesirable.
8. Learn how to converse with, and work with different kinds of people.
9. Work actively to help the teaching profession deserve and attain a higher status than it now enjoys.
10. Express hostile feelings once in awhile. Repressing them may lead to anxiety.
11. Make a plan for your life, but do not be overly ambitious. Overambition can be just as harmful as underambition. Cut the world down to

your size. Do not aspire for things beyond the level where you have a reasonable chance for success.

12. Develop a satisfying philosophy of life. Believe in something.

13. Be yourself. Although there is always room for improvement in personality, you are probably not too bad a person as you are. No one is perfect. Excessive attempts to ape other people kill individuality and lead to unhappiness.

SUMMARY

Psychology is a basic tool in the work of the teacher. Much of this book has shown how the principles which this discipline offers may be used in improving teaching and learning. But psychology can also help teachers solve personal and emotional problems. All evidence suggests that teachers, although relatively stable when compared with other professional groups, need assistance in improving their mental health. This need takes on added importance when the undesirable effects upon pupils of teacher maladjustment are considered.

Research dealing with the incidence of maladjustment among teachers has shown that about a fifth of teachers have personal difficulties, the solution of which would improve their teaching, and that as many as five teachers out of a hundred are sufficiently maladjusted to warrant immediate professional help.

The effects of mentally unbalanced teachers upon pupils is to be found in the instability, anxieties, dislikes and feelings of inferiority which are found among pupils who are unfortunate enough to have a maladjusted teacher. Some of these characteristics and behaviors of children are inevitable, but there is little denying that such children and behavior traits are found in greater numbers in the classrooms of unbalanced teachers. On the positive side, there is little question that well adjusted and stable teachers have helped many disturbed children achieve good adjustment.

The causes of maladjustment among teachers have been shown basically to be the same as the causes for maladjustment of children, viz., frustrated drives and needs. In addition, however, it has been noted that special hazards occur in teaching. Stringent demands by the community for strict codes of conduct, low salaries, poor materials and teaching facilities, and the pressures of handling the emotionally toned activities of children are among the many conditions which may disturb teachers. Most teachers are able to handle these pressures, but some succumb and vent their insecurity and emotion upon children. The fact remains, that there are still teachers who scream, cry, threaten, and who subject children to bizarre forms of humiliation and punishment.

Adjustment is a relative matter. No one is entirely free from some peculiarities and eccentricities. The successful teacher, however, should strive to maintain as high a level of personal adjustment as possible. Suggestions for doing this include the development of appropriate personal and professional goals, and a philosophy of life which gives direction and meaning to teaching and living.

REFERENCES FOR FURTHER STUDY

Bernard, Harold W., *Mental Hygiene for Classroom Teachers*, New York, McGraw-Hill Book Company, Inc., 1952, Chapter 6.

Cook, L. A. and E. F. Cook, *A Sociological Approach to Education*, New York, McGraw-Hill Book Company, Inc., 1950, Chapter 18.

Fenton, Norman, *Mental Hygiene in School Practice*, Stanford University, California, Stanford University Press, 1943, Chapter 16.

Horney, Karen, *The Neurotic Personality of Our Time*, New York, W. W. Norton and Company, 1937.

Kaye, Lawrence, "Are Teachers Neurotic?" *High Points*, Vol. 34, March, 1952, pp. 41–45.

Morgan, John J. B., *How to Keep a Sound Mind*, New York, The Macmillan Company, 1946.

N.E.A., Department of Classroom Teachers, *Fit to Teach*, Ninth Yearbook, 1938.

Redl, Fritz, and William W. Wattenburg, *Mental Hygiene in Teaching*, New York, Harcourt, Brace and Company, 1951, Chapter 16.

Synnberg, Margaret, "Why Teachers 'Blow Their Tops'," *The Nation's Schools*, Vol. 41, March, 1948, pp. 47–48.

Young, Kimball, *Personality and Problems of Adjustment*, Second Edition, New York, Appleton-Century-Crofts, Inc., 1952, Chapter 15.

INDEXES

AUTHOR INDEX

Ackerson, L., 418
Adams, C. R., 564
Adams, O., 148
Adkins, D., 455
Adler, A., 39, 328
Aiken, W. M., 524, 525, 526, 530
Allen, L., 46
Allport, G. W., 394
Almy, M. C., 144, 297
Altman, E., 380, 562, 563, 564
Amatruda, C. S., 23
Anastasi, A., 136, 148
Anderson, G. L., 112
Anderson, H. H., 266, 267, 535
Anderson, I. H., 322
Anderson, J. E., 46, 62, 209, 418
Anderson, L. D., 445
Anderson, R. G., 401
Andrews, T. G., 258, 261
Arthur, G., 428
Asch, S. E., 404
Ausubel, D. P., 62, 89
Averill, L. A., 89
Axline, V. M., 56, 389

Bachhaus, V., 392
Backus, B., 384
Backus, O., 322, 323
Bailard, V., 390
Bain, A., 97
Baker, H. J., 28, 401
Baker, H. L., 283
Baker, J. N., 86, 189
Baldwin, A. L., 50
Baldwin, B. T., 49
Barker, R. G., 14, 62, 66, 69, 75, 110,
    264, 270, 376, 530
Barlow, M. C., 261
Baron, D., 355, 378
Baron, S., 392

Barschak, E., 89
Baruch, D. W., 369
Bateson, G., 37
Bauer, W. W., 63
Bavalas, A., 521
Baxter, B., 559, 566
Bayley, N., 43, 90
Beale, H. K., 569
Beasley, J., 322
Beck, B. M., 87
Beck, S. J., 439
Beebe, G. W., 73
Beecher, D. E., 559
Bell, R., 189
Benedict, R., 50
Benne, K. D., 281, 290, 292, 549, 550
Bennett, A., 443
Bennett, G. K., 137
Bentley, J. E., 418
Berman, I. R., 57
Bernard, H. W., 342, 355, 369, 392,
    418, 574
Bettelheim, B., 392, 418
Betts, E. A., 108, 148, 322
Bibby, C., 86
Bieker, H., 413
Blair, A. W., 62
Blair, G. M., 4, 89, 94, 120, 121, 136,
    211, 300, 311, 313, 316, 322, 387,
    388, 396, 455, 562, 563
Block, V. L., 82, 83
Bogardus, E. S., 436, 437
Bolles, M. M., 59
Bollinger, R. H., 292
Bond, G. L., 559
Bonney, M. E., 59, 276
Borow, H., 185
Bossard, J. H. S., 62, 292
Bovard, E. W., 287
Bowles, J. W., 107

Bowman, P. H., 156, 157
Boynton, P., 566
Bradford, L. P., 269, 290, 552
Bradshaw, F., 402
Brady, E. H., 273, 274, 275, 293
Breckenridge, M. E., 129
Brewer, J. E., 266, 267
Brickman, W. W., 87
Brink, W. G., 230, 232
Bronner, A. F., 380
Bronstein, I. P., 23
Brown, A. W., 23
Brownell, W. A., 103, 211, 223
Brozek, J., 155
Brumbaugh, F. N., 418
Bruner, J. S., 155, 156
Bryan, R. C., 542
Buckingham, B. R., 215
Buhler, C., 189, 384, 385, 392, 402, 414, 418
Bullis, H. E., 292, 386
Buros, O. K., 423, 433, 435, 445, 457
Burton, W. H., 62, 233, 239, 519, 520
Busby, L. M., 49
Buswell, G. T., 237, 318
Butterfield, O. M., 84

Cameron, A. T., 40
Cameron, N., 65 334, 349, 351, 355
Camp, K. L., 510
Cannon, W. B., 16, 25
Cantril, H., 190
Carillo, L., 144
Carmichael, L., 39, 55, 61, 133
Carr, A., 323
Carroll, H. A., 136, 137, 138, 148, 328, 338, 355
Carter, H. D., 186, 194
Castore, G. F., 282
Cattell, P., 49
Cellar, S. L., 369
Chall, J. S., 216
Challman, R. C., 54, 345
Chamberlin, D., 530
Chapman, P. E., 364
Chreitzberg, J., 499, 514, 516, 531
Christensen, T. E., 248
Clark, W. W., 140
Cohen, F. J., 418
Cohen, S. S., 392
Collings, M. R., 171
Collister, E. G., 292

Combs, A. W., 31, 111, 190
Conrad, H. S., 74
Cook, E. F., 574
Cook, L. A., 574
Cook, S. W., 474
Cook, W. W., 130, 135
Coover, J. E., 254
Cottrell, L. S., 404
Courtis, S. A., 115, 116, 132, 295
Cox, W. M., 209
Crawford, A. B., 185
Cresci, G., 209
Crewson, W., 502
Cronbach, L. J., 258, 261, 439, 456, 480
Crow, A., 369
Crow, L. D., 369
Cruickshank, W. M., 57
Crutchfield, R. S., 292, 559
Cruze, W. W., 90
Cryon, E. W., 267
Culotta, C. S., 23
Cummings, H. H., 292
Cunningham, R., 62, 289, 292, 456, 469, 480
Cureton, T. K., 120
Curtis, F. D., 215

Dale, E., 216
Dallenbach, K. M., 224
Daly, M., 90
Daniels, L., 369
Dashiell, J. F., 21, 113
Davis, A., 14, 38, 60, 62, 292, 430, 431
Davis, F. B., 452
Davis, R. A., 212
Dearborn, W. F., 322
Deese, J., 112
Dembo, T., 110, 169, 530
Denemark, G. W., 203, 210
Dennis, M. G., 117
Dennis, W., 37, 62, 117
Derrick, C., 444
Deutsch, M., 288, 292, 418
D'Evelyn, K. E., 506
Dewey, J., 216, 217
Dixon, W. R., 219
Dolch, E. W., 145, 215, 216, 223, 305, 306, 308, 312, 313, 322
Dolch, M. P., 145, 206
Doll, E. A., 437

Doll, R. C., 232
Dollard, J., 331
Dolphin, J. E., 57
Donahue, W. T., 456
Doob, L. W., 40, 189, 192, 292, 331
Dorsey, M. W., 257
Douglas, H. R., 214
Dreikurs, R., 39
Dresden, K., 240
Dressel, P. L., 456
Dugger, H., 566
Dummer, F., 24
Duncker, K., 227, 239
Durrell, D. D., 322
Duvall, E., 86
Dyer, J. P., 369

Eames, T. H., 445
Edgerton, H. A., 259
Edmiston, R. W., 145
Eells, K., 430, 431
Eissler, K. R., 418
Ellingson, M., 413
Elliott, E. C., 494
Elliott, R. M., 445
Ellis, A., 209, 437
Ellis, R. S., 148
English, H. B., 62, 116, 166, 404, 410, 411, 414, 418
Erikson, E. H., 63, 180
Eurich, A. C., 527, 531

Faegre, M. L., 418
Farrell, J. V., 217
Fawcett, H. P., 145
Fawcett, K., 389
Featherstone, W. B., 322
Fenton, N., 392, 562, 563, 574
Fernald, G. M., 305, 306, 313, 322
Fetterman, J., 348
Fiedler, M. F., 392
Fields, M., 86
Finch, F. H., 520
Flanders, N. A., 266, 285
Fleming, C. M., 90
Flemming, C. W., 254
Flesch, R., 215, 216
Flesher, W. R., 356, 357
Fleshman, C. F., 72
Flory, C. D., 46
Flotow, E. A., 474, 475
Foley, J. P., 136, 148

Foran, T. G., 322
Forsyth, E., 476
Foster, R. G., 261
Fowlkes, J. G., 320
Frank, L. K., 41, 49, 66, 90
Frazier, A., 72
Freeman, F. N., 46, 395
Freeston, P. M., 197
Frenkel-Brunswik, E., 195
Freud, S., 17, 49
Fryer, D. H., 259
Fuller, J. J., 189

Gage, N. L., 404, 410, 412, 456, 480
Gaier, E. L., 106, 124, 191, 230, 399
Garfield, S., 75, 76
Garrison, K. C., 90, 322
Garside, H. V., 49
Gates, A. I., 54, 112, 117, 124, 313, 322, 345
Gerberich, J. R., 209, 456, 480
Gesell, A., 23, 63
Giles, H. H., 239, 559
Gilkey, W., 141
Gillenwater, V. W., 520
Gillis, J., 122, 138
Glickman, S., 51
Glock, M. D., 148
Glueck, E., 374, 375, 392, 418
Glueck, S., 374, 375, 392, 418
Goff, R. M., 418
Gonick, M. R., 376
Goodenough, F. L., 61, 146
Goodman, C. C., 155, 156
Gordon, H., 35, 36, 37
Gouldner, A. W., 292
Gray, W. S., 468
Green, A. W., 264
Green, R., 553
Greenberg, P. J., 180
Greene, E. B., 412, 452, 456, 480
Greene, H. A., 456, 480
Greulich, W. W., 42, 70
Griffith, C. R., 18, 19
Gronlund, N. E., 273
Grossman, B., 58
Gruenberg, B. C., 86
Gruenberg, S. M., 63
Guetzkow, H. S., 156, 157, 239
Guthrie, E. R., 9, 222

Haas, R. B., 389
Haiman, F. S., 292

Hamrin, S. A., 90
Hand, H. C., 79, 81, 512, 513
Handlan, B., 559
Hanna, D. C., 283
Hanna, L., 531
Hanson, H. B., 57
Hare, A. P., 59
Hare, R. T., 59
Harms, I. E., 32
Harrell, R. F., 30
Harris, A. J., 108, 322
Harris, D. B., 199, 200
Harris, P. E., 357
Harrison, M. L., 148
Harsh, C. M., 52
Hartley, E. L., 41, 52, 293, 559
Hartley, R. E., 63
Hartmann, G. W., 192, 204
Hartog, P., 495
Hartshorne, H., 224, 438
Haskell, R. I., 258
Hassler, J. O., 244
Haugh, O. M., 209
Havighurst, R. J., 44, 60, 62, 69, 393
Hawkes, G. R., 209
Hayes, C., 14, 41
Hayes, K. J., 14
Healy, W., 380
Hebb, D. O., 107
Heck, A. O., 322
Heidbreder, E., 240, 445
Helbing, M. E., 530
Henderson, K. B., 85, 226, 260
Hendrickson, G., 211, 223, 251
Hendrix, G., 258, 259
Henning, C. J., 369
Henry, A. W., 444
Henry, L. K., 226
Henry, N. B., 297, 298
Henschel, A., 155
Herrick, V. E., 539
Herrold, E. E., 267
Hicks, F. R., 562, 563
Hildreth, G. H., 122, 243, 418, 423, 433, 445, 456
Hilgard, E. R., 99, 100, 113, 177, 189, 194, 332
Hilgard, J., 118
Hilliard, F. P., 148
Hobbes, T., 97
Hobson, J. R., 141
Hollingshead, A. B., 90, 397, 402

Holmes, F. B., 53, 55
Holzinger, K. J., 395
Honzik, M. P., 46
Hopkins, L. T., 257
Horowitz, E. L., 56
Horn, E., 240
Horney, K., 338, 350, 570, 574
Horrocks, J. E., 59, 90
Horst, P., 148
Horwitz, M., 292
Hoskins, R. G., 23, 25, 41
Hovland, C. I., 209, 220
Hughes, B. O., 129
Hull, C. L., 161
Hume, D., 97
Hunnicutt, C. W., 178
Hunt, D. G., 138
Hunt, J. M., 3, 30, 168
Hunt, J. T., 148
Hurlock, E. B., 189

Ilg, F. L., 63
Irion, A. L., 112, 189, 218, 220, 248, 254

Jackson, B., 145
James, H. W., 358
James, W., 17, 214
Jamison, O. G., 90
Janney, J. E., 30
Jarvie, L. L., 413
Jenkins, D. H., 289, 293
Jenkins, F. C., 559
Jenkins, G. G., 63
Jenkins, R. L., 51
Jennings, H. H., 275, 476, 531
Jensen, B. T., 148
Jersild, A. T., 53, 54, 55, 63, 196, 200, 202, 203, 531
John, L., 318
Johnson, D. M., 240
Johnson, G. O., 56, 393
Johnson, K. M., 227
Johnson, L. W., 314
Johnson, W., 169, 315, 322, 380
Jones, H. E., 74, 194
Jones, M. C., 90
Jones, R. S., 191, 230, 235, 236, 257, 289
Jones, V., 133
Jorgensen, A. N., 456, 480
Josselyn, I. M., 63
Judd, C. H., 251

Kabat, G. J., 148
Kalish, D., 102
Kanya, J. R., 369
Kaplan, L., 355, 378
Karnes, M. R., 456
Katona, G., 225
Katz, L., 476
Kaye, L., 574
Kearney, N. C., 5
Keliher, A., 86
Keller, H., 306, 307
Kelley, E. C., 551, 559
Kellogg, L. A., 14
Kellogg, W. N., 14, 113
Kennedy, L., 323
Key, C. B., 35, 36, 37
Keys, A., 155
Keys, N., 436
Kilpatrick, W. H., 209
Kingsley, H. L., 112, 209, 213, 221, 227, 240, 261
Kinney, L. B., 189, 240
Kinsey, A. C., 69, 334
Kinzer, J. R., 145
Kirk, S. A., 323, 393
Kirkendall, L. A., 86
Kirkpatrick, M. E., 90
Kirkpatrick, M. S., 444
Klineberg, O., 90
Kluckhohn, C., 41
Knapp, C. G., 219
Knight, F. B., 183
Koenker, R. H., 144
Koffka, K., 101, 170
Köhler, W., 103
Konopka, G., 418
Kopel, D., 149
Korner, A. F., 401
Koshuk, R. P., 51
Kotick, M. L., 434
Kounin, J. S., 14, 270
Kraines, R., 23
Krech, D., 292, 559
Kreezer, G., 224
Krugman, M., 393
Kuder, G. F., 78, 441
Kuhlen, R. G., 47, 63, 90, 292
Kuo, Z. Y., 19
Kvaraceus, W. C., 531

Laird, D. A., 30
Lancelot, W. H., 240

Landis, P. H., 90
Lange, P. C., 243
Lanier, J. A., 264
Laska, J., 165
Lawrence, C. H., 22
Lawson, D. E., 395
Laycock, S. R., 567
Learned, W. D., 131
Lecky, P., 122
Lee, J. M., 140
Leonard, J. P., 527, 531
Levi, J., 90
Levinson, A., 323
Levit, G., 292
Levitan, M., 30
Lewin, K., 39, 97, 110, 168, 268, 288, 521, 522, 530, 531
Lindgren, H. C., 355
Lindquist, E. F., 444, 456, 480
Linton, R., 41
Lippitt, R., 268, 269, 270, 290
Liss, F., 389
Livesay, T. M., 73
Locke, J., 97
Long, L., 240
Loofbourow, G. C., 436
Loomis, C. P., 480
Loomis, S. D., 264
Lorge, I., 215, 216
Lovelass, H. D., 79
Luchins, A. S., 123, 253, 259
Luchins, E. H., 123, 259
Ludeman, W. W., 370
Lurie, L. A., 25
Lynd, R. S., 31

Maas, H. S., 389, 393
Macfarlane, J. W., 46
Mackenzie, L. T., 393
Macmann, E., 149
Macy, M. T., 444
Madden, E. H., 240
Magaret, A., 334, 349, 351, 355
Maier, N. R. F., 3, 189, 240
Maller, J. B., 180
Mallison, G. G., 215
Malloch, J. L., 561
Malm, M., 90
Mann, F. A., 418
Mann, P. E., 143
Marquis, D. G., 99
Martin, C. E., 69

Martin, W. E., 63
Marzolf, S. S., 189
Masserman, J. H., 3
Mateer, F., 22, 23
May, M. A., 189, 224, 438
McAdow, B., 311
McAndrew, H., 57
McAustin, S. D., 220
McConnell, T. R., 54, 113
McDougall, W., 17
McGeoch, J. A., 112, 164, 165, 166, 189, 218, 220, 248, 254
McGraw, M., 117, 118, 148
McNamara, W. J., 456
McNemar, Q., 74, 167
Mead, A. R., 209, 245, 246, 258
Mead, M., 37, 41
Meek, L. H., 16
Melton, A. W., 104, 105, 112
Melville, S. D., 444
Menninger, K. A., 347, 355
Merrill, M. A., 48, 73, 167, 296, 375, 393, 425, 456
Merry, F. K., 63
Merry, R. V., 63
Metzger, H. F., 39
Meyer, E., 58
Meyer, G., 236
Meyer, H. H., 292
Michael, W. B., 267
Micheels, W. J., 456
Michelsen, O., 155
Michelson, B., 90
Miel, A., 287, 288, 292, 559
Miles, J. R., 204
Mill, J., 97
Miller, N. E., 189, 331
Miller, V., 370
Mintz, A., 180
Monroe, M., 126, 142, 148, 384
Monroe, W. S., 104, 192, 258, 480, 527, 531
Montagu, M. F. A., 41
Moreno, J. L., 272, 531
Morgan, D. A., 320
Morgan, J. J. B., 32, 343, 344, 353, 574
Morphett, M. V., 118, 119
Morse, W. C., 293
Moser, W. E., 186, 203
Mossman, L. C., 240
Mowrer, O. H., 189, 331

Muellen, T. K., 499
Munn, N. L., 112
Muntyan, B., 281, 549, 550
Murphy, G., 97, 99, 293
Murphy, L. B., 293
Murray, H. A., 41, 327, 440
Mursell, J. L., 189, 240

Nall, J., 264
Nelson, A. K., 18
Nelson, C. H., 434
Nelson, E., 209
Newcomb, T. M., 41, 293, 559
Newman, H. H., 395
Nichols, M., 566
Nolan, E. G., 123
Norem, G. M., 262
Northway, M. L., 277
Norvell, G. W., 76, 77

O'Brien, J. A., 166
Odell, C. W., 456
Ojemann, R. H., 205
Olsen, E. G., 556, 557, 559
Olson, W. C., 48, 49, 63, 115, 128, 129
O'Malley, E. E., 292
Orata, P. T., 261
Orlansky, H., 50
Osburn, W. J., 304

Parry, D., 393
Partridge, E. D., 28, 71
Pastore, N., 149
Paterson, D. G., 445
Patton, R. E., 215
Paulson, B. B., 90
Pavlov, I. P., 97, 99
Pearson, G. H. J., 393
Peck, L., 563
Perkins, H. V., 286, 288
Peterson, R. C., 204
Peyton, B., 145
Phelps, H., 186
Phillips, L. E., 57
Piaget, J., 63
Pingry, R. E., 226
Pitts, M. W., 39
Plant, J. S., 87
Pollock, T. C., 314
Pomeroy, W. B., 69
Powers, E., 418

Pratt, K. C., 18
Prescott, D., 63
Pressey, S. L., 24, 30, 69, 159, 230, 244, 261, 272, 283, 357
Proctor, C. H., 480
Pronko, N. H., 107

Quasha, W. H., 445
Quillen, I. J., 531

Raimey, V., 418
Ray, A. M., 197
Ragsdale, C. E., 219
Rasey, M. I., 559
Redl, F., 337, 338, 345, 355, 370, 393, 574
Reed, M. F., 267
Rehage, K. J., 286
Reid, C., 90
Reid, J. W., 78
Remmers, H. H., 52, 183, 410, 412, 456, 480
Renshaw, S., 108
Rhodes, E. C., 495
Ribble, M. A., 49, 63
Richardson, S., 392, 402, 418
Richter, C. O., 244
Rinsland, H. D., 215
Ritchie, B. F., 102
Rivlin, H. N., 112
Roberts, A. J., 120
Robinson, F. P., 24, 69, 159, 226, 230, 240, 261, 272, 406, 407
Robinson, H. M., 323
Robinson, J. T., 273, 274, 275, 293
Roeber, E., 75, 76, 414
Rogers, C. R., 169, 389
Rokeach, M., 209
Rorschach, H., 439
Rosen, I. C., 56
Rosenbaum, M., 52
Rotter, J. B., 168
Roule, L., 20
Rowan, W., 19
Rubinfine, D. L., 3
Russell, D. H., 177, 189, 194, 332
Ryans, D. G., 189

Salisbury, R., 254
Sandiford, P., 98, 258, 261
Sanford, E. C., 164
Sanford, R. N., 155, 195

Sargent, S. S., 293
Sarhan, E. A., 198
Sayles, M. B., 418
Scantlebury, R. E., 201
Scheinfeld, A., 41
Schlosberg, H., 3
Schmidt, H. O., 189
Schoggen, P., 264
Schonfeld, W. A., 73
Schrammel, H. E., 443
Schrickel, H. G., 52
Schroeder, W. H., 251
Schwartz, S., 52
Sears, P. S., 167
Sears, R. R., 167, 190, 331, 485, 495
Seashore, H. G., 137
Segel, D., 90
Sellery, C. M., 371
Semmelmeyer, M., 216, 217
Senden, M., 107
Shacter, H., 63, 390
Sheats, P., 552
Sheldon, W. D., 144
Sheldon, W. H., 376
Sheridan, M. C., 121
Sherif, M., 41, 43, 157, 190, 263, 293
Sherman, M., 35, 36, 37, 119
Sheviakov, G. V., 370
Shock, N. W., 30, 194
Shuman, S. N., 393
Simpson, R. H., 230, 240, 293, 456, 469, 480, 510, 539, 541, 543, 553, 554, 559
Sims, V. M., 440, 441, 454, 499, 514, 516, 531, 538
Sipola, E. M., 253
Skeels, H. M., 32
Skinner, C. E., 192, 295
Skodak, M., 32, 33
Slavin, S., 293, 393
Slobetz, F., 359
Sloman, S. S., 51
Smith, C. L., 127, 146
Smith, E. R., 5, 456, 480, 506
Smith, H. P., 295
Smith, M. K., 47, 48
Smitter, F., 392, 402, 418
Snyder, W. U., 567
Snygg, D., 31, 32, 111, 190
Spain, C. R., 204
Spaulding, F. T., 247
Speer, G. S., 32, 33, 34

Spelt, D. K., 32
Spitzer, H. F., 214, 234, 433
Stagner, R., 192, 195
Starch, D., 494
Stauffer, R. G., 309
Steckle, L. C., 355
Stendler, C. B., 63, 370, 490
Stern, C., 41
Stevens, S. S., 189
Stoddard, G. D., 33, 41
Stolz, H. R., 24, 28, 71, 90
Stolz, L. M., 24, 28, 71, 90
Stone, C. P., 69, 75, 190
Stone, L. I., 418
Stouffer, G. A. W., 372, 373, 400
Stoughton, M. L., 197
Strain, F. B., 86
Strang, Robert, 172
Strang, Ruth, 390, 393, 419, 506
Stratton, G. M., 107
Strong, E. K., 75, 76, 77, 78, 187, 194, 209, 442
Stroud, J. B., 166, 262
Sturm, H. E., 215
Swanson, G. E., 41, 293, 559
Sueltz, B. A., 258
Sun, K. H., 18
Sydenstricker, E., 27, 297
Symonds, P. M., 63, 355, 377, 378, 419
Synnberg, M. J., 570, 574

Taba, H., 273, 274, 275, 293, 456, 480
Tappan, P. W., 419
Tasch, R. J., 196, 200, 202, 203
Taylor, G. A., 117
Taylor, H. L., 155
Taylor, L., 370
Terman, L. M., 47, 48, 73, 74, 296, 425, 456
Thelen, H. A., 283
Thompson, G. G., 47, 59, 63, 178
Thompson, L. R., 444
Thomson, M. K., 190
Thorndike, E. L., 17, 74, 97, 98, 161, 178, 190, 210, 214, 215, 242, 246, 249, 309, 323, 423
Thorndike, R. L., 90, 228
Thornley, W. R., 396
Thorpe, L. P., 335, 348, 349, 355, 382, 390
Thurstone, L. L., 135

Thurstone, T. G., 135
Tiedeman, H. R., 456
Tilton, J. W., 112
Tolman, E. C., 102
Tomlinson, H., 444
Toops, H. A., 445
Torgerson, T. L., 396, 400, 409, 413, 434
Townsend, A., 323
Traphagen, V., 401
Travers, R. M. W., 450, 451, 456
Travis, R. C., 220
Traxler, A. E., 323, 413, 443, 456, 480, 495, 507
Tredgold, A. F., 323
Triggs, F. O., 323
Troup, E., 395
Trow, W. C., 293
Tryon, C., 134, 277
Turner, M., 566
Tuttle, H. S., 190, 419
Tyler, L., 133, 134, 149
Tyler, R. W., 5, 212, 443, 444, 506

Van Pool, G. M., 370
Van Til, W., 203, 209, 210
Vaughn, K. W., 444
Vaughn, W. F., 338, 355
Vernon, P., 149
Vickery, W. E., 273, 274, 275
Viele, J. A., 370
Vinacke, W. E., 223, 240
Vincent, E. L., 129

Wailes, J. R., 217
Wallace, W., 499, 514, 516, 531
Wallin, J. E. W., 53, 566
Washburne, C., 24, 118, 119
Washburne, J. N., 436
Waters, E. A., 514
Watson, J. B., 18, 52
Watson, W. S., 204
Wattenberg, W. W., 337, 338, 345, 355, 574
Weaver, H. E., 240
Webb, L. W., 262
Wechsler, D., 149, 428
Weeks, D. F., 149
Weiss, P., 32
Weitzman, E., 457
Welch, L., 240
Wellbank, H. L., 564

Weltman, N., 52
Werner, H., 240
Werner, L. S., 323
Wesman, A. G., 137, 246
West, R., 323
Whipple, G. M., 41
White, R. K., 268, 270
Whiting, J. W. M., 37
Wickman, E. K., 367, 371, 372, 400
Wiles, K., 230, 559
Wilson, F. T., 418
Wilson, V. A., 30
Wilt, M. E., 159
Wineman, D., 393
Wispe, L. G., 265, 284
Withall, J., 293
Witmer, H., 418, 566
Witty, P. A., 149, 267, 419
Wolf, T. H., 180
Wood, B. D., 131
Wood, H. B., 444

Woodring, M. N., 254
Woodrow, H., 254
Woodworth, R. S., 218, 249
Word, A. H., 212
Worthington, J., 566
Wright, B. A., 376
Wright, H. F., 14, 62, 190, 264, 270
Wright, M. E., 530
Wrighter, J., 58
Wrightstone, J. W., 264, 526, 527, 531
Wrinkle, W. L., 507
Wundt, W., 101

Young, K., 181, 284, 355, 414, 419, 569, 574
Young, N., 124
Young, P. T., 107, 190

Zander, A. E., 293

SUBJECT INDEX

Ability
  individual differences in, 114–115, 127–138
  measurement of, 424–432
  organic and environmental basis of, 13–41
Abstractions, 217
  concepts and, 224
Acceleration of pupils, 504–505
Acceptance of pupils, 275–277
Achievement, experimental schools and, 524–526
Achievement tests, 432–435
  use of results, 464–471
Acrophobia, 350
Activity
  sequence of in school, 236–238
  student, 222
Activity drive, use of in school learning, 158–161
Adjustment
  general treatment of, 327–355
  how teachers view problems of, 371–372
  mechanisms of, 331–346
Adjustment programs, 386–388
  Delaware Human Relations Class, 386–387
  films for, 390
  remedial classes, 387–388
  therapeutic techniques, 388–390
  Tulsa Personal Relations Course, 387
Adlerian psychology, 39, 328
Administrators, relations with teachers, 552–553
Adolescence, 64–90
  anxieties and worries, 71–73, 79–82
  death rate, 66
  delinquency, 86–88

Adolescence—*Continued*
  description of period, 64–65
  developmental tasks, 69–70
  family relationships and, 82–84
  interests of, 74–78
  marginal nature of, 66
  mental development in, 73–74
  mental disorders of, 66
  needs of, 67–69
  peer approval in, 184–185
  physical defects and, 71–73
  physical development during, 70–71
  problems of, 79–82, 84
  religious conversion and, 69
  sex education, 84–86
  stresses and conflicts, 66, 82–83
Adrenal glands, 25
Adrenal virilism, 25
Adult education, 502, 555–558
Age
  change of interests with, 77–78
  learning in relation to, 74
  personality change with, 52
  school entrance and, 140–141
Aggression
  as an adjustment mechanism, 331
  displaced, 169, 331–332
  outlets for, 332
  prejudice and, 332
  social class and, 331
  tension release and, 153
Aggressive behavior, 298, 331–332
Agoraphobia, 350
Agricultural education, evaluating effects of, 509–510
Agriculture tests, 432
Alcohol, used as an escape, 342
Algebra
  classroom disturbance in, 361–362

Algebra—*Continued*
tests, 432
transfer of training and, 242
American Adventure Series, 76
American Council on Education, Psychological Examination for College Freshmen, 431
Analysis of teaching process, 538–545
Anecdotal records, 412–413
Anger, 169–170
Animal learning, 3, 99, 103
Anthropology, culture and personality, 37–38
Anxiety
adolescent development and, 71–72
learning and, 106
neurosis, 350–351
repressions of, 337–338
teachers' methods and, 265–266
Apes
Köhler's insight experiments, 102–103
reared in human environments, 14
Appraisal, 423–530
aptitudes and readiness, 138–142
of total school program, 508–531
teacher's self-appraisal, 538–545
Area, teaching the concept of, 123
Art tests, 432
Arthur Point Scale of Performance Tests, 428
Aspiration, levels of, 167–168
Assignment making, 232–233
teacher's self-analysis and, 544
Association, laws of, 97
Associational typing, 399
Associationism, 97
Atonement, 345–346
Attention-getting, 152
Attitudes, 94, 191–210
change of, 203–205
characteristics of, 192–193
definition of, 192
effect on learning, 193–194
how formed, 55–56
learning of, 109–110
origin and development of, 195–201
parents, toward school, 511–513
pupils, toward school, 511–513
relationships between parents and children, 52
school practices and, 201–203

Attitudes—*Continued*
stimulus generalization and, 250–251
Auditory defects, 28, 297
Autocratic leadership, 268–270

Barriers to goals, 105
Basal metabolism, 22–23
Basketball, knowledge of results and success in, 167
Behavior
animal, 3
clues to learning difficulties, 301
encephalitis and, 30
environment and, 30–39
malnutrition and, 30
out-of-school, 509–511
physical defects and, 27–30
problems, seriousness of, 373
rating schedules, 372
social class and, 14
systematic records of, 412–413
Behaviorism, 18, 101
Bell Adjustment Inventory, 372
Belongingness, 98–99
Bennett Use of Library Test, 443–444
Biological bases of behavior, 13
Biology
interest of pupils in, 207–208
organization in, 212–213
tests, 432, 434–435
Blacky Pictures, The, 440
Body build and delinquency, 376
Books for retarded readers, 311–312
Breast *vs.* bottle feeding, 49–50
Broken homes, 375
Bully, case of a, 364–365
Business education tests, 432
Buswell-John Teachers Diagnostic Chart, 318

California growth studies, 46
California Short-Form Test of Mental Maturity, 428–429
California Test of Personality, 59, 372
Canal-boat children, 35–36
Cases of children
Alfred, a boy who could not compete, 179–180
Bill, a "lazy" pupil, 383
Boney, a lower-class boy, 397–398
Carl, an emotionally disturbed boy, 407–408

Cases of Children—*Continued*
Dodie, a withdrawn child, 384–385
Doris, an undernourished child, 395
Gene and Clyde, two poverty stricken boys, 374–375
George, a potential delinquent, 6
George Stevens, a building defacer, 363–364
Grace, a sensitive child, 284–285
Harold, a retarded reader, 7
Jerry, an isolated child, 250–251
Joe, a bully, 364–365
John, a boy helped by play therapy, 389
Johnny, a thyroid case, 22
Luella, a social isolate, 7
Max, a show-off, 361–362
Steve, a retarded reader, 154–155
Tony, a rejected child, 124–126
a teen-ager and narcotics, 184
adolescents with problems, 80–81
an excessive daydreamer, 342
an obsessional neurosis, 348–349
boy with a bad case of pimples, 29
boy with inferiority complex, 566–567
child with arithmetic problem, 244
fifth-grader who hated reading, 54–55
gifted child, 136–137
girls with physical deviations, 72
hysteria in a nine-year-old, 347
regression in a young girl, 343
Case studies
errors in, 415–416
how to make, 414–417
material to include, 414
of classes, 514–518
Case study conference, 386
Catatonic schizophrenia, 353
Character, measurement of, 438
Cheating, 382–383
Chemistry
readiness for, 145
tests, 432
Child rearing, 49–52
autocratic control and, 50–51
consistent discipline, 51
democratic control, 50–51
social class and, 60
Child study, 394–419
children to study, 400–401

Child study—*Continued*
creative activities, 407–409
individual problems, 396
need for, 394–396
pitfalls to be avoided, 396–399
sources of information, 401–409
tools and methods for, 409–417
uniqueness of children, 395
Childhood
definition of, 42
friendships, 58–60
importance of period, 60–61
Children
lazy, 383
orthopedic cases, 297
over-protected, 378
rejected, 377–378
slow-learning, 296–297
social-emotional problems, 298
speech defectives, 297
truant, 383–384
underprivileged, 36–37
who cheat, 382
who steal, 381
with sensory defects, 297
withdrawing, 384–386
Children's Apperception Test, 440
Chorea, 301
Chromosomes, 15
Class case studies, 514–518
Class size, 282–283
Classics for Enjoyment, 77
Classrooms, description of psychological atmosphere, 264–265
Claustrophobia, 350
Cognitive structure, 102
College
admission requirements and, 523
high school methods, 523–524
remedial programs, 145
Comic books, 303
Committees, pupil, 362–363
Community
attitudes toward schools, 511–513
child study and, 402–403
comparisons of, 526–527
effects on teachers' mental health, 569–571
resources in schoolwork, 171–172
teacher's relations with, 555–558
Compensation, 332–334
Competition, 178–182

Complacency of teachers, 544
Completion test items, 453
Composition tests, 432
Compulsions, 349
Concepts
  formation of, 222–224
  teaching and, 223–224
Conditioned reflex, 99–100
Conditioned stimulus, 99
Conditioning
  diagram of, 99–100
  fears, 53
Conference, case study, 386
Configuration, 102
Conflict
  adolescence and, 66, 82–84
  between motives, 170–171
  learning and, 110
Connectionism, 97–99
Consistency of behavior, 224
Constancy of the IQ, 32–37, 119
Contiguity, 97
Control of class activities, 540, 544, 546–547
Cooperative Dictionary Test, 444
Cooperative planning, teacher and pupil, 544, 546
Counseling, errors of beginners, 406
Cramming, 220
Creative activities, 407–409
Cretinism, 22–23
Crippled children, 57, 297–298
Critical thinking, 260
Criticism of schools, 518–520
Cues, 102
Culture
  competition and, 180
  interests and, 197–198
  sub-cultures in one town, 402
Curiosity drive, 158–161
Curriculum, developmental tasks and, 70

Davis-Eells Games, 430–431
Daydreaming, 153, 341–343
Death instinct, 327–328
Defacement, school building, 363–364
Defense mechanisms, 331–346
Delaware Human Relations Class, The, 386–387
Delinquency
  adolescent, 86–88

Delinquency—Continued
  body build and, 376
  broken homes and, 375
  case studies of, 6–7, 374–375
  cause of, 87–88
  family influences and, 51–52
  interests and, 199–200
  poverty and, 374–375
  school and, 87–88
  unhygienic school practices and, 379–381
Delusions of grandeur, 352–353
Dementia praecox, 351
Democratic group control, 268–270
Democratic homes and personality, 50–51
Dentition and maturity, 49
Depression, 353–354
Development,
  mental, 32–37, 73–74
  physical, 70–71
  prenatal, 31–32
Developmental periods, 42
Developmental tasks,
  adolescence, 69–70
  infancy and early childhood, 45
  middle childhood, 45
Diabetes, 26
Diagnosis
  arithmetic, 318–319
  behavior inventories and rating scales, 411–412
  class as a whole, 464–467
  classroom activities, 538–542
  classroom social structure, 274
  creative activities, 407–409
  individual difficulties, 469–470
  information to parents, 490–492
  interviews, 404–407
  miscellaneous tools, 445–446
  pretests, 140–142
  reading difficulties, 304
  social needs of, 273–275
  sociometric testing, 472–476
  sources of information, 401–409
  special difficulties of, 294–323
  tools, 423–457
Diagnostic Tests of Achievement in Music, 434
Diaries, 273
Dictionaries, 215
Dictionary test, 444

Difficulties in learning, 299–300
Directions, test, 450–451
Discipline, 356–368
    guiding principles for keeping, 366–368
    how teachers currently handle, 359
    past school practices, 356–358
    punishment, 357–359
    teachers' problems, 356–357
Discovery and transfer, 258–259
Dishonesty, 358, 381–382
Disorder, study hall, 362–363
Displaced aggression, 169
Distributing learning activities, 220–221
Dolch Basic Sight Vocabulary, 308
Dominative teachers, 266
Driscoll Play Kit, The, 440
Drop-outs, 295
Drug addiction, 184
Dypsomania, 349

Eames Eye Test, 445
Economics tests, 432
Education Index, 468
Education tests, 432, 446
Educational objectives, 5
    and test selection, 446
Educational philosophy, 4–6
Educational psychology
    how to make functional, 8–10
    of the teacher, 535–560
    sources from which it draws, 4
    teacher's work and, 6–10
    textbooks in, 8
    types of research, 4
Effect of the response, 106
Egocentricism, 340
Egyptian children, interests of, 198
Eight-Year Study, 523–525
Einstellung, 253
Embryology, experimental, 31
Emotion
    conflict, 170–171
    impossible tasks, 169–170
    motivation and, 169–171
    negative attitudes, removal, 303
    saturation, 170
Empathy, 403–404
Employers and report cards, 492–493
Encephalitis, 30, 394–395

Encyclopedia of Educational Research, 527
Endocrine glands, 20–29
Engineering tests, 432
English
    errors in, 316–317
    remedial, 316–317
    tests, 432, 444
    transfer value, 243
Enuresis, 373
Environment
    behavior and, 13
    effects on mental development, 32–37
    effects on prenatal development, 30–31
    isolated and backward communities, 34–37
    personality and, 37–40
Epinephrin, 25
Equilibrium, psychological, 153
Escape, 341–343
Escape mechanisms, 331–346
Essay examinations, 454–455
Ethnic frames of reference, 52
Etiquette tests, 432
Evaluation
    out-of-school behavior, 509–511
    self, 486–487
    teacher's self-appraisal, 538–545
    work of the school and, 508–531
Everyreader Library, 77
Examinations, *See* Tests
Experience, 120–121
    concept formation and, 223
    interests and, 199–201
    meaningfulness of material and, 216–217
    preschool and readiness, 142, 144–145
    variety in the classroom, 217
Experimental schools, 523–526
Experimentation in classrooms, 545–546
Expiation, 345–346
Extinction, 162
Eyesight, defects of, 27–28

Faculty psychology, 245–246
Failure
    aspirational levels and, 167–168

Failure—*Continued*
  attitudes and, 194
  motivation and, 485
Family, and the adolescent, 82–84
Fantasy, 341–342
Fatigue, 221
Fears
  childrens, 52–55
  conditioning and, 53, 99–100
  elimination of, 54–55
  examinations and, 53
  learning of, 52–55
  reading and, 54–55
Feeblemindedness, 33–34
Fels Parent Rating Scale, 411
Fernald method, 305
Field theory, 39
Films
  attitudes and, 56
  sex education, 86
  to aid adjustment, 390
  See lists of films at ends of chapters
Flash-card drills, 310
Foreign language and transfer, 258
Foreign language tests, 432
Forgetting, 211–212
Formal discipline, 245–247
Foster homes, 32–34
Free association, 155
Freudian psychology, 49–50, 327–328, 337
Friendships
  childhood, 58–60, 387
  intelligence and, 59
  social status and, 59
  unrequited in school, 272
Froelich's disease, 24
Frustration
  adjustment to, 330–331
  conditions which create, 329–330
  diagram of, 153
  over-idealization and, 168–169

General science tests, 432
Generalization, 258–259
Genes, 15
Genital organs, 73
Genius, written work, 136–138
Geography
  children's concepts of, 223
  tests, 432
Geology tests, 432

Geometry
  critical thinking and, 259–260
  tests, 432
Gestalt psychology, 101–102
Gifted children, talking, 47–48
Gigantism, 24
Glands, duct, 20
Glands, endocrine, 20–27
  adrenal, 25
  parathyroid, 25
  pituitary, 24–25
  sex glands, gonads, 26
  thyroid, 21–24
Goal setting, 167–168
Goals
  differences among, 528
  idealization of, 168–169
  "lazy" child and, 383
  social climate and, 284
  vocational, 185–187
Goals and incentives, 173–187
Gonads, 26
Grades, giving of, 481–503
Group discussion, 288–290
  aiding rejected children, 278–279
  criteria for evaluating, 290
  method of changing behavior, 520–523
Group dynamics, 268–270
Group therapy, 389–390
Grouping, 468
Growth
  differences in rates, 129–130
  general nature of, 42–43
  predictions of, 43
  types of, 43
Guidance
  adolescents and, 73
  clinics, 391
  helping isolates, 279
  vocational choice and, 186
Guilt feelings, 337–338

Habits
  early childhood and, 61
  food, 521–522
  nervous, 372–373
Haggerty-Olson-Wickman Behavior Rating Schedules, 372, 437
Halo effect, 135, 398, 438
Handicapped children
  goal setting of, 168

Handicapped children—*Continued*
orthopedic cases, 297–298
physically disabled, 376
sensory defects, 297
slow learning, 296–297
social-emotional maladjustment of, 57–58, 298
special classes for, 58
speech defects of, 297
Handwriting test, 445
Harvard Growth Study, 46
Health, tests of knowledge about, 432
Health examinations, 300
Hearing, defects of, 28
Hebephrenic schizophrenia, 352
Henmon-Nelson Tests of Mental Ability, 432
Heredity, 14–15
Hereditary typing, 398
History tests, 432
Home economics tests, 432
Homeostasis, 16
Homework, 556–557
Homicidal mania, 349
Homosexual practice, 69
Honesty, 222–224
Honor system, 382–383
Hormones, 21
Hostility
repression of, 338
stealing as, 382–383
tension reduction and, 153
Hyperthyroidism, 23–24
Hypochondria, 350
Hysteria, 344–345, 347–348
Hysteroid reactions, 345

Ideals, 196–197
Identical elements, theory of, 249
Identification, 334–335
Idiot, 47
IFD, 169
Illegitimate children, mental development of, 32–33
Illinois Curriculum Program, 79
Impudence, 373
Incentives and learning, 104–105
Independence, need for, 68
Individual differences, 127–138
intellectual capacity and, 130
interests, 131, 133
marking and, 494

Individual differences—*Continued*
other trait differences and, 133
promotion and, 505
qualitative differences, 136–138
school achievement and, 130–132
within individuals, 135–136
Industrial arts tests, 432
Infant care and personality, 49–50
Inferiority feelings
compensation and, 332–333
teachers' remarks and, 566–567
Insight, 102–103
Instincts, 17–19, 327–328
Insulin, 26
Integrative teacher behavior, 266
Intellectual growth of teachers, 536–538
Intelligence
friendships and, 59
individual differences in, 130–132
tests of, 424–432
Intelligence tests
contents of, 425
cultural factors and, 430
group, 428–432
Interests
adolescent, 74–78
change of, 203–205
classroom atmosphere and, 207–208
cultural influences and, 197–198
definition of, 192
occupational, 77–78
origin and development of, 195–201
reading, 311
school subjects, 202–203
stability of, 77–78
survey of, 202
tests of vocational, 441–442
Interpretation of Data Test, 443
Interviewing
description of interview, 404–405
for diagnostic purposes, 302
opening the interview, 405
parents, 273–274
resistance during, 407
securing information, 405–406
Intrinsic motivation, 172–173, 175
Intrinsic values, 173
Involutional melancholia, 353–354
Iowa Every-Pupil Tests of Basic Skills, 433

IQ
  calculation of, 425
  changes with age, 34–37
  constancy of, 119
  typing, 398
Islands of Langerhans, 26
Items in the Home Index, 410

Journal of Educational Research, 468
Journalism class and motivation, 160–161

Kerr-Remmers American Home Scale, 410
Kindergarten, 144–145
Kinsey report, 69
Kleptomania, 349
Knowledge of progress, 166–167
Kuder Preference Record, The, 78, 441
Kuhlman-Anderson Intelligence Tests, 432
Kuhlman-Finch Tests of Mental Ability, 432

Labeling children, 380–381
Laissez-faire teaching, 269–270
Language development
  first talking, 47–48
  size of vocabulary by age, 47
Language study, 258
Law of effect, 98, 100, 161
Law tests, 432
Laziness, 383–384
Leadership
  grouping in reading for, 468–469
  teaching and, 268–270
Learning
  apes, 14
  associative, 97–101
  attitudes and values, 109–110
  concepts, 222–224
  conflict and frustration, 110
  connectionism, 97–99
  definition of, 93
  discovery and, 258–259
  distributed, 220–221
  effect of attitudes on, 193–194
  effect of social climate on, 284–290
  essential characteristics of, 104–107
  interests and, 205–208
  knowledge of progress and, 166–167

Learning—*Continued*
  meaningfulness and, 213–217
  motivation and, 150–190
  motor, 218–219
  needs and, 108–109
  organization and understanding and, 102–104
  perceptions, 107–108
  perceptual process and, 101–102
  pervasiveness of, 107–111
  problem solving, 225–232
  professional problems and, 538
  purpose or intent in, 164–166
  reinforcement and, 100–101
  relationships and, 102
  retention of, 234–235
  review and, 233–235
  self-concept and, 110–111
  sequence of activities in, 236–238
  size of units and, 218–220
  social, 287–288
  special difficulties in, 294–323
  student activity and, 222
  teachers and, 94–96
  testing and, 235–236
  transfer and application of, 241–262
  ways of studying, 96–104
  whole and part, 218–220
Least group size, principle of, 283
Lecture method, 521–522
Library, test of use, 443–444
Life instinct, 327–328
Listening, 159–161
Literature tests, 432
Logical Reasoning Test, 432
Longitudinal studies of teaching, 523–526
Lower class culture, 38

Machover Draw-a-Person Test, 440
Maladjustment, 298, 372–388
  causes of, 374–381
  cheating, 382–383
  detecting, 372
  effect of teacher on pupils, 565–568
  frequency of, 371
  laziness, 383
  mentally handicapped children and, 56–58
  over-protected children, 378–379
  rejected children, 377–378
  stealing, 381–382

Maladjustment—*Continued*
  symptoms among teachers, 562–565
  teachers, 561–574
  truancy, 383–384
  unhygienic school practices and, 379–381
  unsocial children, 384–386
Malnutrition, 30, 301
Manias, 349
Manic-depressive psychosis, 353–354
Marks and reports, 481–503
  criteria for appraising, 503
  difficulties involved, 493–495
  groups served by, 482–493
  improvement of, 495–503
Marriage, 387
Massed practice, 220–221
Masturbation, 69, 346, 373
Materials of instruction, 320
  readiness and, 122
Mathematics
  diagnostic tools in, 318–319
  kindergarten and, 144–145
  readiness and, 123
  remedial, 317, 319
  tests, 432
  threats and, 176
  transfer in, 244, 257–260
Maturation, 115–120
  limits set by, 119–120
  pre-school, 117
  school learning and, 115–118
Meaningfulness and learning, 213–217
Measurement, 423–531
Mechanical ability test, 445
Medicine tests, 432
Memorization, transfer and, 254
Menarche, 69
Menstrual cycles, 72–73
Mental ability, decline with age, 74
Mental development
  adolescent, 73–74
  childhood, 45–49
  consistency of, 45–47
  environmental factors and, 32–37
  peak of, 74
  sex differences in, 48–49
  yearly gains, 74
Mental discipline, 245–246
Mental health, suggestions for teachers, 572–573

Mental hygiene, 371–393
  classroom techniques, 388–390
  materials, 390
Mental hygienists, 372–373
Mental tests, 424–431
  fluctuations of scores with age, 45–46
  individual differences and, 130
  readiness and, 139–140
  school achievement and, 45–46
Methods of teaching, studies comparing, 520–523
Metropolitan Achievement Tests, 433
Middle class culture, 38, 331
Military service, adolescent worries concerning, 80
Minnesota Paper Form Board Test, 445
Misophobia, 350
Modern *vs.* past education, 518–520
Monotony and distribution of practice, 221
Mooney Problem Check List, 79
Mothering, 49–50
Motivation, 94, 150–190
  assignment making and, 232–233
  community resources and, 171–172
  competition and, 178–182
  definition of, 150–152
  extrinsic, 173–185
  feelings of achievement and, 182–183
  goal setting and, 167–169
  goals and incentives and, 173–187
  intrinsic, 172–173
  knowledge of progress and, 166–167
  law of effect and, 161
  punishment and, 176–178
  reinforcement and, 161–164
  reward and, 173–176
  scale for appraising classroom, 541–543
  school marks and, 485–486
  self-concept and, 167–168
  social approval and, 183–185
  teachers', 459–461
  tests and, 462
Motives
  emotions and, 169–171
  individual behavior and, 151
Motor defects, 301

Motor learning, size of units and, 218–219
Mountain children, 36–37
Movies, attitude change and, 204
Multiple-choice questions, 453
Music tests, 432, 434

Narcotics, peer approval and, 184
National Teaching Examinations, 446
Nature-nurture controversy, 119
Needs
  adolescent, 67–69
  affection, 44
  behavior and, 152–161
  biological, 43
  desire for activity, 158–161
  fundamental child, 43–44
  fundamental human, 327–329
  how operate, 329
  independence, 44, 68
  interests, attitudes and, 195–196
  learning of, 108–109
  perceptions and, 155–156
  personality, 43, 157
  philosophy of life, 68–69
  physical, 15–16
  psychogenic, 327
  security, 44
  sex, 158
  social, 272
  sociogenic, 43
  status, 44, 67–68, 108, 152
  unsatisfied, 157
  viscerogenic, 327
Negative transfer, 249
Negativism, 340–341
Nelson Biology Test, 434–435
Neonate, 15
Neurological disturbances, 301
Neurosis, anxiety, 350–351
Neurotic adjustments, 346–351
Neurotic parents, 39
Newer methods, 528–529
Nocturnal emission, 69
Non-directive therapy, 389–390
Nursery school children, 50–51, 117–118
Nursing experiences and personality, 49–50
Nursing tests, 432
Nutrition, 521–522
Nymphomania, 349

Obesity, 26
Observations of behavior, 403–404
Obsessions, 348–349
Occupational hazards of teaching, 568–571
Ochlophobia, 350
Ohio State University Psychological Test, 431
Old oaken bucket delusion, 344
Open-ended questions, 274–275
Opportunities, interests and, 199–201
Organic foundations of behavior, 14–30
Organismic age, 129
Organization
  basic principles of in learning, 212–222
  horizontal *vs.* vertical, 223
  size of units, 218–220
Orthopedic cases, 297–298
Ostracism in adolescence, 71
Otis Group Intelligence Tests, 432
Ovaries, 26
Overprotection, 339, 378–379

Paralysis, hysteria, 347–348
Paranoia, 353–354
Paranoid schizophrenia, 352
Parathyroid glands, 25
Parent-Teachers Association, 558
Parents
  child study and, 401–402
  Fels Parent Rating Scale, 411
  interviews with, 273–274
  speech disorders and, 315
Part learning, 218–220
Participation schedules, 274
Pediatricians, 49
Peer approval, 183–185
Peer group, 65
Perception, 101–102
  accuracy in observing children, 403–404
  learning of, 107–108
  needs and, 155–156
Personal inadequacies, 376
Personal Index, 436
Personality, 37–40
  changes with age, 52
  family influences, 38–39
  family relationships and, 50–51
  handicapped children, 56–58

Personality—*Continued*
  infant experiences and, 49–50
  inventories and questionnaires, 435–437
  sensory defects and, 57
Personality measurement
  difficulties of, 435,437
  methods of, 435–441
  projective tests, 439–441
  rating scales, 437–438
  situational tests, 438–439
  tests for, 372
Petting, 84–85
Philosophy, educational, 4–6
Philosophy tests, 432
Phobias, 349–350
Phobophobia, 350
Physical ailments and adjustment, 344–345
Physical anomalies, 28–29
Physical defects, 27–30
Physical variations among adolescents, 70–73
Physically handicapped, maladjustments, 376
Physics
  demonstration in, 217
  readiness for, 145
  tests, 432
Pituitary gland, 24–25
Planning by students, 514–516
Play interests and delinquency, 199–200
Play therapy, 389–390
Poliomyelitis, 57–58
Political science tests, 432
Polyanna mechanism, 336
Poverty, 374–375
Prefixes, 309
Prejudice
  aggression and, 332
  children's, 55–56
  how learned, 56
  racial, 55–56
Prenatal development, 31–32
Pretests, 141–142
Primary mental abilities, 135–136
Primitive peoples, 37–38
Principles, transfer of, 251
Problem children, 6–8, 371–386
Problem solving
  evaluation in, 230–231

Problem solving—*Continued*
  how problems arise, 228–229
  importance of, 225–226
  nature of process, 227–228
  primary grades, 286–287
  resources for, 230
  selection of problems, 229–230
  set, 252–253
  social climate and, 285–287
  solution and action, 231–232
Problems, professional of teacher, 538
Profanity, 373
Profile
  of class in reading, 466
  of two classrooms, 264–265
  of student's aptitudes, 137
Progressive Achievement Test, 408
Progressive practices, 523–526
Projection, 153, 336–337
Projective tests, 439–441
Promotion, school, 503–506
Propinquity and friendships, 59
Protoplasm, 13–14
Psychoanalysis, 49–50
Psychodrama, 389–390
Psychoeducational diagnosis, 302
Psychogenic needs, 327
Psychological Abstracts, 468
Psychological Corporation General Clerical Test, 445
Psychological deprivation, 296–297
Psychologist, school, 390
Psychology
  general, 3–4
  of the teacher, 535–574
  tests, 432
Psychopathic child, 377–378
Psychoses, 351–354
Psychoses among teachers, 564
Psychosomatic disorders, 345
Psychotic adjustments, 351
PTA and adolescent problems, 86
Puberty
  age of attainment, 42
  sex differences at, 70–71
  variation in onset, 70–71
Punishment
  aims of, 176
  learning and, 176–178
  sadistic in school, 564
  teachers' maladjustment and, 562, 564

Punishment—*Continued*
threats, 176
types in past, 356–358
unsound practices, 357–358
values of, 177
Pupils. *See* Children and Cases of
children
Purpose, intent to learn, 164–166
Pyromania, 349

Race
prejudice, 55–56
typing and, 399
Rapport, 405
Raters, 411–412
Raths Self Portrait N Test, 57
Rating scales
home and community, 409–411
personality, 437–438
Rationalization, 335–336
Reaction formation, 339–340
Readability, 216
Readiness, 114–149
appraisal of, 138–142
arithmetic, 114–145
building of, 142–146
emotion and, 124–127
experience and, 120–122
factors which determine, 115–127
for new method of teaching, 528–
529
home, community and, 121–122
individual differences and, 127–138
relevance of materials, methods of
instruction and, 122–124
school programs for, 145
self-confidence and, 145–146
sex differences, 133–135
tests of, 138–142
Reading
accelerator, 310–311
case of reading problem, 154–155
case of rejected child, 124–126
case study, retardation, 7
difficulties, 303–311
disabilities among teachers, 553–
554
easy books, list, 312
experience and, 120–121
flash-card drills, 310
games, 206

Reading—*Continued*
Group Word Teaching Game, 305–
306
grouping of pupils for, 468
improvement of vocabulary and
comprehension, 307–308
interest, 311
knowledge of results in, 166–167
masculine role and, 122
maturation and, 117–119
out-of-school, 510–511
past and present comparison, 520
preschool experience and, 143–144
positive reconditioning, 306–307
prefixes, 309
professional by teachers, 553–555
readiness tests, 139–140, 432
remedial, 304–311
retarded readers, 469–471
reversals, 108
speed, improvement of, 309–310
teachers' resource material, 468
test results, class, 465
tests, 432
use of test results in, 464–471
Records
anecdotal, 412–413
class case study, 514–518
cumulative and personnel, 413–414
diagnosis of class activities, 516–518
Referrals, problem children, 400–401
Regression, 153, 343–344
Reinforcement, 100–101, 161–164
Rejected children, special help for,
277–279
Rejection, 275–277
case of, 124–126
maladjustment and, 377–378
Relationships, seeing of and learning,
102–103
Relevance of materials, 171–172
Reliability, 446–447, 463–464
Reliability of teachers marks, 494–495
Religious beliefs and adolescents, 81
Religious education tests, 432
Remedial classes, 387–388
Remedial English, 316–317
Remedial mathematics, 317–319
Remedial reading, 304–311
clubs, 384
Fernald method, 305
Remedial speech, 315–316

Remedial spelling, 311, 313–315
Remedial teaching, 294–323
Report cards
    letters in lieu of, 490–492
    two-way, 489
Reporting
    parental involvement, 489–492
    student self-reports, 486–487
Repression, 337–339
    aggression and, 331
    hostile feelings of teachers and,
        570–571
Research summaries, 527
Resources
    for teachers, 319–321
    teachers' self-evaluation and, 545
    teachers' use of, 547
Response potential, 105–106
Responsibility of pupils, 367
Rest, need for, 16
Retention
    curve of, 234
    factors which influence, 234
    minimum essentials of, 244
    review and, 233–235
Retention in a school grade, 504–505
Retroactive inhibition, 221
Revenge, 381–382
Reversal tendencies, 108
Review, 223–235
Review of Educational Research, 527
Rewards
    intangible, 174–175
    learning and, 173–176
    material, 174
Rheumatic heart, 298
Rigidity, psychological, 57
Rogers Test of Personality Adjustment,
    372
Rorschach Test, 439

Safety education tests, 432
Sarcasm, 364–365, 397–398
Saturation, 170
Scales, for rating teachers, 539–543
Scapegoating, 269–270
SCI Occupational Rating Scale, 410
Schizophrenia, 351–353
School
    age of entrance, 140–141
    criticisms of, 518–520
    difficulties of children in, 400

School—*Continued*
    facilities, adult use of, 557
    psychologist, 390
    staff meetings, 279–282
Science tests, 432, 434–435
Scientific attitude, reporting of, 497
Scoliosis, 28
Security, psychological, 50–51
Secondary schools, experimental, 523–
    526
Selecting the appropriate test, 447–
    449
Selectivity and elimination of re-
    sponses, 106
Self concept
    goal setting and, 167–169
    learner's expectations and, 168–169
    learning of, 110–111
Self confidence
    building of, 145–146
    competition and, 179
    how achieved, 145–146
    readiness and, 127
Self Corrective Handwriting Charts,
    445
Sensory defects, 297
Sequence of activities, 236–238
Set
    assignment making and, 233
    intent to learn, 165–166
    transfer of, 252–253
Sex
    drive, 334
    education, 84–86
    glands, 26
    instruction, 17
    needs, 69, 158
Sex differences
    achievement tests and, 48
    behavior problems, 401
    cause of, 48–49
    mental tests and, 48
    readiness and, 133–135
    reading and, 122
Sex Knowledge Inventories, 86
Show-off, case of a, 361–362
Simple schizophrenia, 352
Sioux Indians, 180
Size of classes, 128–129, 282–283
Skills, study, test of, 442–444
Slow learner, case of a, 364–365
Smoking, 373

Social acceptance, 264
Social approval, 183–185
Social class
  children's behavior and, 60
  typing and, 399
Social climate
  class size and, 282–283
  effect on group discussion, 288–290
  goals and, 284
  leadership and, 268–270
  physical factors in classroom and, 282
  problem solving and, 285–287
  pupil relationships and, 271–279
  staff relationships and, 279–282
  teacher-pupil relationships and, 265–270
Social Distance Scale, 436
Social-emotional climate of the classroom, 263–284
Social isolates
  case study, 7
  methods of aiding, 277–279
Social learning, 287–288
Social psychology, 263
Social relationships, testing and, 472–478
Social studies tests, 432
Society, American culture, 38–39
Socio-economic status and perception, 155–156
Sociograms, 274
  construction of, 472–475
  example of, 474–475
Sociological studies, 374
Sociology tests, 432
Sociometry, 274
  gathering data, 472–474
  mentally handicapped and, 56–57
  negative reactions, 473
  use of data, 476–478
Sour grapes mechanism, 336
Special education, 294
Speech
  defects, 297
  remedial, 315–316
Speed of reading, 309–310
Spelling
  analysis of spellers, 243
  Dolch list of 2000 words, 313
  growth of ability in, 115–116
  remedial, 311, 313–315

Spelling—*Continued*
  tests, 432
  words most often mispelled, 314
Sperm cells, 14
SRA Tests of Primary Mental Abilities, 432
SRA Youth Inventory, 372
St. Vitus dance, 379–380
Stanford-Binet Scale, Revised, 425–427
Starvation, effect on personality, 155–157
Stealing, 381–382
Stimulus generalization, 250–251
Strong Vocational Interest Test, 77–78
Stubbornness, 373
Study hall
  discipline and, 362–363
  examples of control, 162
Study methods
  problem solving and, 230
  tests of skills in, 432, 443–445
  transfer of, 254
  use of library, 230
Stuttering, 315–316
Sublimation, 17, 334
Substitution, 333–334
Success, 182–183
Summaries, research, 527
Superintendent of Public Documents, 320
Survey of Study Habits, 443
Swaddling of children, 50
Sweet lemon mechanism, 336
Symptoms, checklist of handicaps, 301

Taboos, imposed on teachers, 569–570
Tabula rasa, 97
Tardiness, 373
Tattling, 373
Teachers
  adjustment of, 561–574
  community relationships, 555–558
  complacency, 544
  contracts, examples of, 570
  disturbed, case of a, 365–366
  how marks and reports serve, 487–489
  in-service training, 386
  interrelationships, among, 548–552
  knowledge about learning, 94–96
  leadership, 268–270

Teachers—*Continued*
learners, as, 536–538
mental health surveys, 563
occupational hazards, 568–571
pledges, 570
professional growth, 535–560
professional reading, 553–555
pupil's reactions toward, 267–268
relations with administrators, 552–553
relationships with pupils, 265–270
repression of hostile feelings, 570–571
self-appraisal, 538–545
suggestions for keeping mental health, 572–573
symptoms of maladjustment, 564–565
training in school psychology, 263
traits of well-liked, 267
working with peers, 548–549
Teaching
assignment making, 232–233
attitudes and interests, 201–208
concepts, 223–224
construction of tests, 449–455
generalizations, 258–259
improvement of class activities, 545–547
organizations and methods, 232–238
out-of-school behavior and, 509–511
problems to expect, 400–401
rating scales, 539–543
staff relationships, 279–282
stimulation by new methods, 528
transfer and, 241–262
unhygienic school practices, 379–381
use of available resources, 319–321
Temper tantrums
as rated by teachers, 412
as regressions, 344
Tension reduction, 152–153
Tension reservoir, 153
Tensions of teachers, 561
Terman-McNemar Tests of Mental Ability, 432
Test of Critical Thinking, 444
Test on the Use of Books and Libraries:
General Education Series, 444

Testes, 26
Testing
process, 235
study and, 236
Tests
achievement, 432–435
achievement and course goals, 435
administration of, 463
alternate forms, 447
audition, 300
background of learners, 461–463
batteries, 433–434
cautions in interpreting, 458–464
character and personality, 435–441
completion, 453
construction of, 449–455
cost, 447
course objectives and, 449–450
diagnostic value, 449
difficulty, 448, 451
directions for, 450–451
effects on learning, 235
essay, 236, 454–455
factors influencing scores, 459–464
intelligence, 424–432
interest value of, 448
interpreting results, 458–480
multiple choice, 453
principles of construction, 451–452
projective, 439–441
readiness, 139–142
reliability and validity, 463–464
review, 235–236
scoring problems, 447–449, 463
selecting appropriate, 447–449
situational, 438–439
sociometric, 472–476
study skills, 442–444
time required, 448
true-false, 452–453
use for class and pupil improvement, 467–471
use of results, 464–471
use to facilitate social relationships, 472–478
vision, 300
vocational interest, 441–442
Textbooks, vocabulary of, 214–215
Thematic Apperception Test, 439–440
Then and now studies, 518–520
Therapy
group, 389–390

Therapy—*Continued*
  non-directive, 389–390
  play, 389–390
  psychodrama, 389–390
Thinking
  critical, 260
  essay examinations and, 454
  test of, 444
  training for, 259–260
Thorndike Library, 76
Thorndike Word List, 309
Thrashing, 357
Thyroid gland, 21–24
Tics, 301
Toilet training, 49–50
Toxophobia, 350
Traits of concern to employers, 492–493
Transfer
  attitudes of, 255–256
  discovery and, 258–259
  how takes place, 249–256
  identities, 249
  importance of, 241
  meaning in teaching, 242
  method of, 253–255
  misconceptions and, 245–248
  negative, 249
  principles of, 251
  set of, 252–253
  setting stage for, 256–257
  stimulus generalization and, 250–251
  teaching for, 256–260
Tremors, 301
Trigonometry tests, 432
Truancy, 383–384
  unsound treatment and, 360
True-false items, 452–453
Tulsa Personal Relations Course, The, 387
Twins, 395
Typing of children, 396–399

Unconditioned response, 99
Unconditioned stimulus, 99
Understanding, 257–259
University High School Student Progress Report, 496–498, 500–501

Unsocial, withdrawing child, 384–386
Use of Library and Study Materials, 444
Uses of Sources of Information; Iowa Tests of Educational Development, 444

Validity, 463–464
Values, 109–110
Verbalism, 213–214
Vineland Social Maturity Scale, 437
Viscerogenic needs, 327
Vision, test of, 445
Visual aid libraries, 390
Visual defects, 297
Vitamin deficiency, 30
Vocabulary
  basic sight of 220 words, 308
  development in young children, 47–48
  meaningful, 214–216
  tests of, 432
  transfer and, 258
Vocational goals, 185–187
  opportunities and, 201
Vocational Interest Blank for Men, 442

Washburne Social Adjustment Inventory, 436
Waxy flexibility, 353
Wechsler-Bellevue Intelligence Scale, 428
Whispering, 373
White House Conference, 371
Whole learning, 218–220
Wishes, 196–197
Withdrawal, 341–343
  tension release and, 153
Word lists, 215
Work decrement and learning, 105
Work habits, 254
Workshops, 551–552
Worries and problems of youth, 71–73, 79–82
Writing reports to parents, 489–492

Zoophobia, 350
Zygote, 14–15